CorelDRAW® X8
The Official Guide

About the Author

Gary Bouton (Central New York) is an award-winning CorelDRAW illustrator and author of hundreds of expert design and drawing tutorials. Out of the 30 books he has written in his career, almost a third of them have been on CorelDRAW. His other works include coverage of Photoshop, vector illustration packages, the creation of 3D models, and the production of Hollywood-style special effects. For McGraw-Hill, Gary has written *Xara Xtreme 5: The Official Guide* and co-authored *Photoshop CS4 QuickSteps*. He is a former Madison Avenue art director and has been a professional illustrator for 40 years. He currently runs a full-service design graphics firm specializing in video training. Gary has also served on Corel's CorelDRAW feature review board and was a finalist in the Corel World Design contest.

About the Technical Editor

William Schneider (Athens, Ohio) currently teaches computer graphics and digital photography in the School of Visual Communication at Ohio University. He has been a finalist in the annual Corel World Design contest on two occasions and has written numerous magazine articles about photography and computer artwork. William's photographs and graphical designs have been published in a number of venues, including *Italian Renaissance Art: A Source Book*, for which he created hundreds of illustrations and photographs. When not working at the computer or printing in the darkroom, William likes woodworking and ice skating.

CorelDRAW® X8
The Official Guide

Gary David Bouton

New York   Chicago   San Francisco
Athens   London   Madrid   Mexico City
Milan   New Delhi   Singapore   Sydney   Toronto

Cataloging-in-Publication Data is on file with the Library of Congress

McGraw-Hill Education books are available at special quantity discounts to use as premiums and sales promotions, or for use in corporate training programs. To contact a representative, please visit the Contact Us pages at www.mhprofessional.com.

CorelDRAW® X8: The Official Guide

1 2 3 4 5 6 7 8 9   LCR   21 20 19 18 17

ISBN   978-1-25-986020-1
MHID   1-25-986020-5

Sponsoring Editor Hilary Flood	**Technical Editor** William Schneider	**Production Supervisor** James Kussow
Editorial Supervisor Jody McKenzie	**Copy Editor** Bart Reed	**Composition** Cenveo® Publisher Services
Project Editor Howie Severson, Fortuitous Publishing	**Proofreader** Paul Tyler	**Illustration** Cenveo Publisher Services
Acquisitions Coordinator Claire Yee	**Indexer** Jack Lewis	**Art Director, Cover** Jeff Weeks

*This is for Wilma Elkins Mancuso, my spouse Barbara's mother,
who passed away last year, all too early. Wilma refused to be negative.
She was the most outgoing soul I've ever had the privilege of knowing
and saw that everywhere she looked the world was never boring.
Your family misses you a lot, Wilma.*

Contents at a Glance

viii   Contents at a Glance

Contents

PART III   Working with DRAWing Tools

CHAPTER 7   Choosing (and Understanding) the Right Path Tools 165

CHAPTER 8   Exploring Special Shapes, Connectors, and Other Office Automation Helpers 189

PART V   Attributes for Objects and Lines

CHAPTER 21 **Common Image-Editing Techniques Using PHOTO-PAINT......543**

PART IX **Motion Graphics and Halting Thoughts**

CHAPTER 22 **Creating Animations in PHOTO-PAINT.......................571**

Foreword

Whether you're a new user or have lived and breathed CorelDRAW for years, we know that you'll find tremendous benefit in the wealth of information available here in *CorelDRAW X8: The Official Guide*. Thanks to the long-standing relationship we've enjoyed with McGraw-Hill Education and author Gary David Bouton, we're confident that this book will provide you with everything you need to know to become a power user of CorelDRAW Graphics Suite X8.

A pioneer in the graphics industry, CorelDRAW Graphics Suite X8 is a complete collection of graphics tools that helps designers, artists, and business users to bring their creative imagination to life. Combining an extensive toolset for illustration, page layout, typography, photo editing and other design tasks, this suite provides everything graphic professionals and aspiring designers need to turn their ideas into amazing pieces of art. With an emphasis on productivity, as well as unmatched support for Windows 10 and cutting-edge hardware compatibility, the new CorelDRAW Graphics Suite X8 makes your workflow faster and simpler, all while giving you more control—especially when working with fonts and editing images and objects.

With *CorelDRAW X8: The Official Guide*, Gary David Bouton has created the total training package, introducing you to the new features that are unique to the latest release of CorelDRAW X8. This essential resource will show you everything you need to know to become a pro, as well as give you tips and tricks to make you efficient and productive. *The Official Guide* demonstrates the significant enhancements made to many of the suite's essential tools and capabilities to achieve the professional results you want and need. We welcome you to explore this invaluable reference, and to learn why CorelDRAW Graphics Suite X8 is the optimal environment for anyone creating graphics on Windows versions 7, 8, and especially the latest version, 10.

Our compliments to Gary David Bouton, for writing yet another edition of this long running, high-caliber guide. On behalf of the CorelDRAW team at Corel Corporation, thank you for selecting CorelDRAW Graphics Suite X8. We're pleased that you've chosen to expand your product knowledge with this exceptional and insightful resource, *CorelDRAW X8: The Official Guide*.

Happy CorelDRAWing!

Gérard Métrailler
Vice President, Products
Corel Corporation

Acknowledgments

- To Project Editor Howie Severson: If I had a medal, I'd give it to you. And if we had ever physically met, I'd pin it on you. Howie, thanks from the bottom of my heart for this excellent maiden voyage of collaboration. You've been more than everything an author could ask for in getting these thoughts and occasional wisdoms out there to readers.
- To Editorial Coordinator Claire Yee: All through the process of creating this book, Claire has been funny, generous, accommodating, and supportive of what is really a major effort by a group of highly polished talents. Claire, thank you for the e-mails, the tracking, and all the things that add up to making a book possible. If I wore a hat, I'd take it off for you.
- To Copy Editor Bart Reed: Bart has been my "Write Hand Man" (pun intended) throughout the creation of this *Official Guide*, and I can't thank him enough. With a fine-tooth comb used with subdermal precision, Bart got my sentences flowing and making sense so that you, the reader, can focus on the gist of the tutorials and other information. Thanks again, Bart!
- To Technical Editor William Schneider: *Professor* Schneider, actually, but he lets me call him Bill because he pities my life. Bill and I have been responsible—or irresponsible, it's your call—for *The Official Guide* since version X3, almost a decade ago. We still love what we do, and we still love the software. Bill, this is my big opportunity to thank you for your accurate comments, your diligent work, and your positively mercurial speed. When I grow up, I want to be just like you. I mean it. Thanks, Bill!
- To Editorial Supervisor Jody McKenzie: Amazingly, Jody was able not only to locate the occasional squeaky wheel, but to instantly oil the intricate machinery—the group who produced this book—to keep things flowing smoothly. This, in turn, has produced a magnificent tome, and I need to thank everyone who worked on it. Thanks, Jody! I hope the X9 version of *The Official Guide* is at least as easy to produce with your help.
- To Acquisitions Editor Hilary Flood: Hilary took our first conversation about the book and my relationship to it with great appreciation, considering that almost no one gets "passionate" about a software program! We've had nothing but smooth sailing during the course of the creation and production of *The Official Guide*, and I feel as though this is because of your contributions. Thanks!
- To Production Supervisor Jim Kussow: Thank you for your fine work in bringing both the physical and the electronic versions of *The Official Guide* to our readers. It was a privilege to work closely with the production department to make a tight book even tighter! Thank you, Jim.

- To Paul Tyler, for proofreading this book and allowing me the humor and occasional drifts off course for the good of the reader. Thanks, Paul. I've seen first hand what sort of finesse you add to a book.
- To Vice President of Products, Graphics & Productivity at Corel Corp., Gérard Métrailler: I need to thank this man in print, because I felt as though Gérard was standing right next to me while I wrote this book—except for the moments when I felt he was in the kitchen looking for a snack. Gérard answered my questions and provided me with media, usually at a moment's notice. I thank you, Gérard, as well as Corel's engineers for an outstanding product. I hope this is a fun and profound reading experience for us all.

Introduction

Did you know that America gets 75 percent of its fossil fuel from Mansfield, Rhode Island? Probably not, because we *don't*. But it's a great fictitious claim because *now* I've got you reading the Introduction section of the *CorelDRAW X8: The Official Guide* with a minimum of effort.

Instead of forking the wisdom in this book down two paths—the beginner's path and the path for experienced designers—I sought to do something different. I wound the paths around each other to create a single thread. These paths of information travel from the beginning to the end of this book. You're welcome to cross paths, jump off one path like Tarzan, and wind up in a different place of interest. This is not a reference book, and it's not a version of CorelDRAW's online manual. I *do* offer help here and there, but I want you to get excited while you learn, and that requires some doing on your part. Therefore, I've created new tutorials that examine techniques both new and tried but true. You'll notice that this interwoven series of examinations, revelations, and perhaps a laugh here and there is a good way to take in and retain information. I've tried to write examples and documentation that I myself have retained over more than 20 years of CorelDRAWing.

That said, what do I expect *you* to get out of this new *Official Guide?* I expect you to grow an approach to CorelDRAW without definitions, and to receive a well-rounded education in color and vector graphics without going nerd. Hopefully some inspiration along these long and winding paths will lead you to original, stunning work that looks as though you sweated the details a lot more than you really did. Version X8 can help bring your ideas to life a lot faster than the previous versions, and all you need is a little guidance. A *guide* would do the trick, wouldn't it? You know, like an *Official Guide?*

How This Book Is Organized

One of the wonderful things about books, including e-books, is how patient they are with you. You're encouraged to progress at your own speed, and if you're in luck, the book is organized in such a way that you can dive in at any point and come up richer. I feel very strongly that you have a powerful book in your hands. I encourage you to "pick and choose" your way through this summary to find a place to open the book, through which you'll find other places, other kiosks of information. Then, when you're both sated and exhausted from visiting all these fun places, you can bookmark (or not) a section and revisit it later.

- **Part I** is a greeting meant for both first-time Corellians and seasoned pros. Chapter 1 sets the tone and pace with a walkthrough of the new and changed features. You'll be pleasantly surprised that Corel has put more and more digital goodies online for all to download, and an annual membership is no longer required. Resources that couldn't possibly fit on a disc are yours in a click, and Corel keeps the media fresh with community offerings as well as Corel's own ever-changing set of fonts, patterns, and other content. By Chapter 3, I'm going to push you into a full-fledged tutorial, using shading, new features, the whole ball of wax, so that you're up and running with DRAW before you anticipate it.
- **Part II** is the "up and running" part of the book. It even contains a highly guided tutorial that will make you look as though you read the entire book instead of only a chapter or two. If you're just beginning CorelDRAW, this area of the book is a must-read. You'll find an overview of the tools you have at your disposal, and how to make your drawing page and the UI work for you and not against you.
- **Part III** has a virtual ton of "good stuff" in it. Here, I cover the bare-bones, essential features and tools in DRAW. The chapters in this part show why DRAW is a favorite among professional artists as well as those who just want or need to get a simple sign or logo done for a small- to medium-sized business. Basic drawing functions, Boolean operations, and a complete unraveling of that mystery called "paths and nodes" are covered in Part III.
- **Part IV** provides a break from shapes and paths. It gets you comfortable with CorelDRAW's text features. Can you do Desktop Publishing in DRAW? Yes. Can you create swooping, 3D headlines? Yep. This is a big "Can Do" section of the book, using characters of the alphabet you're already familiar with!
- **Part V** is an education in fills and paths and how each one can have color added to it with different properties such as fountain fills and rounded corners on objects. I'll also show you where and how the corners of objects can be rounded, beveled, and changed in artsy, sophisticated ways. It's also the part in the book where we discover color spaces and how to use them to create color-consistent works of art. And finally, blends and contours are covered—yet two more ways to create colors fills as you create objects.
- **Part VI** is the "*Ooooh! Ahhhh!*" special effects part of this book. Learn how to extrude objects and create shapes that have perspective. Also, distortions are covered in this part of the book. The Distort tools are a little like the object-editing tools such as the Smear tool, but plugged into a high-voltage power station!
- **Part VII** is the aftermath of Part VI, because there was so much to cover; we still have some fireworks left over for this part. Learn how to use Lens Effects, a very powerful and flexible set of tools for warping and changing the colors of stuff directly underneath a Lens object. Also, you'll learn how to master the Envelope tool, so you can warp any shape exactly the way you need it to bend, stretch, pucker, flange, or otherwise create mischief. Also, transparencies and shadows are covered in this part of the book. Add photorealistic detail to anything you draw.

- **Part VIII** shows that you can work with bitmap images and edit imported photos in CorelDRAW. You'll work through some pretty incredible compositions in this part of the book. And we'll also get into PHOTO-PAINT, the bitmap-based sibling of CorelDRAW. You'll find an invaluable entry point into retouching photos right here.
- **Part IX** (pronounced *icks* if you don't understand Roman numerals) covers GIF animations. See how to create animated banners *and* the new trend of GIF-animated film clips. See how to copy still frames out of a film clip, and arrange them as objects in PHOTO-PAINT to make a small, visually exciting GIF animation of one of my cats. Trust me, it's more exciting than I've described it here. And Duchess is a really photogenic Siamese. Finally, in Chapter 23, I share with you something that has nothing at all to do with a Pencil tool but everything to do about what to do once you've finished this book, such as how to assess career possibilities. How about getting to meet a whole community of Corellians? I eagerly share with you some of my advice, a fellow artist who has been around the block so many times, I have Frequent Traveler Miles you would not believe.

Tutorial Content: Where to Find It

Tutorial Tutorials are scattered around this book like so many peanut shells on the ground after a circus. Many of these tutorials will go better and more smoothly, and better demonstrate a technique or principle, if you have a working file loaded in the drawing window. That's why I've provided you with several. Before most of the tutorials, you'll be directed to go download a ZIP file that accompanies the written tutorials. Open the file you were asked to download, and you'll be all set to follow (and work) along. To get the tutorial files, go to the following URLs:

- **www.mhprofessional.com**   From this page, click the Downloads link and locate this book's title to get to the tutorial files.
- **www.theboutons.com**   This is a mirror site for the files. Go to the top page, and you can't miss the conspicuous, obnoxious, but superbly designed *CorelDRAW X8: The Official Guide* Download icon.

The editors don't know how I do this, but I can see that I'm heading toward the bottom of this page. And so I must stop with the Introduction. But the good news is that there are plenty of other pages under your right thumb, and I start at the top of most of them with really exciting stuff!

C'mon. There's only one way to make me prove it!

1 Welcome! What's New (and Also Exciting) in CorelDRAW Graphics Suite X8!

If you've just upgraded to CorelDRAW X8, you're going to be in for a thrill. All your dreams have just come true—this version has all the power and features of X7, but the interface now has the look of Windows 10—and that's just the cosmetics! The features you use most frequently, such as the Fill tool, have been simplified to the way *you'd* expect them to work. But this is not the place to enumerate CorelDRAW's new and enhanced features. Right now, it's time to address new users.

If you're new to CorelDRAW but have experience with drawing programs, you're in for the treat of this century, because everything is easy to use and intuitive to discover, and virtually everything that has to do with drawing is right at your cursor tip. If you're totally new to CorelDRAW, do *not* hold your breath, or take a deep gulp or anything! CorelDRAW is feature rich without being overwhelming, and once you understand the conventions covered in this chapter, finding the Pen tool is going to be as easy as finding your favorite ballpoint in the coffee mug designated for writing tools on your desk.

Let's call this chapter "The Pre-Party," where you'll get warmed up, confident, and ready to take off in "The Main Event" chapters to follow.

If You're New to Vector Drawing Programs

If you've been using CorelDRAW since its beginnings back around 1990, you can skip ahead here. This section is for people who were recently gifted with their first copy of the Suite, or just became curious about what this CorelDRAW thing is that everyone is talking about.

What Vector Drawing Is and Isn't

If you purchased the CorelDRAW Graphics Suite (CGS) in expectation of retouching your great-grandparents' wedding photo, CorelDRAW would not be the program to use, but happily Corel PHOTO-PAINT *is*, and it's part of the Suite. The Graphics Suite contains two major programs that cover the two major types of computer graphics—vector and bitmap—and the difference is worth a little explaining. Let's begin with bitmap graphics because they are more commonly used for attachments or embedding in e-mail and on the web than vector graphics.

Bitmap Images

Bitmap images, such as those you take with your mobile phone or other device, are also called *resolution-dependent* images, because they contain a fixed number of picture elements called *pixels* (*pic*ture *el*ements). All the visual information that you can save in a digital photo, a bitmap image, is taken at the time you snap the photo; you cannot increase or decrease the size of the image without introducing distortion. This is because bitmap images, by their nature, shrink in dimensions you'd measure with a ruler when you increase their resolution. Bitmap images also become greater in printable size when you decrease their resolution, which is something you can do in PHOTO-PAINT. The key to understanding some of the inflexibility of bitmap images is that inverse, unchangeable relationship between measured size and the number of pixels per unit of measured size (resolution). The amount of detail always depends on the size of the bitmap image.

Often in desktop publishing, the terms *resample* and *resize* are used to describe, respectively, the shrinking of an image *without changing the number of pixels*, and—quite differently—"blowing up" a bitmap, which does in fact distort the original image information.

Figure 1-1 shows an original *high-resolution* image on the left. You can make out the phrase on the coffee mug, and every detail looks crisp and well defined. This is because the resolution, the number of picture elements per inch, is very high. On the right is a *low-resolution* image of the same coffee cups. You've probably seen this *pixelation* effect when you've zoomed in very close on a bitmap. The elements are more predominant than the image they are supposed to represent; you will get this sort of unwanted effect if you don't capture a scene at high resolution and also if you're handed a low-resolution image and expected to do something meaningful with it.

You'll learn to work with bitmap images later in this book; a good generalization to remember is that bitmap images require a *paint program* to edit and create, while vector illustrations are the product of a vector *drawing program*, which is covered in the following section.

Vector Imaging

Twenty years ago, vector drawing programs required concentration and a little patience because computer processors had a fraction of the power that we enjoy today. One of the most notable characteristics of drawing programs is the "undo-ability" of your composition. For example, when a painter paints a masterpiece, it's also a "set piece"; it's laborious and sometimes impossible to make corrections or enhancements to the painting because the paint is dry and the deed is done. But vector drawing programs let you move objects around as well as decide (and re-decide) on the color, position, and size of any element on the page.

Resolution: 300 pixels per inch   Resolution: 72 pixels per inch

FIGURE 1-1   Bitmap images depend on the resolution—the number of pixels per inch—to display visual information.

There are two elemental characteristics to a vector drawing: all the objects you create have a shape—an outline, often called a *path*—and an interior that you might choose to fill with any of a number of CorelDRAW's exotic collection of fills. This illustration demonstrates how a vector drawing program makes an outline and a fill visually meaningful. The design is made up of a couple dancing with Fountain Fills in their interior, and a whimsical window shape with no fill, but a 4-point outline.

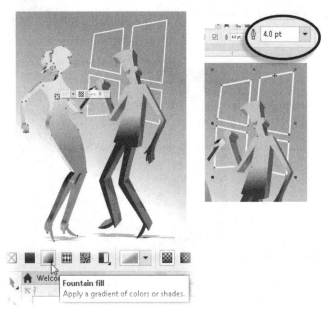

This might come as a surprise, but CorelDRAW is updating your monitor with *bitmap information* every time you create or edit something on a page. There are very few vector monitors still in existence from the 1970s; they were like oscilloscopes, and it was nearly impossible to create something beautiful or even interesting on them. So CorelDRAW deals in math, specifically *geometry*, when you make a design using the tools, and these geometric (and other) calculations can be indefinitely updated and refined—and part of the beauty of working with vector graphics is that you can scale a drawing up or down to any required size, and the elements in the composition remain crisp and scaled to perfectly represent what you originally created.

Here's an example of the flexibility you have when you create a vector design; in Figure 1-2, at left, you can see the Simple Wireframe view of the drawing. Not much to it, right? But when you assign this object a fill and an outline type (a solid white outline), it takes on character and becomes what we commonly call "art." Now at right, this is the same set of circles with a square background, but the fill has been changed to vector artwork from Fill Picker| Content Exchange on the Property Bar when the Fill tool is active. Yes, you can fill a vector design with *other* vectors, and you can even change an outline to a dotted line in different styles—even an

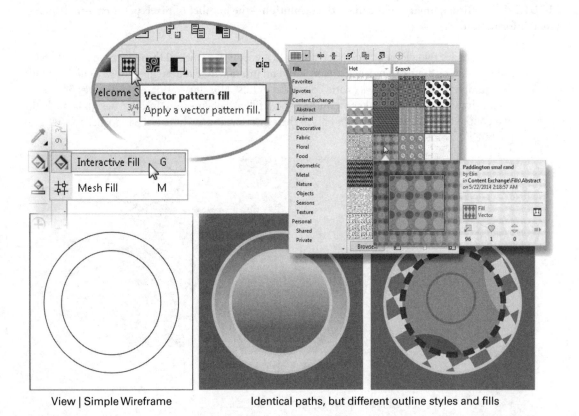

View | Simple Wireframe   Identical paths, but different outline styles and fills

FIGURE 1-2   The underlying geometry of your CorelDRAWing can be simple. Then you dress the object up with fantastic fills and outline styles.

outline style that looks like a brush stroke. All the creativity you can imagine in CorelDRAW is a matter of defining an object and then using an interesting outline style and a novel object fill.

The Vector Sky's the Creative Limit!

By now you're imagining that bitmap images are the sole medium of photographic artwork, while vector artwork is limited to shapes that might make a good pie chart or something. Rubbish—and not at all; for over 20 years CorelDRAW artists have been testing the creative bounds of this constantly evolving program, and everything from photorealistic artwork to menus, catalogs, and even physical license plates are designed in CorelDRAW every day.

Open White pear.cdr from the Chapter 1 download file if you like and then choose View | Simple Wireframe from the menu. Figure 1-3 shows both the vector drawing in wireframe and at a different size, and on the left you can see the original image the drawing was based on. You can also see the advantage of the vector illustration over the bitmap version when a large copy is needed. At left, there is noticeable pixilation when the bitmap version is enlarged, but when it's visually represented as a collection of objects with different colors and transparency values, all CorelDRAW has to do is calculate the final scale of the elements, and the resolution-independent artwork retains all the visual value of a smaller version.

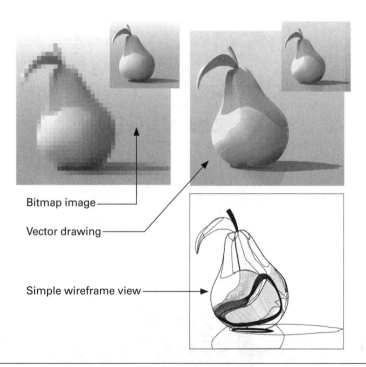

Bitmap image

Vector drawing

Simple wireframe view

FIGURE 1-3   Vector drawings can have the warmth and attractiveness of a bitmap photo when you learn how CorelDRAW's tools work.

You're going to have the time of your life with CorelDRAW, just as soon as you get an intellectual handle on the tools, the interface, and other items that you can add to your work—which "goodies" seems to adequately describe at the moment!

Right now is a good time for novices and experienced CorelDRAW users alike to get a gander at what's new in this version.

Your One-Stop Shop for Extra Content: CorelCONNECT

For users of CorelDRAW X7, you'll be delighted to know that the Premium account is gone, and now you can load every texture, typeface, and media designed by the Corel Community free of charge. The CorelCONNECT button is gone from the Property Bar. This CorelCONNECT is a very thorough implementation of what we read in tech magazines as "cloud computing." In less techy language, Corel Corp. has put a community of users' presets as well as Corel's own work at your fingertips. The new deal with CorelCONNECT is that as long as you own version X8 (IOW, you don't plan to upgrade next year), you'll get special deals on plug-ins and other goodies that relate to productivity, as seen in the following illustration. However, if you don't upgrade to version X9 after it's released, there is no upgrade path for bonus content released after version X9. It's sort of like Microsoft's 365 plan, except you can download and have unlimited access to items found in X8's content area.

You establish your Internet connection with CorelCONNECT—there are no URLs to remember. The Corel Graphics Suite gets you to where you want to go through its menu—and guarantees that you have all the fonts and clipart and other media that used to come with the physically delivery of the program on disc. The only real requirement is that you register your copy of CorelDRAW in the box that comes at the end of the software installation. Get your registration to CorelDRAW via the web, and you'll get everything you paid for. Corel calls the process *authentication*.

Get Started from the Get-Go

Once you've launched, Corel Corp. offers you a rich table of contents from which you can watch tutorial videos before getting down to work or set up the workspace to suit your needs.

Let's take a look at your options for a moment. Figure 1-4 shows the left (the business) side of the Get Started screen. The right side has sample illustrations by terrific artists and occasionally an ad for a great and inexpensive plug-in. You can browse the plug-ins at any time, which is something this chapter gets to shortly. But back to the Get Started screen, and as luck would have it, you want to get started. The icons on the left are annotated in Figure 1-4, and

FIGURE 1-4   Customize CorelDRAW and take in some learning and outstanding art before you begin drawing.

you can also hover your cursor over a particular button to see a tooltip. The "goodies" (Get More) button shown here has an arrow leading to the box you get when after click it.

- **Get Started**   This icon shows the most common options to pick from when you want to start a drawing or open one you've saved. You can find these options under the File | Document Properties menu, and you can also start a new document and override the Welcome screen by clicking the New Document icon on the Standard Bar (the page icon on the far left).
- **Workspace**   When you click this icon, you're given the choice of starting a Lite workspace, which has fewer calories than Regular—and I'm just kidding. It produces a very limited Toolbox and other features. You might want to "hold back" on using all the new features now because you have this book to guide you. The X6 and Default interfaces are similar, except the Default interface provides more intuitive selections of features and tools. Under Specialty, you can set up CorelDRAW to make Page Layout (Desktop Publishing) or Illustration features more prominent and accessible. You can even set up CorelDRAW to remind you of Adobe Illustrator if you're coming to DRAW from that or a similar program.
- **What's New**   You can learn about new features in a well-written, fairly comprehensive but brief document, center-screen, when you click this icon. The Jump In, Craft, and Personalize regions toward the "What's New" headline are jumps on one long document, to get you to an area of interest quickly. Experienced users might want to jump to the Craft section for new feature details.
- **Learning**   Corel offers a very useful collection of video tutorials on the basics. The Quick Start Guide helps novices to orient themselves to a vector workspace and tools. Also, there is a list of good third-party resources for learning and support for CorelDRAW and PHOTO-PAINT, as well as a link to the Corel Community, an online forum packed with experienced, helpful fellow artists.
- **Inspiration**   Here you can enjoy images created by other CorelDRAW users, many of them contestants in Corel's annual art contest. The gallery is updated frequently. Remember that you're cloud computing with DRAW; when a web page changes on the net, you're watching the result of those changes, so you might want to visit the Gallery often to see newly posted work.
- **Product Details**   Clicking here lists the version of CorelDRAW you're using and whether the product is authenticated or not. You have your chance to register the product and establish a name and password for the community—if you've not already done so—each time you launch CorelDRAW. Also, you can check for updates and opt for the Upgrade Program (read the text below this item) in Product Details.
- **Get More**   Clicking this button takes you to a screen that tells you that plug-ins, applications, and extensions to DRAW and PHOTO-PAINT are available, and you click to continue, but only if the CGS is authenticated first. Clicking Get More (on the right) takes you to a pop-up menu of apps and plug-ins, but not extra content—more on that later in this chapter. Many of the plug-ins on this pop-up menu are free, so if you read about one here that looks useful, go for more!

There's just one more eensy matter to settle before you get down to work for the first time: CorelDRAW needs you to tell it what type of new document you'd like it to create for you.

The following illustration shows the Create a New Document dialog; you can check the Do not show this dialog again checkbox, and not be shown this dialog every session—but you really *should* let the dialog appear all the time. Why? Because without this dialog, you'll start a new document *all the time* with default settings, and this is will play havoc with page size and color settings. CorelDRAW is very color sensitive; for example, a document set up for RGB color mode will look hideous if you try to print it with commercial CMYK inks. An explanation of your choices is in order right here in the *Official Guide*:

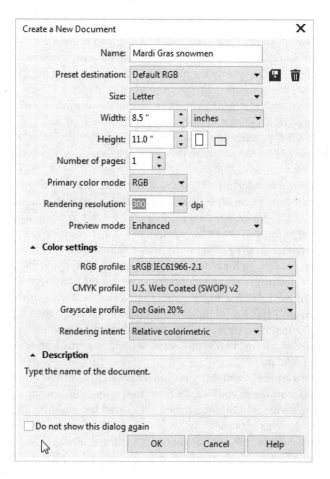

- **Name**   Any time you save a document, you can name it, but by naming the document at the beginning of a session, all you need to do is press CTRL-S at any time, and DRAW saves your document (by default) to the Documents folder in Windows.
- **Preset destination**   This can be a confusing and potentially misleading set of words to the newcomer! A *destination* in computer graphics terms is "where the design you draw will ultimately be displayed." Your work could be going to a commercial printer, to a web page, or anywhere that colors in your document might display incorrectly. It's often best to set the destination to Default RGB from the drop-down list. Your other choices are mostly

CMYK color based. These are onscreen simulations of subtractive CMYK pigments, and your screen might be inexplicably dull—especially the color palette—if you choose a workspace that displays in the CMYK color space.

- **Size, Width, and Height boxes**   This is the area where you set your page size. Your page size can be changed at any time from within CorelDRAW, but it's nice to get this one out of the way before getting creative. There's a units box to the right of these fields, so if you're accustomed to millimeters instead of inches, or typographer's picas, choose the unit you need here. You can also click the little icons of pages to specify Landscape (wide) or Portrait (tall) page orientation.

- **Number of pages**   You can add, subtract, and reorder a multiple-page document at any time in CorelDRAW, but if you know here and now that you're going to create a font, or a leaflet, you can specify the number of pages you want for the file.

- **Primary color mode**   The color mode of a graphics file has a great impact on how you work and how colors are printed, or conversely how they're display on a web page (which is viewed on an RGB monitor). You can choose RGB or CMYK from the drop-down list; if you've never sent a file to a commercial printer, you should choose RGB color mode because RGB is the way human beings perceive color. RGB color mode is predictable; it's like looking at any other scene in the real world.

- **Rendering resolution**   Here's that irritating "resolution" word again! What this value means is how many dots you want the printer (or other output device) to use to render your work to paper. 300 dots per inch, the default, is quite high, and chances are if you work at home, you've got the document set up to as much as a home inkjet or laser printer can render. However, if you don't intend to render at all, but instead want to export a design as a bitmap for e-mail attachments, 72 or 96 dpi is fine; in this instance, the "dots" are actually pixels—for example, 96 pixels per inch has been a typical screen resolution for years. If you're outputting to a web page, you might want to consider 72 pixels per inch, because this is the resolution web professionals render their graphics to in 2016. And if you're sending a bitmap copy of your work to a friend with a high-resolution tablet, consider rendering to 300 dpi, because high-resolution screens are becoming more and more popular.

- **Preview mode**   Without question, choose Enhanced. It's the maximum viewing quality, it won't slow down your work unless your computer is using a processor from an ATM bank machine, and there's a reason, discussed later in this *Official Guide*, for the other viewing quality modes.

- **Color settings**   Digest this set of explanations slowly; take your time, this *Official Guide* has got nowhere to go, and color management is a vital feature that protects the way your artwork looks when printed. The first three settings will work just fine for most people in the Western Hemisphere at their defaults. *Profiles* are collections of settings that make up the optimal "environment" for a graphics file, as it is sent to a printer or other rendering device (such as an imagesetter, a high-resolution printing device). The profile for an RGB color space in which you design something is, by default, sRGB, which is terrific for most inkjets because most of them today are calibrated to the sRGB color space, and sRGB is the color space of the web. The CMYK profile by default is U.S. Web Coated (SWOP, or Standard Web Offset Printing) v2. This is a very common set of color characteristics, so in theory if you do work for output by a commercial printing house, the final print should look something like your original RGB image in CorelDRAW onscreen. Countries in Europe and the Pacific Rim have other standards to choose from in the drop-down list. The Grayscale profile really has only one parameter that could be adjusted and that is Dot Gain (at 20 percent, a very generous compensation). Dot Gain is a compensation a commercial printer uses when printing black ink on any number of different types of paper, all with different rates of absorption. In principle, if you make the halftone dots in the printing plates (or in the direct-digital process) a specified amount *smaller,* the ink will spread (gain) just the right amount to make your halftone copy of your art look good on the page.

Rendering intent is misunderstood by 11 out of 10 people. Seriously, this term means you need to choose between four well-established conversion processes when your artwork uses colors that cannot be expressed using the combination of cyan, magenta, yellow, and black (CMYK) pigments. In essence, your monitor uses red, green, and blue light to show you what you've drawn, while printing uses different colors; as a result, RGB color with a larger color space than CMYK has colors CMYK inks can't express accurately, and something needs to be done—and it's called *color conversion*—so your CMYK print looks more than vaguely like what's on your monitor! The four choices are as follows:

- **Relative colorimetric**   This setting is all around probably the best conversion for most of your CorelDRAW drawings, and even photographs you import to a DRAW document. Relative colorimetric doesn't preserve the whitest whites (the *White Point*), but instead shifts all colors and all brightnesses to the nearest colors that the CMYK color space can express. Relative does clip (exclude) certain colors that are widely out of range, so two different reds, for example, in your onscreen original might be forced to render as the same red. However, the relationship of one color to another is preserved during this conversion, so the human eye sees this conversion as well balanced and even very close to the onscreen original. It's also a good choice for commercial printers to pull a color proof of work before a large press run.

- **Absolute colorimetric**   The White Point and Black Point, unlike Relative, are preserved in Absolute rendering intent. This guarantees that highly identifiable colors (such as Coca-Cola red and Federal Express purple) are reproduced accurately, at the expense of shifting other colors. If you need specific color accuracy for certain colors, this is your choice.

- **Perceptual**   This rendering intent takes the entire expressible range of colors (the *gamut*) available from one device (such as your screen) and compresses it to fit with the gamut of the destination device (such as an inkjet printer). The result is that all the colors in the print have shifted somewhat, even if only one or two colors were out of CMYK's range (gamut), but the relationship among all colors are preserved. If you're obsessed with color accuracy, this wouldn't be your first choice of conversion methods, but if you're most concerned with the relationship between the original colors—grass green contrasted against sky blue in a photo, for example—you'd choose this method.

- **Saturation**   This setting is for highly stylized comic-bookish artwork, charts, graphs, and any time you're free to totally forget about color accuracy and relationships between colors in a document, and you just need garish hues on a page to make a sales pitch or accurately render a Marvel Comics hero in uniform.

Finally, you can and probably should save your Custom settings. This is done by clicking the little 3.5" floppy disk icon to the right of the Preset Destination box and then giving the preset a unique name.

Now that you have a new blank page before you, it's time to choose your tools for creating your future masterpiece—all of which deserves its own section, as follows.

The CorelDRAW Application Window

The application window is mainly what you see when CorelDRAW is open. The "Big Deal" is that the application *interface* has been extensively updated and simplified so that you can almost work at the speed of thought. Predictability and intuitiveness are the foundation of this version, and you'll immediately notice that this version has the Windows 10 "flat" look and feel. *Drawing windows* (sometimes called *document windows*) contain the drawing page or pages that hold the graphics and other content you create.

It's ridiculous and unnecessary to provide a figure here that lists every single element in the application window. Corel Corp. had done a terrific job of doing this task in the Owner's Manual. This *Official Guide* provides you with the quickest way from point A to Point B, and therefore Figure 1-5 points out the new features and features you'll want to understand if you're just beginning vector graphics. CorelDRAW obeys Microsoft Windows conventions, so a page icon means "new document," a floppy disk icon means "save," CTRL-P means "print," and so on. You have CTRL-S, CTRL-C, CTRL-V, and many of the other standard File and Edit menu commands. If you already know all this, you're way ahead of the game.

- **Tabbed document interface** One innovation experienced users will immediately notice is the tabbed drawing windows. You can have more than one drawing window (sometimes called a *document window* in other applications) open in the application window, but only one can be active at a time. The specific settings you see displayed on the Toolbar, Property Bar, dockers, and other application window interface elements are those assigned to the currently active drawing window. They change if you make another drawing window active by clicking on the desired drawing window.

Tip This new tabbed document arrangement isn't a hard-wired feature. If you're used to seeing documents side by side so you can drag a selection from one document to the other, drag the title bar of the document off the tab and it will float in the drawing window. You can also choose Window | Tile Horizontally or Vertically to see more than one document at a time.

- **Menu bar** Although CorelDRAW has a standard menu bar, common to almost all Windows programs, what's in the menu is extraordinary, delightful, and important to achieving complex artwork. Working left to right, it's a fair generalization that the leftmost menu items have to do with arranging shapes, viewing complexity onscreen, and other important workaday commands, but no flashy graphics effects. The center of the menu bar is where you'll find effects, effects you can apply to imported images (but not as easy or as refined as retouching in PHOTO-PAINT), and Desktop Publishing goodies under the Text menu. Toward the right, you'll find commands to change global settings, color

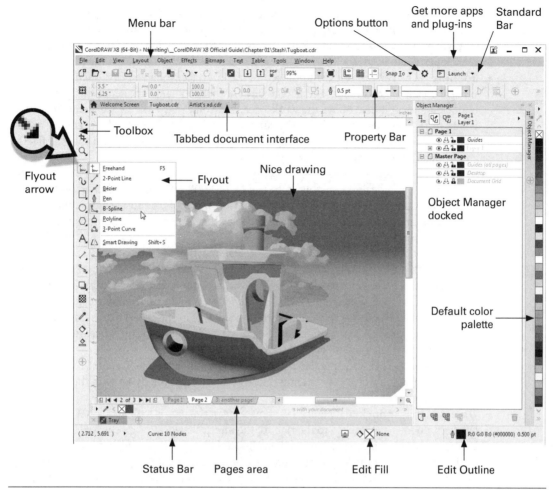

FIGURE 1-5 The CorelDRAW application window provides a highly organized, intuitive workspace.

controls, and commands that make the dockers appear. Dockers are panels that can float in the drawing window or be docked directly to the left of the vertical color palette. Dockers provide options for an effect or a tool that cannot be fully listed in a menu command. You might call them miniature dialogs for a function.

- **Standard Bar** The bar that lies across the interface, below the menu bar, provides some very basic controls, some of which are under the File and Edit menus. You can start a new document, go to Options (where just about everything in CorelDRAW can be modified), import and export content, and undo the last move you didn't want to make.

- **Property Bar** Unlike the Standard Bar, the Property Bar is *context sensitive,* meaning you what is offered on it changes based on the current tool you've selected. For example, you've chosen the B-Spline tool for drawing some open paths. On the Property Bar, you can add arrowheads, set the outline width, and other functions specific to paths and closed objects. Choosing the Pick tool and clicking on a blank part of the page results in controls for Nudge distance, duplicate distance, page orientation, and your choice of units. If you're ever at a loss for what a tool does, or how to modify it, your first stop should be the Property Bar.

- **Toolbox** The column docked to the left of the interface when you first open this new version is called the Toolbox, and it's actually another toolbar in the sense that you can undock it and let it float above the workspace, and you can use the new Customize feature to add or remove items to or from it to suit your work needs. In general, the editing tools are toward the top of the Toolbox, shape creation is toward the center, and special effects and outline/fill properties are toward the bottom.

Note If you're not a designer and want to use CorelDRAW for graphs and charts—for technical purposes—you'll find connector drawing tools, almost magical shape-creation and table tools toward the center of the Toolbox, within groups that contain similar tools for drawing.

- **Flyout** What an umpire at a ball game calls—and I've wanted to use that joke for three versions of this book now. Seriously, the Toolbox is just too small to show all the features that it offers, so tools with similar or related functions are grouped with a single tool icon "on top of" the rest of the group. When you want a tool in the group that is not the top tool, you click-hold on the flyout arrow (see next) to expand the group, release the mouse button, and then click on the desired tool.
- **Flyout arrow** This is the precise point on a tool group icon—the triangular tick mark at the bottom right of the icon—you must click-hold on to get the flyout with the rest of the group tools to show.
- **Object Manager docked** Figure 1-5 shows one of the panels in CorelDRAW called Dockers, opened, yet docked to the right of the interface. Dockers are covered in this book as a specific feature (such as the Lens Effect docker) is discussed, but generally the docker itself and not the features within it are brought to the workspace in a 1-2 move: first, you choose Window | Dockers and then you click on the docker you want to access. Some dockers have shortcut keys (such as Object Properties, which is ALT-ENTER), while others need to be called the long way—although you can set a shortcut key of your own via Options | Workspace | Customization | Commands. The docker appears at the right edge of the interface, and the second part is getting it opened and perhaps even moving it about. To undock and float a docker, you click-drag the docker's title bar from the right window edge into the drawing window. You can also dock a docker in various other places in the interface; if you drag it around the edges of the drawing window, eventually a dark preview rectangle appears. You then halt movement and release the mouse button. Dockers have a common close button to the right of their title bar, and to retract and expand a docker, you click the title bar while it is docked in its original position in the interface.

The reason why the Object Manager docker is shown here, and not, for example, the Fillet/Scallop/Chamfer docker, is because CorelDRAW offers drawing layers, and it is from this docker you can arrange, hide, lock, and create new layers—a *very* important feature in CorelDRAW for complex drawings.

- **Default color palette**   There are many ways to fill an object with a solid color in CorelDRAW, but the fastest is by the convention that many graphics programs offer; there's a set of swatches, vertically, at the far right of the interface. To apply a color to an unselected shape, you left-click-drag a swatch (called a *color well*) on top of the object on the page and then release the mouse button. To fill a selected object, you left-click a swatch. The color palette is determined when you create a new document (by choosing the color mode), and colors are covered later in this *Official Guide.* Clicking the down arrow at the bottom of the palette scrolls the colors up to reveal hidden ones, and the arrow at the top does the inverse. Clicking right-facing arrows at the bottom of the palette expands the palette to reveal all the colors on the palette.

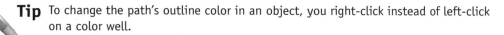

Tip To change the path's outline color in an object, you right-click instead of left-click on a color well.

- **Options button**   Clicking this button is your one-stop shop for customizing your copy of CorelDRAW. In this Options dialog, divided into three main categories, you can adjust units of measurement, the default width for objects drawn, how and when you're alerted to things, and so on. Basically, you can trust the statement that if it's in CorelDRAW's application window, it can be customized. Figure 1-6 shows the Options dialog with some of the categories extended to show subcategories and commands.

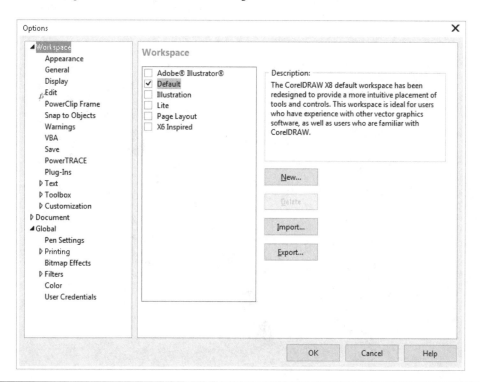

FIGURE 1-6   **DRAW's Options box makes the workspace and your toolset as individual as your own work preferences.**

- **Edit Fill**   When a object is selected, double-clicking this area of the UI displays a box with every fill type imaginable in CorelDRAW. Set your fill type, scale of patterns—you name it.
- **Edit Outline**   Double-clicking this area when an object is selected offers the outline version of what the Edit Fill box does for objects. You can recolor, make dashed lines, add custom heads and tails to open lines—the sky's the limit.
- **Status Bar**   The area toward the bottom of the interface continuously updates to describe an effect or what is selected in the program.

Taking Customization to the Max

In the Options dialog, under Workspace|Customization|Commands, is a feature more powerful than Thor's contract for sequels at Disney. You can add (and later remove) commands found under CorelDRAW's main menu to the Property Bar as buttons. Suppose you need the nonbreaking space command under Text because you're reformatting a document, and you need a quicker way to get to the command than by menuing. First, you choose the Text tool so that the Text tool's Property Bar is visible. Then you click the Options button, choose Customization | Commands from the menu on the left, and then choose Text from the drop-down toward the center of the Options dialog. Scroll down to the Non-breaking Space command and then, with your cursor, drag the command up to the Property Bar (or even the Standard Bar), as shown in this illustration.

It's easy enough to remove the custom button; you hold ALT and then drag the button off of the bar.

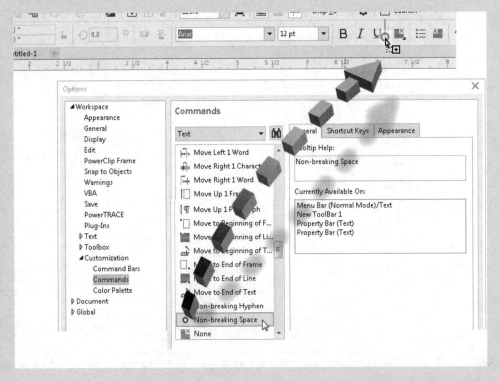

Should you get into trouble with excessive customizing, you can always "reset" all of CorelDRAW *as a last resort.* Exit the program, and then while you launch CorelDRAW again, hold F8 to reset the program to its factory defaults. Factory defaults might *overwrite* any *wanted* modifications you've made, so this is somewhat of a life-changing decision to get up and running with DRAW again.

- **Pages area**   In this area, you can add pages to your current document, delete pages, and reorder pages in your multipage document. These commands and more can be executed as menu commands from the Layout menu. If you want an *overview* of your book, manual, pamphlet, or other multipage document, this isn't done in the Pages area but instead from View | Page Sorter View, where you can drag and drop pages to reorder them.

Tip   You will run into a number of predictable UI elements in CorelDRAW, such as number boxes, radio buttons, and others that are featured in many Windows programs. However, spinner buttons might be new to you. *Spinner buttons* can do one of several things. *Spinners* (also known as *spin boxes*) are similar to combo boxes; they're used to specify values by typing *or* using mouse actions. Single clicks on the up or down arrow button increases or decreases the value incrementally, but you can *also* click-drag on the divider between the two arrow buttons—up to increase or down to decrease the value. *Command* buttons perform commands instantaneously, but *toggle* buttons control (and indicate) a specific feature's On and Off states, using a pressed or not-pressed appearance. Generally, a *pressed* state indicates On, while the *not-pressed* state indicates Off. *Shortcut* buttons open dialogs to further options, while *selector* buttons open lists of preset selections. See the following illustration.

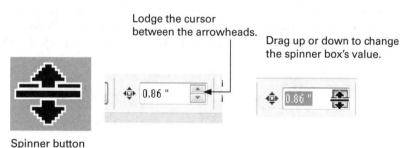

Lodge the cursor between the arrowheads.

Drag up or down to change the spinner box's value.

Spinner button cursor

- **List selectors**   *List selectors* differ from combo boxes in that you cannot enter a value, but instead pick from a predefined list of values or graphic samples that show the way that a style or arrow (or similar) will be applied or created. Clicking on one of the entries in the list chooses and applies a value, size, state, mode, or style to the currently selected object. These lists are occasionally called *drop-down* or *pull-down lists* in other applications.

Click to access preset values.

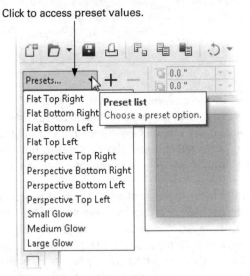

- **Selection icons and option boxes** These two interface devices are slightly different, not just in shape, but also in the choices they offer, as shown next. Selection icons look more or less like regular interface icons, except they are usually smaller. Also, in keeping with Windows 10's "minimalist" look, they're usually grouped, and you're supposed to make one selection per group and not more. An example of this is the alignment options. In previous versions of Windows and of programs like CorelDRAW, a radio button accompanied a small illustration of a choice—now, we have only the illustration. *Option boxes* are square and let you choose an option or state to be either on (with a check mark) or off (without a check mark). You'll find in many areas of the Options pages that you can choose more than one option (that is, more than one box can be checked).

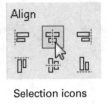

Selection icons

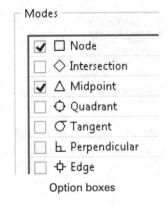

Option boxes

Note Left-handed artists are not uncommon; if you're a southpaw, the order of your mouse buttons is not defined in CorelDRAW, but instead in the operating system's Control Panel | Mouse menu. Just mirror the instructions in this chapter: if a step tells you to left-click, it's the right mouse button, and vice versa.

CONNECTing to Your Workspace

Earlier, the importance of registering and authorizing your copy of CorelDRAW was stressed (okay, it was *suggested*). Here's the reason why: CorelCONNECT and the Corel Content Exchange have been developed for years, and they're fully integrated with the software. When you have an Internet connection active, all you need do is choose Window | Dockers | Get More, and a world of goodies is at your beck and call, as shown here.

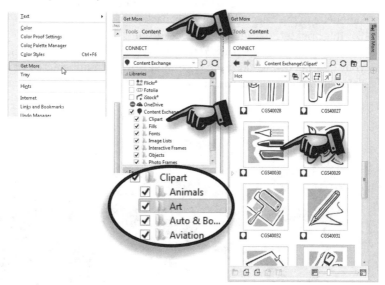

Using Your Universal Connection

It's quite easy now to integrate media from a remote server across the Internet with content you've created and stored on your hard drive. After you've chosen Get More, the Get More categories are Tools and Content. As you saw earlier on the Get Started screen, the tools Corel offers are plug-ins, small applications, and add-ons, ranging from totally free to a few bucks. However, Corel Content, from the Content Exchange, will amaze and delight you. Rather than depending on a CD, or loading tons of digital media on your hard drive, you can pick and choose in this Content field.

There are two different ways to get Corel Content from a server, located somewhere over the rainbow, to your hard disk so you can permanently include the art, background, preset fill, and even some typefaces in your work.

Here are two brief run-throughs (let's call them tutorials) on how you'd download a neat-looking nature-theme background vector, the ideal setting for a cartoon character to sing to the animals.

Tutorial From Corel Content to Your Content, "Add to Page" Style

1. With CorelDRAW open, open a new page and then choose Window | Dockers | Get More.
2. From the menu at the left of the docker, double-click the Content Exchange, which opens to reveal categories. Double-click the Clipart title, and from there, double-click the Backgrounds title.
3. In the following illustration, the author has chosen Top as a subcategory—the top-rated backgrounds chosen by the Corel Community—and the author has settled on the silhouette of the trees against a sepia background.
4. For this brief tutorial, choose any background that tickles your fancy, and then drag the thumbnail onto the page. You might see a status line, depending on the speed of your Internet connection. The bottom line of the thumbnails contains the More from Selected List command, which you can use to gain access to even more content.

5. That's it! There is no step 5. You've just downloaded some art that was not part of the X8 package. You can now begin drawing your singing princess and appreciative animals on a new layer, and you can close and reopen the file. The file is yours to use privately or commercially, and no one is going to come to your house and repossess it—or hurt you, unless you try to resell the art, which is forbidden according to your user agreement.

Here's a different, and perhaps better, way to download and save goodies—especially if you want to drink deeply from this well and download a lot of stuff you'll be using in a project.

Tutorial # From Corel's Content Server to CorelDRAW's Tray

1. Pick some art from the Art category. Let's pretend your name is Bradley Bennet (even if you're a girl), that you're an artist, and you need a business card or poster for advertising.
2. Go to the Get More docker first. By the way, you might want to undock the Get More docker and then drag either of its vertical edges away from its center. Why? Because there are certain docker elements such as the forward and backward buttons that aren't visible when the docker is docked.
3. Under the Art category, there's a swell graphic of art materials you can see in the following illustration. The author was particularly struck with art labeled CGS 40030. And if you hover over certain Corel-created pieces of clipart, you'll see details and keyword tags for future reference. You want this clipart—but don't drag it to the page. Instead, click the button on the Get More docker marked in the next illustration. If you have tooltips turned on, it will tell you that this toggles a tray on and off, at the bottom of the interface. This tray is a neat-as-can-be storage space for downloaded files; it's like setting up all your resources on your drafting table before you begin an award-winning project.

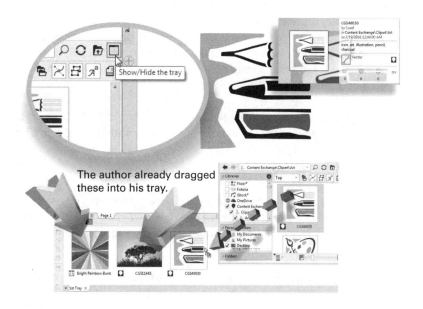

In the final illustration here, you can see that you (Bradley) have gone to town and customized the clipart; it's all vector, so you can edit clipart you've downloaded as objects using the Toolbox tools. Fonts that you put in the tray can be loaded by right-clicking over their thumbnail.

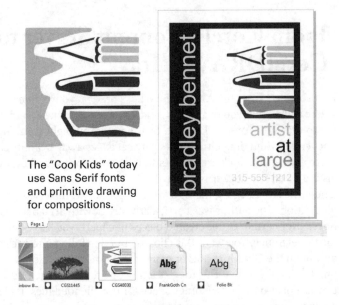

The "Cool Kids" today use Sans Serif fonts and primitive drawing for compositions.

Tip The Get More command is so named because you're getting more content than you originally purchased with the Graphics Suite. You already have a lot of Fountain Fills and fractal textures you can access without an Internet connection, and the new Corel Font Manager can snag a whole base collection of wonderful typefaces without a Get More command. Perhaps Corel might have named this command "Above, Beyond, and in Addition To."

For experienced users, you'll find using the new workflow to be much faster to arrive at a graphical idea, and new users will feel right at home with the intuitive UI properties.

So What Else Is New?

Corel Corp. coded a lot of enhancements to previous versions in the spirit of "logical evolution." As just one example, you can now *select adjacent nodes along an object* merely by holding SHIFT as you use the Shape tool, as you can see in this illustration.

Select and hold SHIFT.   Click here.

Adjacent nodes are selected, the Shape tool is dragged, and Big Hair is the result.

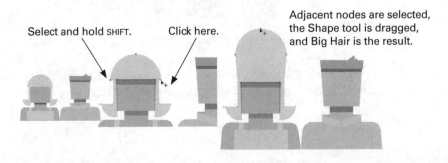

The Elliptical Fountain Fill

Although you can still make a Circular Gradient, the past version of DRAW grew the tool to include elliptical fountain fills. If the boon to artists is not apparent, check out the following illustration. The drawing of the water molecule looks as though it has edge lighting and, as a result, the circle looks a lot rounder, offering a more photorealistic look at the fundamental parts of this wet substance. The color handles can still be used for positioning and rotating the fountain fill (also called a *color gradient*). The illustration here shows you how a radial fountain fill is changed to an elliptical one, in one step. In this example, the fountain fill's end color handle is a tiny circle, and pulling on this handle is what transforms the fountain fill. Also in this illustration, not one but several colors make up the atoms. You do this by double-clicking on the start color handle to add another color node and then fill it with the color palette or the little pop-up mini color picker. More on fountain fills later in this book. Note that the molecule shown on the right has a soft, Gaussian Blur–style drop shadow that's cast on a ground plane. This is controlled by the Feather slider on the Property Bar when the Drop Shadow tool is selected.

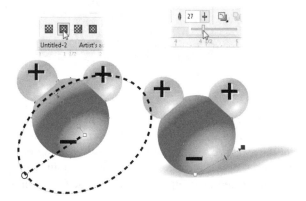

An Improved Knife Tool

You're in for a treat if you need to slice objects as part of your work. The Knife tool is easier to use and can now leave a gap between split shapes (and groups of shapes) as well as an "overlap," in case you need to make objects appear aligned but you don't have time for precision. In the following illustration, you can see the Knife tool in action, slicing a banana drawing made of 58 objects. The Knife tool slices the banana with the finesse of one of those knives you see in TV ads. The banana would go great on a bowl of cornflakes, but the author forgot to peel the banana before slicing it.

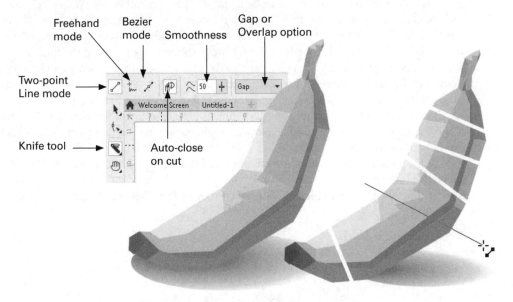

Copying Paths

Think about this: you've spent a great deal of time with the Polygon tool, drawing a stylized sun. A little later you draw a gentleman tipping his hat, but you want him to have a hip hairdo, and don't want to spend the same amount of time as you did drawing the sun.

Not a problem. A new feature in DRAW is the capability to copy a path segment and then close the path or just extend it using one of the Pen tools. This illustration shows the content and the problem.

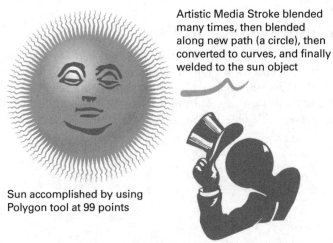

Artistic Media Stroke blended many times, then blended along new path (a circle), then converted to curves, and finally welded to the sun object

Sun accomplished by using Polygon tool at 99 points

Target gentleman who needs hair

The steps here to run through are only the procedure for copying paths and then doing something useful with them. You probably don't own a sun and a gentleman with male-pattern baldness, so just follow along with the steps and the illustrations. This is a non-tutorial tutorial, as the editors have creatively named it.

Tutorial Making Use of the New Copy Segment Feature

1. You create the sun object as described in the callouts in the previous illustration. Mastering the Polygon tool is thoroughly covered in chapters to come.
2. You create a person in need of hair.
3. You choose the Shape tool, and probably hold the ALT key, which lets you lasso some curves on the sun, instead of trying (unsuccessfully) to use the default rectangular selection mode.
4. Press CTRL-C to copy the selected path segment, and then move the sun away from its original position because the pasted path will land directly over the sun.
5. Press CTRL-V to paste a copy of the selected path segment. Now, the sun has no outline, so neither will the pasted path segment. Give it a narrow outline so you can see it, so you can work with it! Refer to the following illustration.

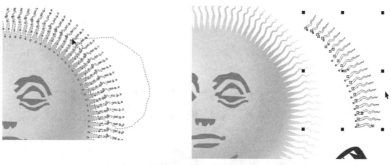

Lasso a good amount of spikey curves and then press CTRL-C to copy.

Move the sun so the pasted path is easier to find, press CTRL-V to paste the segment, and then give it a thin outline because the sun has no outline, so the pasted object will be hard to see.

6. With the Pick tool, drag the open path to a position that is aesthetically and Rogaine-ishly stylish. Rotate and/or scale the path if necessary. It depends on which part of the sun you copied.
7. From the Object menu, choose Join Curves. A docker appears, and the only command you need to use here is to click Apply. As you can see in the following illustration,

there's a golden set of closed, joined curves with a thin outline as an object separate from the gentleman, but the next step fixes that and concludes this non-tutorial.

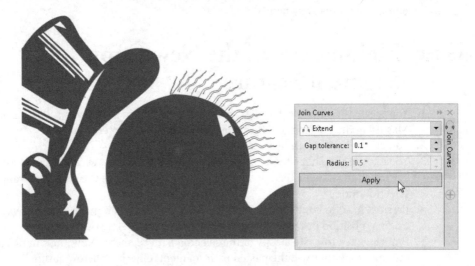

8. Select both the gentleman object and the hair, and then go up to the Property Bar and click Weld. Your gentleman now has hair that might need a little combing; unfortunately, CorelDRAW X8 doesn't have a Comb tool, but it *will* in version X9— and I am totally kidding about this. See the following illustration.

Certainly, if you're just beginning to use CorelDRAW, you might be totally unprepared and a little confused about the ton of stuff thrown at you in this chapter. Well, previous users have gone through the same thing, so don't sweat it.

You could call this chapter "foreshadowing," but this literary device is usually reserved for novels you buy at the airport, and not technical tomes. Kidding aside, there are a lot of pages under your right thumb, and it's all good stuff. Your next stop is to look under the hood and kick the tires of this brand-new model, as your guided tour of the Corel Graphics Suite becomes more "hands on" and pretty productive, considering this will be only the second chapter! But believe it or not, the hands-on work also comes with a helping hand in the form of the author's expert step-by-step guidance. So if you're good at math, you just realized that you're going into the next chapter with three hands.

Don't worry, three hands are more than enough for the fun and learning coming right up!

2   The Roadmap to Features and Productivity in DRAW

To say that CorelDRAW is a drawing program is like saying Mount Everest is tall—it's a phenomenal understatement. In addition to the drawing tools, you also have filters and panels (*dockers*), offering everything from color samples to the revamped Align and Distribute object feature. You'll find effects for bitmap imports, typography tools for Desktop Publishing, and more. In fact there's so much to explore, it could fill a book—specifically, *this* book.

To make the most of your valuable time, there are a lot of ways to perform just about everything in CorelDRAW—and there are hard ways and *easy* ways. Guess which way you'll learn in this chapter? There aren't secrets or mysteries to unravel with CorelDRAW. There's just stuff you might not be prepared to find, or to use. Let's get down to some serious exploration of the fun features in this new version right now.

 Note Download and extract all the files from the Chapter02.zip archive to follow the tutorials in this chapter.

The CorelDRAW Workspace

Once CorelDRAW has loaded and you've specified a default document, the sheer wealth of options and tools can make a beginner (and many experts) feel more than a little intimidated and lost. You have more help than you'd imagine, though, beginning a drawing. Suppose you want to change the page size, or hide all the guides you dragged from the rulers. Or maybe you need a more detailed explanation of the B-Spline tool as you're trying to use it. You can refine, redefine, and customize your document and your view of the document with a few well-placed clicks, and you always have a tutor right within the workspace, as covered in the sections that follow.

The Page Shadow: It's a Command Control

Although the page shadow—the medium gray trim around the right and bottom edges of the drawing page in the drawing window—might be seen as an artistic interface embellishment, it's actually a shortcut to all the options one could ask for that are specific to the page. Double-clicking the page shadow with the Pick tool opens the Page Size tab in the Options dialog. What is the orientation you want for the page? What rendering resolution do you need (for printing and when you import bitmaps)? Although some of the page layout options are available on the Property Bar—and only when the Pick tool is chosen—the Page Size tab in the Options dialog (see Figure 2-1) is a comprehensive resource.

   Now that you know how to get to page options in lightning time, let's breeze through a short tutorial that demonstrates how useful the Page Size options can be.

Tutorial   Defining and Saving a Custom Page Size

1. In a new document, with the Pick tool, double-click the page shadow. The Page Size Options dialog appears.
2. Bear with us Americans for a moment; the default page size you see in Figure 2-1 is measured in *inches*, and it's a default printer size of 8½" by 11". Let's make a square page; type **8.5** in the field that currently says "11.0".

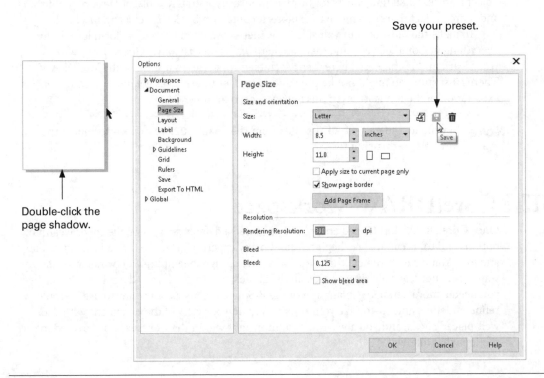

FIGURE 2-1   The quickest way to access all options for the drawing page is by double-clicking the page shadow with the Pick tool.

3. Let's also pretend that this is a multipage document, and we only want the first page to be square. Put a check in the Apply Size To Current Page Only check box. Because you've moved fields within this Options page, the 8.5 value you put in the num box in step 2 has now been accepted.

4. Suppose we want to design something that is *exactly* 8½" by 8½". Well, a page frame would expedite this need, so click the Add Page Frame button. There is now an object exactly 8½" square on Layer 1, Page 1, with no fill and a black outline dead-centered on the page.

5. Let's say you're growing weary of this supervised experimentation, and you want to conclude this mini-tutorial. Save this custom page layout by clicking the floppy disk icon shown in Figure 2-1. In the Custom Page Type dialog, type an evocative name in the text field, such as **square 8.5**. Click OK, and you're done.

Try out your new page preset now. Create a new document, and then with the Pick tool chosen, go to the Property Bar and click the Page Size drop-down list. As you can see in the following illustration, the preset created in the previous tutorial is right there, and if you choose it, a square page appears in the drawing window, there's a square outline object on the page, and the document has the other page attributes you declared in the tutorial.

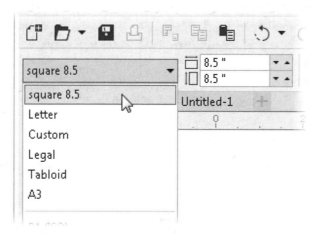

Page Options on the Property Bar

Don't be fooled by the terms "page type" or "page size" when it comes to options specific to your current document in DRAW. You have control over more cool and useful things than you'd imagine if you just switch to the Pick tool for a moment, to display the properties on the Property Bar, which is *contextual,* just as the right-click pop-up menu (also called *the context menu*) is.

Figure 2-2 shows the rightmost controls on the Property Bar when the Pick tool is the active tool; the bar has been split so you can see a larger detail of it in this book.

The following explains the purpose of, and at times the inspired use of, the features; they can save you time and frustration if you know why they were put there:

- **Dimension num(ber) boxes**   These are numerical entry fields for the units you've selected for the current page size. Although an abbreviation for the units follows the numerical entry, you don't have to type, for example, the double-prime character (") denoting inches to enter a value—DRAW puts it in there after you put the cursor in a different field, because the software understands you've specified inches when you created a new document. Therefore, you can change the page size at any time in a document merely by typing in a new value. Only when you're done resetting the values should you press ENTER to confirm the current entries.

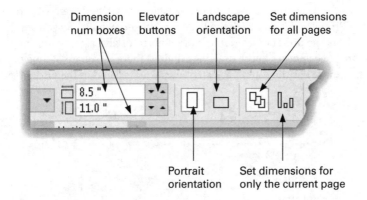

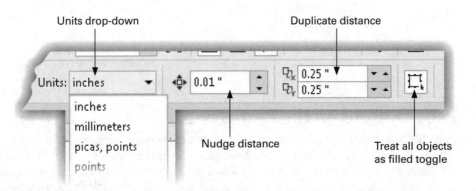

FIGURE 2-2   The Property Bar changes with the active tool, to extend the features of the tool you're currently using.

Tip   Even though there is a Units button on the Preferences Bar for changing, for example, centimeters to inches, if you type an abbreviation for a value into a num box after typing the number value and then press ENTER or move your cursor to a different field, CorelDRAW will enter the value with the new unit and then return the num box display back to the original units. For example, suppose your document is set up for inches and a co-worker pokes his head into your cube and tells you the boss wants the width of the document to be 3 feet, as improbable as that seems. In the Width num box, you type **3 ft**, press ENTER, and the document is 3 feet wide now. Then the Width num box returns to inches for units and reads 36.0".

- **Elevator buttons**   Most of the time in CorelDRAW, where there's a num box, there are *elevator buttons* directly to the right of the fields. You click the up button to increase the current value and click the down button to decrease the current value in the corresponding box. For the Dimension boxes, the value (in inches) for increasing or decreasing the amount is 0.05".

Note   If you put your cursor directly between the up and down elevator buttons on any of these "combo boxes" (a box that accepts number entry and clicking/dragging on elevator buttons), you'll see that the cursor changes to a two-way arrow with a divider in between the arrows. Drag up or down to *significantly* change the value of a nudge, a page dimension, or any value box that features elevator buttons.

- **Portrait and Landscape orientations**   With a simple click of either of these buttons, you rotate your page by 90°. A wide page becomes a tall one, and vice versa. *Portrait* is tall and *landscape* is wide.
- **Set dimensions for all pages**   You should only click this button *after* you've set a new page size. Then, all the pages in your multipage document are identical in orientation and size.
- **Set dimensions for only the current page**   If you've made a different sized page, perhaps for printing scrapbook content, and want only this page uniquely sized, click this button while viewing the page. All other pages will remain the same size.
- **Units drop-down**   Clicking this button reveals a drop-down list of units, from which you change all features that display and use units. For example, if your current unit of measurement in DRAW is inches, and for some whimsical reason you choose Feet from the Units drop-down, a standard U.S. Letter page size will be displayed as .917' wide instead of 11". Similarly, if you had a nudge distance set on the Property Bar of 1", the distance displayed will be the same absolute value, but it will read 0.083' now.
- **Treat all objects as filled toggle**   A *toggle* is just a fancy computer term for an on/off switch, but this feature itself is a genuine boon to artists, who are able to select objects just by touching their edge. When you switch (*toggle*) on to the state where the icon has a slim outline around it (see Figure 2-3), you can use the Pick tool to move an unfilled object by click-dragging on its edge or anywhere in its unfilled interior. This is terrific when you want to keep an object unfilled but the outline width is so thin that the object is hard to select. This figure shows a side-by-side comparison of dragging the left, unfilled object, and in CorelDRAW you see both the current position and the original position of an

object you drag. Micro-hint: the object you're moving is in "preview" mode, and you'll see a thin blue outline in the workspace instead of the original colored outline.

- **Nudge distance**   The keyboard ARROW KEYS can be used to move a selected object by a predefined distance, called the *nudge distance*, although you can also shove, push, and propel a selected shape, depending on the distance you specify in this box. Alternatively, you can use the elevator buttons to nudge an object up, down, and across in increasing increments of 0.05" per ARROW KEY hit. This is a very useful feature for moving an object out of the way and then returning it to its original position when you've finished editing some other object.

 Note   You can push two ARROW KEYS simultaneously to nudge an object diagonally. What's really happening is that CorelDRAW is understanding two sequential commands, but for you, the effect is a diagonal move and it can save time.

In addition to this guided tour of the Standard bar in the *Official Guide*, you also have an automated guide in the form of Hints in CorelDRAW. Let's locate, survey, and embrace this feature next.

 Tip   Use CTRL while you press a nudge ARROW KEY. This is called a *micro-nudge*, a fraction of the nudge distance determined by what you specify in the Options | Workspace | Document | Rulers tab. If you hold SHIFT, this is called *super-nudging*, and it's a multiple of the nudge distance, again, set in the Rulers tab of the Options dialog. This dialog is easily accessed by clicking the Options icon on the Standard Bar (covered later in this chapter).

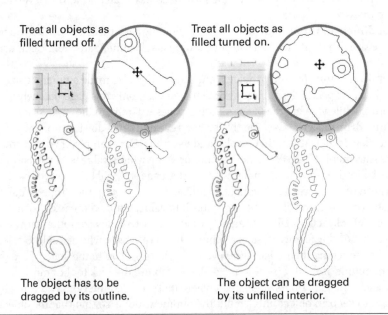

FIGURE 2-3   Moving unfilled objects is simple in DRAW: you toggle the "Treat all objects as filled" button on the Property Bar.

Can You Give Me a Hint?

There's an unbelievable number of tools on the Toolbox, and many of the tools are only the top face of a tool group flyout—the pen tools, the edit tools, and the fx tools all contain several different neighboring tools on their respective flyouts. Suppose you want to draw a freeform shape and are unsure of which tool is the best to use? You'd click-hold on the face of the Curve (tools that produce curves, mostly pen tools) to reveal the flyout, and then choose a tool. But which tool will be best for your goal? Let's say you want to create a shape consisting of both arcs and straight lines. There are several drawing tools that are suitable for your task, and let's suppose for a moment that you choose the Bézier pen tool, a good overall choice for drawing. Now, there are only two drawing techniques you use with the Bézier tool, but you're not sure what they are.

You choose Help | Hints, and as soon as you click a tool on the Toolbox to choose it, the Hints docker is at the ready with a succinct explanation of the workings of the tool, as shown in Figure 2-4.

Ctrl, Alt, and Shift Are Your Friends

The modifier keys CTRL, ALT, and SHIFT are used by many programs to extend a command; even the simple Windows Copy command uses the modifier key CTRL, for CTRL-C. In CorelDRAW, you should learn to reflexively reach for a modifier key when using a tool to change its function.

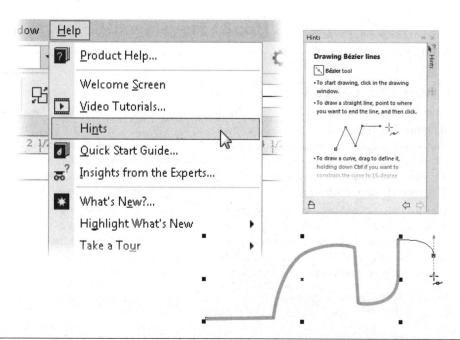

FIGURE 2-4   When you want to quickly learn the basics of a tool or feature, use the Hints docker.

Although no two tools are the same in CorelDRAW, the most common functions of these three modifier keys are as follows:

- **CTRL**   An abbreviation for "Control," you should think of this term as similar to "Constrain." For example, when using the Rectangle tool, if you hold CTRL while you drag, it constrains the dimensions of the object to a perfect square. Similarly, if you put an object into Rotate/ Skew mode (you click with the Pick tool on an object that's already selected) and then hold CTRL while you drag on a rotation handle, the rotation is constrained to the number of degrees you've specified in Options | Workspace | Edit. You can also constrain node control handles while you're drawing by holding CTRL. This is useful for creating objects whose angle at nodes are all identical.

- **ALT**   You can think of this key as offering Alt(ernatives) to the basic command you're executing or tool you're using. For example, when dragging with the Bézier tool, you usually wind up with curved path segments, but if you hold ALT while click-dragging, a straight line segment is the result. Similarly, the Eraser tool switches from freehand style to straight lines when you click a start point and then hold ALT and click your end point. ALT is not as common a modifier key as CTRL or SHIFT, but the point is that when you believe a tool or command has more than one way to work, you try out these three keys before stopping your work to find help.

- **SHIFT**   SHIFT can be thought of as "Add to." For example, if you hold SHIFT while using the Eraser tool, the nib becomes larger. When drawing shapes with object tools such as the Polygon, Ellipse, and Rectangle tools (and others), holding SHIFT before you click-drag draws the object from its center outward instead of from the corner.

And remember that modifiers can also be used in combination. If you hold CTRL-SHIFT while you click-drag a rectangle, the rectangle is drawn from its center outward, and it is also constrained to a square at the same time.

Choosing Tones from the Color Wells

On the color palette, you have a lot of choices of colors with the default palette, but you have still more variations of these colors by using a simple technique. Although digital color is an additive process, when contrasted against the subtractive color process of painting with traditional pigments, we still use the term *tone* to mean a lightness or brilliance characteristic of a color. The way tones were traditionally mixed was to add white (producing a *tint*) or to add black (producing a *shade*). In CGS X8, you have a much faster and accurate way to refine the color well you choose before you apply the color to a shape. In the following illustration, you can see a selected object, and the Pick tool is over a color well; the trick is to click and then hold on the color well, and a tones mini-palette will appear. While holding, move your cursor over to the mini–color well you want, and then release the mouse button to apply the color to the selected object. However, you need to do this motion with a little alacrity; hold, but don't hold too long, because a numerical readout will pop up and obscure your view of the tints on the palette.

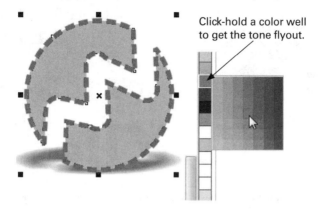

Click-hold a color well to get the tone flyout.

Surprises When You Right-click and Use the Wheel

If you're using the traditional mouse for drawing in CorelDRAW, there's more power to tap into when you understand what right-clicking and setting up the mouse wheel does. Let's take these hardware features one at a time; digitizing tablet users can take advantage of the same power by using pressure and the buttons on your stylus.

Tapping into the Power of the Right-click Menu

It's called different names by different companies, but for ages Windows has supported a pop-up menu called the *context menu* or *contextual menu*. What it does is a lot more important than what it's called! *Contextual* means that the menu commands on this pop-up menu change, depending on which tool is currently chosen. As an exercise, choose the Pick tool and then right-click over an empty area of the drawing page. The menu gives you commands for undoing the last edit, creating a new object, and other commands specific to helping you out when the Pick tool is chosen and you right-click over an empty page area, not an object or an effect. These are purely commands useful when you use the Pick tool. Particularly important when the context menu is used in combination with the Shape tool, you can turn selected nodes and path segments from straight and sharp to smooth and curved, respectively. Figure 2-5 shows the context menu when you right-click over an empty page area, when you right-click over an object, and when right-click over an effect (a drop shadow).

If you can't remember, find, or think of the command you need while drawing, simply right-click, even with a drawing tool active. Chances are the command you need is right there on this menu. If you haven't drawn a CorelDRAW masterpiece yet, it's okay—we're only on Chapter 2. If you'd like to try copying stuff, you can find T-shirt.cdr in the ZIP archive.

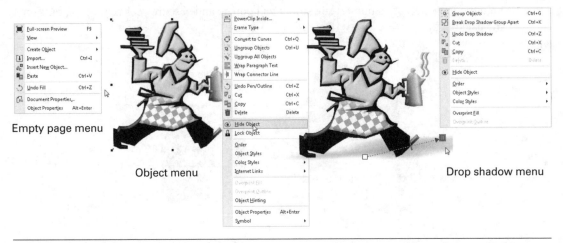

Empty page menu

Object menu

Drop shadow menu

FIGURE 2-5   The right-click menu serves you up commands pertinent only to the area or object over which you click.

Dropping a Copy of a Selected Object

When you're using the Pick tool, left-button dragging moves a selected object, but right-button dragging can do something entirely different, especially when you use the right-button drag in combination with the left button, other keys, and the SPACEBAR. Here are the three methods for making a copy—and several copies—without using the Copy and Paste commands, the Duplicate command, or the Step and Repeat command:

- **Right-click and then drag, release, and use the pop-up menu**   If you're just getting the hang of using a point-and-click device, this is the most surefire way to quickly copy an object. See the following illustration.

Right-click and drag, then release
the button to reveal a pop-up menu.

- **Left-click and drag, click both buttons, and then release**   This is the traditional CorelDRAW "drop a copy" technique, and if you get used to this series of maneuvers, it's perhaps the fastest way to precisely position the copy while creating it. See the next illustration.

Left-click and drag, then tap
both buttons and release.

- **Hit the** SPACEBAR **key over and over while left-dragging a shape to make several copies**   This method for duplicating the selected object (or objects, or groups of objects) is not only a quick method for populating a page with duplicates, but it's also silly fun. Try it with a simple shape such as a rectangle, and before you know it, you have a page of confetti. See the following illustration.

Left-button drag. Every time you press SPACEBAR, a duplicate is placed.

Tip You can also left-button drag and then press the numerical keypad + (plus) key to drop a copy.

Page Navigation: Panning and Zooming the Smart Way

There are dozens of shortcut keys in CorelDRAW, and you can also set your own (explained in Chapter 1). However, there are only a handful you'd really be wise to commit to memory, and they are listed later in this chapter. One of the CorelDRAW shortcuts that is good but not critical to remember is, while you are using any tool—*except the Text tool*—pressing SPACEBAR toggles you to the Pick tool, and another SPACEBAR press returns you to the last-used tool. Many users remember that H is the shortcut for the Pan tool, and after using the tool, a press of the SPACEBAR toggles the current tool to the Pick tool, and not a previously used tool; not when the Pan tool is selected via the shortcut method.

You can elect to ignore memorizing the shortcut for the Hand tool (although it's easy to remember) if you merely remember that the wheel on your pointing device—usually a mouse—serves as both an immediate panning and zooming tool:

- If you press down on the mouse wheel while dragging it, this is a temporary toggle to the Pan tool, and you can drag your view of the document window in any direction you see fit. See the following illustration.

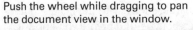

Push the wheel while dragging to pan the document view in the window.

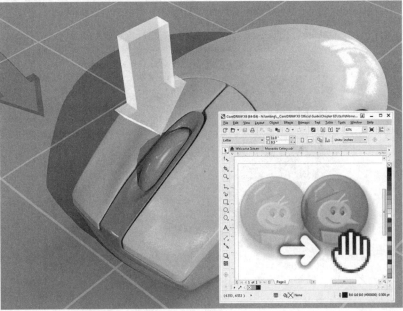

- If you push the mouse wheel away from you, causing a counterclockwise rotation of the wheel, you zoom into the current document. If you pull the mouse wheel toward you (a clockwise rotation of the wheel), you zoom out. Additionally, when you zoom in, you can direct the zoom point by hovering your cursor over the desired area of the document (many programs that offer zoom don't do this). See the following illustration.

Push away from you to zoom in.

Pull toward you to zoom out.

Use the cursor to point to the zoom-in area.

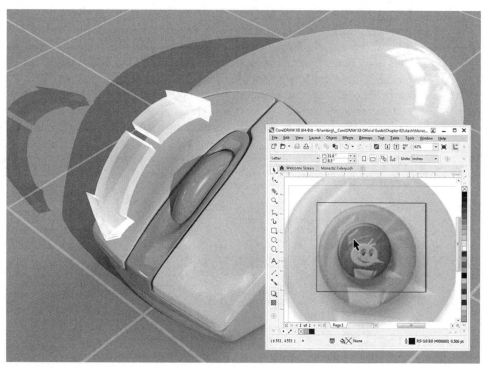

Tip If you choose To Fit from the Zoom Levels dialog, you're taken to the closest view in the window that includes all drawn objects. Now, if you zoom in or out, the objects will always be viewed in the center of the window. If you choose a zoom level when objects are not centered in view, and don't first choose To Fit, subsequent zoom levels you choose or type in the combo box will not display all objects centered in the view.

Not to be Overlooked on the Standard Bar...

The Standard Bar is a permanent screen element (unless you deliberately detach it and/or hide it); it always displays the same features regardless of which tool you choose. Corel Corp. has reworked and simplified the Standard Bar in version X8 to bring you the most needed features at a click. Therefore, you'll have to dig through the menu commands less often and seldom have to interrupt your work for "Adventure Time."

The following list calls out and describes some of the features you'll want to familiarize yourself with, as shown in Figure 2-6:

- **Import** If you're new to computer graphics, "Import," at least as far as CorelDRAW is concerned, means *to bring a copy of something into the drawing window without the original being touched.* Adobe Illustrator, just for reference, calls this action *placing* a file. This is not the same action as opening a CorelDRAW file, although you *can import* a CDR file. Both Open and Import commands are under the File menu. CorelDRAW comes with an exceptional collection of import filters, both for text and graphics files, so bringing in a text document you need to lay out and a JPEG photo for a brochure are as easy as pie.
- **Export** This is the opposite of importing something. Also, exporting is not the same as saving a file. CorelDRAW has extensive export filters—*including* exporting objects as typefaces. As an example, if you need a PNG file made from your Corel drawing, you can

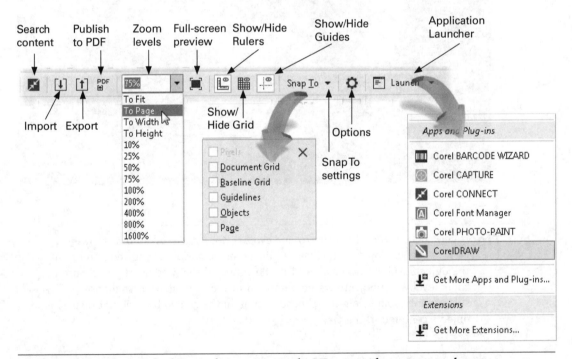

FIGURE 2-6 The Standard Bar is always at top in the UI to provide common and necessary command shortcuts.

do so in the Export dialog, and you can choose a resolution (see Chapter 1) and whether or not you want transparency supported. When you export, you're *not* sending your Corel artwork *original* anywhere; it's a copy, usually in a different file format, that is leaving the drawing window.

- **Publish to PDF**   New to version X8, Corel sees the need for many graphics designers and Desktop Publishing professionals to quickly create a high-fidelity document for the web. You can choose Settings from the Publish to PDF box, or just click Save. Using either option, you now have a time- and energy-saving button on the Standard Bar all the time.

- **Zoom levels**   This is a combo box that offers preset resolutions, and you can also type in a custom value (and then press ENTER). 264,583% is the maximum value you can enter, and 1% is the minimum. You'd be hard-pressed to exceed those levels of magnification in your work, and at each extreme it's very difficult to navigate and see objects.

- **Full-screen preview**   Clicking this button removes the entire UI, and you are presented with your drawing at whatever magnification you had before clicking the button. This is a great feature for making a presentation and for taking uncluttered screen captures. Although in full-screen preview you can see the printable page and its drop shadow, the guidelines and the grid will not display. A click anywhere returns you to the UI and your work.

- **Show/Hide Rulers**   This button toggles on and off the display of the rulers on the top and left of the drawing window border.

Tip   You can move the rulers anywhere in the drawing window by SHIFT-dragging a ruler. The rulers still hide and show when you use the Show/Hide Rulers button, and you need to manually put them back at their default locations if you put them in the drawing window. SHIFT-double-click will return the rulers to their original position.

- **Show/Hide Grid**   This toggles the visibility of the different grids on and off, although a grid can continue to "snap to" objects you move around, even if the grid is hidden. There are three types of grids in CorelDRAW, and you choose which one to hide and display via the View | Grid command. The Document grid is the default grid in all documents, and you can change its spacing and whether it appears as lines or dots through the Options | Document |Grid command. The Baseline grid has no line/dot options, but you can change its spacing and the color with which it displays. The Pixel grid is not visible until you've imported a bitmap—a pixel-based graphic—and View | Pixels is your current choice of viewing the page. You can set the color, the opacity of the Pixel grid, and whether it appears onscreen after you've zoomed in more than 800 percent—an unchangeable value, for reasons apparent when you're at 800 percent and all you can see is the grid!

- **Search Content**   Clicking this button takes you to the Get More docker, also accessed by using the Window | Dockers menu. You can add content to your document or a tray. See Chapter 1 for more details on the Get More docker.

- **Show/Hide Guides**   This setting hides/shows any guidelines in a template or guides you've added to your document; this button has no effect, naturally, if there are no guidelines in your document. There is another way to hide guides if you have the Object Manager open. You click the Show/Hide eye icon for the Guides entry on the Object Manager list.

- **Snap To settings**   This drop-down list offers a check mark area to make each interface object become magnetic ("sticky") or not, which is useful when you want to enable the stickiness of the pixels in a photo you imported, or the guides, or the grid, or other objects. In general, you probably don't want *any* item enabled for "snapping to" if you're simply drawing things freehand and have no need for precision in creating nodes or moving objects.
- **Options**   The Options dialog is the nerve center for customizing the way your documents behave and look, but also how CorelDRAW behaves and looks. This is probably the most important dialog you'll need for overriding default settings, and therefore this button is a welcome alternative to hunting for the command in the main menu (it's under Tools, who would have known?) or memorizing CTRL-J.
- **Application Launcher**   This drop-down list affords access right within DRAW to all the other modules in the Graphics Suite, including additional apps, extensions, and plug-ins for DRAW and PHOTO-PAINT.

Caution   You'll notice that CorelDRAW is listed in the Application Launcher list, although you're working in CorelDRAW, so ostensibly you've already launched it. You can launch another session, or two, or five of the same program, but just because you can, doesn't mean you want to. Saved versions of open documents become impossible to manage, and your computer's memory resources might not appreciate your testing how many copies of DRAW you can load.

Shortcut Keys You'll Want to Memorize

Here's the short list of important key combos, modifiers, and other shortcuts in CorelDRAW that you'll want to memorize. If you do, before long, CorelDRAW will seem more transparent, and the only thing you'll need to concentrate on is the work that you're doing. This list is organized by task first, followed by what you press and/or click.

- To move an object upward by one level in the stack of objects on a layer, press CTRL-PAGEUP.
- To move an object to the front of a layer, press SHIFT-PAGEUP.
- To move an object to the top of all layers (you're actually moving objects to a new layer), press CTRL-HOME.
- To move an object downward by one level in the stack of objects on a layer, press CTRL-PAGEDOWN.
- To move an object to the back of a layer, press SHIFT-PAGEDOWN.
- To move an object to the bottom of all layers, press CTRL-END.
- To convert a text object or other object possessing advanced properties (such as a Polygon object) to a simplified set of paths and curves, press CTRL-Q.
- To break apart a compound object, one made up of two or more different paths within one object such as a donut or the letter *B*, press CTRL-K.
- To join two or more objects together (to combine them) to create a single object, press CTRL-L.
- When the Shape tool is chosen, to add a node to a path, double-click the path or press the + (plus) key on the numeric keypad.

- When the Shape tool is chosen and a node is clicked on, to delete the node, press the – (minus) numeric keypad key. Alternatively, you can then right-click and choose Delete (with a special icon telling you the node and not the entire shape will be deleted). It's also good to remember that when you do delete a node in an object, the neighboring path segments will resize and change to represent the new geometry. This is good advice here: if you're going to delete a node, it might be good first to convert or make sure the surrounding path segments are straight lines so the overall object shape doesn't change significantly.
- If you've drawn an outline that has no fill because the path is open or the object is unfilled, and you want to turn the outline path into an object, use CTRL-SHIFT-Q. This is an exceptionally cool feature for making elegant objects that couldn't be filled as a series of paths, as shown here.

Eight disconnected lines

Convert line to object, CTRL-K to break apart, add different fills and effects

- To start a new document without bothering (much) with the Create a New Document dialog, press CTRL-N and then press ENTER.

Global versus Local

This section is a brief one, intended to familiarize you with the terms *global* and *local* as they apply to options in CorelDRAW. A global change, as expected, changes everything; specific to CorelDRAW, a *global* change refers to how much memory you want dedicated to DRAW out of your computer's memory pool, printer settings (how CorelDRAW addresses your printer), managing the filters CorelDRAW has to load and offer (text import and export, JPEG import and export, and so on), and other program "housekeeping-related" issues. Global settings will have an impact on the way you work, but mostly don't alter or help what it is you're designing. Global settings aren't "creative" settings.

Global resources are also persistent ones. For example, the library of colors you find on the color palette are global resources; they're available to you with each and every document.

Local resources are objects and settings specific to a document, and the local settings you make can disappear unless you *save* your document. Where you added guidelines to a document, a specific symbol you've created (which is local but can be made global), the current nudge distance—these are all *local* settings.

Additionally, the Options dialog is quite specific about where the local and global settings are changed. Document (which means local) and Global are both features and main entries on the Options tree in the left panel.

Tip You can open more than one document window showing the *same* document, so you can work on one document in multiple windows. Choose Window | New Window. Both windows are "live," so you can edit in either of them and all the changes you make editing in one window will also appear in both windows. To switch views, click on the title bar of the document window.

A Brief Anatomy Lesson on Dockers

Dockers are panels—palettes—where many different commands and controls related to specific tasks are grouped together in one handy location. Dockers put more of Corel's power right at the tip of your cursor without forcing you to dig through lots of dialogs or flit between various toolbars and menus. In general, if you display a docker such as Window | Dockers | Effects | Extrude, this might initially seem as though it's just a duplication of what's on the Property Bar when the (interactive) Extrude tool is your current tool. It's not, and here's the important difference: you can work on refining the extrude properties of an extruded shape indefinitely when the Extrude docker is open or minimized—it's simply *there.* You set it down on the counter, but you didn't put it away, in a manner of speaking. In contrast, when you use the Extrude tool to work with the Extrude features on the Property Bar, you will lose those features if you need a different tool for a moment, because the Property Bar is context sensitive—it offers commands specific to the current tool. In the following illustration, you can see all the features found that are needed to refine an extrude on a unique docker.

New Sign Proposal for Webster's Inn

These controls can be anchored to the edge of the screen and reduced to tabs by clicking on those little double-arrows toward the right side of their title bar. You can tear them off (*undock* them) and float them right next to where you are working in the interface. You can make your own groups of commonly used dockers. And, if you have a multimonitor setup, you can even drag them out of the application window and stick them on a different monitor so that you have the maximum amount of space for your drawing windows. It all begins on the Window | Dockers menu.

Opening, Moving, and Closing Dockers

Dockers can be opened using shortcut keys (if your memorized list isn't complete!), through menu commands, or through toolbars. For example, to open the Contour docker, choose Window | Dockers | Effects | Contour, or press CTRL-F9.

Dockers open to their last-used screen position and state, either docked or undocked. While *docked*, they are by default attached to the right side of your application window. Alternatively, dockers can be positioned on the left side of the screen or anchored on both sides of the screen with your document window in the middle.

While *undocked*, dockers float above the document window and can be positioned anywhere on your monitor screen(s). Docked or floating is *not* an all-or-nothing choice; you can have some dockers docked and some floating at the same time. The only situation you *can't* have is more than one copy of a specific docker open at one time.

Nested (Grouped) Dockers

When more than one docker is open, they often appear *nested,* meaning that multiple dockers overlay each other on the right side of your application window. While dockers are nested, clicking their individual title bars or name tabs brings them to the front of the interface.

A very quick way of building your own group of dockers that you can float is by beginning with one docker (display it by using the Window | Dockers command) and dragging it by its tab into the drawing window to float it. Then click the Quick Customize button at bottom right of the floating docker. As you can see in the next illustration, the Quick customize button offers an incredible wealth of additional docking palettes.

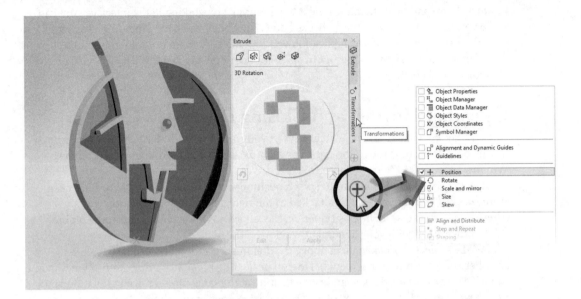

By default, the new docker you put a check next to appears in the right-side, docked position. You then click-drag the docker by its tab (not its title bar) and then drop it into the right column where the first floating docker's tab is located. See the following illustration.

Drag the tab, not the title, to the grouped tabs area.

To separate a docker when it's nested is the reverse operation. You drag the tab away from the group until you see a gray preview box of where the docker is going to land.

Tip To set whether title bars in floating dockers are visible, open the Options dialog (press CTRL-J) to the General page of the Workspace section, where you'll find an option called Show Titles On Floating Dockers.

Finally, if you want to maximize your drawing window area but still keep docked and nested dockers handy, you click the >> arrow guys at top right of the title bar, and the entire collection of dockers collapses to a neat column of titled tabs. To access any of the dockers once again, you click the tab of the docker you need, and the group extends again with the selected docker open and the others tabbed in the right column, which is an improvement over docker behavior in previous versions of DRAW.

It's Reality Check Time now: you bought this book as your guide to CorelDRAW, so it's a safe bet that you want to learn how to (a) draw, (b) draw with CorelDRAW, and (c) not have to read 14 chapters before getting to some of the "good stuff." Fair is fair. Chapter 3 puts you into the thick of it. You're going to create a fairly complex drawing in CorelDRAW, even if you've never owned a previous version or used a vector drawing program before. If this sounds unlikely, you'll be proven wrong shortly, because the author will sit invisibly on your shoulder, call out commands, and explain why the tools you're asked to use are the quickest and provide the best results.

C'mon. It'll be as thrilling as when you were a kid, the folks weren't around, and you checked out dad's rotary saw. And nothing in Chapter 3 will in any way take a corner off the dining table. Promise.

3 Diving In to DRAW!

Whether you're reading a tech book (*this* is a tech book) or an engaging work of fiction like a detective novel, a good author will bait you for the first few chapters and then—*BANG!*—you're off and running on a high-speed adventure by Chapter 3. In short, this departure from a standard teaching method is called "learning by *doing*."

Even if you're an intermediate-level user, you have to admit that the drawing in Figure 3-1 is pretty rich in detail and perspective.

This chapter shows you step by step, process by process, how to reproduce this scene, and along the way you'll become more familiar not only with the location of the tools you might use most often, but also with how they work together in a synergy that produces outstanding artwork in the time it takes to read a chapter in a book!

So let the author be your co-pilot; from here on in, you do the steering. It's going to be an exciting and educating journey—from File | New all the way to File | *Definitely* Save! Okay, that's not a menu item, but you *will* be pleased with how far you get in this amazing program with a minimum of coaching.

Working with the Star Tool to Build a Pattern

As you saw in the first figure, the child's ball is decorated with stars, all the same color, but of different sizes and angles of rotation. Additionally, the pattern of the stars suggests a bulge at the center, perfectly in keeping with the roundness of an actual ball—but this is a step we'll address later. For now, in the following steps, you'll grow acquainted with one of the tools in the Shape Tools group, the Star tool, and then you'll move on to editing a star, duplicating it, and eventually making a fill for the ball illustration. Follow along here.

FIGURE 3-1   By following through this chapter, you'll have a ball.

Tutorial ## Making the Background: Putting the Star Tool to Work

1. You'll use the Rectangle tool first to create a background, because you're not going to be able to see very light yellow stars against paper white to edit them! Choose the Rectangle tool from the Toolbox (or press F6). Then, while holding CTRL (to constrain what you draw to a perfect square), drag diagonally until the rulers tell you the square is about 4" and then let go of the mouse button.

2. On the color palette, click a light blue color to fill the square with a solid color. Pastel Blue is a good choice, and if you have tooltips enabled, hovering over the collection of blues will produce a callout confirming it's Pastel Blue your cursor is over.

3. It's star time. The Shapes tool group is directly beneath the Ellipse tool on the Toolbox. Any time you see a tick check mark at the lower right of an icon, that means it's part of a group and there are others in the group to access if you click-hold on the top icon. So click-hold and then move your cursor over to the Star tool to choose it.

4. As with the Rectangle tool, holding CTRL will constrain the star shape you click-drag to be perfectly symmetrical. Within the rectangle, marquee-drag a star about one-half the size of the rectangle now.

5. Click on the yellow color on the color palette docked to the right of the interface to fill the star with a solid fill.

6. By default, objects are created with a black outline, a very thin width and no fill. The outlines on the star and the background shape don't look very artistic, so choose the Pick tool (the top tool on the Toolbox), select the blue background, and then right-click on the "X" swatch, as shown in the following illustration. Then remove the outline around the star the same way. In this illustration, you can see a summary of steps 1–6, and the star has a white outline around it just so you can see it better in this book. It will actually have a thin black outline when you draw it.

7. Save the file (CTRL-S) and then find a location on your hard drive where it won't get lost. Don't close the file; we've hardly *begun!*

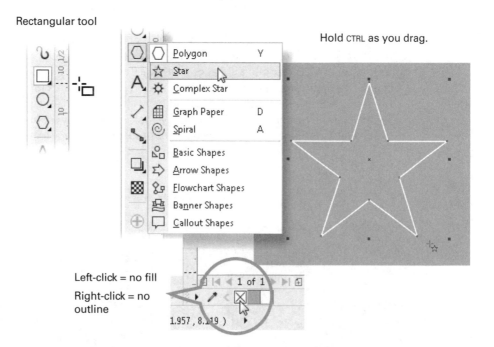

Rectangular tool

Hold CTRL as you drag.

Polygon Y
Star
Complex Star
Graph Paper D
Spiral A
Basic Shapes
Arrow Shapes
Flowchart Shapes
Banner Shapes
Callout Shapes

Left-click = no fill

Right-click = no outline

1 of 1

1.957 , 8.119)

Tweaking the Star Object

Like many "special" objects that are fast and convenient to create in DRAW, objects you produce using the Star tool can be modified at any time; even after you close the program and open it a week later (don't do this now). One of the unique properties of a star object is the capability to change the number of points or sides—from 5 to 11, for example—at any time, even if you extruded the star. Another special property, which you'll use next, is the degree of sharpness the points of the star have. When you first create a star shape, it has a value of 53, which is the sort of star shape you see on military craft and well-written third-grade papers. For this chapter, we want the stars on the ball to look a little inflated and cartoonish, which is more fun and light-hearted, so we'll decrease the Sharpness value before we get into duplicating and populating the blue background with stars. Here are two different approaches to modifying the star.

Tutorial Reshaping a Star: Technique 1

1. After click-dragging the star with CTRL held, filling the star with a solid yellow, and removing the outline width, put your cursor between the elevator buttons next to the Sharpness area on the Property Bar.
2. Drag downward until the star looks a little puffed up, or you've arrived at a Sharpness value of about 36. Hang on; there's also a manual way to do this, which involves getting to know another tool in DRAW.

Tutorial Reshaping a Star: Technique 2

1. Choose the Shape tool, the top tool in the Editing group, just below the Pick tool on the Toolbox.
2. Drag one of the convex nodes along the outline of the star slightly outward, as shown in Figure 3-2. You don't have to hold CTRL while doing this manual edit; there is no way to turn the star into a spiral or anything. The Shape tool is often used to change the appearance of "special" objects in CorelDRAW. For example, a rectangle produced with the Rectangle tool (and not hand-drawn) can have curved corners if you pull on the corner nodes with the Shape tool. As you grow more experienced with CorelDRAW, the Shape tool will become your tool of preference for editing.

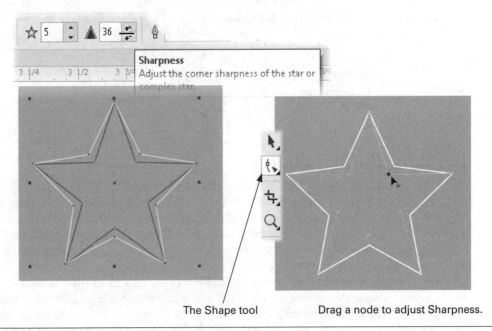

The Shape tool   Drag a node to adjust Sharpness.

FIGURE 3-2   Here is one way to stylize a star produced with the Star tool.

Making a Pattern of Stars

Let's think about how this star pattern should be designed. Stars of the same size, rotational value, and spacing would make a boring kid's toy and they'd soon abandon it and go back to their Xbox. So let's take this opportunity to make a visually interesting pattern by unevenly spacing duplicates of our plump star. You're going to learn the now-classic "drop a copy" technique for duplicating and moving objects, and you'll do a little proportional scaling along the way. You put these moves together, and no one will suspect that all the stars in the pattern on the ball began as one single copy.

Ready?

Tutorial ## Creating More Stars Than a Hollywood Agent

1. With the Pick tool, drag the star you just modified to a different location on top of the light blue background. It can go a little outside of the background rectangle if you're artistically inclined to add a bit of chaos to this ball's design. This is step "a" in the following illustration.
2. When you've arrived at the location where you want a duplicate of the star, with the left mouse button still pressed, tap the right mouse button. This drops a copy of the original where your current cursor location is. This is callout "b" in the illustration.
3. Release both mouse buttons, and the operation is complete; this is "c" in this illustration. You can do this as many times as you like, but you'll learn some steps to make the distribution and spacing a little more random next.

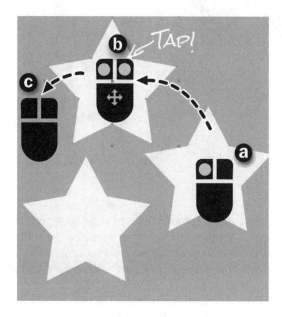

4. Press CTRL-S, but keep the document open.

Okay, it's on to refining and completing the pattern for the ball. Again, you can "drop a copy" or move a star so it's slightly outside of the background rectangle because the areas outside will be clipped eventually by a circle shape, representing the ball. We give the scaling and rotation features a workout next.

Tutorial Rotating and Scaling to Populate the Pattern Area

1. By the time you've dropped more than three copies of the star shape, you'll be running out of room on the background to make an intricate pattern! With the Pick tool, select one of the stars so you can see the eight bounding box handles, and then drag one of the corner handles—*not* one at 3, 6, 9, or 12 o'clock—toward the center of the star, as shown in this illustration. CorelDRAW provides a preview of what the final size of the scaled star will be; when you think it's an artistically appropriate size, release the mouse button and you've scaled the star, as shown here.

Drag a corner handle of the star toward its center.

Tip When you grab a corner handle to scale an object, the position of the scaled object changes—it moves to the corner opposing the control handle you're manipulating. If you'd like to scale an object from its center inward so its final position is the same as before scaling, hold SHIFT and drag any corner control handle.

2. Let's try out the rotation feature in DRAW now, so all the stars don't look like clones of each other, even though they are. When an object is not selected, there's no

screen element around it. When you select it, you'll see eight little dots bounding the selection, called selection handles, and you just used one in step 1. Now, when an object is selected and you click on it, rotation handles appear at the corners and skew handles appear at top bottom, left, and right. So click any of the stars right now, and then click the selected star to make the rotation handles visible.

3. Click-drag any of the four rotation handles to rotate the selected start, as shown in the following illustration.

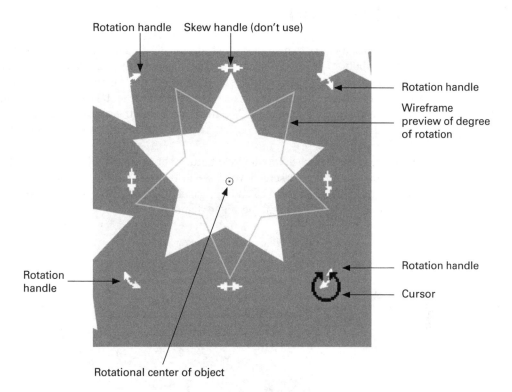

4. Okay. That's all you need to know to make about 14 stars of different sizes, different distances between one another (this is called *distribution,* and it's a feature in CorelDRAW's Object menu), and different degrees of rotation. Press CTRL-S, go get a refreshing beverage of your choice, and then read on to see how to turn a bunch of stars into a bulging bunch of stars—like the stars on the ball, except without the ball.

Shaping Operations and Combining Objects

Grouping objects requires very few brain cells: the shortcut is CTRL-G. However, in the steps that follow, you don't want to group the stars, leaving them as distinct objects, more or less like 14 passengers in the same bus. Instead, you want to perform the Weld operation, available on the Property Bar when more than one object is selected. This operation combines all the paths that make up the stars into one path whose components just happen to have spaces between them. This effect is sort of like the letter *O* when you type it. *O* is a combination of two circles that don't touch one another.

The reason why you're going from star-maker to welder will become evident after a few steps.

Trimming the Stars to the Background and Beyond

1. With the Pick tool, try to marquee-select (diagonally drag the cursor while holding the mouse button) only the stars on the page. If you see a small origin node on the background rectangle, that means it's selected, too, a natural mistake during precision work. To retain the selection of the stars but deselect the rectangle, hold SHIFT and then click on the background rectangle. You might notice on the status bar at the bottom of the workspace that "x number of objects selected" has decreased by 1, which is both a confirmation and a reassurance.

2. On the Property Bar, click on the Weld button, shown in the following illustration. If you look closely at your screen, you'll see little origin markers (nodes) on each star. This means you welded them all and this galaxy of stars is now one discontinuous object (there are spaces within the single shape).

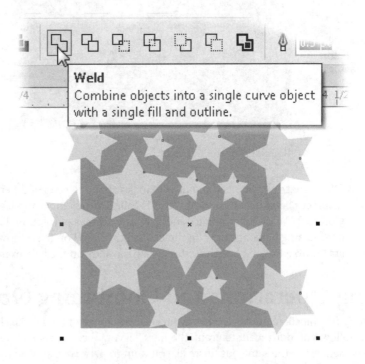

Weld
Combine objects into a single curve object with a single fill and outline.

3. Let's get rid of the star portions that lie outside of the rectangle background now; they won't be featured in the final composition. Select the background rectangle using the Pick tool and then press CTRL-C (Copy) and then CTRL-V (Paste). You now have a duplicate resting on top of all the other shapes. When you paste, the order of the new object is always on top of the others, unless you paste to a different layer (explained in Chapter 6).

4. Select the single star object (there should be a few places where the welded stars stick outside of the top rectangle), hold SHIFT (to additively select), and then click the Intersect button on the Property Bar, as shown in the following illustration. It will appear that nothing has happened, but this is because by default when you command DRAW to create an intersection between two or more objects, it does so, but it also leaves behind the original objects (unless you use the Object | Shaping docker, which can do very obvious and destructive editing).

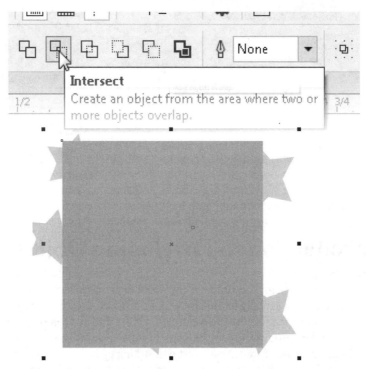

5. First, with the Pick tool, select and delete the top blue rectangle. This leaves the original welded stars, with the intersection result underneath. So click on any of the top stars and press DELETE. The illustration that follows shows what the Intersect object looks

like when it's moved away from the background—but this is only an illustration, not a step, so don't move the Intersect shape! All parts outside of the duplicated rectangle have been removed.

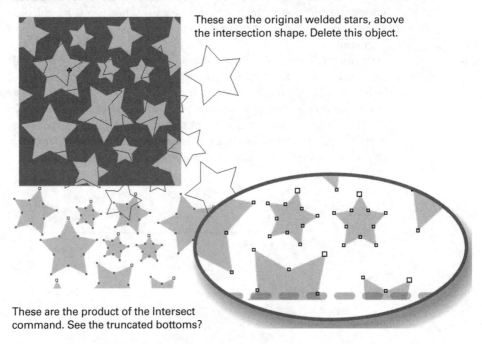

These are the original welded stars, above the intersection shape. Delete this object.

These are the product of the Intersect command. See the truncated bottoms?

6. Choose File | Save, and probably refill that glass with more refreshing beverage. The heavy-duty stuff is coming up next.

An Introduction to Enveloping Objects

The Envelope tool/docker (CTRL-F7) is perhaps the most sophisticated feature of its kind in any graphics program. You can turn any shape or group of shapes into Goofy Putty (we're not allowed to use the actually brand name here). You can stretch and twist at a number of control bounding nodes, yet this feature is not destructive. You can remove an Envelope effect at any time when the tool is active by clicking the Property Bar's Clear Envelope button.

In this next set of steps, you won't be working with the core feature of the Envelope tool—the control points—but you *will* use a preset (Circular) to make the stars conform to a round beach ball you haven't created yet.

Tutorial   Enveloping and Trimming the Welded Stars

1. With the Pick tool, select the intersected, welded stars.
2. Choose the Envelope tool from the Effects flyout group on the Toolbox. You'll immediately notice a bounding box with several control nodes, but don't touch them.
3. On the Property Bar, click the Presets List drop-down at the far left and then choose Circular. Figure 3-3 shows this and the previous step in sequence, and you have to admit the Circular envelope preset makes the stars look pretty darned cool!
4. You need to drag two guides out of the rulers now to establish the exact center of the background square, so you can create a circle on top of it—the stars finally get their well-deserved and much-anticipated ball. First, select the background rectangle; you'll see a very small "x" in the center, and this is the absolute center mark for both the rectangle and the stars, because the star-welded shape was intersected with a copy of the background, so they're both equal (more or less) in orientation and size.
5. Drag from the vertical ruler over to the little "x." You now have a vertical guide for the center of this composition.
6. Because you dragged a guide out of a ruler, the rectangle became deselected, so select it again and now drag a horizontal guide to the little "x" from the top horizontal ruler. See the following illustration.

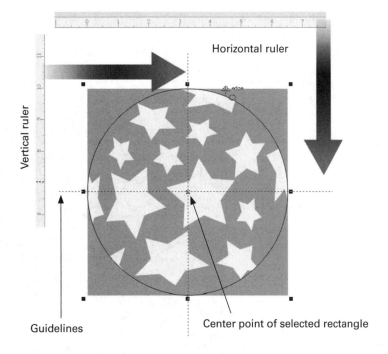

Horizontal ruler

Vertical ruler

Guidelines

Center point of selected rectangle

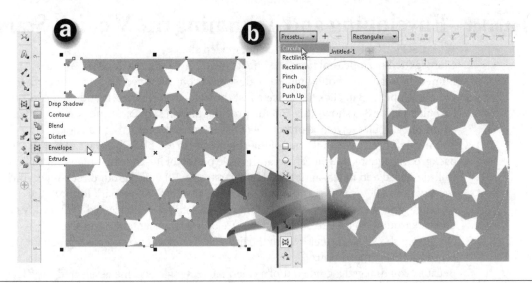

FIGURE 3-3   Use the Circular preset with the Envelope tool to make a "fisheye lens" treatment out of any group of DRAW vector shapes.

7. Choose the Ellipse tool from the Toolbox, put the cursor at the intersection of the two guides in the center of the square, and then while holding CTRL-SHIFT, drag away from the center, in any direction, until the circle produced is just a fraction smaller than the background rectangle, as shown in the next illustration. CTRL in this instance constrains the ellipse to a perfect circle, and SHIFT makes the direction of the oval created begin at the center point and expand outward.

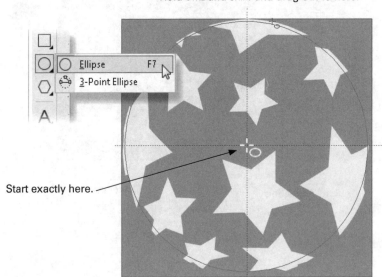

Hold CTRL and SHIFT and drag out to here.

Start exactly here.

8. Choose the Eyedropper tool from the Toolbox and click to sample the background rectangle for its exact color. The eyedropper cursor now turns into a paint can, ready to fill the next object you click over.

9. Click over the circle you created in step 7, being careful not to position your cursor over any part of the "stars" object. Now, the stars are hidden by the filled circle, but this is as planned.

10. Choose the Pick tool, select the blue background rectangle, and then press DELETE (or CTRL-X).

11. With the Pick tool, select the blue circle, and then on your keyboard press CTRL-PAGEDOWN. This is a shortcut command to Object | Order | To Back of Layer, and now the stars are on top of the circle. Be sure to remove the outline around the circle by right-clicking the No Outline swatch on the local color palette at the bottom of the page, or the global one on the color palette docked to the right of the interface.

12. You probably want to move the background object away from the circle and stars right now. With the stars selected, choose Object | PowerClip | Place Inside Frame. With the targeting arrow cursor, click on the background circle, and you now have stars on a ball, no actually trimming necessary; a PowerClip is nondestructive. Figure 3-4 shows all of this graphically.

13. Press CTRL-S, as usual!

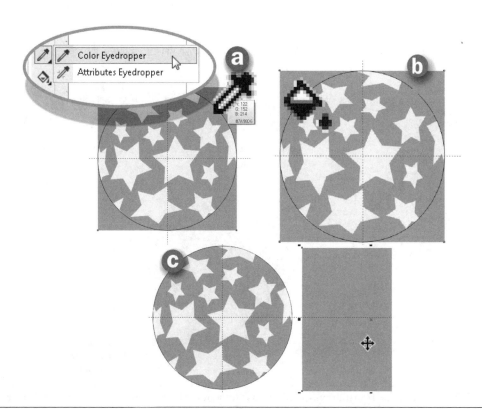

FIGURE 3-4   Pick up the color of the background and apply it to the shape that contains the stars.

Adding Shading to Your Composition

The perspective, choice of colors, and the general shape of a beach ball are all fine and in place. However, the quality of lighting is missing from this scene, and *lighting*—highlights and shading (and sometimes shadows)—is the quality and technique of classic painters (and has been for centuries). And you didn't buy CorelDRAW to become anything less than a modern-day classic Master now, did you?

The first thing you'll do is make a significant change to the beach ball's solid blue color by overlaying a tinted circle using X8's enhanced Transparency features—it's only proper that if the ball has shading, the stars should, too. Even experienced DRAW users should follow along here—in X8, it's easier than ever to set up a very complex fountain fill.

Tutorial Adding Lighting to the Beach Ball

1. With the Pick tool, click any part of the blue background and then press CTRL-C (Copy) and then CTRL-V (Paste). You once again have the stars hidden by a duplicate of the blue beach ball shape.
2. Choose the Transparency tool from the Toolbox. Drag from about 11 o'clock to 4 o'clock, as shown in Figure 3-5. You'll notice that the sphere appears to be solid at the top left, and the stars appear at the bottom right, where the Transparency Linear fill type is 100 percent transparent. This figure should get you acquainted with the elements, the

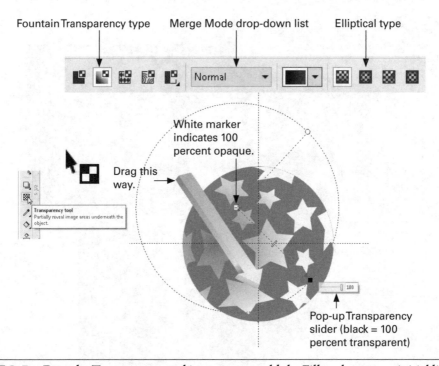

FIGURE 3-5 Drag the Transparency tool just as you would the Fill tool, to set an initial linear progression from a start color (or opacity) to an end point with different values.

controls, and *why you're getting the results that you are from these steps*—which is the most important part of this tutorial and of this book. The next stop is the Property Bar and a little assistance from the pop-up Transparency slider to create dramatic changes to this piece.

3. Although a duplicate of the result of the following steps can be seen on the right in Figure 3-6, you do not have to move or duplicate the object currently on top of your blue circle with the stars on top. First, click on the Elliptical Fountain Transparency button on the Property Bar, and the transparency values are going to be precisely wrong. Let's make corrections here.

4. Change the Merge Mode from Normal to Multiply. Doing this will intensify the shading you're going to perform.

5. The color node markers along the axis of a transparency fill are represented by white as totally opaque, black as totally transparent, and shades of gray indicating partial transparency. Click the beginning point marker, let the pop-up slider appear, and then drag the slider all the way to the right, making the marker black and making the beginning point of an elliptical (in this case, circular) transparency totally transparent.

6. Click on the end marker, the point you dragged to, and then on the pop-up slider set the value to 0, all the way to the left, making this area totally opaque.

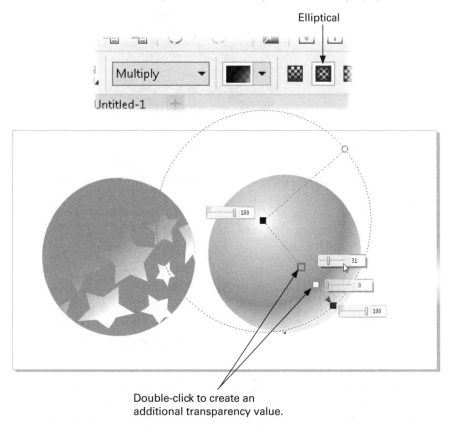

Double-click to create an
additional transparency value.

FIGURE 3-6 The ball will get its color detail from your drawing. It will get its tonal detail from this transparent object overlay.

7. At this point, you may be asking yourself, "What on Earth is the author doing here!?" Bear with him: you *add* transparency nodes by double-clicking the transparency line, that dashed guy that connects the Start and the End points. Double-click a point close to the end point, allow the pop-up slider to appear, and then drag the slider to anywhere from 12 to 0. Do you see what's happening? The bottom transparent area will serve as "rim lighting," making the beach ball look even that much rounder. This is a trick artists have used for centuries to make palace facades look more opulent and the royal family's children's faces look less flat.

8. One more double-click above the previous (zero value) marker. Give this new transparency marker a value of about 31.

9. Don't be afraid to experiment and move the markers along the transparency handle (the dashed blue guy) to increase or decrease contrast between neighboring transparency values (see Figure 3-6).

10. Let's assume you didn't move the duplicate circle to which you applied these various transparency values at different intervals. You should have a fairly dimensional illustration, like the one shown here.

Tip Don't be afraid to reposition—in fact, by all means *do* reposition—the beginning and end points of the transparency overlay if the beginning point isn't at the upper left and the end at about 5 o'clock. The rest of the composition depends on this lighting direction. Shadows and other elements need to be in synch and not contradict one another.

Adding Highlights and a Shadow

The beach ball doesn't look as shiny as new ones do, so the solution to illustrating this is to use a circular transparency inside of a circle whose size is larger than the end point of the transparency. The visual effect is that the highlight is feathered, like so:

1. With the Ellipse tool, drag an ellipse at the upper left of the ball, as shown in this next illustration. You can and should remove the outline width and fill the ellipse with pure white.

2. Choose the Transparency tool, drag it across the white ellipse, but do not let the beginning or end point of the fountain fill go outside of the ellipse. Put it in Screen merge mode from the drop-down on the Property Bar.

3. Increase the size of the ellipse using its control handles and the Pick tool if necessary. In the following illustration, you can see on the left the solid ellipse and on the right the ellipse with the Elliptical transparency applied. The white outline is there simply to demonstrate the bounds of the ellipse when it has no outline width and its transparency handles stay within the ellipse outline. On the far right, you can see the somewhat phony effect caused when you don't keep the transparency handles inside the outline of the object. What is supposed to be a soft highlight looks like a frosted glass oval with its outer dimensions clearly visible.

4. A good way to intensify this highlight without doing any amount of recalculations of values, midpoints, or any of that other jazz is to simply, now, select the highlight ellipse with the Pick tool and then press CTRL-C and then CTRL-V. See the following illustration, where there are duplicates of the ovals above the ball for comparison's sake.

Blending Yourself a Cast Shadow

CorelDRAW has its own Shadow tool, and it's covered in Chapter 18, but for now it would be good to try a manual technique for making a shadow beneath the ball. This ball is going to be resting on the floral pattern provided in the pattern for floor.cdr file. And as shadows go, they are never 100 percent opaque in real life. The solution? At least the one in this chapter?

You're going to create a small dark ellipse at partial opacity and put it almost underneath and to the right of the beach ball, and then create a larger ellipse that eventually will be 100 percent transparent and then blend the two. This way, there's not only a highly photorealistic off-center shadow beneath the ball, but in some areas, you'll be able to see the floor pattern. *Don't* get the idea that this is the last chapter in this *Official Guide* you'll need to read before becoming CorelDRAW Master (or Mistress) of the Galaxy. But what you're going to accomplish *is* pretty sophisticated and exceptionally cool.

Tutorial Making a Cast Shadow with Blends

1. With the Ellipse tool, create a small ellipse to the right of the ball, give it about an 88 percent black color, and give it a solid Transparency setting of about 94 percent. You achieve solid transparency by clicking the Uniform Transparency button on the left side of the Property Bar. Press CTRL-PAGEDOWN to make this circle go behind the one you'll create next.
2. Make a much bigger ellipse (see the following illustration), and give it a 30 percent black fill and about a 75 percent solid transparency.
3. With the larger transparent object selected (which might be a challenge without going to View | Wireframe), press SHIFT-PAGEDOWN to put the larger ellipse to the very back of the page, for the sake of a correct transparency-enabled blend. A dashed outline has been added to the larger, nearly invisible object in the following illustration so you have a reference as to where the ellipses go.

4. Choose the Blend tool from the flyout group above the Transparency tool, and then drag from the nearly invisible large ellipse to the small one, as shown in Figure 3-7. On the left, you can see the Blend tool being applied to the two ellipses—you'll notice a white node marker at each end of the Blend line, and a pair of acceleration handles in the center of the line. These handles perform a "preference" of one end of the blend over the other, and the effect when you drag the handles toward the ball is that more darker tones become visible, while at the outskirts of the cast shadow there is a gentle drop-off in color and opacity, which looks quite natural and photorealistic.
5. Press CTRL-S!

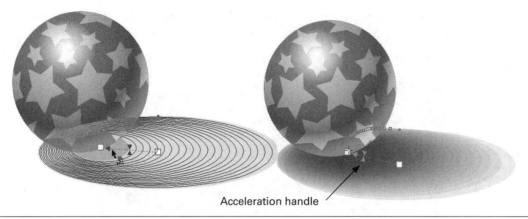

Acceleration handle

FIGURE 3-7 You have a lot of power and control over shadow-making when you choose to combine Blend steps with transparency.

Tip Even while two objects are blended together, the start and end objects *can* be *moved*. You might have to go to Wireframe view to select one of the objects, but once you do, you can create fine or coarse changes to the shape of your Blend object.

Adding a Background and a Floor in Perspective

Let's do the floor first because it's an exciting adventure into the Perspective tool—and there aren't a lot of exciting tech books out there. Select and copy the pattern from the pattern for floor.cdr document, and then paste it into the ball composition. From there, follow the steps outlined in the tutorial.

Tutorial A Starry Ball Sitting on a Floral Rug

1. If the author messed up when building these files and the pattern is on top of the ball, press SHIFT-PAGEDOWN to put it to the back of the layer. *Now* we're talkin'.
2. The shadow might be too light against the pattern, or too dense. If this is the case, select one of the control objects—perhaps the inner one is responsible for the shadow's imperfection—and then double-click on the Fill icon toward the right of the Status Bar, the one that has a red slash through it because it can't figure out a solid color within the Blend group. This displays the Edit Fill box and, in real time, you can lighten the

percentage of black of the chosen control object, and accept the change only when the Blend result looks good onscreen. See the following illustration.

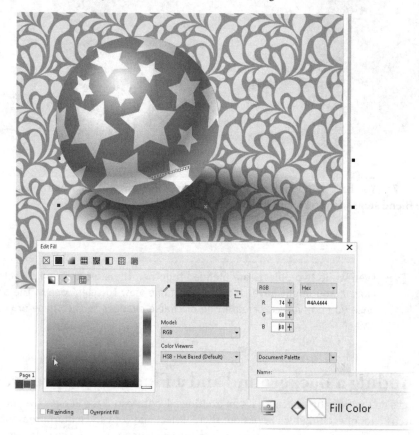

3. With the pattern selected, choose Effects | Add Perspective, and four black squares (handles for you to manipulate) appear around the four corners of the group of objects.

 Note Vector fills will not accept the Perspective command, and bitmaps distorted as much as you're going to distort them would make them suitable only for confetti. However, the author designed one of four tiles to create this large pattern—and as a vector and not a special object of any sort. So, you can pretty much do whatever you want in terms of distorting it.

4. This step is really easy and marginally fun: with the Shape tool, pull the bottom two control handles of the Perspective floor away from each other, and then drag the top two handles nearer to each other—but not by a lot, because by this tutorial's conclusion, you'll frame the piece and don't want bizarre empty triangles peeking through the background. See the following illustration for reference—and ignore the page border entirely.

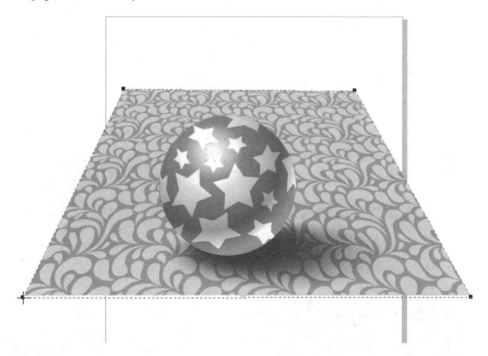

Completing the Composition with Embellishments

If the composition looks rough around the edges, that's because *it is!* The bottom edges of the floor look as though they belong on a 747, and the composition ideally should be portrait mode and all the superfluous and unnecessary elements should be hidden. Also, a simple frame around the ball and floor will truly complete the scene and your first project in this *Official Guide.*

Let's first extend the background's height by taking a black rectangle that fits over the ball and the narrowest section of the top of the pattern. And then you'll use linear transparency to seamlessly blend the top of the pattern's end with a gentle light falloff.

Framing Your Composition

1. With the Rectangle tool, draw a tall, moderately wide rectangle that covers the ball entirely and obscures the top of the pattern. Remove any outline width or color, and make it 90 percent or 100 percent, so it sort of reminds you of that monolith in *2001: A Space Odyssey*.

2. Take the Transparency tool and drag downward on this rectangle. Now comes the challenging part: you need to make the exact point at the top edge of the pattern 100 percent opaque, and then let the opacity gently fall off so you can clearly see the ball with no shadow casting on it. Today is your lucky day, though: you can select both the ball's components and its shadow and then press CTRL-PAGEUP to lift the order of the ball and shadow above the transparent rectangle without affecting the pattern. The illustration here shows all the action.

Linear Transparency is 100 percent opaque where the top of pattern ends.

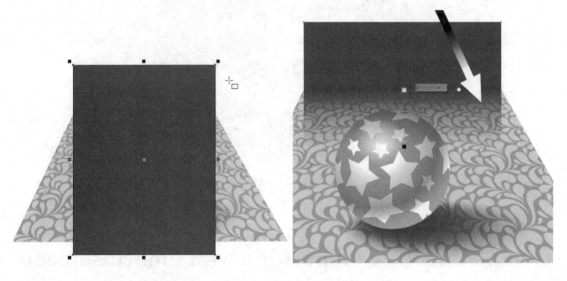

3. A frame around the piece is a no-brainer at this point; you already know how to use the Rectangle tool. However—and this is a big however—there's a new feature you're not familiar with yet (unless you're a Corel Pro, in which case don't spoil this one for the others) called the PowerClip feature, which we breezed through without explanation earlier in the chapter. A *PowerClip* puts things you select into another object, and the effect is like a door that's open, but can be moved around without anything spilling out of the closet. With the Rectangle tool, draw a rectangle around only those areas you want to be visible in your finished piece. A 16-point outline width is good and is used with a dull bluish-green outline to make the composition look a lot like the following figure.

4. Press CTRL-A to "select all." The frame is going to be the PowerClip container, so we don't want it in this selection. So with the Pick tool, SHIFT-click on the frame to exclude it from the selection.

5. Choose Object | PowerClip | Place Inside Frame. See the following illustration.

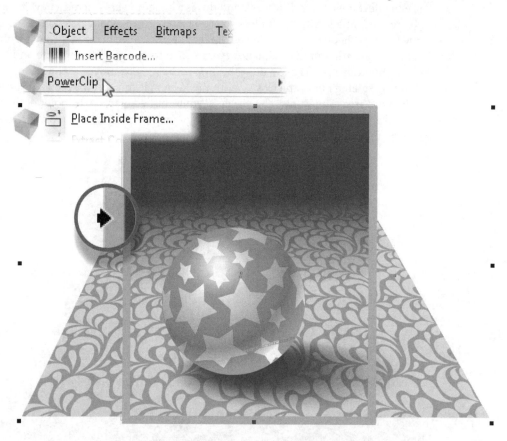

6. Your cursor turns into a right-facing arrow, and you click the frame object. BANG! All your hard work is perfectly framed with no unwanted areas sticking outside of the frame—and it should now look like Figure 3-1 at the beginning of this chapter.

You've done well. You should use CorelCAPTURE to make a copy of your finished product and e-mail it to everyone in your address book to prove you're getting results out of CorelDRAW and this *Official Guide*.

Hopefully, you'll enjoy the more relaxed pace when you flip to the next page. Let the book cool down for a moment; Chapter 4 is *not* going to be the 350-mph, "I don't know what I'm doing but it's sure fun!" chapter this was has been, because we need to shift back into first gear and take a comprehensive look at shape tools. You'll learn how you can transform special shapes to wind up with exactly the shape you need, and this will be without the benefit of getting into the drawing tools in Chapter 7.

But believe it or not, this test drive has shown you a lot of essentials for getting the most out of this program. Now relax, take deep breaths, find some Smooth Jazz on Spotify—the incline we're going to take to get to our destination isn't quite as vertical from here on out!

4 Working with Single- and Multipage Documents

You have an idea for promoting your product or service; you have your graphics, and you have some body copy and a snappy headline in mind. The next step is to define the dimensions within which you express your promotional idea. And this is where an understanding of CorelDRAW's Guides comes in handy.

Do you need a flyer, or perhaps a four-page booklet? This chapter covers the beginning of any graphics project: setting up pages in CorelDRAW. You'll learn about layout styles, page dimensions for your screen and for printing, and page reordering, and in the process, you'll gain a good working knowledge of what you need to do—and what you can tell CorelDRAW to do—to create a page that suits your ideas.

 Note Download and extract all the files from the Chapter04.zip archive to follow the tutorials in this chapter.

Setting Up Your Document Page

Every new file you create has its own set of *page properties* that have two attributes: physical properties and display preferences. The *physical properties* refer to the size, length, and color of each page as you'd define a physical page in the real world. *Display preferences* control how page values are *viewed*. Let's begin with the most common options and then move on to the more specialized features.

Controlling Page Size and Orientation

If you've unchecked the Always Show The Welcome Screen At Launch check box, the default size of a new document is CorelDRAW's default, which might depend on the language version of CorelDRAW you use. For this U.S. author, it's U.S. Letter, 8 1/2" by 11", but this can be changed. The quickest route for document size change is through the Property Bar while the

Pick tool—and no objects—are selected. The Property Bar features options for setting your page to standard and custom sizes as well as its orientation, as you can see in Figure 4-1. If you have a multipage document, the Property Bar also has ways to change all pages at once or only the currently visible page.

The Paper Type/Size and orientation options control the format of your document. When you have a specific format for a design you need to print, the following sections cover the options available to you in CorelDRAW.

Paper Type/Size

To make sure your CorelDRAW page matches the paper in your printer, clicking a Paper Type/Size option from the Property Bar is the quickest method. From the drop-down box, you can choose Letter, Legal, Tabloid, or other common sizes. Once you've made a selection, the dimensions are automatically entered as values in the Page Width and Height boxes on the

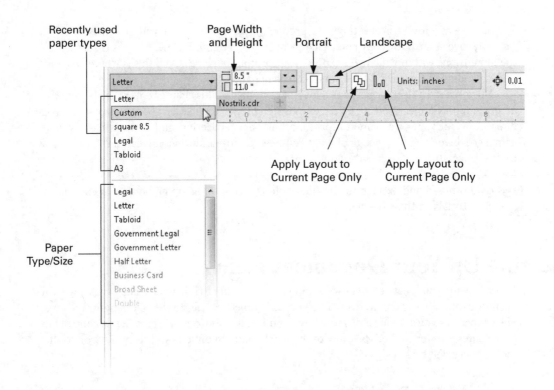

FIGURE 4-1 You change page size and orientation by using the Property Bar.

Property Bar. If you have a limited need for different paper sizes, click the Edit This List button at the bottom of the drop-down list, and you can delete seldom-used sizes: with the preset highlighted, click the trash can icon in the Options dialog. Here's a list of your paper type options; you'll surely find one or more that suit a specific need.

- **Page Width and Height**   You are not limited to a page size that's the same as the paper in your printer; page width and height values can be freely adjusted to match just about any paper size. For a custom page size, type specific values directly into the Page Width and Height boxes and then press ENTER.
- **Landscape/Portrait orientation**   Clicking either Portrait or Landscape on the Property Bar while using the Pick tool (with no objects selected) sets the page orientation. If the page width you enter is less than the page height entered, the orientation is automatically set to Portrait, and vice versa for Landscape. Changing from one orientation to the other automatically switches the values in the Page Width and Page Height fields.
- **All Pages/Current Page**   You can create a document up to 999 pages long, with different pages set to any size or orientation. The All Pages and Current Page buttons operate in "either/or" fashion—like the orientation buttons—so you can set the page size either for all pages in your document at once (the default) or only for the current page. To set only the current page to be different from the others in your document, click the right of these two buttons on the Property Bar (directly to the left of the Units drop-down) and set your new page size and orientation as needed. Other pages in the document aren't resized when you choose this option.

 Note   If you've unintentionally removed a page size you need later, you can re-create it. Click the Paper Type/Size drop-down list on the Property Bar and then choose Edit This List. Create, name, and save the page in the Options | Page Size dialog.

Page Viewing Options

With CorelDRAW at its default settings, when you select File | New, you'll see a rectangle in the workspace. This rectangle represents your document page in height and width. However, what you *won't* see is how your page will be printed to a personal printer or to a commercial press. Whenever you print a page, you'll see two areas called the *printable area* and *bleed area*, and you can add nonprinting guidelines to provide a page preview. This way, objects and text at the edges of your work don't get partially printed. You certainly want these features visible when designing for print; the grippers on printers often prevent edge-to-edge prints. To have CorelDRAW add Bleed and Printable Area (*safety*) guides to your page, press CTRL-J, choose Document | Guidelines | Presets, and then check Printable Area and Bleed Area, as shown in the next illustration. The bleed area extends to the edge of the page, and this is correct for personal printers, as explained in the following Note.

Note A *bleed* is the part of the printed image that extends beyond the edge of the page. When you're printing to a personal printer, there is no bleed because bleed is only relevant when a page on a commercial press is trimmed to final book size. For example, if a commercial press uses 12"×14" paper and the final trim size is 8½"×11", you could set up a bleed area of 10"×13" to make a design extend to the edge of the page the audience reads.

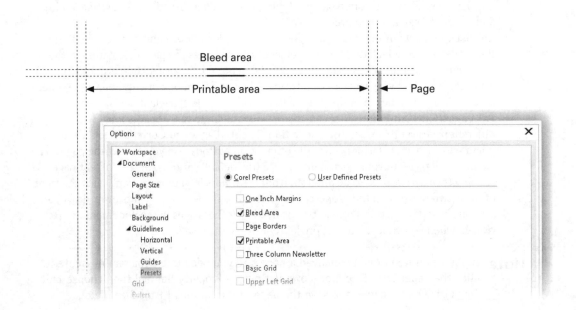

Note If you are printing to a borderless photo printer, your printable area will be the same size as your page border.

The Printable Area and Bleed Area properties depend on the printer options you choose in the Print dialog; this is an easy-access and logical location for print preferences in CorelDRAW. It's important that you have an element on the page before you can access CTRL-P (File | Print). Once you're in the Print dialog, you access the printer you want to choose along with basic options on the General tab. The Preferences button, shown next, takes you to the native print driver options, which is, for example, dependent on Canon's inkjet features, not Corel. To check out the trim, image positioning on the page, and other options, click the Layout tab.

Click to choose the printer's
page size and other features.

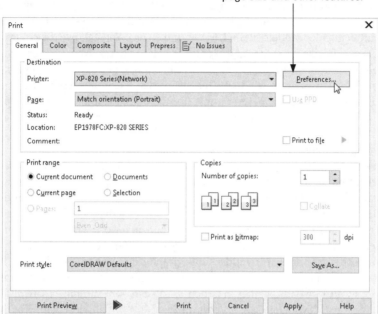

 Tip Setting a bleed amount is done using the Tools | Options | Document | Page Size area, using the Bleed num box. The bleed amount can be defined anywhere between 0 (which is the exact edge of your page) and 900.0 inches (which is silly). Be sure to put a check in the Show Bleed Area box before clicking Apply so you can see how your document is set up onscreen.

Controlling Page Background Color

To specify a page background color for your document, choose Tools | Options | Document | Background. Also, there's a convenient button on the Standard Bar that opens the Options dialog. By default, No Background is chosen in this dialog.

Tip You can skip the step of going to the main menu to choose Tools to get to Options. The Options button is located on the Standard Bar (which means it's always visible), with a tiny picture of check marks on it.

Page backgrounds are great for groups of objects that look like they're stranded in a sea of white. Also a background on the page can't accidentally be moved. Let's take a look at the various options you have before you:

- **Solid** Choose this option and a color from the selector to specify any uniform color as the page background. Click the drop-down list in the color selector to use a color picker in different color models (RGB, CMYK, and so on). You can use the color viewer to mix your own, or select swatches from specific color palettes. And handiest of all, use the Eyedropper tool to choose any color anywhere on your monitor; the Eyedropper can leave CorelDRAW's program window. This means that if CorelDRAW's UI is not maximized, you can use the Eyedropper to sample the color of an icon on your desktop! Once a color has been chosen, the page background is set to that color, but the bleed area and the workspace are not.

- **Bitmap** Choose this option to use a bitmap as the page background. Click the Browse button to open the CorelDRAW Import dialog and then locate and choose a bitmap. Background bitmaps are tiled as many times as needed to fill the page. You can also scale the number of repeating tiles by clicking the Custom Size radio button and entering values. The best bitmaps to use for patterns are ones that have been designed to tile seamlessly. In Figure 4-2, you can see a design you'll work with in a moment. Swimwear Sale.cdr uses an embedded muted ocean waves pattern, one of several you can use in the downloaded ZIP archive, to add a subtle graphical theme to the sale flyer. The Bitmap option is terrific for creating several different signs or stationery that contains different text but must be tied together in a theme. You can, for example, create different text on layers such as "Swimsuit Sale," "Vacation Sale," and "Inflatable Theme Toy Sale," and then print the various signs by hiding all but one layer for printing. You can't accidentally move the background, and this technique is quick to set up when you have 12 different messages that need a common background.

- **Source** The Source options let you establish an external link to the bitmap file or store a copy of it internally with your CorelDRAW document file. Choose Linked to maintain an external link or Embedded to store the bitmap with your document. While Linked is selected, the file path to the bitmap is displayed, and the bitmap itself must be available to CorelDRAW during printing. This option is very useful when you need to conserve on saved CorelDRAW file sizes; additionally, you can modify the background bitmap in PHOTO-PAINT or Painter, and then reload the edited bitmap in the future.

- **Bitmap Size** This field contains "either/or" radio buttons. If you choose Default Size, the background appears on the page because the bitmap's original dimensions allow it to tile as many times as needed to fill the page. However, if you want a smaller bitmap as the background (more tiles), you click the Custom Size button. The Maintain Aspect Ratio option is checked by default; you probably don't want the bitmap background to look smooshed or stretched—with Maintain Aspect Ratio turned on, all you need to do is enter one value in either the H or V field, and CorelDRAW automatically fills in the remaining field. Note that bitmaps are resolution dependent, unlike vector drawings. Thus, you can usually scale a bitmap down—but don't try to enlarge it, because the bitmap will go through something called *resampling*, and blurriness is often the result. Remember: scale down = yes; scale up = no.

FIGURE 4-2   Use a bitmap as a background for your design and text.

- **Print and Export Background**   Use this option to control whether the page background you've added to your document page is included when you export your drawing files or when you print the document. It's available when either Solid or Bitmap is selected for the page background; by default, it's active.

Open Swimware Sale.cdr now, and work through the Background options to change the waves background to something else you prefer for the piece.

Tutorial Changing a Background Bitmap

1. If you haven't already extracted the contents of the ZIP archive for this chapter, do so now, and create a folder for the PNG images and place them there.

2. With Swimwear Sale.cdr open, click the Options button on the Standard Bar (the gear icon) and then choose Document | Background in the Options dialog.

3. Notice that the Bitmap button is chosen (there is already a bitmap as the background), and that the bitmap is embedded. This means that unless you own the bitmap on your hard drive, the next step will forever overwrite this file (waves screened.png), something to consider when you embed a bitmap. Often, you might find it useful to simply externally link the bitmap background so you don't have to remember whether you have a spare copy of the image. Click Browse now to locate the folder of PNG files from Step 1.

4. Choose one of the PNG files, or you could choose your own image. With the file selected, click Import.

5. You can't preview the imported image as it will look; you can only click OK now to see how the new background has affected the composition. Before doing this, though, try setting Custom Size to something other than the default. If you're using one of this chapter's sample bitmaps, try setting the Height to about 2.5" and then put the cursor in the V(ertical) field; the amount should automatically turn to *a proportionately scaled amount* because by default the Maintain Aspect Ratio box is checked. Click OK, and the layout has a new background.

6. Optionally, you can open the Object Manager (Window | Dockers | Object Manager) and click the Visibility icon for the "Swimwear" layer so the little eye icon is closed. This clears everything from the page except the background image and the logo at the top. Now you can design a different flyer using the same background bitmap and logo by clicking, for example, "Vacations" to set the current layer.

Alternatively, when you want to perform variations on a page layout, see Chapter 6 for the details on working with Master Layers.

Tip If a bitmap background appears to have a white seam in an area, this is a visual effect of the bitmap trying to blend (*anti-alias*) with the page itself, which is white. If you zoom in and out, the thin white edge will disappear because at certain viewing resolutions the anti-alias blending matches the resolution of the tiling bitmap background. The design *itself* will print with no visible white edges; this is simply a page viewing issue.

Using Layouts and Labels

The Property Bar is used to set up basic page and paper sizes and orientation, but designers often need to lay out designs for items such as labels, booklets, tent cards, and greeting cards *that are printed on standard size paper*. These items are definitely *not* laid out like a single-page flyer. Happily, CorelDRAW provides specialized layouts that are just a few clicks away, so you don't have to sit at your workstation all day folding paper to try to figure out exactly where the fold lines are and where the text needs to be upside down. These timesavers are not on the Property Bar—you need to open the Options dialog to select the one you need from the Layout drop-down box.

Choosing Specialized Layouts

On the Layout page of the Options dialog, you can choose from seven specialized layouts for your document, including Full Page, Book, Booklet, Tent Card, Side-Fold Card, Top-Fold Card, and Tri-Fold Brochure.

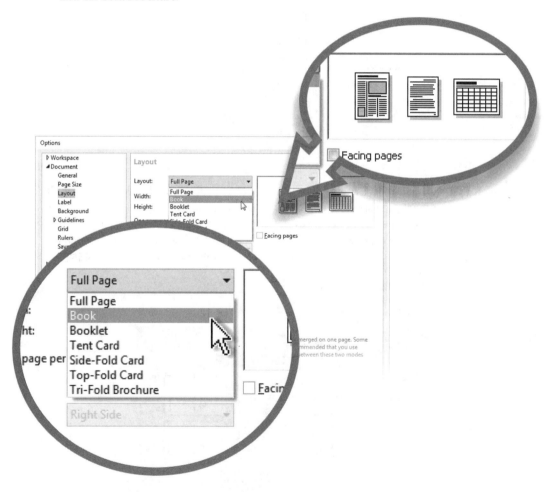

- **Full Page**   This layout style is the default for all new documents, and it formats your document in single pages, like those shown in the previous illustration.

- **Book**   The Book layout format, shown in the following illustration, divides your document page size into two equal vertical portions, and each portion is considered a separate page. When printed, each page is output as a separate page.

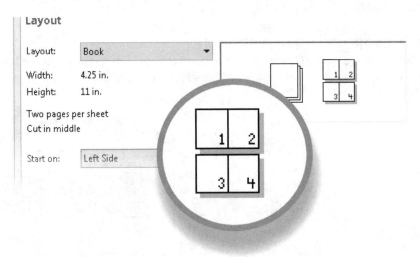

- **Booklet**   In a similar arrangement to the Book layout, the Booklet layout format divides your document page size into two equal vertical portions. Each portion is considered a separate page. When printed, however, pages are paired according to typical imposition formatting, where pages are matched according to their final position in the booklet layout. In a four-page booklet, this means page 1 is matched with page 4, and page 2 is matched with page 3, as shown here.

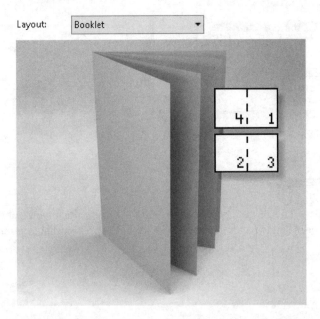

- **Tent Card**   The Tent Card layout format divides your document page size into two equal horizontal portions, although each portion is considered a separate page. Because tent card output is folded in the center, each of your document pages is printed in sequence and positioned to appear upright after folding.

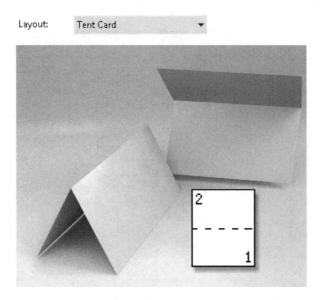

- **Side-Fold Card**   The Side-Fold layout format divides your document page size into four equal parts, vertically and horizontally. When printed, each document page is printed in sequence, and positioned and rotated to fit the final folded layout. Folding the printed page vertically and then horizontally results in the correct sequence and orientation.

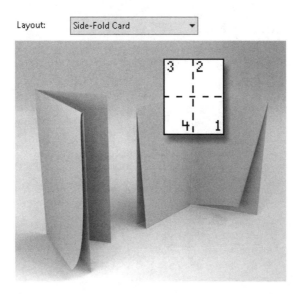

- **Top-Fold Card**   Like the Side-Fold layout, the Top-Fold layout format also divides your document page size into four equal parts, vertically and horizontally. When printed, each document page is printed in sequence, and positioned and rotated to fit the final folded layout.

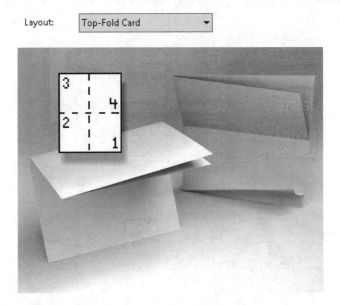

- **Tri-Fold Brochure**   Set your page orientation to Landscape by clicking the Landscape icon on the Property bar—using the Pick tool while nothing is selected. You now have the ideal layout for travel brochures and restaurant tabletop stand-up menus. You can print both sides for a total of six panels, with live space measuring about 3½" wide and 8" high on the end panels.

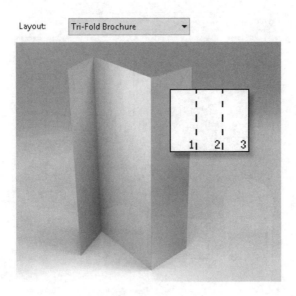

Using Preformatted Labels

CorelDRAW has a comprehensive collection of label formats for preformatted paper stock, from vendors such as Avery, Ace, and Leitz. To use most of these label formats, your document page should be set up for Portrait orientation. Once you've clicked the Label entry under Document in the left column, click the Labels button on the right panel, and then the Size page turns into the Label page, offering access to the label collection. After you've selected a specific label format, the preview window shows its general layout and indicates the number of rows and columns available, as shown here.

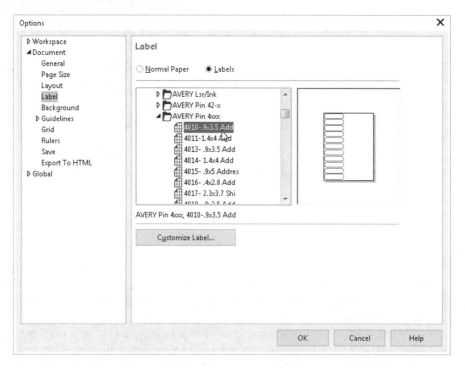

After you choose a label format and return to your document, each of your document pages will represent an individual label. You'll need to add the exact number of pages to accommodate all of your labels. If you don't see the exact manufacturer for your specific label type, you can create your own from scratch or base it on an existing label format (see Figure 4-3). Choose an existing label from the list of label types, click Customize Label, set the number of rows and columns, and then set the label size, margins, and gutters according to your own label sheet. Once you've created the format, you may save your label by clicking the plus (+) button next to the Label Style drop-down list or delete a selected label from the list by clicking the minus (–) button.

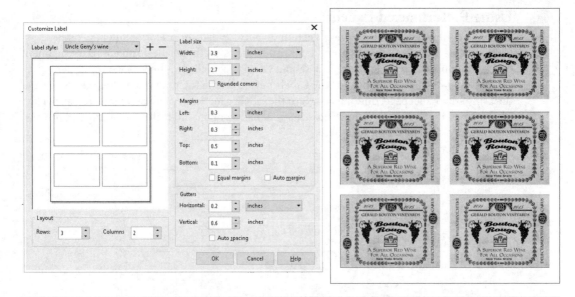

FIGURE 4-3 If you don't find the label you need, modify an existing label using the Customize Label options.

Naming Pages

Whenever a new document is created, CorelDRAW automatically creates the names, such as "Page 1," "Page 2," and so on. These default page names can be customized using several different methods.

When creating web page documents—where each document page is a separate web page—adding a unique name to the page creates a title for the exported page. When your document is printed, page names can also be printed in the margins, can indicate the contents of the page, and can provide other page-specific information. To do this, you use the Pre-Press tab in the Print dialog, choosing File Information options.

Tip Use the PAGE UP (previous page) or PAGE DOWN (following page) keyboard keys for fast navigation.

Using the Rename Page Command

Use the Rename Page command to assign a unique name to pages. Choose either Layout | Rename Page, or (more quickly) right-click the Page tab of your document window and then choose Rename Page from the pop-up menu to access the command. Using the Rename Page dialog, shown here, you can rename a page with a name of up to 32 characters, including spaces.

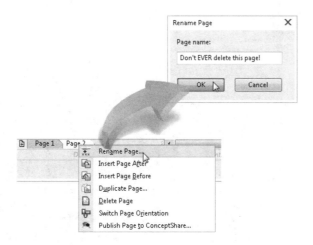

Saving Details with Your File

Document Properties is a CorelDRAW feature that provides details about a document you save without having to type in the margins. To access Document Properties—to both enter and view information—right-click on a blank part of the page. In addition to typing yourself little reminders, you can use Document Properties as a convenient method for tagging designs you export to JPEG and other bitmap file formats. As you can see in Figure 4-4, the same information you type in Document Properties is available to Windows users when they right-click your image in a file folder and then choose Properties | Details.

 Note Users who don't own CorelDRAW cannot access Document Properties info you've embedded in a native CDR file by right-clicking. The solution to this problem is to make them buy CorelDRAW!

Navigating a Multipage Document

To go to different pages in a document, click a Page icon at the lower left of the document window. If the page isn't in view, you can scroll to locate it, or (for lengthy documents) open the Go To Page dialog, shown next, by clicking between the Next Page and Previous Page buttons at the lower left of your document window. It's the field that lists the pages ("2 of 4,"

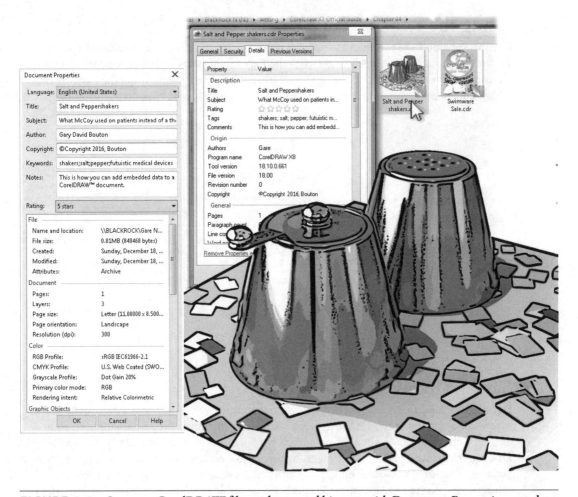

FIGURE 4-4   Save your CorelDRAW files and exported bitmaps with Document Properties metadata.

for example). The field turns light blue when you click on it. You can move quickly to a specific page in your document with this feature.

Click here to open the
Go To Page dialog.

Using the Object Manager

The Object Manager docker offers the advantage of mass-editing page names from within a single docker. To open the Object Manager, choose Windows | Dockers | Object Manager. Once the docker is open, you want to be able to see all the pages in your document, so first make sure the Layer Manager View (the third button at top—see the following illustration) is set to All Pages, Layers, and Objects. Then click the first of the three buttons at top, Show Object Properties.

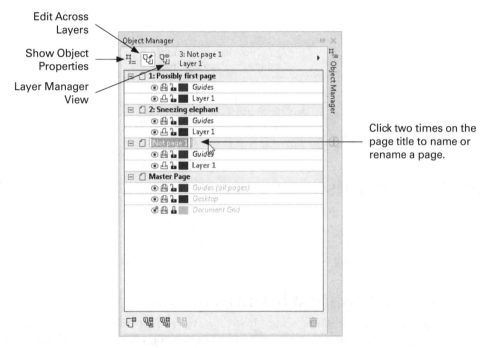

Edit Across Layers

Show Object Properties

Layer Manager View

Click two times on the page title to name or rename a page.

Tip The Object Manager is easily docked to the right edge of the UI, but you might accidently close it on occasion, and it's a pain to go through three menu levels to fetch it again. Try this instead: there is no key combo for Object Manager, so open Options (the shortcut is a button on the Standard Bar and also the keyboard combo is CTRL-J) and then go to Workspace | Customization | Commands. In the Commands area, there's a drop-down you want to set to Object. Scroll about three-quarters down the list until you find Object Manager. Click the Shortcut Keys tab and then insert your cursor in the New Shortcut Key field. Next, *hold* (do *not* type!) CTRL, keep holding CTRL, then hold ALT, then hold M. *As soon as the shortcut appears in the box, release the keys.* Don't go to sleep on them—make a definitive and quick entry, or multiple entries will go into the field. Click Assign, click OK, and you're done. Object Manager is easy to remember with the *M* you used in the shortcut, and in no time, you'll be able to call up the docker in its floating state, all ready to use.

In this view, all page and object names are displayed. To rename any page (or any object), click once directly on the page title to select the page you want to name or rename, click a second time to highlight the page name text, then type a name, and finally press ENTER. Page names appear in the Page tabs at the lower left of your document window, accompanied by a numeral indicating the page's order in your document.

Tip To see more (or less) of the pages of your document in the Page tab area of your document window, click-drag on the vertical divider between the Page tabs and the horizontal scroll bar.

Click-drag to expand/
reduce the Page tab area.

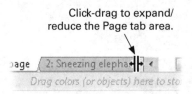

Page Commands

There are several ways to add and delete pages from a document; using menu commands, shortcuts while holding modifier keys, and certain page views are three methods. However, quick is best, and in this section, you'll see the most convenient way as well as methods that are easier to remember. You can decide for yourself which best suits the way you work.

Inserting Pages and Setting Options

From the main menu, choose Layout | Insert Page to open the Insert Page dialog, which has a host of options for specifying your new page properties and where you would like to add the new page in relation to your existing pages. Look ahead to the next illustration to get a better visual on the explanation to come.

In the Insert Page dialog, enter the number of pages needed in the Number of Pages box and then choose to add them either before or after your current page, or between specific pages in your document using the Existing Page box. You are not limited to the orientation or size of your current page when you add pages, unlike the constraints imposed by traditional printed books and magazines!

Tip To quickly add a new page to the beginning or end of your document, go to the first or last page and click the plus (+) symbol on the left or right of the page buttons at the lower left of your document window. To add a page before or after your current page, right-click the Page tab to the right of these buttons and choose either Insert Page Before or Insert Page After from the pop-up menu.

Deleting Pages

Deleting document pages can be done by choosing Layout | Delete Page from the main menu; you can delete one or more of the existing pages in your document. By default, the dialog opens to display the current page as the page in the Delete Page box, shown on the right in the following illustration, but you may select any page before or after your current page if you choose. To delete an entire sequence of pages, click the Through To Page option, which enables you to delete all pages in a range between the page specified in the Delete Page dialog through to any page following your current page. Pay careful attention to the word "Inclusive" after the last page number: if you type, for example, 10 when you want to delete pages 1–9, well, oops—there goes your day unless you press CTRL-Z immediately!

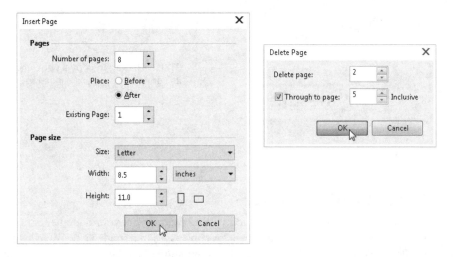

Tip To delete the current page, right-click the page name on the Page tab and then choose Delete Page from the pop-up menu. *There is no confirmation* when you delete a page, so make sure you've had your second cup of coffee in the morning before doing this.

Moving and Duplicating Pages

You're going to create such fantastic content in CorelDRAW that you might not even want to delete it. Instead, you might want to move and/or copy pages. To move a page, use a click-drag action on the Page tab to drag it to a new position. To copy a page—*and all its contents*, thus creating a new page order—hold CTRL while click-dragging the Page tab, moving the page to a new position. You can see this in the next illustration. CorelDRAW does not duplicate the name of a user-named page; you'd wind up with an organizational nightmare if it did, so it's a good practice to name a duplicate page after you've created the copy.

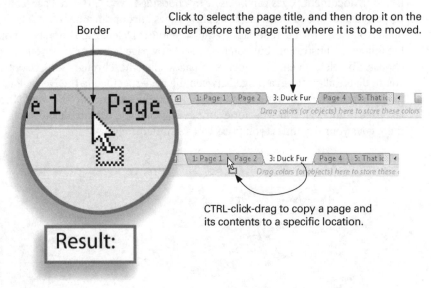

Click to select the page title, and then drop it on the border before the page title where it is to be moved.

Border

CTRL-click-drag to copy a page and its contents to a specific location.

Result:

Using the Page Sorter

Page Sorter is a view that provides you with a broad look at your document and all its pages. In this view, you can add, delete, move, or copy pages in a single view. You can also change the Paper Type/Size setting and the page orientation of all the pages or just selected pages. A CorelDRAW document can contain pages of different sizes, which can be very handy when you are designing matching business cards and letterhead or other similarly related materials. To open your document and all its pages in Page Sorter view, choose View | Page Sorter View. Page Sorter displays all pages in your document.

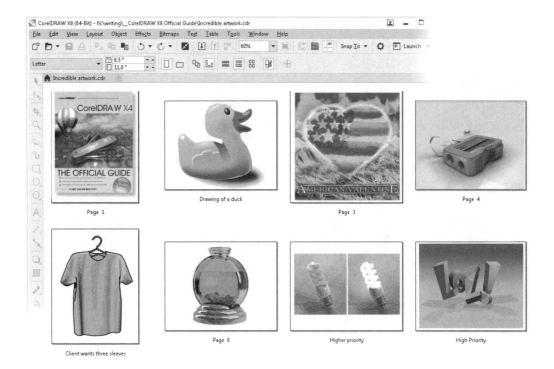

Tip Using Page Sorter, you can export either your entire document or only selected pages quickly. Click to select the page you want to export and choose File | Export, or click the Export button in the Standard Bar to open the Export dialog. To export only specific pages, click the option Export This Page Only, which, by default, is not selected. Exporting is *not* to be confused with *saving;* exporting pages is usually done to get your work into bitmap format, Adobe Illustrator file format, or Corel Media Exchange (CMX). Note that with some file formats such as PNG, it is not possible to "batch export" individual pages to a file.

In Page Sorter view, a single click selects a page. Holding SHIFT while clicking pages enables you to select or deselect multiple contiguous pages. Holding CTRL while clicking enables you to select or deselect noncontiguous pages. The following actions enable you to apply page commands interactively to single or multiple page selections, as seen in Figure 4-5:

- **Move page(s)**   To move a page and change its order in your document, click-drag the page to a new location. During dragging, a vertical I-beam appears, indicating the insertion point for the page or the first page of the selected sequence of pages.
- **Add page(s)**   To add pages to your document, right-click any page and choose Insert Page Before or Insert Page After from the pop-up menu to insert a page relative to the selected page.

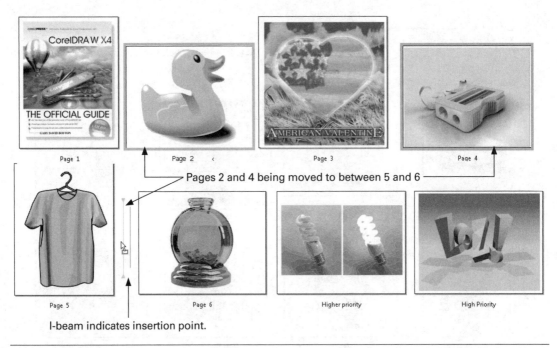

Page 1   Page 2   Page 3   Page 4

Pages 2 and 4 being moved to between 5 and 6

Page 5   Page 6   Higher priority   High Priority

I-beam indicates insertion point.

FIGURE 4-5 Page Sorter helps you manage your document pages interactively while viewing all page properties.

- **Copy page(s)** To copy pages—and their contents—hold CTRL while click-dragging the page to a specific location. During dragging, a vertical I-beam appears, indicating the insertion point for the page copy or the first page of the selected sequence of pages.
- **Name or rename a page** To add a new name or change an existing page name, click the page itself and then click the name below the page to select it. Click a second time to highlight the page title and then enter a new name. Finally, press ENTER. You can also rename a page by right-clicking a specific page and choosing Rename Page from the pop-up menu to highlight the page name for editing.
- **Change page size/orientation of all pages** In Page Sorter view, the Property Bar displays typical page property options for applying standard or custom page sizes and changing the orientation between Landscape and Portrait.

  If you want to change the orientation of *all* the pages in the document, click the All Pages button on the Property Bar and *then* click either the Portrait or the Landscape button to change all pages to that orientation.
- **Change page size/orientation of selected pages** If you only want to change the orientation of some of the pages, click the Current Page button. Select the pages you want

to change and then click the Portrait or Landscape button to change the page(s) to the desired orientation, as shown here.

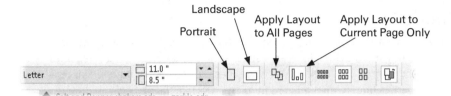

Landscape

Portrait

Apply Layout to All Pages

Apply Layout to Current Page Only

Page 1

Page 2

Page 3

Page 4

Changing the orientation in Page Sorter view not only changes the view but also how the pages themselves are oriented in the document. As you can see in this illustration, the first and last pages have drawings that look better in Portrait view; you CTRL-click pages 1 and 4 in this example, click the Current Page button, and both the Page Sorter view and the pages themselves are reoriented. If you want to rethink this dynamic change, repeatedly press CTRL-Z (Edit | Undo Edit Properties) to restore your document.

Exiting Page Sorter view is easily done; click the Page Sorter View button. Any changes applied while in the Page Sorter are applied to your document.

Tip To exit the Page Sorter view and immediately go to a particular page in your document, double-click the page.

Working with Guidelines and Guide Layers

Now that you have a handle on page setup, multipage particulars, and page dimensions, it's time to turn to perhaps the first thing you *put* on a page: a guide. Guides help you design with accuracy and give you a perspective on a composition so you save time second-guessing where items should be in relation to one another.

CorelDRAW's page guides, dynamic guides, and objects you put on guide layers don't print. Guides are just like the blue lines some of us used to draw on drafting tables before computer graphics. With CorelDRAW's digital tools and electronic guidelines, you have the precision only a cutting-edge computer application can offer; plus, you can place your guides with the same speed and ease as any object you draw on a page.

The following sections are the operator's manual for guides: how to use them and how to customize them.

Using Guidelines

Guidelines placed on your document page extend between the top, bottom, left, and right edges of the document window. Guidelines appear as vertical and horizontal dashed lines, but guidelines can also be *rotated.* In CorelDRAW, guidelines are considered unique objects—they have their own properties but are manipulated in many ways like the objects you draw.

To view or hide the display of guidelines in your document window, right-click a blank area of the page and then choose View | Guidelines. By default, a new document doesn't have any guidelines—you need to create them. To have objects *snap* to the guidelines you create, choose Snap To | Guidelines on the Standard Bar, as shown here.

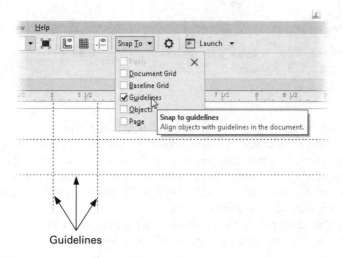

Guidelines

Manipulating Guidelines

The following steps guide you (pun notwithstanding) through the tasks you'll need most often when working with guides:

- Make sure the rulers are visible; they're where many of the guides live. With the Pick tool selected, and no objects selected, right-click and then choose View | Rulers. Then, using any Toolbox tool you like, click-drag beginning on a ruler and then release the mouse button anywhere in the workspace. Although dropping a guide on the page is most useful, you can certainly create a guide on the pasteboard area to measure and align objects not currently placed on the page.
- To move a guide, you need to select the Pick tool. Then hover the cursor over the guide you'd like to move; when the cursor turns into a double-headed arrow, you're all set and all you need to do is to click and drag the guide.

- If you want to eliminate a guide, hover over it with the Pick tool until you see the double-headed arrow cursor (to indicate you've selected it), click the guide to confirm it is "in focus" in the interface, and then press DELETE or CTRL-X.
- If you need a guide that travels diagonally, you create the guide first. Next, click it to select it and then click a second time; you'll see a center and rotation handle. One of the neat things about rotating a guideline is that you can move its center point before dragging on the rotation handles to, for example, rotate a guide around the corner of a shape you have on the page. You move a slanted guideline exactly as you do a perfectly horizontal or vertical guide—you click-drag it to reposition it. In the illustration of the maze, where the design needs shafts of light emanating from a center point, that is *not* the default center of a guide that's put into slant mode. No problem; you change the center of rotation and then drag a rotation handle clockwise or counterclockwise. See the illustration; it should shed some light on guidelines. Sorry.

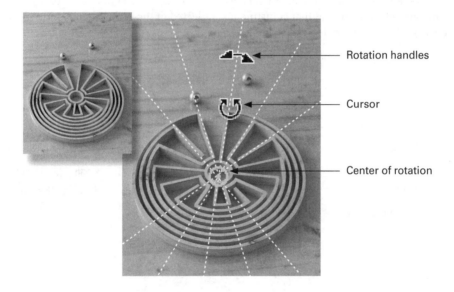

Rotation handles

Cursor

Center of rotation

Tip   Treat a guide like any other object on the page. You can move and rotate several guides by SHIFT-selecting them. You can also drop a copy of a guide, like you do to duplicate objects.

Controlling Guideline Properties

If you want to place several guidelines at an exact spacing, you manage them all via Tools | Options | Documents | Guideline. Separate subsections are here for controlling the vertical, horizontal, and slanted guidelines. You can also right-click either of the rulers and choose

Guidelines Setup, and a Guidelines docker appears. Additionally, while a guideline is selected in a document, you can open the Guidelines docker by clicking the Guidelines button on the Property Bar.

Tip You can also double-click a guide in the drawing workspace using the Pick tool or the Shape tool to display the Guidelines docker.

The engineers at Corel have simplified the process and centralized your options for guidelines placement, all through the Guidelines docker. You first choose Horizontal or Vertical Guides from the drop-down list; the Y box becomes active, and you type in a value and then click Add. Remember, the Y measurement is, by default, the same as the rulers: values increase from bottom to top. You also have a lock option. You can change a guide's value on the page by typing in a new value after you've clicked the guide in the list and then clicking the Modify button. Additionally, at any time, your cursor can "step out of the box"; you can make a manual adjustment, and that adjustment is reflected in the inches value on the Guidelines docker's list. Try it out; it's quite a cool feature.

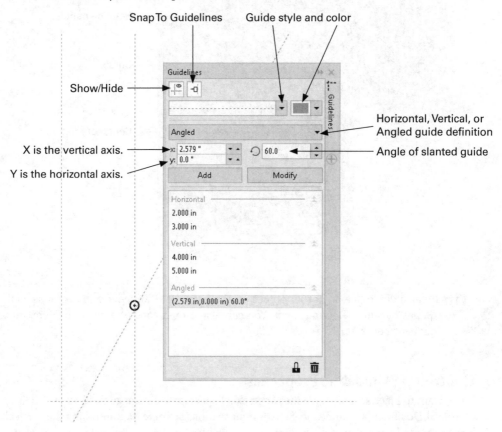

Tip Changing the color and style of guidelines is quite handy, for example, if you're designing a series of medium blue rectangles. You'd certainly want to choose a contrasting color for the guides! Choose Tool | Options | Document | Guidelines to do this.

Adding, Deleting, and Moving Guidelines

You can adjust guides using the Guidelines docker's Modify feature. The list below the main area on this docker contains the position of the existing guidelines on your document page. Here are steps to perform common tasks:

1. To create a new guideline, first choose Horizontal or Vertical from the button drop-down. Now, enter a value in the Horizontal, Vertical, or Angled num box, according to the position where you want the new guideline to be created, and then click the Add button. A new guideline is created where you want it.
2. To move an existing guideline, click it in the list, type the new value in the x or y num box, and then click the Modify button. The selected guideline has moved, and on the list you can see that its new location is correctly entered.
3. To delete a specific guideline, select it in the list and then click the trashcan button in the lower-right corner on the docker. The selected guideline is gone from the page and your document is immediately updated, as you can see on the page from your current view.
4. To remove all guidelines in the list, marquee-select all the entries on the list and then click the trashcan button.

Locking and Unlocking Guidelines

All guidelines are editable by default; you can move or delete them using the Pick tool. But occasionally a guideline that moves accidentally is as welcome as a friend holding your ladder sneezing accidentally. You can lock a guideline simply by selecting it with the Pick tool (the cursor should turn into a double-headed arrow straddling the guide) and then choosing Lock Object from the pop-up menu when you right-click. Unlocking a guideline is the inverse process of locking one. With the Pick tool, right-click over the guideline and then choose Unlock Object from the context menu.

Working with the Guides Layer

Guides belong to a special layer—named Guides on the Object Manager—reserved just for these assistants. To view the layers in your document, open the Object Manager by choosing Window | Dockers | Object Manager. There are two Guides layers: if you click the Guides (All Pages) entry on the Object Manager list under Master Page, every guide you create will be featured on this page and on every page you create in the future in this document. On the other hand, every new page, including the first page, comes with its own Guides layer, and guides specific to a layer will not show on other pages. By default, all guidelines on the Guides layer are set as visible, nonprintable, and editable. You can change any of these options by clicking the symbols to the left of the Guides layer in the Object Manager docker, as shown here.

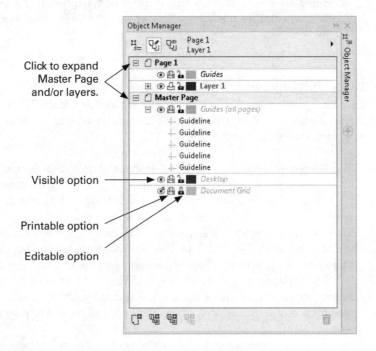

To set all options for a layer at once—including the display color of objects on the Guides layer in the Object Manager docker—right-click the layer name (for example, the Guides layer) and then choose Properties from the pop-up menu. Doing this opens the Guides Properties dialog to reveal further options.

Making an Object a Guideline

You can make almost any drawing shape into a guideline. Going the other way around, you can also turn a guide into a drawing object, and moving any guideline to a drawing layer automatically makes it a printable object. You use the Object Manager docker to move objects between layers. Moving any object to the Guides layer makes a guideline, with all the same properties as a typical guideline, except it doesn't have to be a *line*—spirals and trapezoids make useful guides. After an object becomes a guideline, anything you draw in its proximity snaps to it, as long as the Snap To Guidelines option is active. Think of the artwork you can clean up and refine when you're tracing over the original with a drawing tool that snaps to the original.

To move an object to the Guides layer, follow these steps:

1. Create or select at least one drawing shape that you want to use as a guideline.
2. Open the Object Manager docker by choosing Window | Dockers | Object Manager.
3. Expand the tree directories in the Object Manager docker to locate both the Guides layer on the Master Page and the shape you want to make into a guideline so that both are in view.

4. In the Object Manager docker, click-drag your shape icon (not the shape on the page) from its current page and layer to on top of the Guides layer title on the Master Page. As you drag, your cursor changes to an arrow pointing at representations of layers, indicating the shape's current position as it is dragged. You then release the mouse button, and the operation is a success. The following illustration also shows a "before and after" of a freeform object when it's moved to the Master Page Guides layer. Unlike guidelines you drag from rulers, a user-defined guide doesn't have the look of a dashed line; it's a solid line with no fill.

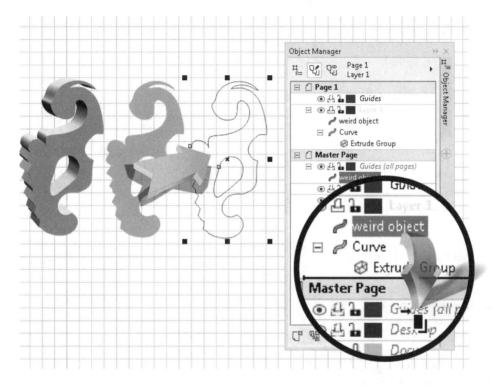

Generally, after you move a shape to the Guides layer, it's a good practice to lock the layer. A guide that moves when you don't intend it to is as useful as putting a stepladder on a pair of roller skates.

The New Alignment and Dynamic Guides Docker

Dynamic Guides now feature alignment and margins between objects as an additional perk in CorelDRAW. You'll find the Alignment and Dynamic Guides docker under Window | Dockers. The docker actually has three areas of functions—Alignment, Guides, and Margins—and you can enable all of them (although your screen might become cluttered with data you don't need), or uncheck one or more of the functions to use only what you need. The following sections take you through the features and buttons as well as how and why you'd use these features, by way of example.

Alignment Properties on the Docker

Before moving forward, do *not* mistake the Alignment feature on this docker for the Align and Distribute docker (CTRL-SHIFT-A). The Alignment and Dynamic Guides docker is a manual feature—it reports to you and offers suggestions, but it does *not* align things *for* you. It's a really sophisticated ruler, not a pocket calculator, as analogies go.

Figure 4-6 shows the Alignment features in action. To begin at the beginning, you must check the box for Alignment Guides on the docker before you can do anything with the Alignment and Dynamic Guides docker.

Okay, the author is trying to renovate North Carolina Avenue by adding affordable housing (a $200 house fits most people's budgets). The goal here is to align the house at the

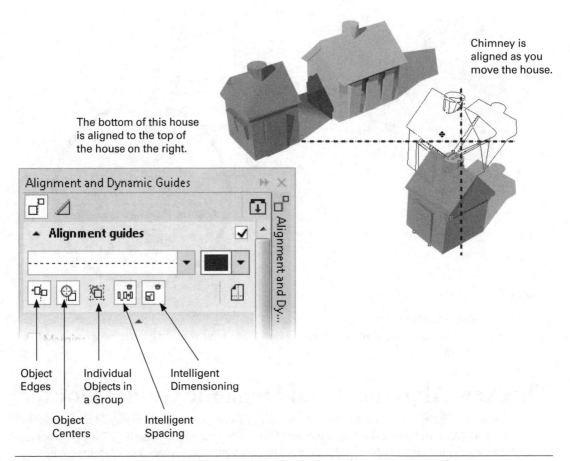

FIGURE 4-6 The Alignment and Dynamic Guides docker helps you in precise design measurements and placements, and it disappears when you're done.

bottom right of the housing.cdr file (open it and try this yourself). By simply using only the Alignment features (Margins and Dynamic Guides are disabled), you don't have to hold CTRL to constrain movement, and all you do is drag up and a little to the left until you can see that the chimney hasn't moved horizontally at all as it has moved up vertically—the dashed light-blue alignment guide demonstrates this when your object is aligned. Also, the guide disappears if your object is moved out of alignment or if you release the mouse button.

Figure 4-6 also shows the option buttons in the Alignment area, and they're new—and important—so a little time is devoted to their function in the following list.

- **Object Centers** Click this button if you want these temporary guides to appear when the object you're moving becomes aligned, vertically or horizontally, with the center of other objects on the page. This option is really good for quickly making an accurate distribution of several objects that you need to space apart equally.
- **Object Edges** This option is good to use in combination with Object Centers, so you can see exactly where in relationship to another object your desired object lies. In the case of aligning a square with another square, you will see two guides: one indicating top-edge alignment and the other indicating bottom alignment.
- **Individual Objects in a Group** When you need to align grouped objects, it's not necessary to ungroup them and then use either the Alignment and Dynamic Guides docker or the Align and Distribute docker. Nope. Instead, you can use the Pick tool to CTRL-click the lucky object to be aligned to something else in the drawing, and then move it around until the temporary guides tell you that your object is now realigned, as shown in this illustration.

CTRL-click with Pick tool to move one object in the group.

The object horizontally aligned (top, center, and bottom) to itself

The object vertically aligned to the left of the large circle

Group of three weird objects

- **Intelligent Spacing** This feature is sort of like an equidistant distribution function. In the following illustration, you can see that the diamond is selected, and the goal is to place it an equal distance between the club and the spade. You'll see these unique divider guides when the object is in the desired position, and the Intelligent Spacing option even tells you onscreen what the distance is between objects; in this case, the x-spacing (horizontal) is 0.115 inches. Naturally, if you have units set up to a value other than inches, Intelligent Spacing will report picas, centimeters, and so on.

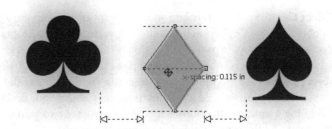

- **Intelligent Dimensioning** Ordinarily, you'd want to hold CTRL to proportionately scale a selected object larger or smaller, but this is unnecessary when you've selected an object and clicked the Intelligent Dimensioning button. Open Brochures.cdr and give this feature a try. The left pamphlet is smaller than the one at right; also they are identical copies of each other. Suppose your boss unreasonably demands (at a quarter to five) that the left pamphlet be the same size as the larger one on the right. No problem; as shown in this illustration, you click the Intelligent Dimensioning button in the Alignment area of the docker, and then with the Pick tool you drag any corner control handle away from the center of the tiny pamphlet. Once the special blue guides appear for either the height or the width, you can release the mouse button, and both objects are identical out to three decimal places.

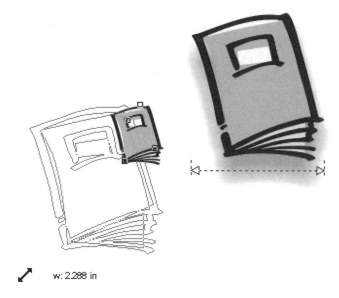

Adding Margins to the Mix

Aligning things can be an exciting sport, especially on rainy days, but artistically, there are often times when you not only need to align objects but also add space—a margin—between the objects. And this is where the Margins area of the Alignment and Dimensioning docker comes into play.

Like the Alignment options, margins can be set to any color and be dashed or solid in appearance, so there's zero chance that what you're aligning will be the same color as these guides. The feature is simple to use and to explain. You should have Align Edges and/or Align Centers enabled in the Alignments area first, or the margins won't be awfully relevant to your aligning efforts. Enable margins you want between the aligned objects. Pick one of the objects and then start dragging it toward the other object. See the following illustration; it can't hurt. You'll see by the alignment guides when the tops and/or bottoms are aligned, but then you'll see markers, shown in the illustration, that tell you when you've reached the desired margin between the objects.

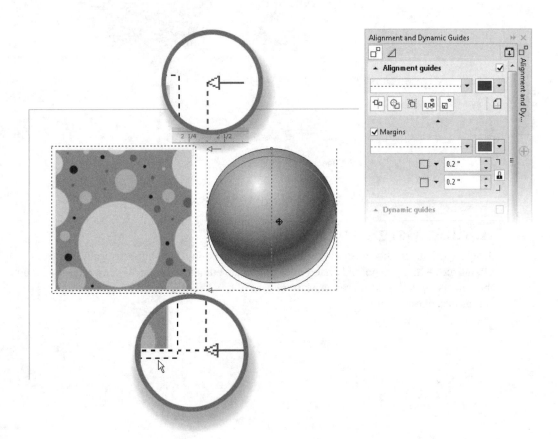

Dynamic Guides

Okay, this is the weird and wonderful part of the Alignment and Dynamic Guides docker. Dynamic Guides can actually help you draw technically accurate objects because your cursor snaps to the nearest of angles that you enable on the docker.

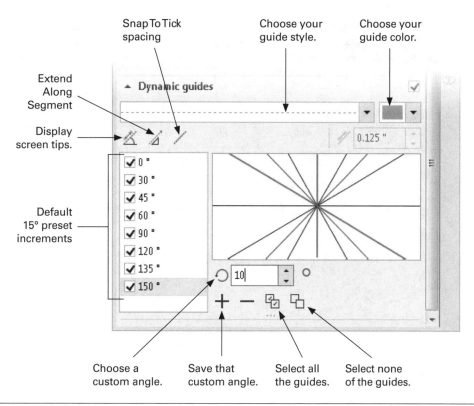

FIGURE 4-7   Dynamic Guides can be one of the most useful upgrades for DRAW users who need architectural precision.

Figure 4-7 shows the bottom portion of the docker where all the Dynamic Guides features are located. Let's do a rundown, and along the way you'll see illustrations demonstrating some of the creative uses of Dynamic Guides.

- **Default angle increments**   You have a number of degrees, spread out in 15° increments, that you can use (or not use by unchecking their boxes) when the Dynamic Guides feature is enabled. This means that every time you draw a straight line (let's say you use the Polyline tool), end the path segment, and begin another, when you come to a 15° or 30° angle relative to the angle of the first path segment—DRAW pops up onscreen info called a tool tip, informing you that you are beginning this next segment from the edge of the preceding one, the number of degrees off the original path's orientation, and how far you're traveling away from the end of the first path.

Note   Tooltips only pop up when the Display Screen Tips button in the Dynamic Guides area is active.

- **Extend Along Segment** Without needing to pull a guide out of a ruler and rotating it so it's perfectly aligned with a path you've drawn, you can activate Extend Along Segment, and the temporary Dynamic Guide will keep you on the straight and narrow, as shown here.

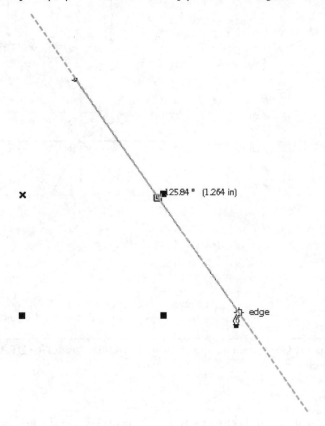

- **Snap To Tick spacing** There are invisible tick marks when you drag a path segment; you'll "feel" some resistance when you use your mouse to pull the onscreen cursor a specific distance. Tick spacing is found in the Alignment and Dynamic Guides docker. First, click the rightmost icon, and then the num box becomes active for Tick Spacing tweaks. You enable and disable this feature by using this button on the docker.
- **Creating a custom angle and saving it** You might find that 15° increments aren't what you need—for example, to make a five-sided polygon (yeah, yeah, you could use the Polygon tool, but play along with me here), you'd need an angle of 72° to start with, which is not to be found on the preset list. So you type in this value, click the + button to add it to the list, and off you go.

If you have any doubt that Dynamic Guides can make quick work of shapes that are exceptionally complicated, check out this next illustration. It was created entirely using Dynamic Guides at default preset values and paying attention to how long each segment was using the tooltips.

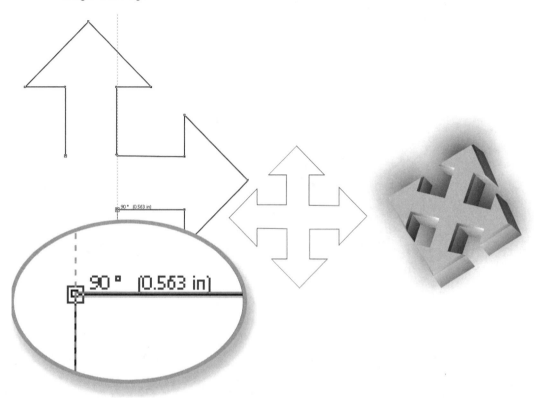

Page definition, sorting pages, margins, bleeds, and enough other options have been discussed in this chapter to fill a book! Now that you know how to set up a page, how about filling it with some artwork? Chapter 5 takes you through how to create and modify basic shapes and how to transform them—scale, rotate, move, and all that good stuff. Page setup meets page content right around the corner of the next page.

5 Creating Basic Shapes, Applying Transformations

You have to begin *somewhere* with the DRAW part of CorelDRAW—and this is the chapter. The creative process within this program usually requires that you build objects that you then customize and refine through fancy fills and elegant outlines, which are covered in later chapters. Therefore, it's important to know the steps to create simple geometric shapes, and to know basic editing moves to create exactly the shape you want to fill and stroke.

 Note Download and extract all the files from the Chapter05.zip archive to follow the tutorials in this chapter.

Using the Rectangle Tool and Property Bar

The Rectangle tool is simple enough to use, but it doesn't just create a four-sided, right-angled polygon—it creates a rectangle that has *special properties* in CorelDRAW. You'll find the Rectangle tool in the Toolbox; you can quickly select it by pressing the F6 shortcut key.

 Note Rectangles drawn with the Smart Drawing tool—covered in Chapter 8—have special editing properties, too.

Rectangle shapes offer you the option to apply corner "roundness," based on a percentage value. Roundness can be set either manually by dragging a corner with the Shape tool—the most common technique experienced Corellians use—or by using the Property Bar Corner Roundness option available while a rectangle is selected. By default, you round all four corners equally and together. However, if you unlock the Edit Corners Together toggle button, you can manually enter different values for each of the four corners, as discussed in the following section. There are several more features for changing the shape of a rectangle object that are reversible (no destructive changes are made) on the Property Bar. Figure 5-1 shows the features and some of the results you can achieve with this seemingly basic shape-creation tool.

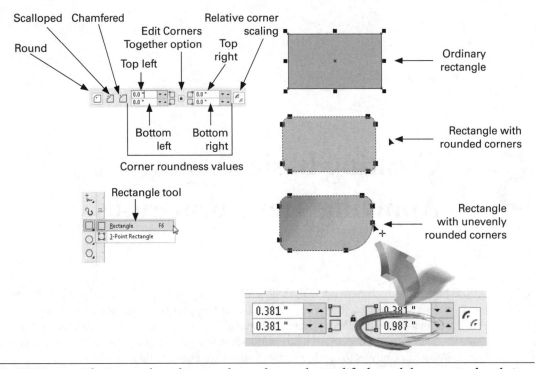

FIGURE 5-1 The Rectangle tool creates shapes that can be modified—and then returned to their original state at any time.

Tip You can also choose the Rectangle tool while any shape-creation tool is selected (the Ellipse tool, for example) by right-clicking a blank space on the document page and choosing Create Object | Rectangle from the pop-up menu.

Drawing a Rectangle

To create a rectangle, choose the Rectangle tool from the Toolbox and then click-diagonal-drag in any direction to define its corner positions, as shown next. The act of click-dragging begins by defining the first two corners; as you drag, the corner positions can be redefined, depending on where your cursor is on the page. Then, before you release the mouse button, you've defined the position for the remaining two rectangle corners.

Begin here

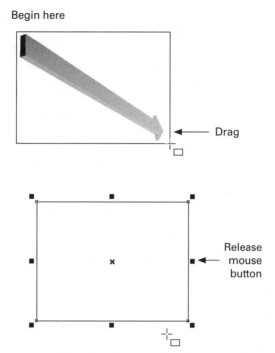

Drag

Release
mouse
button

While the Rectangle tool is selected, notice that the cursor is a crosshair with a small rectangle shape at its lower right. As you click-drag using the cursor, you'll also notice that the Status Bar and Property Bar show the coordinate, width, and height properties of your new object shape.

Setting Rectangle Corner Properties

Corner roundness is one of three different effects you can apply and dynamically edit when you're into rectangles. Corner Roundness, as well as the Scalloped and Chamfered corner styles, can be applied to a rectangle using a value of 0 to about one half the overall length of one of the rectangle's sides. If you think about this, a 2" rectangle *can't* have more than a 1" rounded corner on each side! The Corner Roundness amount can be changed at any time, while the shape remains a native rectangle; that is, it has not been converted to curves. By typing 0 into any of the size boxes while the rectangle is selected, you remove the corner style. Corner Roundness, Scalloped, and Chamfered can be set uniformly for all corners (the default) or independently when the Edit Corners Together lock option is in the unlocked state.

Tip Double-clicking the Rectangle tool button in the Toolbox instantly creates a rectangle border around your current document page.

While a rectangle is selected, use any of the following operations to change corner properties according to your needs:

- Click the type of corner style you want on the Property Bar and then either type in the size for the corner values or drag the elevator buttons up or down to adjust the size of the corners.
- Set your rectangle's corners manually, using the Shape tool, by first unlocking the Edit Corners Together toggle button and then CTRL-dragging any corner control point away from its corner (toward a side that makes up the rectangle). Enabling the Edit Corners Together option causes all corners to be rounded or scalloped in an equal amount by dragging any of the control points.
- Use the Object Properties docker; press ALT-ENTER, click the Rectangle icon to go to the Rectangle Properties tab on the docker, and then edit any property you so choose.

Figure 5-2 shows rectangles with different types of corners; this is an ideal feature for building interesting signs, borders, and frames for documents.

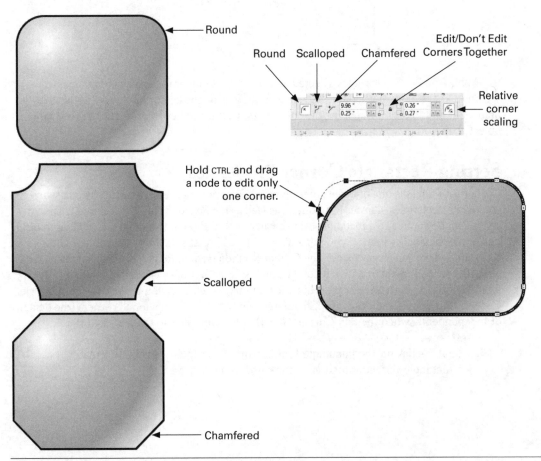

FIGURE 5-2 Rectangles can have almost any type of corner you can imagine.

Creating 3-Point Rectangles

If you want to create a rectangle and have it rotated all in one fell swoop, you can use the *3-Point Rectangle tool*. You'll find it grouped with the Rectangle tool in the Toolbox.

Using this tool, you can draw new rectangles at precise angles, as shown in Figure 5-3. The rectangle you create is a native rectangle shape, so you can round its corners and manipulate it as any other shape.

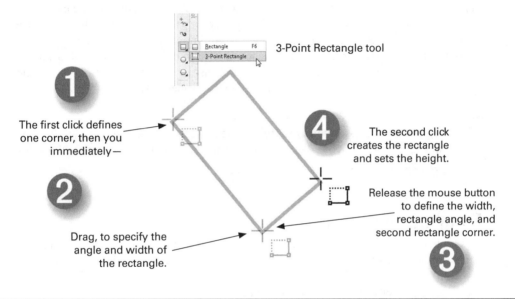

FIGURE 5-3   Draw new rectangles at precise angles with the 3-Point Rectangle tool.

To create a rectangle using the 3-Point Rectangle tool, you click-drag. Clicking sets the first point of the rectangle, and the subsequent distance you drag determines both the angle and length of the rectangle. As soon as you release the mouse button, you move your cursor (*without* clicking; this is called *hovering*) to determine the height of the rectangle. A final click seals the deal—you now have a rectangle. You can now round its corners and perform other operations on your work.

Using the Ellipse Tool and Property Bar

Ellipses are a staple of commercial design work, and essentially an ellipse is a circular shape that is not perfect. The Ellipse tool can be used to draw both circles and ellipses, but in CorelDRAW an ellipse shape has additional, special properties, just like a rectangle can be a round-cornered rectangle. Ellipse shapes can be edited to create dramatically new shapes while retaining their elliptical properties. In contrast, a shape you might draw that *looks* like an oval, using the Bézier tool for example, will have no special properties and always remains an oval.

Ellipses are easy enough to draw with the Ellipse tool and can be set in several different states: as oval or circular closed paths, pie wedges, and arcs. Pie wedges are the portions of an ellipse—like a single slice of a pie, or conversely a whole pie with a slice removed. Arc shapes are open paths, exactly like pie wedges, except the two straight line segments are missing.

To create an ellipse, choose the Ellipse tool from the Toolbox (as shown in Figure 5-4) or press F7, followed by a click-drag in any direction. While the Ellipse tool is selected, the Property Bar shows ellipse-specific options that enable you to control the state of your new ellipse shape before or after it has been created. Choose Ellipse, Pie, or Arc. A complement is reserved for pie and arc shapes: for example, if you specify a 15° pie wedge, clicking the Change Direction icon changes the shape to a 345° wedge. Additionally, if you want a pie or arc to travel in a different path direction, double-click the Ellipse tool icon on the Toolbox, which takes you to Options, where you can choose a clockwise or counterclockwise path direction. Figure 5-4 shows your options and the features on the Property Bar when the tool is chosen.

Tip   You can also choose the Ellipse tool while any tool is selected by right-clicking in an empty space on your document page and choosing Create Object | Ellipse from the pop-up menu.

Drawing an Ellipse

Let's walk before running; before creating pie and arc shapes, begin with creating circles and ovals. Start with these brief steps:

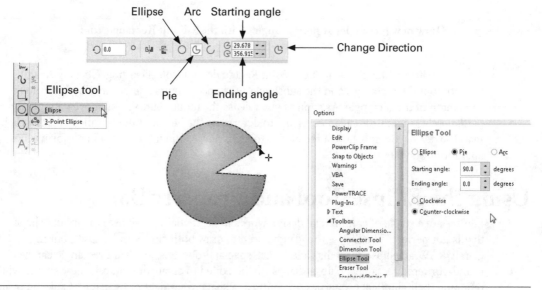

FIGURE 5-4   The Ellipse tool produces an object you can edit to make different shapes.

Tutorial # Round 1 with the Ellipse Tool

1. Choose the Ellipse tool (F7) and use a click-diagonal-drag action in any direction. As you drag, an outline preview of the shape appears. An ellipse shape has two overlapping control nodes (so onscreen it looks like only one node); if you drag down and left or right, the nodes will be located at 12 o'clock. Conversely, if you drag up and left or right, the control nodes will be located at 6 o'clock.

2. Release the mouse button to complete your ellipse shape creation.

Controlling Ellipse States

All ellipses have two control points (*nodes*—a start and an end) that overlap each other and are visible when the ellipse is selected. When these control points are separated, they create either a pie or an arc state, and each control point determines either the *starting* or *ending angle* of the pie or arc.

You can separate these control points either by using Property Bar options or by dragging the points using the Shape tool. Dragging *inside* the ellipse's shape creates the Ellipse Pie state. Dragging *outside* the shape creates the Ellipse Arc state, as shown here.

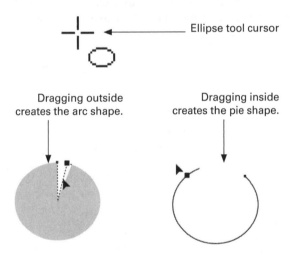

Ellipse tool cursor

Dragging outside
creates the arc shape.

Dragging inside
creates the pie shape.

Tip Even though pies and arcs appear as if sections or path parts are missing, the portions are still there. They're just hidden from view.

To draw a new pie or arc without drawing an oval-shaped ellipse first, click either the Pie or Arc button in the Property Bar before you start drawing. You can also switch any selected ellipse between these states using these buttons. By default, all pies and arcs are applied with a default Starting Angle setting of 0° and a default Ending Angle setting of 270°. Starting and ending angles are based on degrees of rotation from −360° to 360°, which is counterclockwise in orientation.

Creating 3-Point Ellipses

The *3-Point Ellipse tool* is the key for creating ellipses while setting a rotation angle (perfect circles show no possible rotation angle; we're talking *ovals* here). You'll find it grouped with the Ellipse tool in the Toolbox (see Figure 5-5). This tool's operation is very much like the 3-Point Rectangle Tool.

You can create ellipses at precise angles without the need to create and then rotate an existing one, as shown in Figure 5-5. The shape you create is still an ellipse with all associated properties, such as optional pie and arc states.

To create an ellipse using the 3-Point Ellipse tool, choose the 3-Point Ellipse tool, click to set the begin point of the ellipse, and then drag to specify its width and rotational angle. Release the cursor and then position your cursor where you want the maximum height of the oval defined. Click, and your ellipse is complete.

Using Polygons and the Property Bar

The *Polygon tool* (the shortcut is Y) is unique to the category of vector drawing software. Although competing applications offer a polygon tool, CorelDRAW's Polygon tool produces shapes *that can be edited* for making dynamic changes, just like CorelDRAW rectangles and ellipses. The shapes you create with the Polygon tool can have as few as three or as many as 500 points and sides; by default, all polygon sides are straight paths. You'll find the Polygon tool, together with the Star, Complex Star, and other group tools. While the Polygon tool is selected, the Property Bar offers the number of sides for the polygon you'll draw.

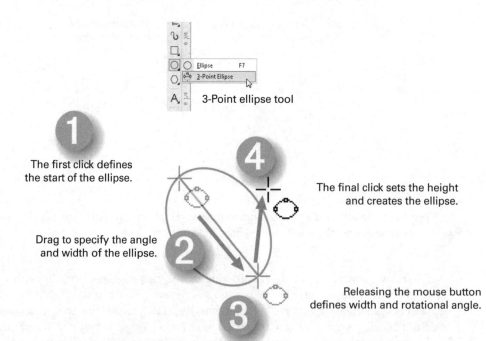

FIGURE 5-5   You can create ellipses at precise angles using the 3-Point Ellipse tool.

Drawing and Editing Polygons

Most of the trick to creating symmetrical, complex shapes with the Polygon tool lies in the *editing* of them. Read the Shape tool section in Chapter 9 before getting too involved with the Polygon tool, because you really need to know how to use the Shape tool in combination with the Property Bar to make the most of a polygon shape.

To create a default polygon, you use the same click-diagonal-drag technique as you use with the Rectangular and Ellipse tools. This produces a symmetrical shape made up of straight paths. Because you'll often want a shape more elegant than something that looks like a snack food, it helps to begin a polygon shape by holding SHIFT and CTRL while dragging: doing this produces a perfectly symmetrical (not distorted) polygon, beginning at your initial click point and traveling outward. Therefore, you have the shape positioned exactly where you want it and can begin redefining the shape.

Here you can see the Polygon tool cursor and a symmetrical default polygon. Because the Polygon tool can be used to make star-shaped polygons, there are control points that govern the polygon points and nodes in-between these point controls that are used to alter the coves between points. When you edit a polygon, the position of these points can be reversed. These control points have no control handles because they connect straight path segments. However, in the following tutorial you'll get a jumpstart on advanced shape creation, and really get down in very few steps to creating a dynamite polygon shape through editing.

Polygon tool

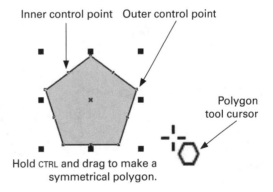

Inner control point   Outer control point

Polygon tool cursor

Hold CTRL and drag to make a symmetrical polygon.

Tip To create a polygon object started at the center of your cursor and make the polygon equilateral (that is, not "smooshed"), hold both CTRL and SHIFT as you drag.

Here is a brief tour of how to create and then edit a polygon to design any symmetric object you can imagine, and possibly one or two unimaginable ones:

Tutorial   Reshaping a Polygon

1. Choose the Polygon tool from the Toolbox, and before you do anything else, set the number of sides to 12 on the Property Bar.
2. Hold CTRL to constrain the shape to a symmetrical one, and then click-diagonal-drag on the page. Release the mouse button after you have a polygon that's about 3" wide.
3. To better see what you're doing, left-click over the color palette with the polygon selected to fill it. By default, polygons are created with a small stroke width and no fill.
4. Choose the Shape tool from the Toolbox. Click any of the control points on the polygon to select it, but don't drag yet. Hold CTRL and then drag outward, to constrain the movement of the cursor so that the polygon doesn't take on a lopsided appearance (although you can create interesting polygons by dragging in any way without holding CTRL). You should have a star shape now, as shown here.

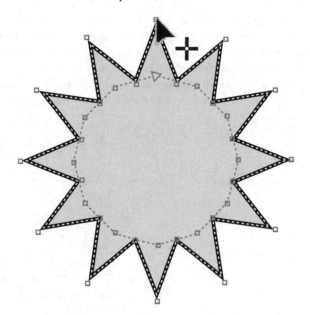

5. Notice that on the Property Bar you now have a lot of icons that control how line segments pass through nodes and whether the segments are straight or curved. Click on any line segment that makes up the polygon; your cursor should have a wiggly line at the lower right, as shown next, meaning that you've clicked on a line. Then click the Convert to Curve button on the Property Bar, converting not only the line, but all the lines in the polygon that are symmetrical to the chosen line, to a curve. Or perhaps more simply, use the same command by right-clicking a point and using the pop-up contextual menu.

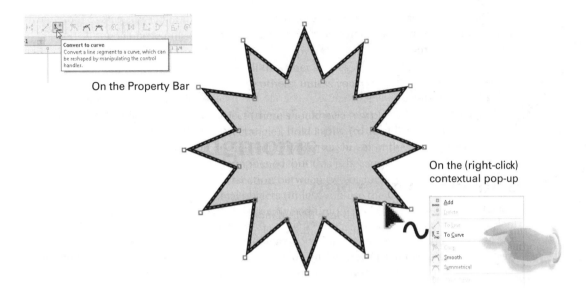

On the Property Bar

On the (right-click)
contextual pop-up

6. There are now two control handles, but they lay exactly on the segment that appears to be a line but now has curve possibilities. First, click an inner or outer original node along the polygon path, as shown next. This reveals the handles, and it is now possible to create a curve by dragging on the segment *between* the control handles. Doing this, as you can see here, creates a very interesting and complex symmetrical shape, and you can now see the control lines and handles for the curves segment much more easily and can manipulate the control handles to further embellish your creation.

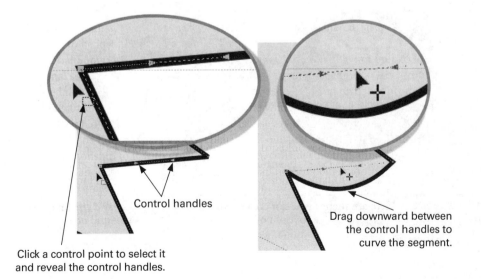

Control handles

Drag downward between
the control handles to
curve the segment.

Click a control point to select it
and reveal the control handles.

Figure 5-6 shows just a few creative examples of polygon editing: from gears to those vinyl flowers you put over shower stall cracks. You have immense design power at your disposal with the Polygon tool.

 Tip After editing a polygon, you can change the number of sides. For example, suppose you've created a 12-petal flower polygon and then decide you want only eight petals. You can select the edited shape with the Pick tool and then decrease the number of sides using the elevator buttons to the right of the num box on the Property Bar.

Stars and Complex Stars

You have variations on polygons at the ready in CorelDRAW, in the same group as the Polygon tool. The Star tool can be used to create pointy polygons with anywhere from 3 to 500 points. The Complex Star tool creates a number of combined polygons to make a star shape; you can create interesting symmetrical shapes by filling a complex star object—the result contains both filled and vacant polygon areas as the component paths intersect one another.

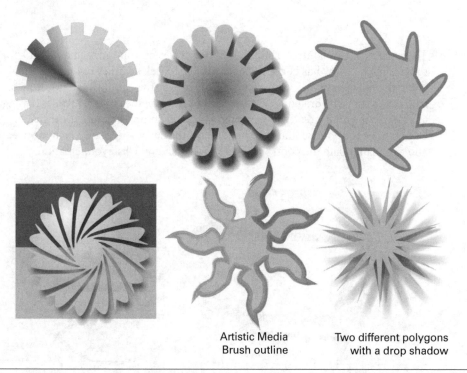

Artistic Media
Brush outline

Two different polygons
with a drop shadow

FIGURE 5-6 Here are shapes you can create using a **Polygon** object and the **Shape** tool.

Working with the Star Tool

The Star tool produces objects by using the click-diagonal-drag mouse technique; CTRL-SHIFT dragging creates symmetrical stars beginning at the initial click point traveling outward.

On the Property Bar, when the Star tool is chosen, you have options for the number of points for the star and the "pointiness" (sharpness) of the resulting object—how severe the indents are between points. At a setting of 1, the star object isn't pointy at all—you'll see that it looks quite like a Polygon tool object. So, if you can make a star using the Polygon tool, why would you ever choose the Star tool? The answer is because the geometric structure of a star shape is always perfectly symmetrical. Although you can use the Shape tool to manually tune the sharpness of a Star tool object's points, the angle between points is always consistent. In the illustration here, you can see a Star tool object compared with a Polygon tool object that has been clumsily edited. You can't perform this goof with the Star tool; its interior angles are always mirrored and symmetrical.

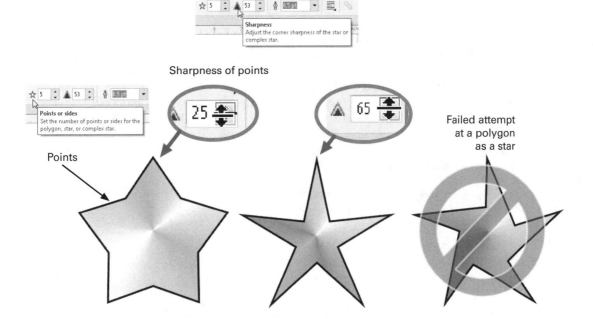

Using the Complex Star Tool

Think of the kaleidoscope images you enjoyed as a child (or still do) when you choose the Complex Star tool, because with only an edit or two using the Shape tool, you can create mesmerizing symmetrical shapes, unlike with any other tool in CorelDRAW.

To use the tool, you know the drill if you've read this far! You click-diagonal-drag to create a shape; by default, the Complex Star object has nine points, with a value of 2 on a 1- to 3-point sharpness scale (which can be defined on the Property Bar, as shown in the following illustration).

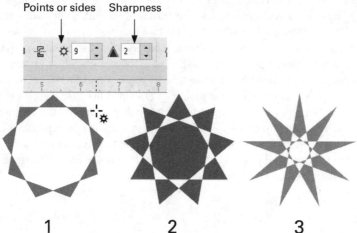

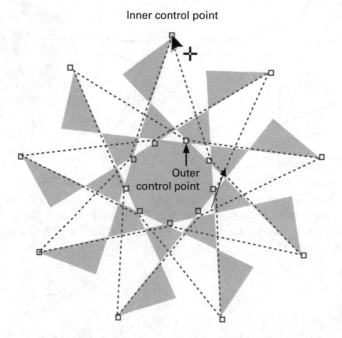

CTRL, SHIFT, and CTRL-SHIFT offer the same modifiers as they do with other shapes. One unique characteristic of Complex Stars is that they have two control points: one for the inner, negative space, and one for the points. When you edit using the Shape tool, holding CTRL causes your edits to be symmetrical, but if you want a spiral treatment of a Complex Star, don't hold CTRL and drag any way you like on both the inner and outer control points. You'll probably want to assign a fill to a Complex Star as your first edit because unfilled Complex Stars aren't as visually interesting. The following illustration shows what you can create by moving the inner control point to outside the outer control point. Imagine the snowflake patterns you can build; and like snowflakes, no two Complex Stars are alike.

Here you can see other examples of simply playing with the Shape tool on a Complex Star object. Also try assigning a wide white outline to a Complex Star as a property to create still more variations.

Using the Spiral Tool

With the Spiral tool (press A as the keyboard shortcut), you can create circular-shaped paths that would be tedious if not impossible to create manually. Spiral objects are composed of a single open path that curves in a clockwise or counterclockwise direction. They can also be designed to expand in even-segment distances or in *increasing* distances as the spiral path segments travel away from the center (called a *logarithmic* function). You find the tool in the Toolbox, grouped with the Polygon and Graph Paper tools.

Spiral tool options share space in the Property Bar (shown next) with the options for the Graph Paper tool and include the Spiral Revolutions, Symmetrical and Logarithmic Spiral modes and a Spiral Expansion slider.

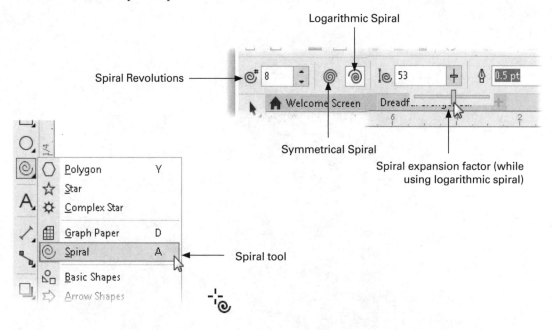

The objects you create can have between 1 and 100 revolutions, each of which is equal to one complete rotation around its center point. The direction of the revolutions is set according to the click-diagonal-drag action during the creation of the initial shape, as shown here.

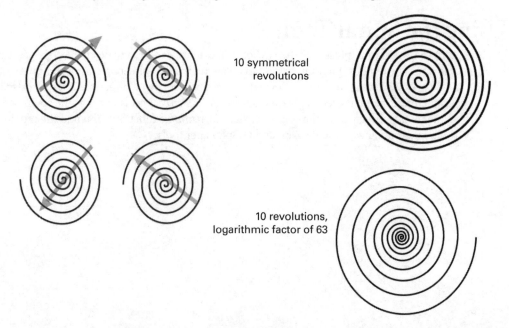

10 symmetrical
revolutions

10 revolutions,
logarithmic factor of 63

Note Spiral objects are *not* dynamic; no special editing or redefining is possible once the spiral has been created. This means you must set their properties before they are created. Other than using the Pick or Shape tool to edit their size or shape, spiral objects are a "done deal."

By default, all new spiral objects are set to Symmetrical. If you choose the Logarithmic Spiral, the Spiral Expansion slider becomes available. Here's how the modes and options affect the spiral objects you can create.

- **Symmetrical vs. Logarithmic** A symmetrical spiral object appears with its spiral revolutions evenly spaced from the center origin to the outer dimensions of the object. To increase or decrease the rate at which the curves in your spiral become smaller or larger as they reach the object's center, you may want to use the logarithmic method. The term *logarithmic* refers to the acceleration (or deceleration) of the spiral revolutions. To choose this option, click the Logarithmic Spiral button in the Property Bar before drawing your shape.
- **Logarithmic Expansion option** While the Logarithmic Spiral mode is selected, the Logarithmic Expansion slider becomes available—as well as a value field you can type in— and you can set this rate based on a percentage of the object's dimensions. Logarithmic Expansion may be set from 1 to 100 percent. A Logarithmic Expansion setting of 1 results in a symmetrical spiral setting, whereas a setting of 100 causes dramatic expansion. If you need a shape that is reminiscent of a nautilus, increase the Logarithmic Expansion option to 50 or so.

Using the Graph Paper Tool

The Graph Paper tool (the shortcut is D) is used to create a grid containing hundreds (even thousands) of rectangles—an emulation of graph paper. Graph paper is invaluable in chart making as well as artistic uses. You find the Graph Paper tool, shown next, grouped with the Polygon and Spiral tools. This tool's options on the Property Bar let you set the number of rows and columns for your new graph paper object. As with the Spiral tool, you must set options *before* drawing your graph paper object; a Graph Paper object cannot be edited dynamically.

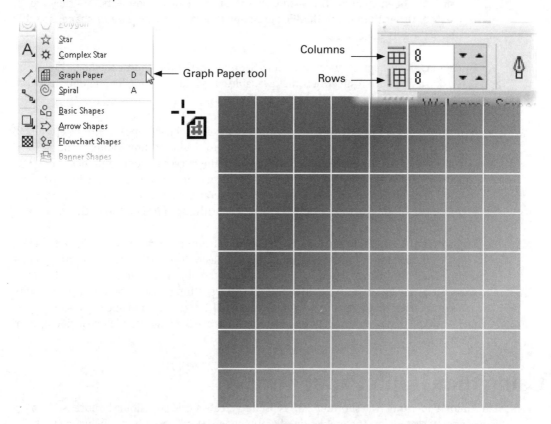

Let's explore one of the many ways to create and use the group of rectangles the Graph Paper tool builds for you. This next assignment uses the Add Perspective Effect to make a dimensional chessboard beneath a drawing of chess pieces, as well as one or two tricky editing techniques—but you're guided step by step all the way. Watch how you can dramatically improve the look of a composition just by using the Graph Paper tool and some minor editing.

Tutorial   Power-Drawing a Grid with Graph Paper

1. Open Chess set limited edition.cdr. Your assignment is to put a chessboard behind the drawings of the pawn and rook. Choose Window | Dockers | Object Manager if it's not already docked and visible.
2. Select All (CTRL-A) and then with the Selector tool, scale the objects down to about 35 percent; you'll see you've arrived at the correct percentage toward the left of the Infobar.
3. On the Object Manager, click Layer 1 to make it the current editing layer, and then lock the layer.
4. Click the New Layer button on the Object Manager. The title "Layer 2" appears over the Layer 1 title. Click-drag the Layer 2 title to beneath Layer 1. This is now your current editing layer, the guy upon which you'll create the chessboard.
5. Choose the Graph Paper tool from the Toolbox (or press D).
6. Using Property Bar options, set the number of rows and columns to 8 for your new graph paper object.
7. Using a click-diagonal-drag action, hold CTRL and drag to create the new object. Release the mouse button when the graph paper is about 4 and ¾ inches high. See the following illustration.

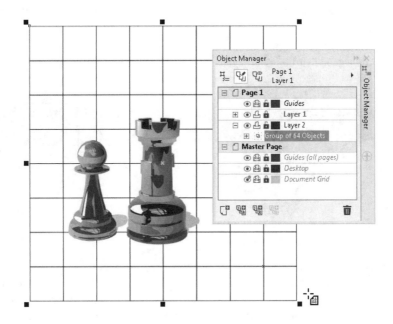

8. Look at the Status Bar; it tells you that a group of 64 objects is selected. All the Graph Paper objects can take on a new fill and outline color in one fell swoop: click the 80% Black color well on the Color Palette, and then right-click white to make the outlines white.

9. The white grouting that the outlines represent on this chessboard are a little too thin. No problem: with the grouped objects selected, set the outline width to 2 points now. The ability to set the outline width of grouped objects directly from the Property Bar comes in handy for stuff like this!

10. Choose Effects | Add Perspective. You'll see a red dashed outline with four control points surround the group, but it's not time yet to apply a perspective.

11. Using the Pick tool, click on the selected Graph Paper object to reveal the rotate and skew handles. While holding CTRL to constrain rotation, rotate the grouped rectangles by 45°. By default, CorelDRAW constrains rotation to 15° increments; therefore, two points of resistance as you CTRL-drag does the trick.

12. Choose the Shape tool (F10); the grouped shapes again feature the Perspective control points.

13. Choose the top control point and then drag it down until you have a chessboard in perspective. You will know when you've dragged enough—the drawing of the chess pieces will visually fit right into place.

Hold CTRL and rotate 45°.   Use the Shape tool to drag the top node down.

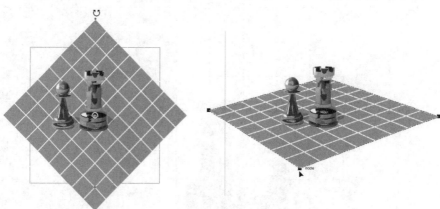

14. With the grouped chessboard in its final perspective aspect, you really should make the chessboard look *checkered*, and not like the tile work in your kitchen. Press CTRL-U (or select Object | Group | Ungroup Objects). Fill every other rectangle with a lighter color; try orange, and you'll have a hit chessboard for Halloween.

15. A clever shortcut to filling every other square with orange (or the color of your choice) is to fill one square with your color and then use the Color Eyedropper tool to sample the orange square. The cursor immediately turns into the Apply Color paint bucket, and all you do is click on every other square to apply the sampled color, as shown in the following illustration.

An attractive, contrasting color combination enhances the overall illustration, and also makes the cast shadows from the chess pieces more apparent.

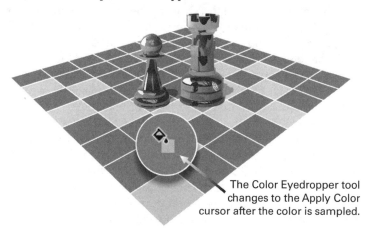

The Color Eyedropper tool changes to the Apply Color cursor after the color is sampled.

 Tip Holding CTRL while you drag constrains the shape of the Graph Paper object, but not the cells in the graph. Therefore, you could, for example, create a five-row, two-column graph whose overall proportions are square, but the cells within the graph paper object are distorted to rectangles.

Note You can ungroup a bunch of rectangles on the graph paper after applying the Perspective command, then redefine the perspective, and then *move* individual cells around the page *with a newly applied perspective*. With the Pick tool, marquee-select all the ungrouped objects. Then choose the Shape tool and click one of the rectangles to select it. When the Perspective overlay appears, you can click-drag any of the Perspective handles. The selected rectangle takes on a different perspective from the other affected rectangles, and you can create some wonderfully bizarre three-dimensional compositions.

Converting Shapes to Curves

Any of the shapes discussed in this chapter can be converted to curves by using the Object | Convert to Curves command (CTRL-Q). Using this command removes any dynamic-editing properties. For example, an ellipse shape may be converted to a pie or arc (and vice versa); but after it is converted to curves, you'll no longer have the option of turning the object into a pie wedge. The same applies to rectangles, polygons, and so on. With the exception of the Undo command, once an object is converted to curves, there is no way to return the object to its dynamically editable state.

Using the Convert Outline to Object Command

A lot of the shapes covered in this chapter—the spiral in particular—have outline properties but no fill. So what do you do, for example, if you want a gradient-filled spiral? The Object | Convert Outline To Object command converts any shape's outline properties to a closed path. To apply the command to a selected object, choose Object | Convert Outline To Object, or use the shortcut CTRL-SHIFT-Q. Once the outline is converted, the resulting closed path looks exactly like the shape of the original, except it can be filled because it's not an outline. Instead, it's a closed path object whose shape is based on an outline.

When an outline is converted to an object, CorelDRAW performs a quick calculation of the Outline Pen width applied to the object and creates a new object based on this value. When you apply this command to objects that include a fill of any type, a new compound-path object is created based on the outline width. If the object includes a fill of any type, the fill is created as a new and separate object applied with an outline width and color of None. When you're converting open paths, only the path itself is created as a single outline object of the path according to the Outline Pen width applied. Figure 5-7 shows a spiral shape with a thick red Outline Pen width that is converted to an object using the Convert Outline to Object command.

Things are certainly shaping up now, aren't they? You've learned how to create basic shapes as well as how to edit them to create scores of original and visually interesting items. This isn't the half of it. In Chapter 6, you learn to move, rotate, scale, and put your new objects anywhere you like on the page, on a new layer, in a group, or on a bus to Cleveland. Okay, that might be stretching a joke as well as the length of the book. Arranging and organizing objects is your next destination, and you'll find it to be a moving experience.

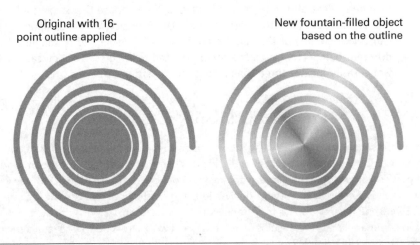

Original with 16-
point outline applied

New fountain-filled object
based on the outline

FIGURE 5-7   When an outline is converted to an object, CorelDRAW performs calculations that create a new object.

6

Arranging and Organizing Objects

When you create or import an object, it might not be *exactly* where you want it on the page. Or the position might be fine, but the object's a little too large. It might also be rotated by a few unwanted degrees, or it's part of a group or on the wrong layer—you get the picture. This chapter covers the techniques to use in CorelDRAW to *transform* objects—both the manual approach and the "pinpoint precise numerical entry" approach are covered. You'll soon have the skills to compose elements on a page the way you want them, and then you can stop cursing at the cursor.

 Note Download and extract all the files from the Chapter06.zip archive to follow the tutorials in this chapter.

Basic Object Selection

The Pick tool—by default, the tool at the top of the Toolbox—can be used to move, scale, and make other transformations when you click an object to select it and then drag to move the selection, for example. Use the SHIFT key as the modifier when you're selecting things on a page; you *add* to your existing selection by SHIFT-clicking other objects. If you've selected an object unintentionally, SHIFT-click on the object (which is already selected) to deselect it.

With one or more items selected, you'll notice that information about the selected shapes is displayed on the Status Bar. The other workspace area to watch is the Property Bar; it shows the position, size, and rotation of the selection. In addition to seeing info about your selection, you can also change transformations by entering numbers directly into the info boxes and then pressing ENTER. Also, if you press ALT-ENTER when something is selected, the Object

Properties docker provides you with not only details about the object, but also the opportunity to quickly *change* many of the object's properties.

Pick Tool Selections

The Pick tool can be used for several things; the two most important are to choose an object (or several objects) and to create a *change* in the selected object(s) by moving it and adjusting its selection handles.

Clicking an object once selects it. While an object is selected, *selection handles* appear—the eight black markers surrounding the object, as shown in Figure 6-1. Additionally, depending on the type and properties of an object, you'll see *nodes* at various areas around the object, which indicate the first node in an object path or sub-path (of combined vector objects) when a vector object is selected or the edge of an object when a bitmap is selected. A small *X* marker appears at the centermost point of the object, indicating its center origin. This origin can be moved and is quite useful for defining a center of rotation for an object, and it's discussed later in this chapter.

Note Nodes are edited using the Shape tool, covered in Chapter 9. The Pick tool has no effect on nodes.

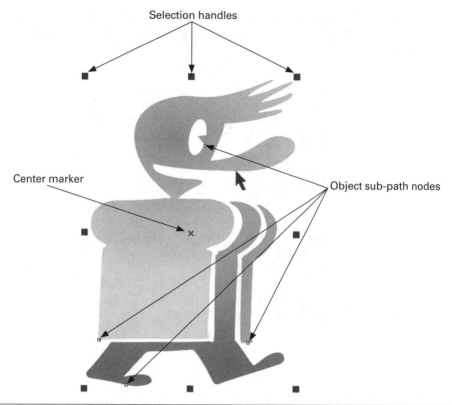

FIGURE 6-1   Select any object with a single click using the Pick tool.

 Tip Occasionally you'll create a shape with an outline stroke that's very narrow and has
no fill, and you have trouble selecting the darned thing with the Pick tool. You're in
luck because, by default, Treat All Objects As Filled is turned on. You don't need to
select the outline because, with this option, you can click on an empty interior and
the object is selected anyway. If you don't care for this option, go to the Options
dialog (CTRL-J) and select Workspace | Toolbox | Pick Tool from the tree on the left.
Clear the Treat All Objects As Filled check box and then click OK to close the dialog.

Picking and Freehand Picking

The Freehand Pick tool is located in the Pick tool group, and both new and experienced
CorelDRAW users might want to give this selection tool a try; the Freehand Pick tool behaves
exactly like the (regular) Pick tool after an object is selected, so you can move or perform other
transformations without switching tools.

The main difference between these tools is that with the Pick tool, you must click-drag
to define a rectangle that the desired objects are completely within. The Freehand Pick tool is
used more like a shape-creation tool than a rectangle-creation tool; you can click-drag around

objects, selecting some and avoiding others, regardless of how closely the objects neighbor one another. The illustration here visually demonstrates the different properties of the Pick and Freehand Pick tools.

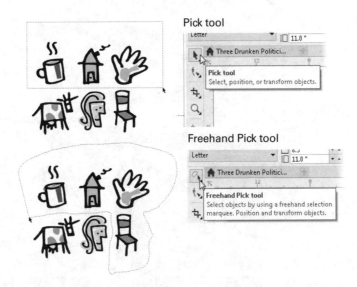

Selection Techniques

You can use mouse and keyboard combinations while navigating through a collection of objects and for selecting more than one object at a time using the Pick tool. Many of these object-selection techniques can also be used in combination with each other. Here's how to select more than one object in one fell swoop:

- **SHIFT-clicking to select** Holding the SHIFT key while clicking an unselected object adds it to your current selection. This also works in the reverse: holding SHIFT while clicking a selected object *deselects* the object. This technique works with both the Pick and Freehand Pick tools.
- **Marquee-selecting objects** To select all objects in a specific area, use the (regular) Pick tool and click-drag diagonally to surround the objects; a dashed blue outline representing the rectangular area being selected appears until you release the mouse button. When you do so, all object shapes completely within the area you define are selected.
- **Holding ALT while marquee-selecting** If you come to CorelDRAW from Adobe Illustrator, you can use the convention of selecting objects by merely touching a shape in a marquee-selection technique. Holding the ALT key as the modifier while click-dragging to marquee-select a specific area selects all objects within—and even ones whose *edge* you touch. Holding SHIFT-ALT while marquee-selecting causes the reverse to occur— deselecting any objects that are already selected.

- **Pressing TAB to select the next object**   Suppose you have a bunch of objects in a document, but some of them overlap, and you're getting nowhere by attempting to click the one you need. Pressing the TAB key alone while the Pick tool is active selects a shape and selects the next single object arranged directly behind your current selection (whether or not it overlaps the current object). Holding SHIFT while pressing the TAB key selects the single object arranged directly in front of your current selection. This tabbing action works because each new object created is automatically ordered in front of the last created object. Tabbing cycles through single object selections on a page, whether you have a current object selected or none at all. The key is to begin tabbing *after* you've chosen the Pick tool.
- **ALT-clicking to select objects covered by other objects**   To select an object that is ordered in back of and hidden by other objects, hold the ALT key while the Pick tool is selected and then click where the object is located. Each time you ALT-click with the Pick tool, objects that are ordered farther back in the stack are selected, enabling you to "dig" to select hidden objects.

The Pick Tool's Shape Tool State

If you're getting an idea that the Pick tool has a host of hidden features, you're right. One of these is its alternate state—the temporary Shape tool state. The Pick tool can temporarily act like the Shape tool while a single object is selected and when held over object nodes, but this isn't its normal behavior, and first you need to activate this feature in Options; choose Workspace | Display and then check Enable Node Tracking.

The temporary Shape tool state lets you move object nodes without changing tools, conveniently giving you control to modify selected characters in a line of Artistic text, to edit open and closed paths, and to modify an ellipse, star, polygon as star, graph paper object, and even a bitmap. The next illustration shows Enable Node Tracking in action. When the Pick tool is outside of a shape, it looks like an arrow cursor. After an object is selected and the tool is over an object node, however, the tool changes to the Shape tool and you can move nodes.

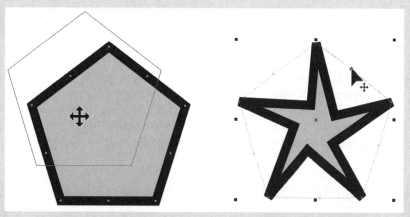

Pick tool moving
selected object

Pick tool in Shape tool state selecting object
with object node selected and moving the node

Tip Although you can select nodes with the Pick tool when Enable Node Tracking is active, you can't perform editing operations other than moving a node. To create curves from straight path segments and work with node control handles, you need to use the genuine Shape tool.

Selecting Objects by Type

So far, you've learned to select any objects on or off your page. But you can also select objects by their type (such as text objects, guidelines, and path nodes) using commands from the Select All menu, as shown in the following illustration. All text objects shown here are selected, and CorelDRAW is being very clever—it didn't select the *O* and the *a* because they are drawings and not text. You can extrude, add a perspective, and put any type of fill you like on text—*and it's still text.* See how effortless sifting through a page of objects can be? Each time you use a command from the Select All menu, a new selection is made (and any current selection of objects becomes *not* selected).

Caution You can't select what's locked or hidden. Check the status of layers with the Object Manager if an object is apparently welded to the page. Also, if click an immovable object and its selection handles are tiny lock icons, right-click over it and choose Unlock Object from the pop-up contextual menu. Any and all objects can now be locked on an object-by-object basis in X8.

Here's how to use each of the commands:

- **Select All Objects**   Choosing Edit | Select All | Objects selects all objects in your current document window. Quicker is the CTRL-A keyboard shortcut, which accomplishes the same thing and is easy to remember.

Tip Double-clicking the Pick tool in the Toolbox instantly selects all visible objects in your current document window view.

- **Select All Text**   Choosing Edit | Select All | Text instantly selects all text objects both on and off the current document page. Both artistic and paragraph text objects are selected after this command is used (unless they have been grouped with other objects, in which case they are ignored). Text objects that have effects (such as Contour and Extrude effects) also are selected using this command.
- **Select All Guidelines**   Guidelines are actually a class of document page objects, different from objects you draw, but objects nonetheless. To select all guidelines on your document page, choose Edit | Select All | Guidelines. Selected guidelines are indicated by a color change (red, by default). To select guidelines, they must be visible and cannot be locked. Probably the fastest way to unlock or unhide a bunch of guidelines is to double-click one using the Pick tool to display the Guidelines docker (*only* if the docker is closed and not docked to the Pasteboard edge). The Guidelines docker has options for locking/unlocking and hiding/revealing existing guides. If guidelines you've placed merely aren't visible on your page, and you're sure you laid some down in your last session, try choosing View | Guidelines.

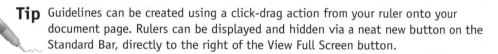

Tip Guidelines can be created using a click-drag action from your ruler onto your document page. Rulers can be displayed and hidden via a neat new button on the Standard Bar, directly to the right of the View Full Screen button.

- **Select All Nodes**   You can have the Shape tool or the Pick tool (which will magically change into the Shape tool) and an object selected (closed or open paths qualify) when using this Select command. Choose Edit | Select All | Nodes to select all the object's path nodes, as shown next. For a quicker method in the same situation, use the CTRL-A shortcut when the Shape tool is your current tool. Special CorelDRAW objects, such as rectangles, ellipses, and polygons, can't be selected this way because their shapes are defined dynamically by "control points" instead of nodes.

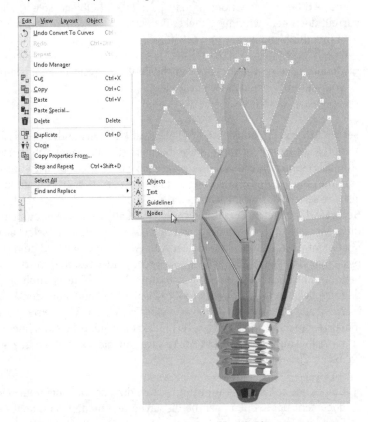

Tip Shapes are often made up of two or more paths that are combined. To select all the nodes on a combined path, first select the object and then double-click the Shape tool on the Toolbox.

Moving Objects

When you're moving objects, it's important to lift using your legs and position yourself carefully to avoid back injury. However, when you're moving objects in *CorelDRAW*, it's a lot less stressful and heavy. You basically have two options for moving objects directly: using the Pick tool and dragging, and using the keyboard arrows to precision nudge objects in any of the four directions.

> **Tip** For information on moving and transforming objects, see the section "Applying Precise Transformations," later in this chapter.

Using the Pick Tool

Holding the Pick tool over certain areas of a selected object activates the tool's positioning cursor, as shown in the following illustration. This means a click-drag action on the area will move your selected object(s) in any direction. As you drag your object, you'll see a preview outline, indicating its new position. When you release the mouse button, the move is complete.

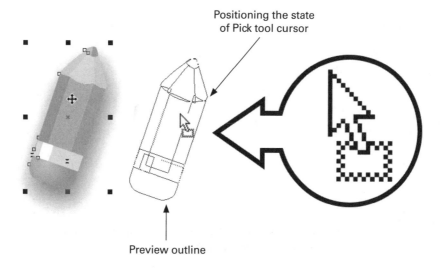

Positioning the state
of Pick tool cursor

Preview outline

> **Tip** If you're having difficulty selecting and/or moving an object because it's too small, you can increase your view magnification using the Zoom tool or you can use the keyboard nudge keys, covered next.

Using Nudge Keys

As an alternative to using the Pick tool, you can also move selected objects by a distance you specify by nudging them using your keyboard arrow keys. To nudge a selected object, press the UP, DOWN, LEFT, or RIGHT ARROW key. Your object will be moved by the nudge value specified on the Rulers page of the Options dialog. You can customize the Nudge distance by opening the Options dialog (CTRL-J), clicking to expand the tree directory under Workspace and Document, and clicking to display the Rulers options page, as shown here:

Nudge increment options

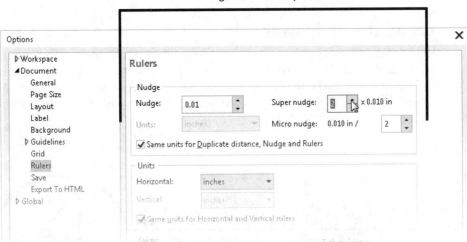

 Tip You have eight possible directions in which to nudge your artwork. In addition to using an ARROW key, you can also press two neighboring keys—such as LEFT and UP ARROW—to perform a *diagonal* nudge.

Using nudge keys, you can perform moves according to the Nudge value or by using larger or smaller values. These are referred to as *Super* and *Micro nudges*. Like "normal" nudges, these values are set on the Ruler options page. Here are the techniques for using Super and Micro nudges:

- **Super nudge** This action moves a selected object in larger increments than a normal nudge. To use Super nudge, hold SHIFT while pressing the UP, DOWN, LEFT, or RIGHT ARROW key on your keyboard. By default, this moves your selected object by twice the default value for a "normal" nudge distance, although as you can see in the preceding illustration, you can change that 2 to a larger value in the Super Nudge num box.
- **Micro nudge** The pint-sized version of a typical nudge is the Micro nudge, which moves your object in smaller increments. To use a Micro nudge, hold CTRL while pressing the UP, DOWN, LEFT, or RIGHT ARROW key on your keyboard. By default, Micro nudges move the selected object by one-half the default nudge distance, but again, this value's in the Micro Nudge num box and you can make it even smaller.

Transforming Objects

A *transformation* is any type of object shape or position change, short of actually editing the object's properties. This includes changing an object's position, size, skew, and/or rotating or reflecting it. Dragging an object directly in a document is more intuitive than precision transformations—but both approaches have their own special advantages. In this section, you'll learn how to apply transformations using both techniques.

Transforming Objects Using the Cursor

For the intuitive method, the Pick tool is what you need to transform objects by the simple act of click and dragging. Depending on the type of transformation you need to apply, you can click-drag any of the four black, square selection handles that surround the selected object or group of objects to change the size *proportionally*—by width only and by height only. Dragging any middle selection handle or side handle scales the object *disproportionately*—"smush" and "stretch" are the more common terms for disproportionate scaling, as shown in Figure 6-2.

During transformations, CorelDRAW keeps track of the object's transformed size, position, width, height, scale, and rotation angle. CorelDRAW remembers your object's original shape from the time it was created, regardless of how many transformations have been applied to it. You can remove all transformations and restore the object to its original state in

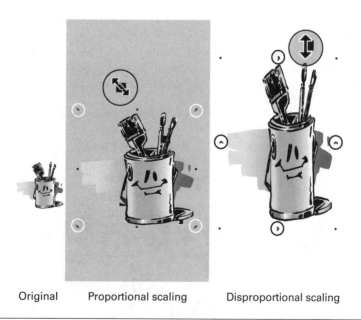

Original   Proportional scaling   Disproportional scaling

FIGURE 6-2 Dragging these handles changes the size of an object proportionately or otherwise.

a single step: choose Object | Transformations | Clear Transformations to return your object to its original shape immediately.

While transforming objects, you can constrain certain shape properties by holding modifier keys. Here are the effects of holding modifier keys for constraining a transformed object's shape:

- **To change object size (scale)**   Click-drag any corner handle to change an object's size *proportionally*, meaning the relative width and height remains in proportion to the original object's shape. Hold ALT while dragging any corner selection handle to change an object's shape *disproportionally*, meaning width and height change, regardless of original proportions.
- **To change width or height only**   Click-drag any side, top, or bottom selection handle to change the size of the object in the drag direction. Hold SHIFT while doing this to change the width or height from the center of the object, or hold CTRL while dragging to change the width or height in 200 percent increments.

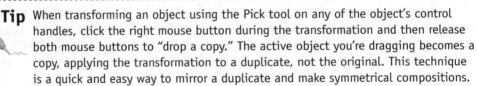

Tip   When transforming an object using the Pick tool on any of the object's control handles, click the right mouse button during the transformation and then release both mouse buttons to "drop a copy." The active object you're dragging becomes a copy, applying the transformation to a duplicate, not the original. This technique is a quick and easy way to mirror a duplicate and make symmetrical compositions.

You can also rotate or skew an object using Pick tool states that become available after you click a selected object a second time—you click an object that is *already* selected once to display rotation and skew controls around the object. This action causes an object (or group of objects) to look like the illustration of the 45 here, an ancient analog sound device best known to listeners who remember Little Anthony and the Imperials.

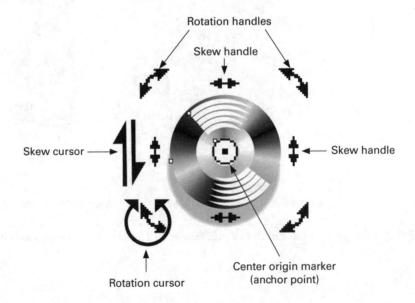

Rotation handles

Skew handle

Skew cursor →

Skew handle

Center origin marker (anchor point)

Rotation cursor

You control the point around which objects are rotated or skewed by *moving* the center origin marker or anchor point of an object or group of objects. Your cursor will change to display either the rotation or skew cursor when held over a corner or side handle. A good creative example of offsetting the original center of an object is covered in the following tutorial, where you'll make a circular pattern from a group of objects.

Tutorial Off-center Object Rotation to Create a Design

1. Open Art Nouveau Ornament.cdr. The page has guidelines that you'll use and a single grouped object, the source for the radial pattern you'll build.
2. With the Pick tool, click the object to select it, and then click the selected object (again) to put it into rotational and skew mode.
3. Drag the center rotation origin to the intersection of the guidelines.
4. Click-drag the top-right (bent double-arrowhead) handle downward until the light blue object preview is touching the original object at the middle of the red wing portion of the group of objects. Ideally, you'll wind up with a copy every 45 degrees or so.
5. Before releasing the mouse button, press the other mouse button, and then release both buttons to "drop a copy" of the original object. (Unless you've configured your mouse or other pointing device to accommodate left-handers, the primary mouse button is the left one, and the button you click briefly to drop a copy is the right one.)
6. Repeat steps 4 and 5 with the copy of the object, working clockwise until you've made a circle from copies of the pattern, as you can see in this next illustration.

Note If steps 4 and 5 seem like a lot of manual effort and you accept the idea that computers are supposed to be timesavers, instead of repeating the steps, you can use Edit | Repeat (CTRL-R) to quickly rotate and copy the rest of the grouped objects.

Drag, then right-click to drop a copy.

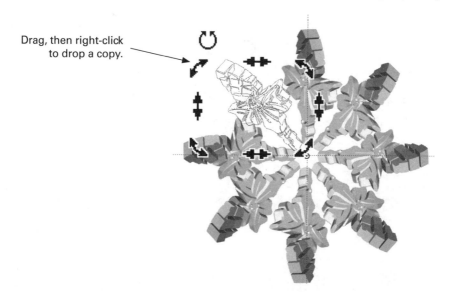

Tip To flip a selected object quickly, either vertically or horizontally, use the Mirror Vertical and Mirror Horizontal buttons on the Property Bar while using the Pick tool.

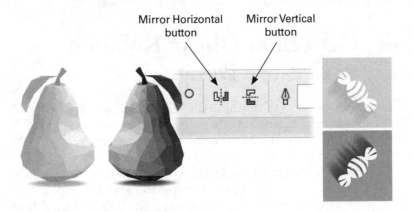

Mirror Horizontal button

Mirror Vertical button

Using the Free Transform Tool

The Free Transform tool is the middle ground between controlling transformations entirely with mouse gestures and using the hands-off controls of the Transformation docker. When you use the Free Transform tool, the Property Bar offers four transformation modes: Free Rotation, Free Angle Reflection, Free Scale, and Free Skew. The Free Angle Reflection mode is shown here to mirror the drawing's original location and left-to-right orientation.

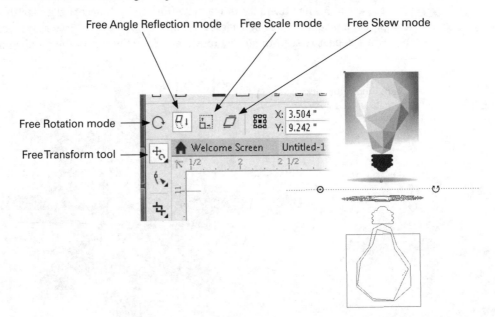

Free Angle Reflection mode

Free Scale mode

Free Skew mode

Free Rotation mode

Free Transform tool

To transform a selected object in one of these four modes, click to select the mode and then use a click-drag action on your object. A live preview of the new object's shape appears. While you're using Rotation or Angle Reflection mode, a reference line appears as you drag to indicate the object's angle transformation from its original state.

Using the Free Transform tool and then applying a little transparency can yield compositions that contain believable reflections. The Free Transform tool works with bitmaps as well as native CorelDRAW vector objects.

Copying Effects with the Attributes Eyedropper Tool

In addition to properties such as outline color and effects such as perspective (covered in later chapters), you can copy transformations between objects using the Attributes Eyedropper tool. To do this, choose the tool, have both the objects in view, and then click the Transformations button on the Property Bar. Then check the individual properties you want to sample. For example, if you want to copy the scale of an object to a different object, put a check in the Size box in the Transformations list, making sure no other transformations, effects, or properties are checked. Click OK to close the flyout and save your choices. You then click the Attributes Eyedropper tool over an object whose scale you want to apply to a different object; the cursor turns into a paint bucket shape and you click over the target object to apply the transformation. The cursor will remain a bucket until you either click the Select Object Attributes button on the Property Bar or you change tools. Because of the persistent state of the applied (the paint bucket cursor) transformations, you can click over several *objects* with the cursor until you've finished your work and your need for the tool.

There are limitations to what the Attributes Eyedropper tool can copy and apply:

- You need to be careful to select the attributes you need copied and applied to other objects; the Properties, Transformations, and Effects drop-down selectors can, for example, copy a single color and then apply it to a single object, but the Attributes Eyedropper cannot sample several colors in a group and apply them in order to another group or single object. What it *can* do with single (compound or simple) objects, however, lies in the Transformations List. If you pick Scale and then sample from, as an example, a large object and then apply the tool to a single object, the target object will indeed scale in proportion to the sampled object.
- You can copy an attribute and apply it to a contour object because CorelDRAW sees this as one object. Similarly, a PowerClipped group of objects is seen as one object, as is an extruded shape. Blend objects are seen as two (or more) objects, so don't try applying an attribute to blend objects.

In the following set of steps, you'll get a better idea of the power of applying copied attributes. You're going to rotate a drawing of a knife (a PowerClipped group of shapes) and its shadow based on the angle of rotation of a different piece of flatware in the composition. Dig in!

Straightening Objects via Attributes

Open Table Setting.cdr. Now, understand that the trick to "unrotating" the knife and its shadow lies in the fact that it was originally rotated, and CorelDRAW can read the information about the previous transformation. You cannot duplicate a transformation using an object that has had no transformation to begin with.

1. Choose the Attributes Eyedropper tool from the Toolbox. Click the Transformations drop-down list on the Property Bar and then ensure Rotation is the only option checked. All other boxes should be unchecked, including those in the Properties drop-down box.
2. Click the fork.
3. When the cursor is a paint bucket, click exactly over the knife. You'll see, as shown in Figure 6-3, that the knife almost magically straightens itself. By the way, you could also choose Object | Transformations | Clear Transformations to accomplish this with a selected object, but the Attributes Eyedropper tool proves faster a lot of times.
4. Click over the shadow of the knife. You can now consider yourself a perfect host.

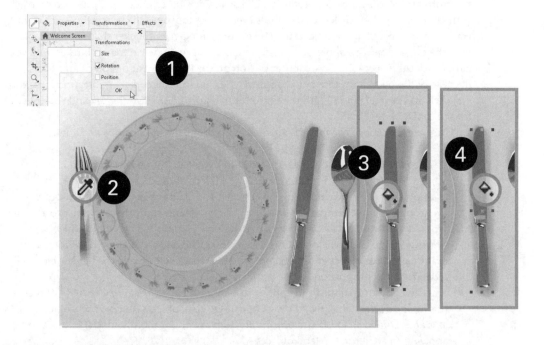

FIGURE 6-3 Sampling and pasting attributes is a quick way to change scores of elements dramatically in a composition.

Applying Precise Transformations

The Transformations docker is terrific for applying multiple transformations with a single command. The docker has five Transformation buttons: Position (Move), Rotation, Scale and Mirror, Size, and Skew, as shown in this fantastic illustration, which you can open and experiment with. It's named Pushpin.cdr.

To open the Transformations docker, choose Window | Dockers or choose Objects | Transformations. When you click any submenu command, the entire docker appears docked to the right edge of the drawing window. The docker has been detached in this illustration.

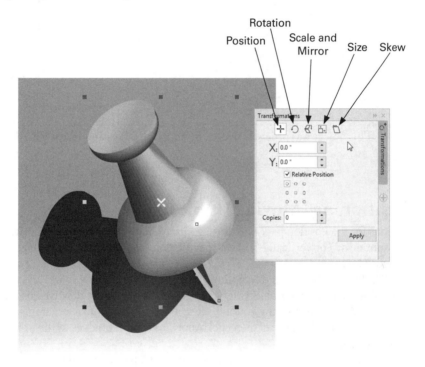

For all transformations, the procedure is the same: click the button for the type of transformation, enter the values you need, and then click the Apply button in the docker to transform the selected object(s). In this section, you'll learn what each area does for you and the options offered for each.

 Note Options in the Transformations docker vary by transformation type. Over the next few pages, the examples show only the specific transformation being discussed.

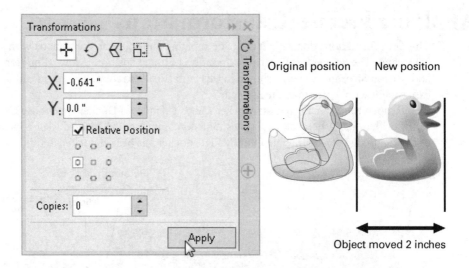

Original position   New position

Object moved 2 inches

FIGURE 6-4 This object was precisely moved by applying a Position transformation.

Positioning (Moving) Objects

Options for the Position page will move your object selection a specified distance, either horizontally (x) or vertically (y), to a specific point on your document page, as shown in Figure 6-4.

While the Relative Position option is selected, entering new values and clicking the Apply button moves your objects by a specified distance. If the Relative Position option is *not* selected, you'll be moving your object to a specific location; for example, if you type **11** in the x (horizontal) field and then click Apply, your object moves to the 11" mark on the horizontal ruler.

If you specify a value greater than zero in the Copies field and use the Relative Position option, you create a duplicate object for every increment of the x value you've typed in.

Rotating Objects

On the Rotation page, you can enter exact angles of rotation based on degrees and in default increments of 5 using the spin boxes. Here, you see two very different results when using relative and absolute positioning and two copies of the lobster.

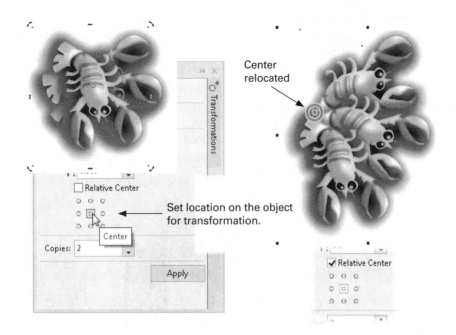

Center relocated

Set location on the object for transformation.

Relative Center

Copies: 2

Apply

Relative Center

Entering negative values rotates an object clockwise, whereas positive values cause counterclockwise rotation. Selecting the Relative Center option cause the object to be rotated around its center marker position. By default, the marker is at position x=0 and y=0; this is the object's geometric center. Entering new values has the same effect as moving the center marker position with the Pick tool, but with the advantage of mathematical precision. When Relative Center is not selected, the x and y values represent fixed page coordinates for the center of rotation.

Tip You can change the initial transformation point on an object by first clicking any of the nine mini-boxes above the Copies field. So, for example, if you want an object to rotate by 15 degrees, making seven copies, and you want to commence the process from the lower left of the object's bounding box, you first click the lower-left mini-box. This Windows 10 Metro ("flat") look makes it a little hard to see what you're doing: the selected mini-box takes on an outline box around it when selected instead of taking a check mark, but if you need this feature, this is a fast and easy option.

Scale and Mirror Objects

The Scale and Mirror transformation has features for entering precise changes in object size. You can also flip the object on either the x- or y-axis (or even both simultaneously), by clicking one of the two mirror buttons, as shown here.

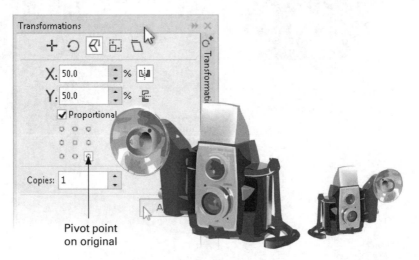

Pivot point
on original

Original drawing   New drawing scaled 50 percent
and mirrored horizontally

When the Proportional option is selected, width and height scaling operations are locked to each other. This means that scaling the width or height by a given percentage value causes the adjacent value to be calculated automatically to preserve your selected object's original proportions. When the Proportional option is unselected, your object's new horizontal and vertical scale values are unlinked, meaning you can apply scaling commands to either the width or height, independent of each other. Remember that the final position of any copies is determined by which of the mini-boxes above the Copies field you selected before clicking Apply.

Sizing Objects

This transformation type gives you the option to change either the x or y measure (or both) of an object selection based on the values entered. For example, entering **2** (inches) in the Width box and clicking the Apply button scales the selected object to a width of two inches. When the Proportional option is not selected, the width and height values can be changed independently. While it's selected, both width and height values are linked and calculated automatically to alter the size of the object proportionally.

Precision Skewing

The term *skew* means to change the position of two sides of a shape in a parallel fashion while leaving the other two sides alone; *slanting* is a more common synonym for skew. The Skew transformation also gives you the chance to apply both vertical and horizontal skew independently or simultaneously by entering degree measures, in turn, transforming the object on either the x- or y-axis. As with rotation commands, negative degree values produce clockwise skews, whereas positive values cause counterclockwise skews. Choosing the Use Anchor Point option lets you specify a left, center, right, top, bottom, side, or corner point as the point around which your objects are skewed, as shown here. The skewed copy more or less looks like a cast shadow of the original symbol, doesn't it?

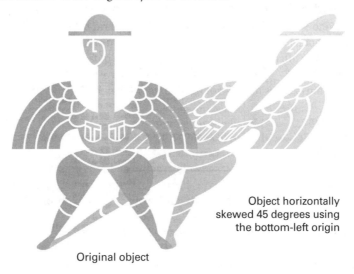

Object horizontally
skewed 45 degrees using
the bottom-left origin

Original object

Controlling the Order of Things

How your objects are ordered is another consideration when organizing drawing objects in a composition. The order of objects determines whether an object appears in front of—or behind—another object. Your page and the Pasteboard (the area surrounding your document page) are always the *backmost* point, whereas your screen is always the frontmost point. All objects are layered between these two points.

When overlapping objects are ordered, they appear in front of or behind each other, according to their order. As you create each new object, it is put in front of all existing objects *on the current document layer*. Changing the object order lets you rearrange overlapping objects without changing their position on the page. To do this, CorelDRAW has a series of order commands that let you shuffle the order of objects in various ways. You'll find them in the Object | Order submenu, but you can also apply them using shortcut keys or the To Back Of Layer and To Front Of Layer buttons, available toward the far right on the Property Bar, when an object is selected.

Note The *hierarchy* of object ordering on a layer is very different than *object layers*. Although each layer has its own collection of objects that can be ordered in a sequence, the layers *themselves* can *also* be ordered. This means that if you're trying to control the ordering of two or more objects, check the Status Bar to make sure they're on the same layer.

Here's how each of the object order commands works:

- **To Front of Layer**   This command shuffles your selected object(s) to the very front of the current layer. Press SHIFT-PAGE UP or choose Object | Order | To Front of Layer to apply it. The To Front command is also available as a Property Bar button when an object is selected.
- **To Back of Layer**   This command shuffles your selected object(s) to the very back of the current layer. Press SHIFT-PAGE DOWN or choose Object | Order | To Back of Layer to apply it. The To Back command is also available as a Property Bar button while an object is selected.
- **Forward One**   This command shuffles your selected object(s) forward by one in the object order of the current layer. Press CTRL-PAGE UP or choose Object | Order | Forward One to apply it.
- **Back One**   This command shuffles your selected object(s) backward by one in the object order of the current layer. Press CTRL-PAGE DOWN or choose Object | Order | Back One to apply it.
- **In Front Of**   This command is interactive and puts your selected object directly in front of any object you specify in the current layer order. A targeting cursor will appear, and you use it to choose which object to shuffle your selection in front of. Choose Object | Order | In Front Of to apply it.
- **Behind**   This command also causes a targeting cursor to appear, enabling you to specify which object you want your object selection to be shuffled behind in the object order on the current layer. Choose Object | Order | Behind to apply it.
- **Reverse Order**   This command effectively shuffles the order of your selected object so that it's in the reverse of its current order on the layer. Front objects become back objects, and vice versa. For example, if your objects are numbered 1, 2, 3, and 4 from front to back, applying this command would reorder them to 4, 3, 2, and 1. Choose Object | Order | Reverse Order to apply it.

Tip   When you change the object order using the Reverse Order command, grouped objects are considered a single object, so their relative order in the group will be preserved. To reorder objects within a group, you'll need to ungroup (CTRL-U) the objects first before applying the command.

Working with Views of a Document's Depth: Layers

CorelDRAW's layer feature provides invaluable ways not only to organize but also to view complex drawings. You can create several layers and move shapes among layers. You can also name layers, control their order and appearance, change object ordering within layers, group objects, and quickly see object information. One immediate advantage to adopting layers in your composition work is that you can hide layers; suppose you have a lot of objects that need labels, and you need to print the objects with and without the labels. Put all the labels on a layer, hide the layer, print just the objects, and then unhide the layer and make a second print!

Exploring the Object Manager

The Object Manager docker is your resource for viewing layer content and using layer options. With the Object Manager, you can perform a whole range of actions: navigate document pages, create and name layers, select and move objects among layers, and set layers as editable, printable, and visible. To open the Object Manager docker, choose Windows | Docker | Object Manager. As mentioned in Chapter 4, a keyboard shortcut such as M is a good idea to assign to the Object Manager, unless you want it docked to the workspace window for all time.

The Object Manager shows a listing of the layers, each accompanied by options and a flyout menu. A Master Page also appears and includes default layers for controlling guides, the desktop, and grid objects. If more than one page is in a document, you can specify whether you want odd, even, or all pages in the file to have Master Pages; more on this later in the chapter. Figure 6-5 shows a drawing and what the Object Manager reports for this composition. There is only one page; the drawing was created on two layers on Page 1, and you can see a main entry below Layer 2 that indicates a group of 10 objects. Actually, many more objects make up the paper cup illustration, but they are in subgroups within the entry that says "10 Objects"— as far as the Object Manager goes, you need to expand all the + boxes to see what really exists in the drawing aside from grouped objects, whose number is unknown until you look. As you dig through the groups on the Object Manager, you will see individual entries named curve, rectangle, polygon, and so on. The Object Manager is quite explicit about objects in groups, making locating an object a much easier task than in most other drawing programs.

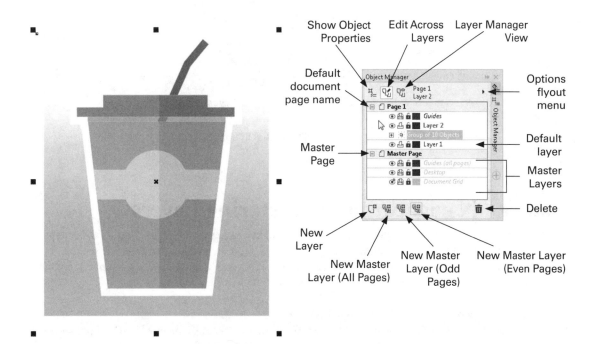

FIGURE 6-5 View information, as well as name and alter it, with the Object Manager.

Note Having Master Pages for odd- and even-numbered pages in a multipage document makes page numbering and special elements belonging to a facing page easier than ever to compose.

Navigating Pages, Objects, and Layers

The best way to use the Object Manager docker to navigate through your document, select layers, and control layer options is by experimenting yourself; the following steps are a guide. You'll learn exactly how these operations are performed; look at the next illustration, which shows a default layer structure for a new document.

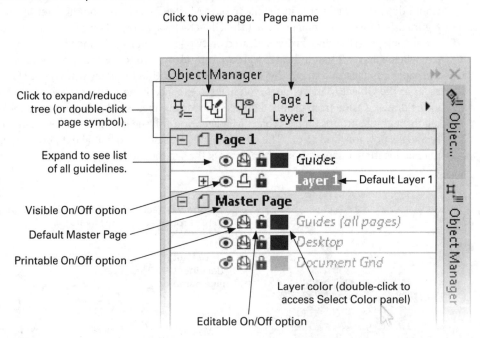

Tutorial Navigating and Mastering Layers

The next steps have no right or wrong execution, but rather they're simply exploration steps to get you comfortable working with layers. This is why an illustration has already been created for you; you just work the steps and see how any of several techniques can be applied to your own work, future and present.

1. Open Alarming.cdr in CorelDRAW.
2. Open the Object Manager docker: Window | Dockers | Object Manager. Look at the status of the layers. The background—the pattern fill of the clocks—is locked so it

cannot be moved at present. Also, there's a layer on top with a default name, and it's hidden, which also means it's locked. Investigate a little now; unhide the top layer to see what's inside.

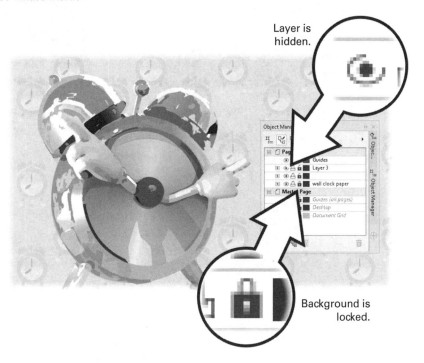

Layer is hidden.

Background is locked.

3. Okay, I'm trying to be funny here—and hopefully succeeding. The layer contains a third hand; yet within the context of an alarm clock, it's really a "second hand." It's possible now to select the group of objects on Layer 3 by clicking them with the Pick tool, and if you click a second time, you can rotate the hand by dragging the rotation handles, and crank Time itself back to 1289 A.D.! Click twice (slowly, don't double-click) on the name of Layer 3 on the Object Manager and then type a name in the field that's more descriptive than "Layer 3" for future reference. Try **extra hand**, because why not?

4. Double-click the "extra hand" layer title to open its contents. The hand is several grouped objects, and they can be moved to the "clock" layer. First, rename the group: click twice on the "Group of 36 objects" and then type **third hand** in the field. Notice that control nodes are visible when a group or a single object is selected. Press SHIFT-F2 to "Zoom to Selected." Selecting items from the Object Manager is an easy way to select and then zoom into an object you want to work on.

5. Double-click the "clock" layer title to open it, and then drag the "third hand" group below the layer title, but above the "Group of 233 objects" entry. Layers have

a hierarchy, and if you put the group below the "Group of 233 Objects," the third hand would be hidden from view by the 233 other objects.

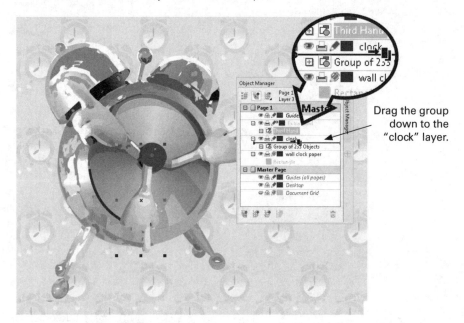

Drag the group down to the "clock" layer.

6. Double-click the "extra hand" layer title. This action produces precisely nothing, which indicates that there is nothing nested within the layer. So it's okay to delete it—with the layer title highlighted, click Delete (the trash icon). Poof!

Caution There is no confirmation box with the Delete trash icon; it's similar to pressing the keyboard DELETE key. Be careful how you use it. To undo an inadvertent deletion, you need to click the workspace to put the document (and not the Object Manager) "in focus," and then press CTRL-Z (Edit | Undo).

7. Similarly, the background is expendable in this composition. Click the rectangle object on the locked layer; you can't because the layer is locked. Click the Lock or Unlock pencil icon with the red slash over it to make the layer editable, and then click the Delete button.

Tip Every object, down to single objects, on the Object Manager's list can be renamed. Consider giving a very important object a custom name in your own work. Then, at any time, you can locate the object by conducting a search with the Edit | Find and Replace feature, or just by scrolling through the list of objects.

8. Create a new layer by clicking the New Layer button. Name it and then drag its title to the bottom of the layer stack on this page.
9. Lock the clock layer.

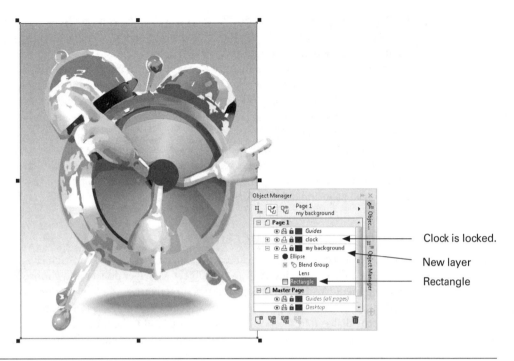

Clock is locked.

New layer

Rectangle

FIGURE 6-6   Working with layers takes full advantage of CorelDRAW's search capabilities and makes it easy to modify only certain elements in a complex drawing.

10. Click the new layer highlighted on the Object Manager list, choose the Rectangle tool from the Toolbox, create a rectangle as a background for the clock, and then apply a fill. Figure 6-6 shows a linear gradient fill (covered in Chapter 12) and a blend with transparency added to the new background layer. See Chapter 14 for the scoop on blends and contours.

Using Object Manager Editing and View States

Objects can be on different layers, and you can edit across layers in CorelDRAW. Create a new file that has objects on, let's say, three layers. This way, you can better learn through example about the editing and view states of CorelDRAW layers. Open the Object Manager docker. You'll see three view state buttons at the top of the docker—that's where information about viewing and editing behavior are set. Clicking each button toggles its state on or off. Each button has the following effects:

Tip   You can use the Combine, Group, or Convert To Curves command on objects in the Object Manager docker by selecting the objects, right-clicking them, and choosing a command from the pop-up menu.

- **Show Object Properties**   Click the Show Object Properties button to set whether you want to view a detailed name for a layer's contents (color, type of object, and so on) or just the name (either the default or your own custom name).
- **Edit Across Layers**   Click the Edit Across Layers button to set whether objects can be selected, moved, and copied between layers. While cross-layer editing is disabled, objects appear grayed out, allowing only objects on your current page layer and/or the desktop to be selected or edited. While cross-layer editing is enabled, you can select, move, or edit any object on an unlocked layer.
- **Layer Manager View**   The Layer Manager View button toggles your view to show only your document's layers. When you're working with complex drawings that have many pages, layers, and objects, using this view can make managing layer properties a lot easier. In this state, all page and object information is omitted.

Controlling Layer Properties

Using the Layer Properties dialog, you can control specific properties for each layer. To access these options, right-click a specific layer in the Object Manager docker and choose Properties from the pop-up menu. You can access properties directly from the pop-up menu or display a modeless dialog for defining the properties of a specific layer. There is a minor difference between using the dialog and the pop-up: the pop-up (right-click) menu has the Delete, Cut, Copy, and Paste commands. However, in X8, you can now rename layers in the Layer Properties dialog in addition to the Object Manager.

Options in this dialog control the following layer properties:

- **Visible**   This option enables you to toggle the view state of a layer between visible and hidden. You can also control the visibility of objects on a layer by clicking the Eye symbol to the left of the layer name.
- **Printable**   This option toggles the printing state of objects on the layer on or off. You can also set whether layer objects are printable by clicking the printer symbol beside the layer in the Object Manager docker to toggle the printing state of objects on the layer.

 Note   Nonprinting layers will also not export. If you need objects selected on a nonprinting layer to be included when exporting, you need to turn on the layer's Printable option.

- **Editable**   Use this option to lock or unlock all objects on a layer. While a layer is locked, its objects can't be edited (or even selected), which is a little different than the Lock (object) command. You can also set whether layer objects are editable by clicking the padlock symbol beside the layer in the Object Manager docker to toggle the editing state of objects on the layer.
- **Master Layer(s)**   You can have layers for odd, even, and all pages in the Master Page entry on the Object Manager docker. You can create a new Master Layer, and you can

also drag an existing layer from a page to the Master Page entry. Changing a layer to a Master Layer makes it part of the Master Page structure. Any objects on a Master Page appear on all pages. For details on working with Master Pages and Master Layers, see the next section.

- **Layer Color** This selector sets the color swatch as it appears in the docker listing directly to the left of a layer name, for easy recognition. Layer Color also determines object colors when viewed using Normal or Enhanced view while the Override Full Color View option is selected. You set the color coding for a layer by double-clicking the color indicator next to a layer name to open a typical color selector menu and then clicking any color from the drop-down color picker.

Working with Master Page Layers

Whenever a new document is created, a *Master Page* is automatically created. The Master Page isn't a physical page in your document, but instead a place where document objects can be placed so they appear on every page of your document. Objects on a Master Page layer are visible and printable on every page in your document, making this an extremely powerful feature. For example, placing a text header or footer or a company logo on a Master Page layer is a quick and easy way to label all the pages in a pamphlet or brochure.

Moving any object onto a layer on the Master Page makes it a Master Page object and causes it to appear on each page. Let's try out this feature.

Tutorial Working with Master Page Items

1. Open the Object Manager docker by choosing Window | Dockers | Object Manager.
2. Click the New Master Layer (All Pages) button—the second in the row of buttons at the bottom of the docker. A new layer is automatically added to the Master Page with the default name "Layer 1."
3. With this new Master Layer as your current layer (click the entry to make sure it's selected), create the object(s) you wish to appear on every page in its final position and appearance. By creating the object while the Master Layer is selected, the object automatically becomes a Master Layer object. You can also move objects from other pages onto the Master Layer by click-dragging them in the docker list from their position under a layer name to the Master Layer name.
4. Click to select the new Master Page object(s) on your document page. Notice that you can still select, move, and edit it. To toggle the lock/unlock state of your Master Layer object(s), click the Edit button (the padlock icon) beside the Master Page in the docker. Locking prevents any accidental editing of the Master Page object(s).
5. Add pages to your document by clicking the + button at the lower left of the workspace. As you browse through the pages, you'll see the same object on all pages.

Several default layers already exist on your document's Master Page for controlling special items that appear in your document, such as guides, Document Grid, and Desktop. These layers have the following purposes:

- **Guides Layer**   This is a global layer for guides you create; if you click the Guides (all pages) entry on the Object Manager to select it, and then drag a guide onto the page, all pages in the document will display this guide. If you need a guide on only one page, you choose that Guides entry on the page you're working on, drag a guide from the rulers, and that guide belongs to that page and is not a Master Page item.

Tip   You can move a local guide, a guide you created on a page, to the Master Guides entry on the Object Manager to make it global—it will then appear on every page of your document.

- **Document Grid**   This controls the appearance of grid lines. You can control the grid color and visibility, but you can't make the Grid Layer printable, nor can you change its editable objects or add objects to that layer. Options in the Document Grid Properties dialog enable you to control the grid display color and to gain quick access to the Grid page of the Options dialog by clicking the Setup button in the dialog. To open the Document Grid Properties dialog, right-click the Document Grid under the Master Page in the Object Manager docker, and choose Properties from the pop-up menu.

Tip   Document Grid visibility can be toggled on or off by clicking its eye icon on the Object Manager docker.

- **Desktop Layer**   This is a global Desktop, the place outside of your drawing page. If you want to keep objects handy but don't want to print them on your page, drag the object to this entry on the Object Manager. If you put an object on the Desktop from a layer, you can't hide it or keep it from printing, but if it's explicitly placed on the Master Desktop, you can hide it, keep it from being edited, and keep it from printing.

Hopefully, this chapter has shown you how to transform not only objects, but also your skill level with CorelDRAW. You now know how to move, scale, rotate, and perform other operations on page objects and their duplicates. You also know how to manually transform and use the dockers and other features for precisely moving and aligning the elements you need for a terrific design. Chapter 7 takes you into *creating* these shapes that you now know how to move; you put Chapters 6 and 7 *together,* and your family's going to start missing you because you'll be having too much fun designing to sit down for regular dinners!

7 Choosing (and Understanding) the Right Path Tools

If you thought learning to create basic shapes and modifying them in Chapter 5 was a fun learning experience, then hold on: basic shapes will basically get your work only so far. CorelDRAW's path building and editing tools are at your disposal to create *exactly* what you envision. The Curve Tools group on the Toolbox has tools that make any shape you can imagine (and some you *can't*) a snap to design. In the following sections, you'll work through the *editing* process of lines and their nodes, so there's no reason to draw something that's *close* to what you need. This chapter is the "DRAW" part of CorelDRAW. Incidentally, the Artistic Media pen is no longer part of this Curve Tools group; it has its own icon on the Toolbox, and the Smart Drawing tool is covered in Chapter 8 because it's of enormous use to novices whose jobs require them to instantly become graphics designers. *Experienced* users will enjoy Chapter 8, too!

 Note Download and extract all the files from the Chapter 7.zip archive to follow the tutorials in this chapter.

Sidling Up to CorelDRAW's Curve Tools

The most basic shape you can draw in CorelDRAW (and any vector drawing program) is a *line:* a line is a path that passes through at least two *points,* called *nodes* in CorelDRAW. A line is actually a mathematical equation, and as such, it doesn't necessarily have an outline color and a width, and it doesn't even have to be a *straight* line. However, a line *does* have a *direction;* that is, the direction in which you draw the line. This might seem obvious or trivial, but vectors *do* have a direction, and you can get arrowheads on the wrong end of a line, and all sorts of unwanted stuff, if you fail to remember the basic properties of a vector graphic.

There are scores of different properties to which you can assign a line, such as arrowheads and a dashed outline around clip-out coupons. You can also assign solid colors and varying widths to complete any assignment. Joining the beginning and end points of a line (a path) closes the path. If the beginning doesn't meet the end point, the shape is called an *open path.*

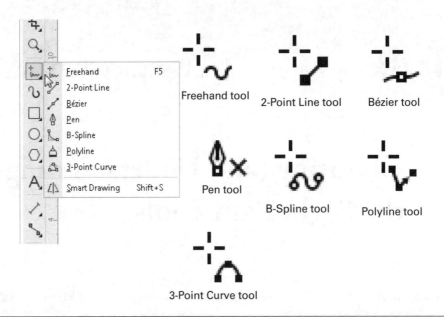

Freehand tool   2-Point Line tool   Bézier tool

Pen tool   B-Spline tool   Polyline tool

3-Point Curve tool

FIGURE 7-1 For visual reference while you work, each of the different drawing tools has a unique cursor.

CorelDRAW X8's Curve tools are task-oriented tools; although they all produce paths, your choice of tool(s) for a task depends on what it is you want to draw. For example, do you need to produce an object whose curves are flawless—like those of a physical French curve? This task calls for the B-Spline tool. You can also "mix and match"; that is, you can begin an object with one tool and then finish it with a different tool. Your choices depend on the object you want to create. Some of these tools work similarly, so it's best to become acquainted with what the cursors *look* like, as shown in Figure 7-1.

How to Fill an Open Path

When you draw a path and the beginning and end points don't meet, it's called an *open path*, and ordinarily you cannot apply a fill to its interior. However, you can *indeed* fill an open path—just like in Adobe Illustrator—when you know where to turn this option on.

To change CorelDRAW's behavior so that all open paths are filled—without the need to close the path first—follow these steps:

1. Open the Options dialog. Click the Options button on the Standard Bar (alternatively, press CTRL-J).
2. Expand Document and then click General to display the associated options on the right side of the dialog.
3. Click the Fill Open Curves option so that it is selected, and click OK to close the dialog.

After choosing this option, the open paths you draw can have an interior area.

How to Draw in CorelDRAW

Although you can use the Artistic Media tool and its variants to "paint" in DRAW, this nicety is covered in Chapter 13. Right now, we're talking technique and proficiency with vector shapes made of straight lines and curves and connected by nodes. In the Curve Tools group, you'll find CorelDRAW's path and node-creation pens; they're used for both accuracy and artistic expression, and they have varying degrees of ease of use that correspond directly to their power.

Drawing with Freehand and Polyline Tools

The *Freehand* and *Polyline tools* share a common function, giving you the freedom to draw as if you were sketching by hand on a physical sketchpad, but the tools work in slightly different ways. Sketched lines can create a single open or closed vector path. Both tools are located in the Toolbox, grouped with other line-creation tools.

For mouse users and stylus users alike, click-dragging initially produces a start node for a path segment, and then a node is placed when you release the mouse button (or stylus), setting the end of the path segment. Here's how to use these tools:

1. Begin by selecting the Freehand tool.
2. You can create a continuous line by click-dragging a path shape. As soon as the mouse button is released, the line is complete, as you will see on the left in Figure 7-2.
3. To *extend* this path—that is, to *add* a path segment after the first segment's end node—you position your cursor over either the beginning *or* end node. The cursor now features a tiny bent arrow, as shown in Figure 7-2. To continue with a freeform path, you just start click-dragging again.
4. Now, let's say you want to extend this path with a straight line segment or two. Instead of click-dragging on the end node of the previous segment, you click and then release the mouse button; the cursor turns into a little line segment icon, and wherever you want to end this segment, you single-click.
5. If you want to keep going with straight line segments, don't just click an end node and move your cursor; instead, *double-click* an end node, and you are now creating a new line segment that is joined to the previous line segment by a node.
6. To create a path that only has straight lines, you single-click and then move the cursor and double-click each time you want the line segment ended and a new one begun. Figure 7-2 shows the result on the right, and what the cursors look like and do depending on their position over the page or the path. Do not freak out at the apparent complexity of this figure! It's a treasure map to mastering the Freehand tool.

The Polyline tool, on the other hand, can be used similarly to the Freehand tool, except only a single-click adds a node, and you can continue to add path segments. You'll notice that

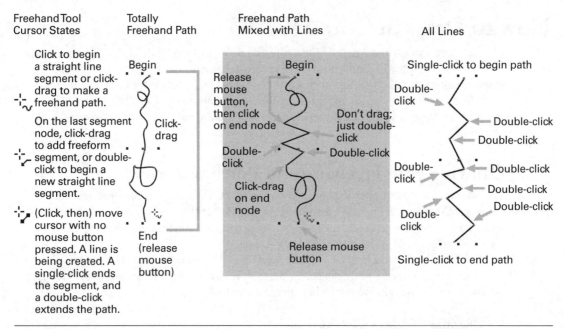

Freehand Tool Cursor States   Totally Freehand Path   Freehand Path Mixed with Lines   All Lines

Click to begin a straight line segment or click-drag to make a freehand path.

On the last segment node, click-drag to add freeform segment, or double-click to begin a new straight line segment.

(Click, then) move cursor with no mouse button pressed. A line is being created. A single-click ends the segment, and a double-click extends the path.

Begin

Click-drag

End (release mouse button)

Release mouse button, then click on end node

Double-click

Click-drag on end node

Begin

Double-click

Don't drag; just double-click

Release mouse button

Single-click to begin path

Double-click

Double-click

Double-click

Double-click

Double-click

Double-click

Double-click

Single-click to end path

FIGURE 7-2   Straight lines and freeform paths are the strong points of the Freehand tool.

when you click-drag with the Polyline tool, your curves appear smoother, and this, like the Freehand tool, might serve digitizing tablet users the most. The following illustration shows the standard method for using the Polyline tool.

The Polyline Tool: Standard Method

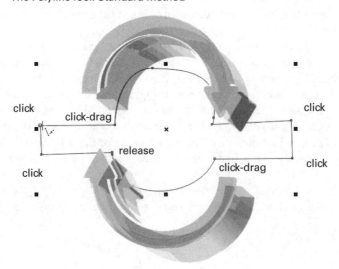

click   click-drag   click

click   release

click   click-drag   click

Note A *single*-click using either the Freehand tool or the Polyline tool at the beginning of a path closes the path, and it then becomes an object that can be filled, extruded, or perhaps even sold as Fine Art.

There is an *extended* function of the Polyline tool that lets you draw straight lines, mixed with perfectly circular arcs if you single-click the end of a straight line segment, hold ALT, release the mouse button, move the cursor position (this is called *hovering)*, and then single-click. The illustration here shows that with a minimum of patience and a good idea in your head, you can easily create French-curve-like abstract objects. If you want your work to be an open path, double-click when you're done with the pen.

The Polyline Tool: ALT Method

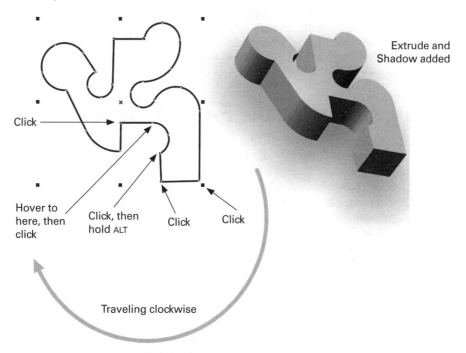

Extrude and
Shadow added

Click

Hover to
here, then
click

Click, then
hold ALT

Click

Click

Traveling clockwise

Tip You can use the Property Bar options to make any open path begin with an arrowhead, make the line—open or closed—into a dashed line, and change the stroke width.

Using either of these tools, you have control over the smoothness of path shapes drawn using click-drag actions by adjusting the Freehand Smoothing option in the Property Bar *before* drawing your path. You can control smoothness after *drawing* a path by selecting nodes with the Shape tool and then using the Reduce Nodes slider. Reduce Nodes has a range between 0 and 100 percent; lower values apply less smoothing, and higher values apply more smoothing, as shown here.

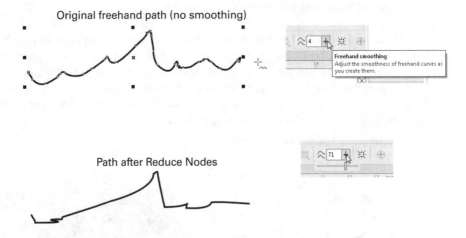

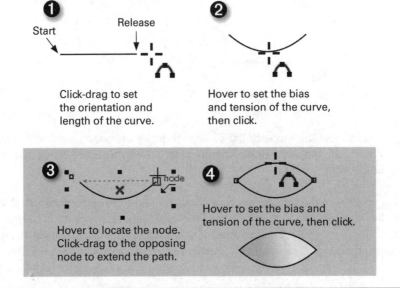

Drawing Arcs with the 3-Point Curve Tool

The *3-Point Curve tool* was created for artists to build perfectly smooth arcing line segments, with complete control over the direction and steepness of the curve between two points. First, you hold-drag the tool to set a straight line that defines the angle of the curve. This sets the start and end points for the curve. Then you release the mouse button and hover the cursor to define the slope and degree of the curve; you're provided with an onscreen preview until you decide and click a point and thus create the curve. Figure 7-3 shows the process, and

FIGURE 7-3 A 3-point curve can be adjusted at every step of its creation.

additionally how to extend the curve with a second segment to close the path so it can be filled. This is the basis for the tutorial to follow, where you'll create flower petals on an almost-completed illustration. Let this figure be your graphical guide.

Terms such as *angle* and *slope* don't adequately describe the characteristics of a curve to anyone other than a geometry professor. Therefore, here are two additional, slightly nerdy but highly accurate terms describing the characteristics of a curve:

- **Bias**   When you draw an imaginary straight line through the end points of any curve, *bias* describes which of the two end points the curve leans toward.
- **Tension**   Similarly, when a straight line runs through the two points that define a curve, *tension* describes how close or how far the curve's farthest point is from the line.

The following illustration shows examples of tension and bias. When you click on a control point (a node) on a CorelDRAW path, the curve's node sets the tension and bias, while the control handles address the heading of the path—the vector direction in which the path is going.

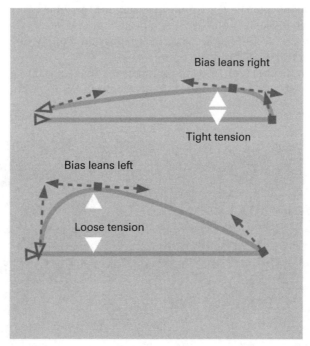

You'll quickly discover that part of the power of the 3-Point Curve tool is its use in building a series of connected arcs; you can design French curves and ornamental borders by creating a 3-point curve, positioning your cursor over the end point until you see the cursor signifying an extension of the last-drawn curve, and then building another 3-point curve.

In the following steps, you'll create a cat's eye object that will serve as both a leaf and a flower petal to complete an illustration.

| Tutorial | # 3-Point Curves and Closed Objects

1. Open Flower and Vase.cdr. The white outlines are where the petals should be drawn, and this overlay is on the Guides layer, which is locked. The center of the flower is on a layer above the current layer, and it and the background illustration are on locked layers, so there is nothing to accidentally move.

2. With the 3-Point Curve tool, click-drag across any of the Guides, beginning at one point of the petal guide and ending at the other. Release the mouse button and then hover below the line until the curve basically matches the curve of the guide; then click to make the 3-point curve.

3. Hover over the right node of the curve until your cursor features an arrow and the word *node*. Then click-drag to the opposite point on the underlying curve. You're extending this original curve. Release the mouse button when the cursor signifies that it's over the second point with a tiny arrow.

4. Hover and let the curve arc upward until it matches the underlying curve guide; then click. You now have a closed path that can be filled (see the left side of Figure 7-4).

5. With the Interactive Fill tool, drag from the tip to the base of the petal object (look ahead to Figure 7-4). Then drag a brown color well from the color palette to the left (the From color) marker, and, finally, drag and drop a yellow-orange color well to the right (the To color) marker.

6. With the Pick tool, move the object center marker to the center of the brown object—the disc florets of my attempt to draw a Black-Eyed Susan.

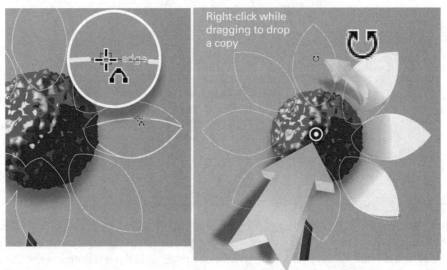

FIGURE 7-4 You can create smooth, connecting arcs quickly using the 3-Point Curve tool.

7. Click the selected object to put it into rotation mode. Drag the top-right selection handle down; before releasing the mouse button, tap the right button to drop a copy of the object onto another unfilled guide object. The process is shown on the right side of Figure 7-4.
8. Repeat Step 7 until you have all seven petal guides filled with duplicates of your object.
9. Drag and (right-click) drop an extra petal near the empty leaf guide on the illustration's stem. Rotate it into position and fill it with a linear gradient of two different shades of green. Save your work and be sure to water it about every two to three days.

Here's the finished drawing:

The 2-Point Line Tool

This is the most self-explanatory tool in the Pen tool group: you click-drag at any point on the page, and when you release the mouse button, the line is completed. Although this might seem like a "toy tool" compared to the others, it's actually very useful for callouts in technical manuals, and it was used extensively in this book. For callouts, create a line, assign a 2-point weight, and add an arrowhead—end of task.

Using the Bézier and Pen Tools

The *Bézier tool* and the *Pen tool* are variations on the same theme of drawing connected curves and straight segments through the action of first clicking to set a path point and then either dragging to define a curve behind the click point or clicking (no dragging) to define a straight path segment behind the click point. You'll find these tools grouped together with other line-drawing tools.

One of the less obvious differences between the two tools is that the Pen tool offers a "look-ahead" point when you draw with it: before you click or click-drag a point, the proposed path between the point before you click and the previous (already defined) point on the path is shown in light blue. Although control handles (those guys sprouting off the nodes, discussed later in this chapter) are displayed when a curve is defined with the Pen tool, the Pen tool doesn't afford you as much control in steering the shape of the curve as the Bézier tool. Unlike the Pen tool, the Bézier tool always uses a click-drag mouse gesture to produce curves. The Pen tool, on the other hand, lets you hover your cursor before clicking to set the preceding curve in an object's path segments. When you're just beginning with CorelDRAW, the Pen tool is useful because it provides a preview of the next segment you'll create. However, after you gain some experience, you might want to skip the previews, pick up some drawing speed, and use the Bézier tool.

Pen tool   Bézier tool

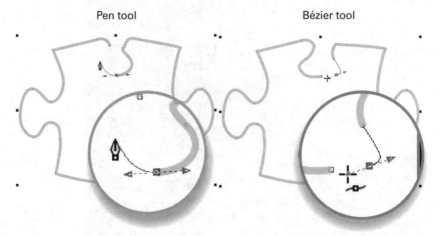

Hover the cursor between the previous click and the next click to see a "look ahead" of the path you're drawing.

Drags control the handle from the node created when click-dragging.

Getting a Handle on Béziers

The product of both the Bézier tool and the Pen tool can be curves between two nodes whose connection to a neighboring node is smooth and symmetrical. Control handles are revealed on smooth, symmetrical nodes when you click one using the Shape tool. These handles are used for intuitively reshaping the curve.

Because straight line segments and curve segments share so much in their fundamental anatomy, there is almost no distinction between the terms *line* and *curve* in the discussions in this chapter. The shapes of Bézier lines are controlled in part by node properties and the position of curve handles. Two paths can have nodes in the same relative page position but have completely different shapes, as shown here.

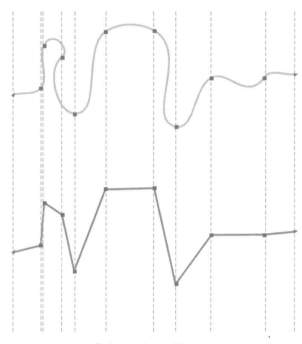

Same node positions

Nodes and Control Points

When a vector path describes an arc, *nodes* (points) connect the beginning and end points, and the nodes have *control handles,* at the end of which are *control points,* the screen element you use to manipulate curves. The number of control handles and points depends on the segment connected by each node. For example, an arc (a curve) connected to a straight line segment has one control handle visible, and it controls the slope of the curve segment. When two curve segments are connected, you'll see two control handles if you click the connecting node with the Shape tool, and this node can have different connection properties (such as Cusp and Smooth—described later in this chapter). A straight path segment can be described as two nodes connecting the segment, and the control handles for the nodes coincide in position with the node itself. For all intents and purposes, the control handles can't be seen; they become visible when the segment is changed to a curved segment: the control handles appear on the segment, and you can move them away from the launch point of the curve and then freely manipulate the slope of the curve by dragging the control points.

Nodes can be defined as *cusp, smooth,* or *symmetrical* by using the Shape tool in combination with the options on the Property Bar, as shown in the following illustration. *Cusp* nodes can be used to create a discontinuity in direction between two line segments; in English, the two segments connect in a "non-smooth" fashion. Think of the moon being on the cusp; it's crescent shaped, and this is the sort of shape you can create using cusp node connections. *Smooth* nodes cause the path slope and direction to align on either side of a node; their relationship is in 180° opposition, which has the effect of creating a smooth transition at the node point itself. Control handles surrounding a smooth node may be unequal distances from the node. *Symmetrical* nodes not only are smooth, but the control handles are of equal distance from the node. You'll immediately appreciate the effect of a symmetrical node; when you drag one control point away from a node, the opposing control handle moves an equal distance from the node in exactly the opposite direction. The artistic effect is that the two joined path segments take on an almost circular appearance, which is very useful for technical illustration work.

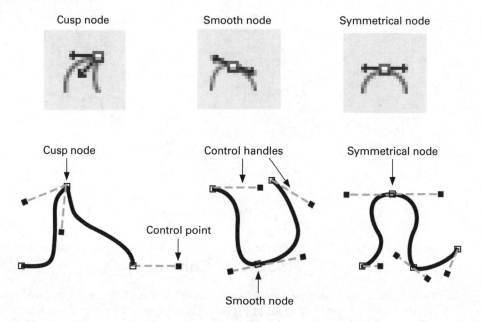

Tip When drawing with the Bézier tool, hold CTRL as you click to force new node positions to align vertically, horizontally, or within constrained angles relative to the last created node position. Holding CTRL while dragging curve handles constrains their angles to 15° increments relative to the last node created.

We try out a new drawing method in the following tutorial.

Tutorial # Drawing Curves and Straight Line Segments

1. Choose either the Bézier tool or the Pen tool and use a single-click action to define the first node position of your path. Click again to define a second point somewhere else on your page. The two nodes are now joined by a straight line.
2. Using the click-drag mouse technique, click to define your next node position, but continue dragging in any direction. As you drag, the second and third nodes are joined by a curved line.
3. If you chose the Bézier tool, you'll notice that two control handles appear joined by a dotted line. The point you are dragging is the control point that steers the control handle. The farther you drag the control point from the node, the larger the arc of the curve becomes. Release the mouse button and notice that the control handles remain in view; your path is complete unless you'd like to move a node or refine the position of its control points some more.
4. If you chose the Pen tool, you'll notice that a preview of your next curve appears as you move your cursor, which remains active until the next node is defined. To specify a node as the last in the path, use a double-click action to define the current node as the last point.
5. Using either tool, click your cursor directly on the first node you defined. This action closes the path and automatically joins the first and last nodes.
6. You can now fill the object; regardless of the settings in CorelDRAW's General options, the curves are filled. Export after 10–12 minutes at 450°. Allow to cool. Serves one to four. I'm just kidding here, of course—but not about the closed paths.

Editing Bézier Paths

All lines are controlled by properties of the nodes they include, which are edited using the Shape tool (F10). You'll find this tool, shown here, grouped with the Knife, Eraser, and Freehand Transform tools.

Using the *Shape tool,* you can change node positions and curve shapes by click-dragging the nodes, their control points, and by directly click-dragging on a path segment. While you're using the Shape tool, icons appear on the Property Bar when one or more nodes are selected; you can select several nodes to change by marquee-dragging them or by SHIFT-clicking a few. These icons are used to set node attributes to Cusp, Smooth, and Symmetrical, to join nodes and break nodes to create individual path segments, and to create straight lines from curves (and vice versa) when you've selected a segment or a node connecting segments. There are additional options, and the

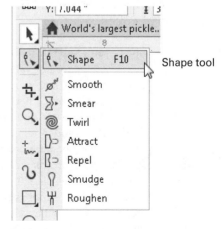

Shape tool

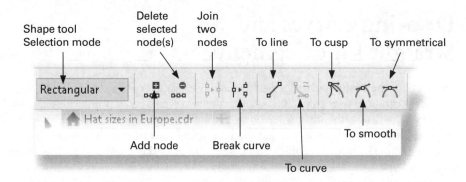

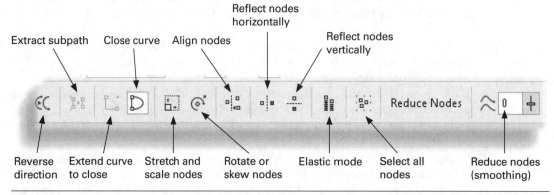

FIGURE 7-5 The Property Bar offers comprehensive control over path and node properties.

bevy of functions on the Property Bar provides exceptional control and flexibility in your design work. In short, you should *get to know the functions* for the Shape tool. The options are called out in Figure 7-5.

Obviously, being able to alter the connections between line segments is an important aspect of creating sophisticated artwork! Each of these buttons changes the selected nodes, lines, and curves in specific ways. The following is a description of what the icons do and what they're called.

- **Shape tool, Selection mode** You can marquee-select nodes the way users always have, by click-dragging a rectangular shape around the nodes you want to select, or you can use freehand style, which produces a lasso-like marquee you can use to be very careful and exacting about which nodes in a group you want to edit. In freehand style, you might also want to use SHIFT to add to the selected nodes.
- **Add/Delete Nodes** These buttons give you the power to add new nodes to a curve or delete selected nodes after you've drawn a path, using the Shape tool and clicking at specific points on a path. To add a node, click any point on a line to highlight the new position and then click the Add Node button. You can also add a new node to a line by clicking on one or more nodes and then clicking the Add Node button to add a node midpoint between the selected node and the next node on the path. To delete a node, click to select it with the Shape tool and then click the Delete Node button. You can also

marquee-select (drag diagonally with the Shape tool to create a rectangle surrounding the nodes) and then delete all the selected nodes in one fell swoop. Pressing the minus (–) key on your numeric keypad or the DELETE key also deletes the selected nodes.

> **Tip** Pressing the plus (+) key on your numeric keypad with the Shape tool touching a path segment might be a quicker way to add a node. You can also double-click anywhere on a path segment to add a node.

- **Join Nodes/Break Curve**   When two unconnected nodes on an open path are selected (for example, when the start point is close to the end point), clicking the Join Nodes button connects them to create an unbroken path. On single paths, only the unjoined beginning and ending nodes may be joined. On compound paths (paths that aren't necessarily close to one another, but have been joined using the Object | Combine command; CTRL-L is a shortcut worth memorizing), the beginning and ending nodes selected on two existing—but separate—paths can also be joined. While a single node is selected or while a specific point on a segment is clicked, clicking the Break Curve button results in two nodes becoming unjoined, breaking a closed path into an open path.

> **Tip** Unjoined paths are *not* the same as separate objects. Two paths, for example, can be located *nowhere near* each other on a page and yet still be part of a single path. If you want to break a path into its component subpaths, you first select the nodes using a marquee-selection technique with the Shape tool, click the Break Curve button, and then choose Object | Break Curve Apart. CTRL-K is the shortcut, and it's another shortcut you'll want to commit to memory.

- **Line to Curve/Curve to Line**   These two buttons are used to toggle the state of a selected straight line to a curve state, and vice versa. A single-click with the Shape tool selects a line or curve, indicated by a round black marker on the line. When curves are converted to lines, the path they follow takes on a shortcut: "the shortest distance between two points." When you convert a straight line to a curve, the path remains the same shape, but control handles appear directly on the "line." The quickest way to get the control points visible is to drag on the line to force it into a curve shape.
- **Extend Curve to Close**   For this command to be available, you must have both the beginning and ending nodes of an open path selected (marquee-select the points or SHIFT-click to select them both). Under these conditions, clicking the Extend Curve to Close button joins the two nodes by adding a straight line between them, thus closing the path.
- **Auto-Close Curve**   While an open path is selected, clicking this button joins the beginning and end nodes to form a closed path by adding a new straight line between the two nodes; it's a similar command to Extend Curve to Close, but depending on the closeness of the start path node to the end path node, you might not even see a visible straight line connection. You can also join the end points of a selected curve using the Close Curve option in the Object Properties docker's Curve tab. Press ALT-ENTER to open the Object Properties docker. The start and end nodes don't even have to be selected to use the Object Properties method.
- **Reverse Curve Direction**   While a curve path on a line is selected, clicking this button has the effect of changing the direction of the path. By doing this, the start point of the

path becomes the end point (and vice versa). The results of using this command button are most noticeable when the start or end of the line or path has been applied with an arrowhead, meaning the arrowhead is applied to the opposite end of the line or path. You may also notice subtle changes in the appearance of line styles applied to a path after using this command button.

- **Extract Subpath**   This option becomes available only when a compound path is selected. After you click the Extract Subpath button, the selected path is separated from the compound path, converting it to a separate path. Using this command on a compound path composed of only two different paths is essentially the same as using the Break Apart command. It's more useful when you need to extract a specific path from a compound path made up of three or more paths.

- **Stretch and Scale Nodes**   This is a very powerful CorelDRAW feature not available in competing applications. When at least two nodes on a path are selected, clicking the Stretch and Scale Nodes button allows for the transformation between nodes using their relative distance from each other vertically, horizontally, or from the center. Eight selection handles become available, just like object selection using the Pick tool, and you can use a click-drag action from any corner or side selection handle toward or away from the center of the node selection. Holding SHIFT constrains the stretch or scale operation from the center of the selection. As an example, if you draw a cartoon portrait of a man in profile, you could select the nose nodes and enlarge the fellow's nose without significantly affecting any other curve segments in the drawing.

- **Rotate and Skew Nodes**   Similar to Stretch and Scale Nodes, when at least two nodes on a path are selected, clicking the Rotate and Skew Nodes button lets you rotate and skew the selected nodes; this is a great feature for refining a shape just a little, and also for creating more dramatic appearance changes (see the following illustration). Eight selection handles become available, enabling you to use a click-drag action from any corner selection handle to rotate the nodes in a circular direction, either clockwise or counterclockwise. Dragging from any side handle lets you skew the node selection either vertically or horizontally.

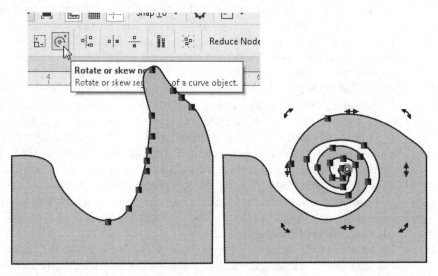

- **Align Nodes**   When two or more nodes are selected, clicking this button opens the Align Nodes dialog, from where you choose either the Align Vertical or Align Horizontal option to automatically align your node selection accordingly. In addition to these options, while only the beginning and ending nodes of an open path are selected, you can also choose to align control points. This has the effect of moving the two end points of the line to overlap each other precisely. This is a wonderful command for quickly sketching a zigzag (perhaps for an illustration of a saw blade), and then in one step aligning the nodes to create a precise illustration.
- **Reflect Nodes Horizontally/Vertically**   These two buttons become available when two or more nodes are selected. You use these options to move nodes using the nudge keys (the UP, DOWN, LEFT, and RIGHT ARROW keys on your keyboard) or click-drag actions in opposite directions.
- **Elastic Mode**   With this command, you move selected nodes according to their relative distance from each other; the effect is like experimenting with a rubber band. For example, while a collection of nodes is selected, dragging one of the nodes causes the others to be dragged a shorter distance in relation to the node that is being dragged. While Elastic mode is off, all the selected nodes are moved by an equal distance. Try this option to add a more organic and natural feeling to a drawing you might feel looks a little too studied and stiff; it adds expression to a path.
- **Reduce Nodes**   When you use this command, CorelDRAW evaluates the overall shape based on the nodes you've selected, deletes nodes that deviate from a predictable course along the path, and then repositions the remaining nodes—the effect is to smooth the curve. To use this feature, select the nodes controlling the segments you want to smooth and drag the Reduce Nodes slider control position toward 100. As you drag the slider, the shape of the curves becomes smoothed and you'll notice that superfluous nodes disappear from the curve. This option is useful for smoothing lines drawn using the Freehand tool with either the mouse or a digitizing tablet stylus.
- **Select All Nodes**   This button selects all the nodes on a path (or compound path) using one click. It's a great feature for users who aren't experts with the marquee-selection dragging technique yet. You may also select all the nodes in a path with the Shape tool by holding CTRL-SHIFT and clicking any node on the path.

Are you ready to test-drive the Shape tool? Follow along in the upcoming tutorial.

Tutorial   Editing Paths with the Shape Tool

1. Choose the Ellipse tool (F7) and create an ellipse of any size. Convert the ellipse shape to curves (CTRL-Q) to create a closed path with four nodes joined by four curved lines.
2. Choose the Shape tool (F10). Notice that the Property Bar now features all the line and node command buttons. Click the Select All Nodes button to select all nodes on the path.
3. With the nodes still selected, click the Add Node button (or press the + button on your numeric keypad). Notice that four new nodes are added midpoint between the four original nodes.
4. Click any of the segments once and click the Convert Curve to Line button. The curve is now a straight line, and the curve handles have disappeared.

5. Click a node on one of the other existing curves, drag either of the curve handles in any direction, and notice how they change the shape of the path.

6. Using a click-drag action, click near the middle of the curve segment and drag in any direction. As you drag, the curve handle positions at either end both move, and the shape of the curve is changed accordingly.

7. Click the Make Node a Cusp button and then perform the same action. Notice that the lines on either side of the node can be curved in any direction independently of each other. Now click any node on the path to select it and then click the Make Node Smooth button. Drag the curve handle of this node in any direction. Notice that the curve handle can be dragged only in a single direction.With this node still selected, click the Break Curve button to split the path at this point. Although it may not be obvious, two nodes now exist where the original node used to be. Drag either of these nodes in any direction to separate their positions. The nodes are now control points because they break the path to form beginning and end points.

8. Select one of these nodes, hold SHIFT while clicking the other, and click the Extend Curve to Close button. Notice the curve is now closed again, while the two nodes have been joined by a straight line.

9. Undo your last action (CTRL-Z) to unjoin the nodes and, while they remain selected, click the Align Nodes button to open the Align Nodes dialog. If the nodes aren't already selected, click to select all three options (Align Horizontal, Vertical, and Control Points) in the dialog and click OK to align the points. Notice that they are positioned to overlap precisely. Click the Join Two Nodes button in the Property Bar. Your path is now closed, and the nodes are joined.

10. Hold SHIFT and click to select two or more nodes on your path. With your nodes selected, click the Stretch and Scale Nodes button and notice that eight selection handles appear around your node selection. Hold the SHIFT key (to constrain from the center) and drag one of the corner handles toward or away from the center of the selection. All node positions are scaled relative to each other's position, and the lines joining the unselected nodes also change shape.

11. With the nodes still selected, click the Rotate and Skew Nodes button in the Property Bar. Notice that eight rotate and skew handles appear around your selection. Drag any of the corner rotation handles either clockwise or counterclockwise to rotate the nodes. Notice that they are rotated relative to their current position and that the lines joining the unselected nodes also change shape.

The preceding tutorial is only a sampling of what can be accomplished when editing nodes using the Shape tool. You'll want to invest some quality time practicing your editing skills using all the available node-shaping command buttons, because the payoff is better artwork—artwork that's closer to what you have in your head. Also, in the long run, you'll save time creating wonderful pieces.

Tip To set the drawing behavior of the Freehand tool and/or Bézier tool, double-click either of the tool buttons in the Toolbox to open the Options dialog for the Toolbox group. Then you can click on the Freehand/Bézier tool title to open its page in the right pane. Options are discussed in the next section.

Copying and Pasting Subpaths

New to CorelDRAW X8 is the ability to use the Shape tool to select a subpath of a more complex object. This new feature will come in very handy when you need to copy only part of a drawing, but the part you want is joined to a larger path.

Take a moment to open Swiss Cheese.cdr and get some serious hands-on entertaining experience in the digital dairy business. On the *hole* (sorry!), this tutorial will be fun and educational.

Tutorial   # Increasing the Number of Holes in Swiss Cheese

1. Zoom into the two holes on the facing side of the drawing in Swiss Cheese.cdr and then choose the Shape tool from the Toolbox.
2. Marquee-select all eight of the nodes on both subpaths, as shown in Figure 7-6. Then use the Windows standard shortcuts CTRL-c to copy and then CTRL-v to paste.
3. The copies of the paths do not belong to the front subpath of the cheese. Choose the Pick tool from the Toolbox, and then move the compound path (that you freed from the cheese subpath) to the left, and with the object selected, click the object to put it into Skew/Rotate mode. Then rotate the piece as shown in Figure 7-6 so the new holes don't look as though you just cloned over an area in the drawing.
4. Choose the Attributes Eyedropper from the Toolbox—and, yes, we're getting a little ahead of ourselves in exploring CorelDRAW (it's covered in detail in Chapter 12). However, this is a guided tour, and your guide promises not to tax your patience or skills for more than two minutes, so why not continue?
5. On the Property Toolbar, click the Properties drop-down list, leave only Fill checked, and then click OK to confirm your setting.
6. Click the Attributes Eyedropper on the bottom of the hole, where it looks like a circular gradient in Figure 7-6. Now you're ready to apply the attributes to the new holes. Your cursor is now a paint bucket; click over either of the circles and, except for perhaps a little modification of the circular gradient using the Interactive Fill tool, you now have a darned nice wedge of cheese, with fewer calories because there are more holes now. You should get out the crackers and the red wine you have in the kitchen.

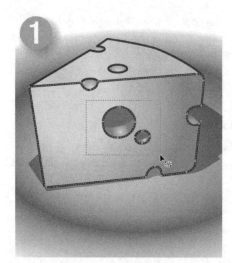

Marquee-select both holes with the Shape tool.

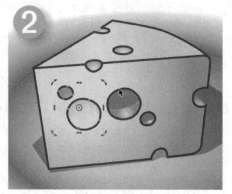

Press CTRL-C and then CTRL-V. With the Pick tool, move the copy, click the selection, and then rotate the holes.

Choose the Attributes Eyedropper, set it to only sample Fill, and then sample the large original hole. Then fill the new holes.

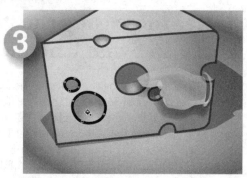

FIGURE 7-6 Easily select a subpath and make a copy using the extended features of the Shape tool in version X8.

Controlling Freehand and Bézier Tool Behavior

The settings to control how the Freehand and Bézier tools create the curves and lines you draw are set using a series of options in the Freehand/Bézier Tool pane of the Options dialog, shown next. To access these options, click the Options button on the Standard Bar, expand the tree subdirectory under Toolbox, choose the Freehand/Bézier Tool entry, and you're there. The *quick* way to get to this box, however, is to double-click the Freehand or Bézier tool button after choosing it from the Curve Tools group.

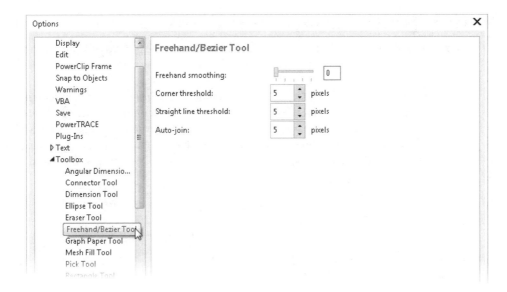

Here's how the options work:

- **Freehand Smoothing** The Freehand Smoothing option enables you to set the default value of the Freehand Smoothing option in the Property Bar while drawing with the Freehand tool. Smoothing may be set based on percentage within a range between 0 (minimum smoothing) and 100 (maximum smoothing).
- **Corner Threshold** This option is for setting the default value for corner nodes when you're drawing with the Freehand or Bézier tool. Lower values cause nodes to be more likely set to cusp nodes, and higher values cause them to more likely be smooth nodes. The range may be set between 1 and 10; the default is 5.
- **Straight Line Threshold** This option pertains to how the shapes of lines or curves are created when you're drawing with the Freehand tool. Lower values cause nodes to be more likely set to straight lines, whereas higher values cause them to be curved more frequently. The range may be set between 1 and 10; the default is 5.
- **Auto-Join** This option sets the behavior of the Freehand or Bézier tool while you're drawing closed-path objects. This value represents the distance in pixels your cursor must be when you click *near* the first node of a newly created path to close the path automatically. Auto-Join can be set anywhere within range between 1 and 10 pixels; the default is 5, which is probably the best overall choice for the large screen resolutions we all run today.

Working with Compound Paths

Compound paths have at least two separate paths (either open or closed) composing a single shape. To examine an example of a compound path, use these steps:

1. Choose the Text tool (F8), click once to define a text-insertion point, and then type an uppercase *Q* character. You can assign the character any typeface you like; the more ornamental the character, the more obvious the compound path soon will be. The character shape shown in the illustration has two paths that are combined: one represents the "positive" space and one represents the "negative" space shape.

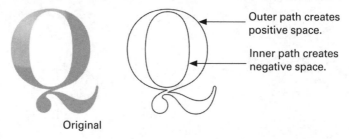

Outer path creates positive space.

Inner path creates negative space.

Original

2. While the text object is selected, convert it to curves (CTRL-Q). The Status Bar now indicates the object is a curve on Layer 1.
3. Change your view to Wireframe; choose View | Wireframe.
4. Press CTRL-K (Object | Break Curve Apart). With the Pick tool, click on one of the shapes and drag it to move it; clearly the two paths are now separate. You have just converted a compound path featuring two subpaths into two individual objects, as shown here.

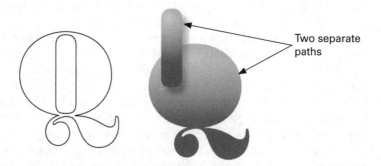

Two separate paths

Combining Objects

When separate objects are combined, they behave as a single object. While two or more closed paths are combined, they form positive and negative spaces within the object. Applying a fill to this type of object causes the positive shapes to be filled, and the negative shapes remain clear, as shown next. The Combine command does this: choose Arrange | Combine, or use the CTRL-L shortcut. You can also click the Combine button in the Property Bar, or choose Combine from the pop-up menu.

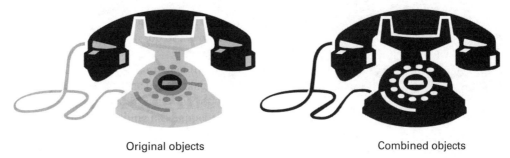

Original objects   Combined objects

Combining objects that normally feature unique properties—such as rectangles, ellipses, polygons, and perfect shapes—permanently converts them to curves.

Breaking Paths Apart

You can separate the individual paths in a compound path using the Break Curve Apart command (CTRL-K). This command is available when a compound path composed of at least two subpaths is selected. (Using the Extract Subpath command button in the Property Bar also does this, but only for the *selected* path.)

Converting Objects to Curves

Converting special types of objects to curves—such shapes auto-created with the Rectangle and Ellipse tools—frees them to be manipulated with the Shape tool as if they were ordinary paths. Choose Object | Convert To Curves, press CTRL-Q, click the Convert To Curves button in the Property Bar, or right-click the object and choose Convert To Curves from the pop-up menu.

Converting an object to curves removes any special editing properties; for example, text loses its editing property as text, and rounded rectangles can no longer be edited to refine the curvature of the rounded corners. Convert To Curves applies to Polygon, Ellipse, and Artistic Text objects as well as certain effects objects such as envelopes and perspective effects.

You saw in this chapter that there are different tools for creating paths, but the results are more or less always the same; objects have path segments and nodes, and paths can be open or closed. You also learned how to edit paths using the Shape tool. You'd be well served to bookmark this chapter; there's an awful lot of power in CorelDRAW's drawing and editing tools, and this chapter can be a good reference in the future. After all, the program isn't called CorelFILL or CorelRECTANGLE—*drawing* is what good artwork and vector design is all about.

8 Exploring Special Shapes, Connectors, and Other Office Automation Helpers

Not everyone is a born artist. But try telling this to your boss, who has elevated you from the company's nominally talented artist to the resident Art Director. You've shown a little design flair, helped out stapling a flyer or two, and, right or wrong, your boss's presumption now is that you're a digital da Vinci.

This chapter is the Corel version of a Non-Artists' Rescue Kit. As you unpack and read through this chapter, you will gain experience with the features most sought by your business—tables, clean and crisp dimensioning callouts for tech work, banners, and perfect polygons—even though you think that *vector* is the kid's name down in the mailroom.

Seriously, CorelDRAW is so all-encompassing as a creative suite that it includes something for just about every need. And this chapter is "all business"—with a healthy serving of fun, as you've come to expect from these *Official Guides*.

CorelDRAW's Smart Drawing Tool

Even if you use a graphics tablet and stylus, you're still drawing freehand, and using a mouse introduces still more flubs when it comes to freehand drawing. Fortunately, the Smart Drawing tool takes the guesswork out of drawing polygonal and rounded objects—in a nutshell, you click-drag *an approximation* of what you intend, tune the options for the Smart Drawing tool based on your first drawing, and in a jiffy you have a precise object with the proportions you need. Pictured next on the Toolbox, the Smart Drawing tool instantly translates rough drawings into shapes you'd usually consider drawing with the Rectangle tool or Ellipse tool— or with other tools that require more effort and skill.

When the Smart Drawing tool is selected, the Property Bar displays Shape Recognition Level and Smart Smoothing Level options (shown next) for setting the sensitivity CorelDRAW uses to translate your roughs into precise shapes.

Recognition and smoothing options

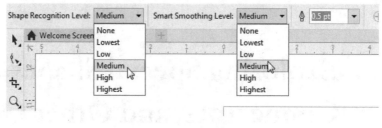

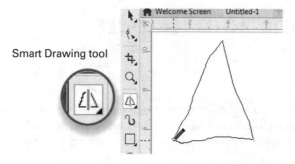

Smart Drawing tool

You control how well your sketch shape is translated into a precise shape by setting these options:

- **Shape Recognition Level** This option determines how precisely your sketched shape is matched to a recognizable shape. You can set it to one of five levels, ranging from Lowest (sketched shapes are not easily recognized) to Highest (sketched shapes are easily recognized), with Medium being the default; None off turns the feature.
- **Smart Smoothing Level** After you've completed a sketch by releasing the mouse button, a level of node smoothing is applied to make object recognition more, or less, precise. This option gives you total control over the smoothing action, much in the same fashion as using the Reduce Nodes spin box on the Property Bar when a path is selected with the Shape tool. Choose from five options ranging from Lowest (less smoothing applied) to Highest (more smoothing applied), with Medium as the default; None turns off the feature.

Tip You can control the delay time interval between the moment you release the mouse button and stop drawing to the moment CorelDRAW determines a recognizable shape. By reducing the delay time, you can sketch several separate lines or shapes one after the other, and DRAW then recognizes them as a single compound path. Double-click the Smart Drawing tool icon on the Toolbox to open Options. The *Drawing Assistance Delay* slider can be set between 0 and 2.0 seconds. The longer you set the delay time, the more time you'll have to keep drawing before CorelDRAW steps in to assist you.

Try the following steps to get an immediate leg up on drawing flawless objects.

| Tutorial | # CAD: CorelDRAW-Assisted Drawing

1. Choose the Smart Drawing tool and use a click-drag action to sketch the shape of a square or rectangle. Try to keep the sides of the shape vertical and horizontal as you draw; if the square shape looks like a melted ice cube, don't worry. When you release the mouse button, CorelDRAW automatically translates your sketch into a rectangle shape.
2. Choose the Pick tool next and check your Status Bar display. The shape you sketched is specified as a Rectangle, and the Property Bar shows options associated with shapes created with the Rectangle tool, including the rounded-corner options. Try dragging a corner node with the Shape tool to make the rectangle a rounded-corner rectangle.
3. Choose the Smart Drawing tool again, and sketch the shape of an oval or circle. Try to keep the shape parallel to the page orientation, although CorelDRAW can also intelligently refine a sketch of an oval that's rotated. When you release the mouse button, CorelDRAW translates your sketched shape into an ellipse shape.
4. Choose the Pick tool and check your Status Bar. The shape you sketched is specified as an Ellipse, and the Property Bar shows options associated with shapes created with the Ellipse tool, such as the Ellipse, Arc, and Pie properties.

 Tip You can alter your sketched shapes on the fly using the Smart Drawing tool to backtrack and erase the path you're drawing. Hold SHIFT as the modifier key to reverse and erase. Release the SHIFT key to resume sketching normally.

The shapes you draw also have special editing properties:

- Rectangles and ovals produced by using the Smart Drawing tool become CorelDRAW objects, with the same editing properties as the objects you draw with the Rectangle and Ellipse tools.
- Trapezoids and parallelograms produced with the Smart Drawing tool become Perfect Shapes, explained in a moment.
- Other shapes you draw—triangles, arrows, stair-steps, and so on—become regular curved objects, but the Smart Drawing tool intelligently smooths out curves and straightens nearly straight line segments.
- *Perfect Shapes* are a special category of CorelDRAW objects, and they have special properties. They feature "glyph" nodes (by default, a red-filled diamond)—which are different from regular nodes along a path. These nodes—covered in the next section—can be manipulated to modify the shape without destroying any of its unique geometric properties (see Figure 8-1).

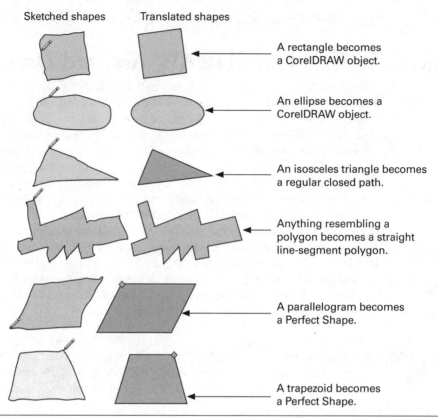

Sketched shapes   Translated shapes

A rectangle becomes
a CorelDRAW object.

An ellipse becomes a
CorelDRAW object.

An isosceles triangle becomes
a regular closed path.

Anything resembling a
polygon becomes a straight
line-segment polygon.

A parallelogram becomes
a Perfect Shape.

A trapezoid becomes
a Perfect Shape.

FIGURE 8-1   Perfect Shapes retain their properties even when you extensively edit their appearance.

Try these next steps to create variations on the basic appearance of a Perfect Shape.

Tutorial   Reshaping a Perfect Shape

1. Using the Smart Drawing tool, sketch the shape of a trapezoid (refer to Figure 8-1). In a trapezoid, two sides are parallel and the other two sides converge. When you release the mouse button, CorelDRAW translates your sketch into a Perfect Shape.

2. Choose the Pick tool and then look at the Status Bar. The shape is identified as a Perfect Shape, a special category of shape. Use the Shape tool next to click-drag the glyph node. You'll see that the parallel sides remain parallel, and the converging sides slope away and toward each other. By duplicating this Perfect Shape, you can edit with the Shape tool and create an array of trapezoids, all different in appearance but all editable indefinitely, and all retain the geometric structure of a Perfect Shape.

Each of the translated shapes has its own special properties, which you'll learn in detail in the sections that follow.

Using Perfect Shape Tools

CorelDRAW gives you the power to create objects called *Perfect Shapes*. This group of tools (see Figure 8-2) helps you to draw shapes, many of which would be a challenge to draw manually, and some of which can be edited dynamically.

Perfect Shapes often (but don't always) offer one or more control points called *glyph nodes*. These nodes allow you to edit specific parts of a specially formatted object dynamically, according to the shape's design. For example, the shape representing a dog-eared page features a single glyph node that changes the amount of curl to the page shape, or a glyph on a beveled rectangle shape enables you to set the bevel depth, as shown in Figure 8-2.

In Figure 8-2, you see a group of Basic Shapes tools beneath the Graph Paper and other manual shape tools (covered in Chapter 5). Once you've selected a specific Perfect Shape tool, a collection of shapes becomes available on the Property Bar. Choose a specific type of shape from the Property Bar's Perfect Shapes flyout selector, shown next, *before* drawing.

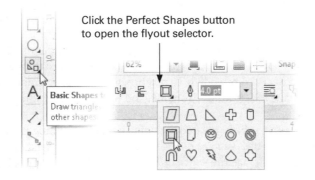

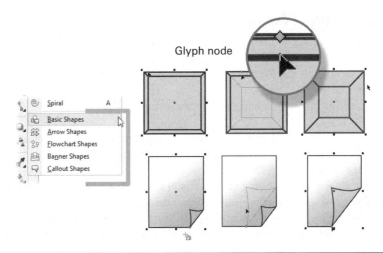

FIGURE 8-2   Glyph nodes can be used to control specific parts of these specially formatted objects.

Note As you work through the shapes, you will see that not all the presets have glyph nodes and therefore do not offer variations, once created, using glyph nodes. The shapes in the Flowchart Shapes group, for example, are not adjustable Perfect Shapes. If you need to adjust a preset shape manually, you're better off selecting it and then pressing CTRL-Q to convert the shape to a curve, which makes the preset shape infinitely editable with the Shape tool.

Walk through the following simple steps to arrive quickly at a level of perfection in your CorelDRAW design work.

Tutorial   Creating Perfect Objects

1. Choose a Perfect Shape tool by clicking the Toolbox flyout and selecting a category.
2. On the Property Bar, click the Perfect Shape selector and choose a symbol. Use a click-drag action to define a size and position. For all symbol types, except Callout, the direction of your click-drag won't matter because the symbols are created using a fixed orientation. For Callout shapes, the direction of your click-drag determines the object's orientation.
3. Once your shape has been created, you may notice it includes one or more glyph nodes that control certain symbol properties. In cases where more than one glyph node exists, the nodes are color coded. To position a glyph node, choose either the Shape or the Perfect Shape tool from the Toolbox, and then use a click-drag action directly on the node itself.
4. Once your object has been created and any glyph node editing is complete, your other Basic Shape properties (such as outline and fill) can be changed in the usual way. For example, you can change the width or height of your new shape using the selection handles available.

Editing Glyph Nodes

Glyph nodes are edited similarly to the control points on a polygon. As they are moved, the glyph nodes often have the effect of resizing, changing proportion, or dynamically moving a certain part of an individual symbol. Complex symbols can include up to three color-coded glyph nodes.

To explore glyph node editing, take a moment to try this:

1. Choose the Banner Shapes tool from the Shapes group on the Toolbox.
2. On the Property Bar, click the Perfect Shapes flyout button to expand the list and then choose the second preset shape.
3. Using a click-diagonal drag action, create a new shape on your page. Notice the shape includes two glyph nodes—one yellow, one red.
4. Click-drag the yellow glyph node up or down to reposition it several times. Notice that its movement is horizontally constrained; as it is moved, the vertical width of each portion of the banner changes.

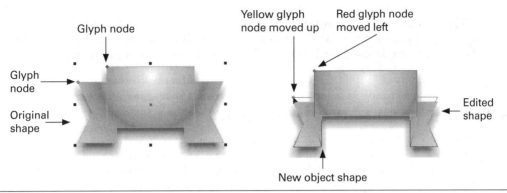

FIGURE 8-3   When movement is vertically constrained, the width of each portion of the banner changes.

5. Click-drag the red glyph node left or right to reposition it several times. Notice that its movement is vertically constrained; as it is moved, the horizontal width of each portion of the banner changes to match your movement, as shown in Figure 8-3.

Glyph nodes can be edited using both the Perfect Shape tool you used to create the shape and the Shape tool (F10). You can also edit glyph nodes by using the Object Properties docker for a selected Perfect Shape, as shown in Figure 8-4. This docker offers precise control over glyph node position; just right-click your shape and choose Object Properties from the pop-up menu, or press ALT-ENTER. Depending on the Perfect Shape you've selected, the Object Properties docker might display one, two, or more controls.

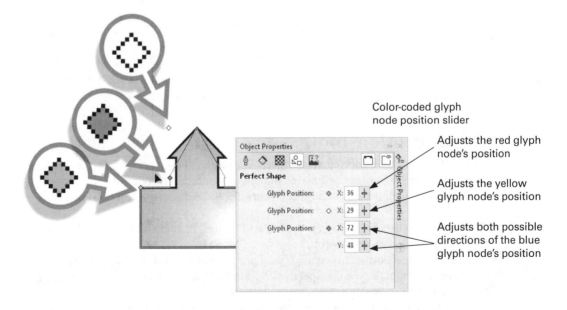

FIGURE 8-4   Use the Object Properties docker to edit glyph nodes.

Tip You can adjust the glyph nodes of the Perfect Shapes you create using either the tool you used to create the shape (you can edit a selected Perfect Shape arrow with the Banner Shapes tool) or the Shape tool (F10) at any time in the future.

Working with the Dimension Tools

If you need to annotate a drawing or an imported bitmap image with dimensions or labels calling out, for example, different parts of a machine, you'll want to use the Dimension tools (shown next), which are expressly for this purpose. The lines you create with the four Dimension tools will tag the bracketed area with the units of measurement of your choice, and they dynamically update when you scale them. The 3-Point Callout tool is for adding text to a wide selection of arrowhead lines; you can choose a line style for the connector as well as a width, a type of arrowhead, and any style of typeface you have installed on your system. The text labels for callouts are also upright, regardless of whether you rotate the line, and a Callout Control line can be edited at any time with the Shape tool (F10).

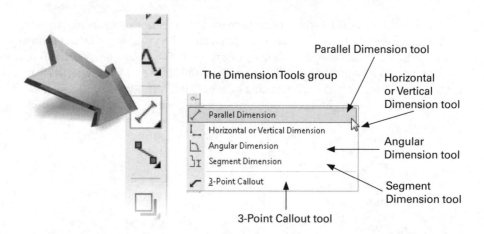

Using Dimension Tools

When a Dimension tool is selected, the Property Bar displays options to specify the style, precision, and unit values of your displayed dimensions, and to control the display and appearance of the labeling text, as shown in Figure 8-5 and detailed in the following list.

- **Dimension Style** This option is used to set Decimal, Fractional, or Standard measuring conventions; the default is Decimal.
- **Dimension Precision** This option is used to set a level of precision. When using Decimal as the measuring style, you can specify precision up to ten decimal places. When using Fractional, you can specify precision using fractions up to 1/1024 of a selected unit measure.
- **Dimension Units** This option specifies the measurement unit with which to display your text labels. You can choose any of the unit measures supported by CorelDRAW.

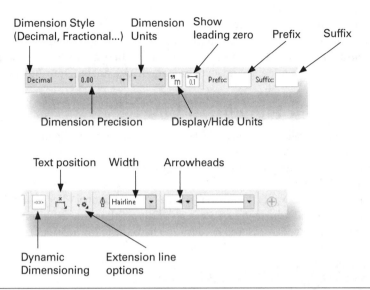

FIGURE 8-5   The Property Bar offers specific modifications to your Dimension lines.

- **Display Units**   This is a toggle button. If you don't want units appended to a dimension, leave the button turned off before you create a dimension line. Alternatively, you can click the dimension line itself—not the dimension numbers—to change the visibility of the units. If you accidentally click the text instead of the units, you'll get the option to change the font and other text-related options.
- **Show Zero Leading**   When a dimension has a value of less than 1 (a tenth of an inch, for example), you can add a 0 before the decimal or choose to leave it off by toggling this button (the non-depressed state). If you have a series of columns of dimension lines, adding the leading zero will help keep the values aligned to the left or right.
- **Prefix/Suffix for Dimension**   With this feature, you can enter your own text so it appears before and after the text label for your dimension line. For example, you can specify a style of merchandise, such as "Plastic" or a "Children only"–sized garment. Prefix and suffix text may be any character you want and may be applied before or after the dimension line has been drawn.
- **Dynamic Dimensioning**   This option lets you specify whether your measurement values are updated automatically as the size of the dimension line is changed. By default, this option is turned on for all new dimension lines. If you plan on resizing or changing the scale of your drawing after creating the dimension lines, disabling this option freezes the values being displayed so they remain fixed, whether your dimension lines are resized or not.

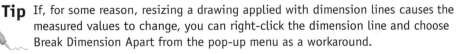

Tip   If, for some reason, resizing a drawing applied with dimension lines causes the measured values to change, you can right-click the dimension line and choose Break Dimension Apart from the pop-up menu as a workaround.

- **Text Position**   This drop-down list lets you specify a position for the text labels applied to your dimension line. You can choose Text Above Dimension Line, Text Through Dimension Line, or Text Below Dimension Line. There are additional choices: Center Text Between Extension Line, Force Text Horizontal, and, finally, Draw Box Around Text.

Checking Out Dimension Lines

The following steps walk you through the techniques used to build dimension lines. Let's pretend in the Ancient Vase.cdr file that the drawing of the antique vase is to size: it's 6¾" tall if it existed in the real world. Your assignment is to respond to an antique dealer who wants to know the overall height of the vase, the height of the neck, and the angle between the top of the bowl and the base. Moreover, she wants the drawing marked with fractional values and thinks metric amounts are for nerds and scientists. People go a little overboard when it comes to cataloguing antiques, but your success is ensured because you have the following steps to guide you.

Tutorial   Using Dimension Lines

1. Open Ancient Vase.cdr and then select the Horizontal or Vertical Dimension tool from the Toolbox.
2. Click-drag from the top of the vase to its bottom, where you release the mouse button. With this tool, direction is set to vertical or horizontal by the direction in which you first drag.
3. On the Property Bar, set the Dimension Style to Fractional. If you'd set the Dimension Style as the first step, DRAW would assume (without a line already created) that you want this style to be the default (hint: you probably don't).
4. Move the cursor to the right without holding either mouse button. Doing this defines a position for the control text, so make sure your cursor position is far to the right of the vase drawing. You need to leave space for other dimensioning data you'll create.
5. Click. You're done, and the number value is called out now.
6. Choose the Parallel Dimension tool; the neck of the bottle is slightly slanted, so this is the appropriate measuring tool.
7. Click-drag from the top of the neck to the part that joins the neck with the bowl; release the mouse button at this point.
8. Move the cursor to the right, away from the drawing but to the left of the first dimensioning line, and then single-click to add the dimension line and number value.
9. Choose the Angular Dimension tool.
10. Click-drag from the junction of the neck and bowl on the left (you're creating a perfectly horizontal line) and then drag to the left. Release the mouse button when your cursor is about 3 inches left of the junction.
11. Move your cursor up and to the right so it touches the top-left point of the vase's neck.
12. Click. You're not finished yet. You now have the opportunity to set the position of the arc. Move your cursor toward or away from the vertex of the two angular lines and then click.

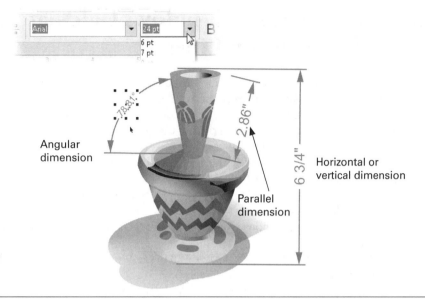

FIGURE 8-6   Use dimension lines to annotate drawings and images quickly and accurately.

13. If any of the text elements are too small in your judgment, click on the text with the Pick tool. Then, on the Property Bar, type in a new font height or even change the font if you so choose. Figure 8-6 shows the completed assignment.

Segment Dimensions

Whether you need to discover a value for technical comparison's sake or just want to make sure a part of a personal illustration is an exact length, the Segment Dimension tool is your ticket. This tool measures the distance between nodes on a path, whether the nodes are on a straight line or a curve.

To use this tool, first select a line in your composition with the Pick tool. Choose the Segment Dimension tool and then marquee-select the two nodes you want to discover the distance between. Move the cursor away from the selection to create handles that bound the selected nodes and then click.

An Exercise in Dimensioning to Scale

All of the preceding information and examples are fine in theory; now, you're going to put the theory into practice in the next tutorial. Let's say you've been handed a CorelDRAW document with a photo in it. Your boss—or any other person who is intimidating—wants the parts of the toy water pistol called out, but here's the catch: the image of the water pistol is *not* 1:1. So how does one measure all the parts of a 7½" long toy that is 5¾" on the CorelDRAW page?

Tutorial Drawing Scale, Windows Calculator, and Dimension Lines

1. Open the file The Martian Soaker.cdr. This toy is an exact replica of what NASA let Mark Watney take with him, except he lost it in the sandstorm.
2. Choose the Horizontal or Vertical Dimension Line tool and drag it from the left edge of the green water reservoir to the right of the green nozzle on the other end of the water pistol. Write this value down.
3. The boss says the body is 7½". In this example, the body length should be 4.75". You launch Windows Calculator (or use the physical home version next to your saved coupons in the kitchen). Divide 7.5 by 4.75, which equals 1.578. This is the value by which this document's drawing scale must be adjusted.
4. Right-click over a ruler, choose Ruler Setup, and then in the Ruler Options box click Edit Scale.
5. Page Distance should be 1 inch. Type **1.578** in the World Distance field, and then click OK to apply this new scale (see Figure 8-7).
6. Use the Horizontal, Vertical, Parallel, or Angular Dimension tool to measure anything asked of you in this, or your own, drawing.

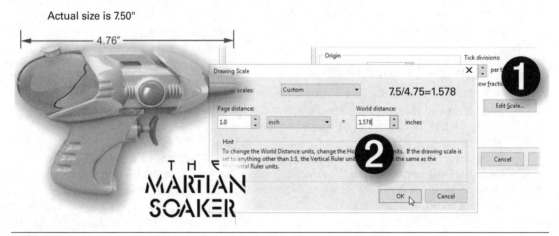

FIGURE 8-7 Adjust the World Distance scale to make measuring areas in photos and drawings accurate to scale.

When Fractional styles are combined with reassigning line and fill colors for text, you'll have a highly detailed, picture-perfect presentation for the manufacturing department and even print ads, as shown here.

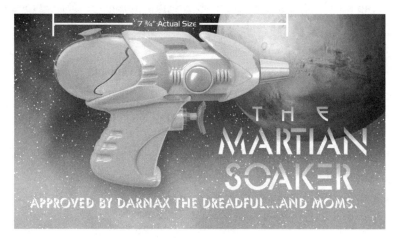

Working with Callouts

When using the 3-Point Callout tool, you produce two elements: a line composed of two segments (the "Callout," as it's displayed on the Status Bar) and the control text. Callouts are not bound to an object; they can be moved anywhere on the page. However, the text and the line are linked and are not moved independent of one another. You have a number of options on the Property Bar:

- **Callout line width**   By default, you always begin a callout with a Hairline width in blue. It's not such a good idea to adjust the width before drawing a line, because doing so triggers an attention box that asks whether you want the default line width—for any object you draw, not just callouts—to be changed. Instead, create your callout and *then* adjust the width while the callout is selected. Because the callout belongs to the general class of line objects in CorelDRAW, you can change the color of the callout line by right-clicking a color well on the color palette while the line is selected.
- **Start arrowhead**   This drop-down list will seem familiar if you've ever applied an arrowhead to a line using the Property Bar. The same basic styles are available as they are on the Start Arrowhead collection. You can even use an arrow *tail* for a callout.
- **Line style**   Like any other line you draw with the Pen or other drawing tool, the callout can be solid, dashed, or a series of dots. Choose a style by clicking the pop-up box and then click a style thumbnail.
- **Callout shape**   You set the style for the callout text from this pop-up list of presets. The symbol doesn't affect the font—it's a style, such as a rectangle bounding the text or a straight line butted above or below the text. The symbols add an element of polish to your presentation.
- **Callout Gap/End size**   This setting determines the distance between the tail of the callout line and the beginning of the text. It happens when the default Callout shape at the top of the list is chosen as a preset shape for the callout text. If you use a circle or other shape, this spin box sets the size of the circle, box, or other shape that surrounds the text.

After creating a callout, you can select the text with the Pick tool, right-click to choose Object Properties from the contextual menu pop-up, and use the newly enhanced and redesigned Object Properties docker to edit all aspects of the text, from font to size to color. You can even apply a gradient fill to your text right from the Object Properties docker (if you want your text to be illegible).

To use the 3-Point Callout tool, follow these steps:

1. If you like, open the Bric a brac.cdr file. There are different shapes, colors, and sizes on the objects in the picture, ideal for getting some exercise working with the Callout tool.
2. Click-drag to create a point where you want the callout to end (the node will eventually have the arrowhead). Move the cursor to where you want the "elbow" of the callout line and then click.
3. Move your cursor to where you want to place the control text and then click.
4. Begin typing the callout text.

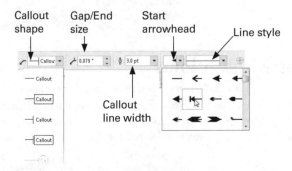

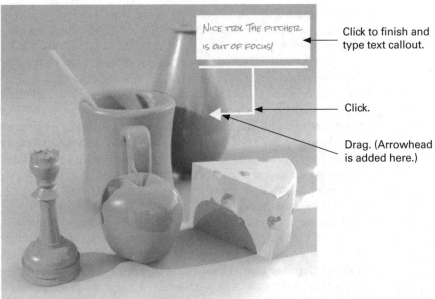

The Connector Tools

The Connector Tools group is so self-explanatory, it's almost not necessary to cover how they work here. Connector lines come in one straight segment, a right-angle, and a rounded right-angle, and there's also an Editor tool, shown in the following illustration, to modify the exact location of the connector line relative to the object (or group of objects) to which the line is anchored.

Connector tools

There are more uses in everyday work for Connector tools than you might imagine. Everything from mapping genealogies, to org charts, to seating arrangements at receptions—these all need text in boxes and some sort of connecting line to establish relationships. The marvelous thing about DRAW's Connector tools is that once you've connected two objects, regardless of where you move an object, the connector line preserves the connection. This makes arranging and laying out complex hierarchical maps and charts a snap. Here, I am building my own genealogy chart.

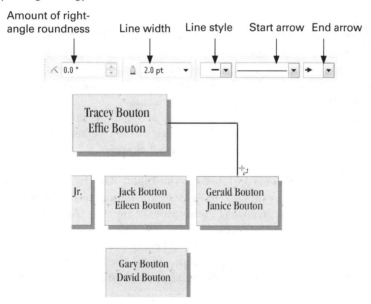

As with dimension lines, you set connector line properties— arrowheads, line widths, colors, and others—after you've created the connector line.

Tables

With CorelDRAW's Table tool tucked into the Toolbox, you no longer have to struggle to present tabular data neatly and attractively in your documents. Creating data sheets or directories or displaying spreadsheet data no longer hinges on setting up elaborate networks of guidelines or paragraph text blocks with a generous handful of tab and column settings thrown in. Drag out a table with the new Table tool, or import a table from your word processor or spreadsheet program, and you're all set to use CorelDRAW's tools to make the data look good.

Creating a Table

You can create a new table with either the Table tool in the Toolbox or from the Create New Table command on the Table menu. If you use the Table tool to create the table, you can click-drag to position and size the table exactly where you want it to be inserted. If you create the table using the menu command, the table will be inserted in the center of the document. In either case, you can drag the table to a new position or resize it just as you would any other object, such as a rectangle that you create with Toolbox tools.

Using the Proper Tool for the Job

Customizing a table happens on several levels: the entire table, a single cell, and a range of cells. The content you place inside a cell, such as text or graphics, is controlled with the same tools and settings that would affect the content if it were not inside a cell. Which tool is active, and what you've selected with that tool, if anything, determines what customization options are available to you at that moment from the Property Bar or the menus.

Table Options When the Pick Tool Is Active

With the Pick tool, click anywhere in or on the table to select the entire table. You can use the Pick tool to select, move, resize, stretch, skew, or rotate the entire table. When the Pick tool has been used to select the table, the commands and options shown in Figure 8-8 appear on the Property Bar. These options apply to the entire table.

The table's position on the page and the overall dimensions of the table use the same common entry fields on the left of the Property Bar that other objects such as rectangles and polygons use. Other important options are as follows:

- **Number of Columns and Rows in the Table**   Use the top control to enter the number of rows you want your table to have and the bottom one to enter the number of columns you require. You can change these entries at any time. For example, if a table currently has two columns and two rows, entering **3** in the column field and **4** in the row field immediately reconfigures the table so it contains the new number of columns and rows. If you reduce the number of columns or rows, they are removed from the bottom up and from the right to the left. Any content you have in the columns and rows is lost, so do this with forethought!

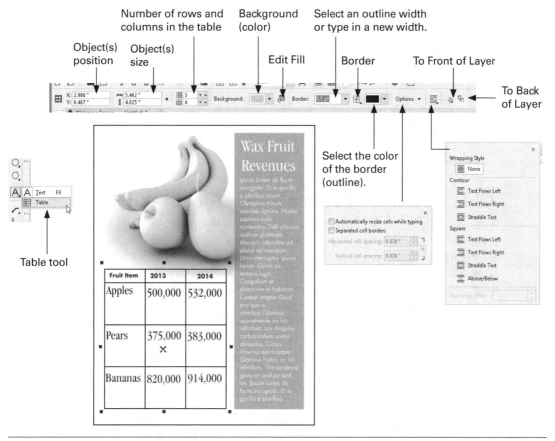

FIGURE 8-8 Use the Property Bar to customize the look of a table.

- **Background** Choose a uniform color for all the cells from this drop-down list. You can also accomplish the same thing by choosing a color from the color palette.
- **Edit Fill** If you've given the table a background fill, you can go directly to the Edit Fill dialog by clicking this icon. By default, tables are filled with a Uniform fill. If you want your table to have any *other* fill type, such as Fountain or Pattern fill, you can choose it right from the Edit Fill dialog.
- **Border** *Border* refers to the outline of each cell and the table as a whole. You can show or hide the interior cell outlines and/or combinations of the top, bottom, left, and right sides of the table.
- **Border Outline Width** This field applies a point outline width to the entire table, to a cell (CTRL-click to select one), or to the border specified in the Border drop-down.
- **Options** The options that can be set here are Automatically Resize Cells While Typing and Separated Cell Borders. The former is useful when the amount of content you need to enter in each cell is not uniform. Enabling this prevents your content from overflowing and moving out of view. The latter option lets you space out your cells horizontally and

vertically so each cell is still contained in the table but is not in immediate proximity to the adjacent cell.

- **Wrap Text**   This important option determines how *Paragraph Text* flows around the table and how close the Paragraph Text box can get to the table—this option has nothing to do with the text content of the table. Tables are objects; text can be made to flow around them or over them or under them. Artistic Text is not affected by the Text Wrap setting.
- **To Front of Layer and To Back of Layer**   These icons become available if another object is layered on top of or below the table. Clicking these icons changes the position of the table in the stacking order.

Table Options When the Shape Tool Is Active

When you want to select a single cell or multiple cells in a table, use the Shape tool. To select a single cell, click in it with the Shape tool. To select adjacent cells, click-drag across the row(s) or column(s) that you want to select. To select nonadjacent cells, hold the CTRL key and click in the cells you want to select. Diagonal blue lines shade the cells you've selected. These lines are an onscreen visual indicator and not an actual fill.

Once cells are selected with the Shape tool, you can use the options available to you on the Property Bar, as seen in Figure 8-9, to customize the cells. The attributes you apply to

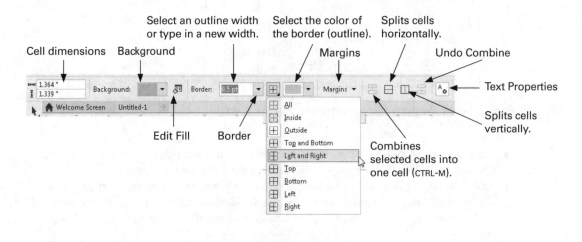

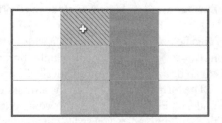

FIGURE 8-9   These options are available for customizing your tables when the Shape tool is active.

cells override any you set for the table. The first control group on the left now will set the dimensions of the selected cells as opposed to those of the entire table. The Background and Border options work the same as before, but making changes with them now only affects the selected cells. New to the Property Bar are the Margins drop-down, which sets the top, bottom, left, and right margins within the cell's bounds, and a group of controls to merge or split the selected cells into fewer or more cells.

You can also use the Shape tool to select an entire column or row. With the Shape tool, click the left border of the table next to the row you want to select. When the cursor turns into a small arrow, click again to select that row, or click-drag to select additional adjacent rows. To select columns, click the top table border over the column you want to select, wait for the arrow to appear, and click again to select the column, or click-drag to select additional columns.

To select nonadjacent rows or columns, follow the preceding procedure, but hold the CTRL key and then click next to or over the rows and/or columns you want to select.

Editing a Table When the Table Tool Is Active

You use the Table tool to create a table by click-diagonal-dragging in your document, but you can *also* use it to edit the table once it is created. Right-clicking in a table row, column, or cell and then choosing the appropriate option from the Select menu in the context menu is a quick way to select a single row, column, or cell. To select the entire table, choose Table from the Select command on the pop-up menu.

The Table tool can also be used in the same way the Shape tool is used to select multiple columns and rows, but it is easier to use the Shape tool and avoid the possibility of creating a table instead of a selection.

You can insert or delete columns or rows in your table by clicking in a row or column and then choosing Delete | (Row or Column) from either the Table menu or the right-click context menu. You can insert a row or column by right-clicking at the juncture between two existing rows or columns and then choosing Insert | (whatever you like from the submenu) from the contextual pop-up menu.

Working with Text and Graphics in a Table

Entering text in a table is easy; just use the Table tool to click in a cell and enter text using any text-entry method. You can type text directly into the cell, import text from the File menu or from the Edit Text Box dialog (CTRL-SHIFT-T), or paste text into the cell from the Clipboard.

Text in tables is handled as Paragraph Text and can be proofed, edited, and formatted in the same ways. If you want to draw a Paragraph Text box within the table cell, you can do so by click-dragging the Text tool in the cell.

You can paste any graphic into a cell, but which tool you use to select the cell that will hold the graphic makes a huge difference. If you use the Shape tool to select the target cell, the graphic will be pasted into the center of the cell as a graphic object. If you use the Table tool to select the cell and then paste the graphic into the cell, the graphic will be pasted in as an inline graphic whose size matches that of the default or current font size being used in that cell. This operation can take some time if the size reduction is great.

Once a graphic object has been placed in a cell using the Shape tool, you select it by clicking it with the Pick tool. You can then use the control handles to resize, rotate, and skew it. You can even extrude it if you like. If you want to move the graphic to another cell, select it with the Pick tool and drag it into a different cell in the table. You can drag a graphic *out* of a table, but you cannot drag a graphic into a table. However, if the graphic was placed using the *Table tool*, the object can be modified (scaled and so on) using the Type tool. When you place a graphic with the Table tool, the Pick tool will be of no assistance in working with the graphic.

Converting a Table to Text

You can convert a table into a single Paragraph Text box at any time by selecting the table and then choosing Table | Convert Table To Text from the menu. The Convert Table To Text dialog that appears offers you the option to separate the contents of each cell with a delimiter—a comma, a tab, a paragraph, or the character of your choice. If you choose to separate the cell contents with a comma, a tab, or one of your own choice, each row of cells will be saved to a paragraph with the individual cell contents separated in that paragraph by the delimiting character you choose. If you choose to separate cell contents by paragraph, you will get a paragraph for each cell.

Converting an Existing Text to a Table

Existing Paragraph Text can be converted into a table in a process that is basically the reverse of the process outlined in the previous section. Select the text you want to convert and then choose Table | Convert Text To Table from the menu. From the Convert Text To Table dialog, choose the delimiter you've used to break up the text into the chunks that you want to go into each cell. CorelDRAW analyzes the selected text and guesses what will work best as a delimiter. Because commas and tabs are frequently used within a section of text as delimiters, they might create many more cells than you were expecting. At the bottom of the dialog, you can see how many rows and columns will be created. If the number sounds wrong, cancel and go back to your original text in a text editor or a word processor. Mark the end of each piece of text you want transferred into a cell with some other character—an asterisk or a tilde, for example. Then choose User Defined and enter the character you choose as a delimiter into the field.

This chapter has demonstrated that DRAW can lend you as much—or as little—automated assistance as you need to get an assignment finished. That's one of the neat things about this program: just about every arena of business, or level of experienced artist, can find what they need easier than ever in this version, and do what everyone wants to do—reach the goal!

Chapter 9 catapults you from object creation into some creative and advanced object *editing*. See how to subtract one shape from another (this is great for drawing bolts and washers), how to perform some welding on a car, and how to make a virtual nutcracker. Is Chapter 9 going to be seriously educational or out-and-out fun?

The answer is, *yes*.

9 Editing Objects, Rearranging Paths, and Using Boolean Ops

Let's say you've drawn an object and you're fairly pleased with it, *except* for that little corner that you couldn't draw *just* right. This chapter shows you various techniques to massage that almost-perfect shape into *exactly* the shape you envisioned. Because every object you draw on a page can be broken down into rectangles, ovals, path segments, and so on, this chapter covers the tools and features for doing exactly this: breaking down shapes, combining them, subtracting a little of this, adding a little of that. Often, arriving at a design of your dreams can be realized by creating an approximation of the shapes you seek. Then, with a pull and a tug here and there, erasing a tiny area perhaps, you'll get your desired results faster than by creating the drawing from scratch. You'll also see in this chapter that you can add visual complexity and embellishments through editing that would be hard to achieve using other methods.

 Note Download and extract all the files from the Chapter9.zip archive to follow the tutorials in this chapter.

Shaping and Reshaping Object Shapes

You have a choice of two places to begin when you want to edit an object: you can use operations (commands you make with the click of a Property Bar button) or the hands-on approach. Both approaches are covered in this chapter and will serve you well; your choice largely depends on what you need to edit and then what type of operation is required.

CorelDRAW has great shaping commands to speed the object-creation process, such as Trim, Weld, Intersect, and Create Boundary. You'll also find four other shape commands at your disposal: Simplify, Front Minus Back, Back Minus Front, and Create Boundary. In this section, you'll learn exactly how you can use these commands to shape and reshape your objects. Before getting into the specifics of each type, though, let's take a look at where you can find them in X8.

Shaping Commands and the Property Bar

X8's Property Bar provides shaping command buttons that let you shape selected objects instantly. These Property Bar options become available only while at least two objects are selected—and they make shaping commands available, whether or not the objects are positioned to overlap. Property Bar shaping buttons are shown here:

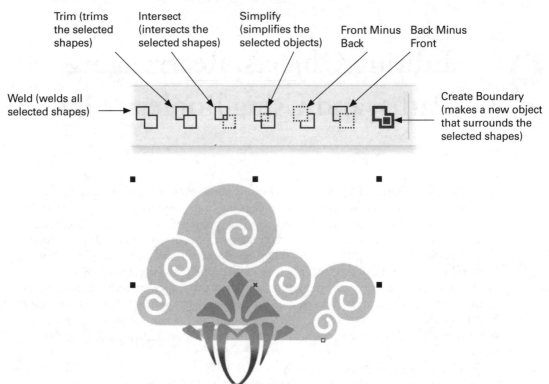

Trim (trims the selected shapes)

Intersect (intersects the selected shapes)

Simplify (simplifies the selected objects)

Front Minus Back

Back Minus Front

Weld (welds all selected shapes)

Create Boundary (makes a new object that surrounds the selected shapes)

When you use the Property Bar's shaping buttons, shapes are subtracted, added, and so on, but the original objects go away. To keep your original objects, use the Shaping *docker*, which offers options to specify that the *source object* (the one performing the operation—that is, the "scissors") and/or the target object (the object receiving the operation—that is, the "paper") should remain after shaping.

Tip When using the Shaping docker and the Weld and Intersect operations, you have an additional helper at the bottom: the Intersect With or the Weld To button. When only one object is selected, naturally it's hard for CorelDRAW to perform these operations. The idea behind this option is that if you have several objects nestled closely together (making a target object hard to select), you click the Weld To or the Intersect With button, your cursor changes to a unique shape, and you then click on the desired target object to complete the operation, as shown next.

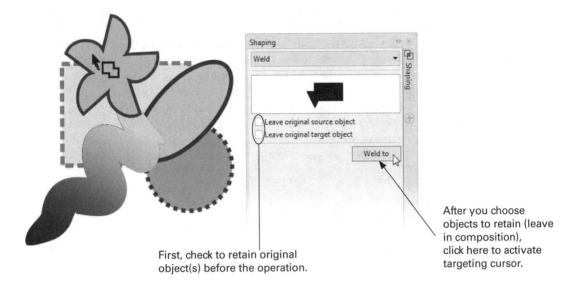

First, check to retain original
object(s) before the operation.

After you choose
objects to retain (leave
in composition),
click here to activate
targeting cursor.

Now that you know where to find the buttons to launch these commands quickly, it's time to examine what you can do with them. The following section explains the results of applying each command to at least two selected objects:

- **Weld** The Weld command creates a new shape based on the outline shape of two (or more) overlapping objects, as shown on the right in the following illustration. You can specify via the Shaping docker whether or not the *original* shapes remain on the page.

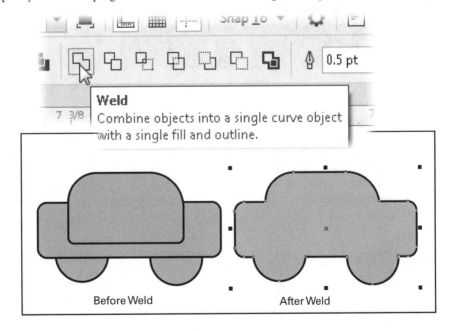

Before Weld   After Weld

This illustration shows a couple of circles and two modified rectangles so their edges are rounded. The car is going to be welded (because that's the way cars are manufactured), and the image on the right is the result of how the different colored objects weld together. Not only did the Weld operation create a single object, but it also gave the result object the *color* of the *bottommost* object, the wheels. This is an important thing to know when welding objects.

- **Trim**   The Trim command removes any area of the backmost object that overlaps the frontmost object, as shown here—the rectangle used in this operation is *not* deleted and has been moved to make the result more obvious. No color change takes place; the back object does not inherit the front object's color, transparency, or any other trait.

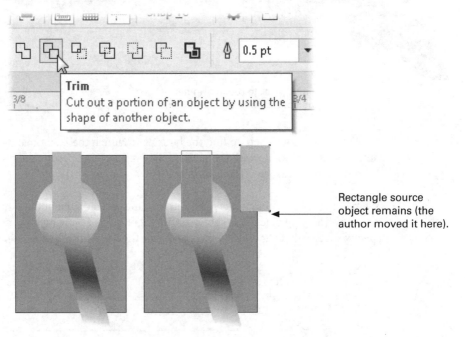

Rectangle source object remains (the author moved it here).

- **Intersect**   The Intersect operation creates a new object based on the overlapping areas of two or more objects. The original objects remain on the page, and the result is not obvious because the new object is in the same position as the overlapping parts of the original objects. In the following illustration, the square was on the bottom, and the resultant object takes on the color of the bottom object. Intersect is a great operation for creating difficult crops of complex objects. The new sun shape would make a nice logo for a tanning salon!

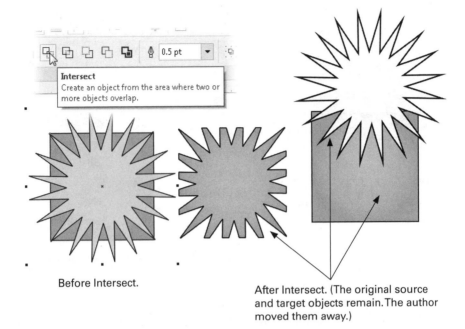

Before Intersect.

After Intersect. (The original source and target objects remain. The author moved them away.)

- **Simplify** The Simplify command removes all hidden areas of objects that "underlap" the foreground object. This command is great for simplifying an intricate drawing, and it can also make a design that otherwise might not print to PostScript correctly print just fine. Different order and arrangements of objects will result in slightly different results.
- **Front Minus Back** When two or more shapes are selected, applying the Front Minus Back command removes the hidden area of the object in back from the shape in front. When more than two shapes are selected, it removes all portions where the shapes in back are overlapped by the object in front, leaving only the object in front remaining, as shown in the following illustration.
- **Back Minus Front** This shaping command is the opposite of Front Minus Back. While at least two shapes are selected, applying the Back Minus Front command removes the portions of the shape layered in front from the shape in back. When more than two shapes are selected, it will remove all portions where the shapes in front overlap the shape in back, leaving only the shape in back remaining. The following illustration shows the

results of Front Minus Back and Back Minus Front, when applied to two objects, in the same front-to-back order.

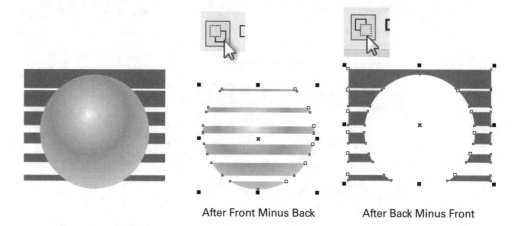

After Front Minus Back   After Back Minus Front

- **Create Boundary**   This is similar to the Weld operation, except it leaves the target objects on the page. Also, if there are empty spaces between objects, Create Boundary ignores them when making the combined single object. Here is an example of several objects selected and, below them, the result shape. By default, the new object has no fill and is ordered on top of the target objects. Just click a foreground color on the color strip, and the new object will become immediately apparent. This operation provides particularly good results when you have an easily recognizable figure, and you want a silhouette version in one click.

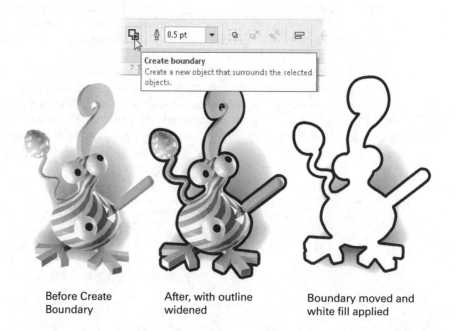

Before Create   After, with outline   Boundary moved and
Boundary   widened   white fill applied

Tip   When you're using the Shaping docker instead of the operation buttons on the Property Bar, there are two important differences in the results you'll get. You can choose to keep or delete the target and source objects. When the Source Object(s) option is selected, the object you selected before the shaping operation remains after the command has been applied. With the Target Object(s) option selected, the object you trim, weld to, or intersect with remains after the command has been applied.

Working Examples of Object Shaping

If you've seen some stunning CorelDRAW artwork and said to yourself, "Wow, that must've taken that artist ages to do all that work," nope, it probably didn't: the artist put *object shaping* to work. The following examples show just three of the thousands of creative possibilities for shaping operations; these are just a few examples to kindle your efforts.

Figure 9-1 shows a sample problem and a solution using the Trim operation. The peanut shell is whole, there appears to be a peanut outside instead of inside the peanut shell, and it would be a swell artistic touch if you took part of the shell off the top and let the peanut poke out of the shell. The peanut drawing is composed of several grouped sub-objects, and fortunately the Trim operation trims all objects in a group. Walk through the next set of steps to see how the Trim operation solves a lot of the manual effort of editing dozens of objects to create a more visual story for the scene. All the shapes needed to perform the Trim operation have been added for you; just focus on how to use the Trim operation.

FIGURE 9-1   Creating the illusion that something is inside or behind some other object is usually a job for the Trim operation.

Getting Nutty With the Trim Operation

1. Open Nutty Tutorial.cdr. The goal is to visually slice off part of the top of the shell, put that piece near the rest of the shell, and then to move the peanut so it appears to be nestled in the shell.
2. With the Pick tool, drag the Nutcracker group of objects to a position that covers almost the top half of the peanut shell. (See callout 1 in the following illustration.)

Choose the Nutcracker grouped objects; then check the boxes on the Trim docker and click the peanut group of objects.

Move trimmed peanut to the side, but leave the Nutcracker shapes and original peanut in place.

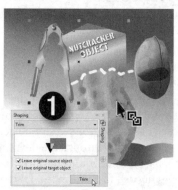

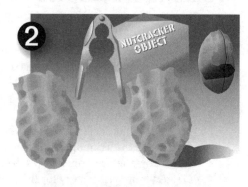

Intersect creates the top of the peanut shell.

Position the nut and then position the back part of the smaller shell.

3. Choose Object | Shaping | Shaping to display the Shaping docker.
4. Select the Nutcracker object group of shapes. The illustration is overly embellished; you can perform the next steps just using a single four-sided shape, but it seemed like more fun to include a badly executed pun in this tutorial. If you were designing this composition from scratch, the Pen tool is ideal for drawing such a shape. The white

dashed outline is not in the file but only in the illustration, meant as a suggested guide for your object drawing—the shape can be any outline color or style.

5. Choose Trim from the drop-down list on the docker. Put a check in both the Leave Original Source Object and Leave Original Target Object fields. You'll need to reuse both the peanut shell and the Nutcracker object in the following steps.

6. Only one object is selected, the Nutcracker object, which becomes (because you've selected it first) the *source* shape, the shape that performs the operation on the following object you click on. Now click Trim on the Shaping docker to then prompt the docker to query you on what you want trimmed. Your cursor takes on a new shape.

7. With the special cursor, click over the peanut shell. Because you've elected to keep both the original target and source objects, apparently nothing has happened. It has, though.

8. The trimmed peanut is already selected, so move it to the side temporarily, but leave the Nutcracker object in its position over the original peanut shell. (See callout 2 in the above illustration.)

9. Choose Intersect in the Shaping docker. (See callout 3 in the above illustration.) Uncheck the Leave Original Source Object and Leave Original Target Object boxes. Click Intersect With, and then use the special cursor to click on the original peanut. This leaves just the top of the peanut shell behind.

10. Move the trimmed peanut back to its original position, using the shadow on the ground plane and the trimmed top as a reference.

11. Now that you have both the top and bottom of a broken peanut shell, move the top shell to the lower right. Select the peanut itself to the right of the first shell piece, and then put it "in the top of the peanut," poking through. To rotate the removed top shell, select it and then click the selection one more time. Do this, and rotate the peanut itself until its degree of rotation suits your artistic sensibilities.

12. Take that mysterious piece on the far right of this document and move it over to the right side of the small, rotated peanut shell. (See callout 4 in the above illustration.) This piece makes the whole composition look more dimensional because logically, if you split a peanut shell, the back side of one of the pieces would be partially visible.

Fillet/Scallop/Chamfer

The Fillet/Scallop/Chamfer docker can be displayed by choosing it from Window | Dockers, and with it, you have your choice of truncating sharp corners of an object you draw. This docker will not alter a curved path segment: a shape that consists of straight paths is the best to use with this feature; objects with a combination of curved and straight segments will only be affected along the convergence of two straight path segments.

When Fillet/Scallop/Chamfer evaluates sharp direction changes along a path, it "rounds off" the point of a convex area toward the inside of the path and then adds to concave areas. This is a terrific feature for quickly building elegant objects such as furniture pieces, machine parts, and simply nice ornaments for desktop publishing documents. You enter a positive value in the Radius field (or use the elevator buttons on the docker), you see a faint outline preview in your document, and then you click Apply when you're happy with the preview.

Fillet/Scallop/Chamfer is a destructive operation, unlike the shaping operations, so if you want to keep your original object, duplicate it before using this docker.

- **Fillet**   Rounds the corners of an object.
- **Scallop**   Trims a semicircle from the corner of an object.
- **Chamfer**   Lops a straight angle off a corner, perpendicular to the interior angle of the corner.

Figure 9-2 shows the effects of the Fillet/Scallop/Chamfer docker on the same zigzag object created with a single click and the Pen tool. Because the radius of this trimming effect is measured in page units, it's usually a good idea to keep rulers visible in your document, and to refer to them to achieve the exact degree of corner truncation you need.

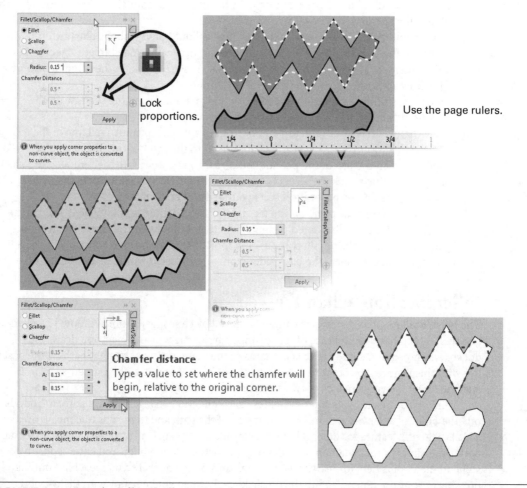

FIGURE 9-2   Use the Fillet/Scallop/Chamfer docker to take the corners off an object with intricacy and classic style.

Down and Dirty and the Shape Tool

Up untill now in this chapter, you've learned how to reshape objects using docker features and menu commands. The Shape tool in CorelDRAW gets right to the heart of object editing; it's used to do the following:

- Connect the beginning and end nodes of a path to close the path, so it becomes an object you can fill.
- Add nodes to an object so you can alter part of the object's outline.
- Remove (delete) nodes to smooth out a very rough object.
- Move nodes to alter the shape of an object.
- Change a straight line—a standalone line, or a line that's part of an object—to a curve.
- Change the amount of curve that a curve segment has.
- Make the node that joins two curves in an object sharp, smooth, or even symmetrical.

 Note The Shape tool responds differently and creates different effects depending on the type of object on which you use it. The examples in this section use the Shape tool in combination with ordinary objects consisting of nodes and path segments. Text handling with the Shape tool is covered in Chapter 10, and special objects such as those drawn with the Ellipse and other preset shape-creation tools can be modified using the Shape tool and the directions in Chapter 5.

You might say that the Shape tool is to editing what any of the Pen tools is to drawing. The Shape tool's use is covered in other chapters during tutorials, but right now it's time for a taxi driver's tour of what you can do with the Shape tool—and what the results look like. Follow along in this whirlwind exhilarating (but hardly overwhelming!) series of participatory events in tutorial style.

Tutorial # Reshaping Objects With the Shape Tool

1. Open the Shape tool playground.cdr file, which contains sample objects to work with during the steps here. Pan over to the strange (and open) path to the right of the whimsical pointing hand.
2. Select the path with the Pick tool and then try to fill the shape by clicking a color well on the Color palette. Nothing happens, right? This is because the path is almost, but not quite closed. Zoom in to the upper-left corner of the shape; if necessary, to see where the start and end points are, go to View| Wireframe.
3. Choose the Shape tool from the Toolbox (the group directly below the Pick tool), and while the shape is selected, click-drag on either end of the shape and then drag the node over to the opposing node. When your cursor looks like that shown in the

following illustration, it means when you release the mouse button, the shape will then be closed.

4. Now, what gives with the dull purple fill in this newly closed object? Aha! This is *another* trick found in CorelDRAW: the author closed the shape, filled it, and then reopened it in preparing this CDR file, and DRAW remembers the fill to an object that was previously closed.

5. Let's move on to the rectangle to the right of the closed object, the one filled with red fish scales or something. You can tell that this is a rectangle, and as such has editing properties we do not seek using the Shape tool—you just select the object and look at the status line, and the Status Bar says it's a rectangle. The object needs to be converted to a simpler object, one with no special editing properties. So, with the rectangle selected, press CTRL-Q (Object | Convert to Curves).

6. With the Shape tool, double-click a point on the top center line of the rectangle. To remove this point, you can double-click on this node and it disappears, but don't do this now (it's sort of a Tip). Now the closed rectangular series of straight paths has five nodes, and each can be moved. But let's explore just a little more here.

7. Press the plus (+) key on your keyboard. Surprise! A new node has been generated, and its position on the top path segment is equidistant between the first node you added and the left corner node. Quit after you've grown about four nodes.

8. Try clicking the top-right corner of the object and then press the plus key a few more times until you have about eight nodes in total.

9. With the Shape tool, marquee-select the new node at left on this top line. Then, while holding CTRL to additively select, select every other new node across the top of the line of the rectangle. See the following illustration.

10. Press DOWN ARROW on your keyboard several times, to nudge the selected nodes down, until your shape looks like that shown in the lower right of this illustration.

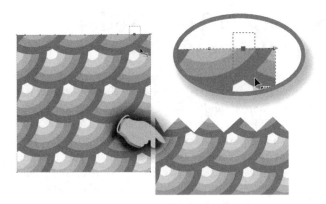

11. For the grand finale to our mini-tutorial, select the star shape at the right in the document, and then press CTRL-Q to convert this polygon shape (which has special editing properties when the Shape tool is used) into an ordinary shape composed of a straight path and nodes connecting the lines.

12. With the Shape tool, marquee-select all the nodes, and then click the Convert to Curve button on the Property Bar. It's okay to look ahead to the following illustration, where the button is called out. You could also have right-clicked and chosen To Curve from the contextual pop-up menu, but it's good to learn more than one technique for accomplishing a CorelTASK!

13. The path segments have control handles on them, and technically they are now curves, but they aren't curve shaped because all you've done is add control handles—you haven't moved the handles to create curves. Fortunately, there's a real easy way to make all the control points force the handles to become in opposition to one another, and what this does is… oh, just watch! Click the Smooth Node button, and you'll probably see something like a form of aquatic sea life on your page now.

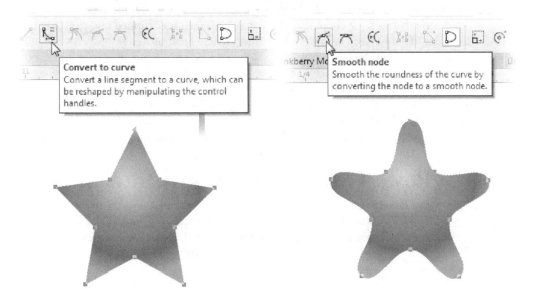

Editing Shapes via Their Nodes and Control Points

Because you only worked through three examples of the power of the Shape tool when editing the basic components of an object, a little more discussion is worthy here. Because *nodes* and *control points* and *control handles* sound more like parts in a 1979 Chrysler LeBaron than the building blocks of objects you draw in CorelDRAW, a few definitions and explanations are provided here. They are low-cal and won't fill up your brain, so not to worry!

When a vector path describes an arc, *nodes* (points) connect a beginning and end point, and the nodes have *control handles,* at the end of which are *control points,* the screen elements you use to manipulate curves. The number of control handles and points depends on the segment connected by each node. For example, an arc (a curve) connected to a straight line segment has one control handle visible, and it controls the slope of the curve segment. When two curve segments are connected, you'll see two control handles if you click the connecting node with the Shape tool, and this node can have different connection properties (Cusp, Smooth, or Symmetrical). A straight path segment can be described as two nodes connecting the segment, and the control handles for the nodes coincide in position with the node itself. For all intents and purposes, the control handles can't be seen; they become visible when the segment is changed to a curved segment: the control handles appear on the segment, and you can move them away from the launch point of the curve and then freely manipulate the slope of the curve by dragging the control points.

You can read more about creating curves and producing (and editing) the nodes that connect these curves in Chapters 7 and 17. For now, let's get back to easier and more dramatic reshaping procedures.

PowerClips

CorelDRAW PowerClips change the appearance of a shape by *hiding* certain areas of its exterior using a different shape. This, unlike other reshaping operations, is completely nondestructive, and the clipping object can release the inner clipped object(s) at any time. Consider the usefulness of PowerClips: You can hide most of an object from view and put other objects behind the PowerClip. You can play a dozen possible scenarios for the composition you have on a page and never commit to any of them, unlike trimming an object.

To give you an idea of the creative power of PowerClips, follow these steps with a document whose objects have already been created for you. The assignment is to put a design on the bottom of a flower vase, stencil-style, so parts of the vase's original color still show through in different regions. It's not hard work when you're familiar with PowerClips.

Tutorial PowerClipping a Design Onto an Object

1. Open Flower and Vase.cdr. To the left you'll see a grouped pattern with transparency. Below it is the same pattern with an Envelope effect applied to make the pattern look bulged, as it would when viewed on the surface of a round shape such as the vase drawing here. On the right in Figure 9-3, over the vase is a thin yellow outline shape

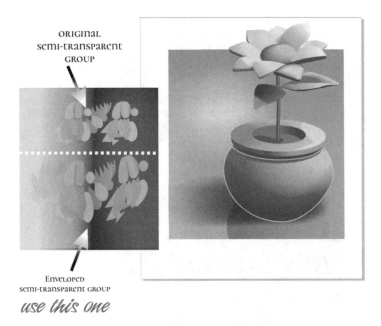

ORIGINAL
semi-transparent
GROUP

ENVELOPED
semi-transparent GROUP

use this one

FIGURE 9-3   Using a PowerClip can simulate the painted texture on an object.

that is a fairly accurate trace over the vase. This will be your PowerClip shape for the pattern—it will hide all shapes outside of it. If you'd like to experiment with the non-enveloped grouped pattern with the Envelope tool, Chapter 14 provides additional documentation on this feature.

2. Select the bottom pattern with the Pick tool, and then drag it over so it's on top of the yellow outline object, making certain that all parts of the pattern overlap the outline. You don't want gaps in the pattern as it's displayed on the vase.

3. Choose Object | PowerClip | Place Inside Frame.

4. A huge arrow becomes your cursor. Click the cursor over the yellow outline, and the pattern scoots inside the container object.

5. The container object is now selected, and a control bar appears below the PowerClip object, with buttons and a flyout menu that cover all the commands you'd otherwise have to go up to the Object menu to access. More about these later.

6. Right-click over the No Fill color well on the color palette to remove the outline. Alternatively, choose None for the Outline Width from the drop-down list on the Property Bar (see Figure 9-4).

Right-click to remove the
outline of the PowerClip.

FIGURE 9-4 Let empty areas in patterns and other complex drawings show through a PowerClip object.

Although the preceding example shows how to mask the exterior of a group of shapes, a PowerClip container can also have an outline width, color, and fill. In any case, the nondestructive property of PowerClips will serve you in a number of design situations.

- **Edit PowerClip** This button takes you to a unique view of your document, where the contents of the PowerClip are available for you to rotate, reposition, scale, and recolor. You can even create a new shape and put it inside the outline of the "frame," the container shape as it is represented in this Edit state. When you're done editing, there will be a single icon below the PowerClip called "Stop editing contents"; click it, and you're done adjusting the PowerClip.
- **Select PowerClip Contents** You can rotate, scale, and move the contents of the PowerClip after using this command, but the contents always stay *inside* the PowerClip object. Attempts to move the contents outside the container will result in hiding them. This is a terrific command, for example, if the pattern in the preceding flower vase tutorial didn't line up exactly the way you wanted it to with the vase.
- **Extract Contents** This command takes the objects out of the PowerClip container. The container now features an "x" through it, indicating it's an empty PowerClip frame, and the objects on your page have no relationship to one another. However, if you want to do some editing on your formerly contained objects and then put them back inside the PowerClip

shape, drag the first one (if there's more than one object you extracted) and then drop it inside the boundaries of the PowerClip object. You can put other objects back inside the PowerClip, but you need to hold w on the keyboard before letting go of the mouse button to bind the second, third, or other object to the interior of the PowerClip.

- **Lock Objects to PowerClip** This is possibly an ambiguous name for the function. If you use this command in its unlocked state, the objects inside the container object are "nailed" to the drawing page, and by moving the container object, you are changing what parts of the inner objects are seen. In the command's locked state, the contained shape(s) travel wherever you move the PowerClip container object. This is a good feature to use if the contained objects are the right size and in their ideal relative positions, but the container object isn't where it should be on the page.

Figure 9-5 shows the mini-toolbar and the flyout extended.

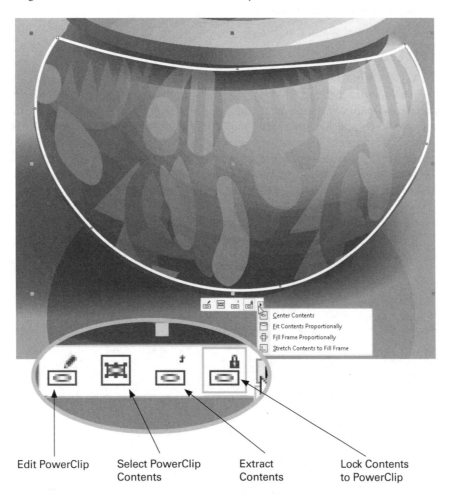

Edit PowerClip   Select PowerClip   Extract   Lock Contents
                   Contents   Contents   to PowerClip

FIGURE 9-5 In CorelDRAW X8, a lot of menu commands can be more easily accessed through a context-sensitive mini-toolbar right next to where you're working.

On the flyout of this floating mini-toolbar are four commands that are almost self-explanatory. First, Center Contents will completely reveal the contained objects within the frame (the container shape). This is useful when you've edited the contents in such a way that you can no longer see a specific object. Next, Fit Contents Proportionally resizes the contents so that all objects can be seen, none are completely outside of the frame, and no disproportionate scaling (commonly called "smooshing") is performed. Similarly, Fit Frame Proportionally increases the size of the contained shapes until each shape occupies the same volume within the container. Sometimes, in order to perform this operation, shapes might disappear outside the frame object to retain everything's proportions.

Finally, Stretch Contents to Fill Frame will distort the shapes "inside" the PowerClip and usually give you a pattern within that's a consistent combination of objects and the frame (container) color, if it originally had one. With this option, imagine a rectangular bounding box that encompasses the container, and contained objects are scaled to fit within the boundary box, not the PowerClip container itself.

The Knife Tool

The Knife tool functions like a knife you'd use in the real world—except you can run with it, and it requires no sharpening—and feels quite natural to use. You begin by hovering over an object area where you want to begin the cut; your cursor changes its appearance to signify it is ready, and then you click-drag to the end of the cut, the other side of the object. The result is two separate closed objects. As with many of CorelDRAW's tools, SHIFT and CTRL can be used as modifier keys as you work with the Knife—and in the case of the Knife tool, these modifier keys add precision to your cuts. You'll find the Knife tool in the Toolbox grouped together with the Crop, Eraser, and Virtual Segment Delete tools, shown here.

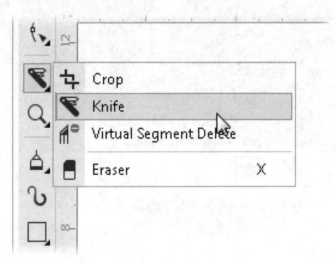

Types of Cuts With the Knife Tool

New to version X8 is a simplification to making cuts with the Knife tool. Gone is the required precise placing of the tool to make cuts on an object. You just make sure the object isn't right next to a different object (your target object doesn't have to be selected), you drag across the target shape, and it's now two shapes. Depending on the options you choose on the Property Bar, there are three ways to cut a shape with the Knife tool, and each one requires a little different approach, as covered next:

- **Straight cuts**   If you want to slice an object into two separate shapes as you'd do with a workshop saw, to produce straight lines on sides of both objects, you aim the cursor on the near side of the object, release the mouse button, and then click on the far side of the object, as shown in Figure 9-6.

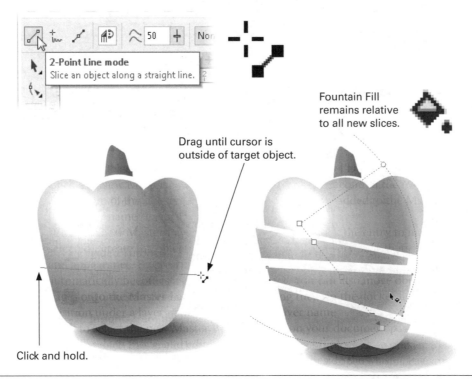

FIGURE 9-6   The Knife tool's 2-Point Line mode makes it a snap to make straight cuts through objects.

- **Freeform cuts**   This mode of slicing can be used, for example, to quickly create an illustration of a sheet of paper roughly torn in half—or in this example, a broken promise. Sorry! You begin your drag at the near side of the object, and then drag until you reach just a little outside of the far side of the shape, as shown here.

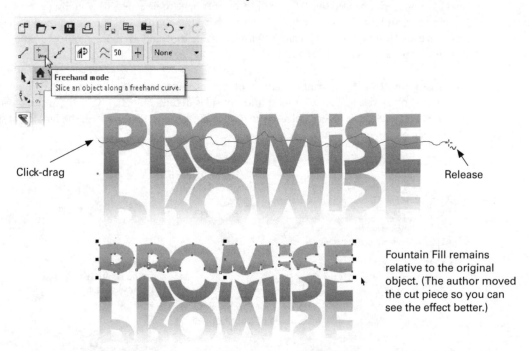

Click-drag

Release

Fountain Fill remains relative to the original object. (The author moved the cut piece so you can see the effect better.)

- **Bézier mode**   If you need to guide the Knife tool to make smooth jigsaw-like cuts, use the Bézier mode of the Knife tool. The operation of this tool is just like the Bézier drawing tool: click a point and then a second point, and a straight line segment is produced. When you click (and hold) and then drag, the segment behind the cursor is a curve. To end the line (or in this case, the cut), you double-click. In the following illustration, the rectangle background is locked. If it weren't, the Knife tool would also divide this object. Remember that to cut a shape with the Knife tool, both the beginning and end points of the cut you draw must lie completely outside of the target object.

Here is where a setting has been changed on the Property Bar for the Knife tool that you might want to explore in your own work.

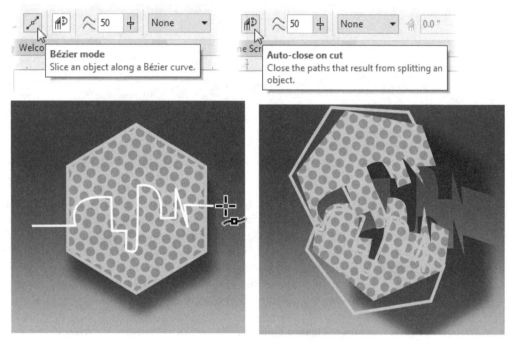

Click-click = line segment.

Click-drag = curve segment.

New split outline is closed, two shapes.

Shadow is split, two shapes.

If Auto-close is active when you use the Knife tool in *any* mode, as long as Close Options is set to Automatic on the Property Bar, any outline is split into two new closed outlines along with separate objects for the cut object. In the illustration, note that the Drop Shadow (Lens effect) is applied to two separate objects.

Although you cannot adjust the Bézier cut's path as you *make* the cut, you can indeed use the Shape tool later to alter the nodes the Knife tool left behind.

Setting Knife Tool Behavior

Using the Knife tool results in just what you'd expect—several objects out of a single one. However, you *do* have options: the two Property Bar options shown here are of the most importance. Each of these options is a drop-down list of approaches to the cutting act on shapes.

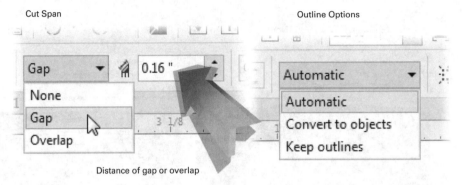

Cut Span

Outline Options

Distance of gap or overlap

- **Cut Span**   The three options you have on this drop-down determine the width of the cut, and whether a cut duplicates the edge of the object and tucks it under the other resultant shape. The amount of offset is determined when you choose Gap, Overlap, or None (the default). This option can be very useful if you've designed a poster that's too large to be printed on your home printer. You calculate how many pages need to be printed to assemble one whole poster, and then set Overlap to, say, a quarter inch. Then you cut up the poster to make physically cutting and taping the complete poster together after printing a snap.
- **Outline Options**   This is a truly neat feature, as demonstrated earlier. If your target shape has an outline, and you want only the exterior of the outline to remain—not around the cut itself, but just around the original shape's profile—choose Convert to Objects. This produces four shapes and no paths with a color width. The shapes are the two parts of the original object, and two parts of the original outline, except they are now shapes—the same result as if you chose Object | Convert Outline to Object (CTRL-SHIFT-Q). The option Keep Outlines will produce two outlines around the sliced object, with both outlines entirely around both shapes. Automatic is recommended before you master this admittedly complex feature.

Using the Eraser Tool

The Eraser tool, shown next, completely removes areas of selected objects you click-drag over—just like a real art eraser, but without the stubble landing in your lap. The Eraser comes in two different shapes, and you can define the size by using the Property Bar. You'll find it in the Toolbox grouped with the Knife, Virtual Segment Delete, and Crop tools.

Eraser tool options

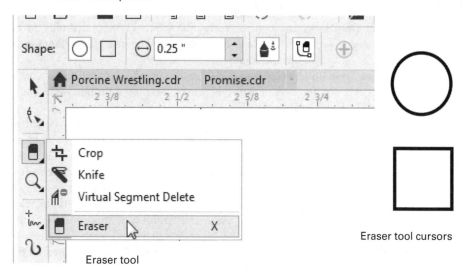

Eraser tool cursors

Eraser tool

Working With Eraser Operations

With this tool, you can remove portions of shapes in four ways:

- **Double-clicking**   When you double-click a selected shape, you remove an area that is the shape of the cursor. Therefore, if you double-click a lot with the circular cursor chosen, you can quickly design a town sign in the Old West.
- **Single-click two points**   If you single-click, move your cursor, and then click a second time, the Eraser tool erases a straight line through the selected object.
- **Click-drag**   This is the most common method of erasing, and the results are totally predictable and usually look like hand-painted strokes. If you click-drag, you erase the area you've dragged over on a selected object.

Note   Grouped objects do not qualify for use with the Eraser tool. However, if you CTRL-click an object in a group to temporarily isolate it, you can indeed erase part of that object.

- **Click, hover over a different area, and then press TAB**   This technique creates several connected straight-line segments, and after you get the hang of it, it will feel like you're painting with an eraser, and you'll be able to quickly produce phenomenally expressive and complex drawings.

Walk through the following tutorial to see the power of this hover-TAB erasing technique and make it your own.

Tutorial Power Erasing

1. Open *Don't Litter.cdr*, an incomplete international symbol that tells the audience, "Put refuse in the appropriate place; don't be a pig." The pale blue outlines are guides for you; they're locked on the Guides layer.

2. Select the main object. Choose the Eraser tool and then set the nib style to rectangular by clicking on the default nib style (the circle) on the Property Bar. For this example, set the nib size to about 0.15".

3. Single-click at the top left of the wastebasket guide. Move your cursor over to the bottom left of the wastebasket guide, but don't click. Notice as you move the Eraser tool that a path preview follows the cursor.

4. Press TAB, but *don't* click your mouse button. Notice that a new erasure appears between the first single-click point and the point where you pressed TAB.

5. To define a third point, move your cursor to a new point (without clicking the mouse button) and then press TAB again. A third point is defined, and the path between the second and third points is erased. Now single-click to end the progressive erasing feature.

6. When you're done with the wastebasket, set the nib style to round, and then add limbs to the thoughtful international guy. Use the TAB technique, for example, to extend a forearm from the guy's shoulder. Once this segment has been erased, double-click where you think his hand would be to extend the erasure. Single-click to end an erasure. Figure 9-7 shows the work in progress.

Single-click

TAB defines points; single-click defines the end.

FIGURE 9-7 Press TAB to define intermediate points between your first and last erase path points to create connected, straight-line erasures.

Setting Eraser Tool Properties

The width and shape of the Eraser tool are set using Property Bar options, as shown next. The complexity of the removed shape, the number of path segments, and the connecting nodes created during an erase session can also be controlled. These properties significantly affect the shape of erased object areas.

 **Tip**   As with most of the Toolbox tools, you can get to the options for the Eraser in Options by double-clicking the button on the Toolbox.

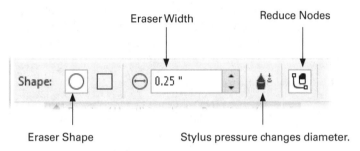

Eraser Width

Reduce Nodes

Shape: 0.25 "

Eraser Shape

Stylus pressure changes diameter.

Tip   Use the keyboard to change the cursor size while you erase. Press UP ARROW and/or DOWN ARROW on your keyboard while click-dragging, and the result can be a tapered brush. After you release the mouse button, the Eraser tool resets to its original size, so you don't have to worry about starting out a new erase stroke with a yard-wide tip!

The Reduce Nodes Option

Enabling the Reduce Nodes option (also called *Auto-Reduce Nodes of Resulting Objects* in the Eraser tool options) lets you reduce the complexity of erased area shapes at the price of what's usually trivial inaccuracy. The importance of removing unneeded nodes is two-fold: First, fewer nodes along paths makes editing easier and provides more predictable results. Second, having too many nodes (and we're talking hundreds of thousands of nodes) can occasionally cause a failure when trying to print to older PostScript printing technology. Depending on the shape, the speed at which you erase an area, and the shape of the Eraser cursor, you might produce 45 or 125 nodes when you make a complex erasing stroke. The option is better than having none, but auto-node reduction also requires a vigilant eye to ensure the feature is doing what you want it to be doing with your artwork.

Using the Virtual Segment Delete Tool

The Virtual Segment Delete tool is used to delete specific portions of objects—specifically, overlapping areas. Additionally, this tool removes portions of an object's path where it intersects the paths of *other* overlapping objects.

To use this tool to delete path segments where an object intersects itself, use these quick steps:

1. With the Freehand tool, draw a path that loops around and crosses itself.
2. With the Rectangle tool, create a rectangle that overlaps a little of the freeform path you drew in Step 1.
3. Choose the Virtual Segment Delete tool.
4. Let's see how much of the rectangle remains when you click on its top segment. Hold your cursor over the segment to delete—you don't need to have the objects selected to use this tool. You'll notice the cursor becomes upright when an eligible segment is hovered over. Now click. As you can see in this illustration, the fill of the rectangle disappeared because it's not a closed path any more. But the segments that did remain are inside the freeform shape you drew.

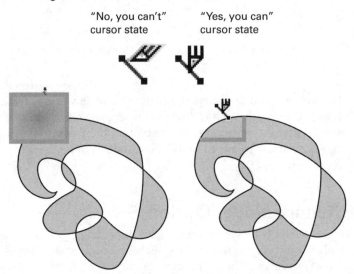

After you delete portions of a path with this tool, what remains is either an open curve with just one path, or a compound curve with two or more subpaths. For example, if the object you're deleting segments from is a closed path, deleting one segment will result in an open curve. Deleting a segment from a rectangle, ellipse, or polygon object will convert the resultant shape to curves and remove the dynamic object properties. To delete segments that are hidden behind an overlapping object, temporarily set its Fill to None.

Cropping an Illustration

The Crop tool, located in the group with the Knife and the Eraser, brings a bitmap effect to vector drawing. If you have experience with Corel PHOTO-PAINT or another photo-editing program, you already are familiar with a crop tool: you select an area within a photo, perform a command such as clicking inside the crop area, and the result is that the area outside the crop is deleted and the image is resized.

The Crop tool in CorelDRAW behaves exactly like an image editor's crop tool. Objects do not have to be grouped; you just drag a rectangle around the area of your design you want cropped, double-click inside the proposed crop area, and all object areas outside the crop box are deleted. On the left in Figure 9-8, you can see a chrome cartoon character photo-bombing a real estate photo. The prudent countermeasure is to isolate the house in the picture, so the house is worth its sticker price when this photo sells it. You drag the Crop tool around the desired area, and then you double-click inside the crop area to permanently alter the imported image.

This is a powerful and potentially very destructive tool, but fortunately you can work with the crop box *before* cropping: you can drag a *corner* crop box handle before cropping to proportionately resize the crop; dragging a *middle* handle disproportionately resizes the crop area. Additionally, once you've made a proposed crop, clicking and then clicking again inside the box puts the box in rotation mode, and you can actually crop a diagonal shape such as a diamond. If you want to cancel a crop operation, press ESC—or click the Clear Crop Marquee button on the Property Bar—and the crop box goes away.

This chapter has taken you through several processes by which you can create minor and big-time alterations to just about anything you draw; additionally, many of the operations apply to bitmaps you bring into the workspace. Use the command that best suits the task you have in mind, and use your judgment as to which operation will get you to your goal fastest. Personal computers are productivity enhancers: there's no need to labor over something when CorelDRAW and your PC can do it for you in less time.

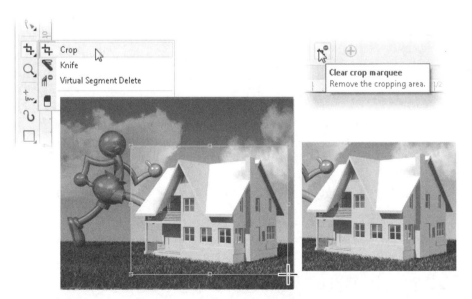

FIGURE 9-8 The Crop tool removes all areas of every object that lies outside the crop box.

Now that you have one, or two, or a dozen shapes on your drawing page, it would be nice to mix them up with some honest-to-gosh text: a headline here, a little body copy there. Shapes and words live together—practically no one publishes an image-only website. Chapter 10 of this guide gets you into the language of typography and the features in CorelDRAW that make your keyboard a professional communications tool.

10 Paragraph Text, Artistic Text, and When (and How) to Use Them

CorelDRAW is a great facilitator of communication and self-expression, and that includes text as well as graphics. This chapter gets you started with the Text tool and other CorelDRAW type features and puts them to use in order to make your thoughts and ideas inviting and presented in a clear fashion. Text and graphics go hand in hand in presentations, and as you'll witness in the following pages, you have many tools at your disposal. This chapter shows you how to access them and how to work with them.

Note Download and extract all the files from the Chapter10.zip archive to follow the tutorials in this chapter.

CorelDRAW's Text Tool

All the text you want to enter on a page in CorelDRAW is created with the Text tool, the tool with an *A* as its icon in CorelDRAW's Toolbox. To begin, click its button in the Toolbox or press F8. If there's *already* text on the page, double-clicking the text with the Pick tool switches the current tool to the Text tool and makes an insertion point for adding text. The Text tool cursor is a small crosshairs with an *A* in the bottom-right corner, which becomes an I-beam (a text-editing cursor) when it's over a text object. You click anywhere on the page or the pasteboard to create an insertion point, and then you get to work with your keyboard.

Note Text copied from the Clipboard can be pasted when the Pick tool is your current tool. Usually, unformatted text—text from a TXT file you copied from TextPad, for example—will import as Paragraph Text. Text copied from word processors will import as a document object; double-clicking the object offers in-place editing exactly as you'd edit a WordPerfect or Microsoft Word document. It's usually best to choose Edit | Paste Special when pasting Clipboard text to ensure correct formatting and the original fonts are used, and to use the Text tool's I-beam cursor to insert pasted text.

Tip A shortcut to reselect the Pick tool while the Text tool is selected is CTRL-SPACEBAR—for all *other* tools, you can press either SPACEBAR or CTRL-SPACEBAR.

When you use the Text tool, you can produce two different types of text objects in a document: Artistic Text and Paragraph Text. Figure 10-1 shows a layout that uses Artistic Text in combination with the Text | Fit Text To Path command—the path is hidden in this illustration. The smaller body copy text uses Paragraph Text; the top paragraph wraps around the top of the image by use of a CorelDRAW Envelope (see Chapter 17). Artistic Text and Paragraph Text have different properties but are added to a document using the same Text tool. Artistic Text, by the way it's produced in a document, is easy to reshape and distort—you'll find it simple to do artistic things with it, such as creating a company logo. Conversely, Paragraph Text is optimized for longer amounts of text, and it's a great text attribute for quickly modifying columns of, for example, instructions, recipes, and short stories. In short, Paragraph Text is best used for several paragraphs of text in a composition while Artistic Text should be reserved for headlines and just a few lines of text you might want to curve along a path, extrude, or do something else unique and fancy with.

FIGURE 10-1   Artistic Text and Paragraph Text have different attributes, and each is suited for different text treatments in a design.

Although there are similarities between Artistic and Paragraph Text, you're best off using one or the other depending on the type of text element you want in your design.

Entering and Editing Artistic Text

Artistic Text will serve you best for illustration headlines, callouts, and on any occasion when you want to create text that has a special effect such as extrusion, an envelope, text on a path, and so on. To add a line of Artistic Text to a document, with the Text tool you click an insertion point and then type your phrase; alternatively, after clicking an insertion point you can press CTRL-V to paste any text you have loaded on the Windows Clipboard. To create several lines of Artistic Text, you type and press ENTER to put a carriage return at the end of the line; you then continue typing. By default, all Artistic Text is set in Arial, 24 point; later in this chapter you'll see how to change the default.

Artistic Text is also easy to convert to curves so you can modify a character in a word: for example, Microsoft's logo has a tick missing in the second *o*. To duplicate this effect (but not Microsoft's logo), you begin with Artistic Text for the company name, press CTRL-Q (Object | Convert to Curves), and then edit away using the Shape tool. Artistic Text can be fine-tuned using the features on the Property Bar when the text is selected using either the Pick tool or the Text tool. The options are shown in Figure 10-2.

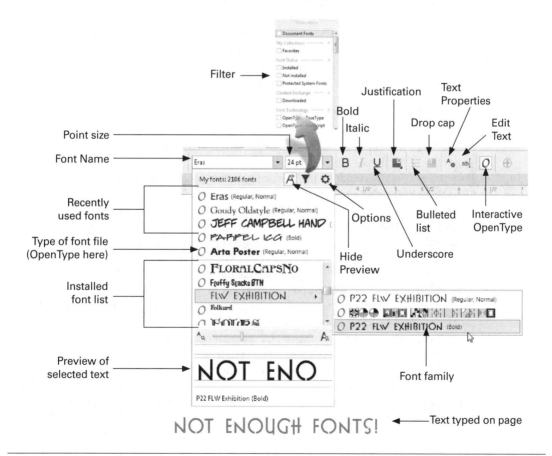

FIGURE 10-2   Use the Property Bar to get Artistic Text exactly the way you want it looking.

 Note Many of the options covered in the following section are *also* available on the Object Properties docker, covered later in this chapter.

 Tip Mirroring buttons on the Property Bar (in addition to creating special text effects) are also useful when, for example, you want to print a T-shirt transfer with your company name. The name needs to be reversed (mirrored horizontally) to print on the transfer paper so that the un-reversed print on the T-shirt reads correctly (or at least without the need for a mirror).

- **Type of Font (File)**   To the left of the font name displayed in the drop-down box is an icon signifying what file format the chosen font uses: OpenType, Type 1, or TrueType. This is a nicety when you're using the Filter List feature, covered later in this section.
- **Font Name, Font Family**   The font name is the name of the typeface you decide upon. By default, you're using Arial 24 point. You change fonts in a new document by selecting text you've typed with the Pick tool and then choosing a different font from the drop-down list. If a font has family members, a right-facing triangle can be seen to the right of the font name when the drop-down list is extended, and you can choose one by hovering above the triangle to reveal the flyout and then clicking the family member title. You can also perform a speed-search by clicking the current name in the font name box and then typing the first few letters of the font you want. The drop-down list immediately scrolls to the neighborhood of installed fonts, making your selection a fast and effortless one. Note also that on the Font List, at the top, above the divider bar, are the fonts you've chosen recently, from previous documents and even from previous CorelDRAW sessions.
- **Point Size**   Text has traditionally been measured in points; with current digital typeface technology, the measure is 72 points to the inch. Artistic Text used as a printed headline can be anywhere from 18 points for a flyer headline to 72 points for an impactful newspaper headline, to 300 points and up for headlines that fairly shout at the reader.
- **Bold and Italic**   These buttons on the Property Bar are shortcuts to defining a whole line of text or only selected characters as bold and italic members of the typeface shown in the Font Name box. If a specific font has no family members, CorelDRAW *doesn't* "fake" a bold or italic look, and the buttons are dimmed. If you need an italic treatment of a font that has no italic family member, a quick fix is to use the Transformation docker and then set Skew to about −12° to apply to the Artistic Text.
- **Underline**   An underline is an effect available for every font you have installed—you click the button when text is selected and CorelDRAW renders an underline. You can modify the style of the underline to your choosing by highlighting the underlined text and choosing Object Properties. Then on the Character area of the Object Properties docker, you click the Underline flyout and choose the type of underline style you prefer.

Note   Underlines are great for professional documents, particularly legal ones, but an underline *isn't* the cleverest way to emphasize a phrase in an advertisement. Use a bold font instead, or a colored outline, or a gradient fill to attract attention artistically. Although underlines are effects, they're very real, and if you convert an underlined phrase to curves (CTRL-q), the underline becomes a simple, four-node object.

- **Justification**   Also called "Horizontal Alignment" in balloon help. This drop-down offers how lines of text are aligned relative to one another. Although Justification will serve you best when using long columns of Paragraph Text, Artistic Text takes on a more polished look, too, when you apply, for example, Center justification to two or three lines. By default, there is no Justification for newly entered Artistic Text, but for all intents and purposes, this is left-justified text. Full Justification creates a splendid, professional look for columns of Paragraph Text, but tends to generate an awkward look for two- or three-line headlines. Left Justification is quite common and acceptable in Desktop Publishing, and Right Justification should be reserved for extreme design circumstances in Western countries, because we read text from left to right. There is a slight difference between Full and Forced Justification, your last two choices on the drop-down list. *Full Justification* ensures that both the left and the right margins are flush to an imaginary line at the width of the text column. Forced Justification creates the same flush-left and -right column edges, but it will also create extra space between words and characters if a line has only a few characters. In the illustration here, you can see an awkward presentation of a few lines. You might actually *want* a wide character-spacing effect, and to do this, you put a soft return at the end of a line (press SHIFT-ENTER).
- **Text Properties**   Clicking this button displays the Text Properties docker. Text Properties is very similar to the top area of the Object Properties docker. Essentially, anything you need to do to customize one or more characters in a text string can be done using the

Full Justification   Forced Justification

Also called "Horizontal Alignment" in balloon help. This drop-down offers how lines of text are aligned relative to one another. Although Justification will serve you best when using long columns of Paragraph Text, Artistic Text takes on a more polished look, too, when you apply, for example, Center justification to two or three lines. By default, there is no Justification for newly-entered Artistic Text, but for all intents and purposes, this is left-justified text. Full Justification creates a splendid, professional look for columns of Paragraph Text, but tends to generate an awkward look for two or three line headlines. Left Justification is quite common and acceptable

Also called "Horizontal Alignment" in balloon help. This drop-down offers how lines of text are aligned relative to one another.   Although Justification will serve you best when using long columns of Paragraph Text, Artistic Text takes on a more polished look, too, when you apply, for example, Center justification to two or three lines. By default, there is no Justification for newly-entered Artistic Text, but for all intents and purposes, this is left-justified text. Full Justification creates a splendid, professional look for columns of Paragraph Text, but tends to generate an awkward look for two or three line headlines. Left

features on the Text Properties docker. You can access the features of the Text Properties docker by clicking the button when text is selected with the Text tool and Pick tool, or by pressing CTRL-T when the Shape tool is the active tool.

- **Interactive OpenType**   Explained shortly, Interactive OpenType shows alternative characters in highlighted OpenType text you've typed. OpenType fonts sometimes contain scores of custom characters that are very hard for average users to access and add to text. The Interactive OpenType button shows and hides alternatives, allowing one-click addition of special characters when a specific OpenType font contains them.
- **Edit Text**   This button displays a text-editing box, which also appears when you click the Text tool on text that has an effect such as Envelope or Extrude. CorelDRAW is designed with text editing flexibility in mind, so in order to transform text using just about any feature—and to allow the text to still be editable—you work in a proxy box so you don't have to start over when you make a typographic error. You can also display the Edit Text box by clicking a line of text that has, for example, an Envelope effect, using the Text tool. The Edit Text box just pops up, with the text selected and ready to edit.
- **Bulleted List**   With text selected (with the Pick tool) or highlighted (using the Text tool), clicking the Bulleted List button creates a bulleted list from your text, using a standard bullet symbol, a hanging indent for the text, and a new bullet wherever you've put a hard return in Paragraph Text. This button is inactive when Artistic Text is chosen. This feature is covered in Chapter 11.
- **Drop Cap**   By default, when Paragraph Text is highlighted and you click this button, a three-line-tall drop cap is auto-created. Options to adjust the drop cap height and spacing, as well as whether a hanging indent is used or not, are found under the Text menu. This feature is covered in Chapter 11.
- **Hide Preview, Filter, Options**   These three buttons can be seen when the font list has been rolled down. The Hide (or Show) Preview button shows the first few characters of the text you want to use, displayed with the selected text on the page. The Filter option lets you choose whether the Installed Font List shows only OpenType fonts, shows font "favorites," or only fonts shown in the current document. It's handy. Finally, the Options button lets you choose how the fonts on the list are displayed—fonts displayed by name, show/don't show the recently used fonts, and so on.
- **Recently Used Fonts**   When this option is turned on in Options, a list of fonts you've used in the current and previous documents is displayed.

Options for Formatting Characters

The Text Properties docker takes the place of other UI features in previous versions and includes more comprehensive features to change selected characters.

If you're new to CorelDRAW, changes can be made to Artistic Text characters in three different ways:

- *Use the Shape tool in combination with the Property Bar.* This method gives you control over character positioning, rotation, and other properties, as covered in the next section.
- *Use the Text tool or the Shape tool in combination with the Character section of the Object Properties docker.* Using this method gives you more control through more options than the Property Bar. Using Object Properties with characters is covered later in this chapter.

- *Use the Text tool, the Shape tool, or the Pick tool (which works but you cannot select individual characters) in combination with the Text Properties docker.* You have the same comprehensive options with Text Properties and the Character area of Object Properties, but for experienced users this feature might be easier to remember by its historic shortcut, CTRL-T.

Use the Property Bar to Change Characters

As you can see in Figure 10-3, you have some options using the Shape tool to select characters, but a more complete set of options when you highlight a character with the Text tool and then click the Character Formatting button on the Property Bar. For quick and simple reformatting, use the Shape tool, and for extensive reworking of your Artistic Text, use the Text tool. You have additional options for lines running under, over, and through selected characters, and if, for example, you've used the Character section in Object Properties to put a double thin underline beneath your text, you can remove this underline later using the Property Bar while character nodes have been selected using the Shape tool. Character nodes appear black when selected (as shown in Figure 10-3), and your cursor is a clear indication you're editing text with the Shape tool and not an object path node.

Tip When a character node is selected with the Shape tool, you can drag the character any which way. You don't *have* to rely on the Offset numerical entry fields on the Property Bar to create offset changes.

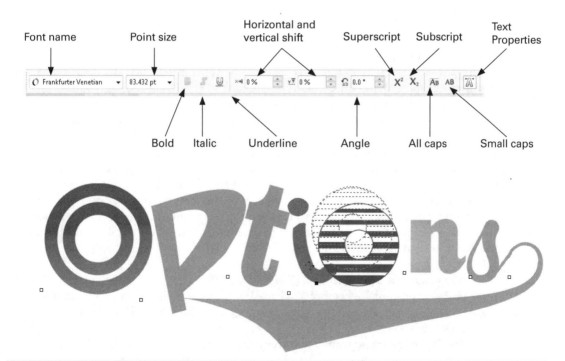

FIGURE 10-3 Format and reformat text characters using the Character Formatting box and the Property Bar.

Selecting and Moving Characters with the Shape Tool

To select arbitrary characters in an Artistic Text object, select the Text object with the Shape tool (F10). With the Text object selected in this way, a small, empty box (a *control handle)* appears at the lower-left corner of each and every character.

To select any character, click on its control handle using the Shape tool. To select nonconsecutive characters, hold SHIFT (*not* CTRL as you'd anticipate) while clicking. You can also marquee-drag around the nodes you want to select with the Shape tool. With the control handles selected, you can modify the text formatting, fill, outline, and position of those characters.

To move one or more characters selected with the Shape tool, click-drag one of the selected control handles. Alternatively, you can nudge the selected characters with the keyboard ARROW keys. It's usually a good idea to keep the characters you move horizontally aligned: hold CTRL while dragging—vertical moves do not accept the CTRL key for constraining movement.

Moving characters with the Shape tool changes the horizontal- and vertical-shift values of them, and the new values can be seen in the Character Offset fields on the Property Bar. Moving characters with the Shape tool is useful for manually adjusting the position of characters visually to improve the kerning, the intercharacter spacing. It's useful if you own a "bum font," a digital typeface that is coded poorly and, as a result, certain characters neighboring other characters are too tight or too loose.

Using the Object Properties Character Options

Everything you can do with the Shape tool in combination with the Property Bar for editing characters within a text string, you can also do on the Object Properties docker, by selecting one or more text characters with the Shape tool *or* the Text tool. Additionally, there is an area in the Character field on the docker where you can quickly access special characters in OpenType fonts you use. This feature is *not* the same as the Insert Character docker, discussed later in this chapter. Many of the OpenType typefaces you find today, both as commercial fonts you buy and ones that comes with Windows and applications, are capable of holding far more than the 256 characters TrueType fonts used to offer. DRAW uses and organizes OpenType data to offer you custom fractions, special ligatures, alternate characters, and other professional typesetting features when a specific font holds the special data.

Whenever you need to change a character in an Artistic Text string, select the character's node with the Shape tool or highlight the character with the Text tool, and then right-click and choose Text Properties (or press CTRL-T), and all the character options are displayed.

Here's a minimal guided tour of where character formatting features have been relocated and a brief example of how to use ligatures (characters that are specially linked together) in text. Refer to Figure 10-4 as you read on.

1. **The Underline button flyout**   You have six different styles of underline for a selected character or word. Remember, a tick mark at the lower right of a button means there are more options on the button's flyout. You click the button to reveal the flyout and then click your choice.
2. **The OpenType typography features area**   If you've chosen an OpenType character or phrase (there should be an italicized *O* to the left of the font name), and the OpenType font was coded to include special characters, you can do some professional and fancy

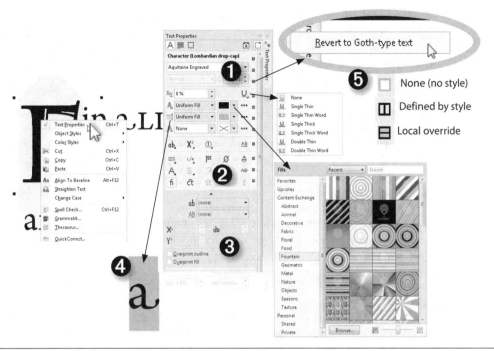

FIGURE 10-4   This figure is your roadmap to CorelDRAW's formatting options.

stuff with your text on a page. As explained shortly, when a character, word, or phrase is highlighted, you'll see some or all of the 15 options turn black in this area, which means CorelDRAW has checked out your font, and, yes, it does have, for example, the capability to build custom fractions (such as 5/16) or ligatures such as a dotless *i* to the right of a lowercase *f*, which looks a lot more professional and is easier to read than the stem of the *f* banging into the dot of the *i*. If none of the options turn black, your OpenType font doesn't have any special features.

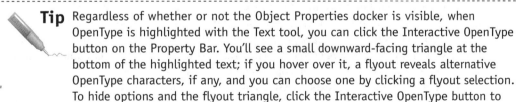

Tip   Regardless of whether or not the Object Properties docker is visible, when OpenType is highlighted with the Text tool, you can click the Interactive OpenType button on the Property Bar. You'll see a small downward-facing triangle at the bottom of the highlighted text; if you hover over it, a flyout reveals alternative OpenType characters, if any, and you can choose one by clicking a flyout selection. To hide options and the flyout triangle, click the Interactive OpenType button to return it to its off state.

3. **Advanced options**   The down triangle on the bar below the OpenType features reveals offset and rotation features when you click it, the same features as presented on the Property Bar when you've selected a character node with the Shape tool. You also have Overline, and the option to specify overprinting if you send this document to commercial printing and a character or other object has both a fill and an outline width.

4. **Background fill**   Characters you've selected can have a solid fill, fountain fill, or other type of fill behind them. The effect is like highlighting passages on a printed page. Any background fill will take up the entire font character height (which usually exceeds the height of capital letters in a font) plus the line spacing. Therefore, you can create background fills for characters that are seamless with the following line of text that has a background fill.

5. **Style modifications**   Because the Object Properties docker is integrated—and objects are treated the same as text—everything on the page can be styled, the styles can be overridden with the Object Properties docker features, and this docker can also change your re-styled object back to its original styled self again. If you see an empty gray square to the right of any feature on the Object Properties docker, it means the selected text (or object) has not been styled in any way; it's an unstyled object. When you see a light blue vertically divided square to the right of a property, the text is styled—and you might want to think twice about modifying your work. If you have modified a styled piece of text, you can change it back to its original style by clicking the Local Override icon and then choosing Revert to Style.

Here's a set of steps you can walk through to get an idea of the ease and power of working with Object Styles. Let's imagine that you worked with a Paragraph Text frame months ago to achieve a beautiful antique look with a custom color and a drop cap. You just received a multidollar contract to work on Ensign Doug's Hot and Spicy Rum, and the label for a bus stop poster needs to carry a legend on the bottle label. You think your fancy text you previously created would work well in this assignment, so your task in this tutorial is to create a style from your saved text and then apply it to the text that goes on the poster.

Tutorial   Using Object Styles with Paragraph Text

1. Open Ensign Doug's rum.cdr. You'll see that in addition to the JPEG image on the page, there is some text above it in Arial and a Paragraph Text block to the left, nicely formatted in Times New Roman, which contains a passage from the U.S. Bill of Rights amendments. If you have a more elegant, perhaps antiqued typeface than Times, select the Paragraph Text now with the Pick tool and then choose your ideal font from the drop-down list on the Property Bar.

2. With the Text tool, highlight a few characters of the Paragraph Text, and then right-click to access the Object Styles menu item. This is much faster the menuing your way to Windows | Dockers | Object Styles. The keyboard shortcut to Graphic and Text Styles from previous versions of CorelDRAW is still the same: CTRL-F5.

3. With the Paragraph Text chosen (using the Pick tool), right-click and then choose Object Styles | New Style Set From. You're choosing to define an entire style set and not simply a style because the Paragraph Text has formatting and also a unique color that you'll want to define and apply shortly to the Ensign Doug's text.

4. On the New Style Set From dialog, type the name of this new style set in the text field, and notice that in the future, you can display the Object Styles docker right after you

define a style by checking the box in this dialog. Your screen should look like the illustration shown here. Click OK.

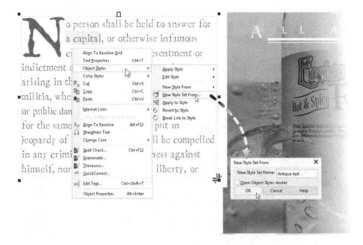

5. On the Object Styles docker, you'll see a new entry below the Style Sets heading. Select the text above the advertisement, and then click the Apply to Selected button. It's that easy to apply two defined styles to a different object, and this updated docker can spare you minutes of work (minutes are considered *hours* in Internet time!) over using the Attributes Eyedropper tool.

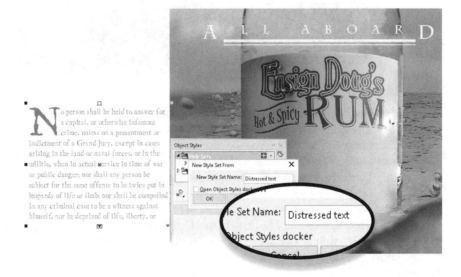

6. In the following illustration, you can see the result of your work. This is a feature well worth investigating in your spare time because it will *save* you time. There's a little added touch or two to the text, and you'll see how to put an envelope around text and other objects in Chapter 17. This is why the text looks as though it's *on* the label and not simply on top of the image.

Here's a working example of using OpenType features—the fast and professional way. In Figure 10-5, I went to some professional expense and bought the Rennie Mackintosh collection of typefaces from ITC in OpenType file format. The fonts were chosen because they are text for a print ad featuring the furniture of the famous Arts and Crafts designer, and as you can see in this figure, the font and the furniture are highly similar. The *fi* characters in "The finish" look awkward, but happily, when the whole phrase is highlighted and the Object Properties docker is open, a down arrow appears below the highlighted text, offering alternative character choices. There are not a lot of features in this OpenType font, but the *fl* and *fi* ligatures and a special picture glyph or two are supported. If there's a special character in OpenType, CorelDRAW will find and offer it for you.

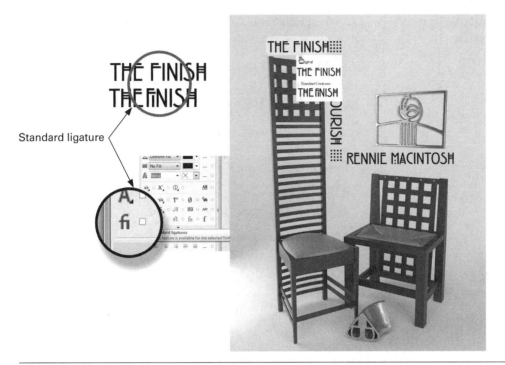

Standard ligature

FIGURE 10-5 Use OpenType features on the Object Properties docker to access characters you couldn't otherwise.

 Tip Try typing a line of text and then using Gabriola, an OpenType that comes with Windows 7 and later. You'll see that just about all the options for OpenType light up on the docker, and several pre-styled combinations are offered when you click the down triangle below the text.

Adjusting Spacing with the Shape Tool

When an Artistic Text object is selected with the Shape tool, two additional handles appear at the lower-left and lower-right corners of the object, as shown in the following illustration. These two handles modify the line spacing and character spacing for the entire block in one go.

To increase or decrease the word and character spacing between words only, hold SHIFT while dragging the handle at the lower-right corner of the selected Text object right or left with the Shape tool. To increase or decrease the line spacing (also the before-paragraph spacing), drag the handle at the lower-left corner of the selected Text object down or up with the Shape tool.

All spacing values modified with the Shape tool can be viewed and edited in the Paragraph Formatting box.

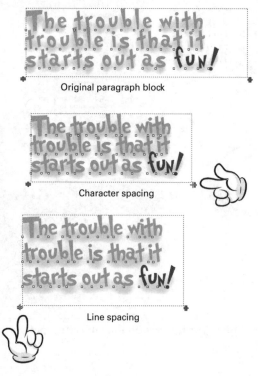

Original paragraph block

Character spacing

Line spacing

Combining and Breaking Apart Artistic Text

You can combine several Artistic Text objects into a single Artistic Text object; you select all the Artistic Text objects with the Pick tool, and then choose Object | Combine or press CTRL-L. Each Text object starts a new paragraph in the new Text object.

The Text objects are combined *in the order in which they are selected*—if you select several objects in one go by dragging a marquee around them, they will be selected from front to back. Text objects that do not contain spaces are combined onto a single line. If any of the selected objects is *not* a Text object, all the Text objects will be converted to curves and combined with the non-Text object.

Tip If the text doesn't combine in the order you want or expect, you can reverse the stacking order of the original Text objects by choosing Object | Order | Reverse Order.

To break apart Artistic Text, choose Object | Break Artistic Text, or press CTRL-K. With multiline Text objects, the breaking apart command results in one Text object for each line or paragraph from the original object.

Also, using the breaking apart command on single-line Text objects results in one Text object for each word, and breaking apart single-word Text objects results in a new Text object for each character.

Converting Artistic Text to Curves

Many effects can be applied directly to Artistic Text, but you might want to apply effects that cannot be applied as a "live" effect to editable text. Artistic Text objects occasionally need to be converted to curves. To do this, choose Object| Convert To Curves, or press CTRL-Q. Text that has been converted to curves is *no longer editable with the Text tool*. Text converted to a plain object with paths and control nodes is a good way to begin creating logos.

Entering and Editing Paragraph Text

The largest difference between Artistic Text and Paragraph Text is that Paragraph Text is held in a container—a frame—so *you don't directly edit*, for example, the width of characters in a Paragraph Text frame simply by yanking on a bounding box handle with the Pick tool. The top of the following illustration shows duplicate Paragraph frames. They're easy to differentiate from Artistic Text; even when not selected, they have a dashed outline around them—a Paragraph *frame*. The version at the top right has been scaled so it's wider than the one of the left. The lines of text flow differently but *the characters themselves* remain unchanged, as does the spacing between characters and words. At the bottom of the illustration, the same text has been entered as Artistic Text and then a bounding box handle was dragged to the right using the Pick tool. What happens is that the characters themselves are stretched. That's the biggest difference between Paragraph and Artistic Text: if text doesn't have a frame, then you're scaling the text.

Four score and seven years ago our fathers brought forth on this continent, a new nation, conceived in Liberty, and dedicated to the proposition that all men are created equal.

Now we are engaged in a great civil war, testing whether that nation, or any nation so conceived and so dedicated, can long endure. We are met on a great battle-field of that war. We have come to dedicate a portion of that field, as a final resting place for those who here gave their lives that that nation might live. It is altogether fitting and proper that we should do this.

The Pick tool modifies *the container* for Paragraph Text.

The Pick tool *directly modifies* Artistic Text.

Once you get the hang of working with Paragraph Text (and the following sections are your guide), you'll find this type of text indispensable for business designs, and your brochures will look as slick as can be.

To create a Paragraph Text object, choose the Text tool from the Toolbox, and then click-drag diagonally to create a rectangle into which you'll enter the text. The upcoming illustration shows to diagonally drag to create a Paragraph text frame as well as the result of this action. The sample text inside the Paragraph frame is simply a placeholder; it disappears after you've added text. There are resizing handles on a Paragraph Text frame as well as kerning and leading handles (Artistic Text features these as well), as discussed later in this chapter. There are three ways to fill a Paragraph Text frame with text:

- *Type in the frame manually.* You probably want to run Spell Check (Text | Writing Tools | Spell Check, or press CTRL-F12) when you're finished typing, because only three people on Earth have perfect spelling from memory, and one of them was your third-grade teacher. Don't disappoint her.
- *Paste from the Clipboard.* You'll see a dialog before you can paste if you press CTRL-V or choose Edit | Paste (or Edit | Paste Special). It is here you can choose to keep or discard the formatting of the text on the Clipboard.
- *Import a text file.* This move is performed by choosing File | Import or using the keyboard shortcut CTRL-I. Depending on the text file type, you might be prompted to install a compatibility pack, especially for older Microsoft Word documents. With a broadband connection, the process takes about three minutes, you don't have to quit CorelDRAW, and you can paste after the compatibility program is installed. In contrast, a plain TXT file with no font or paragraph attributes will import perfectly after you choose a style of import from the Importing/Pasting Text dialog.

The frame you drag for imported Paragraph Text might not accommodate the amount of text. As a result, the *overflow* text is hidden; the frame is a dashed red outline instead of black. To reveal the text, you drag down on the "window-shade handle," the small square tab, bottom-center, on the text frame; when there's hidden text, the handle has a down arrow in its center.

You always have the option to *link* Paragraph Text frames. Instead of spoiling a design by increasing the size of a frame, you can create a second, third, or any number of additional frames, and then flow the excess text into the new frames as you create them. You can move the linked frames around in your design, and the *content* (the *meaning* of the typed text within Paragraph Text) remains in perfect order. For example, suppose you break a paragraph into two frames in the middle of the text "Now is the time for all good people to come." Then, in the future, if you need to resize the first Paragraph Text frame, the excess of words will "pour" into the second frame, regardless of their position on the page. This is too neat to simply describe with words, so let's try creating linked text frames in the following steps.

Tutorial Creating Linked Paragraph Text Frames

1. In a word processor or plain text editor, copy some existing text to the Clipboard; it doesn't matter what the text is. Highlight a few paragraphs and then press CTRL-C.

2. In CorelDRAW, choose the Text tool and then perform a diagonal-drag to define a Paragraph Text frame. Try to make the frame smaller than the text on the Clipboard (eyeball it).

3. Insert your cursor in the frame and then press CTRL-V to paste the Clipboard text. If you copied from a word processor, CorelDRAW will flash you the Import/Pasting Text box, where you have the option of retaining the formatting (if any) created in the word processor—font choice, point size, justification, and tabs are all attributes of text formatting. Go with it; click the Maintain Fonts and Formatting button and then click OK.

4. Click the bottom-center text handle (the box with the black triangle arrow), and your cursor is now loaded with all the text that was hidden from view because your frame is smaller than the text you pasted into it. Your cursor takes on a new look, as shown in the following illustration.

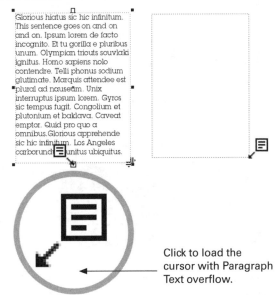

Click to load the cursor with Paragraph Text overflow.

5. Click-hold-drag diagonally to create a new, linked text frame. The excess text from the first frame automatically flows into the new frame, as shown here. A light blue line with an arrow indicates the relationship between the text in the first frame and the second frame (this screen element does not print, don't worry). Try repositioning

the two frames now using the Pick tool. Then try resizing the first frame. You'll see, dynamically, the second frame takes the overflow from the first frame.

Wrapping Text Around Other Shapes

You can apply text wrapping to shapes in CorelDRAW so that any Paragraph Text placed close to the shape will flow *around* the shape instead of over or under it, as shown in the examples in Figure 10-6.

FIGURE 10-6 There are six contour and square text-wrapping options available and one non-wrapping option (None).

All you need to do is have some Paragraph Text superimposed upon an object, press ALT-ENTER to display Object Properties, click the icon of the question mark inside a picture frame, and you're all set to do some text-wrapping, as shown here.

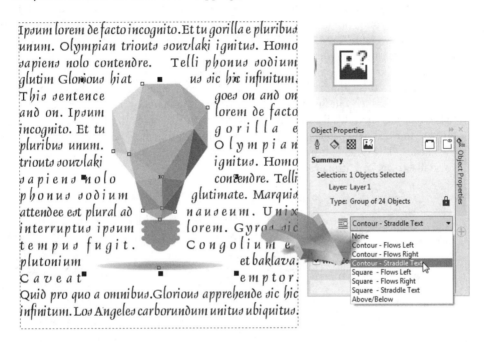

Text conforms to a shape in two different ways:

- **Contour wrapping**   The text is wrapped a line at a time *around* the outline of the shape.
- **Square wrapping**   The text is wrapped around an imaginary rectangle that bounds the shape with the wrap (its *bounding box).*

In either case, the text can be made to flow down the left or right of the object, or straddle it (flow down both sides). Square wrapping also supports Above/Below, where no text flows to the sides of the object.

To apply Contour Straddle, right-click the shape and select Wrap Paragraph Text from the pop-up menu. To set a different wrapping type, select it from the Summary tab of the Object Properties docker (ALT-ENTER is the shortcut). Then set the text wrap offset (the margin distance), which is the gap between the outline or bounding box of the shape and the Paragraph Text wrapped around it.

Fitting Text to Curve

Wrapping text around an object has its alter ego: putting text inside a shape, so it looks as though the text itself forms the shape. A third variation involves fitting text to a curve—you can have Artistic Text follow an arc, a freeform line, or an open or closed shape, and you have options for the style in which the text follows your line.

The simplest way to form text so it appears to have a geometry other than rectangular is to first create a shape, copy some text to the Clipboard if you don't have a message in mind, and then carefully position your Text tool just inside the line of the shape (perhaps 1/8th of a screen inch inside) until the cursor turns into an I-beam with a tiny text box at its lower right. Then, click to start typing, or click and then press CTRL-V to paste your Clipboard text. Text inside a shape is Paragraph Text, and it obeys all the Paragraph Text formatting conventions covered in this chapter and Chapter 11.

In the following illustration, you can see sample Paragraph Text on the left. This text has been copied to the Clipboard, and then the Type tool is placed close to the white ellipse; it makes no difference whether the container object is selected or not. When the cursor changes to the one shown in this illustration, it's time to start typing (or in this case, press CTRL-V), format your text, and probably assign the container outline no color and no width to complete the illusion. The Orange Innertube file is provided in the ZIP archive for this chapter, in case you'd like to get in a little practice.

Type tool

Copy (CTRL-C)

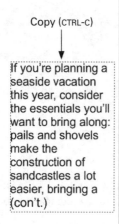

Note   Orange Innertube.cdr and Yield sign.cdr are in the ZIP archive you downloaded. You can use them for practice, pouring text into the predefined shapes in the files.

One very popular treatment for text "bound" to an object is the arc of text. This is accomplished by first creating the arc shape (a circle usually works well) and then instead of clicking inside the shape, you hover above the shape until your Text tool cursor becomes an I-beam with a tiny swooping curve beneath it.

Follow these steps to flow text in a semicircle.

Text Along a Curve

1. Open Toon Valley Milk cartoon.cdr. The graphic of the cow could use some text revolving around the outer circle.
2. Create a circle using the Ellipse tool.
3. With the Shape tool, drag the Ellipse node away from the center of the circle to create an open arc. Adjust each node until you have an arc centered above the cartoon. See Chapter 9 if you're unfamiliar with editing CorelDRAW objects.
4. With the Text tool, position the cursor just above the outline of the circle and then click an insertion point and begin to type. You'll see that the text follows the curve. What you type is up to you, but "Toon Valley Farms" is a solid starter for graphics that involve a cow and possibly a milk carton logo!
5. If the text isn't aligned to your liking, use the Offset spin box on the Property Bar to correct it.
6. If you'd like the text to be a little off the curve, use the Distance from Path spin box.
7. If you'd like a truly wild and interesting style (a *treatment*) of the text, such as a 3D ribbon look, check out the drop-down list on the left of the Property Bar. Click any of the styles to apply them. The circle still has an outline, but it takes one right-click on the X in the color palette to fix that. Figure 10-7 shows an example of the finished label, and how it can be placed over a photo—covered in Chapter 16.

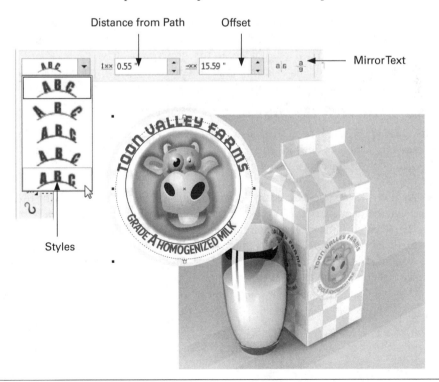

FIGURE 10-7 Use Fit Text to Curve to make your message a flowing one.

Tip Don't overlook the Mirror Text button when fitting text to a curve. If you want text arcing in a semicircle beneath a graphic—as the text was created in Figure 10-7 at the bottom of the logo—you can't fit the text into a lower arc in the graphic without mirroring the text vertically first.

Embedding Objects into Text

Graphic objects and bitmaps can be embedded into blocks of Artistic and Paragraph Text—in the layout profession, this is called an *inline graphic.* This is great for adding special symbols to text, such as logotypes, bullet points, and horizontal separators, or for embedding instructional graphics, such as mouse cursor images.

You embed an object into text in two ways:

- **With the Clipboard**   Copy or cut the object to the Clipboard (CTRL-C or CTRL-X), click the Text tool in the text where you want the object to be placed, and then paste the object (CTRL-V).
- **Drag and drop**   Using the Pick tool, select the object with the mouse and then drag it with the *right* mouse button to the position in the text where you want it to appear—a vertical bar between characters in the text indicates where the object will be placed. Release the mouse button and select Copy Into Text or Move Into Text from the pop-up menu.

Embedded objects are treated as "special characters"—they can be selected only with the Text tool or the Shape tool. To resize an object after it has been embedded, select it and set its point size on the Property Bar as if it were a typographic character.

To delete an embedded object, select it with the Text tool and then press DELETE.

Using the Insert Character Docker

CorelDRAW, via Text | Insert Character (CTRL-F11), removes the guesswork in locating a character or symbol in any font you have installed. When you choose this command, the Insert Character docker appears, and you have two ways to insert a character:

- **As text**   If you need, for example, a fancy bullet that is inline in existing text in your document, you place the Text tool cursor at the location in the text where you want the character, click the character on the docker to select it, and then drag the character into the line of text (or double-click the thumbnail of the character). You might not always want to choose this method; the advantages are that the character is editable text and stays aligned to the text that comes before it and after it. However, the disadvantage is that as a designer, you might want to move this ornamental character around on the page—but as inline text, the inserted character is bound to the line of text you added it to, as shown here.

- **As a collection of editable shapes**   To add a character to your document as a shape that you can immediately edit with the Shape tool, use either the Text or the Pick tool to drag the thumbnail of the symbol you want onto the page. Then press CTRL-Q to convert the Artistic Text to an editable object. It's easy to spot the difference between an inserted symbol on a page and an editable symbol (object): shapes display start nodes along paths when selected, while Artistic Text only has a beginning node you use with the Shape tool to move, rotate, and so on, using the Text Properties docker (CTRL-T). You have an endless supply of special characters at your cursor tip with the Insert Character docker, so mistakenly adding the type of symbol you don't want to a document is corrected in a flash.

A new and important feature is a button titled simply Entire Font, which opens a context-sensitive drop-down list. Depending on the typeface you've chosen to pick characters from, clicking on this button can help you focus and narrow the selection of glyphs in the preview window you drag into the line of text. For example, the font Arial contains almost 1,000 characters, but you only want a character that pertains to currency. So you click the button, put a check next to Currency, and the symbols for the euro, yen, British pound, American dollar, a generic currency glyph, and so on are displayed, removing hundreds of visual distractions from your search.

Using the Symbol Manager

Now that you've located the perfect symbol for a design by using the Insert Character docker, it would be nice to save the symbol so you can reuse it in the future instead of hunting for it again! This is where the Symbol Manager (CTRL-F3) under Windows | Dockers is an invaluable resource. The Symbol Manager provides you with information about symbols contained and saved only to a document you have open and also provides User Symbols, an area on the Symbol Manager where you can duplicate a catalogued symbol into any document at any time.

Let's say you've found a great symbol for a layout, you've placed it in your document, and you decide you want to reuse it tomorrow. Here are the steps for cataloguing the symbol and for accessing an *instance* of it (a duplicate that takes up less saved file space in a document) tomorrow.

Tutorial   Creating, Saving, and Using Symbols

1. With an object selected, choose Object | Symbol | New Symbol.
2. In the Create New Symbol box, type a name you'll remember later in the Name field and then click OK. As you create more and more new files using CorelDRAW, you'll definitely want to stay tidy in your cataloguing work. Cross-referencing is a good practice; in Figure 10-8, the name of the symbol refers what the author named his drawing as it was added to the symbol collection. Later, it's easy to look up the name of the symbol and use it in a program outside of CorelDRAW.
3. Open the Symbol Manager and then click on the Untitled-1 title. A thumbnail of the symbol you just saved appears.
4. A tiny Export icon becomes active. Click it—it's the Export Library command. This is not much of a library, but you need to start somewhere!
5. In the Export Library box, it's best to save the new library to where CorelDRAW recommends (to better allow the program to locate it in the future; "symbols" is a good location). Name the library and then click Save. You're done.
6. In any new document, open the Symbol Manager, click the Local Symbols + icon to open the collection, and then click the name of the library you saved in Step 5. Now all you need to do is drag the thumbnail into a document, and you have an instance of the symbol you saved.

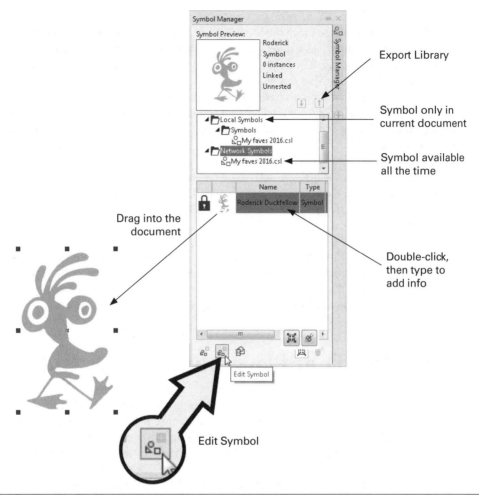

Export Library

Symbol only in
current document

Symbol available
all the time

Drag into the
document

Double-click,
then type to
add info

Edit Symbol

FIGURE 10-8   Define a symbol and then save it to a symbol library.

In Windows 7 and later, your saved symbol library will be in C:\Users\(your user name)\ AppData\Roaming\Corel\CorelDRAW Graphics Suite X8\Symbols. This is good to know when you want to load your collection by clicking Add Library on the Symbol Manager docker, to add symbols to a local document.

Tip   With the Pick tool, right-click over any object you create, and you can then choose Symbol | New Symbol from the context menu.

Symbols saved to a library are always *instances* and, as such, duplicates you add to a document cannot be edited using the Shape tool or other shape-editing features. You can apply transformations such as scaling and rotating, but you cannot edit the nodes of a shape instance. However, you *can* edit a local symbol, one you have not saved to a library but rather to the current document. Now this editing technique is more dramatic and fun if you've dragged several saved symbols on to the page and rotated and scaled them and stuff, so do this right now. To edit a symbol, with the Pick tool you right-click over any symbol you've added to the page (to display the context menu) by dragging the locally saved symbol thumbnail into the page. On the context menu, you choose Edit Symbol, and then on the page you'll see a single object, ready to edit. You can use the Shape tool, recolor the symbol, and even use the Boolean operation to subtract an ellipse you add to the page to slice the symbol—whatever goes. After you've edited the shape, you right-click over it in the document window and then click Finish Editing Object. *Bang! Whoo-wee! Gosh-a-rooties!* Every instance is updated to reflect your edits.

Tip It's easy to tell the difference between an instanced symbol and one that can be edited in any document. Choose the shape using the Pick tool. If the bounding box dots are blue, it's a shape *instance*. If the bounding box handles are black, it's a regular shape, and you can perform any CorelDRAW operation on it.

CorelDRAW's Font Playground: Take a Ride!

To end this chapter on the lighter side, let us look at a utility Corel Corp. added to DRAW that's both useful and *fun*. The Font Playground is an onscreen panel that looks like any other Corel docker, but aside from copying and pasting text, its purpose is *not* to enhance drawings or modify text but to *preview* and *compare* a phrase or word when set in different font styles. Try this: type some Artistic text, something like "Flash Sale! 8 hours only!", or something similarly anxiety provoking for customers. Then Choose Text | Font Playground. The illustration that follows is a composite of the Font Playground docker, showing multiple views of it to visually clue you into your options.

Single-line display   Multiline display   Waterfall display Installed font list   Sample size

Copy text on the
page, then press
CTRL-V after clicking
on a sample

Sample
preview
window

From left to right, here are your display options for the Font type and the preview you've
entered (covered in a moment):

- **Single-line display**   Clicking this button displays part of a phrase once, in as many font
  styles as you like.
- **Multiline display**   Clicking this button displays a longer phrase you might choose as the
  display sample—again, in any number of font styles you choose.
- **Waterfall display**   This button option shows you only the text sample you've clicked on
  in the preview window, at various increasing point sizes. This is useful for predetermining
  whether your chosen font is legible at, say, very small point sizes.

Additionally, you have a type size slider toward the top left of the docker, but perhaps the neatest part of the Font Playground is the option to copy a phrase into the Playground so you can compare it in several styles, and then copy the chosen phrase and typeface to the drawing page.

To put a phrase into the preview window of Font Playground, you select the text with the Pick tool on the drawing page, copy the original text first (CTRL-C), click an entry in the preview window, and then press CTRL-V. This is a shortcut to remember, because the docker doesn't have a "Paste" command or button.To put your phrase in your dream font on the page, all you do is click it in the preview window to select it and then click the Copy button.

Typography is such a large part of human communications, and type features are such a large part of CorelDRAW, that we can't just say, "Nice lecture, thanks. *Next*...." Paragraph margins, column widths, setting dot leaders for fancy menus, creating bulleted lists—this is all important stuff, too, unless you're certain you can convey any message with your drawings alone. Advanced typesetting features and CorelDRAW's proofing tools are your next stop in Chapter 11, because fancy text layouts just don't cut it if you've used an expensive font, extruded it, colored it magnificently, and the headline reads, "SUPER-SAL 2TODAY ONLY. EVERTHIN MUST GO!"

We can do much better. Turn the page....

11 Intermediate Desktop Publishing and Proofing Tools

After reading Chapter 10, you should be up and running and getting some handsome results from *some* of CorelDRAW's Type tool features. But like the child in all of us who wanted to skip the bicycle riding and get straight to Formula 1 racing, this chapter is intended to train you up on professional typesetting, Desktop Publishing, and the proofing tools CorelDRAW offers so that your typed ideas are as easy to understand as the way these typed gems *look* on a page. Bring an idea and an open mind, and let's explore some of the more advanced typographic tools that version X8 has to offer.

 Note Download and extract all the files from the Chapter11.zip archive to follow the tutorials in this chapter.

A Few Paragraphs Covering Advanced Paragraph Features

When you set type in a text-intensive document, you'll certainly have special needs for the formatting of the text. You might want a set numbers of columns, moving sections around to make an article read better; perhaps you even have a need for a bulleted list such as you'd find in a fancy restaurant's outrageously priced menu. The following sections take you through the mechanics of accomplishing special formatting requirements with DRAW's tools.

Working With Columns

Although you can manually create flowing columns of Paragraph Text, it's often less time-consuming to use the automated Columns feature in CorelDRAW. Text columns divide Paragraph Text frames into several vertical columns separated by *gutters* (margins). Multiple columns can be created only in the Text | Columns dialog, shown next. The following section describes how to adjust columns with the mouse. Naturally, you need Paragraph Text on a page to start with before creating columns; you diagonally drag with the Text tool to create a Paragraph frame. Also, you must have Paragraph Text selected with the Text tool to work with columns: the tabs do not show on the rulers using other tools.

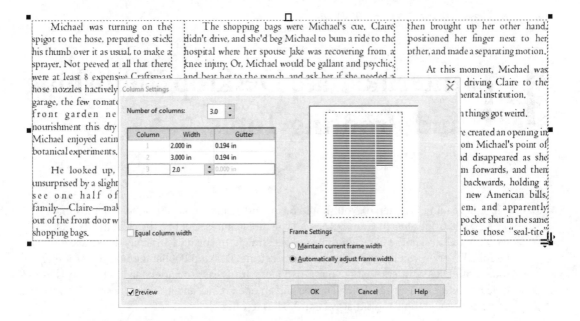

Select the frame in which you want to place columns, open the Text | Columns dialog, and then set the number of columns in the Column Settings dialog box. It is always a good idea to keep the number of columns balanced, so each column is neither too wide nor too narrow. A good rule of thumb for legibility is, each line of text should be no wider than six inches or 16 words, but it should be wide enough to have *at least* four words per line. Anything else becomes hard for your audience to read, and the look of your layout seems unprofessional.

To change the width of the columns and margins, drag the column guides, column-boundary markers, gutter handles, and horizontal-resize handles, as shown in Figure 11-1. When you're dragging the column guides or boundary markers, if the Equal Column Width option is selected in the Format Text dialog, all the gutters will be resized together; the gutter handles are available only when this option is not selected.

Note Columns can be applied only to entire Paragraph Text frames and cannot be applied to individual paragraphs or Artistic Text.

Column Settings

Once you've created a Paragraph Text object with columns, you can refine and make precise columns and gutter widths through the Text | Columns | Column Settings dialog, shown in Figure 11-2.

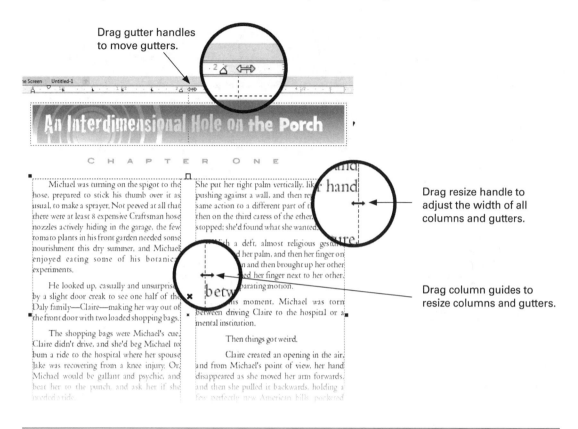

FIGURE 11-1   Column widths can be edited directly by dragging with the mouse.

To add extra columns, first set the number of columns and then set the widths of the columns. The Gutter value is the distance between the selected column and the next one. If Equal Column Width is selected, changing the width of any column or gutter changes the width of all columns or gutters to the same value. If Maintain Current Frame Width is selected, changing the width of any column or gutter will not change the overall width of the frame, so the other columns and gutters will be resized to accommodate the change. A preview of the column settings is shown in the preview frame on the right side of the dialog.

Text in columns (even if only one column is used) can be justified via the Alignment button on the Property Bar, the Text Bar, and the Object Properties docker when you click the Paragraph tab.

Tip   You can have more control over columns by laying them out as multiple text frames, each one containing a single column.

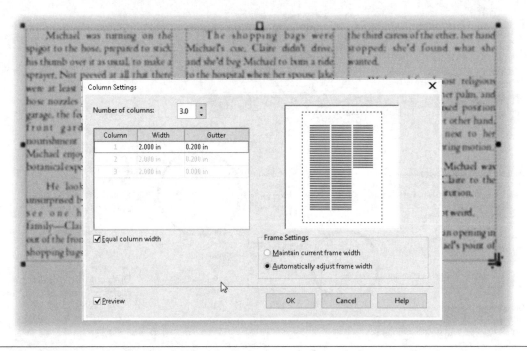

FIGURE 11-2   Under Text | Columns, use the Column Settings dialog to apply columns to Paragraph Text.

Moving Text Within a Paragraph

You can move a selection of text with the mouse by dragging and dropping; select the word or phrase you want to move, and then click-drag the text to its new location in the current text object—or any other text object—with the primary mouse button. A vertical bar indicates the insertion point at the new location; the cursor becomes the international "no" sign (a circle with a slash through it) if it is not possible to drop the text at the current location. Dragging with the *right* mouse button causes a pop-up menu to appear when you drop the text, with options for what to do with the text. The options are Copy Here and Move Here (Add To Rollover doesn't do anything unless you have a web page rollover defined). You can use this editing gesture to copy and move words within Paragraph and Artistic Text, but you can also put the copied or moved text outside of the body of Artistic and Paragraph Text. In this event, the text is no longer inline with the text from which you copied or moved, so use this command (particularly Move Here) with a *very* good reason in mind.

Tip   If you click on the Paragraph Text box with the Pick tool and then change justification, all paragraphs included are changed. If you click on one paragraph with the Text tool, then only that one paragraph is affected.

Converting Between Artistic Text and Paragraph Text

To convert a block of Artistic Text to Paragraph Text, right-click the Artistic Text object with the Pick tool; then choose Convert To Paragraph Text from the pop-up menu. The menu command is Text | Convert To Paragraph Text, and the keyboard shortcut is CTRL-F8. All the text formatting is maintained as closely as possible each time you convert between the two text types, although some formatting, such as Paragraph Text Columns and Effects, cannot be applied to Artistic Text and is lost.

Going the other way is similarly simple; however, all the text in a Paragraph Text frame must be visible: it cannot be hidden, and you cannot convert a linked Paragraph Text frame. With the Pick tool, right-click over Paragraph Text and then choose Convert To Artistic Text (CTRL-F8 works, too).

The Text Bar and Special Paragraph Formatting

Because of the large screen resolutions we enjoy today, we can view pages at almost a 1:1 resolution as they would print, but this also means we might need to scroll and mouse around a document more than is healthy for the wrists. The solution in CorelDRAW is simple: if you're working extensively with text, you *float* the Text Bar close to the area of the document in which you're fine-tuning. Right-click over any area of the Property Bar and then choose Text from the pop-up menu. You can drag the Text Bar to hover over any area you like.

The Text Bar can be used to edit single characters in Artistic Text and Paragraph Text, but its real strength is in the offering of options for making Paragraph Text look polished and sophisticated. When the Pick tool or the Text tool is active, all the features are active and at your disposal. There are additional modifications to the available options, described a little later in this chapter.

 Tip The Text Bar and the Text options on the Property Bar are essentially identical for text that has been selected using the Pick tool or the Text tool. The Text Bar is simply a more portable device for working closely with text.

Formatting Bulleted Lists

Bulleted lists are commonly needed for page layouts: restaurant menus, assembly instructions, and just about anything that's a list that doesn't need to be a numbered list! In the following sections, you'll see not only how to create a bulleted list but also how to choose any character you like for the bullet and even create a hanging indent for the bullet.

Making Bulleted Paragraph Text

Like the toggling Drop Cap button, the Show/Hide Bullet button can be your one-click stop for creating bulleted lists; however, you'll surely want a custom bulleted list that looks as artistic as your document layout. On the Text menu, you'll find the Bullets command: it's straightforward, and you'll quickly achieve great results. Find or create a list of something and follow along to see how to work the options for Bullets.

Creating a Bullet Motif

1. There's no real harm in simply using the Pick tool to select the Paragraph Text you want to make a fancy bulleted list: every line break in the list begins a new bulleted item, so select the text and then click the Show/Hide Bullets button on the Property Bar or the Text Bar.
2. Choose Text | Bullets, as shown in the following illustration.

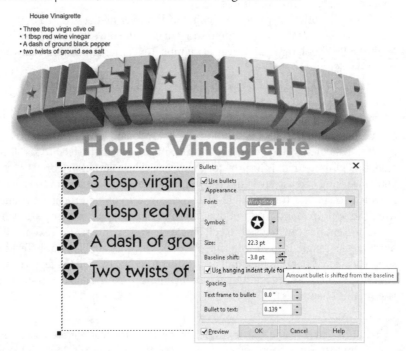

3. Choose a typeface that contrasts, yet is compatible, with ITC Machine, the font used in the extruded headline text. Kabel Book BT comes with the Graphics Suite, and is used in these illustrations.
4. The illustration here is an "All-Star Recipe," and the interiors of the A's are stars, so a bullet shaped like a star is appropriate.

5. Microsoft's Wingdings font is installed with every copy of Windows, and it features some nice symbols: choose Wingdings from the Font drop-down list in this example, and then click the Symbol drop-down button and locate a good star shape.

6. Click the Use Hanging Indent Style For Bulleted Lists check box to get a polished look for the list.

7. Increase the point size of the bullets by dragging upward in the center of the spin box control labeled Size.

8. Most likely, the baseline of the enlarged symbol won't look right compared to the text in the list (it'll be too high). Drag on the Baseline Shift spin box control until the bullets look aligned.

9. Optionally, if your symbol is crowding into the list text, increase the Bullet To Text spacing. Similarly, the Paragraph Text frame might be too tight to the left of the bullet; in this case, you increase the Text Frame To Bullet amount.

10. Optionally, you can color the bullets by selecting each one individually and then choosing a color from the mini-swatch pop-up. See the following illustration for the completed design.

Changing Text Case

Occasionally you'll receive text from a client who doesn't know where the Caps Lock key is on the keyboard, or you have a really, really old plain-text file created using a DOS application. In any event, all caps in a text message, unless it's a very brief headline, can be a real eyesore.

To change the case of text you have typed, insert the Text tool cursor in text, right-click the text, and then choose an option from the Change Case submenu. Changing the case of characters replaces the original characters with new characters of the correct case.

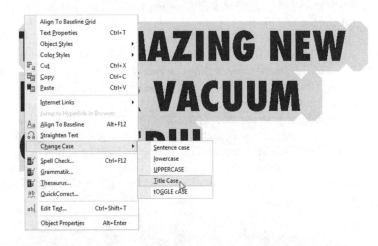

Formatting Paragraph Text

Stepping inside the frame and column formatting of Paragraph Text, you'll see that CorelDRAW has extensive options for specifying how lines of text look compared to one another, how tightly characters and words are spaced, and how you want individual paragraphs to separate from each other. The following sections cover the use of the Paragraph features on the Object Properties docker.

Paragraph Alignment

The Alignment settings on the Paragraph section of Object Properties affect the spacing for the entire selected paragraph; you can choose the entire Paragraph Text object using the Pick tool, or only pages by highlighting them with the Text tool. You have left, right, center, full, and forced as alignment settings (called *justification* in the publishing world), and None at far left, which removes the current alignment.

Spacing

Below Alignment are controls for indent preferences, how much space should go before or after a paragraph, line spacing (leading), and finally intercharacter and interword spacing. It should be noted here that proper typographical form dictates that separate paragraphs are usually indicated by either a first line indent or a line space between paragraphs, but not both. It's also important to understand that character and word spacing apply to the entire paragraph, whether you have only a portion highlighted with the Text tool or not. See the following illustration.

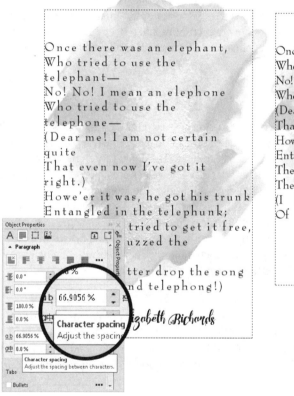

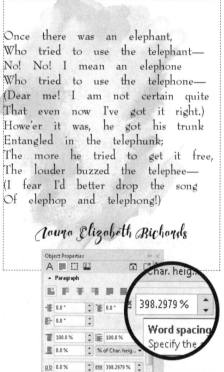

Paragraph and Line Spacing

You might choose to separate paragraphs by using the Before Paragraph or After Paragraph spin box, but not both. By default, the spacing between paragraphs is the percentage of the character height, the *total* height of a character in a digital font. The *actual* height of a character in a font can vary—some uppercase characters are 650 units for example, while others are 750 units. You cannot always know the absolute height of a capital letter, but typically CorelDRAW puts in 30 percent more line spacing than a capital letter in the average font.

However, you can always choose Points or Percentage of Point Size from the drop-down list to create custom inter-paragraph spacing. This is an option you want to experiment with, depending on the typeface you're using. Anywhere from 125 percent to 200 percent can work from an artistic standpoint.

Tip Although *you* measure text in points, when you create typefaces, each character lies on an imaginary grid, measured in *units*.

Line Spacing is used to let some "air" into paragraph text and is especially useful when you have a font whose ascenders or descenders are unusually tall. You can also use very wide Line Spacing to create an artistic effect when starting, for example, a magazine article. It has been fashionable in layout for several years now to put about 300 percent line spacing in the opening paragraph: it lightens the page when using a bold font and also allows the reader to see more of any decorative background you've used.

Language, Character, and Word Spacing

If you're typesetting, for example, an article using an Asian font, Language Spacing will be useful to space non-left-to-right sentences; otherwise, you'll have very little use for this option. You can set how much extra space is added to the default intercharacter space for the paragraph as a whole by using Character Spacing. The values are a percentage of a normal space character for the current font. You can also modify the interword spacing—this has the effect of adjusting the width of the space character. As a rule, if you need to adjust typeface kerning to all the contents of a paragraph frame, you use Character Spacing in the Paragraph area of Object Properties. If, however, there is only a bothersome line or two in a paragraph, you highlight only those lines and then adjust character spacing with the Range Kerning spin combo box in the Character area of the Object Properties docker.

Tip Remember the control handles on the bounding boxes of Paragraph Text. Also remember that the Shape tool is the only tool for editing Paragraph Text. They offer less precision for character and line spacing than the Paragraph Formatting dialog, but they're quick to use and provide a good coarse view of how your layout is shaping up.

Indentation and Margins of Paragraph Text

You can set the sizes of the indents of the left and right margins, as well as the size of the first-line indentation, just as you do in a word processor. These can be set precisely from the Paragraph Formatting dialog, or you can set them with a little less precision using the triangular markers on the ruler, which are shown next:

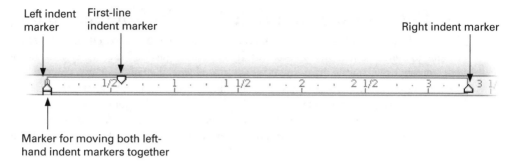

Left indent marker

First-line indent marker

Right indent marker

Marker for moving both left-hand indent markers together

Formatting Tabs

Tab stops for Paragraph Text can be edited either directly in the ruler or in the Text | Tabs | Tab Settings dialog, as shown in the following illustration. CorelDRAW supports left, right, center, and decimal tabs, just like most word processors.

Alignment

Add tab

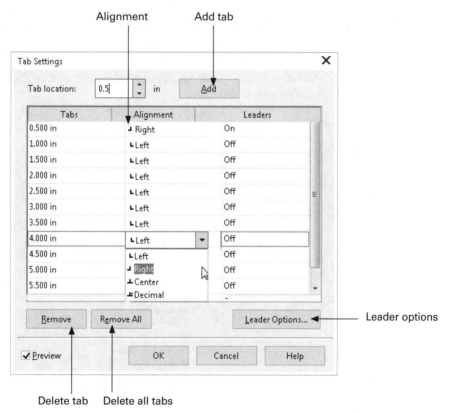

Leader options

Delete tab   Delete all tabs

Adding, Moving, and Deleting Tabs from the Dialog

Tabs can be added to the current paragraph in the Text | Tabs | Tab Settings by first entering a value in the Tab Location spin box and then by clicking Add. To set the type of the new tab, you choose from the drop-down list associated with the tab. Similarly, you can adjust an existing tab by clicking its position (thus opening the value for editing) and then typing in a new value. To delete a tab, select it in the list and then click the Remove button.

When you create a new paragraph, unless you have modified the default paragraph style, tab stops are positioned every half-inch. To remove all the tabs, click the Remove All button.

Formatting Tab Leaders from the Dialog

You can choose whether text positioned to any tab has a leader between the tab settings from the Leader Settings box, which you can go to by clicking the Leader Options button in Tab Settings. *Leading characters* are often used in tabulated lists, such as tables of contents and menus, to join the section titles or menu items on the left with their respective page numbers or prices on the right.

Leaders are usually displayed as a series of dots, but they can be changed to any of the characters shown in the Character drop-down list. Unfortunately, you can't make a leader using a font other than the one used in the Paragraph Text. To change the leader character, select a character from the Character drop-down list, as shown in this illustration. The distance between the leader characters is set with the Spacing setting: this value is the number of space characters to insert between each leader character.

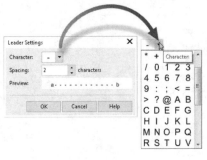

PRE-FLIGHT CHECKLIST

Hobbs / Tach time - - - - - - - - - Check
Weight and C.G. - - - - - - - - Check
Charts and Navaids - - - - - - - Check
Phone w/ ABBA's Greatest Hits - - - - Check
Woods Path® Trail Mix-Sweet 'n' Salty - - Check
Fuel Quantity - - - - - - - - - Check
Lights (Night) - - - - - - - - - Check
Lapel Pin - - - - - - - - - - Check
Flaps - Down - - - - - - - - Check
148 oz. After Shave - - - - - - - Check
Flight Controls - - - - - - - - Check
Circuit Breakers - - - - - - - - Check
Oil Pressure - - - - - - - - - Check
Brakes - - - - - - - - - - Check
Carb Heat - - - - - - - - - Check
Engine Instruments - - - - - - - Check

Using the Ruler to Set Tabs

To edit tab stops on the ruler, you must make sure the ruler is visible (choose View | Rulers), you use the Text tool in selecting the Paragraph Text, and you click to set or edit the tab stops. To view tab characters in the body of your Paragraph Text, press CTRL-SHIFT-C (Text | Show Non-Printing Characters). Before creating new tabs, you should delete all the tabs that are already in place—select Remove All from the Tabs Settings dialog.

To create new tabs with the ruler, use the Text tool to select the paragraphs to which you want to add tabs and then click on the horizontal ruler where you want to add the new tab stop. The type of the tab can be set by right-clicking over the tab. There is also a selector button where the ruler origin usually is when working with Paragraph Text. Clicking the selector button cycles between the four tab states: left, right, center, and decimal. Note that clicking the selector button doesn't change existing tabs; instead, it only sets new *successive* tabs.

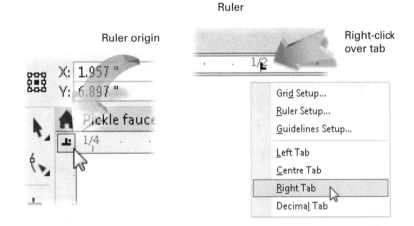

To move a tab, drag it to its new position on the ruler. To delete a tab, drag it off the ruler and into the workspace. To change the type of a tab, you have three options: delete it and create a new one of the correct type, right-click it in the ruler and select a new type from the pop-up menu, or change its type in the Tab Settings dialog. Tabs cannot be added to Artistic Text.

Here's a practical example of the value of knowing how to set up tabs: create a folding menu design and then create Paragraph Text with menu items and their corresponding prices on the same lines (make up anything you like—have fun here!). Here's how to create a dot leader so the guests can see the prices at the far right easily, based on the menu items on the far left.

Tutorial   Take Me to Your Leader

1. Open the One Café menu.cdr file. Notice that all the prices are directly after the menu item with no space in between. This is done deliberately so when you add leaders, the prices will align to the right. The headline text (Gillies Gothic) and all elements except the menu text are locked. With the Text tool cursor inserted in the body of any of the linked text blocks, press CTRL-A to select all the text. Now choose Text | Tabs.

2. Click Remove All; you don't want the default evenly spaced tabs in this menu. If you look closely at the ruler in the tabs region above the document, you'll see that the paragraph box is a little more than 4" wide. Therefore, type **3.75** in the Tab Location box at the top and then click Add.

3. The first entry in the list, as shown in the following illustration, is 3.75", but its alignment is by default to the left, which is wrong for making a tab leader layout. Click the Left entry in the Alignment column, and it turns into a drop-down box—choose Right from the list. If you haven't checked the Preview box in the Tab Settings dialog, do so now so you can watch live updates on the page as you work. Also, you probably want to set Leaders to On; this is done the same way as you chose Right alignment for the 3.75" tab. Finally, the shortcut for toggling visibility of nonprinting characters is CTRL-SHIFT-C; use this to be able to tell leader dots from spaces marked in the text. See the following illustration.

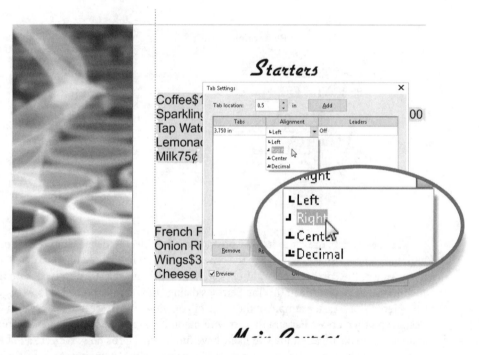

4. Click Leader Options.

5. Choose a period as the character. If you want something fancier, you might try a caret (^) or a tilde (~) instead.

6. Set the spacing for the leader character.

7. Click OK, and then place the Text tool between the price and the menu item, and then press TAB. Figure 11-3 shows the nearly complete, easy-to-read, somewhat underpriced menu. Notice that your document updates in real time, so you can preview how your dot leader looks before clicking OK.

FIGURE 11-3 Tab leaders help guide the eye from an item to its price.

Spelling and Grammar

You want your text to look as good as your drawings, and the same powerful grammar and spelling tools offered in Corel WordPerfect Office suite are right inside CorelDRAW. A spell-checking system, thesaurus, and grammar checker—in 25 different languages—are at your fingertips. This means you can both compose in CorelDRAW and import writing to CorelDRAW—and be assured your words are perfect.

CorelDRAW also has the same QuickCorrect feature that's in WordPerfect, for correcting common typos and spelling mistakes *as you type.* This is extremely helpful for words that you commonly mistype and for common extended characters such as © and ™.

CorelDRAW and WordPerfect use the same writing tools, dictionaries, word lists, and configurations. If you add a word to your User Word List in WordPerfect, it is there for you in CorelDRAW. If you're a Microsoft Word user, CorelDRAW's proofing tools are as easy to learn as Word's—the dialogs and labels are a little different in appearance, but you'll soon get the idea. It's time now for you to step up to the title of Literary Wizard in addition to CorelDRAW Design Guru.

Using CorelDRAW's Writing Tools

With text proofing in 25 different languages available right out of the box, CorelDRAW makes it easy for you to get your sales language proofed perfectly regardless of the world destination for your products or services. When you install CorelDRAW, choose the languages you are most likely to use, and you are ready to check the spelling and grammar of anything that comes your way.

By default, CorelDRAW assigns a language code and checks all text using the proofing tools that correspond to the language your operating system uses. If you use a U.S. English copy of Windows, CorelDRAW automatically installs English–U.S. proofing tools and assigns all text to U.S. English (ENU).

Assigning Language Codes

If your document contains text in a language other than the default language, you need to select the foreign language text and assign the proper language code to the text so CorelDRAW will use the appropriate proofing tools. The language currently assigned to selected text is noted by a three-letter code in parentheses next to the font description in the Status Bar—for example, by "(ENU)" shown in most of this book.

To change the language assignment of any character, word, or paragraph of Artistic or Paragraph Text in a document, select the text and then choose Text | Writing Tools | Language. When the Text Language dialog opens, you can choose any one of the 122 different language and language variants that appear in the list (see the following illustration). Click OK to make the change.

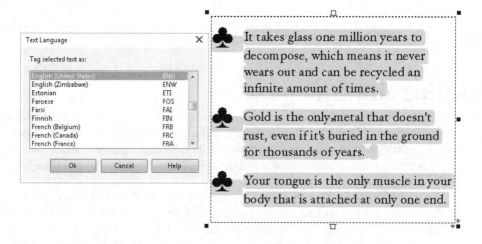

Using the Proofing Tools

To use CorelDRAW's spell checker, thesaurus, or grammar check, select the text with the Pick tool or the Text tool, and then choose the appropriate writing tool from the Text | Writing Tools menu. Alternatively, you can right-click a text object with the Text tool and then choose a proofing tool from the pop-up menu. CTRL-F12 is the shortcut for opening the Writing Tools dialog to the Spell Checker tab, as shown here:

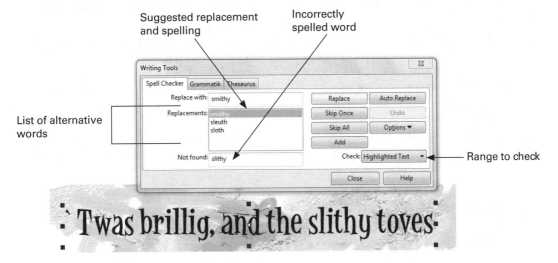

Suggested replacement and spelling

Incorrectly spelled word

List of alternative words

Range to check

Common Buttons

The Spell Checker and Grammatik tools share common buttons in the Writing Tools dialog. These buttons perform the functions described here:

- **Start**   The Start button starts the Spell Checker or Grammatik. This button is visible only if Auto Start is off—it is on by default. To enable or disable the Auto Start option, in the Writing Tools dialog, click the Options button and then select Auto Start.
- **Replace**   As the check is performed, when a misspelled word or grammatical error is found, the Start button changes to Replace, and the misspelled word or grammatical error is highlighted. Select the suggested correction from the list and then click Replace to apply it. You can also edit the replacement word in the Spell Checker's Replace With box, or type in a new word before replacing it. After the replacement has been made, the checker rechecks the replacement and continues checking.
- **Undo**   The Undo button reverts the last correction to its previous state.
- **Resume**   After you correct a mistake, if you move the insertion point—for example, to a different part of the text—the Start button changes to the Resume button. Simply click it to recheck any selected text and to continue checking from the insertion point.
- **Skip Once and Skip All**   If the word or sentence that a checker has queried is actually correct—for example, a brand name such as Pringles or Humvee—you can click one of the Skip buttons to have the checker ignore it. Skip Once causes the check to continue, but future instances of the same problem will stop the checker. Skip All tells the checker to ignore *all* instances of this spelling or grammatical error.
- **Add**   Add allows you to add a word to the current User Word List. Many unusual names and technical terms are not included in the Spell Checker's dictionary, and these can be added to the User Word List for the current language. In the future, these words will not

be queried. If a word appears in the Replace With box or in the Not Found box, clicking Add immediately adds the queried word to the default User Word List. Otherwise, if no word appears in either box, clicking the Add button opens an input box, where you can type the word you want to enter into the User Word List.

- **Auto Replace**   If you choose an alternative spelling for a queried word, the Auto Replace button becomes active. Clicking this button will add the misspelled word and its replacement to the default User Word List, *and* if QuickCorrect is enabled, then the next time you type the same mistake, the correct word will be automatically substituted.
- **Options**   The Options button displays a drop-down menu that contains various settings for the current Writing tool.
- **Range of Text**   By using the options from the Check drop-down list, you can set the range of text for performing a spell check or a Grammatik check. The available options depend on whether text is selected with the Text tool or the Pick tool.

Setting Spell Checker Options

You can click the Options button on the Spell Checker page of the Writing Tools dialog to access various settings that affect how the Spell Checker works.

Using Word Lists

CorelDRAW's writing tools maintain Word Lists that contain all the valid words and phrases for spelling checks. If a word in your document is not in one of the active lists, it is flagged as being incorrectly spelled. CorelDRAW has two types of Word Lists:

- **Main Word Lists**   These lists are provided by Corel and contain the most common words and spellings in each language. One Main Word List exists per language, and this list is not editable.
- **User Word Lists**   These lists contain words that are not in the Corel-supplied lists but rather are made up of words you have added during a spell check by clicking the Add button. Words and phrases that are common to an industry are very useful to create. It is up to you to ensure that the words you add to a User Word List are spelled correctly! User Word Lists also contain the QuickCorrect entries for the text's language. Each language has at least one User Word List.

You can also use third-party-created lists. Specialized User Word Lists, such as those containing medical, legal, engineering, scientific, or other professional terms, can be created and then shared.

Using Main Word Lists

The Main Word Lists are predefined by Corel and cannot be edited by CorelDRAW. However, they can be edited by the WordPerfect suite's Spell Utility if you happen to have a copy. Main Word Lists contain only words used by the Spell Checker—no QuickCorrect word pairs are included.

Which Main Word List is currently being used changes according to the Language setting. Click the Change button (Writing Tools | Spell Check | Options | Main Word Lists), choose a different language, and CorelDRAW will use the Main Word List for the new language you chose. Changing which word list CorelDRAW is currently using does not change the language code of the selected text but rather temporarily proofs that text using the new Main Word List.

You can also switch spell checking, for example, to check a language other than the default in the CorelDRAW document. For example, some U.S. English users might want their U.S. Spell Checker to include Spanish words. When a U.S. English user adds the Spanish word list, the Spell Checker will first check words against the English list. Then, if the words are not found in the English list, the checker compares against the Spanish list. Only if the check fails against both lists will the Spell Checker display an error. Using this method, you don't have to specifically set a language code for the Spanish text.

Other Spell-Checking Options

Some other options available from the Options drop-down menu of the Writing Tools dialog are described here:

- **Auto Start**   The Spell Checker and Grammatik start the check automatically when the Writing Tools dialog is opened or when that checker's page is opened in the Writing Tools dialog.
- **Check Words with Numbers**   Checks or ignores words that include numbers.
- **Check Duplicate Words**   Flags words that appear twice in succession.
- **Check Irregular Capitalization**   Checks for words that have capital letters in places other than the first character.
- **Show Phonetic Suggestions**   Makes *phonetic* suggestions—replacement words that *sound* like the unrecognized word.

Main Spell-Checking Options

The Workplace | Text | Spelling section of CorelDRAW's global Options dialog (CTRL-J) also includes various options that modify how the writing tools work:

- **Perform Automatic Spell Checking**   Check this if you want to check spelling as you type. When it is turned on, unrecognized words are underlined with a red zigzag line while you're editing text with the Text tool.
- **Visibility of Errors**   Choose here to have all errors underlined in all text objects or just the text object being edited.
- **Display Spelling Suggestions**   You set the number of suggestions to display in the pop-up menu after right-clicking a misspelled word with the Text tool. The maximum and default number of suggestions is 10.
- **Add Corrections to QuickCorrect**   When this option is checked, CorelDRAW will add a correction pair to the User Word List based on a correction made from the right-click pop-up menu.

- **Show Errors Which Have Been Ignored**   When you right-click a word, the pop-up menu includes an Ignore All command, which tells the Spell Checker to ignore this word. With this option set, CorelDRAW will still show ignored errors, but it will use a blue zigzag line to indicate that they have been ignored.

Using Grammatik

Spelling errors aren't the only proofing goof that can make your work look unprofessional. Poor grammar is a big, red flag that reflects on your education and communication skills. CorelDRAW includes the Grammatik grammar checker in many of the languages that spell checkers are available in.

Grammatik is a flexible, powerful tool for checking your work. What Grammatik excels at is calling your attention to parts of your text that *might be* grammatically incorrect; it second-guesses you. Grammatik encourages you to stop and think about what you've written and offers helpful suggestions to fix the problem it *thinks* is a thorn in your rosy prose. The day-to-day operation of Grammatik is not difficult to manage, as you'll see in the next section, where the basics are covered.

Checking and Correcting Grammar

To check your grammar, select the text objects to check with the Pick tool, or select sentences with the Text tool; in the Writing Tools dialog, open the Grammatik tab, shown in Figure 11-4, by choosing Text | Writing Tools | Grammatik. As with all of the other writing tools, you can also select text and then use the right-click pop-up menu to launch the tool you want to use. It's common to use a word that sounds like the word you want. For example, "affects" is indeed a real word, but it's a homonym—a word that *sounds* like a word you might intend to use, such as "effects."

Grammatik highlights potential grammar problems with light blue on the page. Occasionally when it finds more than one space between words, the white space is underlined. This is very helpful; modern rules of good digital typography call for only one space between sentences and not the two that were required in the days of typewriters.

If Auto Start is enabled, Grammatik will immediately start checking the text; otherwise, you must click the Start button.

If Grammatik finds something that breaks the rules of grammar using the current settings, it displays an explanation of the problem next to the name of the broken rule—the "Rule Class" that has been broken. Grammatik may make one or more suggestions of better grammar, and if you click an option, the new sentence is shown so that you can decide if that's what you meant to say. Click Replace to apply the change and continue checking.

Turning Grammatik's Rules On and Off

If you don't want Grammatik to check a certain kind of grammatical error, you can tell it to ignore it. As soon as Grammatik pops up a grammar query, the Add button in the Writing Tools dialog changes to Turn Off. If you click Turn Off, the specific grammar rule that is currently being used will be deactivated for as long as the Writing Tools dialog is open. If you

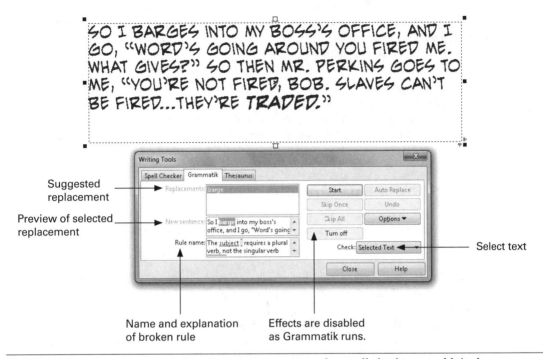

SO I BARGES INTO MY BOSS'S OFFICE, AND I GO, "WORD'S GOING AROUND YOU FIRED ME. WHAT GIVES?" SO THEN MR. PERKINS GOES TO ME, "YOU'RE NOT FIRED, BOB. SLAVES CAN'T BE FIRED...THEY'RE *TRADED.*"

Suggested replacement

Preview of selected replacement

Select text

Name and explanation of broken rule

Effects are disabled as Grammatik runs.

FIGURE 11-4 Grammatik catches errors in your writing that spell checking wouldn't alert you to.

want to turn it back on again, choose Options | Turn On Rules, which brings up the Turn On Rules dialog. Choose those rules that you want to reactivate and click OK. The next time you perform a check, these rules are included.

After you have pared down the rules to the one you want to keep, you can save this new "profile" for future use: choose Options | Save Rules. The Save Rules dialog opens, and you can either click the Save button to update the current style or click Save As to create a new checking style.

Using the Thesaurus

When the word you're using doesn't convey exactly the right shade of meaning or if you've already used it three or four times, check out the available synonyms with the Thesaurus Writing tool. Right-click with the Text tool on the word you want to replace with a better word, and then choose Thesaurus from the pop-up menu. Alternatively, choose Text | Writing Tools | Thesaurus. The Writing Tools dialog opens with the word in the look-up word box.

The look-up word box contains the word you want to look up. The suggestions area of the dialog contains a folder-like tree view list of alternative words and meanings for the word you are looking up. Find one that matches the message you are trying to present and click to expand the entry. If you find the word you want to use, select it and click the Replace button to insert the word into your text. You can also choose *the opposite meaning* of a word in case inverting a sentence is a style of writing you like—*antonyms* are available for the word you chose in the expandable tree in the suggestions area.

If you find a word that is close, but not exactly the right word for you, double-click on the word to automatically open another suggestion area in the dialog that makes suggestions for words that are similar to the selected word. Up to three panes of suggestions are visible at once, but you can keep clicking on suggestions and open up more panes that you can navigate through using the left and right navigation buttons at the top of the dialog. To use a word in one of the alternate panes as your replacement word, select it and click the Replace button.

Setting Thesaurus Options

You can set various options for the Thesaurus by clicking the Options button in the Writing Tools dialog and clicking the Thesaurus tab to view the drop-down menu; the most useful ones are described here:

- **Auto Look Up** This option speeds up your work by starting the process right away.
- **Auto Close** When turned on, this option closes the dialog as soon as the Replace button is clicked.
- **Spelling Assist** When this option is enabled, if the word that you selected to check in the Thesaurus is not recognized, a list of similar words from the Thesaurus is shown. Click the word that best matches the correct spelling of the word you typed, and then click Look Up. The suggestions area will contain alternatives.
- **Synonyms** This option displays synonyms of the look-up word in the list of suggested alternatives.
- **Antonym** This option displays antonyms of the look-up word—a lifesaver for those times when you can't think of an opposite for the word you want.
- **Language** Choose this to change which language's Thesaurus is used for the current session. This does not change the language of the text in your document, but any replacements will be set to the new language. This only works with languages you have currently installed.

Finding and Replacing Text and Special Characters

All too often you may find yourself in the situation of having to locate a specific piece of text so you can change the font or formatting or even the content of the text itself. CorelDRAW has terrific tools for searching for and replacing text—and text attributes—regardless of whether your layout is a paragraph or a multipage document.

Finding Text

To find a word, phrases, and other marks such as dashes, hyphens, and special characters like tabs, paragraph breaks, and spaces, open the Find Text dialog by choosing Edit | Find And Replace | Find Text. In the Find box, enter the word or exact phrase you want to find.

You can include special characters such as an em or en space or dash, a ¼ em space, a nonbreaking space, a nonbreaking hyphen, a column/frame break, an optional hyphen, a space, a tab, or a hard return in your search. To enter the search tag for a special character into the Find box, click on the right arrow next to the Find drop-down and then choose the character you want to include in your search.

If you know the exact character case of the word or phrase, enter it and check the Match Case check box—if the Match Case check box is cleared, all matching words will be found, regardless of the case of the characters (a case-insensitive search). The Find Text dialog is shown here.

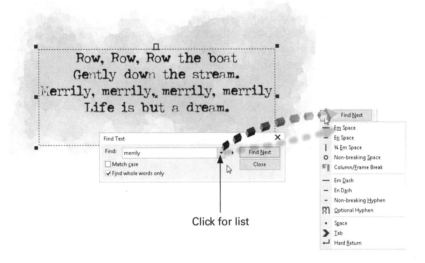

Click for list

Click the Find Next button to find the next instance of the searched text within the document. All the text objects in the document—Paragraph, Artistic, and Fitted Text—will be searched, starting with the current page and working to the end of the document. You will be asked whether you want to continue from the start of the document when you reach the end: clicking Yes takes the search back to page 1, and it will continue through to the start position, so the whole document is checked once. If the search text is not found, CorelDRAW tells you.

Replacing Text

If you want to replace a word, phrase, or special character in the text with another word, phrase, or special character, use the Replace Text dialog, which is accessed by choosing Edit | Find And Replace | Replace Text.

You enter the word or phrase you want to find into the Find box, and enter the replacement word or phrase into the Replace With box using the same process as described for finding text in the previous section. Click the Find Next button to find the first instance of the search text. When the search text is found, click the Replace button to replace it with the replacement text, or click the Find Next button to skip over the found text and to find the next instance to replace.

If you are sure that you want to replace *all* instances of the Find text in the current document with the Replace With text, click the Replace All button.

 Note The ability to search and replace special characters in addition to text is incredibly useful when you are cleaning up imported text, changing five spaces into a tab, and removing column/frame breaks (soft returns). It is also a useful feature if you want to tweak your typography; for example, you can search for a hyphen between numbers and replace it with an en dash. You can also give your text some breathing room and search for all the em dashes in your text and put ¼ em spaces on either side of the em dash.

And this is the last word on typography in CorelDRAW! You now know how to spell check, grammar check, and find and replace text. Our next stop is setting properties for filling objects and outline properties for paths. Let's get your objects—*including* text objects—looking as visually captivating as you'd like them to be.

12 Options for Filling Objects

A shape without a fill on your drawing page is like a brand-new coloring book. To make a coloring book—and your CorelDRAW artwork—more complete, you need to *fill* your shapes with colors and textures. CorelDRAW has more than a half-dozen types of fills you can apply to your shapes, and these types have hundreds of variations. In computer graphics, you have over 16 million solid shades of color at your disposal; imagine what you can do with *blends*, *patterns*, and *textures* of colors! The worst part of filling CorelDRAW objects will be deciding on a style of fill. The *best* part, as you explore filling shapes in this chapter, is that it's very difficult to color outside of the lines.

 Note Download and extract all the files from the Chapter12.zip archive to follow the tutorials in this chapter.

Examining the Fill Types

Each type of CorelDRAW fill has its own special characteristics:

- **Uniform** Uniform fills apply flat, solid color.
- **Fountain** Fountain fills make a color transition from one color to another, in different directions—sometimes also called a *gradient fill*. You can also create a fountain fill composed of more than two different colors. CorelDRAW ships with many preset fills, and this chapter demonstrates how to pick and apply them.
- **PostScript** PostScript fills are good for repeating patterns. Although PostScript is a *printing* technology, you don't need to print a CorelDRAW document to see a PostScript fill, and you can indeed export a PostScript-filled object to bitmap format and the fill will look fine. PostScript fills support transparency and are ideal for exporting to EPS file format to use in desktop publishing programs. And, naturally, a PostScript fill is valid for printing to a PostScript printer.
- **Pattern and texture** Pattern and texture fills can fill shapes with bitmaps, including photographs, and a large supply of preset bitmaps is included with CorelDRAW.

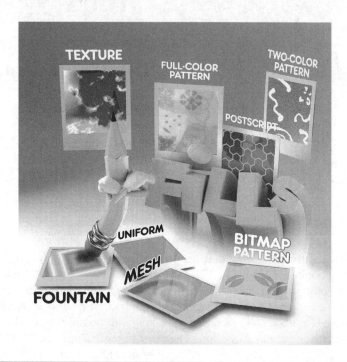

FIGURE 12-1 Fill your shapes in a composition with the fill type that draws attention to your design work.

- **Mesh**   Mesh fills take multicolored fills and present you with the option of "smearing" colors within the fill, much like finger painting.

Every fill type is applied in a slightly different way through the use of onscreen tools, docker windows, or the Interactive Fill and Mesh Fill tools (see Figure 12-1).

Using the Color Palette

For color selection, the color palette is an excellent starting point, and to apply a uniform (solid) fill to a selected object, just select an object with the Pick tool and then left-click a color on the color palette. You can also drag a color swatch from the color palette, drop it onto a shape—which *doesn't* have to be selected—and the object is filled.

You can choose not only a color from the color palette, but also a *shade* or a *tone* of that color. To pick a shade of a color on the color palette, you first select the object you want to fill, click-hold on a color swatch, and a small pop-up menu of shades and tones of that color appears, as shown next. While holding the mouse button, drag to the exact shade you want, release the mouse button, and the object is filled. This pop-up features shades that vary in *hue* from top to bottom, and in *brightness* from left to right. You have 49 possible colors at your cursor tip when you choose one color.

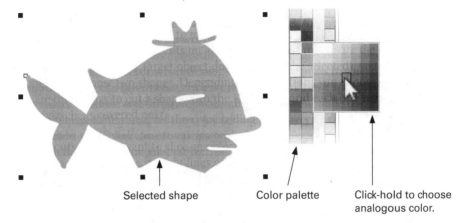

Selected shape   Color palette   Click-hold to choose
                                               analogous color.

Uniform fills can also be assigned to all objects right from the get-go. With no objects selected in the drawing window, left-click a color you want to use for future Artistic Media (such as calligraphic pens), Artistic Text, callouts, dimension lines, graphics, Paragraph Text, or QR codes. CorelDRAW then displays a dialog that asks what sort of object you want filled as it's created from now on. Your choices for any properties you select when nothing is selected are objects, text, and both. You can also elect to cancel out of this operation.

From Uniform to Non-Uniform Object Filling

The quick way to apply any of the fill types is to use the Interactive Fill tool, shown next. You'll find it at the bottom of the Toolbox; to select it quickly, press G. You'll see a hint here that the Interactive Fill tool is also a selection tool—the cursor is an arrow cursor with a paint bucket. You don't have to have already selected the object you want to fill when you use this tool. You can click an unselected, solid-filled object with the Interactive Fill tool to select it, and then a click-drag on the object, by default, applies the Linear-style fountain fill, making a transition from the current solid color to white. You can then change the colors used, or choose a different fill type from the Property Bar—and here's where CorelDRAW today makes applying different types of fills much easier than previous versions.

Interactive Fill tool   Interactive Fill tool cursor

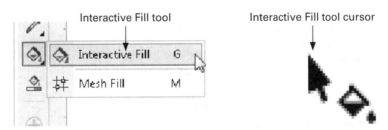

Suppose you just filled an object with the default Linear-style fountain fill. In version X8, there's more than one control node on the fill: a mini color and transparency picker pops up when you click over a color node. And all the fill types you can imagine are on the Property Bar. Additionally, you can change some controls for the fountain fill parameters, so this streamlined,

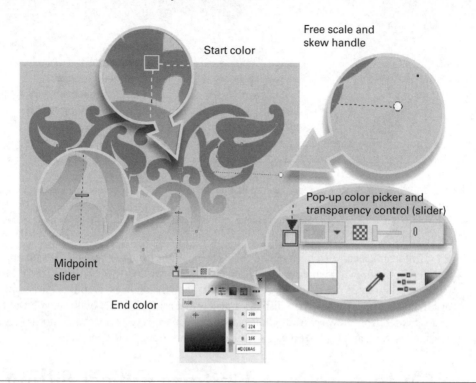

FIGURE 12-2 The Fill tool properties include onscreen interactive features.

fortified Fill tool will get you where you need to go in a jiffy. Figure 12-2 shows you what you'll see on your page when you click-drag with the Fill tool to create a linear gradient. The element names and what they do are described in a moment.

- **Start and End color nodes** With an object filled with a fountain fill (also called a gradient), the fountain fill begins at a Start color node and transitions toward the End color node inside the object. With the Interactive Fill tool, you can click either the Start or End node and then choose a different color for them by using the pop-up mini color picker, by clicking a color on the color palette, or by click-dragging a color well from the palette onto one of the color nodes. In addition to defining a color, the Start and End nodes can be moved like little handles using the Fill tool in a click-drag gesture. Click-dragging the Start node moves the entire gradient; it's repositioned within the object. Click-dragging the End node does two things. If you drag in a circular motion, you change the angle of the fountain fill. If you click-drag toward or away from the Start color handle, you increase or decrease the contrast of the transition between the two colors.

- **Free Scale and Skew handle**   The result you achieve by moving this round node is more obvious with, say, the Elliptical fountain fill style than Linear (see the following illustration). You can now skew and disproportionately scale a fountain fill. One of the most obvious benefits to this capability is that making an elliptical fill for elliptical objects is a breeze. If you drag the Free Scale and Skew node toward or away from the Start node, fill types such as elliptical and rectangular become obviously disproportional in their fountain fill characteristic; that is, not circular and not perfectly square. If you drag the Free Scale and Skew node in a direction other than a 90° angle to the line between the Start and End nodes, the fountain fill takes on a skewed appearance. This handle node operates independent from the Start/End nodes. If you drag the End node, the Free Scale node moves with it both distance-wise and rotationally. It stays parallel to the Start node if you move that one, as well.

Free Scale and Skew handle dragged down.
It is shorter now than the fountain fill transition line.

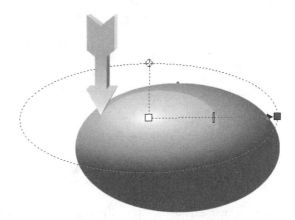

- **Midpoint slider**   You drag this slider toward one color node or the other to establish where, within the filled object, the 50/50 blend of each color has arrived. Therefore, if you want the filled object to feature more of the Start color than the End color, you drag this slider toward the *End* color, so the distance is greater between the Start color and midpoint.
- **Pop-up color picker and transparency control slider**   The pop-up color picker and transparency control slider only appear with fountain fill types of fills. When you click a color node—and an outline appears around it, indicating it's selected and can be changed—you'll see a mini toolbar with a drop-down button that leads to a color picker and a transparency slider to the right. You can now set transparency values every time you select a color node in a fountain fill. This is definitely a feature you want to explore, because, in addition to an Eyedropper tool on the color picker, you can choose color modes (for example, HSB and CMYK; see Chapter 15 if you're unfamiliar with color spaces), and you can work with a click-drag color field or enter numerical values for color components.

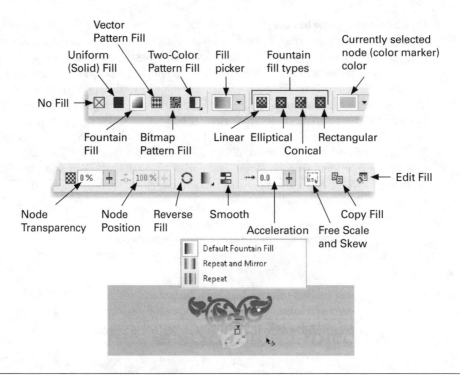

FIGURE 12-3 The properties for fountain fills are available when the Fill tool is active. You can *change* fill types using the Property Bar.

While you're using the Interactive Fill tool, the Property Bar displays options that change depending on the type of fill you choose from the Fountain Fill types or which style of fill is the current one (fountain, bitmap, two-color—all covered later in this chapter). If your selected object features no fill color at all, the selector displays the type as No Fill and the Property Bar displays no options. Figure 12-3 shows the fountain fill options on the Property Bar; what these options do is discussed next. There are options for fill types *other* than fountain fills, which are also covered in this chapter, but let's discuss one type at a time.

Let's walk through the relevant options on the Property Bar now for fountain fills, and then practice what you've learned in a tutorial to follow.

- **Fountain Fill button**   Only options for fountain fills are available when this button is depressed. If you click a different fill type, such as Vector Pattern Fill, fountain fill options disappear from the Property Bar. If you select an object that already has a fountain fill and you use the Fill tool to select it, the Fountain Fill button will immediately appear on the Property Bar in its depressed (on) position.

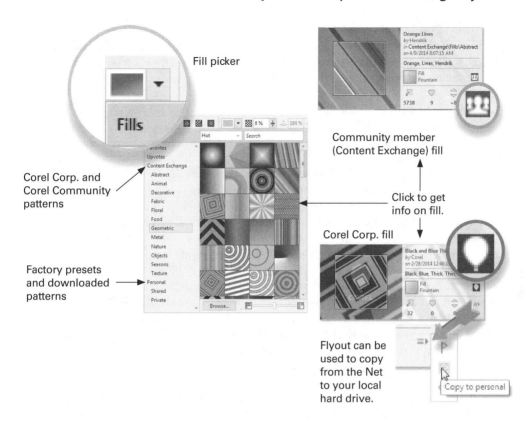

FIGURE 12-4   With an Internet connection, you can download scads of presets from the eight types of CorelDRAW object fills.

- **Fill picker**   Read Chapter 1 if you're not familiar with Corel's community sharing and downloadable content. When you click to open the fill picker, the flyout reveals a mind-boggling collection of fills in different categories—for each fill type. As you see in Figure 12-4, there are two basic types of authors of these presets, and two locations where you acquire and use them.

When you choose a fill type from the Property Bar and then click the down arrow next to the fill picker preview icon, you're presented with a number of themes of fills, within which you have numerous entries. Understand that if you purchased the download version of the Corel Graphics Suite, you don't have nearly as many preset fills at your disposal on your hard disk as you do when you download some from the Net. And because (again, see Chapter 1) you can connect to the Content Exchange, which is constantly updating and adding to themes, you might want to consider downloading fills you see potential for, or just apply them to an object you want to save and copy attributes from in the future.

Corel Corp. and the Corel Community are the two sources that created content in the form of fills. There's no difference in the functionality of the contributions, but you will find Corel-created fills in your *Personal* and *Private* folders because these fills are on your hard drive, and not on the Net.

- **To choose a fill you want to download to your Personal fill folder**: Click the fill thumbnail to reveal the large fill info dialog. Click the More options flyout icon at the lower right and then click the Copy to Personal icon. Alternatively, you can choose Window | Dockers | Tray and then drag a fill thumbnail directly into the Tray for future use locally—you won't need an active Internet connection.
- **To add a fill to an existing object on a page**: You drag a thumbnail to the center of the object on the page. Performing a preset download like this downloads the fill to the document, but not to a collection on your hard drive. You can always propagate more of the fill later by using the Attributes eyedropper, but this might be a hard approach for beginners, who will surely curse the author for suggesting this.

Strive for a balance between fills you've saved locally to your hard drive and those you'll want to use in the future. You can waste a lot of time copying thousands of different fills to your hard drive, but the upside is you'll be able to use them faster with no Internet between the artist and the fill. If you're in a rush at work (and who isn't), use the Favorites (the heart) icon on the More Options flyout to tag the preset to your Favorites folder, and then access the file at any time by choosing Favorites and waiting a moment while the program fetches the fill from Corel's servers.

- **Fountain fill types (Linear, Elliptical, Conical, and Rectangular)**   Figure 12-5 shows the four types of fountain fills, along with callouts for the interactive options available for click-dragging screen elements. The *Linear* style is fairly self-evident: moving the Start node sets the beginning point for the Start color, and moving the End color node changes the angle, the end point, and to a certain extent the acceleration of the fill from one color to the other. Acceleration is covered shortly in this chapter. *Elliptical* fountain fills begin as circular fills, and they can take on the elliptical appearance when you shorten or lengthen the distance between the Start node to the Free Scale and Skew handle. The *Conical* fountain fill is the only type whose Start and End nodes are precisely over one another, and this cannot be changed. You can choose to repeat and mirror the fill from the Property Bar, and you can also add intermediate color nodes (covered later) to soften the abrupt transition in this fill type. The *Rectangular* fountain fill is closely related to the Elliptical fill, except it has four corners within the design. It begins as a square pattern, and you can use the Free Scale and Skew handle to distort and create a rectangular and/or skewed color transition.
- **Currently selected node (color node) color**   To change the Start or End color in an applied fountain fill, it needs to be selected onscreen using the Interactive Fill tool. Because the color nodes serve more than one purpose—they mark both the color and the position of the color within the object—you'll be unintentionally confused in this guide when the term *node* is also called *marker, handle,* and, occasionally, *Phillip.* If you want to change the color when a node is selected, you can use the Property Bar or the color palette; if you want to move the node, you need to click-drag it to the desired position.
- **Node Transparency**   Corel has gone all-out in this version, so every time you click a color node to alter its color, you can also change its opacity via a transparency slider. You can, in fact,

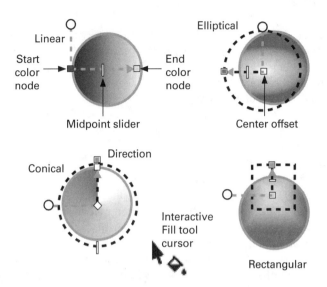

FIGURE 12-5   There are four basic fountain fill choices, but there are many permutations when you use fountain fill options.

have fountain fills that change opacity from left to right or from center to exterior, as shown here. You can see that the circle, sandwiched between the triangle and the squiggle, is not only lighter in color toward the 11 o'clock position, but it also allows parts of the underlying and obscured triangle to appear through. All you do is drag the pop-up slider from left to right.

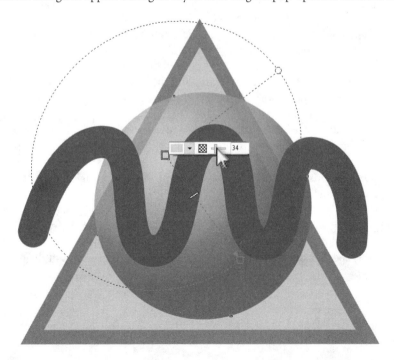

Tip An object that has any of the four fountain fill types can also contain transparencies that are also any of the four fountain fill types. You can, therefore, build an elegantly shaded object by, for example, applying an Elliptical fountain fill to an object and then giving it a Linear transparency property. See Chapter 18 for more details on transparency.

- **Node Position**   This combo box is only active when there are more than two color nodes along a fountain fill. When you've created several intermediate color nodes, you select one with the Fill tool, and this box can be used to reposition it precisely. To add a color node, you double-click the line between the Start and End color nodes.
- **Reverse Fill**   If you've created a multicolor elliptical gradient, for example, it would be a royal pain to have to change all the nodes if you wanted to reverse the appearance of the colors. But you don't have to! All you do is click this button on the Property Bar to reverse color node order immediately.
- **Smooth**   Because fountain fills are mathematically calculated as step progressions from one color to another, occasionally you might see the steps—called *color banding*—if the colors change dramatically over a very short distance. Enabling (depressing) this button makes an attempt to add more intermediate colors to make the steps less visible.
- **Acceleration**   Acceleration might be called *contrast*—how fast toward the center of a fountain fill does the 50 percent blending point occur. Corel has called this the *Edge Pad* in previous versions of DRAW. When you need an abrupt change from the Start color to the End color, you increase the acceleration.
- **Free Scale and Skew**   This button enables/disables the Free Transform function in fountain (and other) fills. By default, it's on, and you can see and work with the node onscreen within an object. Disabled, the screen element disappears and you're left with only Start and End color nodes (and the midpoint slider).
- **Copy Fill Properties**   This option is common to many object fills in CorelDRAW. To use this feature, you have to have a target object (the object to which you want to apply a fancy fill) and an object with the desired fill. You first select the object you want to fill, then choose the Interactive Fill tool, and then click this button. You're presented with an oversized arrow cursor onscreen; click over the object you want to copy the fill from, and the action is completed.
- **Edit Fill**   Gone is the dialog you used to have to drill down to by choosing the Fill Properties icon from the Toolbox. Clicking this button provides an onscreen dialog where everything you might want to do using the Property Bar is presented to you, but with more options and a more precise way to fill objects through number boxes with fractional amounts out to three decimal places.

Tip If you want to change the fill properties of an object, but you're working with a tool other than the Fill tool, with the object selected, press ALT-ENTER and the Properties docker includes all the features from the Edit Fill dialog.

Customizing Your Fountain Fills

A default fountain fill features two colors, but you can *add* colors to customize any type of fountain fill. When you make multicolored fountain fills, the appearance of your artwork can change dramatically. To add a node, double-click with the Fill tool on the dashed line connecting the Start and End color nodes. The position of added colors is shown by node positions on the dashed line guide joining the two default colors. After you've added color nodes and clicked to select them on the object, the Property Bar will display their position and color.

You can add, move, and delete fountain fill colors you've added to a default fountain fill type in several ways, but you *must* have both the object and the Interactive Fill tool selected, or you'll wind up editing the object and not the fill. To explore doing this, follow the steps in this tutorial.

Tutorial   Editing a Fountain Fill In-Place

1. Select the object to be filled, choose the Interactive Fill tool (G), and then apply a fountain fill by choosing Linear, Elliptical, Conical, or Rectangular from the Property Bar.
2. With this fill applied, double-click a point on the guide between the two existing color nodes where you want to add a color node. Doing this adds a color that is based on an average of two existing node colors, so your custom fountain fill probably looks the same as the default fill.
3. Decide on a new intermediate color (choose one in this example from the color palette) and then drag a color from the color well (drag the swatch) onto your new node. You have a three-color gradient now.
4. Try a different technique to add a color node position and color at the same time: drag a color swatch directly onto the same fountain fill guide, but at a different location.
5. To reposition an added color, click-drag it along the guide path. As you do this, the color's node position changes, as indicated by the Node Position percentage value on the Property Bar.
6. To change any fountain fill color, click to select it and then choose a color from the Property Bar selector or click a color swatch on the color palette.
7. To delete an added color, right-click or double-click it on the guide. End and Start color nodes can't be deleted, but they can be assigned different colors, and you can make them invisible by choosing 100% transparency from the mini pop-up color mixer.

You can also add color when a color node position is selected; choose from the color selector to the right of the fountain fill types on the Property Bar.

Although fountain fills are useful and fun, we need to return to uniform colors for a while because color models, color components, and standards such as PANTONE colors, which are important for commercial print designers, haven't been addressed yet. The following section takes you way beyond the color palette and into the Edit Fill dialog.

Uniform Color Fill Options on the Property Bar

Uniform fills are like the paint chips at the hardware store; they're solid colors, no variations. A uniform fill floods an object within the boundaries of its outline with the color you choose. The color palette is a fast, easy way to assign a uniform color; however, when you choose the Fill tool, you have several different color models from which to choose. See Chapter 15 for some details on color theory; if you're already familiar with the CMYK printing color model, the intuitive HSB color model, and others, you'll feel right at home using the Property Bar to mix up color values and, better still, entering values a client might give you for that big advertising job. Figure 12-6 shows the Edit Fill dialog, and if any of the callouts seem unfamiliar, a plain and frank discussion follows that'll get you from novice to expert in no time.

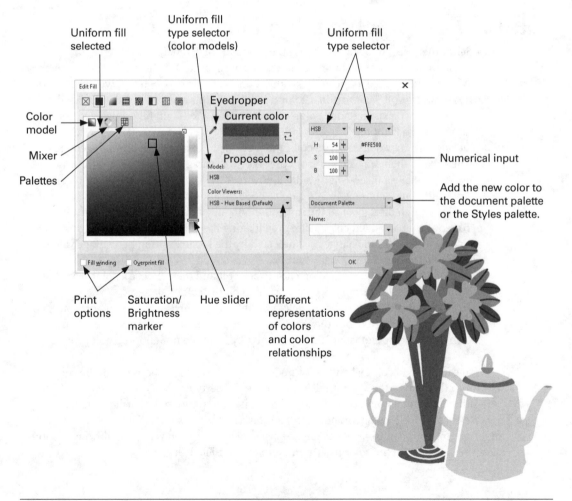

FIGURE 12-6   The Edit Fill dialog is where you specify an exact color and an exact color space for that color, such as printing CMYK and web page RGB models.

Tip   HSB and RGB color models occupy the same *color space*, the extent to which a color can be expressed onscreen. Therefore, you can arrive at an identical color using either color mode. This means you can switch color models for a filled object, and between RGB and HSB there will be no real color change.

When a uniform color is filling a selected object and you enter the Edit Fill dialog, you'll see the following areas and controls:

- **Color model**   Figure 12-6 shows the author working in RGB color space; therefore, HSB has been chosen from the color model drop-down list, which offers three different *views* for specifying a color by dragging your cursor through a color field and a color slider. Two additional color selection layouts and two other mixers are covered in this section. In the HSB hue-based color viewer, colors are specified by first dragging the Hue slider to the hue you want, and then dragging a small onscreen marker through the Saturation/Brightness field to the left of the Hue slider.
- **Hue slider**   In the HSB configuration for defining a color, the *H* stands for *Hue,* and the Hue slider is offered in the hue-based color viewer in the Edit Fill dialog. Hue is the predominantly recognizable aspect of HSB color; red is a hue, orange is a hue, but an exotic home-decorating color such as Pale Salmon is *not* a hue but rather a brightness and saturation-altered variation of a red hue. Hues might be described as "pure" colors; they can't get any brighter, and they can't get any more saturated.
- **Saturation/Brightness marker**   This is the small square in the color field when the HSB hue-based color viewer is chosen. Move this around within the field to designate a specific brightness and saturation for the current hue. Dragging the marker to the left makes a hue paler, whereas dragging it to the right makes the hue more saturated. Dragging up and down increases or decreases the brightness of a hue. If you want pure black and forgot that it's on the color palette (I'm kidding here), based on what you've read so far, you'd set the Hue slider to any color you like, and then drag the brightness and saturation marker all the way down (no brightness) and all the way to the left (no saturation).
- **Uniform fill type selector (color models)**   This drop-down list, titled simply "Model," offers HSB, RGB, HLS (basically the same as HSB and RGB), CMYK, Grayscale, and other color models. Depending on your work on a specific piece, you might choose Grayscale for final output to a laser printer or CMYK for commercial output. A *color model* defines a space, an expressible perimeter of available colors. For example, the CMYK color space is smaller than LAB color, and that's why an illustration created in LAB color mode looks dull when printed to CMYK colors—some of the LAB colors need to be shifted into a narrower color space and the "closest match" is chosen by DRAW. More on this in Chapter 15. Always choose your color model, and always set up your document when you choose New Document according to your intended final output.
- **Uniform fill type selector and Numerical input**   This area is basically the same as the color-picking visual input on the left of this dialog, but you use number values instead

of click-dragging to define a color. Not to worry: as you change the values in this area, you *will* see your proposed color to the left. You are shown duplicate fields in this area for a very important reason: you might need to know, for example, what the equivalent of a selected color is in a "different language." For example, suppose your boss tells you a specific color for a logo using RGB values. No problem: you type them into the fields and save the color to the color palette. However, now suppose the commercial printer now wants to know what this logo color is in CMYK values. You can see both sets of color components values if you set one field to RGB and the other to CMYK. Take the rest of the day off; that was easy!

- **Different representations of colors and color relationships** The Color Viewers drop-down list presents different ways to manipulate the components of colors graphically to accommodate the way you work—or the way your client might want you to work. In the illustration here, RGB 3D Additive is selected in the Color Viewers drop-down, and you can see an entirely different way to make up a color, based on red, green, and blue primary color markers that add brightness when dragged away from the center of the hexagon as well as mix with the other primary colors when dragged toward each extreme. Additionally, a slider controls the brightness of all the RGB markers simultaneously. You have several different views of color relationships; pick the one that makes the most sense to you.

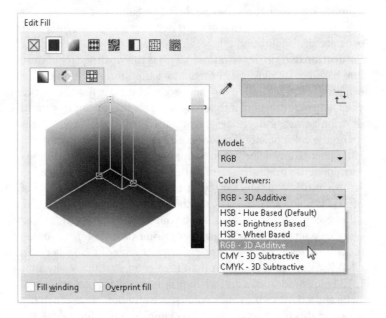

- **Add the new color to the document palette or the Color Styles palette** These are your two choices when you click Add to Palette. When you've arrived at the color of your dreams, you might want to add the color to the document palette—the horizontal strip at the bottom of the interface, not the default color palette that's vertically attached outside of the drawing window. Once the custom color is added to the document palette, you can double-click the newly created swatch on the document palette at the bottom of the window and enter a new name for it. Your other choice, aside from not adding the color to any palette, is to add the color to the Color Styles palette, a vertical strip that pops up to the right of the default color palette when you choose Window | Color Palettes | Color Styles Palette. See Chapter 15 for more details.

- **Color Mixer** The Color Mixer tab (enlarged in the following illustration so you can find it) provides an artistic way to define a color, not based on empirical values but instead on how colors compare and relate to one another. You have your choice of the uncomplicated Complementary color arrangement that shows the "color opposite" of the current color, along with variations of both colors in a selection box below the arrangement of colors. The Variation drop-down offers Lighter (to define tints of a specific color), Warmer, Darker, and other options. For a more complex arrangement, you can choose Rectangle from the Hues drop-down, and drag any of the white makers at the corner of the rectangle to skew toward a narrower selection of hues and drag the black triangle node around outside of the circle to set the baseline hue to then create variations and other harmonic comparisons of colors. Although it's initially a challenge, you might grow to love working with harmonies as a color basis because you're choosing colors by emotion—how they impress you—instead of by numerical values.

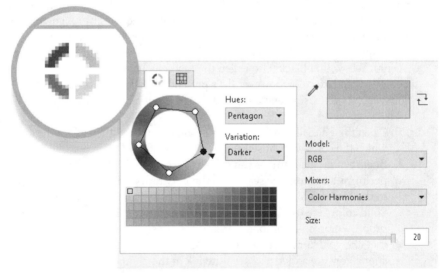

- **Print options** Two checkboxes, Fill Winding and Overprint Fill, pertain to commercial printing and not web work or personal printing. *Fill Winding* refers to the *Winding Path Rule:* if you follow a combined path, the fill should go to your left. This means that, potentially, a combined path such as a donut could have its inner subpath going in the same direction as its outer path. You might not even notice this, but when printed to PostScript technology, the donut would wind up being filled—and not with raspberry jelly.

Checking Fill Winding helps alleviate this potential problem. *Overprint Fill* usually has the opposite effect that artists want when printing artwork. By default, overlapping colors are knocked out—colors printed after the latest color in multicolor printing do not mix together. If you enable Overprint Fill, overlapping colors (cyan and yellow, for example, in CMYK printing) will produce green when areas overlap accidentally or intentionally. Unless you have experience with commercial presses, leave this box unchecked.

- **Current color and proposed color**   This handy feature is for visually comparing the current color you've chosen against the color you've mixed up and intend to use to replace the current color. To the right of these fields is a little recycle icon: it swaps the colors onscreen so you can preview what the object will look like before making a final decision to click OK and apply the new color.

- **Eyedropper**   You will find instances of the Eyedropper tool all over the place in DRAW, and it's quite welcome in the Edit Fill dialog because the dialog isn't *modeless*—your cursor can't "step outside of the box" to adjust something on the page. But the Eyedropper tool can be moved anywhere to sample a color in your drawing, on the page, on the interface, and even outside the interface in a different program or on your desktop.

Swatches and Preset CMYK "Color Chips"

Spot color is the printing process used to add a color to packages—for example, that cannot be reproduced using standard press inks, such as that reflective silver logo on a box of cereal. The third tab in the Edit Fill dialog is for viewing preset swatches from several preset catalogs—from simple grayscale values to PANTONE. Not all the libraries here are based on the Cyan, Magenta, Yellow, and Black (also called the *Key* color) color model. If you or your client has specified a standard color, however (let's pretend it's from a PANTONE Color Bridge process color swatch book), using that color in a design is not a brain-teaser:

1. Open the Edit Fill dialog, click the Swatches tab, and then select the color library from which the color was chosen.
2. Begin typing the number value of the PANTONE color in the Name field; doing this performs an automatic search. In the illustration following these steps, **241** was typed in the Name field, and the swatch book immediately went to that swatch.
3. Solid colors are used as an *additional* color to the Cyan, Magenta, Yellow, and Key *process* colors in traditional commercial press printing. They're used as spot colors—a metallic gold burst of pigment that says "New!" on a cereal box, for example. Because spot colors are added as a separate ink in the composition, you can choose a tint of these colors by using the Tint slider to specify the amount of this color expressed as a halftone screen on the printed page. Again, Chapter 15 has more info on printing than can be presented in this chapter on color, but the two are related.

As you can see here, color swatches, similar to those paint chips you see in hardware and home improvement stores, are presented as names in the color field as well.

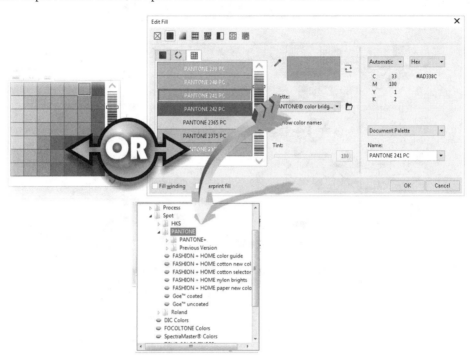

Applying Pattern Fills

Pattern fills are rectangular-shaped tiles that repeat vertically and horizontally to fill a closed-path object completely. They come in three different varieties: two-color, vector, and bitmap patterns. Each has its own unique qualities, shown here.

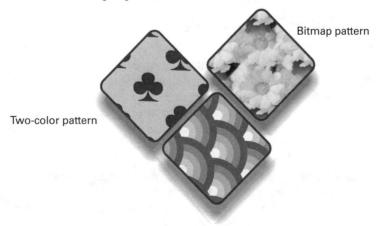

Bitmap pattern

Two-color pattern

Vector pattern

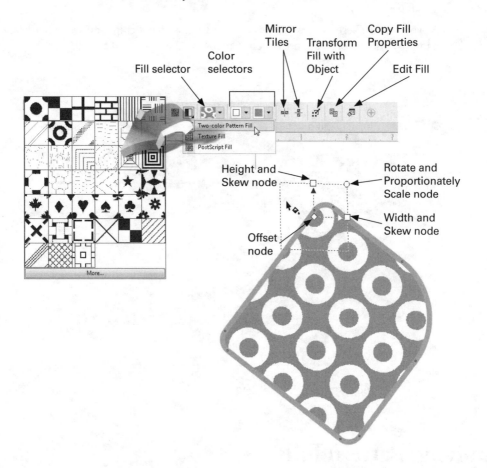

FIGURE 12-7 Two-color patterns are ideal for filling clothing on cartoons and for simple walls and other structures in drawings.

Two-Color Pattern Fills

When you decide that a two-color fill will suit your object, the Property Bar displays a host of options you can use to apply dramatic changes to the fill's appearance. Figure 12-7 shows what the control handles look like for the pattern fill, and it details the options offered on the Property Bar for two-color fills.

The Property Bar offers options for the type of pattern, colors used, and general appearance of the two-color pattern. The interactive control nodes around the pattern control the pattern's frequency, degree of rotation, and other things covered right now:

- **Fill selector** Use this drop-down box to choose from existing pattern fill libraries. Notice that there is a More... button at the bottom of the Selector flyout. Clicking this takes you to a pattern-making utility where you can create an original two-color pattern that you can save and apply later.

- **Color selectors**   When you've chosen a two-color pattern, these two selectors let you set colors other than black and white for the pattern.
- **Transform Fill with Object**   When this option is active, transformations applied to your object will also be applied to your fill pattern. This feature is useful when you need to scale an object larger and don't want your pattern to "shrink"! Stretching and squashing a pattern within an object is possible when you specify that the fill should be reproportioned according to what you do to the object itself.
- **Mirror Tiles**   You have your choice of vertical or horizontal mirroring (or both), and the result is most apparent when the two-color design does *not* feature symmetrical objects. The circle pattern shown in Figure 12-7 doesn't change when horizontal mirroring is applied because the circles are both vertically and horizontally symmetrical. However, choose a pattern featuring a horizontally asymmetrical pattern element such as a club from a pack of playing cards. Then if you choose vertical mirroring, every other row of clubs is turned upside down. Mirroring is a good feature for producing symmetrical patterns but also is great when you want a more visually interesting fill than, say, polka dots.
- **Copy Fill Properties**   This is a persistent button when the Fill tool is selected. As with fountain fills, you select an unfilled object, click the Copy Fill button, and then click the cursor over an object on the page whose fill you want to copy to the unfilled object.
- **Edit Fill**   As with most pattern-filled options, the Edit Fill dialog has almost identical features to those found on the Property Bar, except it has numerical fields for precise size, rotation, skew, and other pattern properties.
- **Offset node**   Within the filled shape when using the Fill tool, you drag on this node to establish a center to the design. This feature is terrific if the pattern appears just a little lopsided within the "window" that is your object through which the pattern peeks.
- **Stretch and Skew node**   These two node handles, arranged at right angles to each other, by default, control how much the pattern inside the object is stretched or skewed. Moving one node controls the vertical stretch and skew, and the other controls the horizontal. If only one node is moved away from the default position, the pattern's shape is disproportionally altered. Although they are not true perspective controls, they can be used as a simple way to change a brick-wall fill into a brick road.

 Note   Two-color patterns are limited to *exactly* two colors, with no additional edge colors to create antialiasing. This means the edges of the design will be harsh if you export your work to a bitmap format such as TIFF and PNG. The best way to cope with this limitation is to export to high resolution, such as 300 dpi. Then the rough edges will still be there, but harder to make out at a 1:1 viewing resolution.

Vector Pattern Fills

You have access to scores of beautifully designed vector shapes created by the Corel staff and the Corel Community when you click the Vector Pattern Fill selector button on the Property Bar. However, the pattern itself already has color applied and cannot be altered. Additionally, these full-color fills cannot be extracted as vector shapes from the pattern. Therefore, when making your own vector fill, save a copy of your pattern to CDR file format for editing in the future, and forget about the Break Apart and Convert To Curves commands in an attempt to reduce a full-color pattern to its vector component shapes.

Bitmap Pattern Fills

Bitmap patterns are carefully edited bitmaps; some of the presets are taken from photos, others are paintings, and all of them are relatively small in dimension. The difference between a full-color fill and a bitmap fill is that the vector-based pattern tiles for the full-color fills can be resized without losing design detail or focus or introducing noise. However, enlarging bitmap pattern tiles carries the same caveat as enlarging any bitmap—the more you enlarge it, the better the chances are that the component pixels will eventually become visible. You can scale bitmaps down but not up—computers are "smart," but they can't create extra visual data from data that wasn't there to begin with.

Controlling Pattern Fills Interactively

Knowing what you do now about the editability of patterns when applied to objects, it's time for a little hands-on tutorial to demonstrate how to edit the look of an applied pattern fill by adjusting the interactive markers and using the various Property Bar options common to a pattern style.

The interactive handles surrounding a pattern fill help you to set the tile size, offset, skew, and rotation of the pattern. To experience this firsthand, open Platonic.cdr and work with the uncompleted group of objects. The image on the right is just for reference.

Tutorial Customizing a Pattern Fill

1. Select an object in the group on the left, and then choose the Interactive Fill tool (G).
2. Choose Two-Color Pattern from the Fill Type selector. Choose the first sample entry, the polka dot pattern. Because the object you selected was already filled with a uniform color, the polka dot pattern is probably very light gray against white. Don't worry; you'll change this shortly.
3. Click the Front Color button on the Property Bar and—just so we don't drag this tutorial out into next week—rather than trying to define an appropriate gold polka-dot color with the color picker drop-down, click the Eyedropper tool and then go sample the color used in the corresponding finished design on the right. If you have the spare time, experiment with foreground and background colors as applied to your own pattern work.
4. Repeat step 3 with the Back Color button, choosing a medium purple with the Eyedropper and applying it to your current pattern fill.
5. Drag the Rotation/Tile Size handle toward the center of the selected object until the polka dot pattern repeats about four times.
6. Drag the diamond-shaped center origin handle slightly in any direction. Notice that the center origin of the pattern changes.
7. Drag the Stretch and Skew node to the right to stretch the polka dots a little, creating perspective within this composition.
8. Use the right Stretch and Skew node to skew the pattern a little to the left, so it is about the same angle as the selected object. Then, use the Scale/Rotate node again to achieve the proper angle for this object.
9. That's all you need to know about editing to finish this composition! Repeat steps 3–8, varying the front and back colors to complete filling in other objects.

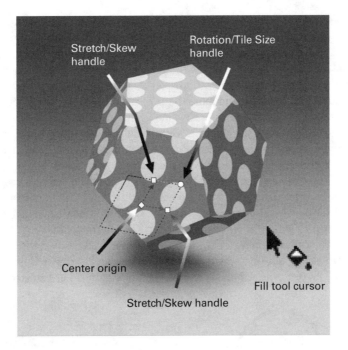

FIGURE 12-8   The nodes surrounding a two-color pattern fill are there for you to control the pattern's colors, size, and skew.

Figure 12-8 shows the node handles around a two-color pattern fill.

> **Tip** One important feature found in the Edit Fill dialog that *doesn't* appear on the Property Bar is Row and Column Offsets. By default, pattern tiles join to appear seamless. However, you can *intentionally* ruin the pattern (or just create an "interesting" one) by offsetting the pattern seams through either of these two options. To apply an offset, choose either Row or Column as the offset option, and enter a value between 0 and 100 percent.

Create Your Own Two-Color and Full-Color Patterns

Two-color patterns are harder to think up than they are to create, and the details are covered right after this section. Full-color vector or bitmap patterns are created by sampling an area on the page. With your desired pattern created, draw a new object outside of the pattern area and make sure it's selected. Open the Object Properties docker (ALT-ENTER) and click the Fill button at the top. Select either the Vector Pattern Fill or the Bitmap Pattern Fill option. Click the New From Document icon located to the right of the pattern list. Move your cursor into the document and drag a selection around the desired pattern area, but don't include the new object you created. It will have a default fill automatically applied to it when you click the Vector or Bitmap Pattern Fill button. After the pattern area is selected, click the Accept icon floating underneath the box. If you clicked the Vector Pattern Fill button, you now click the Save As New button in the docker, where you can name it, tag it with keywords, and elect to share it with Content Exchange. If you clicked the Bitmap Pattern Fill button when selecting your pattern, click the floating Accept icon to display a Convert To Bitmap dialog. Here, you can assign resolution, color mode, and more to the pattern. Saving a bitmap pattern is the same as for vector patterns—click the Save As New button in the Object Properties docker. To apply a custom pattern, click either the Vector or Bitmap Fill Pattern button and the Fill Picker drop-down list on the Property Bar. Click the Browse button at the bottom and navigate to your saved pattern. Saved patterns are located in My Documents\Corel\Corel Content\Fills. Note that both vector and bitmap fills are shown, and that your fill type will change to a vector pattern fill if you choose a saved vector file, and to a bitmap pattern fill if you choose a bitmap pattern. Both kinds of pattern fills have the same file extension (.fill), so it might be wise to include the word *vector* or *bitmap* in your filename when you initially save a pattern as either type.

Two-color patterns, on the other hand, are created using a special editor box displayed by clicking the More button at the bottom of the First Fill Pattern or Color button on the Property Bar. As you can see in Figure 12-9, two-color patterns are created by choosing a tile

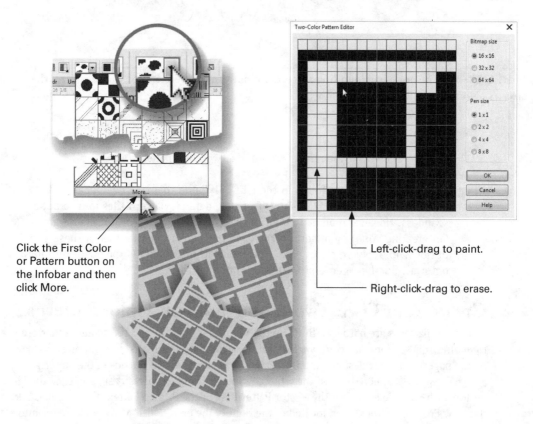

Click the First Color
or Pattern button on
the Infobar and then
click More.

Left-click-drag to paint.

Right-click-drag to erase.

FIGURE 12-9 Create your own two-color pattern in the Two-Color Pattern Editor.

size, a cursor size, and then left-dragging and/or clicking to set the foreground pattern; right-clicks and right-click-drags act like an eraser. Two-color patterns you create are immediately applied to a selected object, unlike full-color patterns, which are saved to a .fill file on hard disk. Although you are creating a black-and-white pattern in the Editor, two-color patterns can be any two colors; you apply the pattern and then use the Property Bar's mini-palettes to define the two colors.

Tip You can also create patterns by using the Tools | Create | Pattern Fill menu command. This command lets you capture a screen area and use it as an RGB Color (24-bit), Black and White (1-bit), 16 Colors (4-bit), Grayscale (8-bit), Paletted (8-bit), or CMYK Color (32-bit) pattern. And it is here you can elect to share it with Content Exchange—part of the Corel Community—or not.

Applying Texture Fills

PostScript and (fractal) texture fill types aren't "out in the open" in version X8—they're still available, but you need to click Edit Fill with the Fill tool active to locate these fill types. For users new to CorelDRAW, draw a rectangle, select the Fill tool, apply any type of fill just so the Edit Fill button appears, and click the Edit Fill button on the Property Bar. Let's review texture fills. Here's the Edit Fill dialog when the Texture Fill type has been selected, along with a labeled layout of the options.

Tip Although it's one more thing to remember in this feature-filled program, you can also access PostScript and texture fills on the Property Bar by click-holding the Two-Color Pattern Fill button.

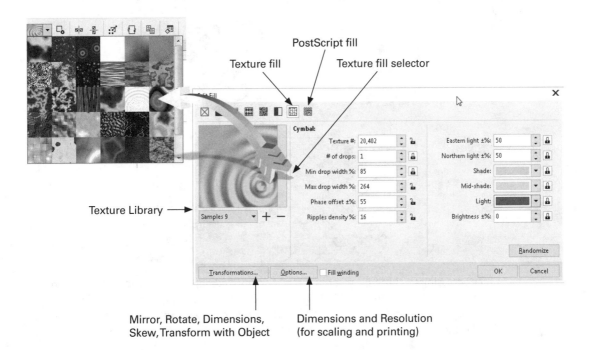

Texture fill

PostScript fill

Texture fill selector

Texture Library

Mirror, Rotate, Dimensions, Skew, Transform with Object

Dimensions and Resolution (for scaling and printing)

The strange and wonderful thing about Corel's texture fills is that they are math-based bitmap images that can be scaled without any loss of detail because the math belongs to the *fractal* family of imaging. Fractal fills are resolution independent in a certain way—the closer you zoom in, the more detail you'll see in any one given shape. The textures are based on more than a hundred different styles, ranging from bubbles to clouds.

For the artist, all you really need to know about fractal (texture) fills is that you have an awful lot of customization controls that change as you choose various samples from different collections. In the previous illustration, the "Cymbal" preset was originally a fairy hideous color combination, so I experimented with different colors and a slightly different Ripples Density setting and then I clicked the plus (+) button—a button common to most content collections in DRAW that's used to add and save a custom texture or whatever to a collection for later use.

The interactive nodes surrounding a texture fill are the same as those for pattern fills; they're there for you to set the size, offset, skew, and rotation of the texture. If you have experience manipulating pattern fills by click-dragging the control nodes above the object, you'll discover bitmap fills are exactly the same. However, because these are *bitmap-based* textures, rotating or scaling them to a larger size will degrade the image. This is a moot point, though, if you use the Options button at the bottom of the Edit Fill box to set the fractal resolution to a high value such as 300 dpi.

Applying PostScript Fills

PostScript fills are vector based and use PostScript page-descriptor language to create a variety of patterns, from black and white to full color. Each PostScript fill included with CorelDRAW has individual variables that control the appearance of the pattern, much the same way as you can customize texture fills. PostScript pattern styles come in a variety of patterns, as shown here, and they also come as nonrepeating fills.

Like accessing texture fills, you must select an unfilled object, choose the Fill tool, and then click the Edit Fill button on the Property Bar to get access to the PostScript fill type and the available options—presets, line widths, pattern element size, and color options, depending on the specific preset.

The image you see onscreen is an accurate representation of the actual pattern that will be printed; again, PostScript is a printing technology, but Corel Corporation has made the technology viewable in CorelDRAW and printable without the need for a PostScript printer. On that note, it should be mentioned that PostScript fills will print exceptionally well to any PostScript device; that's what the fills are intended for, but you don't necessarily have to use PostScript. However, you *must* be using Enhanced View to see it (choose View | Enhanced).

To apply a PostScript fill, follow these steps:

1. Create and then select the object to apply any PostScript texture fill to, and then click-hold the Two-Color Pattern Fill button on the Property Bar. The first in a collection of fills immediately fills the object, and you can choose other preset patterns from the PostScript patterns drop-down list.

Tip For fill types such as PostScript that have no More... button, go to the Edit Fill box and double-click the Edit Fill dialog's fill icon on the status bar, toward the right of the bar below the local color palette.

---

2. Click the Edit Fill button on the Property Bar—you can only modify the PostScript fill so much from the Property Bar. In the Edit Fill dialog, click the PostScript button.
3. There is a Refresh button that forces a redraw of the current pattern when you make changes, but you will see an unchanged preset right away when entering this set of options in the Edit Fill dialog, and if you move the Edit Fill dialog to the side, you can see a preview of the fill in the selected object on the page.
4. Notice that each fill has its own set of parameters that can be changed. For example, the GreenLeaves preset is chosen in the next illustration; however, the leaves are too small and there's not enough variation in the greens to suit a specific assignment. The solution is to decrease the number of leaves per square inch, thus increasing each leaf's relative size, and to lower the Minimum Green setting, so a wider expression of the preset's green color is visible.
5. Click Refresh to refresh the preview. If it looks good, you can click OK to get back to your work!

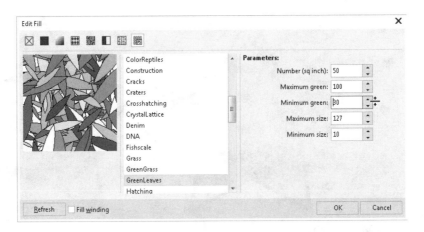

PostScript fills are great for schematic and roadmap illustrations, and if you use no background color when you customize many of the fills, the fills support transparency. So you can actually apply, for example, crosshatching over a color-filled object to enhance the shading.

Working with Mesh Fills

Mesh fills can be used to create the effect of several blending-color fountain fills over a mesh of vertical and horizontal Bézier curves. Editing a mesh grid creates a sort of fill that doesn't really look like a fountain fill but instead looks very much like a *painting.* Mesh fills make it easy to create, as you'll see in the following illustrations, most of the visual complexity of a reflective sphere—*using only one object and one fill.* Add to the visual complexity the capability to set transparency levels to each patch of a mesh fill individually, and in no time you'll be creating scenes that look like paintings, using a fraction of the number of individual objects you'd imagine. You'll find the Interactive Mesh Fill tool in the Toolbox grouped with the Interactive Fill tool, or you can press M for speedy selection.

With the Mesh Fill tool selected, the Property Bar features a number of options, shown next, for controlling this truly unique fill type. Many of these options will look familiar to those who work with the Shape tool to edit paths because, essentially, a mesh fill defines different color areas in a vector, resolution-independent way. Use these options to set the vertical and horizontal size in the mesh grid, to change node and path properties, and to set the smoothness of curves.

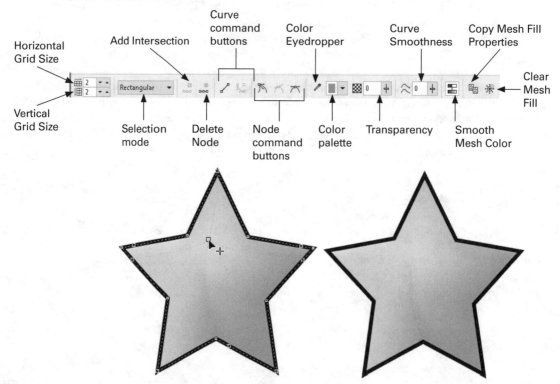

Believe it or not, the star in the previous illustration has one scalable fill, made up of nine colors that blend into one another according to how the color nodes are moved around the interior of the circle. Acceleration between color nodes is done by dragging on the color node handles. It might not be apparent in the black-and-white edition of this guide, but if you try it out on your copy of DRAW, you'll instantly see and understand the complexity of the result of this tool!

Applying a mesh grid to an object is a quick operation. Mesh fills are dynamic, so they can be edited and reedited at any time. Editing the shape and color of a mesh grid can be a little bit of a challenge your first time out, but being able to smear and almost paint on a fill will make the effort worthwhile to you and your work. Node- and curve-editing actions needed to move fill areas are the same as for Bézier curves. For information on how to do this, see Chapter 9.

Mesh Fill Options

On the Property Bar, when the Mesh Fill tool and an object are selected, you have control over the following attributes:

- **Frequency of the patches** By default, a new mesh fill is created on an object with two horizontal and two vertical sets of patches. These patches are linked at the edges by paths and at their vertices by nodes. You can use the numerical entry fields or the spin boxes with these fields to increase or decrease the number of columns and rows of patches. Manually, if you left-click and then right-click the icon created, you have the option to create a node or an intersection by choosing from the pop-up menu.

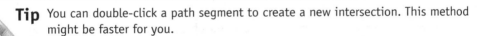

Tip You can double-click a path segment to create a new intersection. This method might be faster for you.

- **Add Intersection/Delete Node** When you've clicked on a path segment and a node appears, you can add an intersection, either by clicking the Add Intersection button or by pressing + on the numerical keypad. When you add an intersection, you add a row or a column to the mesh fill, depending on whether you've added a point to a vertical or a horizontal mesh path segment. You must first select a node to then delete it. Clicking the Delete Node button or pressing DELETE on your keyboard removes both the mesh node and its associated intersecting path segments—reducing the number of columns or rows of mesh patches. Deleting nodes can yield unanticipated results, so give some thought before you delete a node.
- **Curve and Node command buttons** By default, path segments that make up the mesh fill are curves, bound by nodes that have the Smooth property. To change a path segment to a line, you use the Convert To Line command button; click Convert To Curve to create the opposite property. Nodes can be changed to a Cusp, Smooth, or Symmetrical property by clicking the associated Property Bar button; the commands can also be found on the right-click pop-up menu when you select a node with your cursor.

- **Curve Smoothness**   Suppose you've added far too many nodes to a path segment and your mesh fill looks like a bad accident in one area. If you marquee-select the nodes that bind this path segment, the Curve Smoothness slider and numerical entry field act like the Node Reduction feature in CorelDRAW. You reduce the number of superfluous nodes (CorelDRAW decides on the meaning of "superfluous"; you yourself have no control) by entering a value or using the slider.
- **Selection mode**   By default, you can select nodes in Rectangular mode, which means you marquee-drag a rectangular shape with your cursor to select nodes and then change their properties, such as color, position, and transparency. Your other selection choice is Freehand; in this mode, your cursor behaves like a real-world lasso, and you are unconstrained by a selection shape for nodes. Additionally, you can SHIFT-click and select non-neighboring nodes to edit. When using Freehand mode, you can't select patches—selecting patches by clicking within them is only available in Rectangular selection mode.
- **Smooth Mesh Color**   This toggle on/off button can produce smoother color blends in your fill without changing the position or properties of the mesh nodes and curve path segments.
- **Color Eyedropper**   When a patch or node is selected, you can choose a color anywhere on screen by dragging the Color Eyedropper tool over to any point.
- **Color palette**   The mini color palette flyout on the Property Bar lets you select colors for selected nodes and patches. Click the flyout button to access the default color palette or choose from other preinstalled CorelDRAW palettes. Clicking a color well on the (regular) color palette applies color, too.

When working with the mesh fill, you'll get far more predictable results if you apply colors to the nodes instead of dropping colors onto patches. Also bear in mind that regardless of how you create a shape, the mesh fill makes the object "soft"—the control nodes that make the closed path of the object are also mesh fill nodes. So, unavoidably, if you want to move a node you've colored in *at the edge* of the object, you're also *moving the associated path segment*. This is fun and creative stuff, actually, and if you need the fill to be soft with the object's original shape intact, you can put your finished object inside a container by using the Object | PowerClip | Place In Frame feature.

Sampling Fills

With an Eyedropper tool, you can click on a color on the page, and the sampled color immediately becomes the foreground color on the toolbar. You can then use this sampled color somewhere else in your drawing.

CorelDRAW has two Eyedropper tools, though, and each one has a specific purpose.

Applying the Color Eyedropper

The Color Eyedropper is your "standard" Eyedropper tool, and it operates as you probably anticipate, with one or two notable enhancements that Corel has given it. To sample a color and apply it to one or more other objects, you select the tool from the Eyedropper group on the Toolbox. Now here's where something cool comes into play: bitmap images can have millions of colors, but high-resolution images impress us as having a predominant color in an area, such as the leaves on a tree, when, in actuality, at a pixel level, there are dozens of different green colors that leave the human eye with but a single color impression.

The Color Eyedropper offers Sample Size on the Property Bar. You can choose from a precise 1×1 pixel sampling size, a 2×2 pixel average, and a 5×5 pixel average color sample. When sampling from bitmap images and even fountain fills, increase the Sample Size on the Property Bar to capture the color your brain sees, not the precise color under your cursor.

With the Color Eyedropper, unlike many other graphics programs, once you've sampled, it's not a one-pop deal to then fill another object. The filling part of the Attributes Eyedropper is persistent—you'll see a bucket icon on the Property Bar that stands for "Fill," and you can continue to fill two or a hundred objects on your page until you want to reset the sample color, in which case you click the Eyedropper button to the left of the paint bucket icon.

Using the Attributes Eyedropper Tool

The Color Eyedropper's cousin tool, the Attributes Eyedropper, is used to sample and apply fills such as fountain and texture fills and some the others, excluding the mesh fill. Choose the Attributes Eyedropper from the Toolbox, and three drop-down categories are presented to you: Properties, Transformations, and Effects (as shown next). Just as a point to ponder and revel in: if you've dressed up a rectangle with a fountain fill, a dashed outline, and a drop shadow, it would take about two clicks to apply all these same trappings to one or several "ordinary" objects you've created on the page. What a timesaver, eh?

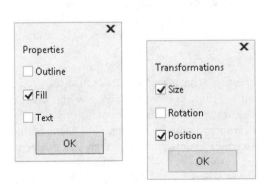

Tip As an alternative to using the Attributes Eyedropper tool, you can drag an object using the right mouse button and then drop it on top of an object to which you want to apply any fill style. A pop-up menu appears when you've released the right mouse button, and you then can choose Copy Fill, Outline, or All Properties. The position of the source object does not move when you use this drag technique.

Here's a brief tutorial to demonstrate the utility of the Attributes Eyedropper.

Tutorial Dropping a Property

1. Open Fancy Circle.cdr. You'll note that in front of a small locked bitmap background, there's an elegantly decorated circle to the left of a minimalist star. Your mission—should you decided to accept it, Jim—is to make the star look like the circle without changing its shape.
2. Choose the Attributes Eyedropper tool from the group in the Toolbox.
3. Click the Eyedropper cursor over the circle. Good—the circle's outline and fill properties are copied, as shown in callout "a" in Figure 12-10, and your cursor is now a paint bucket, all set to fill that star.
4. Click over the star. No, wait a moment. That circle has a drop shadow under it, doesn't it? (See callout "b" in Figure 12-10.) Also, that's not an attribute property, but rather an effect, and I told you earlier that, by default, none of the attributes in the Effects list are checked.
5. Go up to the Property Bar and then click the Effects button, marked as "c" in the figure. Put a checkmark beside the Drop Shadow entry *and then click OK*. If you don't click OK, the box will close without registering this change in sampling parameters.
6. Well, darn. Because your list of attributes has changed, you need to go back to Eyedropper mode (click the Eyedropper icon on the Property Bar) and sample that circle again.
7. Click over the star shape with the Attributes Eyedropper tool's paint bucket cursor and, yep, the star looks related to the circle. You can create new objects and even bold text now, and fill them the same way you just dressed up the star with the circle's attributes— or not. Figure 12-10 shows the steps you've run through here, with the grand finale marked with a "d" (for DONE!) .

If you've had your fill, it's okay, because so have your objects. You've learned in this chapter how to tap into CorelDRAW fills, and, hopefully, you've also seen how important fills can be to your drawings. Fills can actually contribute to the visual robustness of a composition more than the shape of the objects. Take a cardboard box, for example. The shape of the box isn't that interesting and takes only a few seconds to draw. But the *texture* of a cardboard box is where the object gets its character and mood.

Outline properties and attributes are covered in the following chapter. Believe it or not, you can do as much with customizing the thing that goes *around* an object as with the object itself.

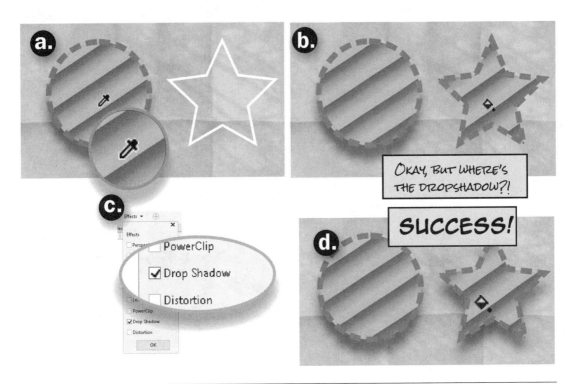

FIGURE 12-10   Use the Attributes Eyedropper to copy and add several different custom properties from one object to another. And another. And...

13 Applying Strokes to Paths

Chapter 12 covers only half the story about how you can flesh out a visual idea by using CorelDRAW. Although an object can usually live its life just fine without an outline, the attributes you can apply to a path can add a touch of refinement to an illustration. The right outline color can visually separate different objects. Additionally, you can simulate calligraphic strokes without using Artistic Media when you know the options on the Object Properties docker. You can even make a path a dashed line, complete with arrowheads for fancy presentations and elegant maps. In fact, an outline, especially an open outline, can live its life in your work just fine without defining a filled object. You don't have to draw the line with fills and effects in your CorelDRAW artwork. This chapter shows you the ins and outs of properties you apply to your paths, from beginning to end.

 Download and extract all the files from the Chapter13.zip archive to follow the tutorials in this chapter.

Applying Outline Pen Properties

By default, when you create an open or closed path, it's given a 0.5 point width in black (and this has been known to change from version to version), with mitered (90° angle) corners, square line caps, and no fancy extras. Part of the rationale for this default is that vector paths can't really be seen without some sort of width. In contrast, bitmap artwork, by definition, is made up of pixels, written to screen and file; so when a user draws an outline, it always has a width (it's always visible). Happily, vector drawing programs can display a wide range of path properties, and unlike with bitmap outlines, you can change your mind at any time and easily alter the property of an outline.

In CorelDRAW, you can apply properties such as color, stroke width, and other fun stuff to an open or closed path (and even to open paths that don't touch each other but have been unified using the Object| Combine command). The following sections explore your options and point out the smartest and most convenient way to travel in the document window to arrive quickly at the perfect outline. When an open path or an object (which necessarily has to be described using a path) is selected on the page, the Property Bar offers many options for outline properties. You can also dig into the Outline Pen dialog, now accessed by double-clicking the Outline box on the Status Bar; there is no longer any Toolbox button for this dialog. And you also have the Object Properties docker, accessed from the pop-up menu when you right-click a path; ALT-ENTER also gets you there. Some shortcuts for performing simple property adjustments are covered on the long and winding path through this chapter.

Outline Pen Options and the Property Bar

Although it doesn't offer *all* options for path properties, the Property Bar is probably the most convenient route to the most often-needed outline properties. It actively displays a selected path's *current* properties, which you can change when a path is selected and the current drawing tool is still active. Some options are persistent and are available when you choose a drawing tool but have not drawn a path yet, such as the Outline Width box. The Property Bar—shown here for the Freehand Pen tool at the top and the Pen tool at the bottom—offers outline width, style, and arrowhead options. You can make an open path with a head, tail, two heads—it's up to you. Other options give you control over wrapping text around a path, showing or hiding a bounding box around a path, and items not directly related to the outline's look. Closed paths, naturally, can't have arrowheads, but your options for dashed lines and other attributes are available for rectangles, ellipses, all the polygon shapes, and for freeform closed curves you've drawn by hand. You can see that when using the Pen tool, you have two tool-specific options: Preview mode and the capability to use the tool to add or remove nodes along the path you're drawing. The Freehand tool doesn't have these options, but it does offer the Auto-Smoothing option, which the Pen tool does not (because it is irrelevant).

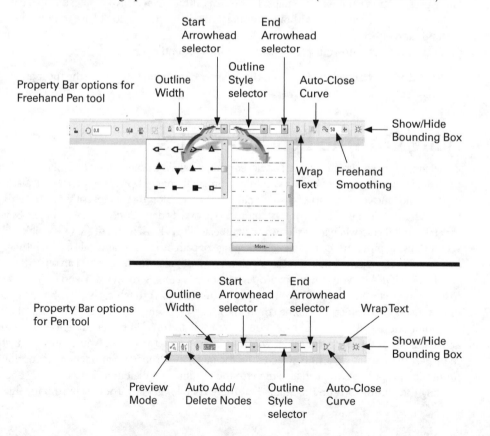

In the following tutorial, you'll use the Property Bar when you draw a path.

Tutorial   Going Long and Wide

1. Choose any drawing tool—the default Freehand Pen tool is fine—and just drag a squiggle and then press SPACEBAR to switch to the Pick tool; the path is selected now.
2. On the Property Bar, choose an outline thickness using the Outline Width selector, or enter a value and then press ENTER. If you're zoomed out of the drawing page, try choosing 8 points or greater so it's easier to see the effects in the following steps.
3. For arrowheads (on an open path), click the Start or End Arrowhead selectors, and then choose an arrowhead style from the pop-up. The Start option applies an arrowhead to the first node of the path; the End option applies it to the most recently created. However, this might not be the direction in which you want the arrow to point. If this is the case, you have to perform a little mental juggling; the head of your arrow will be the *last* node on a path you create, not the first.

> **Tip** You can reverse the direction of an open path by choosing the Shape tool (F10), right-clicking over any of the path segments, and then choosing Reverse Subpaths from the contextual pop-up menu.

4. To apply a dashed- or dotted-line pattern to the path, click the Outline Style selector and then choose from one of the presets. Creating custom dashed patterns is covered later in this chapter.
5. Try increasing and decreasing the outline width, and see what happens to dashed-line styles and arrowheads; they scale proportionately to the width of the outline.

As you apply outline properties from the Property Bar to your object or path, the effect is immediately visible, making this method both quick and convenient to use.

> **Tip** To set the color of a shape's outline quickly, right-click over any color palette swatch.

Outline Tool Features on the Object Properties Docker

You can define a path's properties by accessing three levels of features: The Property Bar is always available when you select a line, providing basic outline attributes. The Object Properties docker has taken over most of the duties from your third option, the Outline Pen dialog (formerly the Outline tool). The redesigned Object Properties docker can modify virtually everything about a drawn line except editing the path itself (covered in Chapters 7 and 9). These features, shown in Figure 13-1, are covered in the following sections.

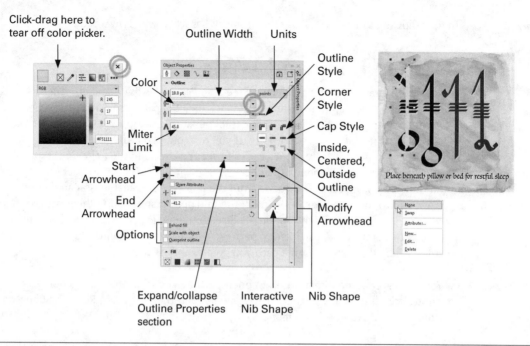

FIGURE 13-1 You have complete control over how an outline looks when you use the Object Properties docker.

Tip In various areas on CorelDRAW X8, you'll discover that you can tear a color picker off a dialog after clicking the expand button in the dialog. This is true of Outline Properties' Color picker, and you might want to do this if the screen is getting too crowded or too bunched up in an area where you need to see things. The torn-off picker will disappear and return to its normal position if you click outside of the picker. Just drag at the top of the picker, to the left of the close X icon.

To display the Outline section of the Object Properties docker, right-click over a selected outline on a page or press ALT-ENTER. Make sure the docker is fully extended so you can see all the outline properties.

Exploring the Outline Pen Features

The Object Properties docker is virtually your one-stop shop for modifying all attributes of a selected path, whether open or closed. Although some of the options for path outlines on the Object Properties docker are self-explanatory, even with Tooltips turned on, other features in DRAW might not strike you immediately as useful. Therefore, a survey is in order, as follows.

Draw a *closed* path (you'll see why in a while) with the tool of your preference. As soon as it's drawn, you can right-click over it with your current drawing tool, and then choose Object

Properties on the contextual pop-up menu. This pop-up toggles the visibility of the Object Properties docker, so don't accidentally move to a different page and right-click because it will toggle to *removing* visibility. This can be a source of confusion, so either bookmark this passage or remember it.

Setting Outline Color

The Outline Color mini flyout on the Object Properties docker affects only the color of the object's path; object *fills* are not changed. Outline color can be set only to CorelDRAW's Uniform colors from the drop-down palette. To access *every* color collection and color model for outlines, click the wide swatch to drop the color models down, and then work in the Color Mixer, Model, and Palettes tabs. You can also click the ellipses (…) button (which indicates more options) and choose from a specific color collection, such as PANTONE process colors. The Outline Color Properties features are nearly identical to the ones you use for fills, as covered in Chapter 12.

If you want color control and don't need to fuss with dashed outlines, arrowheads, or other outline attributes, don't choose Object Properties. Instead, right-click a color well on the color palette to set an outline color.

Choosing Outline Styles

For a quick way to apply a dashed- or dotted-line pattern to the path of a selected object, use the Line Style selector, which offers 28 different preset variations.

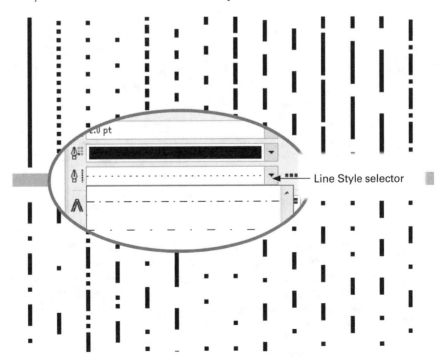

Line Style selector

Applying an outline style causes a pattern to appear along the entire path, which is a must for anything you need to suggest visually to readers—for instance, that they should go running for the scissors to cut out coupons, tickets, you name it. *Styles* are repeating patterns of short, long, and combinations of dashes that apply to the entire path. Line styles can be applied to any open- or closed-path object, as well as to *compound paths*—such as a donut object or an *O*. The quickest way to apply a dashed-line style is to use the Pick tool and the Property Bar's Outline Style selector when one or more paths are selected, as shown here.

 Note Circles, rectangles, and polygons do not show the Outline Style selector on the Property Bar. Happily, you can press ALT-ENTER and edit the properties of these objects using the Object Properties docker.

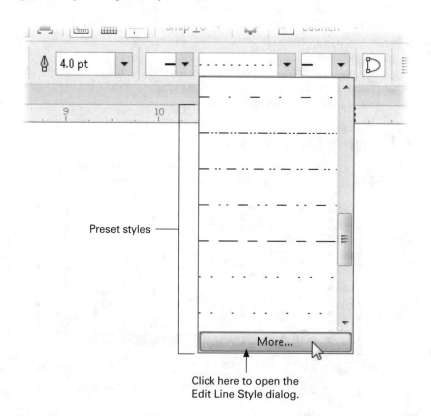

Preset styles

Click here to open the
Edit Line Style dialog.

 Tip Once you have a nice custom outline set of properties defined and want to apply all the parameters to a different path, you can copy outline properties from one path to another by right-clicking and dragging one path on top of the target path (this doesn't move your original path; it's a special editing technique). Release the mouse button when a crosshairs cursor appears over the target path. Then choose Copy Outline Here from the pop-up menu.

Creating and Editing Outline Styles

If you're looking for a special dashed-line style (one of your own invention), you can always *build* it. Click the Settings icon directly to the right of the Style selector in the Object Properties docker while an unfilled line or object with a outline width is selected to open the Edit Line Style dialog, shown here.

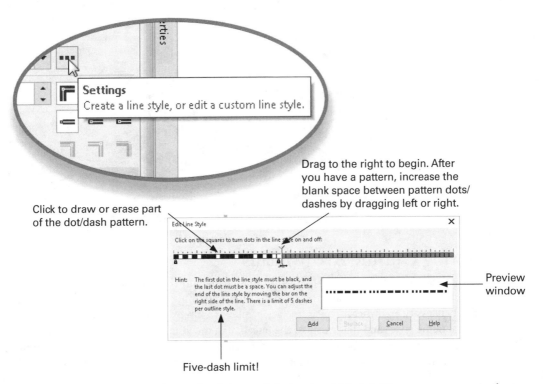

Creating a custom line style of dots and dashes is a fairly intuitive process, very similar to drawing a line in a paint program; your cursor serves as both a pencil and an eraser—click a black dot to erase it, click a white (space) dot to add to or begin a line. If you practice a little care and patience, you can also click-drag to draw and erase multiple dashes or dots. Once you save a style by clicking Add, it becomes available throughout CorelDRAW wherever outline styles are offered. Your only limitation—*read the legend at the bottom left of the editor*—is that you can't create a sequence consisting of more than five dashes or dots; adjoining marks count as a single dash.

If the pattern applied to a path doesn't exactly match its length—for example, the pattern is longer than the path it's applied to—you might see a "seam," especially when applying outline styles to closed paths (as shown next). There are two ways to cure the problem. One is to go back to the Edit Line Style editor and increase or decrease the length of the pattern; this is a trial-and-error edit, but it doesn't change the path to which the style is applied. The other method (a desperate measure) is to lengthen the path by using the Shape tool or to scale the path by using the Pick tool. With either of these edits, you change your design and not your custom preset—it's your work, so the call is up to you. However, editing the style is usually the best way to avoid seams on a case-by-case basis with compositions you create.

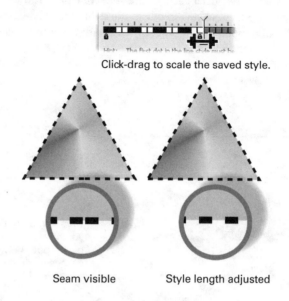

Click-drag to scale the saved style.

Seam visible   Style length adjusted

Setting Outline Arrowheads

Arrowheads are both heads *and* tails on an open path, and although DRAW has a handsome collection of preset arrows, an arrow can be almost anything you decide to draw. Most of the preset styles are arrowheads, but some are symbols that represent a tail. Here, you can see several of the styles and that many of the tails match the visual style of the arrowheads. When applied, arrowheads can be set to appear at the start and end points of open paths, at both ends, at one end, or, by default, at neither end.

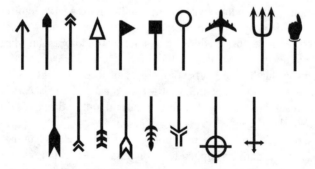

Here's a trick to defining the size of an arrowhead or tail: you increase or decrease the size of an arrowhead by adjusting the outline width using the Property Bar or the Outline dialog. The quickest way to apply an arrowhead is by using the Start and/or End Arrowhead selectors on the Property Bar when an open path is selected. Incidentally, applying an arrowhead to a closed path has no visible effect unless the path is broken at some point.

Creating Custom Arrowhead Styles

Realistically, CorelDRAW will not always have the ideal arrowhead (and tail) preset for your (and every other user's) assignment—or the preset selector would need a head and a tail itself, from here to the moon! That's why you have the Tools | Create | Arrowhead command—don't choose the command yet; you need to *draw* the arrowhead first, as covered in the following tutorial. The best arrowhead should be simple in its construction and needs to be a single or compound path—fill makes no difference in creating the arrowhead because a finished and applied custom arrow style gets its color from the outline color you use on the selected path in your drawing. The orientation of the arrowhead needs to be in landscape, too, before you select the Create command. In other words, the top of your custom arrowhead design needs to face right, not the top of the page.

To create a new arrowhead and save it, follow these steps; if you'd like a jump-start, open Shovel.cdr first. It contains the elements needed to make both a head and tail.

Tutorial Drawing, Saving, and Editing an Arrowhead Style

1. Give some thought and planning to what would make a good arrowhead and tail. Shovel. cdr has a drawing of the ends of a common garden shovel. This design works for garden planning (an arrow pointing to "dig here"), treasure hunts, and certain civil engineering diagrams. Allow about 3" for your arrowhead symbols; this size gets you around the need to edit later. When you've drawn your arrowhead (a tail is optional for this tutorial), rotate it so it's pointing toward the right of the drawing page.
2. With the shovel head object selected, choose Tools | Create | Arrowhead.
3. Type a name in the upper-left field for future reference. If you like, the Create Arrowhead dialog gives you the chance to set a size for the arrowhead; by default, it's the size of your drawing on the page, as shown in the illustration here. Click OK, and your arrowhead is saved at the bottom of the Arrowhead selector list.

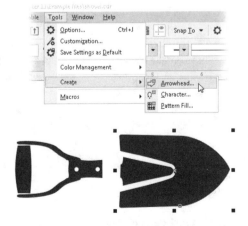
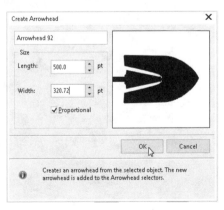

4. If you like, you can perform these steps for an arrowhead *tail* by selecting the shovel handle on the page. Possibly you're done now. Let's check, before calling it a day, to see how the arrowhead shovel looks when applied to an open path.

5. Using the 2-Point Line tool, click-drag a two-node path. Straight is good for checking out the arrowhead, but in the future a curved path might be more visually interesting.

6. With the path selected, on the Property Bar, choose the 10 pt. outline width so you'll have a clear view of the arrowhead you defined (or the shovel head if you used the Shovel.cdr file).

7. On the Property Bar, choose the arrowhead from the Start Arrowhead drop-down selector. Let's suppose you're not 100 percent happy with the look of the arrowhead; you now access additional options for modifying the saved arrowhead. With the path selected, double-click the Outline Color icon (either the pen icon or the color swatch) on the Status Bar to display the Outline Pen dialog. Click the Options button beneath the thumbnail of your arrowhead and then choose Attributes from the pop-up menu.

8. Here's where you can correct a number of problems with your arrowhead; you cannot, however, edit the path of the arrowhead itself. If, for example, your arrowhead is pointing the wrong way, select Mirror | Horizontally. You also have the option to rotate the arrowhead, for corrective or creative reasons, as well as to move the head away from its parent line (the Offset options) and to smoosh or stretch the selected arrowhead proportionately or disproportionately. If you made a mistake drawing the arrowhead, you cannot change it in the editor; instead, you need to revise your drawing and then redefine the arrowhead. See Figure 13-2 for the visuals for these steps.

9. Click OK to overwrite your saved arrowhead, or rename it to add it to your collection. The Arrowhead Attributes dialog can also be used to modify *existing* preset arrowheads, but only to the extent that you've just modified your custom arrowhead in step 8. End of tour!

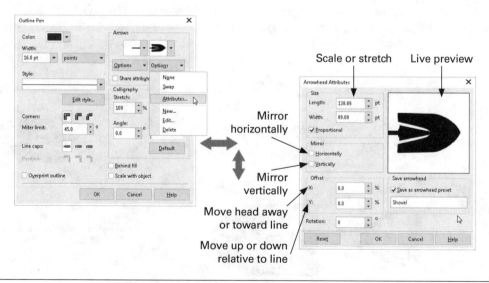

FIGURE 13-2   Edit an arrowhead (or tail) in the Outline Pen dialog.

Here you can see a few uses for a shovel. Don't be hesitant to mix and match outline styles; in the middle illustration, a dashed outline style happily coexists with a custom arrowhead.

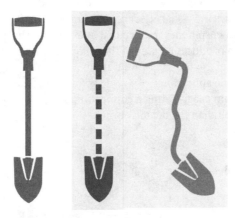

At work   Under construction   Uri Geller was here...

Other Arrowhead Options

Other convenient options are available in the Outline Pen dialog when applying an arrowhead style. Just below each Arrowhead Style selector are two Options buttons. Click either the start or end Options button to open a drop-down menu that features—in addition to Edit and Attributes—the following commands:

- **None**   Choose this command to clear the arrow style you selected from your path. You can also do this from the document window using the Property Bar.
- **Swap**   This command switches the styles currently selected for the start and end arrowheads. You can also reverse the path; select the path with the Shape tool, and the Reverse Direction button appears on the Property Bar.
- **New**   Choose this command to open the Edit Arrowhead dialog and create a variation on a default style to add to the existing collection. New does *not* offer custom arrowhead creation; you need to use Tools | Create, as you learned earlier, to make a truly new arrowhead.
- **Delete**   While an existing style is applied, choosing this command permanently removes the selected style from the collection.

Note   The Share Attributes check box on the Object Properties docker lets you specify that the head and tail should be the same size, offset distance, and orientation.

Setting Corner Shape

You'll frequently create a path whose segments join at a node in a cusp fashion; the connection is *not* smooth—for example, a crescent moon shape has a least two sharp cusp connections between path segments. When shapes have *discontinuous* connections—that is, when a path abruptly changes direction as it passes through a node—you can set the appearance of the node connection through the Outline Pen dialog and the Object Properties docker. The illustration here shows the visual effect of selecting Round, Beveled, and Mitered (the default) joints on a path with cusp nodes. Notice that at extremely sharp node connection angles, the Beveled joint option produces an area of the outline that extends way beyond the path—an exaggerated effect you might not always want in a design. You can use Corner Style properties creatively to soften the appearance of a node connection (Round works well) and also to keep a severe cusp angle from exaggerating a connection. Mitered corners can often keep a path more consistent in its width than the default corner.

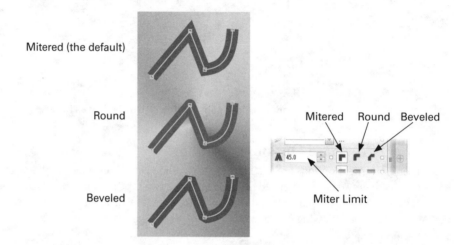

Also, you'll note a num box near the Corner Style settings; this is the Miter Limit angle, which you can set to suit your line needs. By default, if the angle of the line segments meeting at a path node is less than 45°, the Miter connection is automatically replaced by the Bevel connection type. If your *intention* is to have connections that overshoot, you might want to increase this value. Many artists who work with thick lines, however, choose to decrease this Miter Limit setting.

Setting Line Cap Shape

Line caps, the beginning and end of an open path, can look like their counterparts, the corners, covered in the previous section. One of the greatest visual differences you can create is extending the true width of a path using the Round and Extended choices—the outline width overshoots the true path's length, proportional to the width you choose for an outline. Here are visual examples of your Line Cap options.

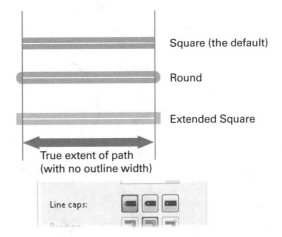

Applying Line Cap options to the end points of an open path affects not only the first and last nodes' appearance on an open path, but also dashed- and dotted-line styles. If you want a string of pill capsules, one way to do this quickly is to make a dotted line with short dashes, widen the line, and then apply the Round line cap.

Tip　Line caps are not "mix and match"; for example, if you choose Round, both end caps in a two-node path are rounded—CorelDRAW has no facility for a two-node path that begins Round and ends Square.

Outline Pen Calligraphic Effects

The term *calligraphy* has come to be accepted today as a handwriting craft, the result of which is text and ornaments that have a varying width along strokes due to the popular use of a flat-edged pen nib held at an angle. The same effect can be achieved using the Calligraphic options in the Outline Pen dialog.

Calligraphic options—let's refer to the Object Properties docker here—are applied using a set of options and an interactive preview window to define the shape of the nib that affects a path you've drawn. *Stretch* controls the width of the nib using values between 1% and 100%. *Tilt* controls the nib rotation in 360° (the minimum, −180°, produces the same "12 o'clock" stroke angle as the maximum, 360°). Click the Default button to reset these parameters to their original state. Stretch and Tilt values work together to achieve the nib shape. Set them numerically by entering values or, better still, set them interactively by placing your cursor in the Preview window and then click-dragging to shape the nib. By default, all paths in CorelDRAW are created using a Stretch value of 100% and a Tilt value of 0°. As you can see in Figure 13-3, varying the stretch and degree of a calligraphic nib changes the look of an outline, but the *shape* you begin with also has an impact on the final look of the design. For example, these three pairs of interwoven B-spine paths are identical, but the one on the left is perhaps more visually interesting and elegant with its 45° angled nib. The point is that if you have an object you think will look more refined and elegant with a calligraphic stroke, keep changing the angle until you're happy with the finished artwork.

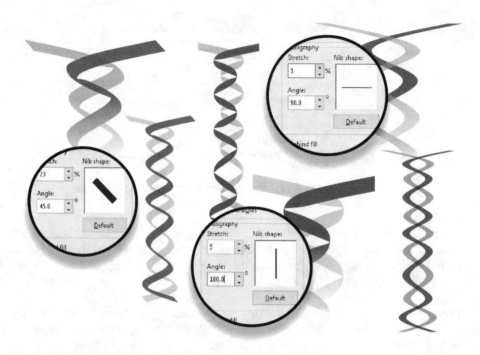

FIGURE 13-3 Calligraphic effects can be used as ornamentations to a piece of work or to imitate handwritten phrases.

 Tip The Artistic Media tool—covered later in this chapter—has a Calligraphic style that can be used as a brush; you just drag on the page, and it immediately produces angled paths.

Scaling and Behind Fill Options

Two more options for controlling how outlines display in particular design situations are available in the Outline Pen dialog. The following sections explain how Scale With Object and Behind Fill work.

Scale With Object

Choose Scale With Object to increase or decrease the outline width applied to an open path or closed object when you scale the object at any time after the outline width has been applied.

For example, a 2-point outline width applied to a path becomes 1 point if the object is scaled in size by 50 percent. However, if you leave the scale constant (leave Scale With Object unchecked), you can duplicate, for example, 50 stars, arrange them on the page at different sizes, and the design looks good because the outline width is consistent from star to star. The illustration here shows copies of a pretzel shape reduced with and without the Scale With Object option selected.

Original object

Reduced using the Scale
With Object option

Reduced without using the
Scale With Object option

Behind Fill

Behind Fill sets outline properties to print and display in *back* of the object's fill. One of the many practical uses for Behind Fill is in a sign or other simple illustration where you need rounded corners along the outline, but sharp and crisp edges along the fill, the most important and recognizable part of many illustrations. Here, on the left, you can see the ubiquitous recycle symbol with a 16-point rounded-corner outline. The arrows are lost in the design. However, on the right, a 32-point outline is used with Behind Fill checked in the Outline Pen dialog. Therefore, the same outline width has been achieved (visually); however, because the outline is behind the fill, the points on the arrows are undistorted, even in weight, and will print crisply.

16-point outline in front of fill:
most edges are soft.

32-point outline behind fill:
edges are crisp and detailed.

Turning an Outline into an Object

A fancy calligraphic property for an outline, arrowhead, and even for dashed outlines can be edited to a greater extent as an *outline* property when you convert an outline to an object. Consider this: an outline is constrained to solid fills, whereas an object that *looks* like an outline, that was originally *based* on an outline, can have any type of CorelDRAW fill. To make an outline into a object, choose Object | Convert Outline To Object—but it will disturb your workflow less if you perform this on a *copy* of the path you slaved over! The shortcut is similar to Convert To Curves; it's CTRL-SHIFT-Q. The path you see in the illustration that follows is fully loaded, using a calligraphic nib, a dashed line, an arrowhead, and a tail. It is about to become a shape that's as editable with Toolbox tools as a rectangle or an ellipse, and will accept all of CorelDRAW's effects, such as contours, fountain fills, and texture fills; even the Extrude tool can turn this shape into elegant, abstract, or bizarre artwork.

On the left in this illustration, you can see the path; in the middle, the path is now a shape that will take, in this example, a Linear Style fountain fill—in contrast, you can't fill an open path. On the right in this illustration, you can see the arrowhead path is now a shape that can be extruded. To come full circle, the new object based on the path can have an outline; in this case, a black outline behind the fill is used artistically to visually separate the linear fill areas.

Using the Artistic Media Tool

The Artistic Media tool treats a path as though it's a skeleton to which you can apply any number of CorelDRAW preset "skins": there are five different types of Artistic Media "brushes" and a number of preset variations for the Preset, Brush, and Sprayer Artistic Media types. It helps to get your mind around a "paintbrush" metaphor; by dragging strokes, you can wind up with anything from complex filigree strokes to elegant calligraphic handwriting.

The underlying path of an Artistic Media stroke can be altered at any time, changing the corresponding look of the media—and you can see the dynamic changes for accurate visual feedback as you work. You can draw while an Artistic Media effect is enabled, and you can also apply these painterly strokes to existing lines.

You don't have to give up the Pen tools in CorelDRAW to add another dimension to outlines you create. The Artistic Media tool—directly below the Pen Tools group on the Toolbox—can be used by itself as a drawing and painting tool, and the media that comes with DRAW can also be applied to paths you've already created using other drawing tools. Use Window | Dockers | Effects | Artistic Media to go about making more expressive artwork the "manual" way, without the Artistic Media tool itself.

With the Artistic Media tool selected, the Property Bar offers five different line-drawing modes, shown in Figure 13-4, each of which has its own options. There are additional options on the Property Bar, directly to the right of your choice of Artistic Media, and the options change, depending on the media type selected.

Applying Presets to Lines

Powerlines—elegant strokes found in previous versions of DRAW—are now called *Presets*. When Presets is selected on the Property Bar, the Artistic Media tool surrounds your drawn lines with specific preset vector shapes that are dynamically linked to the underlying path.

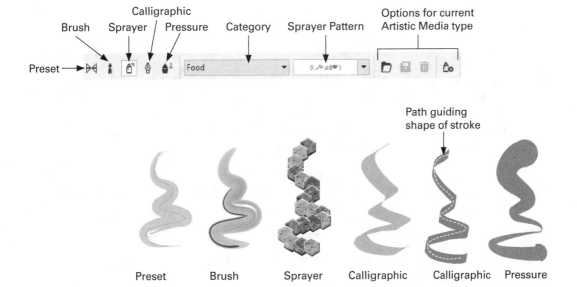

FIGURE 13-4 The Property Bar offers five different line-drawing modes, each of which has its own options.

The smoothness and width of the applied effect is set according to the Freehand Smoothing and Width options on the Property Bar, as shown here.

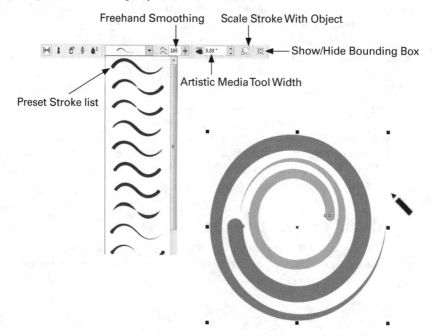

Set the shape using one of the styles in the Preset Stroke list. Smoothing is based on percent values between 0 (no smoothing) and 100 (maximum smoothing). Width can be set on a unit measure within a range of 0.03 to 10 inches. As you draw, a path is created in freehand style and immediately applied to your line.

Ready to take the Artistic Media tool out for a spin? The following tutorial walks you through the completion of an illustration—adding cartoon "reaction lines," the sort of emanations a character has when struck with a revelation—like *you* will be when you discover how the Artistic Media's Preset brush works and feels.

Tutorial Painting with a Drawing Program

1. Open Pinwheel.cdr in CorelDRAW. The objective here is to highlight the different petals on the pinwheel by making different colored strokes emanating from them in an outward direction.
2. Choose the Artistic Media tool and then click Preset, the far-left button on the Property Bar.
3. Click the Preset Stroke selector and choose a style from the drop-down list. For this example, choose a style that has a rounded head and tapers at the end to a point.

4. Think of how you'd draw a cartoon sun; drag strokes so the "sun" is the center of the pinwheel. The target width for the strokes is about .4". If your current stroke width is something different, you now have an opportunity to become familiar with Artistic Media features; while the stroke is highlighted, you can increase or decrease its width on the Property Bar.

5. The head of the Preset Stroke starts where you begin your click-drag. If you drew a stroke backward, you can easily fix this. Press F10 to choose the Shape tool, click to select the stroke (you'll see the underlying path when the stroke is properly selected), and then right-click and choose Reverse Subpaths from the context menu.

6. Click the Artistic Media tool in the Toolbox, and you're ready to continue stroking. The Artistic Media tool is persistent—it "remembers" your last-used stroke settings, styles, and all that good stuff.

7. The Preset Strokes you create are a special instance of an object surrounding a path. You can, therefore, recolor the default black fill. With a stroke selected, try clicking a color swatch on the color palette. The enhanced, quite excited pinwheel is now in color on your monitor and in the e-book version of this Guide, shown in Figure 13-5.

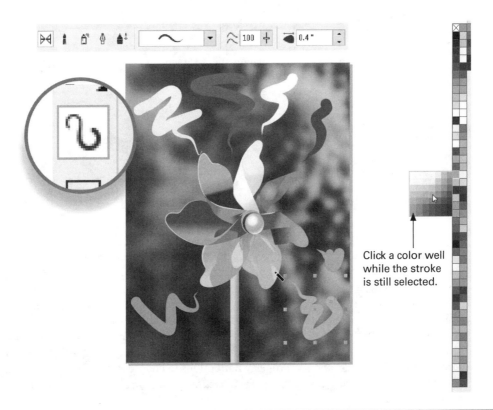

Click a color well while the stroke is still selected.

FIGURE 13-5 When a Preset Stroke is selected, you can change its width, smoothness, and color.

8. Let's say you want to get adventurous and change the Preset for one of the strokes. While the stroke is selected, choose a different Preset Stroke style from the drop-down list. Now, every subsequent stroke you make will have that new style. When choosing it, be sure to click *the outer part* of the stroke and avoid *the underlying central path* itself. If you've deselected a stroke and want to change it, choose it with the Pick tool and then use the drop-down list. Alternatively, you can click (don't click-drag, though) on a stroke on the page to select it and then change the Preset Stroke style. Now go find some meteorological turbulence to put that pinwheel to work!

Drawing with Brushes

In Brush mode, you can simulate the look of traditional natural media, which looks very similar to the brushes in Corel Painter, with a notable exception. Beneath an Artistic Media stroke lies a skeleton path, and the strokes you make can be edited ad infinitum. In contrast, bitmap paint programs such as Corel Painter and Adobe Photoshop feature brushstrokes that can't be edited after you make them. Like the Presets category, Artistic Media brushes extend the full length of every path you create.

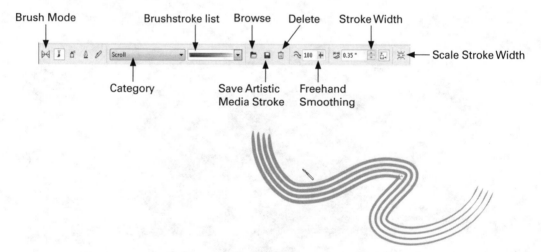

The Brushstroke list offers a variety of different styles. Freehand Smoothing and Stroke Width options are used to change the appearance of the graphical object—the "skin"—applied to the underlying path.

You can draw using a brush style or, alternatively, apply one to an existing line. To draw using a brushstroke, choose the Artistic Media tool and use the Property Bar options to choose a brush style. Begin drawing by click-dragging on your page in a stroking motion. To apply a new brushstroke to an *existing* line, select the line using the Artistic Media tool, choose the Brush mode, and use Property Bar options to choose a width and brushstroke style. The important thing with this technique is to *create a change in settings* on the Property Bar because there is no Apply button or anything to confirm the changes. However, you can make a slight change to the Stroke Width setting on the Property Bar to apply the effect. You can load saved brushes by clicking the Browse button on the Property Bar, and you can save your own objects as brushstrokes and add them to the existing Brushstroke list.

Tip Custom Artistic Media brushstrokes are saved to Corel's CMX file format, which is a limited subset of its native CDR file format. You don't have unlimited options when creating your own brush, but you *can* use a simplified contour or blend to create a graduated color effect that can stretch when used as a stroke.

Applying the Sprayer

The Artistic Media tool's Sprayer mode is used to pepper the drawing page with a sequence of drawings—your *own* that you save as a brush or by choosing a preset from CorelDRAW's Sprayer collections. Changes to the underlying path and the objects used in a spray can be dynamically changed at any time. The sprayer objects repeat uniformly or randomly across the full length of a path. The Size/Scale, Spray Order, Dabs, Spacing, Rotation, and Offset values can be set using the Property Bar, shown in Figure 13-6.

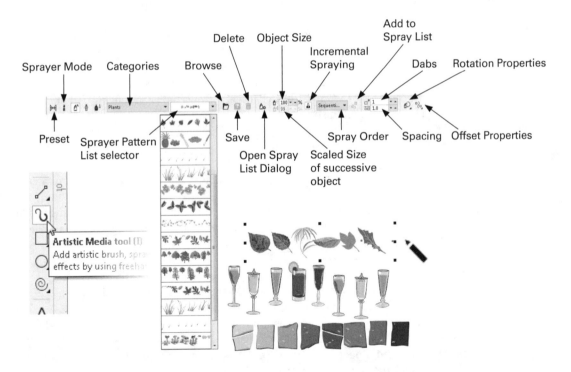

FIGURE 13-6 The Artistic Media tool's Sprayer mode offers a huge number of design variations.

The Sprayer Property Bar options give you control over the following:

- **Object Size and Scaled Size of successive object** Two options control the initial object size of the Sprayer style (that is, the objects that make up a specific Sprayer type) based on a scaled percentage of the original Sprayer object selected. When the Scaled Size of successive object option is unlocked, you can set the scaling size of successive objects to be increased or decreased in scale relative to the size of the first object in the Sprayer style. Some preset sprays offer scaling, whereas some do not, owing to their construction. The Snowflakes preset, for example, offers successive scaling; it's in the Misc. category. The bottom field is dimmed when you've chosen a preset that cannot be successively scaled.

- **Spray Order** This option lets you set the ordering of the Sprayer objects: Randomly, Sequentially, or By Direction. If the Sprayer style features only one object to vary, changing this option has no effect. Try the Mushrooms preset in the Plants category; the spray presets contain several different objects of different sizes, and you can get various looks by choosing Randomly and By Direction.

- **Dabs and Spacing** These two values set the *number of objects* to be placed along a drawn or existing path and *the distance between* the center of each object. *Dabs* are the individual objects in the Sprayer style; *Spacing* controls how many objects appear within a given distance. Think of spacing as "population."

- **Rotation** This option sets the angle for the first object in the Sprayer style. The *Increment* option compounds rotation values for each subsequent object. Rotation angles and increment values can be based on the degree measure relative to the page or the path to which the objects are applied. If you need a circular pattern whose objects are oriented toward the center of the circle, for example, the Rotation option is your ticket.

- **Offset** This option sets the distance between the path you click-drag and the Sprayer objects. *Offset* can be set to Active (the default) at settings between roughly 0.01 and 13 inches. The direction of the offset can also be set to Alternating (the default), Left, Random, or Right. To deactivate the Offset options, uncheck the Use Offset Option in the selector, which sets the Offset measure to 0.

As with other Artistic Media tool modes, you can draw while applying this effect or apply an Artistic Media stroke to an existing line.

With a Sprayer style applied and the line selected, you can use Property Bar options to edit the effect. Doing this edits the style *only as it is applied to your line* and *not* the original style in the Sprayer Pattern List selector.

 Tip To create your own Sprayer brush, first open the Artistic Media docker (Window | Dockers | Effects | Artistic Media). Create several shapes—they can be groups of objects, and they can contain any fill you like—and then arrange them horizontally on the page. Select them, and then click the Save button (the little diskette) at the bottom of the docker. You're then asked whether you want to save the selected objects as brushes (no) or as object sprayers (yes). Saving and choosing sprayers is almost identical to the way you save and use brushes.

Calligraphy Pens and Applying Media

The Calligraphy tool mode produces results similar to adjusting the nib shape with any regular Pen tool; however, you can dynamically change the width and angle when you use the Calligraphy tool. Additionally, your artistic approach with this tool is different from drawing paths—you click-drag to produce an entire stroke instead of click-dragging to set a node and a path segment.

You have three options on the Property Bar when Calligraphic is selected: Freehand Smoothing (the degree of accuracy when you click-drag), Stroke Width (which sets the *maximum* width because calligraphic strokes are alternately thick and thin), and Calligraphic Angle. Increasing values in this field rotate the stroke evaluated from the vertical in a counterclockwise direction. If you're a mouse user, you'll notice that strokes with the Calligraphy pen might not need any refinement work later. Your success depends mostly on how agile you are with a mouse and your click-drag technique.

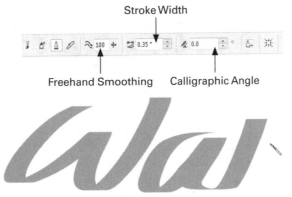

Your experience with using a mouse, however, doesn't have to be an obstacle to creating elegant curves, handsome signatures, and other calligraphic designs. Follow this tutorial to learn how to apply a Calligraphic property—and any Artistic Media except Pressure—to an *existing* path.

Tutorial Defining and Applying Calligraphic Brushstrokes

1. Open the Calligraphy.cdr file. You'll see a thin centerline on the top, unlocked layer. The bottom layer is just for reference. Mistal was used as the typeface and is a good example of calligraphic swoops, curves, and turns.
2. With the Pick tool, select the lowercase *a* after the initial *C*.
3. Choose the Artistic Media tool and then click the Calligraphic tool on the Property Bar. Do not deselect anything.
4. Here's the trick: click either the up or down elevator button to the right of the Stroke Width field (or type **.2** or **.1** in the field instead of using the elevator button). What you've done is get the calligraphic pen to "recognize" that you want to change a value

of the selected path's calligraphic width. The change isn't important; it's the *recognition* that applies the Calligraphic property to the selected stroke.

Create the value change by
clicking the elevator button.

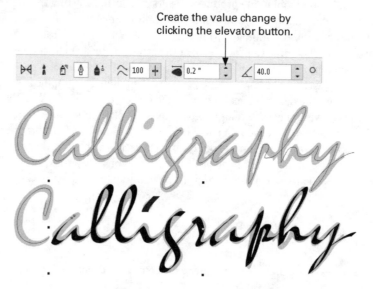

5. Continue to adjust the Stroke Width setting (**.2"** works well at the path's scale here), and then play with the Calligraphic Angle option—anywhere from 35° to 55° looks good in this example.

6. Perform steps 2–5 with the initial *C*, and then with the brush, dot the *i*.

Pressure Mode

The last of the Artistic Media modes was created for digital tablet users; if you own a stylus and tablet, you can set up the drivers for the stylus to apply pressure, and CorelDRAW will read stylus pressure to vary the width of the stroke as you drag across the page. You have Freehand Smoothing and maximum Width controls on the Property Bar.

If you're using a mouse, you can use UP ARROW and DOWN ARROW on the keyboard as you drag to (respectively) increase and decrease the width of the stroke. Honestly, don't expect world-class art using the mouse and arrow keys; you might run into a design situation where you need to vary the width of a stroke, but there are other ways to edit an existing stroke that produce more refined results.

This chapter has taken you through simply assigning one property to a path to applying several, more complex properties to a path. As you gain a better understanding of the options in CorelDRAW, you add to your personal, creative wealth of design options. Dashed lines, arrowheads, and calligraphic strokes will come to your rescue during 11th-hour assignment crunches, just as other features will that have been covered in previous chapters.

Blends and contours are the topic of the next chapter; each has it own use. And you can actually take what you know now about filled objects from Chapter 12 and strokes from *this* chapter and do some ultra-exotic blending and contouring. Will it look weird? Yep. But also *interesting*. Just think of it as building on your knowledge!

14 Using Blends and Contours

Although they're different effects, blends and contours share the common trait of creating many shapes based on control shapes. The additional shapes are dynamically linked to the control object, and the "in-between" objects can vary in size, color, and outline shape, depending on how you set up the effect. Blends and contours are terrific for shading flat color fills in a way that fountain fills sometimes cannot. Additionally, blend objects can be used to illustrate the transition between two objects of completely dissimilar shapes. This chapter takes you through the use of blends and contours so you can create outstanding, intriguing work in addition to what you already know.

Blend and Contour Effects: Similarities with Distinctions

The Blend effects create a series of objects *between* objects using the number of steps you define—an object can be a closed path, a group of objects, or even a line (an open path). The properties of each step can be determined by the objects used in the blend (more on this later in the chapter). The Contour effect also creates additional objects in steps; however, only one object is used to produce a contour. When you imagine a Contour effect, think of a shape surrounded by the same shape radiating outward (or inward) in a concentric pattern, like the circular waves produced when you drop a pebble in a still pond. The following sections explain the properties of the effects you can manipulate, and then you can decide for yourself which effect to reach for when you need a complex graphic or a smooth, shaded fill in an illustration area.

Blending as Illustration Shading

If you've ever tried to add depth to a drawing but the Mesh Fill tool isn't working and a fountain fill doesn't do the trick, the solution is to blend a large shape through transition objects to a smaller object inside the large one. By making, for example, the outer shape darker than the inner one, you can position a soft-edged highlight on an illustration of a shiny object. Similarly, a contour can be used to create a highlight; however, the contour object should be symmetrical to achieve the highlight effect (for example, an ellipse). You'll often see Blend

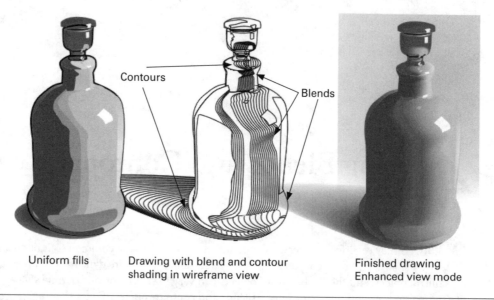

Uniform fills   Drawing with blend and contour shading in wireframe view   Finished drawing Enhanced view mode

FIGURE 14-1 A drawing, especially a perspective drawing of an object, can appear flat until you add shading with blends and contours.

effects used in illustration work for creating photorealistic illustrations, but regardless of whether the visual content of a drawing is real-life accurate or a whimsical cartoon, with blends you can add depth and suggest lighting and the type of material on an object. The left side of Figure 14-1 shows a drawing of a bottle, but you and other viewers will detect that there's something missing from the illustration. On the right, you can see the finished illustration in Enhanced view in CorelDRAW's drawing window after some Blend and Contour effects were added; a wireframe view showing the blend and contour steps is shown in the center. You'll see how to do this stuff later in the chapter.

Smooth shading and highlights accomplished by the artistic use of blends create a visual impression of strength, size, and other qualities that help the audience read an object very quickly: "Oh, that's a *porcelain bottle!* It looks really bright! And it probably contains perfume that's too expensive." Seriously, the more complexity you build into an object's fill, the more readily the audience will pick up on the complete visual idea and fill in *more* details. And before you know it, you've *sustained your audience's attention.*

Blends can also be used to create a lot of similar objects very quickly; the trick is to blend between similar objects that are quite a distance apart on the page. The following illustration shows an example of two groups of objects blended together to create a bar graph; the reference lines were blended from two identical lines. This is a graph with an even, upward progression. However, when you need to create similar blended objects that *don't* follow an even progression, you use the Break Apart (CTRL-K) command to break the relationship between the blend control objects. You then ungroup the blended group and edit the individual blended shapes to create a more random transition from object to object.

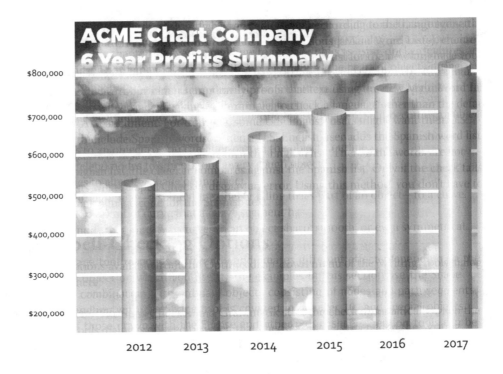

The Interactive Blend Tool and Property Bar

The Blend tool can be found in the Toolbox, on top of the Interactive tool group. When you choose the Blend tool, the Property Bar offers options (shown in Figure 14-2) for customizing the effect. By default, 20 intermediate steps are created between two blend control objects.

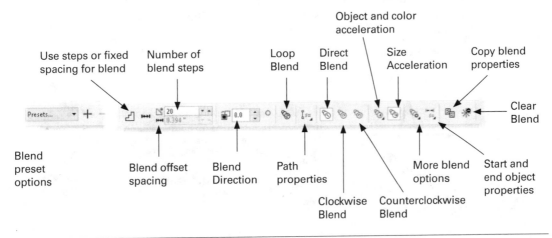

FIGURE 14-2   When the Interactive Blend tool is used, the Property Bar has options to customize your Blend effects.

Creating a Simple Blend Effect

You might want to work with similar objects to create blends that look like repeats—rubberstamped copies of the original objects—but there's another creative use for the Blend tool. You can morph totally dissimilar objects, and the resulting blend will probably contain a lot of interesting and useful transitional shapes. Work through the following tutorial to experiment with a basic Blend effect between a star and an ellipse object.

Tutorial A Basic Blend Between Very Different Shapes

1. Choose the Star tool; it's in the group on the Toolbox with the Polygon tool. Click-drag a star that's about 1" in size at the top left of the drawing page. Fill it with yellow on the Color Palette, and give it a four-point blue outline. First, choose 4 pts. from the Outline Width drop-down box on the Property Bar, and then right-click any blue color well on the Color Palette.

2. Choose the Ellipse tool (F7) and then click-drag an ellipse at the top right of the page. Fill it with blue and give it a yellow outline, but keep the outline width at the default of .5 pts.

3. Choose the Blend tool from the Toolbox. Your cursor changes, and the Property Bar's options are all dimmed because a blend doesn't exist yet on the page.

4. Click inside the star and then drag until your cursor is inside the ellipse. Once you release the mouse button, a series of new objects appears, and the Property Bar comes to life with almost all options available.

5. Twenty steps is too many for this example: type **2** in the Steps field on the Property Bar and then press ENTER. As you can see in the following illustration, the blend shapes make an interesting progression; the outline color makes the transition from blue to yellow; the fill color transitions from yellow to blue; and the intermediate shapes are some interesting stars in stages of distortion as they become the ellipse. These intermediate star-like objects are actually a little difficult to make using the standard drawing tools!

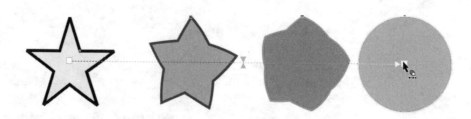

Tip To remove a Blend effect, click the blend portion of the effect to select it and then choose Effects | Clear Blend; or, while using the Interactive Blend tool, click to select the Blend effect portion and then click the Clear Blend button in the Property Bar.

Looking at the Components of a Blend

The Blend effect you built in the previous tutorial creates a fun composition, but to build on your *knowledge*—to be able to create more complex blends—it's a good idea to now examine what really went on, and what properties the objects on your page now have. A two-object blend includes several key components: the original objects become *control objects*; any changes made to either the star or the ellipse will change the blend itself. The effect portion—called a *blend group*—and the *control objects* maintain a relationship as long as the blend exists.

Each of the interactive markers around a Blend effect corresponds to an option in the Property Bar. Figure 14-3 shows the various parts of a two-object blend.

Editing a blend is a little more of a challenge than making dinner reservations, but significantly less challenging than brain surgery. With the Pick tool, click the blend group to begin editing it using the Property Bar options. Single-clicking selects both the blend and its control objects. To select either control object, click only that control object itself. You'll see that the Status Bar tells you that a "Control Object" (or Curve, Rectangle, or *Whatever*) is selected, confirming that the correct object is selected for editing. Double-click on the blend group with the Pick tool to switch to the Blend tool for making adjustments directly to the group. Your cursor becomes a crosshair as you perform an operation. Similarly, when you want to adjust the acceleration, hover your cursor over the central color and object markers and then drag when the cursor becomes a crosshair.

When you attempt to do something not allowed with the Blend tool cursor (such as move an intermediate blend object), an international "no" symbol appears at the lower left of the cursor.

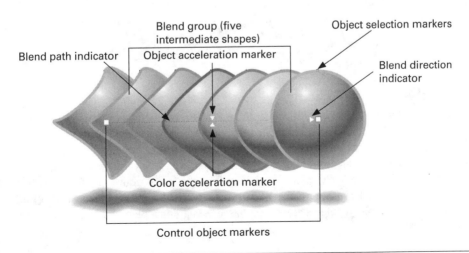

FIGURE 14-3   This blend between two shapes shows the interactive markers controlling the effect.

Editing Blend Effects

You can create a custom Blend effect by directly manipulating markers and objects with your cursor, setting specific values for options using the Property Bar, and occasionally by using a combination of the two interface elements. The following sections take you through the features you'll use most often; then it's on to useful but less frequently used options. Think of this as a journey from mildly amusing, to wonderful, and then on to totally bizarre effects as you progress through these sections.

Setting Blend Options

Options controlling a Blend effect can have an impact on each intermediate step of the blend itself. You can change each step's value, rotation, and color, as well as the acceleration of the blend objects. You can even save the effect you've custom-designed as a preset.

Controlling Blend Steps

The number of steps in the blend group can be set within a range of 1 to 999. To set a number of steps, enter a value in the Property Bar Blend Steps num box and then press ENTER. Notice that as you set higher step numbers, the blend control objects might overlap, depending on their closeness. This is an interesting effect, as shown next, but if you need intermediate blend objects that don't touch one another, you can resize both blend control objects, or move them farther apart from one another.

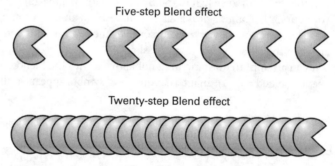

Five-step Blend effect

Twenty-step Blend effect

Specifying Blend Spacing

To set spacing values between blend steps, use the Blend Spacing option, which becomes available *only* if a blend has been applied to a path, as shown in Figure 14-4. This limitation is because the distance between the Blend control objects must be fixed by the length of the path. Using the Blend Spacing option in the Property Bar, enter the value to a specific unit measure. CorelDRAW automatically calculates the number of objects required to fit the path's length. Blend Spacing works within a range of 0.010 inch to 10.00 inches, in increments of 0.010 inch. To learn how to blend objects along a path, see "Assigning a Blend Path," later in this chapter.

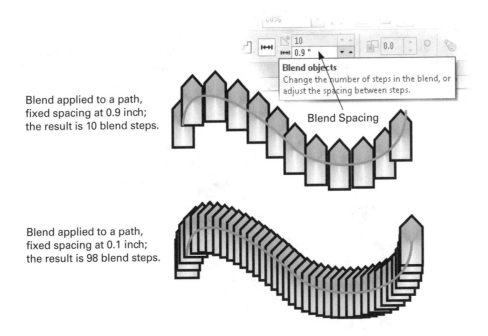

Blend applied to a path, fixed spacing at 0.9 inch; the result is 10 blend steps.

Blend Spacing

Blend applied to a path, fixed spacing at 0.1 inch; the result is 98 blend steps.

FIGURE 14-4   Fixed spacing between blend objects applied to a path can be controlled using the Blend Spacing feature on the Property Bar.

Rotating a Blend

You can rotate the objects in a blend group by fixed degree values using the Blend Direction option, shown here. Enter an angle value (based on degrees of rotation). Positive values rotate the objects counterclockwise; negative values rotate them clockwise. With a rotation value specified, the last object in the blend group is rotated the full angle, with the intermediate steps rotated in even increments starting at 0° rotation—the rotation value of the Start blend control object. This is a handy feature for suggesting action or even an animation. However, rotating a blend cannot be accomplished using a blend on a path.

Blend Direction

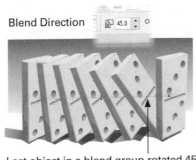

Last object in a blend group rotated 45°

When Blend Direction is set to anything other than 0° on the Property Bar, the Loop Blend option is available. Choosing the Loop Blend option has the effect of applying both rotation and path offset effects to the blend group. Looping a blend works in combination with the Blend Direction value, offsetting the objects from their original direction and rotating them simultaneously. If you then modify a blend control object, as done at the bottom of the following illustration, you can achieve a different loop effect, sort of like one of those children's toys that never really got the hang of walking down the stairs.

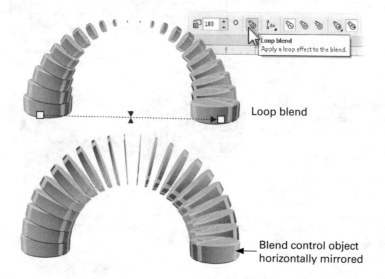

Loop blend

Blend control object horizontally mirrored

Changing Color Rotation

By default, the object colors in your blend group are blended *directly* from one color to the next to create a smooth color transition. However, you can change this using either Blend Clockwise or Blend Counterclockwise on the Property Bar. If you want a rainbow effect, for example, one control object should be red and the other filled with blue so the Blend Clockwise and Counterclockwise can cycle through the visible spectrum.

Acceleration Options

Acceleration increases or decreases the rate at which your blend group objects change shape; think of it as "preferring" one control object over the other. When a default Blend effect is applied, both of these settings are at the midpoint of the blend; the blend group objects change in color and size evenly between the two control objects. You change object and color acceleration rates simultaneously (the default) when the two options are linked, or make acceleration changes independently of one another by clicking the Unlink Acceleration option from the Object and Color Acceleration buttons on the Property Bar. In this illustration, you can see linked acceleration to the right, and then at the bottom, to the left control object.

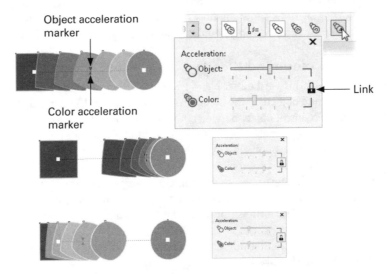

Moving either slider in this pop-out box to the left of the center position reduces (slows) the acceleration from the Start object toward the End object of the Blend effect. Moving either of the sliders to the right increases the acceleration. Interactive acceleration markers can also be used to adjust these values. While the two rates are unlinked, changing the Object Acceleration affects only the progression of shapes.

With Object Acceleration sliders unlinked, changing the Color Acceleration affects only the change in progression of the fill and outline colors between the two objects. Moving the sliders, or the interactive markers, left or right changes the acceleration of the color change.

Tip   Changing the Color Acceleration also affects the width properties applied to outline paths of objects.

Using Blend Presets

It's taken up to now to learn how to change the blend steps, rotation, color, and acceleration rates of Blend effects; naturally, you want to be able to save an elegantly customized blend so you can apply it to other objects in the future. Saving your hard work as presets is accomplished through the Blend Preset list when a blend is selected; you can also tap into some nice *existing* presets on the list.

Blend presets are used the same as other CorelDRAW preset controls and can be saved and applied to two or more different shapes.

Creating Extraordinary, Complex Blend Effects

More advanced blending can solve illustration challenges when a standard, direct blend can't. The following sections show you how to create *multipoint blends,* how to *map* blend control object *nodes,* and how to apply blends to paths. Yes, this is the "good part" of this chapter!

Creating Compound Blends

A simple, straightforward direct blend from one object to another can be split so that one or more of the child objects in the blend group becomes another control object. Once you have a "mezzanine" control object between the *original* control objects, you can reposition it on the page—which can make a blend look like Pablo Picasso's idea of a caterpillar. You can also recolor the new control object as well as edit it with the Shape tool.

You now have *two* different stages of blends within the compound blend object: a transition from the start point to the point you created, and then a transition between this point and the end-point control object. There are two different ways to achieve the same goal when you want to add a transition control point within a simple blend:

- Double-click a blend group object. This is an imprecise method, especially if there are more than 10 blend steps spaced tightly together.
- Click the More blend options pop-up button on the Properties Bar and choose Split Blend. Your cursor turns into a targeting cursor and you can now pick the exact child object in the blend that you want promoted to an intermediate control object.

Here is a visual of both processes:

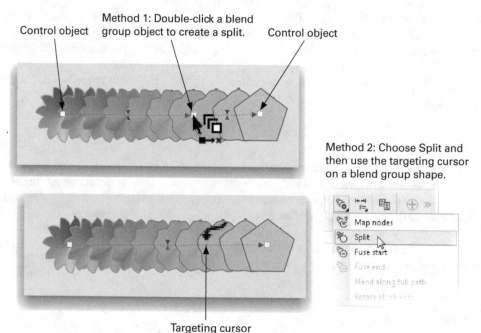

Control object   Method 1: Double-click a blend   Control object
                  group object to create a split.

Method 2: Choose Split and
then use the targeting cursor
on a blend group shape.

Targeting cursor

After you've created a split in a blend, you can edit the intermediate control object—change its fill, change the path with the Shape tool, reposition it on the page, scale it... you name it. To perform edits on the new control object, deselect the compound path—choose the Pick tool and then click on a blank area of the page—then select the new control object and perform your edits. At the top of the following illustration, you can see that splitting and then editing the new control object affects all the child group objects on either side of the control object.

You can split a blend in as many places as you have child blend objects. Alternatively, you can add a new shape to the blend by dragging from any new object you've created to any control object on the blend, while using the Blend tool. You'll achieve some wonderfully bizarre effects should you choose to blend between a new object and the middle of a compound blend, but it can be done. At the bottom of this illustration, you can see a rounded-corner rectangle being blended to the end of a complex blend.

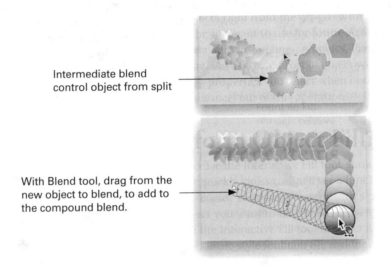

Intermediate blend control object from split

With Blend tool, drag from the new object to blend, to add to the compound blend.

Fusing a Blend

Fusing, as the term applies to CorelDRAW blends, is the opposite of splitting, and it applies to a complex blend made by adding an object to a direct blend. When you apply a fusing action to a blend, you remove a control object. The resulting blend adjusts to reflect the new lack of a control object and its properties. To remove an intermediate control object you created by double-clicking with the Shape tool, you double-click this marker with the Blend tool, and it disappears. To remove, for example, a control object that's part of a complex blend created by adding a control object, you can click the More Blend Options flyout button on the Properties Bar and choose Fuse (Start or End), depending on which end of the blend you added a control object to.

Mapping Control Object Nodes

When a blend is applied, the blend group is built of a series of intermediate objects between the control objects. When you use two completely different shapes as control objects, the chances are that they won't have the same number of nodes connecting path segments; additionally, the position on the page of the first node you draw is usually arbitrary, depending on your style of drawing. By default, CorelDRAW blends two different objects using *node mapping:* the Blend effect makes an assumption that the blend should start with the first node on the Start object and should end at the first node on the End object, and that all objects in the blend itself make the transition based on the same node position on the page as the Start and End control objects.

Occasionally you might get a blend that looks like a parade of crumpled sheets of paper, or something similarly nasty—it's interesting, but not what you had in mind.

Fortunately, you can match the nodes of your control objects in a few clicks. To map the nodes in a blend, click the Miscellaneous Blend Options button and then click the Map Nodes button. The cursor becomes a targeting cursor, which is your signal to click the nodes you want matched. Node mapping is a two-step operation: look for oversized nodes showing on one of your control objects and then click on one with the targeting cursor. Then click on the corresponding node on the other control object, as shown in this illustration.

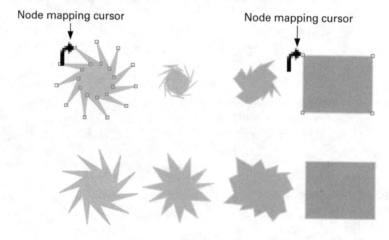

Assigning a Blend Path

Objects can be blended along a path either by using a path you draw before the Blend operation or by ALT-dragging from one object to another with the Blend tool while nothing is selected on the page. Blend objects on a path can also be rotated, offset from the path, and set to fill the full path or only part of the path.

You can see in the following illustration an example of the "ALT-drag a path" technique. If your path is a little shaky or otherwise imperfect, first choose the Shape tool from the Toolbox and then choose Show Path from the Path Properties pop-up on the Property Bar. Once you can see the path, you can edit it, just as you'd do with a drawn path, using the Shape tool.

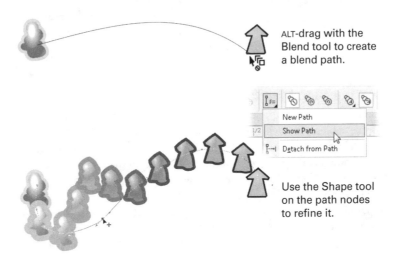

ALT-drag with the Blend tool to create a blend path.

New Path
Show Path
Detach from Path

Use the Shape tool on the path nodes to refine it.

The following tutorial takes you through the more studied and precise approach to binding a blend to a path, again using the Path Properties pop-up.

Tutorial Blending Objects Along a Path

1. With a Blend effect already created and an open or closed path in view on the page, choose the Blend tool and then click the blend group portion of your effect to select it, not the control objects on either end of the blend.
2. Click the Path Properties button and then choose New Path. Notice your cursor changes to a targeting cursor.
3. Click the open or closed path with this special cursor; the blend now follows the path you clicked. Notice also that the blend has changed position to align with the path exactly where it's positioned. The Blend effect and the new path are featured top to bottom in this illustration.

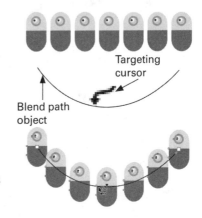

Targeting cursor

Blend path object

Choosing New Path while a Blend effect is already applied to a path lets you assign a new and different object as the blend path. To remove a Blend effect from a path, use the Detach From Path command. If the blend includes so many steps that the path is hidden—or if the path itself is not visible because it has no outline color applied—use the Show Path command to select and highlight it for editing. Show Path is also a good command for editing a path you created. Using the Shape tool as your current tool, use the ALT-click-drag technique described earlier. Remember: as long as the path is visible (in any View mode), you can change its course by using the Shape tool to edit the path's nodes.

 Tip If you don't want a path to be visible in the final effect, set its Fill and Outline colors to None. This way, you can edit the path later.

Rotating Blend Objects

Objects set to follow a path do so using their original, unaltered orientation by default. For example, a blend involving vertical lines when blended to a path results in the centers of objects aligning with the path, but their orientation will remain vertical. If you need your blend group objects to *align* with the orientation of the path itself, choose the Rotate All Objects option in the Miscellaneous Blend Options pop-up menu in the Property Bar, which is available when a blend on a path is selected.

Doing this applies a rotation value to each of the objects in the blend group to align with the direction of the path.

Blend Along Full Path

If the path you've applied your Blend effect to is the right size and length to cover your blend completely, you may automatically set the blend group and control objects to cover the entire path. To do this, choose the Blend Along Full Path option from the Miscellaneous Blend Options pop-up. Using this option, you can move the center origins of the control objects in the blend to the first and last nodes of the path. The illustration here shows the effect when a blend is applied to an open path.

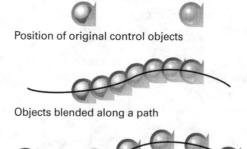

Position of original control objects

Objects blended along a path

Blend Along Full Path chosen

 Tip Once a blend group is bound to a path, you can manually space the blend objects by click-dragging the Start control object or the End control object with the Pick tool. This technique might not get you where you want to go 100 percent of the time, but this is a good feature for visualizing how you want spacing to occur in a blend.

Controlling Blend Object Path Alignment

When a blend follows a path, the point at which all objects align with the path is determined by their center origin. The *center origin* is where all objects are rotated during any default rotation. Controlling how a blend aligns to a path is one of those hidden features you won't find in any dialog or Property Bar. Instead, the center origin is moved manually using the Pick tool, with object rotation and skew handles in view. By moving the center origin, you can control how the objects align to the path.

To perform this alignment operation, you click a blend control object to select it, click again to reveal the center origin and rotation handles, and then move the center origin point. The blend moves in the opposite direction. This trick is a very quick way to reshape and move a blend along a path with a minimum of steps.

Working with Multi-object Blends

Blending between *more* than two objects can produce an effect quite unlike splitting a blend, and it's just as easy to do. You click-drag between different objects on your document page. Each time you do this, a new blend group is created. The dynamic link is maintained between all objects in a multi-object blend, which means you can change control objects, and the blends are instantly updated. Figure 14-5 shows two Blend effects applied to three different objects with the multi-object blend defined in different directions. The one on the left is linear, and the one on the right converges from points to the circle object.

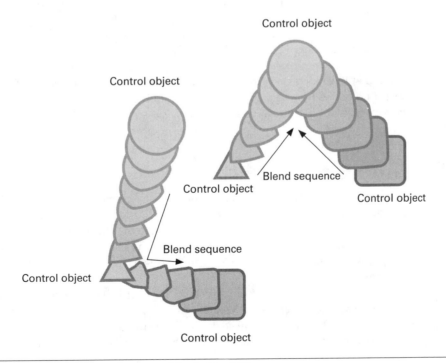

FIGURE 14-5 These three shapes are blended in different sequences.

Each blend of a multi-object blend is considered a separate effect; each has its own control objects with defined Start and End blend objects. You can change the Start and End blend objects using the Starting and Ending Objects Properties pop-out menu commands on the Property Bar. The Start and End blend objects are the key to making blends that change shape all over the place in very intriguing patterns. And the key to selecting blend groups within blend groups is to hold CTRL and then click on a subgroup within the compound object, and then the options on the Property Bar can be accessed.

With a blend selected, you first need to locate the Start or End blend object—choose either the Show Start or Show End command. Choosing New Start changes the cursor to a targeting cursor, so you can then unlink the Blend effect from one object and target a different one. Doing this creates a new effect each time a different object is targeted. Choosing New End works similarly.

After a blend has been made, you might need to dismantle it and break the link between the control objects. This is easily done, but keep in mind that it can't be reversed without using the Undo command (CTRL-Z). To dismantle a blend, choose the Pick tool, right-click the blend group portion, and choose Break Blend Group Apart from the pop-up menu (or press CTRL-K). The control objects then become separate objects, leaving the blend intermediate objects grouped. To further dismantle the arrangement, select only the blend group by using the Pick tool and then choose Arrange | Ungroup (CTRL-U).

Tapping into Contour Effects

Contour effects instantly create perfect outlines of shapes or paths by the dozens or even hundreds. The result is similar to viewing a topographical or *contour* map, hence the name.

During a Contour effect, dynamically linked shapes are concentrically created outside or inside an object's path. CorelDRAW effectively calculates the shape of each contour step and applies progressive outline and fill colors based on the original object's properties and selected contour options.

While a Contour effect is linked to an object, the object itself becomes a control object, and the new shapes created become the "contour group." Changes made to the properties of the original immediately affect the linked group. While the contour group is selected, its properties can be edited at any time—without your having to begin the effect from scratch.

Exploring CorelDRAW's Contour Effects

First, let's see what Contour effects enable you to do. One of the more popular uses is to simulate depth.

Figure 14-6 shows two illustrations of climate zones in the Urals region of Russia. At left, uniform fills (solid colors) occupy the objects; at right, the same objects have Contour effects. In the contour version, the control objects still use uniform color, but the contour uses different colors for the outermost and innermost objects. This is one of the uses of the Contour effect. As with blends, intermediate objects are generated from the beginning object; however, you don't have to draw the end (the inner object) because it's part of the Contour effect function. Because a high number of steps are used in the Contour effect, you can see a smooth color transition in most of the objects. Also note that some of the objects have a low number of intermediate objects, producing banding, which can be useful in your design work. Just use a low number of steps when drawing a map of the Steppes.

Here is a fairly simple hands-on example of how the Contour tool can be used as the basis for an Oxford-style (in other words, "fancy") border around a piece of stationery. Not only will you create a page border, but the border will also curve around the text at the top of the page. The Contour effect was applied to the text before this file was created, the contour was broken at the left and right using the Shape tool, the border was similarly broken at the horizontal middle, the two shapes were broken using the CTRL-K (Break Apart) command, and then the two lines were joined. You'll work through this stuff in the following tutorial, though. By the way, in your own adventures, you do not have to convert text to curves to apply a Contour effect. All the text in this CDR file was broken into curves.

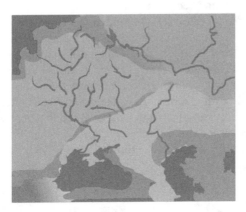

Original filled with solid colors

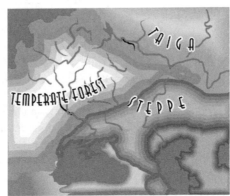

Finished artwork with Contour effects

FIGURE 14-6   Contour effects create a smooth color transition.

Tutorial Creating Expensive Stationery

1. Open Magnificent Stationery.cdr, a base for the stationery you'll create for a company who thinks "Magnificent" is an appropriate or even safe name for a retail company. Choose the Contour tool from the Toolbox, click the Outside Contour button on the Property Bar, and then touch the outer border (as shown in callout 1 in the following illustration) to tell CorelDRAW you're going to make a contour out of the selection.

2. It's possible that the outside contours will have an inside color, which you don't want in this example. If this is the case, go up to the Fill Color box toward the right side of the Property Bar and then choose white.

3. You probably don't want to create this outside border effect manually using the interactive controls shown in callout 2 in the illustration. Why? Because you're applying a relatively small amount of contour, and inevitably when you drag on an interface element, you're prone to apply a quantum error to the effect. Instead, use the controls on the Property Bar. Click the Outside Contour button, set the number of steps to 2, and then type **0.101"** in the Contour Offset box—and then while your cursor is in the number box, press ENTER on your keyboard to apply the effect.

4. Let's not stop at the two-step contour for the finished product. Instead, let's make the contours different colors and widths, very classy like... and stuff. With the contour selected, choose Object | Break Contour Apart, as shown in callout 3 in the magnificent illustration. The former contour pieces are grouped together, so press CTRL-U to ungroup them. Choose the Select tool from the Toolbox and then click a vacant area on the page to deselect everything.

5. Click the outer object; then, on the Property Bar, choose Hairline from the Outline Width box on the Property Bar.

6. Click the middle ex-contour shape. Why not give it an aqua color? Choose 2 points for the outline and then double-click the Outline Pen box at the lower right of the interface. Click the Color drop-down list and then type **#4CD4D4** in the hexadecimal box. Press ENTER to apply the color, and then close out of the Outline Pen box. Apply the same outline (and black as the outline color) to the innermost ex-contour object, just like you did in step 4. In callout 4, you can see a close-up of some very tasty editing you did.

7. Again, if CorelDRAW gets fussy and wants to change the contour object's fills, just return to that fill color button on the right side of the Property Bar and then choose White.

8. Callout 5 in the illustration is an inadequate-sized picture of the final result of your work here. Save the file under a different name, and you just might decide to take this tutorial out for a spin on your own someday. Happy CTRL-P adventures!

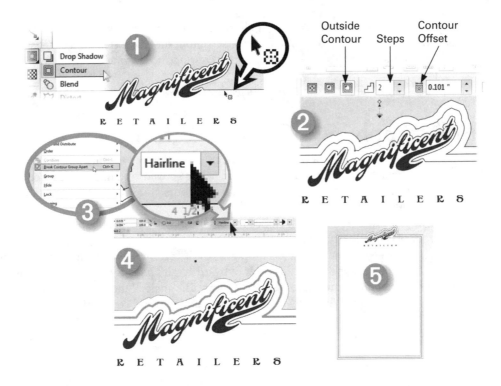

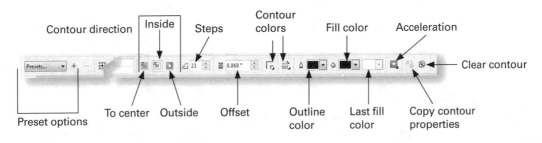

Tip   Letterhead fonts (just do a search on "LHF") were used in the previous tutorial to get an exceptionally professional letterhead look. See Chapter 12 for the inside track on professional typography and the use of appropriate fonts in your work.

Using the Contour Tool and Property Bar

To apply Contour effects, you'll need to use the Contour tool, shown in Figure 14-7, in combination with the Property Bar. You'll find the tool in the Toolbox with other interactive tools: Blend, Drop Shadow, Envelope, Distort, Extrude, and Transparency.

FIGURE 14-7   Use the Property Bar to make the fullest use of the Contour tool.

While you're using the Contour tool, the Property Bar displays options for customizing the effect. These options include contour presets, contour direction, steps and offset spacing, color rotation, outline and fill color, and buttons for copying and clearing the effect, as shown in the figure.

Let's put some of the Contour tool's features to use.

Tutorial Applying a Contour Effect

1. Create an object (a polygon or star is a great seed shape for contours); apply a fill and (optionally) outline properties. If you'd like to go wild with this Contour tool tutorial, try filling the object with a fountain fill—contours produce interesting results with fountain fills.
2. Choose the Contour tool. Notice that your cursor changes and the Property Bar now displays Contour options.
3. Click the object and drag (click-drag) in the direction you want the contour to be applied. Dragging from the center outward creates *outside* contours; dragging in the opposite direction creates *inside* contours. The angle of the drag action has no effect on the contours themselves—only inward and outward count. Notice that as you drag, a silhouette of the final size of the Contour effect appears in inverted screen colors.
4. Release the mouse button, and your effect is finished and ready for customizing.

These steps created a contour in its default state. Adjusting the effect to suit your needs takes a little more work with the Property Bar options. The contours outside or inside the object can also be controlled using the interactive markers surrounding the effect. The next section explains the use of these markers, their purpose, and how to manipulate them.

 Tip To remove a Contour effect, click the contour portion of the effect using either the Contour tool or Pick tool and choose Effects | Clear Contour, or click the Clear Contour button in the Property Bar.

Editing Contours Interactively

The easiest way to edit a Contour effect is by doing it "hands on," using the Interactive Contour tool to change the interactive markers in combination with adjusting Property Bar options. Use them to adjust the direction, spacing, and offset values of the effect.

The black diamond-shaped marker indicates which object is the control object of the effect. The white rectangle marker indicates the final object in the contour group, and its position sets the distance between the control object and the last object in the effect. A slider between these two enables you to adjust the spacing between the contour steps interactively, which, in turn, sets the number of steps by dividing the difference. Figure 14-8 identifies the interactive markers and their purpose.

You'll also notice the Contour tool cursor changes its appearance as you drag outside, inside, or to the centermost point of your selected object, as shown in Figure 14-9. While held over an object, the cursor will also indicate whether the object is valid for the Contour effect.

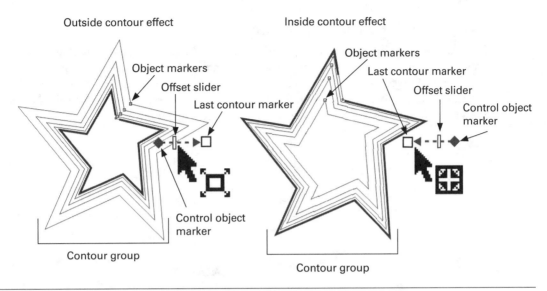

Outside contour effect

Inside contour effect

FIGURE 14-8   These two shapes have contours applied in opposite directions.

> **Tip** To quickly edit a contour, double-click the effect portion of an existing contour with the Pick tool.

Incidentally, the Contour tool is accommodating to a fault. It can apply a contour to an object that has an envelope applied to it; it will even apply a contour to a group of objects. But note that you may not be happy with the results, which are as predictable as a Three Card Monte game a guy hosts on a street corner on top of a cardboard box.

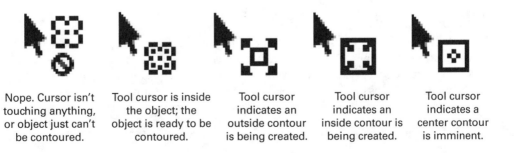

FIGURE 14-9   The Contour tool cursor lets you know what's going on.

Choosing Contour Direction

You've already seen how to create an outside contour, but wait—there are two more types! Choosing either To Center, Inside, or Outside, shown next, causes the contours to be applied in the direction relative to the object's outline path. When Inside or Outside is selected, you can set the number of steps and the offset spacing between the steps by entering values in the Steps and Offset boxes in the Property Bar and then pressing ENTER.

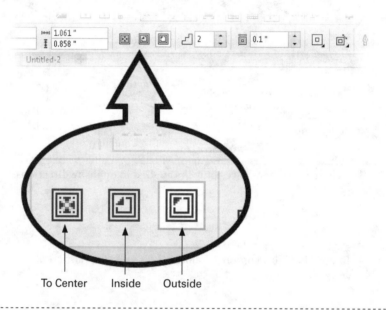

To Center   Inside   Outside

Tip To separate an applied contour and break the dynamic link to the original object, right-click directly on the effect (objects) and then choose Break Contour Group Apart from the pop-up menu.

The effect's contour direction, spacing, and offset values affect one another. In the sections that follow, remember that when you change one parameter's values, a different parameter will probably auto-change.

Contour Inside

With the exception of the 47 clowns that can get out of a Volkswagen, there is a real-world and mathematical limit to how many steps you can use to create a shape within a shape. For contours, if the offset spacing value you enter in the Offset box (on the Property Bar) exceeds the number of steps the distance allows, the Steps value is automatically reduced to fit. Here, you can see some results of applying inside contours to different objects; as you can see, compound paths produce quite elegant contour steps. Remember: open paths are not eligible for Inside Contour effects; it can't be done mathematically, and it can't be done in CorelDRAW.

Contour Outside

Choosing the Outside option creates contours *around* your object—and yes, you can use an open path, as shown in this illustration with outside contouring. It creates an interesting effect you can use for designing everything from neon signs to expensive paperclips. The Steps value can be set as high as 999, and the Offset values travel within a range of 0.001 to 300 inches.

Open path

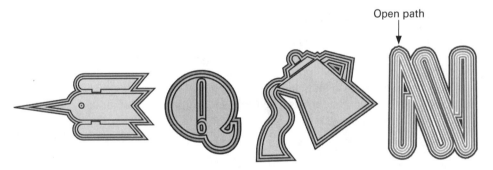

Contour To Center

The To Center direction creates the contour inside the selected object, but it does so using as many steps as mathematically possible. The number of steps depends on the Offset value (editing the number of steps is not available). In any case, your object is filled with a contour. This is a terrific option for illustrating game mazes—with a little editing after making a contour of a bicycle or a flower in a pot, you could fill a book with games like you see on children's menus in restaurants. Here, the Offset value is the only parameter that can be changed;

the number of steps is calculated automatically. This illustration shows contours applied using the To Center option; as with the Inside option, open paths cannot take a To Center contour.

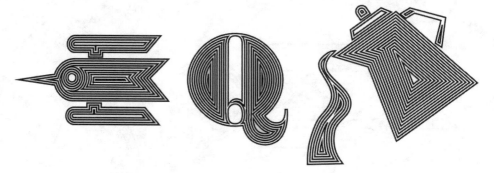

Setting Contour Colors

Controlling the progression of color between your original object and the colors of the Contour effect is important in creating great illustrations; CorelDRAW is a wonderful drawing program, but *you* are the artist! You can set color in several different ways, specify a *nonlinear color rotation*, control the pen and fill colors, and even set fountain fill colors for individual contour steps.

Color Rotation Options

A default contour creates fill and outline colors in a steady progression between the base object and the final contour (the End object if contours were blends). However, you can rotate these colors to create rainbow contours and other special effects. To do this, choose either Clockwise Contour Colors or Counterclockwise Contour Colors, as shown here, which has the effect of applying fill and outline colors based on color positions located around a color wheel—red, orange, yellow... you get the idea!

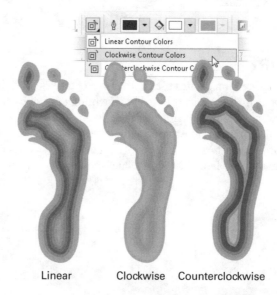

Linear   Clockwise   Counterclockwise

Outline Color

The Outline Color option—the pop-up mini palette directly to the right of the color rotation options on the Property Bar—sets the outline color of the last contour in the effect, meaning the colors change steadily from your original to the last contour object. To set the outline color, click the Outline Color selector and choose a color. If your object doesn't have an outline color applied, this option still displays black as the default color, but no color will be applied to your contours.

Fill Color

If you want to wow your audience, definitely play with Fill Color to create significant changes along the steps of a contour. It's the mini-palette directly to the right of Outline Color on the Property Bar. To set the fill color, click the Fill Color selector and choose a color. If an object doesn't have a fill, although you can set a contour color, the contour will not have a fill. This creates an interesting effect if you have outline width and colors applied to the base object, but with no fill and no outline set for the base object to which you want to apply a contour—it's an exercise in artistic futility.

Creating Special Effects With Contours

Because Contour effect intermediate steps travel concentrically from the control object to the end of the effect, you can accomplish certain things that would take hours or perhaps not be possible using other tools and effects. For example, a Blend effect is simply the wrong choice of tool when you want interior shading in an object, because when you scale an irregularly shaped object (such as the letter *Q*), it scales disproportionately. As a result, when you blend, say, a *Q* to a smaller *Q* you've centered inside the larger *Q*, the intermediate blend objects scale different areas disproportionately. Therefore, a key to creating smoothly shaded objects is to use a Contour effect with many steps and a small Offset value. Here's a sample recipe: With the Artistic Text tool, type the letter **Q** (uppercase), choose a bold font such as Futura, use black as the fill color, and make it about 200 points in height. With the Interactive Contour tool, choose Inside on the Property Bar, set the Offset to about 0.001", create about 150 steps, and choose white as the fill color. The result is a very smoothly shaded piece of artwork that will print beautifully with no banding, because 150 intermediate steps from black to white within relatively small objects is just about the upper limit for laser printers and most inkjet printers.

However, a smooth contour transition might not always be your artistic goal; by using no fill but only an outline width on objects, a small number of steps, and a relatively high Offset value, you can indeed design topographic maps, magnetic fields, and other illustrations in the technical vein. In Figure 14-10, you can see an object with the top edge suggesting a landscape—created by using the Roughen Brush. The Contour objects are white lines, they have a high Offset value so they're clearly visible, and then the Effects | Add Perspective command was used to suggest Contour effects that have depth in the illustration. The text also has a Contour effect; a linear transparency was then added from top to bottom.

Fountain Fill Color

Contour effects also support the use of certain fountain fills in linear, radial, conical, and square modes. The Last Color Fill selector on the Property Bar can be used to change the last color in the contour of the original object, which can produce some very artsy effects.

FIGURE 14-10 Make smoothly shaded Contour effects or make the effect obvious; the technique you choose depends on the illustration assignment.

If you've applied a fountain fill to your original object, the color fill properties of the contour group are also applied with the same fill type. If you've contoured an object that has a fountain fill, use the Property Bar to set the last color in the Contour fountain fill; if the fountain fill uses multiple colors, the Contour fountain fill ignores the transition colors. If an object doesn't include a fountain fill, the Last Color Fill selector on the Property Bar is unavailable.

Controlling Contour Acceleration

Just like blends, contour acceleration options have the effect of either increasing or decreasing the rate at which the contour group objects change shape (and color) as they progress between the control object and the final object. You can choose Object Acceleration and Color Acceleration options on the Property Bar when a Counter effect object is selected in the drawing window. When a default contour is applied, both these settings are at a default midpoint—the contour objects change in color and size evenly. Change both acceleration rates simultaneously (the default) while the two options are linked, or change them individually by clicking the Unlink Acceleration option, shown next.

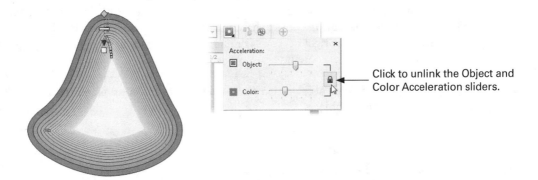

Click to unlink the Object and
Color Acceleration sliders.

To access acceleration options, click the Object and Color Acceleration button in the
Property Bar and then adjust the slider controls and/or choose the Unlink option. Moving
the sliders to the left of the center position reduces (or slows) the acceleration rate between the
control object and the final contour in the effect. Moving the sliders to the right increases the
acceleration. While the two acceleration options are unlinked, changing the object acceleration
affects only the progression of shapes in the contour group. Figure 14-11 shows the effects of
increasing and decreasing acceleration.

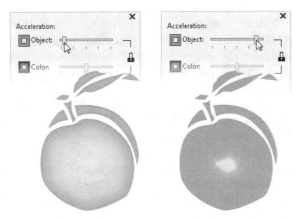

Object Acceleration decreased;
slider moved left of center.

Object Acceleration increased;
slider moved right of center.

FIGURE 14-11 Acceleration rates can dramatically change the look of an object that has a
Contour effect.

When the sliders are unlinked, changing the Color Acceleration slider affects only the change in progression of the fill and outline colors between the control object and the final contour in the effect, leaving the object shape acceleration unchanged. Moving the sliders (or interactive markers) left or right decreases or increases acceleration, respectively, between the control object and the final contour.

Tip   Changing the Color Acceleration slider also affects the color properties applied to outline paths of objects.

Using the Contour Docker

Although the Contour tool is the most intuitive way of applying contours, you can still apply them using the old Contour docker as an alternative. The Contour docker has been redesigned in DRAW X8 to offer you *all,* not just some, of the Property Bar options.

To open the Contour docker, choose Effects | Contour or choose Window | Dockers | Effects | Contour (CTRL-F9). The docker's options are organized a little differently than on the Property Bar, but the same options can be found there. One advantage to using the docker is that, as with the Blend docker, you can choose all your options before applying them.

In this chapter, you've seen where to find the options for controlling and customizing blends and contours, so you know where things are. However, just like with operating heavy machinery, don't take prescription medicines an hour before beginning. And when you turn the key, the real fun begins! Dig into Blend and Contour effects; add shading to simple objects to make creating workaday illustrations an inspiring endeavor and to reap the reward of the automation that's possible within CorelDRAW. Blends and contours are some of the best ways to generate scores of similarly shaped objects, so fill your page with little drawings to make patterns, charts... you name it.

Chapter 15 takes a severe right turn, as we head into color models—those funny initials CMYK, HSL, and so on that you see when you begin to define a color in one of the Window | Color Palettes and the Color Management settings for your document under the Tools menu. After all you've learned so far—and all you intend to create in the future—it's sort of a given that you want the colors you print to be similar to those you see in CorelDRAW's workspace. And you don't want your web graphics to look as though they were taken from the Sunday funny papers. Color management is your next stop in Chapter 15, and it's your insurance that what you create is what you get (WYSIWYG, or something like that).

15 Mixing and Matching with Digital Color Models

Put away those crayons and fling that color wheel out on the front lawn. *Digital* color obeys *none* of the rules we were taught in school, and you use digital color models to fill objects that CorelDRAW, in turn, displays on your monitor. Defining colors, *period,* is an art that even professionals occasionally struggle with. The good news is that CorelDRAW makes applying the color you have in mind as simple as can be, through an extensive collection of industry-standard swatches, intuitive color models, and color mixers that make color definition more like play than work.

If you've ever been faced with picking out a tie to match your shirt at 6:30 A.M. in a dimly lit closet, you'll appreciate the importance of choosing harmonious and intriguing color schemes. Similarly, your color work from DRAW is out there for the public to evaluate; this chapter guides you through the digital process of choosing colors and ensuring that what you print is what you see onscreen. You want your colors to be *consistent* from the screen to the saved file to the final output.

Digital Color Terms and Definitions

Let's say you've created a rectangle on your page; by default, it has no fill. There are two quick ways to fill it. You can left-click on a color on the color palette, which offers a nice selection of preset colors. But let's say you want a specific color. If so, you double-click the Fill icon on the Status Bar (either the swatch or the bucket icon), shown in the following illustration, and you can then see (and work in) the Uniform Fill dialog as long as the selected object has no fill. If it's already filled with a fill *other* than Uniform, click the Uniform Fill style button at the top of the Edit Fill dialog. You're presented with a combination of interface palettes with tabs for models, mixers, and palettes.

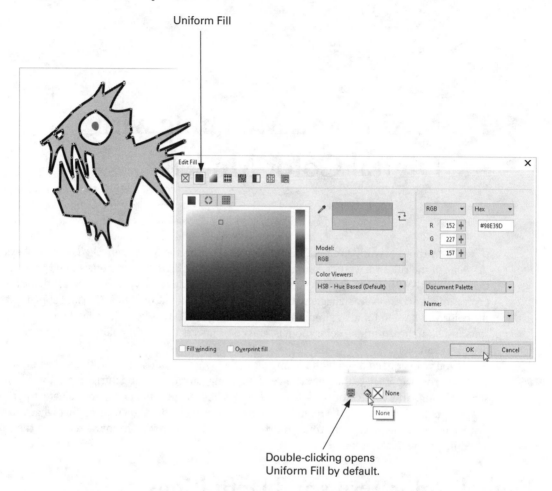

Uniform Fill

Double-clicking opens
Uniform Fill by default.

Palettes are predefined collections of color swatches, which is pretty self-explanatory. Then you have mixers; this is *not* a self-explanatory area, and it's covered later in this chapter. Finally, you have models, an area worthy of some serious discussion here.

The first set of terms, which sets the stage for color exploration in this chapter, describes digital color and also defines the real-world colors you apply to paper, plastic, and so on, giving you a handle on the seemingly overwhelming variety of attributes that colors have. The terms are somewhat interrelated; when you change a parameter for one, most of the time you change a parameter for another.

Color Model A *model* is a representation of something that's intangible or too ungainly in other respects to directly manipulate. For example, a child plays with a model airplane because this representation fits in his bedroom better than an actual airplane, and the passengers feel safer. *Color models* are used in CorelDRAW to make dealing with the relationships between colors easy; without a model of the intangible qualities of the light spectrum, choosing the colors you need would be quite a challenge. Additionally, a color model *scales* all the available colors you have when working in CorelDRAW and other programs, in the same way a model airplane can be rotated to see all its sides—a task that's hard to do with a full-sized airplane. Today, using a 24-bit color space, users have at least 16.7 million possible colors from which to choose in design work. There are still more color values if you work with a 48-bit color space, but we're getting off track here. A color model makes color selection much easier than choosing colors from a palette containing, for example, 16.7 million swatches (if such a thing were possible).

Color Space   Think of a color model as a piece of architecture: it's a structure. Now, if you were having a house built, your structure would need to take up space, usually on some land. A *color space* is the "land" for your color model "architecture." Different color models require different color spaces. To get off of this analogy kick here, let's say you have a CorelDRAW file to print from your inkjet printer. Inkjet printers use the CMYK color model as the basis for reproducing the colors you've used to fill objects within your document (CMYK color is covered later in this chapter). Unfortunately, digital color, the color you see on your monitor, has its structure in a fairly wide color space; RGB colors have a wider range of expression (more possible colors) than the CMYK color space. What can happen (unless you read this chapter carefully) is that some colors you use in your CorelDRAW document look fine onscreen, but they don't print as you anticipate. The reason is that the CMYK color space is smaller than the color space of your monitor, and some of your original design's colors are *clipped* when printed; they've been arbitrarily moved to a color that's *similar* to the color you used, or they just don't print, or you get a nice splotch of muddy brown on the printed page. You certainly want more control over how a CorelDRAW design prints, and that's why CorelDRAW offers a CMYK color picker and also a gamut alarm. *Gamut* is a term that means *the expressible range of color.* In other words, colors that fall into a specific color space. When you choose a color that falls out of range of the color space, it's called an *out-of-gamut* color, and these colors won't print correctly because they are built on a part of the land you don't own.

File Color Capability   If the extent of your CorelDRAW work is to create CDR files, print them, and save them, you have no concerns about a file format that can hold all the colors you've picked and applied to objects. The CDR file format will retain the colors you've used. But if you intend to export a design to bitmap file format, different bitmap file formats have different ceilings of color capability, which relates to color space in many ways. TIFF images, as written by CorelDRAW, for example, can contain 16.7 million unique colors, and this file format can be written to the RGB color model, the CMYK color model, and even some color models such as Grayscale that offer no color at all but instead only brightness values. On the other hand, GIF images continue to be used for the web, and these images can only hold 256 unique colors—pretty meager when compared to 16.7 million colors—so you need to know how to design using only 256 colors, at most.

The sections that follow provide a step-by-step guide to understanding the structure of digital color and the space in which color resides, manipulating color models in CorelDRAW to define the colors you want, and matching color values a client gives you over the phone.

Subtractive and Additive Color Models

Within the world of color models, there are two distinct categories: *subtractive* and *additive* color models. You, the designer, use both: when you print something, you use a device that uses the subtractive color model, and when you design for the web or an onscreen presentation, you use an additive color model. How these models are similar, how they differ, and how you access these models in CorelDRAW is the subject of the following sections.

Subtractive Color Models

From the moment the first caveman depicted an antelope on his family room wall, humankind has been using a *subtractive* color model for painting. Subtractive color is what many artists were brought up on, mixing physical pigments—and as we all know, when you mix a lot of different pigments together, you eventually get black. This is what the traditional subtractive color model is all about: you *remove* part of the visible spectrum as you overlay one color on another. CMYK is a subtractive color model used in commercial printing, and in theory, if you put cyan, magenta, and yellow pigments together at full intensity, you should get black... but you don't. Black ink is abbreviated *K* in CMYK. It's shorthand for "key," the color printing plate to which the other colors are registered, or "keyed." In addition to making it possible to obtain a true black color, using black ink instead of heavy mixtures of CMY saves on overall ink costs and speeds ink drying times

---

 Note If you take your kids to a family restaurant that has crayons and menus that the kids color on, notice that the crayon colors are not cyan, magenta, and yellow. More than likely, they're red, yellow, and blue, and if you're lucky, green also comes in the little box. You might rightfully wonder why commercial presses use CMYK and your kids are using red, yellow, and blue. The answer is that red, yellow, and blue have traditionally been the primary subtractive colors used by painters throughout history—*before* scientific color theory proved that cyan is more of a pure subtractive primary than blue and that magenta describes a component of subtractive color better than red. Green was introduced as a primary subtractive color because of the human mind's perceptual bias that green is a *perceptual* primary color, although it's not used at all in today's commercial printing.

The RGB Additive Color Model

The *additive* color model describes color using *light*, not pigments. A combination of the primary additive colors—red, green, and blue—when combined in equal amounts at full intensity, produces white, not black, as subtractive CMYK color does. RGB is a common additive color model, and it is not at all intuitive to use as an artist; however, CorelDRAW has different views of the RGB color model that makes it easy and intuitive to work with.

Because a color model only does one thing—*it shows a mathematical relationship between values that are intangible*—you can use any color model to visualize the relationship among red, green, and blue, with the goal being to make color picking and color relationships as painless as possible to perform! Figure 15-1 shows the default view of the Uniform Fill dialog. When you first install CorelDRAW, it's optimized for commercial printing, both with your view of the drawing window and the CMYK color model offered on the Uniform Fill dialog. If you do web work and no print work, this chapter walks you through how to customize your onscreen display and your color choices for the RGB color model.

Let's look at these controls in Figure 15-1 one at a time. It's quite likely that a color attribute you're looking for right now can be defined in this dialog.

- **Color Model**   This selector drop-down list includes CMYK, CMY (as explained earlier, black is more a part of the printing process than a part of the color model), RGB, HSB, HSL, Grayscale, YIQ, LAB, and Registration. These models are covered later in this section. If you're in a hurry, CMYK should be chosen for in-gamut colors for printing, and RGB is the color model for doing nonprinted work.
- **Color field and Hue slider**   Here is something tricky, a little confusing, and totally wonderful on the Model tab. A model is a representation of a hard-to-grasp thing or idea. Simply because the default color model is CMYK, there's no real reason to offer a CMYK

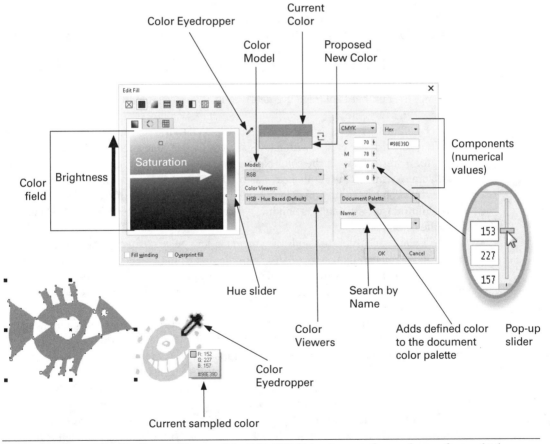

FIGURE 15-1   The Uniform Fill part of the Edit Fill dialog is one of several areas from which you can pick colors in CorelDRAW.

color picker to accompany the color model: CMYK is an intangible item; a model of it is best represented by what works *for the user*. The *HSB* Color field and slider make a terrific and intuitive mechanism for quickly defining colors, even though you're not *choosing* HSB colors. To manipulate brightness, you drag the little rectangle up or down in the Color field. To manipulate saturation, you drag left or right; obviously, you can navigate both brightness and saturation at the same time. The Hue slider to the right of the color field sets the predominant, recognizable attribute of the color you're picking. Users generally set the hue first, and then play with the amounts of saturation and brightness.

- **Current Color/New Color**   The color well at the top shows you the current color of the selected object on the page. The bottom color well shows you any changes you've made, and the two together provide a convenient way to compare color changes. You can also swap these colors by clicking the little circular arrow pattern icon directly to the right of these fields.

- **Components**   The field on the right provides a numerical breakdown of the current color, as expressed in the components of the current color model. Therefore, in Figure 15-1, you can see that the current color is purplish, and if you choose CMYK from the Components area drop-down list, you'll see this color's closest numerical equivalent in CMYK color mode is C: 70, M: 78, Y: 0, and K: 0. However, these values are not static; in fact, when you click the icon to the right of any value (the icon that looks like a slider), a slider does indeed pop up, and you can adjust the color by dragging any component value up or down. This gives you a more precise adjustment of the filled object's color; you can also insert your cursor into the number field (it's a live field), double-click to select the entire value, and then type in a new value.

- **Search by Name**   The color palette, the strip docked to the right of the drawing window, contains colors that are tagged with names such as Desert Blue and Mint Green. To search quickly for a preset color on the color palette, you can choose from the drop-down list, or begin typing a name in the Name field—as you type more characters, the dialog narrows the search. If you have a custom palette loaded, you can't search it using the Model tab of the Uniform Color dialog; you conduct a search using the Palettes tab, the third tab above the color field.

- **Add To Palette**   This button adds the current color you've created to the document's color palette. You can then retrieve this color directly from the palette at the bottom of the interface at any time without visiting the Uniform Fill dialog. This is one way to save a custom color; see "Using the Color Styles Docker" later in this chapter for a more feature-filled way to save a custom color.

- **Color Viewers**   This flyout offers a choice of color selection interfaces for your chosen color model. To show the components of color models, the unique structures of the various color models necessarily need to be graphically represented. Some color models such as HSB are blessed with a structure that is intuitive for us mere mortals to use; others are less intuitive. The next illustration shows the RGB model with various viewers selected. Try the RGB – 3D Additive viewer; you'll hate it—although the model itself is mathematically sound, it just isn't user friendly and a slider is necessary *in addition to* the 3D picking cube because this model is just plain hard to visualize. At the top left is the RGB color model, except this time the HSB – Hue Based viewer has been selected from Color Viewers drop-down list. This viewer is perhaps the best all-purpose color picker from which you can choose colors in any color model. Again, try it; it's very easy to get the color you need quickly. At the bottom left is the RGB color model displayed as the HSB – Wheel Based color viewer. A variation of this color picker is used in Corel Painter; it, too, makes defining colors a joy instead of a chore.

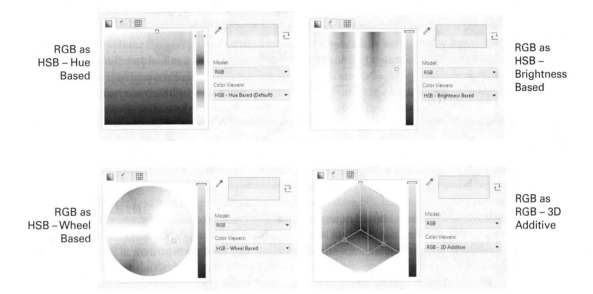

RGB as HSB – Hue Based

RGB as HSB – Brightness Based

RGB as HSB – Wheel Based

RGB as RGB – 3D Additive

The HSB Additive Color Model

The HSB color model is to designers what the RGB color model is to software engineers; HSB serves the non-programming community for intuitively choosing colors. HSB and RGB occupy the same color space but use different components. HSB is the acronym for *hue, saturation,* and *brightness.* It's occasionally called HSV (*V* for *value*) or HSL (*L* for *lightness*), but it all boils down to a user-friendly model for working with digital color. HSB was created by Dr. Alvy Smith, co-founder of Pixar Studios and an accomplished artist. The HSB color model has the same number of colors as the RGB color model. However, HSB organizes the relationship between color differently, and in a friendlier fashion, than RGB. Here are the HSB color components:

- **Hue**   The distinguishing characteristic of color. When you tell a friend, "Oh, that's a very nice blue tie" or "The TV picture is a little orange, isn't it?" you're describing the *hue* component of the color. Hue is usually expressed in degrees on a hue wheel; technically, hue is determined by light wavelength.
- **Saturation**   The presence of color, the purity, the predominance of a hue. We often use the saturation component when we talk about how juicy the colors are in a photograph. If a photo or drawing has a lot of noticeable blues, the blue hue is said to be quite saturated in that color. Conversely, colors you often see on today's household appliances, such as a toaster oven the manufacturer calls *Oyster, Putty, Ivory,* or *Bisque,* are neutral; they have no dominant hue, and they have little saturation. The pages in this chapter have no saturation.

- **Brightness**   The amount of illumination a color has. Brightness, as described in digital color terms, is somewhat elusive, but an analogy from traditional painting with pigments (subtractive color) provides some clarity. When you mix a pure color with white, you increase its brightness; in industries where color description is critical (fashion design, house paints) bright colors are a *tint* of a pure color, also called a *pastel color.* Then there are darker colors: a *shade* is the mixture of a color with black. Mixing with white increases lightness, whereas mixing with black reduces it. In both digital and traditional color, mixing black, white, or a perfectly neutral value in between black and white leaves hue unchanged.

LAB Color

LAB is both a color space *and* a color model. CorelDRAW offers LAB as a color model; however, LAB—the color space—is device independent, and, therefore, it can be used to describe colors you see in the drawing window, on a physical plastic bottle of soda, or even on a basketball. The Commission Internationale de l'Eclairage (the CIE, the International Commission on Illumination) was established about a century ago as a worldwide body for standardizing and exchanging color specifications. They created the LAB color model. It successfully replicates the spectrum of human vision, and this is why if you check out the color space of CIELAB on a scientific website, you'll note that there is a disproportionately large area of green in LAB color space. This is because the human eye responds to this region of the visible spectrum more strongly than other hues. LAB is modeled after one channel of *luminance,* one color channel (named *A*) that runs from magenta to green, and another channel (named *B*) from blue to yellow. When you use LAB to describe a color, you're (theoretically) assured of color consistency. LAB, the color space, is frequently used by software engineers as a conversion space; when you want, for example, to convert an RGB bitmap to CMYK, the LAB color space is larger than both, and, as a consequence, colors are not driven out of gamut when the pixels in such a bitmap are reassigned new component values.

YIQ

The YIQ color model is similar in its components to LAB color; however, its purpose is for working with designs and text that are "video legal," as defined by the National Television Standards Committee (NTSC). YIQ's components are one channel of luminosity and two of *chromaticity* (color). Standard definition TV is brighter than PC monitors, the color range is smaller, and if you get an assignment to draw a logo for a commercial, you'd use this color model.

Grayscale

You use the Grayscale color model (which actually has no hue) if you're designing for one-color commercial printing and for laser-print output. You might find that a color design you've drawn doesn't look right if printed to a laser printer: blue areas seem too faint and reds look much too dark. By using a Grayscale model, you take the influence of hue out of the color equation, and what you see onscreen is what you get on paper.

Registration

You do not design with this color model; it's only one color. Registration is used for an object when you want that object to be printed on all commercial press plates, including spot color plates. As the name suggests, Registration applied, for example, to hairline paths around the border of a design helps a commercial pressman to see and keep all the printing plates in Registration when he or she reviews progressive proofs of the plates.

The following sections bring relevance to all of these explanations of color; you want to put color to *use* in CorelDRAW, so it's only fitting to move to where the palettes and other features are *located!*

Using Color-Related Dockers

If you've been doing some independent exploring, you might have discovered the Edit Fill dialog and the multitude of fill types, including Uniform. But the Edit Fill dialog is not a persistent part of the interface. The good news is that it's not supposed to be; three dockers—covered next—are used to handle almost all commands that specify uniform color: the Color docker, the Color Styles docker, and the Object Properties docker. Let's take a look at these essential items.

Using the Color Docker

The Color docker, shown next, is extremely convenient to work with; essentially, it's the Uniform Fill dialog, just smaller, dockable, and persistent in the workspace. When an object is selected, you can specify whether the color applies to the outline *or* fill color of the object, and any changes to colors are immediately applied. To open the Color docker, choose Window | Dockers | Color. Unlike Uniform Fill in the Edit Fill box, you don't need to have an object selected to call it.

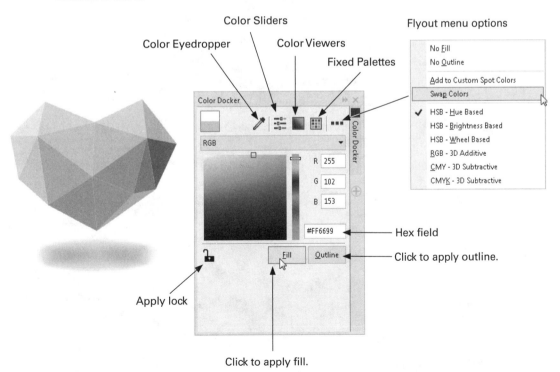

The Color docker is organized into three areas—Color Viewers and Color Sliders (the same as discussed earlier on the Uniform Fill dialog) and Fixed Palettes (actually, they were never broken). You can display each area by clicking one of three buttons at the top of the docker. Each area is geared toward specifying a color using its unique parameters and to then apply that color to the fill and/or outline of a selected object. Here's how each of the three areas is used for specifying color:

- **Color Sliders** By default, CMYK is CorelDRAW's color space, but you can easily change that to RGB in the New Document dialog. You can mix the components of any color model you choose from the drop-down selector at the top by dragging the sliders or entering RGB (red/green/blue) values in the number fields. Notice that the sliders are in color and change dynamically, instantly updating to show you how much of a component affects the overall color as well as the relationship between one component and the others.

 Note Hexadecimal values are shown under the color component fields for RGB colors. This feature is handy when you or a coder needs to use the hex value of the colors you choose for coding web page backgrounds and such. You can copy the hex code by swiping to select it in the box and pressing CTRL-C. Then press CTRL-V to paste the value into a text document.

Color Sliders tab

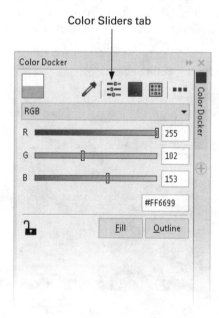

- **Color Viewers**   The color viewers (occasionally called *color pickers* in other programs) on the Color docker basically offer the same options as the Color Viewers drop-drop in the Edit Fill dialog when Uniform Fill is chosen.

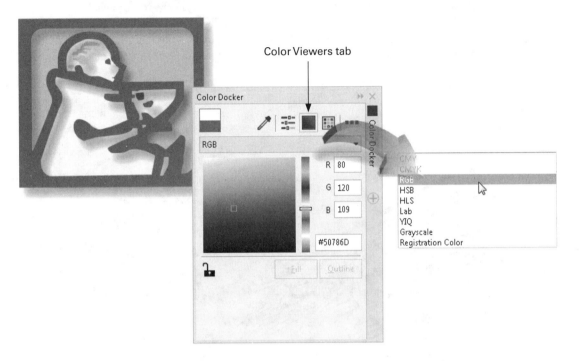

Color Viewers tab

- **Fixed Palettes**   Use this area to choose a color from a swatch collection from vendors such as PANTONE, Trumatch, Focoltone, and others from the palette selector drop-down. Use the flyout options menu to display a color by name; if you have Tooltips turned on, the names of the swatches appear when you hover your cursor over them. The Tint slider at the bottom of this docker is dimmed if you've loaded Uniform Colors or any user or custom palette; this slider is for creating a mathematically precise color tint of an industry-standard solid color, such as any swatches in the PANTONE metallic-coated collection. Solid colors can make use of tints. Tints produce a lighter-appearing halftone of the solid-color ink on paper. Therefore, you can use this Tint slider with solid predefined colors, but not with process colors. Process colors are created in the physical world through separate passes of C, M, Y, and K pigments and, as a consequence, it's impractical to tint the four components. However, CorelDRAW professionals make spot colors for designs by applying a tint to a solid. The technique works because a spot color always requires a separate printing plate. To set up a tint of a solid color quickly, you can click-hold on a swatch and then release the mouse button after the flyout appears. Then you can choose from percentages in 10 percent increments, from solid to white. Tint flyouts appear only from the document palette; click the tint on the flyout, and then click Fill or Outline to apply it.

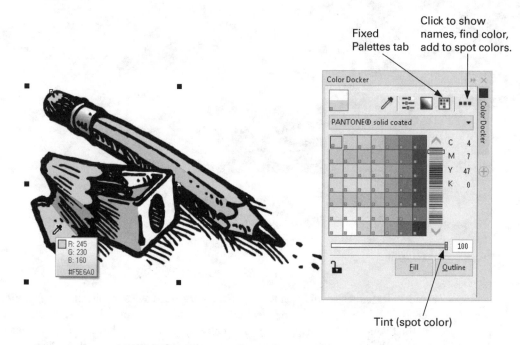

Fixed Palettes tab

Click to show names, find color, add to spot colors.

Tint (spot color)

Tip Swatches on the Color docker are "drag and drop." You can click-drag a color onto an object, selected or unselected, to instantly fill it. If you have good skills with your mouse or other input device, you can set an outline color for an object by dragging and then dropping a color swatch on the edge of an object, even if the object has no outline attributes; the action of drag-dropping a color forces the object to take on a Hairline outline.

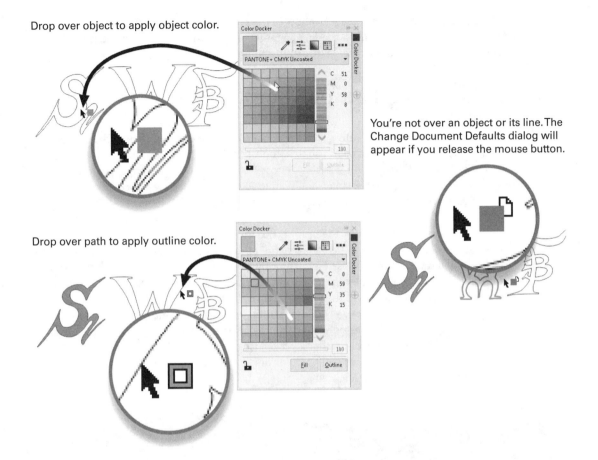

Drop over object to apply object color.

You're not over an object or its line. The Change Document Defaults dialog will appear if you release the mouse button.

Drop over path to apply outline color.

Finding and Applying Fixed Colors (and Tints)

To demonstrate some of the power of the Color docker, the upcoming tutorial shows you how to find a commercial color—specifically a PANTONE color. If you're familiar with physical swatch books, you know that PANTONE has zillions of unique colors, and an equivalent zillion different sets of numbers to name them.

Before beginning, understand that PANTONE is in the business of color and selling color swatch books. It is not reasonable, therefore, to expect 2016's Color of the Year, Serenity, to be offered in its precise value for Textile Cotton Extended values. The good news, though, is that CorelDRAW can automatically choose the *closest match* to any value you type into the Find Color dialog. Additionally, the author went to Pantone.com to view this year's colors and discovered the RGB, CMYK, Hex (web) values as well as the closest match to print on coated paper.

Open Shuz.cdr now and you'll learn how to match numerical values to printed colors, how to work with a tint (and add a shade) of a target color to the document palette, and how to apply colors to elements above the picture in the composition.

Tutorial # Dyeing a Pair of Shoes

1. With Shuz.cdr open, choose Window | Dockers | Color.
2. Click the Color Palettes button, click the Show Color Palettes, and then click the drop-down list. From the list of color palettes, choose Spot | PANTONE | Previous version | FASHION + HOME cotton selector. Choose Show Color Names from the "more options" flyout (...). The TCX suffix stands for Textile Cotton eXtended swatch collection.
3. Note that the number for the Serenity color is typed as editable text on the drawing. With the Text tool, highlight 15-3919 directly above the Plus series line in the text block. Press CTRL-C to copy the numbers to the Clipboard.
4. On the Color docker, click the flyout menu—those three dots directly to the right of the Color Palettes button. Choose Find Color by Name, as shown in the next illustration.
5. A pop-up box appears: place the cursor in the field in the box (the cursor becomes a text insertion cursor) and then press CTRL-V. If an exact match can be found, the Color docker will automatically add the suffix to the color name. If by some chance the box will not accept the pasted value, type the value in manually. In this case, an exact match cannot be found, but rather a very close one, so no suffix is added.
6. Click OK, and the swatches on the Color docker move and the closest match to the color you asked for is highlighted.

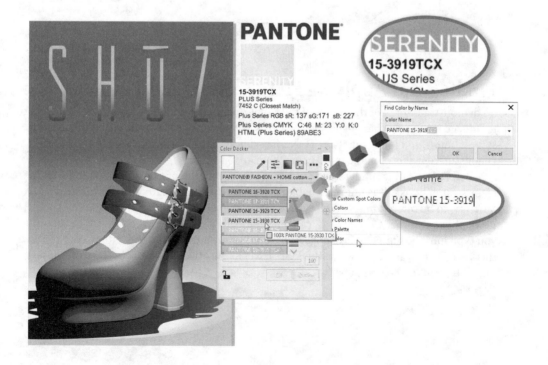

7. Add the current color swatch from the docker to the horizontal document palette at the bottom of the drawing of the shoes by click-dragging it. When you need lighter tones of the Color of the Year for highlights in the drawing, choose the base color, and then use the Tint slider on the Color docker to lighten the color, as shown in the following illustration. From the New Color swatch in the docker, drag a couple of lighter tints to the document palette to add them.

8. The opposite of "tint" in color language is "shade." In a subtractive medium such as physical pigments, a tint is achieved by adding white to a color, and a shade is created by adding black. Therefore, if you switch to the Color Sliders view of the color spectrum, you can drag the black (K) slider a little to the right to add black to the underlying color formula. This will come in as an indispensable technique when you want to replace areas of the shoe drawing with tints and shades within a gradient fountain fill.

9. Using the new swatches you just added to the document palette at the bottom of the drawing, drag and drop them onto various shapes that make up the shoe. There are a few areas that use a color gradient. To recolor a gradient, you need to first click on a color node using the Fill tool to display the color nodes. Drag the appropriate color swatches onto the individual color nodes that make up the gradient.

10. Be patient—or move on to other chapters in this *Official Guide*—because it might take as much as a half hour to recolor most of the shoe to shades of one of 2016's top colors. Feel free to leave the inside of the shoe its original color, and check out the accent colors for Serenity on Pantone.com, especially if you want a two-tone or three-tone expensive shoe.

Using the Color Palette Manager Docker

The Color Palette Manager, shown in Figure 15-2, gives you the option to manage multiple palettes and palette colors. To open the Color Palette Manager docker, choose Window | Dockers | Color Palette Manager. The docker is structured as a tree directory so you can view palettes by folder as your browse, and it includes handy palette command buttons.

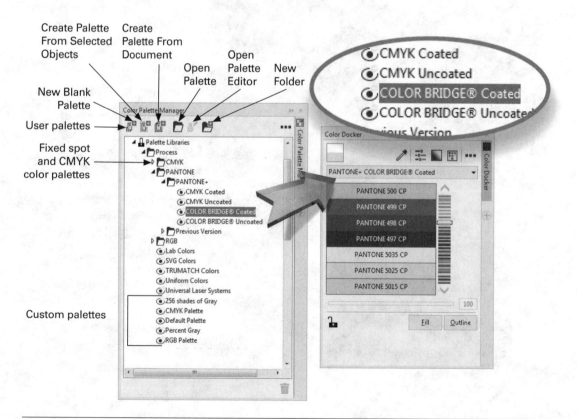

FIGURE 15-2 Choose from a wide selection of palettes with the Color Palette Manager docker.

As you can see in Figure 15-2, any color palette can be accessed by opening its eye icon (clicking it). By default, the palette will dock to the right, vertically, of the current color palette docked to the right of the drawing window, but you can undock it by dragging just above the flyout arrow at top—three faint dots represent a grip for the palette. Palettes remember their previous configuration, so if you've undocked a palette, closed it, and want to reopen it in a subsequent DRAW session, it will appear as you left it, docked or undocked.

Using Fixed and Custom Palettes

A *fixed* palette—such as the PANTONE palette demonstrated in the previous tutorial—is a noneditable collection of ink colors prepared by an ink manufacturer, such as a specific process or spot color. Fixed palettes are like small color catalogs. Even though you'll likely use only a handful of different fixed palettes, version X8 supports the latest available to support Corel's global community of users.

Using Fixed Palettes

Each fixed palette has its own special characteristics. Some palettes comprise spot and process ink colors, whereas others cater to web graphics. Using a specific color palette enables you to specify colors within the capabilities of the reproduction or display technique being used.

While browsing the fixed palettes within the Palette Libraries drop-down menu, you'll notice that CorelDRAW features an enormous number of choices. Here's a quick rundown on each of the fixed palettes available:

- **SVG Colors**   This palette in the collection is specifically formulated for applying Scalable Vector Graphics (SVG) colors using RGB values according to the standardized W3 consortium. For specific information, visit http://www.w3c.org/TR/SVG11/types. html#ColorKeywords.
- **PANTONE**   PANTONE is perhaps the largest color-matching system in the publishing industry. CorelDRAW includes all of PANTONE's digital ink collections, including coated and uncoated versions for spot inks, as well as process colors. DRAW also features PANTONE's metallic, pastel, and other palettes.
- **HKS**   This palette collection consists of spot ink colors based on CMY combinations varied with black. HKS palettes include HKS Colors, HKS E, HKS Z, HKS N, and HKS K.
- **Focoltone**   This 750-color palette designed by Focoltone reduces the need for color trapping using standardized CMYK screen percentages.
- **Trumatch**   The Trumatch process-color palette comprises more than 2,000 easily printable colors. Trumatch has specifically customized its color matching system to suit the digital color industry using the Computer Electronic Prepress System (CEPS). The palette comprises 40 tints and shades of each hue. Black is varied in 6 percent increments.
- **Web Safe**   The Web Safe palette contains the 216 colors of the Web Safe color model. Colors are defined using the hexadecimal scheme, meaning one of six shades of each color (red, green, and blue) are combined to create each color in the palette.
- **TOYO and DIC**   The TOYO and DIC color-matching systems are widely used throughout Asia—especially Japan. Each system contains its own numbering system and collection of different process colors. The TOYO collection of colors has been developed using its own process ink colors.

Creating Custom Palettes

CorelDRAW's custom palettes feature lets you create groups of your own defined colors. By creating a custom palette, you can make these color collections available via your onscreen palette as you work or available for later retrieval.

> **Tip** To create custom color palettes from a selection of objects or from all objects in your document, on the Color Palette Manager docker, choose either Create Palette From Selected Objects or Create Palette From Document, the second and third buttons on the top of this docker, respectively. This opens the Save Palette dialog, so you can name and save the colors you've used as a unique palette.

CorelDRAW offers various ways to access custom palettes—via dialogs, the Color docker, or an open color palette. The fastest way is to click the flyout button on the default palette (the vertical strip where you've been choosing object and outline colors in this *Official Guide's* examples) and then choose Palette | Open. This opens the Open Palette dialog, and you can now browse through what's available. The pop-up menu where you found Open also includes the Save, Save As, Close, and New Palette commands.

In addition to accessing a bundle of fixed color palettes, the Color Palette Manager docker is the ideal place to manage custom palettes. While editing palette colors, you can also access CorelDRAW's other color resources.

To explore this for yourself, use these steps:

1. Open the Palette Editor dialog by choosing Window | Dockers | Color Palette Manager. Choose a palette by first clicking the eye (the visibility) button next to it to display the colors in the palette. Now, not all palettes allow this sort of editing: custom palettes, the document palette, and some of the RGB-themed palettes are all able to be edited. You can then double-click a color in the swatches to open the Palette Editor. To edit an existing custom color, select the color and click Edit Color. The Select Color dialog opens to reveal the color-selection resources.

2. To begin a new palette, click the New Palette button in the Palette Editor dialog to open the New Palette dialog. Enter a name and click Save. Your new palette is automatically opened, but as yet contains no colors.

3. To add colors, click Add Color for access to the Select Color dialog. Proceed by defining your new color and clicking the Add To Palette button. By default, new colors are automatically added.

4. Once your colors have been added, click OK to return to the Palette Editor dialog. If you wish, click to select the new color and enter a unique name in the Name box.

5. To remove a selected color, click Delete Color and confirm your action in the prompt that appears. To reorganize your palette colors, click Sort Colors and choose from Reverse Order, By Name, or By Hue, Brightness, Saturation, RGB Value, or HSB Value.

6. To name or rename an existing color, select the color in the palette, highlight its current name in the Name box, and enter a new name. Existing names are automatically overwritten once a new color is selected.

7. Use the Reset Palette button to restore your palette to its original state before any changes were made, or click OK to accept your changes and close the dialog.

Clearly, there are many ways to mix colors and save them in palettes. Next up is a way to change the *relationship* between colors in an illustration.

Using the Color Styles Docker

In DRAW, using the Color Styles docker is the way to create, name, and apply colors and color *relationships* to objects.

 Note Because all styles are associated with individual documents, you must have at least one document open to use the color tools available in the Color Styles docker.

Color styles are managed completely from within the Color Styles docker, shown in Figure 15-3, which is opened by choosing Window | Dockers | Color Styles. The docker is divided roughly into three areas:

- The Color Style and Harmony drop-downs for existing colors in the document. You can also mix up a new color with no colors on the page.
- The Color Editor. A style can consist of one or more colors. When only one color needs to be adjusted, use the Color Editor.
- The Harmony Editor. This area is where you can change not only a master color in your document (a color that is a color style), but also the relationship between it and other colors in the document that also have color styles. This is perhaps the most interesting part of the Color Styles docker because, as you'll see in the next tutorial, you can make many variations on a design simply by reassigning a predominant color in a color harmony style.

You won't see the Harmony Editor or the Color Editor before you've added colors—what the docker calls *color styles*—to either the Color Styles area or the Harmony Styles area. The text in these boxes is self-explanatory—the benefits to your artwork aren't, so they are addressed in a moment.

Let's begin with a fairly undemanding tutorial, where you are given a drawing and told to change two colors in it. Because the colors are scattered all over the place in the drawing, it's impractical to select each one, or even to use the Find and Replace Edit command to accomplish this given task. Instead, open the file Lots of cubes.cdr, and the following steps walk you through something amazing.

Tutorial Making a Color Style and Changing It

1. Open the file Lots of Cubes.cdr. There is a proliferation of blue, yellow, and red cubes, and guess what? Your boss doesn't like the blue ones. He says, "Make them all yellow or red. Just recolor the blue ones." Bosses like to use the word *just* a lot to belittle the labor of artists; they also like to say, "during your lunch hour," but this is okay. Choose Window | Dockers | Color Styles Docker.

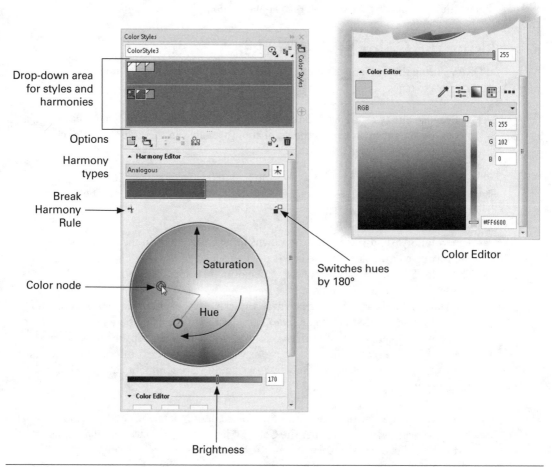

FIGURE 15-3 The Color Styles docker has commands for creating new styles and harmonies.

2. Click the New Color Style button (the orange square with a green dot at its upper right) and then choose New From Document from the menu. This command presents you with a dialog that organizes all the colors in the drawing into harmonic groups of colors. If you want more specific harmony groups, you can drag the Less/More slider below the Group Color Styles Into Harmonies check box (which should be checked). But in this scenario, you'll see that the blues in this drawing all fall into one tidy style, with the diversity slider all the way over to Less.

3. Because the author did this artwork and you didn't, you cannot be sure there are no outlines in this illustration. Click the Create Color Styles From: Both Fill And Outline button. Remember to do this and/or click Object Outline (color) in your own work with the Color Styles docker. Your success depends on whether or not drawings have outline widths. Click OK, as shown in this illustration, and then it's on to color harmonies next.

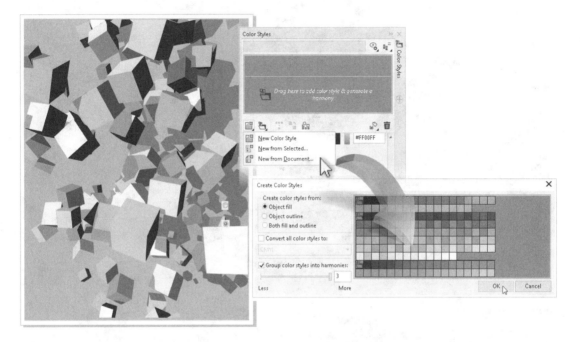

4. Click the Harmony folder that precedes all the swatches on the list, as shown in the following illustration. This is key: the Harmony Editor shows color markers for every color in the style, but, by default, these markers can be moved independently of one another... which makes recoloring all the blue objects to red or yellow a logistical nightmare. However, once the folder icon called out in the illustration is clicked

(selected), you can move all the markers to a new location on the color wheel, and each value will be in proportion to the others.

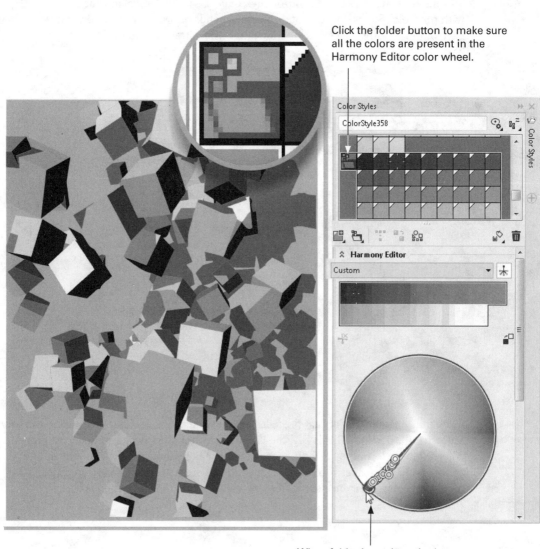

Click the folder button to make sure all the colors are present in the Harmony Editor color wheel.

When folder icon above is chosen, you can drag any color marker to move them all.

5. Here's the fun part: drag a marker over to the area on the color wheel slightly between yellow and orange. Impressive, isn't it? Also try moving all the markers to the red hue. In the following illustration, there is no blue in the image. Your boss should be happier than he usually appears to be, and *you* learned a new trick to speed up humdrum work!

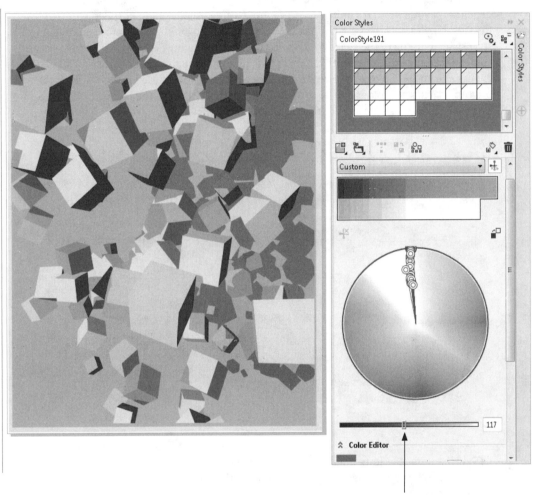

You can elect to brighten all the colors in the style proportionately.

Introducing the New Color Harmony

The parent/child relationship of what used to be called "Master Colors" in previous versions has been reworked into something more intuitive and faster to use. One example of generating several shades of the same color to make a color style group is the new New Gradient command in the New Harmony drop-down in the Options area of the Color Styles docker, shown next. You need to have at least one color harmony swatch to the right of a color style icon in the Harmony Editor to access the New Gradient command. Once you've selected the New Gradient command, you're presented with options for the number of colors you want in the style, whether these colors are closely or loosely similar in brightness and saturation or very different (Shade Similarity), and whether you want lighter variations, darker, or both. It depends on your work. It's quite easy to generate three or four gradient styles and then use the Color Styles docker as a color palette, selecting objects on the page and then dragging a style swatch on top of the shape to color it. Once your drawing is finished, if there's a specific color in the range (the gradient) you don't like, it's easy enough to click that swatch and then change it with the Color Editor. If the entire hue gradient you've used is too warm or the wrong brightness, click the folder icon that precedes the swatches above the Harmony Editor, and then drag all the markers at once to a different hue.

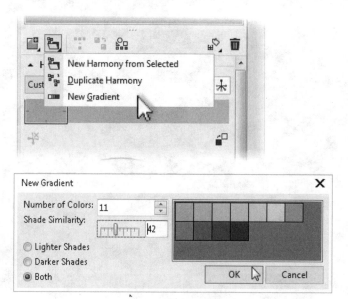

Tip Dragging the joined markers toward the center of the circle desaturates all of them. Dragging them toward the edge of the circle increases the saturation proportionately.

Color Harmonies for Fashion Design

If you've labored for far too long on an illustration of, say, an informal T-shirt, and you'd like to see how the whole color line of T-shirts this season looks, then, once again, this is a job for the Color Styles docker, and the steps are similar to, but not exactly like, the cubes you recolored earlier. Very quickly, open the file Shirt on Hanger.cdr and follow along here.

Tutorial   Changing the Color Harmonies of a Monochrome Drawing

1. With the file Shirt on Hanger.cdr and the Color Styles docker open, from the Options area on the docker, click the far-left drop-down button and choose New From Document.
2. In the dialog, by default, you'll probably notice that because all the colors in the document are minute differences of brightness and saturation, the Create Color Styles dialog wants to lump all the colors together. You want to recolor the shirt hanger to a color very different from the shirt, so drag the Less/More Group Color Styles slider to about 3 in this example. As you can see in this illustration, the silver of the shirt hanger separates beautifully into its own style group, as do the shirt colors.

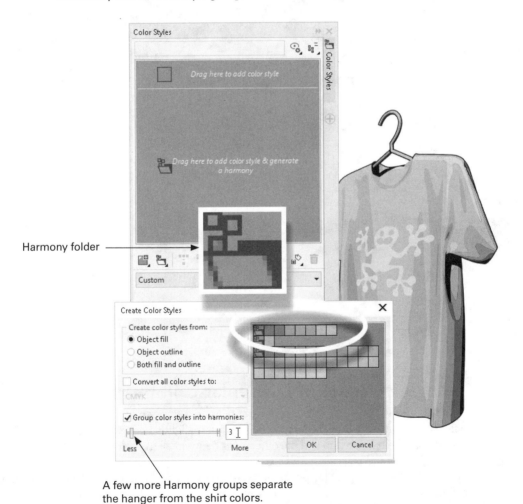

Harmony folder

A few more Harmony groups separate the hanger from the shirt colors.

3. Click OK to return to the Color Styles docker. Click on the top Harmony folder icon, to the far left of the deepest gray color. This selects all the swatches to the right of it in the row.

4. On the Harmony color wheel, click-drag the grouped markers to, say, a dull orange so it looks a little like a gold hanger, thus increasing the price of the shirt. As a bonus, the hanger is now clearly visually separated from the shirt, as you can see here.

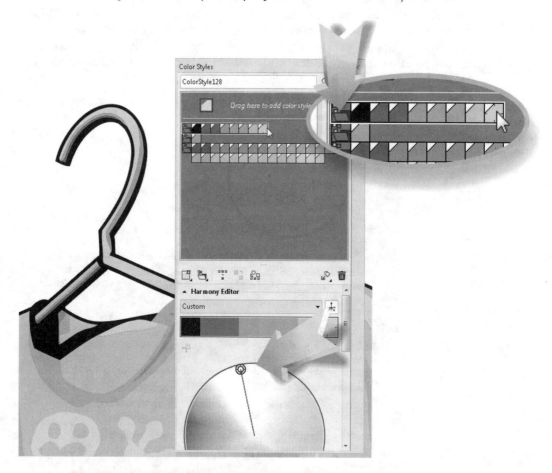

Changing Groups of Dissimilar Colors

We've had some fun with the amazing Color Styles docker; not many graphics programs can intelligently change the hue of a bunch of colors while slightly tweaking the brightness and saturation so the relationship and the differences between all the colors in a style remain visually constant and pleasing to the eye.

Here's a true test, though (spoiler alert: DRAW wins): you've created a logo whose colors are harmonious, but they are not of the same hue; in fact, some contrast with each other. You want to experiment with a different color scheme or two for the logo before submitting it. This is *definitely* a job for the Color Styles docker: open the file Breakfast to go to logo.cdr and get set for some dramatic editing work.

Tutorial Recoloring a Logo with Color Styles

1. The CDR document contains a logo with several different colors but only a few strong hues. The objective here is to recolor the logo with a *different,* eye-pleasing color combination.
2. Choose Window | Dockers | Color Styles and then click the New Color Style drop-down. Choose New From Document (callout 1 in Figure 15-4).
3. Make sure the Group Colors Styles Into Harmonies check box is checked and specify **5** groups. By doing this, you'll have control over every color aspect of the logo when you modify it (see callout 2).

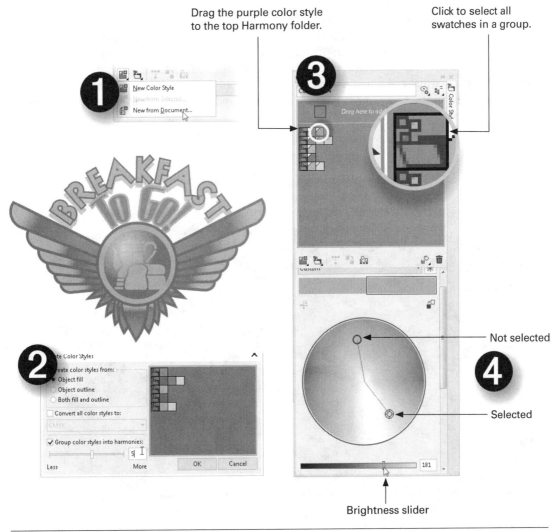

Drag the purple color style to the top Harmony folder.

Click to select all swatches in a group.

Not selected

Selected

Brightness slider

FIGURE 15-4 Create harmonies from a drawing so that selective color and color relationships can be changed.

4. The wings in the logo are a Linear fountain fill, and the gold color has its own color harmony group (see callout 3). To dynamically modify this fountain fill, the last color in the fill needs to be in the same group. Drag the purple swatch to the right of the gold one.

    As a point of information before continuing, the Color Editor (see callout 4) will display two large colors and markers on the color wheel. When a marker is highlighted, the color is selected and can be changed without changing other colors. Depending on how many colors you've put in a style, each of the color handles can be moved independently of each other. However, when you click the folder icon that precedes the swatches, all the colors change relative to each other when you drag one color marker. You do have control, however, as to *how* the colors change when they move in tandem when you adjust one. You use the Harmony Types drop-down list to choose from Analogous Colors, Complementary, Tetrad, and a host of other color relationships.

5. It's time for you to experiment! Click the top Harmony folder to select the gold and purple, and then in the color wheel, drag either of the selected marker handles around.

6. If and when you're feeling adventurous, click the second-from-top folder to select all the purples and blues in the logo, and then move any of the selected markers around the color wheel. Use your artistic judgment, and you'll experience a creative process similar to what's illustrated in Figure 15-5.

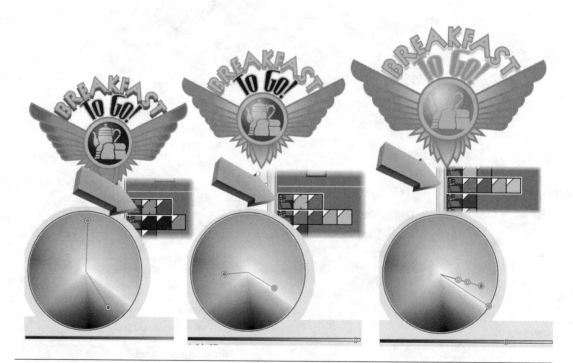

FIGURE 15-5 Changing multiple colors via harmonies can make one design look like a dozen different ones.

Color Relationships

Through color harmonies you can better see the relationships among primary, secondary, and complementary colors. In the additive color model, the primary colors are red, green, and blue. Complementary colors are the color opposites of primaries and lie at 180 degrees in opposition on a color wheel of hues. For example, the complementary color of red is green (more accurately know as cyan in recent years); the opposite of blue is yellow, and these complements are largely responsible for the A and B color channels in the LAB model, discussed earlier in this chapter. Secondary (additive) colors are the result of a mixture of two primary colors: red+green yields yellow, green+blue produces cyan, and red+blue produces magenta, which is the basis for the CMYK (subtractive) color model. It should be noted, however, that color harmonies, relationships that are described based on math, are not necessarily the sort of "harmony" one thinks of when designing a scheme, for example, for the living room. The "color explorer" utilities you can download online typically do exactly what CorelDRAW's mixer does. Usually showing only contrasting colors (color opposites, complementary colors), color mixers have no intelligence; they describe only relationships between hues and, therefore, can choose, for example, high school and college colors. But you truly have to use your own mind's eye when designing an *eye-pleasing* palette of colors to use in your work.

Adjusting and Transforming Color

In CorelDRAW, you can also alter all colors in a selection of drawing objects at once. Certain color adjustments may be performed either to selected bitmap images or to vector objects via filter commands. All the filters are available when a bitmap is chosen—far fewer commands are available when a vector object is selected. The quick solution to that is to *make a bitmap copy* of your vector work first, because the next command irreversibly changes your vector work to pixel-based work and your vector copy is gone. Choose Bitmaps | Convert To Bitmap. Then choose the desired options in the dialog and click OK, and the bitmap copy will take all of the filters described here. Choose Effects | Adjust or Effects | Transform to access the available filters for your selection.

- **Brightness-Contrast-Intensity**   Use this to adjust the brightness, contrast, and/or intensity properties of all colors in a selection of bitmap or vector objects. The brightness, contrast, and intensity properties can be adjusted individually based on the visual appearance of the object. Each value can be set between 100 and −100 percent. Choose Brightness-Contrast-Intensity from the Effects | Adjust menu.
- **Color Balance**   The Color Balance filter can be applied either to vector objects or bitmaps and enables you to adjust colors by RGB-CMY values. You can adjust the color balance of Cyan-Red, Magenta-Green, and/or Yellow-Blue colors specifically to Shadow, Midtone, and/or Highlights, with the added option of Preserve Luminance (brightness). RGB-CMY values range from 0 to 255. The Color Balance filter values range from −100 to 100. Color Balance is available from the Effects | Adjust menu.

- **Deinterlace**   This bitmap-only filter enables you to improve the appearance of bitmaps obtained from the older NTSC standard for video, as opposed to today's progressive video-capturing techniques with digital cameras. You'll find options for reducing either the even or odd horizontal lines seen in video formats. The filter has the effect of optionally filling the tiny gaps between the horizontal lines with either duplicate pixel colors or by averaging the color of surrounding pixels. Deinterlace is located under Effects | Transform.

- **Desaturate**   This option-free and instant bitmap-only filter converts your selected color bitmap to grayscale. Desaturate is located under Effects | Adjust.

- **Gamma**   This combination vector/bitmap filter changes the range measured between the highest and lowest color values of a selection, enabling you to adjust gamma between 0.10 and 10.00. Gamma is located under Effects | Adjust.

- **Hue-Saturation-Lightness**   This combination vector/bitmap filter enables you to adjust color based on the HLS model principles, similar to adjusting color based on color balance—with a twist. Using this filter, the hue, saturation, and/or lightness of colors can be adjusted all at once using the Master option or individually by selecting the Red, Yellow, Green, Cyan, Blue, Magenta, or Grayscale component. You'll find this filter under the Effects | Adjust menu.

- **Invert**   This option-free and instantly applied combination vector/bitmap filter changes the colors in a selection to be the "reverse" of the original colors, meaning colors are transposed in relative position across the standard color wheel. Invert is located under Effects | Transform.

- **Contrast Enhancement**   This bitmap-only filter enables you to change color contrast by adjusting the levels of the darkest and lightest color shades while automatically adjusting the color values between. Eyedropper tools enable you to sample your image's input and/or output values by color channel. A histogram displays the distribution of pixels according to their color values. The Auto-Adjust option averages colors between the lightest and darkest, or you can manually adjust changes to these colors using the Input Value Clipping slider. The Gamma Adjustment slider enables you to control the resulting midtone values. You'll find this filter under the Effects | Adjust menu.

- **Local Equalization**   This bitmap-only filter changes the contrast specifically at the edges to improve image detail. The Width and Height sliders can be set between 5 and 255, enabling you to specify the extent of the equalization effect toward the center of the image. You'll find it under the Effects | Adjust menu.

- **Posterize**   This combined vector/bitmap filter limits the number of colors in your selection to as few as two or as many as 32 colors using a Level slider control. You'll find it under the Effects | Transform menu.

- **Replace Colors**   This bitmap-only filter enables you to substitute one image color with another by choosing old and new colors; specifying hue, saturation, and lightness values; and specifying a color range. Eyedropper tools enable you to perform direct sampling. You'll find it under the Effects | Adjust menu.

- **Sample/Target Balance**   This bitmap-only filter takes color replacement a step further by enabling you to sample the color of a point—or an area—of a bitmap image and replace the color with a chosen color or color range. You'll find a complex set of options for sampling highlight, midtone, and/or shadow areas for replacement. Color changes can be adjusted all at once or by individual channel. You'll find this filter under Effects | Adjust.

- **Selective Color**   This bitmap-only filter enables you to adjust the color based on changes made to specific color spectrums. Adjust color based on color mode; and/or change reds, yellows, greens, cyans, blues, and/or magentas; and/or change gray levels for shadows, midtones, and highlights. This filter is under Effects | Adjust.
- **Tone Curve**   This bitmap-only filter adjusts shadow, midtone, and highlights channels uniformly or selectively or applies a preset tone curve via command buttons. The curve preview can be used to adjust the object's color interactively by click-dragging the curve itself. Clicking one of four Curve Style buttons enables you to apply a preset color adjustment. You can also save your curve or retrieve saved curves, and an Invert button instantly inverts the curve. This filter is found under Effects | Adjust.

 Tip   You can quickly copy color properties between two objects (including groups) interactively by holding modifiers as you right-click-drag one object onto another (meaning click and hold the right mouse button to drag an object). Holding SHIFT copies the fill color, holding ALT copies the outline color, and holding SHIFT-ALT together copies both. With each action, your cursor will indicate the property being copied.

You've seen in this chapter how important color is; color sets a mood for an illustration, and the artistic use of color can actually fix an illustration that lacks visual interest or complexity. And you now know how to define and save not only a color you need, but an entire palette. For still more information on color and other DRAW fills, be sure to check out Chapter 12. This concludes the section on colors and fills; from here, we travel to the land of very special effects—take what you've learned and use what you've drawn to bend it, distort it, and, in general, make it a unique piece by learning how to sculpt vector shapes.

PART VI   Creating the Illusion of 3D Composition

16   The Perspective and Extrude Effects

For centuries, traditional artists have studied and sweated (and sometimes failed) to create artwork that conveys a sense of dimension. Perspective, vanishing point, and angle of view can easily elude all but the most diligent, talented people because the sense of a third dimension on a 2D canvas is, after all, an illusion.

Fortunately, you don't have to go to school for years and you don't have to break a sweat when you want a little photorealism and dimension the next time you sit down to draw because you have CorelDRAW. In this chapter, you'll learn how to lift your graphical ideas right off the page with version X8's perspective effect and DRAW's legendary Extrude tool.

If you want your audience to be drawn *into* your work and not simply to stare at it, fire up CorelDRAW and read on!

 Note Download and extract all the files from the Chapter16.zip archive to follow the tutorials in this chapter.

The Perspective Effect: What Perspective Does to an Object

We've all seen examples of *perspective;* for example, after you make sure a train isn't coming, you stand on the tracks and look toward the horizon. Seemingly, the train tracks converge at the horizon. Naturally, the tracks don't *actually* converge, or it would be difficult to put a train on them. This optical illusion demonstrates the very real optics of the human eye. Any object that has parallel sides (such as a milk carton and most tables) when viewed at an angle other than face-forward will look as though its parallel sides converge at a point somewhere in the distance. This point, whether you can see it on train tracks or imagine it by mentally extending the parallel lines, is called the *vanishing point,* and CorelDRAW's perspective effect offers an

405

onscreen marker for moving a shape's vanishing point when Effects | Add Perspective has been applied to an object or group of objects.

Depending on the angle at which you view an object—to use a cube as an example—you can see one, two, or three sides of the cube. When you draw a cube, face front, in CorelDRAW, you've drawn a square; there is no perspective, and it's not very interesting. If you can see two faces of the cube, you're viewing from a perspective point; the object is said to have *one-point perspective.* Naturally, you can't see more than three sides of a cube at one time, but when you do see all three front-facing sides, this is called *two-point perspective.* It's visually intriguing to pose an object (or draw one) using two-point perspective, and CorelDRAW helps you set up an object for two-point as well as one-point perspective.

Getting a Perspective on Perspective

Now that you understand what a "normal" lens does to perspective, let's take a look at a few abnormal (but artistic and creative) perspectives, beginning with no perspective and working our way up. In Figure 16-1, you can see on the left an *isometric* view (also called an *orthographic* view) of the kid's block. Regardless of the term, it's unrealistic because the parallels of the cube do not converge. Isometric views of objects are quickly accomplished in CorelDRAW by putting an object into Rotate/Skew mode (clicking once and then a second time) and then skewing the object by click-dragging a middle control handle. Isometric views are completely the province of computer graphics and geometry. They don't exist in the real

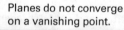

FIGURE 16-1 Example of an isometric view and a fairly wide-angle view of the same object.

world with human eyes, but they are useful in illustration to put equal emphasis on all visible sides of an object. For example, if you want your client to read the side panel of a proposed cereal box design but want the box posed to show more than one side, you'd use an isometric view (occasionally called *isometric perspective*). On the right, you can see the same kid's block using a wide-angle perspective. In CorelDRAW, such an illustration is accomplished by putting the vanishing points outside of the drawing page. It's exaggerated mostly because the human eye does not have a field of view as large as 76 degrees—that is, the view is not entirely in focus.

The following illustration goes way over the top; the vanishing points are quite close to the object, and the result is dramatic, unrealistic, and unsuitable for presenting a product design. As you read through this chapter, you'll learn that, on some occasions, you want a vanishing point on the drawing page, and on other occasions, you want the "normal" human-eye type of perspective.

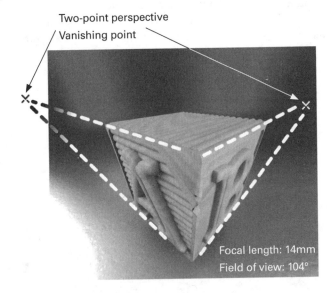

Two-point perspective
Vanishing point

Focal length: 14mm
Field of view: 104°

Experiments in Perspective

Experimenting with the perspective effect is a lot more fun and rewarding than reading about it. The operations are fairly straightforward, and you'll probably get ideas for future illustrations just by playing with it! Single objects and object groups can be put in perspective; you can change the angle of a perspective shape (or group) by click-dragging any of the four control corners or by click-dragging the vanishing point(s), which changes two of the four control corners at once.

Let's begin with a simple perspective, performed on an object that will immediately give you a reference for what's going on: a 12×12-cell graph paper object. The perspective effect displays subdivisions in red-dotted lines on top of the object you're manipulating, which provides good visual feedback; with a graph paper object, you'll see exactly how the grid corresponds to the visual changes in the graph paper cells.

Tutorial Creating Two-Point Perspective

1. Press D, the keyboard shortcut for the Graph Paper tool. On the Property Bar, set the number of columns to **12** and the number of rows to **12**.
2. Hold CTRL while you click-drag to constrain the graph paper object to a square. Make the object fairly large (about 7" is good). Because the perspective effect can appreciably shrink one or more sides of an object, it's a good design practice to create objects that are a little exaggerated in size.
3. Click a deep red swatch on the color palette to set the fill for all the cells and then right-click over a pale yellow to set the outline color.
4. Choose Effects | Add Perspective, as shown here. Your object now has control handles around it, and your current tool has changed to the Shape tool. The Shape tool is used during perspective creation. Additionally, if you intend to edit a perspective effect while you're working on a different area of a design, all you need to do is choose the Shape tool and then click an object that's in perspective.

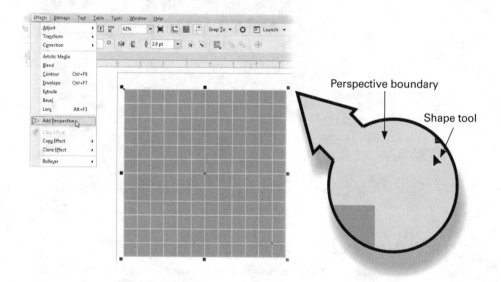

Perspective boundary

Shape tool

5. Click the top-right handle of the Perspective Effect box surrounding the graph paper object. Hold CTRL to constrain the movement of your cursor to the first direction in which you drag, and then drag down to about the second or third cell in the right column. You've created a *two-point perspective* effect on the object, which shows one *vanishing point*. As you can see, the cells align more or less with the effect's red-dotted overlay reference, and a vanishing point appears directly to the right. If the vanishing point lies offscreen—which it will when you use a small amount of perspective—press F3 to zoom out so it shows.

6. Click-drag the vanishing point up and then down, as long as this is an experiment and you are not playing for points. Notice what happens: you've defined a one-point perspective. This is the right side of a hypothetical cube, and one-point perspectives have only one vanishing point. So the left side of the object is anchored; it doesn't change with the perspective change.

7. Click-drag the vanishing point left and right. The left side is still anchored, and what you're doing is making the hypothetical box's right side deeper and shallower, extending to and from an imaginary horizon on the page.

8. Save this document; you'll work with it in a moment, so don't close it. This is only the beginning of the experiment with suggesting depth in a 2D document!

There *has* to be a practical use for what you've just learned; adding one-point perspective to a graph paper object by itself is about as exciting as watching grass grow. Here, you can see the result of grouping some text with the graph paper object before applying the perspective effect. The real point here is that one-point perspective can establish a *ground plane* for a dimensional composition—a ground plane has been suggested in this illustration by the effect, the "scene" has depth, and the illustrator obviously can't read signs.

Working with Three-Point Perspective

Using the perspective effect, any 2D drawing can be made to look as though it extends into space, as you proved in the previous tutorial. It's time to up the stakes, however, and create a *second* vanishing point, thus a three-point perspective. This second point will make this graph paper object look as though it occupies space, suggesting visually that the grid recedes away from the page and that its depth is traveling in a direction. This tutorial is going to be fun; by the end of the following steps, you'll have created a great high-tech, sci-fi background you can use in several design situations.

Tutorial Creating a 3D Ground Plane

1. With the graph paper document you saved in the previous tutorial open, choose the Shape tool and then click the object to reveal its perspective effect control handles and the vanishing point you defined.

2. Click-drag the top-right control handle up and toward the center of the object, until you see a second vanishing point marker at about 12 o'clock on the page. You might want to zoom out to better see the second vanishing point because it is initially defined quite far away from the object. In the illustration after Step 9, you can see how the graph paper object should look. Notice also that because this two-point perspective is so extreme, the graph paper outlines are actually curved to accommodate the severely distorted perspective. This is *not* an optical illusion; the lines are indeed curved now.

3. Choose the Pick tool, and with the graph paper object selected, click it to put it into Skew/Rotate mode. Rotate the object about 45° counterclockwise—stop click-dragging when the Property Bar reports that you've rotated the object by about this amount. Changing the orientation of the object by only changing the vanishing points' positions would be difficult.

4. Choose the Rectangle tool and then click-drag a rectangle to cover the graph paper object.

5. Choose the Fill tool, and then click-drag from top to bottom on the object so the top is black, fading to white at the rectangle's bottom. Then choose a red from the color palette to fill the End color indicator of the fountain fill.

6. Choose the rectangle with the Pick tool and then press SHIFT-PAGE DOWN to put the rectangle on the back of the drawing page, behind the graph paper object.

7. Choose the graph paper object and then right-click the white color well on the color palette. Then double-click the Outline Pen swatch on the Status Bar to open the Outline Pen dialog.

8. Type **4** in the Width field and then click OK to apply this width. You're done and your composition looks like the following illustration.

9. Left-click the No Fill swatch now while the graph paper object is selected.

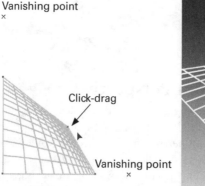

Vanishing point
×

Click-drag

Vanishing point
×

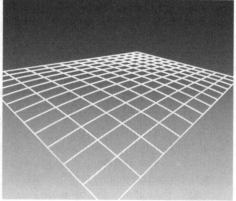

> **Tip** The outline properties of an object possessing the perspective effect do not diminish in width along with the shape of the object. If you need outlines to follow a perspective, you need to first convert the outlines to objects: press CTRL-U, for example, to ungroup a graph paper object, and then choose Object | Convert Outline to Object (CTRL-SHIFT-Q). Then, group the objects once more to apply perspective.

Copying Perspective and Creating a 3D Scene

Like many of the features in CorelDRAW, a perspective can be copied from an object and applied to a different object using the options on the Property Bar. Being able to instantly copy and match perspective between objects in a composition can turn the entire drawing into a 3D event, as the following tutorial demonstrates.

In the Commuters.cdr file you downloaded, you'll see several characters you can use, or you choose to use your own in the following tutorial. The idea is that these fellows are so self-absorbed they're going to miss the train pulling in behind them unless they look to the right a little. So you'll apply a perspective to one guy, copy the instance of the perspective effect to the rest of the gang, and then embellish the composition a little to give the drawing true depth.

Tutorial   Perspective Scenes via Copying

1. Open Commuters.cdr. Select the guy on the left side of the page and then choose Effects | Add Perspective.
2. Click the top-right control handle on the object and then drag down a little. Next, click-drag the bottom-right control handle and then drag up and to the right until the commuter is facing right in perspective, as shown in Figure 16-2. You might not see the vanishing points on the page because this perspective is not severe enough.

FIGURE 16-2   Create just enough perspective to give the shape some dimension.

3. Choose the Pick tool now. Click the guy with his hat in his hand and then choose Effects | Copy Effect | Perspective From. Click over the guy on the left that has the perspective shown here, and the second object adopts the perspective of the first.

4. Repeat Step 3 for the guy holding the writing pad.
5. Create a graph paper object and then give it a deep red fill and a white outline. Put it to the back of the illustration.
6. Put the graph paper in perspective to make a ground plane. Next, drag the top-left control handle to the right and then drag the top-right control handle to the left until you see a vanishing point just above the graph paper object. This object's perspective should be very distorted, suggesting a horizon at about the chest level of the characters.
7. Create a second graph paper object, choose Object | Group | Ungroup, and then choose Object | Combine so the graph paper object is truly a single path.
8. Give it a medium- to light-blue fountain fill, and give its outline a white property exactly like you did with the first object in Step 5. Put it to the back of the drawing (SHIFT-PAGE DOWN).
9. From here on out, the steps will "ground" the characters on the graph paper below them. To begin, click any of the fellows and then choose the Drop Shadow tool from the Effects group of tools on the Toolbox.
10. Choose Perspective Top Left from the Presets drop-down on the Property Bar. With your cursor, click-drag the black control marker for the shadow down and to the right until the shadow looks correct.
11. Repeat Step 9 with the two other commuters. Select a guy, choose Effects | Copy Effect | Drop Shadow From, and then click the first shadow (not the object casting

the shadow) you defined. You can also add a shadow to the train and the cloud group of objects. Additionally, try moving the commuters up or down from their original position to increase the sense of depth in the scene. Your scene should look like the illustration shown here.

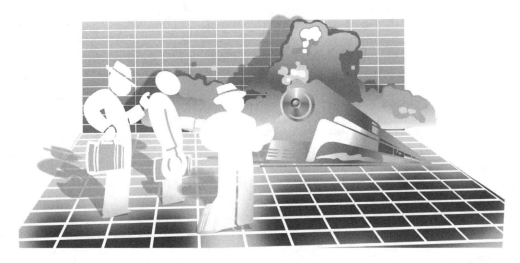

> **Tip** You can quickly put any object that has the perspective effect into Editing mode when the Pick tool is the current tool by double-clicking the object. Also, if you want to mirror the perspective effect—to make a symmetrical perspective—hold CTRL-SHIFT while you click-drag a control handle.

Pre-visualizing Designs in Perspective

Often you'll design something such as a pattern and will want to see what it would look like as a garment, giftwrap, or some other physical piece of art before you pay to have the design printed. You can do this in CorelDRAW with the perspective effect. In the following example, you'll create a simple giftwrap pattern; then, using perspective, you'll virtually wrap a package. The package is provided for you as an image on layers in a CorelDRAW document.

Let's use CorelDRAW's Artistic Media tool to create the giftwrap for the present in the following steps.

Tutorial Pre-visualizing a Design on a Product

After creating a new document (choose Landscape orientation), press CTRL-I to import the file A present.cpt. If you get an attention box that says there's a color profile mismatch, click the

Convert from Color Profile to Document Color Profile button and then click OK. Now, just click at the upper left of the page to place it to size.

1. Open the Object Manager from the Window | Dockers | Object Manager menu. Expand the "A present.cpt" entry to reveal the two image objects.
2. Click the New Layer button at the bottom left of the docker. Doing this creates a new default named "Layer 2."
3. Click-drag the "Bow" entry on the Object Manager and place it on the Layer 1 title. Doing this destroys the list entry "A present.cpt," and the bow and the present objects now both belong to Layer 1.
4. Drag the "Bow" object now from Layer 1 to Layer 2. Layer 1 will only contain the "A present" object now. The Bow object is above the present.
5. Create a new layer, which by default is named "Layer 3." Click-drag it to below Layer 2. Here is where you'll design the giftwrap.
6. Choose the Artistic Media tool located just under the drawing tools group on the Toolbox. Then choose the Sprayer button on the Property Bar. You can use any preset you like, such as one of the Festive Food presets.
7. Create a rectangular area by scribbling up and down, like making several *W*s.
8. Choose Object | Break Artistic Media Apart (CTRL-K works, too). With the Pick tool, select first and then delete the parent black path that's now visible (see Figure 16-3).

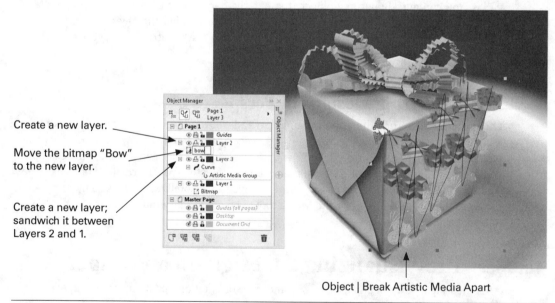

Create a new layer.

Move the bitmap "Bow" to the new layer.

Create a new layer; sandwich it between Layers 2 and 1.

Object | Break Artistic Media Apart

FIGURE 16-3   Create a pattern with the Artistic Media Sprayer tool.

9. Select the Sprayer shapes. Then, choose Effects | Add Perspective. With the Shape tool, drag, one at a time, the control handles for the effect to match the four corners of the face of the present, as shown here.

10. Duplicate the pattern (press CTRL-D) and then use the Shape tool to edit this duplicate (which also has the perspective effect) so it matches the four corners of the top side of the present. Because the bow is on the top layer, you're actually adding the top pattern in perspective below the bow so it looks optically correct.

11. Repeat Step 10 to create the left panel of the pattern on the present.

12. The pattern shouldn't look totally opaque, but instead should take on a little of the shading on the blank present. The quickest way to apply transparency to the scores of objects that make up your Artistic Media stroke is to turn the pattern into a bitmap. First, let's check out the resolution of the present image so the conversion of the giftwrap pattern isn't unnecessarily larger than the present or bow images. After choosing the Pick tool, click either the "Bitmap" or the "Bow" entry on the Object Manager list and then look at the Status Bar. The correct answer is 96 dpi.

13. Select one of the patterned sides and then choose Bitmaps | Convert To Bitmap. In the Convert To Bitmap dialog, choose **96** in the Resolution box, check the Transparent Background box, and then click OK.

14. With the new bitmap selected, choose the Transparency tool on the Toolbox. On the Property Bar, click the Uniform Transparency type, choose Multiply Style, and then play with the amount of transparency your eye tells you looks best and visually blends the pattern into the present. Repeat Steps 12 and 13 with the other two sides of the gift, be sure to include a card, and then send it to someone who deserves a present.

This finished pre-visualization provides you and your client with a view of the goods you've designed, as they will appear from the customer's point of view, which is perhaps the best "perspective" effect of all. This illustration shows a finished version of the tutorial, using the bubbles from the Misc. category of spray patterns.

Extruding Objects: How Extrude Works

Although CorelDRAW is a 2D vector drawing application, the Extrude feature adds a simulated third dimension by adding objects that are shaded and in perspective. This section takes you through the rich feature set of the Extrude tool, offers some creative possibilities for its use, and gets your head around the initial challenges of navigating 3D space in CorelDRAW.

CorelDRAW's extrude effect examines the geometry of an object and then, with your input, creates dynamic extensions to all path segments, suggesting the added objects recede into the distance to a vanishing point. Figure 16-4 shows some finished artwork based on objects that are easy for you to draw in CorelDRAW. The train composition uses *several* extruded objects, and shapes were added manually after the extrudes to make the scene look even better. Specifically, all the shadows you see were manually drawn on top of areas. You need to be imaginative to place the extruded object in context, within a scene, to build a complete graphical idea. The Extrude tool doesn't create "Auto-Art." It's a tool; it needs your creativity to guide it.

Tip When extruding objects, don't limit your perception of an extruded circle as a coin shape. You will see later in this chapter that if you create a deep extrude out of a circle and then rotate the object by 90° from left to right, you have a straw or other cylindrical shape.

When an extrude effect is applied to an object, the original becomes a *control object,* and the extrude effect objects become a dynamically linked group. Any editing you then perform

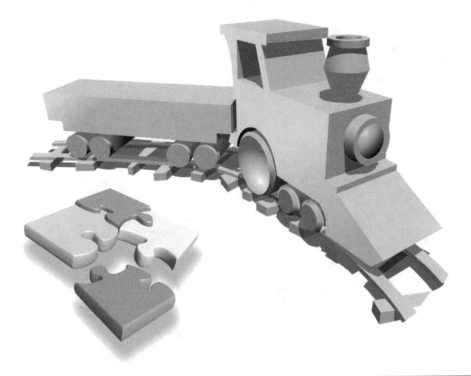

FIGURE 16-4   Imagine what an object looks like when projected into a third dimension and then manually add what's missing.

on the properties of the control object, such as fills and edits to the outline of the control object, are immediately updated in the linked extrude group.

Be aware that both lighting and the control object's geometry impact how many extrude group objects are created. Although you don't usually need to concern yourself with how many objects are dynamically created to make an extrude, the sheer number of objects can slow down redraws of your page when you have, for example, hundreds of objects in the extrude group. When CorelDRAW creates an extrude group, it calculates lighting (when you *use* lighting, covered later in this chapter) and creates extrude group objects based on curved path segments in the control object.

Choosing and Applying an Extrude Effect

The extrude effect can be applied interactively using the Extrude tool, which is located in the Toolbox with other effects tools, or you can choose from the Presets list to create a 3D object instantly.

While you're using this tool, the Property Bar provides all the options for setting the effect's properties. Browse the Property Bar options shown in Figure 16-5. Options are grouped into areas for saving your applied extrusions as Presets, controlling the shape, depth, vanishing point position, rotation, lighting, color, and bevel effects.

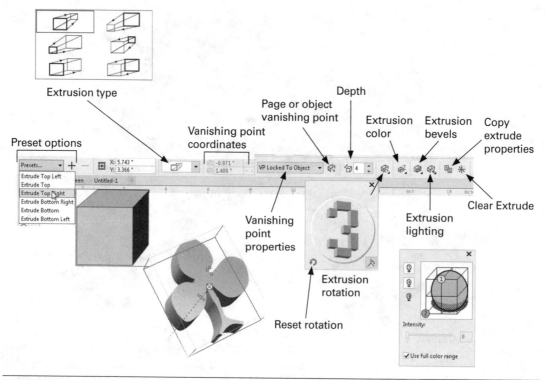

FIGURE 16-5 The Property Bar contains all the options for defining and saving the look of an extrude.

Navigating the Interactive Markers

When you decide to extrude a shape manually, interactive markers appear around the resulting object after you perform the first step in the extrude operation, which is click-dragging on the face of the object you want to be the control object. The interactive markers offer you control over the position, depth, and vanishing point position of the 3D object. You'll create a 3D object by hand in the following tutorial, so familiarize yourself with the elements that surround a 3D extruded shape, as shown in Figure 16-6.

Note If at any time in this chapter you feel like trying out the cathedral radio objects as extrude targets, the file is called (oddly enough!) Cathedral Radio.cdr, and can be found in the Chapter 16 zip archive.

Alternatively, you can apply a Preset extrude effect to get a 3D version of a shape in lightning time; however, you might want hands-on control over creating the extrude effect. Follow this tutorial to get a handle on what some of the Property Bar options do to an extrude effect.

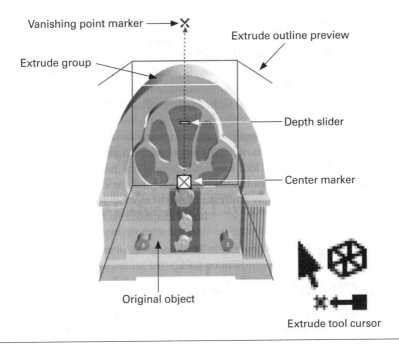

Vanishing point marker ⟶ ✕

Extrude outline preview

Extrude group

Depth slider

Center marker

Original object

Extrude tool cursor

FIGURE 16-6   These control handles are used after an object is initially extruded to change the appearance of the extrude.

Tutorial Going Deep With the Extrude Tool

1. Create an object to be the control object for the extrude. A rectangle produces results that make the relationship between the face of the object and the sides clear, but not very artistic. Try a star shape for more dramatic extrude results. Give the shape a fill (a fountain fill will produce a stunning effect), and give the outline a contrasting color such as white so you can visually track where the extrude objects are created.

2. Choose the Extrude tool, and your cursor changes to the Extrude tool cursor, which is hard to mistake for the Pick or Pen tool. When held over your object, the cursor indicates a Start extrude position by displaying a tiny shape with a direction line below the symbol of an extruded cube.

3. Drag from the center of your object outward in any direction, but don't release the mouse button. The control object now has interactive markers and a Wireframe preview of the front and back boundaries of the extrude; the front of the object is bounded by a red outline, and the back of the 3D shape is bounded by a blue outline. The preview indicates the length and direction of the extrude effect, and the X symbol you're dragging is the *vanishing point*. As discussed earlier in this chapter, a vanishing point is a geometric indicator of where parallel lines on a surface would converge at the horizon if the surface were actually to extend to the horizon. Once you're satisfied with the extrude Wireframe preview, release the mouse button. Now you can edit the extruded object and immediately see the results.

4. Drag the vanishing point X symbol around the page; not only does the preview outline change, but also, more importantly, the view on the 3D object also changes. When the vanishing point is above the control object, you're looking down on the object; similarly, you move your view to expose the side of an object in direct correlation to the position of the vanishing point.

5. As you use the Extrude tool, you define both the direction and depth of the 3D object. Try dragging the Depth slider toward and then away from the control object. Notice how you first make the extrude a shallow one and then a deeper one, all while the sides extend in the direction of the vanishing point. At any time from when you create the object by releasing the cursor, you can also set the object depth by using the Depth spin box on the Property Bar.

6. Click outside of the object, and the extrude operation is complete. However, because extrude is a *dynamic* effect, you can change its appearance at any time in the future by double-clicking the extrude group with the Extrude tool to once again display the interactive handles.

Using the Extrude Tool and Property Bar

Like other effects, extrusions can be set using the Property Bar. However, regardless of your work preferences, version X8's Extrude feature produces the same results whether you use the Property Bar controls or the Extrude tool. The following sections walk you through some of the design options you have when you use the Extrude tool.

Setting Extrude Depth

Extrude depth is based on the distance between the control object and the vanishing point. You will get different appearances using the same depth value but different styles, and you can set extrude depth as high as 99. Here, you can see a shallow and a deep extrude, using two different depth values but the same extrude style. You can control object depth manually by dragging the interactive Depth slider on top of the object, or you can enter values in the num box on the Property Bar (press ENTER after typing a value; the spin box controls update the object without your needing to press ENTER).

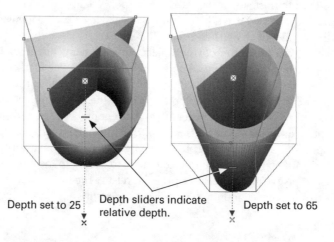

Depth set to 25

Depth sliders indicate relative depth.

Depth set to 65

Setting Vanishing Point Properties

The direction of the vanishing point determines only the point toward which objects diminish; it does not control whether the extruded portion extends from the front or back of the object. Using the Vanishing Point Properties drop-down on the Property Bar, you can lock an extrusion's vanishing point, copy vanishing points from an existing extrusion, and share vanishing points between extruded objects.

Here are the options for vanishing points, including how they can be set and shared between different extruded objects:

- **Locking to the object**   Choosing the VP Locked To Object option (the default setting) fixes the vanishing point to a position relative to the object, regardless of where the original extruded object is positioned.
- **Locking to the page**   The VP Locked To Page option allows you to tack the vanishing point to your page, forcing the extrusion to diminish toward a fixed page position, no matter where the original object is moved. Try it to see for yourself the effectiveness of this setting: lock the vanishing point of an extruded object to the page, and then move the object using the Pick tool; you'll see that the sides of the extrude dynamically update to always show the object's correct perspective.
- **Copying vanishing point from**   The Copy VP From command doesn't define a vanishing point like the other drop-down choices do; instead, you use it to copy an existing vanishing point. Copying a vanishing point lets you set up several extruded objects on a page, and in a few clicks, the objects all appear to be facing the same direction, at a common point of view from the audience's perspective. Immediately after you choose Copy VP From, your cursor changes to a vanishing point targeting cursor (a really, really large arrow), which you use to target any other extruded object on your document page, with the goal of copying its vanishing point position. For this command to be successful, you must have at least one other extrude effect applied to an object and in view. After the vanishing point has been copied, the Property Bar indicates the object's vanishing point as VP Locked To Object, and the vanishing point can now be moved.
- **Sharing vanishing points**   Choosing Shared Vanishing Point lets you share the *same* vanishing point among several objects, but you must have applied at least an initial extrude effect to your objects before attempting to use this command. Immediately after you choose this option, your cursor changes to a vanishing point targeting cursor, so you can now target any other extruded object for the purpose of creating a common vanishing point position for multiple objects. This option creates a similar effect to copying vanishing points, but the overall effect is every object on the page is in the same scene. You can move two or more selected objects simultaneously and change the perspective of all of them.
- **Setting a relative position for vanishing points**   The Page or Object Vanishing Point button on the Property Bar is used to toggle the measurement state of object vanishing points between page and object. When the option is inactive (the button is not depressed), the vanishing point position boxes allow you to specify the vanishing point relative to your page origin—a value determined either by the lower-left corner, by default, or by the zero markers on your ruler origin. When the option is active (the button is depressed), the center of your currently selected object is used as the measurement value, which changes

according to the object's page position. You will see this most noticeably if you have a depth on an object of more than 40 and you drag the object around the page with the Pick tool. The extrude group actually changes to reflect different vanishing point views.

Setting 3D Rotation

Beginning your extrude adventures with the object facing you is a good starting point in your 3D experience, but not always the most visually interesting of poses. You can *rotate* extruded objects after extruding them via the Property Bar or via the interactive control handles. Create an extrude group of objects and then we'll begin with the precise, noninteractive method of rotation you access on the Property Bar when you've chosen the Extrude tool and selected an object. VP Locked To Object is necessary for this trick to work.

The Rotation pop-up menu offers a proxy box that you use by click-dragging on the "3," as shown next. As you drag, a faint yellow line appears on the 3, indicating the current rotation of the object and the proposed new rotation once you release the mouse button. You might not always get the exact look you need using this technique because of the position of the object's vanishing point—your experience can be similar to levering an object seesaw-fashion when the pivot point (the fulcrum) is 15 miles away! To avoid imprecision, you can click the toggle button labeled in the illustration. The value fields have spin box controls that increase and decrease the values by 5; you probably want to enter values manually because a single percent of rotation (from 0 to 100 percent, not degrees) can be quite significant, considering only 100 of them are in this pop-up box. If at any time you find you've gotten too deep in this 3D rotation stuff, clicking the Undo curved arrow icon on the lower left of the selector, as shown here, resets all rotation values to zero.

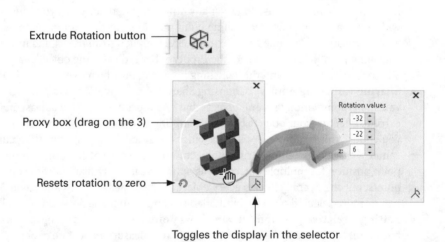

Extrude Rotation button

Proxy box (drag on the 3)

Resets rotation to zero

Toggles the display in the selector

Overall, the best teacher is experience, particularly with manipulating your view of a 3D object in CorelDRAW. Set aside some quality time, and you might even be pleasantly surprised by some of your errors!

Using the Rotation Tools

You don't have to use the Extrude Rotation pop-up box on the Property Bar to rotate an extruded object: you can define a degree of rotation along the X, Y, and Z axes of any object by click-dragging the object directly. To do some manual rotation, the object needs to be extruded and first put into Editing mode—you can double-click on the extrude group of objects with the Pick tool to put the object into Editing mode, and then click a second time to expose the control handles shown here.

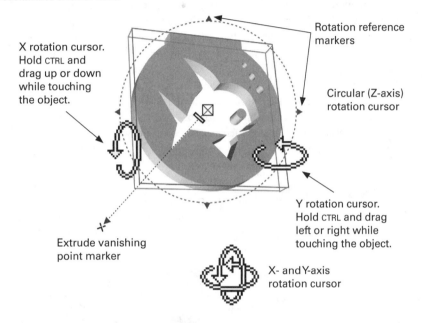

X rotation cursor. Hold CTRL and drag up or down while touching the object.

Rotation reference markers

Circular (Z-axis) rotation cursor

Extrude vanishing point marker

Y rotation cursor. Hold CTRL and drag left or right while touching the object.

X- and Y-axis rotation cursor

Note If either Back Parallel or Front Parallel is selected, the Extrude Rotation controls are unavailable; parallel extrusions have no vanishing point, so there's nothing to pivot with. Also, when the vanishing point is locked to the page, Extrude Rotation cannot be performed.

When an object is rotated, you can't use the vanishing point controls on the Property Bar, mostly because mathematically, the vanishing point is nowhere near your drawing page. If you need to adjust an object's vanishing point, you must work backward; on the Extrude Rotation pop-up panel on the Property Bar, click the Reset Rotation icon. Then the vanishing point options and controls become active (and your object is no longer rotated).

Adding Lights

Adding lighting to an extruded object can spell the difference between an effect and a piece of artwork that truly attracts a viewer with its realistic appearance; many of the figures in this chapter use the Lighting option. To access the lighting controls, click the Extrude Lighting button on the Property Bar while selecting an extrude effect.

Working with the Options in the Lighting Control Window

Three independent light sources can be activated, positioned, and adjusted for intensity and to set whether all the control object's colors are used in the extrude group (the Use Full Color Range option). These lights perform like bare light bulbs. You can reposition them, but not aim them as you would a real flashlight or spotlight. Light intensity is set on a light-by-light basis between 0 and 100 percent by using the slider control when each light is selected. One of the nice things about setting up light intensity and position is that response is immediate—there is no Apply button, and your object's light changes as you make changes in the control window.

When you first open the Extrude Lighting control window, all lights are inactive. To activate a light, click one of the three Light Source buttons—the numbering is for your reference; it's just a label. There is nothing special about light 3 versus light 1, for example, in any of its properties. Once you click a light button, a circle with the light's number inside appears in the front, upper-right position on a 3D grid surrounding a sphere, which represents the extrude object (see Figure 16-7). The lights themselves aren't visible on the drawing page, but the lighting effect

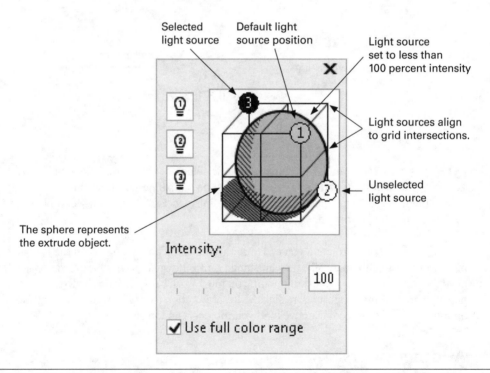

FIGURE 16-7 The 3D grid represents light positions relative to the selected extrude object.

you define displays highlights and shaded areas on your extrude object, particularly evident when the sides of the control object are curved. You can pose the light sources by adding them to the grid and then dragging them—there are over a dozen possible positions for lights; some of the positions can create very interesting "edge lighting" on your object.

Every time you activate a new light, it appears on the grid in the default position of front, top, right. This means if you click to activate two or three Light Source buttons in succession without first moving them, you'll stack them on top of each other and wind up with one extremely intense light source on the object. When this happens, drag the individual lights to reposition them at different points.

A *selected* light is shown as a black circle in the preview; unselected lights are shown as white circles. Lights set to brightness levels less than 100 percent appear in shades of gray. As these light sources are dragged around the 3D grid, they automatically snap to line-intersection points on the grid. You *can* position lights at the back-mid-center or back-center-bottom position—if you're *really* determined and have lots of time to spare—but lights in these positions will not contribute significantly to the shading of the extrude shape.

 Note There is no option to set the color of lights; all lights cast white.

The following tutorial obliges you to put on your stagehand cap as you work the lights in a scene, adding them to the extrude object's properties and learning how to position them and turn the wattage up and down.

Tutorial Working with Extrude Light Options

1. Create a color-filled object and apply an extrude effect to it.
2. Using the Extrude tool, click the Extrude Lighting selector on the Property Bar to open the light source option.
3. Click the Light Source 1 button, and a light source symbol appears in the upper-right-front corner of the grid, shown as a black circle numbered "1." The Intensity slider is activated. Light Source 1 is now active, and the colors of your extrude effect are altered (brightened and possibly a little washed out) to reflect the new light's contribution to the extrude effect.
4. Drag the symbol representing Light Source 1 to a different position on the 3D grid; notice how the coloring of the effect changes in response to the new lighting position.
5. With Light Source 1 still selected, drag the Intensity slider to the left, approximately to the 50 percent position, and notice how the color of the object becomes darker and more saturated.
6. Click the Light Source 2 button to activate it. Notice that it appears in the same default position as the first light source, and the symbol representing Light Source 1 is gray, indicating it is not selected and is not at 100 percent intensity. When an unselected

light is at 100 percent intensity, the symbol is white. Drag Light Source 2 to a different grid position—in classic scene lighting, a secondary light of, say, 50 percent of the main light's intensity is usually positioned directly opposite the main light to make objects look rounder, deeper, and more flattering with more visible detail than when using only one light source.

7. Click the activation buttons for Light Sources 1 and 2 to toggle them off, and the color of the extrude object returns to its original state. To finish editing lights, click anywhere outside the Extrude Lighting selector.

Tip Occasionally in your design work, you might like the perspective you've created for the face of an extrude object, but you might not need the extruded side or the extrude group of objects. You can remove an extrude effect from an object and keep its perspective and position on the page by clicking the extruded portion of the effect and choosing Effects | Clear Extrude. You can also use the Extrude tool by clicking the Clear Extrude button on the Property Bar.

Controlling Light Properties

Two additional options are available when you use lighting, and they have the following effects on your extruded objects:

- **Lighting intensity**   As mentioned in the previous tutorial, the Intensity slider determines the brightness of each light. When a light is selected, you can set the range between 0 and 100 percent; higher values mean brighter lighting.
- **Full color range**   Below the Intensity slider, you'll find the Use Full Color Range option, which directs your display to use the full *gamut* of colors when coloring the surfaces of your original object and its extruded portion. *Gamut* is the expressible range of colors available to CorelDRAW, which depends on the color mode of the original object and the extrusion. When working in CMYK process or RGB color, you might find the shading on an object to have too much contrast; the lighting might look too harsh and might create washed-out surfaces. The remedy is to uncheck Use Full Color Range; the gamut of colors is then limited, and the dynamic range of available colors becomes narrower. You just might wind up seeing areas that are hidden in deeply shaded zones when Use Full Color Range is not checked.

Setting the Extrude Color

In addition to shading an extrude group using lighting, you can further embellish and draw out photorealistic qualities by using color options for the extrude. You might need to perform some technical illustration with extrude objects, and you might need cross-hatching in addition to lighting, for example. In these situations, turn to the Color option on the Property Bar; you can shade an extrude group in three different ways: object fill color, solid color, and color shading (much like a fountain fill transition from one color to a different color).

Going from left to right on the Color Control window, you'll see the color modes you can use.

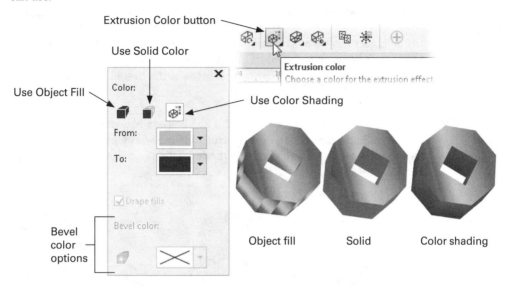

You can achieve effects that range from flat, technical illustrations to highly polished metallic surfaces—which actually can work on their own without your needing to light the object. It all depends on the choices you make in the Color Control window:

- **Using an object's fill**   The Use Object Fill option is the most straightforward to use, but it does not automatically create any sort of shading—if you choose to use the default object fill and the object is filled with a uniform color, give the control object an outline width whose color contrasts with the object fill color. When Use Object Fill is selected, the Drape Fills option also becomes available (and is selected automatically). Drape Fills is discussed shortly; here is an example of a fountain fill control object, with and without Drape Fills.

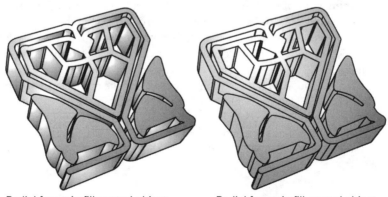

Radial fountain fill control object,
Use Object Fill

Radial fountain fill control object,
Use Object Fill, Drape Fills

- **Choosing your own solid fill** Choose Use Solid Color to set any uniform color to the extrude portion of your effect, regardless of the fill type currently applied to your object. The secondary color option becomes available only when Use Color Shading is selected.

> **Tip** If an object has no outline width/color applied, you might have difficulty seeing the edges between the original and extruded portions. Applying an outline to your original object might help define the edges of the overall composition.

- **Using color shading** Choose Use Color Shading to add depth by using your object's color as the Start color and black (by default) as the End color. Creating visual separation between the extrude group objects and the suggestion of depth is easy with Use Color Shading.

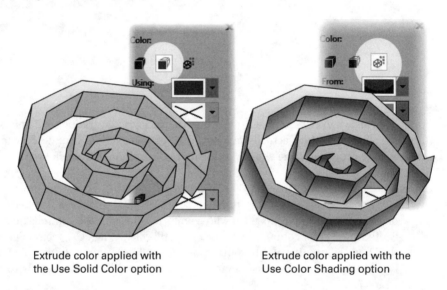

Extrude color applied with   Extrude color applied with the
the Use Solid Color option   Use Color Shading option

- **Draping your object's fill over the extrude effect** *Draping*, as used in CorelDRAW's extrude effect, means "treat each extrude group object's fill as a unique item." Say, for example, you have a patterned piece of cloth, and you drape it over a coffee table: you will see discontinuity in the pattern as each angle of the folds of cloth travels in a different direction in 3D space. Similarly, draping creates discontinuity in a pattern and fountain fill that you apply to both the control object and the extrude group of objects, as shown in Figure 16-8. On the right, with Drape Fills enabled, the polka-dot shape (with some lighting applied) truly looks dimensional, even though the two-color bitmap fill doesn't change perspective (bitmap fills do not take on the rotation angle of extrude objects; they always face forward). On the left, with Drape Fills turned off, the pattern proceeds

Without Drape Fills. Pattern is
continuous (looks hokey).

With Drape Fills. Pattern is
discontinuous (looks realistic).

FIGURE 16-8   **The Drape Fills options can make or break the realism you're trying to illustrate.**

across the object and the extrude group of objects in a continuous pattern, as though it's *projected* onto the surface of the shape instead of *being* the surface of the shape.

- **Using bevel color**   The Bevel Color option becomes available only if you've applied the bevel effect to an extruded shape. Bevel options are located on the Bevels selector on the Property Bar (covered in the next section). This option can be used to give the bevel and the front face of an object the same color, while the extrude shapes retain the original type of fills you specified.

Using the Extrude Docker

If you're a longtime CorelDRAW user, you may have grown accustomed to applying extrude effects using a docker; new users will probably find the interactive editing methods and the options on the Property Bar more convenient to access, but the Extrude docker is available via Window | Dockers | Effects | Extrude. The Extrude docker is organized into five areas: Camera (referring to shape), Rotation, Light, Color, and Bevel.

Although these options are organized differently from the Property Bar, the same options are there. Using the docker method for extruding objects lets you choose extrude settings before applying them.

Assembly Instructions for a Kid's Toy

Now that you've participated in some tutorials, you've learned everything there is to be learned about CorelDRAW extrudes! Okay, this is a bit of an exaggeration, but not by much. It's time, then, to go over the top with a brief, very ambitious survey of what it takes to reproduce the following composition, expressed here as a model rendered in a 3D program.

This is about as photorealistic as you can get, but with a little guidance and a dollop of patience, you can draw something this intricate and dimensional. In the following illustration, I've created a composite view—both Wireframe and Enhanced views—of a drawing that my friend Rik Datta created at my request, using the previous illustration as a reference.

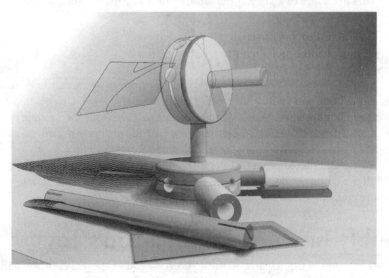

The following is not a group of formal steps as you're used to performing in this *Official Guide*. Instead, I provide some insights on how to reproduce this simple construction kit assembly. Let some of the processes serve as solutions in your own work, and *don't* feel pressured to complete the design.

Tinkering Around.cdr and a Beginning Point

Open the Tinkering Around.cdr file. In it, you'll find a disk and a tube shape; both objects have other objects overlaid to complete a visual effect. First, to create the disk with the hole in the center and an inside bevel halfway along its depth, you want to draw a circle. Hold CTRL while you drag with the Ellipse tool.

Before you begin, make sure that each new extruded shape you create has the Shared Vanishing Point setting applied. You set up your first piece, and then use this button—and its targeting arrow—for each new piece, in order to make sure all objects in the scene are in the same perspective.

Comparing the circle to Rik's drawing, you want to create a linear-style fountain fill, traveling from a light beige to suggest wood beginning at about 11 o'clock, to a slightly darker beige ending at about four o'clock. Doing this also helps out with the lighting of the object, creating lighting fall-off where the extrusion lights might not create this effect.

You could certainly create a smaller circle in the center of the larger one and use the Trim operation, but the inside of the disk will not be self-shaded, as the Extrude feature does not produce shadows. Instead, create the small circle and then use the Circular-style fountain fill, ranging from a deep brown beginning at about 4 o'clock to a lighter beige ending at about 11 o'clock. Drawing plays an important part of completing a 3D design. Do not rely solely on the Extrude tool, unless perhaps you're extruding text for a headline.

Perform an extrude on the circle; then, using the 3D interactive markers, rotate the piece so that its top faces right—use the completed disk in the Tinkering Around.cdr file to get an idea of the best depth (about half what you'd anticipate) and angle of the disk.

Add a small bevel using the Extrusion Bevels button on the Property Bar. Use the Extrusion lighting panel to put a primary light in the upper right of the interactive lighting area, and then add a second light in the opposite direction; make the Intensity setting of this light about 44 so that it adds some detail in shaded areas without bleaching out your extruded shape.

Duplicate the disk using the "drop-a-copy" technique and then move the duplicate to the right so it overlaps most of the original object. This way, you've created the inner bevel in Rik's drawing by using the bevel of the original object. Clever, huh?

The tubular piece at the bottom of this file can be positioned within the composition and created in a general sense (it will need a little refining) by first creating a smaller circle than the first one and then filling it with the same linear fountain fill as the first one—you can use the Attributes Eyedropper to pick up the fill from the first circle.

Then, with the Extrude tool, just drag on the face of the circle to produce an extrusion that is in no way appropriate for reproducing this object! Next, use the Copy Extrusion properties button on the Property Bar to click the extruded side of either of the disk pieces. Presto, the long piece is perfectly lined up in 3D with the disk, and the Copy Extrusion properties also include lighting properties.

You finish this second piece by extruding the circle a little deeper (longer) and adding a handcrafted hole to the end, exactly as you did with the disk object.

Concluding Touches to the Construction

To create a long piece that is angled 90° to support the disks, you can certainly copy the second piece, recolor it, scale the circle, and extend the extrude. You can just use the Rotate/Skew feature in CorelDRAW to change its angle from 0° to 90°. Now, because these pieces all have perspective (a vanishing point), you might not get where you want to go with this or your own composition, not precisely by rotating a piece. You can remedy this by selecting an extruded object, choosing VP Locked To Object, and then manually rotating the object in 3D space. For precision, it's recommended to use the Extrusion Rotation values box and numerical axis entry, because values entered give you immediate feedback on the page—the controls are totally live and interactive.

Any other piece you choose to pursue will probably require inheriting a rotation angle, a shared vanishing point, or both. Remember, for rotations of equal amounts, use the Copy Extrusion From feature on the Property Bar. No kidding, this is an ambitious piece, but certainly if you complete it, it's worthy of an art show award.

The green paddles in the composition can be created using the Perspective feature explained earlier in this chapter. They do not need extruding because in real life they're cardboard thin, but you'll want to use a Linear fountain fill from light to darker green, to suggest the same lighting in the scene as the other pieces.

Figure 16-9 is the author's idea of a panoramic, international-style instruction booklet like those that come with knock-down furniture from Swedish stores.

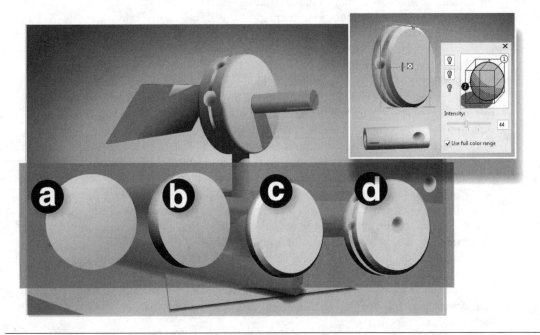

FIGURE 16-9 Extruded objects in combination with those you draw can lend a scene depth that otherwise is hard to draw.

Cleaning Up After Assembling an Extrude Composition

The Extrude feature in CorelDRAW can be an indispensable timesaver when you want to print a quick, astounding drawing. However, the sheer number of individual objects that make up an extrude shape, especially when lighting is applied, can be staggering and unwieldy to work with.

Is there a simple solution to reducing the number of objects CorelDRAW produces? No. Is there a way that requires effort but basically assures you of the objects you need, and is a great way to practice tracing? Oh, yeah….

The following illustration shows a process you can adopt that re-creates a surfeit of individual flat shaded object with one object that has a fountain fill. The Extrude feature does not use fountain fills in its calculations, but *you* can.

Incidentally, the Tinkering Around.cdr file in the .zip archive is Rik's drawing. You'll see some blends, but the extruded shapes have all been replaced using the technique outlined next.

Callout A in this illustration shows two pieces: a scarab beetle shape and a second shape on top depicting the beetle's shell. Callout B shows the beetle and its shell; they were lined up by first using the Copy Extrusion From features, and then the shell was recolored and a bevel applied.

Callout C shows a Wireframe view, a close-up of a part of the extruded beetle, after the Object | Convert to Curves command (CTRL-Q, memorize this one!) has been made. Oh, darn; this beetle consists of over 1,700 individual objects—much more than an actual VW Beetle. You do *not* want to work with this many shapes; the result if you had three or four of these prolific things on a page would be a slowdown in processing and your creativity.

Callout D shows the Pen tool in action, tracing under the front piece of the extrude on a layer I've created under the extruded bug layer. Once a suitable replacement is created for dozens of shapes that represent a single fountain fill, you can delete the original shapes.

As you can see in Callout E, a radical reduction in shapes has been made for the beetle. It's no longer editable as a 3D shape, but if you're done editing a complex extruded shape, you now have the luxury of duplicating twice (or a hundred times) on the page, creating an infestation in this example, and the speed at which you create and edit will be practically unnoticeable.

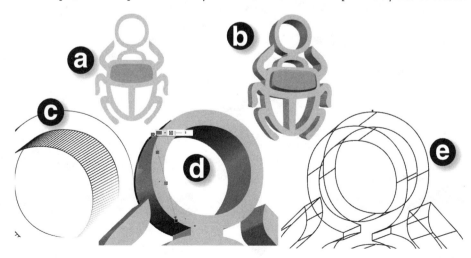

Note The Beetles.cdr file in the .zip archive contains a broken-down copy of the extruded beetle, plus a live copy of the original extruded shapes, in case you'd like to rotate the beetle or otherwise edit it before breaking up the extrusion. Have fun with some tracing practice and making both your life and the beetle simpler.

Extruding shapes is something many artists who compete with you for jobs might not be able to offer, especially if they don't own CorelDRAW! However, it's probably not a career-enhancer to use the extrude effect (or any other effect) as a substitute for your own talent as a designer. Use the Extrude feature with good judgment. Use it when you're in a design rut and need that certain something to perk up a piece. But don't let yourself get branded as the Extrude King or Queen (it even *sounds* rude!).

Chapter 17 continues the *Official Guide*'s Effects Extravaganza, with envelopes, lens effects, and additional fun stuff. Learn to take an object or group of objects from being close to what you want to draw to *exactly* what you want. Just rotate this page 180° counterclockwise along your local X axis.

17 Using the Envelope Tool, Lens Effects, and Bevels

When you feel a design needs an element of realism—or even surrealism—to add attention, complexity, or that "certain something" that makes a shining piece absolutely brilliant, you turn to some of the effects CorelDRAW offers. Specifically, you need the ones not covered yet in this book—and more specifically, you need effects that can add lighting to an object, bend it, twist it, and, in general, modify it as though you are sculpting and not drawing.

This chapter reveals the inner workings of the envelope effect—probably the most advanced effect of its kind in any drawing program—and the Lens Effects docker, which provides some pretty wild variations on your artwork by overlaying it with a lens object. To round out this chapter's collection of neat embellishments, you'll also get hands-on experience with creating beveled objects; you can create anything from an emboss to a 3D starfish shape. These effects are easy to use and apply—the only hard part is deciding which *type* of effect works best in your illustration!

 Note Download and extract all the files from the Chapter17.zip archive to follow the tutorials in this chapter.

What Does an Envelope Do?

You've probably seen this effect in stores a dozen times: for example, the words "Fresh Fish" shaped in the silhouette of a fish. In CorelDRAW, conforming objects to a different shape is done with the Envelope tool.

In CorelDRAW, you can start with a fresh envelope around an object, use presets, and copy a shape to use as an envelope of a different shape. Then, you edit the envelope until the shape suits your need. Envelopes are nondestructive; your original artwork can be restored at any time. The Property Bar includes a Clear Envelope button when an enveloped object is selected with the Shape tool. Once an envelope has been defined, you edit the envelope exactly as you would a path—you can drag on segments and nodes and change the node control points to your heart's content.

Here are two visual examples of how useful the envelope effect can be. At the top illustration, the Artistic Text object is enveloped, and the envelope is based on an existing shape (shown on the right). The bottom illustration shows the envelope control segments and nodes in the process of being edited. It's true: the CorelDRAW envelope effect is just like playing with Silly You-Know-What!

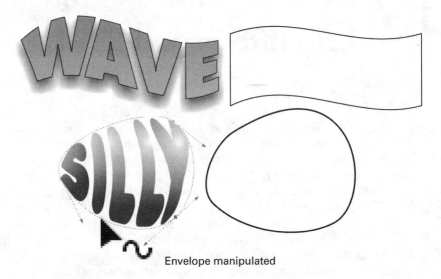

Envelope shape copied from the object

Envelope manipulated

Creating Envelope Effects

When creating envelope effects, you can choose from three different methods. You can shape your envelope from scratch by defining a default envelope and then manually reshaping it. You can copy an envelope shape based on an object on the drawing page, and you can also use a preset shipped with CorelDRAW.

Using the Envelope Tool and Property Bar

Using the Envelope tool along with the Property Bar options is the most intuitive way to apply envelopes. You'll find this tool in the Toolbox with the other effects, such as the Extrude and Drop Shadow tools.

With both the Envelope tool and an object selected, the Property Bar displays the options shown here:

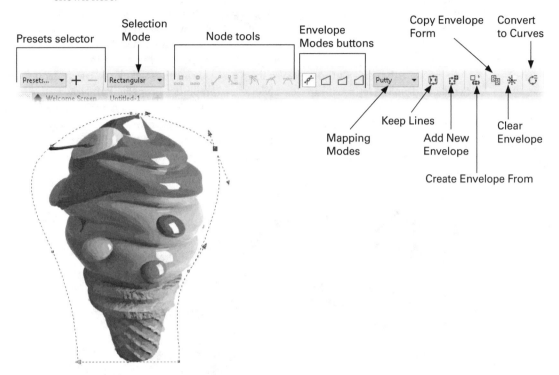

You'll get the best results from the Envelope tool if you follow a sequence of moves in CorelDRAW. Let's work through some basic maneuvers using the following steps.

Tutorial

The Envelope, Please

1. Create or open an object (or group of objects) that you feel would make a good target for the envelope effect, and then choose the Envelope tool from the Toolbox. Notice that the Property Bar shows Envelope options. The more intricate the object, the more noticeable the effect will be. In general, don't choose a rectangular shape to which you want to apply a rectangular envelope; the effect would be more or less defeated.
2. Click the Envelope Mode button that resembles a square with one corner higher than the other—Straight Line Mode—and notice the markers surrounding your shape.
3. Drag one of the nodes on your object in any direction. Notice the direction of movement is constrained and the shape of your object changes to match the envelope as you release the mouse button.

4. Click the next Envelope Mode button resembling a square with one curved side—Single Arc Mode. Drag any node in any direction, and notice the object shape changes, but this time you have some curvature going on with the edges of the envelope and the object(s) inside. Double Arc Mode provides more distortion, most noticeably when you drag a center envelope node instead of one of the four corner bounding nodes.

5. Notice that you can drag an envelope node to reshape the object, but the direction handles on either side of the node are fixed and won't budge. Click the Unconstrained Mode button, the leftmost Envelope Mode button on the Property Bar. Now try dragging nodes and then their direction handles. The following illustration shows the object group in its original state; on the right, it has been worked over a little in Unconstrained Mode (it looks reminiscent of how your packages occasionally arrive on Mondays, doesn't it?). Seriously, though, nothing is hard and fixed in a CorelDRAW drawing, and no changes are permanent.

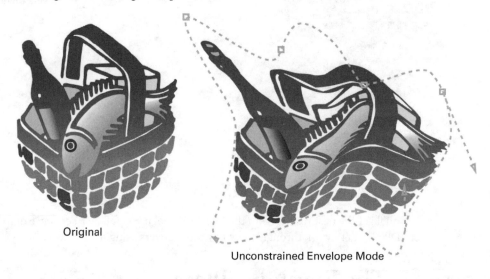

Original

Unconstrained Envelope Mode

 Note For most effects in CorelDRAW, the Property Bar offers presets and the ability to add your own preset by clicking the + button; whereas clicking the minus button (-) deletes the currently selected preset on the drop-down list.

Clicking the Clear Envelope button on the Property Bar removes the last applied envelope, but don't stop reading here! You can apply an envelope to an object that already has an envelope by clicking the Add New Envelope button on the Property Bar. If you want to return the object to its original state, you must click the Clear Envelope button, which returns you to the Pick tool and only reverts one stage of enveloping. You then have to select the Shape or Envelope tool, reselect the shape, click the Clear Envelope button, and then *repeat* this somewhat tedious process until you return the object to its original form. It's far better to choose Windows | Docker | Undo Manager and click on a saved state that precedes an Envelope effect, reverting the object completely to its original state. One click, nice trick.

Caution There is a limit, particularly with grouped objects in an envelope, to how much you can reshape before the paths that make up an object begin to self-intersect. Self-intersecting is usually an unwanted effect, so either use the tool sparingly on a group, or ungroup the group and apply similar envelope effects to individual objects.

Using the Envelope Docker

The Envelope docker provides an alternative to using the Envelope tool in combination with the Property Bar. You can select options before they are actually applied. To open the Envelope docker, choose Effects | Envelope, or press CTRL-F7.

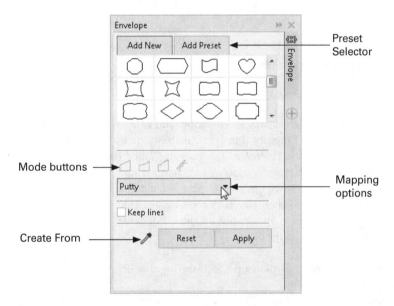

Choosing an Envelope Mode

The Envelope mode you choose has no initial effect on the envelope you apply to an object; however, as you begin to move envelope nodes around, the selected Envelope mode offers

Tip For speedy envelope editing, use the Pick tool to double-click any object that has an envelope. The enveloped object is immediately available for editing, and the Pick tool becomes the Envelope tool. A single click with the Shape tool also opens an enveloped object for editing.

features and limitations. Depending on the mode, corner and segment nodes take on different properties, which result in different capabilities to edit the envelope, as seen here:

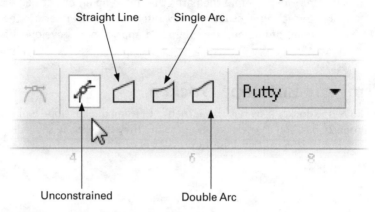

Envelope modes (shown on the Property Bar)

> **Tip** At any time while editing an envelope, you can change its mode just by clicking a button on the Property Bar. This capability gives you control over the overall shape you're trying to create. Any previous mode limitation is inherited with existing nodes, but nodes you've not changed inherit the new node property. For example, if your envelope is in Double Arc mode and you drag a node to make a swooping arc, and then you click the Straight Line Mode button on the Property Bar, the arc remains an arc, but all the other nodes can now only be edited as connectors to straight lines.

These modes have the following effects during shaping operations:

- **Straight Line**   This mode (the default) makes envelope segments be straight lines; in effect, you're manipulating an eight-point polygon when the envelope is in Straight Line mode. Dragging an envelope node creates a different polygon shape, and this mode serves you well for imitating the shape of a traffic sign, a simple house shape, and other outlines you create with straight line segments.
- **Single Arc**   This mode sets the resulting envelope segments to curves, sets side nodes to smooth nodes, and sets corner nodes to Cusp nodes; you can't change the angle of the cusp for corner nodes directly, but you can change it when you reposition a side envelope node. Using this mode, dragging corner nodes creates a curved side on the envelope, whereas side nodes align with the path of the resulting curve.
- **Double Arc**   This mode creates sine-wave-shaped sides. Behind the scenes, corner points become cusp nodes, and side nodes become smooth nodes. However, the curve handles of side nodes remain stationary in relation to the nodes, causing the segments to take on a double-arc shape. The same vertical and horizontal constraint restrictions as with the previous modes apply.

- **Unconstrained**   Unconstrained mode gives you complete control over nodes, segments, and control handles for envelope elements; it gives you almost unlimited freedom to reshape an object. You can position either side or corner nodes as if they were vector path object nodes. In this mode, the Shape tool and Envelope tool let you *severely* reshape objects, and nodes can be dragged in any direction to shape the envelope in any way. Unconstrained mode also allows you to add or delete nodes, change any line segment states to straight or curved, or change the properties of nodes to Cusp, Smooth, or Symmetrical using Property Bar buttons for these tasks.

Here's a visual example of the four modes, with a faint outline overlay indicating the original shape of the extruded phoenix object:

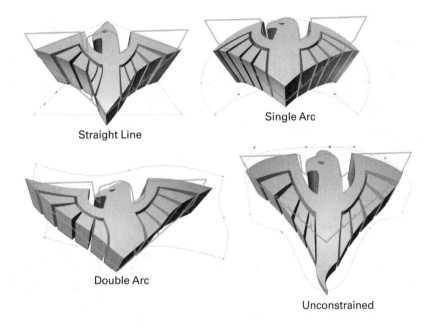

Straight Line

Single Arc

Double Arc

Unconstrained

Note   Modifier keys offer valuable ways to constrain the shaping of an envelope while using *Single Arc* mode. By holding key modifiers, you can quickly shape two sides concentrically or simultaneously. Hold SHIFT and drag any side or corner node to move the corresponding node on the opposite side in the *opposite* direction. Hold CTRL to move the corresponding node on the opposite side of the shape in the *same* direction and by an equal distance.

Choosing Envelope Mapping Options

Envelope mapping options are available from the Envelope docker as well as when you're using the Envelope tool and Property Bar options, which control how the shape of an envelope

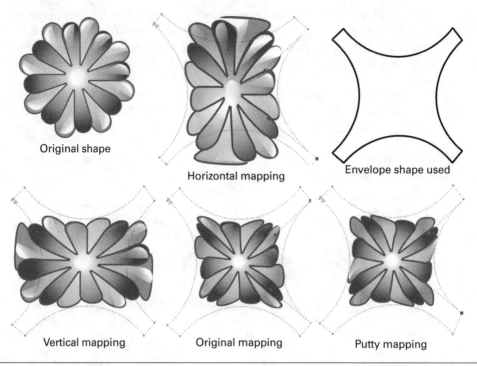

Original shape

Horizontal mapping

Envelope shape used

Vertical mapping

Original mapping

Putty mapping

FIGURE 17-1 This object group uses the same envelope but different mapping options.

changes your object's shape (see Figure 17-1). As you can see, Original and Putty mapping provide almost identical results for this particular group of objects and the envelope shape used here, but Horizontal and Vertical mapping give you the design opportunity to ignore the other envelope axis (Horizontal mapping ignores the vertical aspect of the envelope, and vice versa). This option is handy when you want to limit distortion of an envelope but don't have the time (or need!) to create a unique envelope for several different design purposes.

Mapping options give preference to the shape of your original object's node positions and path shapes. Four types are available: Putty (the default), Horizontal, Vertical, and Original, as shown here:

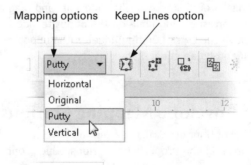

The four Envelope mapping options, plus a special option for text and another to preserve lines, are worthy of explanation:

- **Putty** This option (the default) distorts the shape of your object to match the envelope as closely as possible; the envelope's nodes are given priority over the nodes in the object being enveloped. Putty maps the envelope shape to your object and results in a smoothly mapped effect.
- **Horizontal** This option maps the lines and node positions in your original object to match the horizontal shape of the envelope, without significantly altering the vertical shape of the original object.
- **Vertical** This option maps the lines and node positions in your original object to the *vertical* shape of the envelope, with the horizontal shape mostly ignored.
- **Original** This mapping type is similar to Putty. The main difference is that Original maps *only the outer shape* of your original object to the envelope shape. Corner nodes are mapped to the corner nodes of your original object's shape, whereas node positions and line shapes toward the inside of your object are mapped using an averaging value. The result can be less distorted. If Putty mapping is too severe, try Original.
- **Keep Lines** Using this option changes only the node positions in your object to match the envelope shape being applied, leaving any existing straight lines unaffected. If your object is already composed only of curved lines, choosing Keep Lines has no effect. When Keep Lines is *not* selected (the default), all node positions and lines in your original object are reshaped to match the envelope shape—even if this means changing straight lines to curved lines.
- **Text** This option is the only mapping option available when a Paragraph Text object frame is selected. Text mode applies an envelope to the *frame* properties of a Paragraph Text object; the actual text and line of text are not distorted. This feature presents a wonderful opportunity to walk through a tutorial.

In this tutorial, you'll use the Violin.cdr file, which contains a silhouette drawing of a violin and a block of Paragraph Text attributed to Wikipedia. Your task is to fit the text inside the profile of the violin drawing. It's a class act, and this technique can be used for scores of designs—especially music scores.

Tutorial Creating a Text Envelope

1. In the Violin.cdr document, choose the Paragraph Text object with the Envelope tool.

2. On the Property Bar, click the Create Envelope From button, and once your cursor changes to a targeting arrow, click the violin shape.

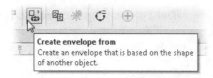

Create envelope from
Create an envelope that is based on the shape of another object.

The violin is sometimes informally called a fiddle, regardless of the type of music played on it. The word violin comes from the Middle Latin word vitula, meaning stringed instrument; this word is also believed to be the source of the Germanic "fiddle". The violin, while it has ancient origins, acquired most of its modern characteristics in 16th-century Italy, with some further modifications occurring in the 18th century.
Someone who plays the violin is called a violinist or a fiddler. The violinist produces sound by drawing a bow across one or more strings (which may be stopped by the fingers of the other hand to produce a full range of pitches), by plucking the strings (with either hand), or by a variety of other techniques. The violin is played by musicians in a wide variety of musical genres, including Baroque music, classical, jazz, folk music, pop-punk and rock and roll. The violin has come to be played in many non-western music cultures all over the world.
—Excerpt credited 2010 to Wikipedia.

3. Click the Paragraph Text object with the Pick tool and then choose the Envelope tool to be able to copy the effect. Click the text using the Paragraph tool. Then click the Create Envelope From button on the Property Bar; your cursor turns into a targeting

cursor. CorelDRAW recognizes this as a change to the Paragraph Text and obligingly pours the text into the violin shape, as shown here.

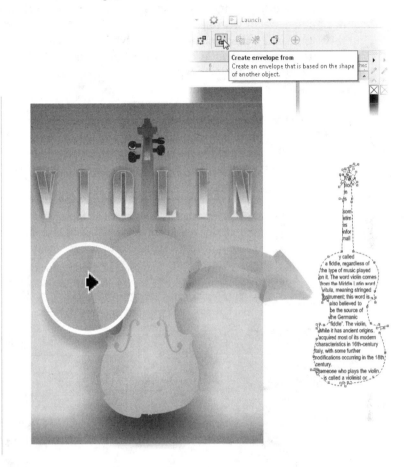

4. Choose the Pick tool and move the text to fit over the violin drawing. You will probably have to scale the enveloped text up a little. When you do this by dragging on a corner selection handle, try to keep the text just a little to the inside of the violin shape so there is a small margin between the text and the edge of the violin shape. You can also click-drag the object selection handles with the Shape tool to fine-tune the flow of the text.

5. With the Text tool, insert your cursor at the beginning of the paragraph and then press ENTER to kick the text down so none of it is in the neck part of the violin, which looks awkward, reads terribly, and makes it hard to play the instrument. See Figure 17-2 as a reference for where your composition should be now.

6. Optionally, choose a more elegant typeface than Arial. Select the text with the Pick tool, and then on the Property bar choose an installed font. In Figure 17-3, Mona Lisa Solid (distributed by ITC) is used. End of exercise—pretty fancy graphic using the Envelope tool!

Tip Once the text has been enveloped, you can add this shape to your Envelope Presets list. Unfortunately, you cannot add an object as a preset envelope, but only the product of enveloping an object based on the shape of a different object.

Let's move now from twisting objects to recoloring, magnifying, and, in general, applying a lens over an object.

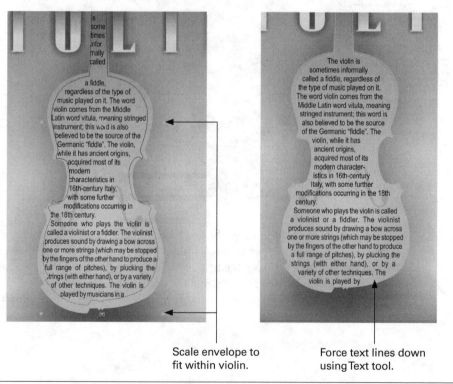

Scale envelope to fit within violin.

Force text lines down using Text tool.

FIGURE 17-2   Perform a little manual editing to make the envelope text fit within the violin drawing.

FIGURE 17-3   Create an elegant symbiosis of text as a graphic combined with a simple CorelDRAW drawing.

Tip   You can apply *several* instances of an envelope, an envelope enveloping an envelope, and so on, if you need a truly gnarly effect. After you've sampled the envelope, click the cursor over the target shape three or four times until your laughter subsides.

What's Behind a Lens Effect

Looking at your drawings with a lens effect object on top is like looking through a window or a magnifying glass. What you see is influenced by the *properties* of the glass. For example, tinted glass in the real world makes objects in the distance appear darker—you can easily simulate this phenomenon with the lens effect set to Color Limit and applied to a 50% black object.

One of the more popular uses of this feature is to overlap a shape partially with a lens effect so you can see both affected and original areas at once. You can also freeze the lens effect object, capturing whatever's underneath the lens, and then move the lens object around, retaining the original view within the object.

Using the Lens Docker

The only way to apply a lens in CorelDRAW is through the Lens docker, opened by choosing Effects | Lens (ALT-F3). Figure 17-4 shows the Lens docker, whose options change depending on the function you choose. Operate the Lens docker by first placing an object—which becomes the lens object—over a *different* object (or several objects, vector or imported bitmaps), choosing a Lens type from the drop-down menu, and then choosing from the different property options.

It's easier to understand lens effects if you just do it, as the manufacturer of running shoes says. Let's take the Lens docker out for a trial spin.

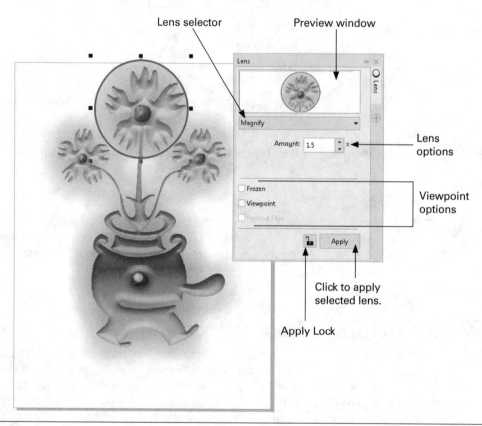

FIGURE 17-4 The Lens docker is where you customize effects to create the specific type of lens you need.

Tutorial   # Working with a Lens Effect

1. Create a rectangle and then, with the Fill tool, click-drag to create a default Linear fountain fill from black to white. This rectangle will serve for this demonstration, but you'll most certainly get better effects using artwork of your own.
2. Create an ellipse and, with the Pick tool, arrange the ellipse so it partially overlaps the rectangle so that you can better see the creative possibilities of applying a lens to the ellipse object.
3. With the ellipse selected, open the Lens docker (ALT-F3).
4. Choose Custom Color Map from the docker's Lens selector drop-down list. Choose a deep blue from the From Color picker and then choose a bright green from the To Color picker.
5. The Apply Lock button, when in the locked position, auto-applies the effect as you adjust the parameters. If you like to review stuff *before* applying it (such as car wax or cosmetic surgery), click the lock icon to unlock the auto-apply state, and then click the Apply button to finalize the effect. The lens effect has remapped deeper shades in the rectangle to blues and lighter shades to greens, but areas of the rectangle not covered by the ellipse are still a black-to-white fountain fill.
6. Move the ellipse around a little to see how the lens effect changes only those areas of the rectangle that the ellipse covers.
7. With the ellipse partially eclipsing the rectangle, click the Frozen check box to put a check mark in it.
8. Move the ellipse around. As you can see, its content colors remain constant, even when you move the ellipse totally away from the rectangle.
9. Show your friends this effect. This is *fascinating* stuff!

Tip   The Apply Lock option on the Lens docker applies lens effects immediately, so you don't need to click the Apply button.

Exploring the Lens Effects

Each lens effect has different properties you set using the docker controls. Each lens type is covered in the sections that follow so you can better judge your starting point when you want to dress up an illustration with a certain type of lens effect.

- **Brighten lens effect**   Colors in objects seen through a Brighten lens can appear brighter *or* darker, depending on the setting in the Rate num box. The Rate setting can be between 100 and −100; positive values brighten up underlying colors, whereas negative values darken them. Brighten is a handy effect when, for example, part of an illustration you've worked on for days looks under- or overexposed when you print it. The solution is to design an object to use as the lens and place it directly on top, perfectly aligned with the area that prints poorly.

- **Color Add lens effect** The Color Add lens fills the lens object with the color you choose by clicking the Color mode color picker and then combining all underlying colors in an additive fashion—the culmination of the three primary colors being white instead of the real-world physical pigment model of subtractive colors, which eventually produce black when excessive amounts of primary colors are mixed. As an example, if you created an object with a red-to-blue fountain fill and then put a red Color Add lens object over it, the red areas will look unaffected at all rates, whereas the blue areas will change to cyan. This effect is good for adding a tint to isolated areas of an illustration and imported bitmaps. Any color can be added within a range of 0 to 100 percent in increments of 5 percent. Higher values add more color; 0 adds no color at all.

- **Color Limit lens effect** The Color Limit lens produces an effect that looks like the opposite effect produced by the Color Add lens. Color Limit tints underlying areas and decreases brightness in all underlying areas *except* for the hues in the color you choose from the docker. Color Limit can be quite useful, for example, to highlight an object in a composition by deemphasizing all other objects.

- **Custom Color Map lens effect** This type of lens object looks at the original colors in the underlying objects based on brightness values and then reproduces the design with the remapping colors you specify on the Lens docker. Usually, you want to choose a deep From color and a light To color; this tints and colorizes a drawing or bitmap in a predictable way. You can also remap your drawing colors in untraditional ways; mapping options include three palette-mapping choices: Direct Palette, Forward, and Reverse Rainbow.

  - Choosing Direct Palette offers two colors (From and To) and maps the colors found in your objects evenly between the brightness values of colors found directly between these two around the color wheel.

  - Conversely, Forward Rainbow has the same effect as Direct Palette, but in this case each of the object colors is mapped to *all* colors between your two chosen colors in a clockwise rotation. For example, if you choose red as the From color and green as the To color, instead of a blend between these two colors throughout your illustration, you'll get greens making a transition to magenta and then purple recoloring the underlying design. If you want the entire spectrum of the rainbow, choose red as the Start color and violet (purple) as the End color.

  - The Reverse Rainbow option has the effect of mapping the colors in your object to the RGB brightness values of all colors between your two chosen colors in a counterclockwise direction. If you choose this option after setting up Forward Rainbow colors, you'll get a chromatic inverse of Forward Rainbow color mapping, a highly solarized look, much like what developed physical film would look like it if you opened the back of the camera before rewinding the film.

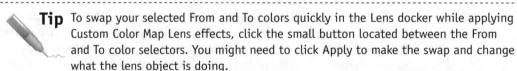

Tip To swap your selected From and To colors quickly in the Lens docker while applying Custom Color Map Lens effects, click the small button located between the From and To color selectors. You might need to click Apply to make the swap and change what the lens object is doing.

- **Fish Eye lens effect** A conventional camera "fish eye" lens has a very wide angle of view. CorelDRAW's Fish Eye lens performs the virtual equivalent; you can produce exceptionally distorted artwork, which can be an interesting, if not an everyday, effect in commercial design. Fish Eye is controlled by setting the rate of distortion within a range of 1,000 to −1,000 percent. You'll probably find these extreme values useless in your work. At lower rates, the effect is subtle while retaining a sense of drama and dynamics.

Note   The Fish Eye lens' strong suite is distorting over vector drawing. If you try to distort a bitmap with this lens, the effect will be subtle to no effect at all.

- **Heat Map lens effect**   The Heat Map lens is similar to the Color Map lens effect, except the colors are predetermined (there are no specific color options). The effect simulates "black body" physics: a hypothetical object (in space) absorbs all light, and the presumption in this hypothesis is that the body is warm. With the Heat Map lens, colors in underlying objects on the warm side of the color wheel (red, orange, yellow) appear in shades of red or orange. Cool colors (green, blue, and violet) appear in shades of white, yellow, purple, blue, and light blue. You can also offset the color mapping by using the Palette rotation spin box. When you use the Palette rotation spin box, values of around 50 usually make colors appear cooler, and as you move to 0, or in the opposite direction (100), colors appear warmer.

- **Invert lens effect**   The Invert lens applies color inversion to the colors of underlying objects. In this case, colors are directly mapped to colors found on the opposite side of a color wheel. Black areas change to white, light grays turn to dark grays, reds turn to greens, yellows turn to blues, and so on. To make a "day and night" composition, follow these steps:
  1. Open the Sundial.cdr image.
  2. Put the black half-circle over the left half of the logo.
  3. Choose Invert from Lens selector list on the Lens docker.

- **Magnify lens effect** Although this lens produces a straightforward and predictable effect, it can make underlying objects larger *or* smaller, depending on the value you enter for the Rate setting. The Rate can be set within a range of 0.1 to 100, where values between 1 and 100 increase magnification and values less than 1 reduce magnification. Try opening Swamp Water.cdr and then magnify the 1-point text at the bottom of the bottle so the public can see what's in this "sports drink." Bitmaps are resolution dependent, so you can only magnify the image of the bottle so much. The text in this composition is, however, a pure native CorelDRAW vector. Place the ellipse over the fine print in the image, and then magnify it 8× or even higher if you like, and the text remains crisp and legible—and, in this example, you'll get a little reminder about what it is you're potentially putting into your system.

- **Tinted Grayscale lens effect** By default, the Tinted Grayscale lens converts the colors of underlying objects to grayscale values, which is terrific if you're into black-and-white photography, but you can use any color you like, thus tinting photos and drawings just by choosing a color from the Color flyout palette on the docker. Remember that digital images use the additive color model, so the lighter the lens color, the fainter the resulting composition. You might want this effect, however; try light grays and light warm browns to make new photographs look like they were originally taken in the 1940s.

- **Transparency lens effect** This lens effect a simplified version of the effects you can achieve using the Transparency tool on the Toolbox. Blending modes are unavailable, and the object itself becomes transparent—not the underlying objects—to varying degrees based on the rate you set on the Lens docker. The perk to using a Transparency lens effect over the Transparency tool is that you can freeze the effect and then move a partially transparent copy of the underlying area anywhere you like on the page.

- **Wireframe lens effect** This lens effect converts the color and outline properties of objects to specific colors; this effect is useful for pointing out the technical details in an illustration. You can set the outline and fill colors of objects beneath the lens to any uniform color you choose by clicking the Outline or Fill flyout palette on the docker. The fill and outline colors of your objects are replaced with the selected colors, whereas outline properties—such as applied widths and line styles—are ignored; Wireframe produces a fixed-width outline.

Although Burger.cdr—the file you'll work with in a moment—is a good illustration, let's say the fictitious client, Mr. Beefbarn, wants to "accentuate" his sixteenth of a pound all-beef special by plumping up the illustration for the advertisement instead of the actual weight of his product. Instead of using the envelope effects (which will not work on imported photographs), in a few mouse clicks, you can create a shape that roughly fits over only the burger in the drawing and then apply the Fish Eye lens.

Tutorial Changing Object Size with the Fish Eye Lens

1. Open Burger.cdr; with a Pen tool, draw a shape that roughly matches the shape of the hamburger, just a little larger so the lens effect works. If you want to cut to the chase, creating an ellipse around the burger provides decent results.

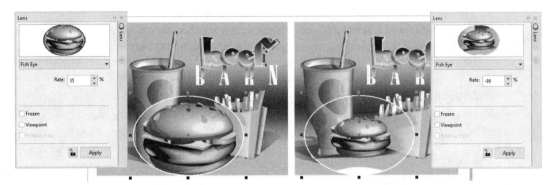

| Fish Eye rate at 35% | Fish Eye rate at –90% |

FIGURE 17-5   Two different Fish Eye lens effects settings are used to bloat and pucker the underlying drawing area.

2. On the Lens docker, with the object selected, choose Fish Eye. Set the Rate to **65%**. If the Apply button is unlocked, click Apply now to see the results. Try moving the lens object around a little if the illusion that the burger is almost twice its original size isn't perfect.

3. Let's say Mr. Beefbarn gets on a health-food kick and wants you to design a leaner burger. You just crank the Fish Eye lens effect to –90 and then click Apply. With just one click (and perhaps moving the lens object a little), you can get today's health-conscious culture to buy the advertisement, if not the burger.

In Figure 17-5, you can see, on the left, the result of an ellipse shape with the Fish Eye lens type defined at a rate of 65%. The burger bulges toward the viewer, and Mr. Beefbarn is happy. On the right, a negative rate (–90%) is defined using the same lens object. Happy client and very little editing work needed.

Using Lens Options

Only one option has been discussed so far with the Lens docker: the *types* of effects. You'll gain more control of your effects when the other options on the docker are explained in the following sections. Locking an effect, altering viewpoints, and controlling whether the page background is involved in an effect open extra doors to this docker.

Using the Frozen Option

The Frozen option "freezes" the view seen through any lens effect—even if the lens object itself is moved. You can then apply and freeze the lens object view and use it for other purposes. A Frozen lens effect object can actually be ungrouped to reveal a set of objects based on the lens you've applied. If the effect is applied above a bitmap, the result is often a complete copy of the filtered image area, and it can be exported as a bitmap.

After choosing the Frozen option, you can ungroup the lens object (CTRL-U). This action converts the effect to a collection of ungrouped vector and/or bitmap objects. Each of the objects representing the complete effect becomes a separate object, including the lens object, the page background, and the objects within the lens view.

Changing a Lens Viewpoint

The Lens Viewpoint option lets you move a lens and keep the view inside the lens constant—like freezing a lens, but this option *keeps the effect dynamic.* When you check Viewpoint on the docker, an Edit button appears. You then click-drag interactively to reposition the viewpoint of the lens effect either using your cursor (indicated onscreen by an X) or by entering numeric values in the X and Y page position boxes.

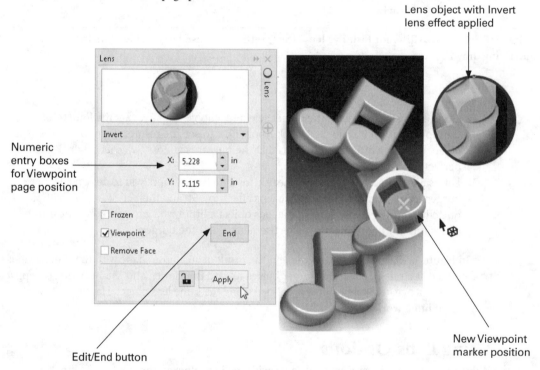

Lens object with Invert lens effect applied

Numeric entry boxes for Viewpoint page position

Edit/End button

New Viewpoint marker position

Tip The view seen through a lens object depends on the object order on a layer—all objects layered below the lens object appear in the lens. When the Viewpoint is repositioned, you may find that an object is not visible. Arranging objects in back of the lens object causes them to be affected; arranging them in front of the lens object prevents the lens effect from changing them.

The default Viewpoint position of a lens effect is always the center of your object, but you can move it anywhere you like. After moving it, unlatch the lock button and then click the Apply button on the Lens docker to set the new position.

Using the Remove Face Option

Remove Face is available for only a few types of lens effects. It lets you specify whether other objects and the page background participate in the effect. By default, whenever a lens effect is applied, the background—your page, which is usually white—is involved in the effect.

If the lens you are using changes the colors—such as with Custom Color Map—and you *don't* want your background to be changed within the view seen through the lens object, selecting this option leaves the background unaltered. The design idea is to remap only the objects under the lens. Without Remove Face, a background on your drawing page is tinted, but after Remove Face is applied, the page background of your composition is unaffected by the tinting effect.

Using the Bevel Effect

The Window | Dockers | Effects | Bevel docker gives you a way to make objects dimensional, but not as completely three-dimensional as the Extrude tool. The Bevel docker offers two different types of engraving effect: Emboss and Soft Edge. The Emboss mode is an automated routine that creates duplicates of an object, offsets them, and gives them different colors to create the effect of, for example, a seal crimped onto a piece of paper like notary publics used to do. Although you can manually create this emboss effect, the Bevel docker creates a dynamic, linked group whose color and position can change when you define different light intensities and light angles.

Here are visual examples of the emboss effect. If you choose to use Emboss mode, create a background for the object because either the highlight or the shadow object might not be visible against the page background. Usually, a color similar to the background will serve you well for the object color. You can use any fill, including bitmaps and fountain fills, for the object you want to emboss, but the resulting emboss objects will not *feature* the fill, only solid (uniform) colors.

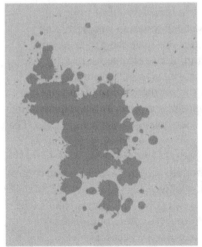

Original

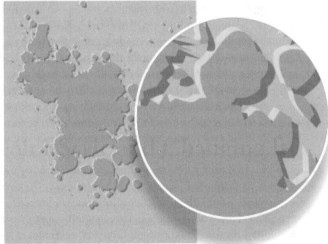

Two offset duplicates create the effect.

Here, you can see the Bevel docker and the options available while applying the Emboss mode.

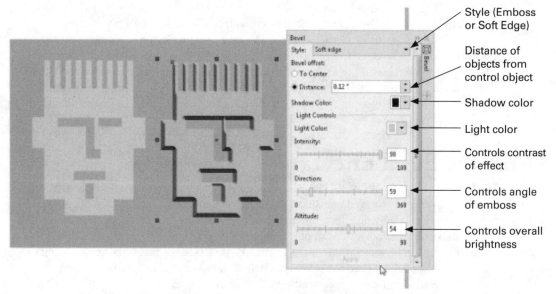

Style (Emboss or Soft Edge)

Distance of objects from control object

Shadow color

Light color

Controls contrast of effect

Controls angle of emboss

Controls overall brightness

Here's a rundown of what the options do on the Bevel docker in Emboss mode:

- **Bevel Offset—Distance**   This combination num box and spin box is used to set the distance of the duplicate objects from the original. You don't gain anything visually by setting a high value for an object; rather, this box is used to set a relational distance, depending on the size of the object to which you apply the emboss effect. For example, a 4" object looks embossed if you use a 0.09" Distance setting, but the effect looks a little phony at greater distances. On the other hand, an 8" object will probably not look embossed with a 0.09" Distance setting—0.16", however, scales the effect proportionately to the object and the emboss effect looks good. If you need to resize an object, plan to redefine the Distance setting for the Emboss mode after you scale the parent object.
- **Shadow Color**   The color of the object has a direct influence on the color of the shadow object behind the control object. For example, if you create an emboss effect with a blue object, the shadow object is a dark blue, even if you set the color to black. You can neutralize the shadow color by defining the color opposite the control object; for example, if you have a cyan circle, set the Shadow Color to red, the color complement of cyan. The resulting color is always duller than the color you define because—well, it's a *shadow!* Shadow Color is unaffected by the Intensity option.
- **Light Color**   This controls the color of the highlight object; it affects neither the control object's color nor the color or brightness of the shadow object. Light Color at full intensity displays the color you choose, and as you decrease intensity, the Light Color blends with the object color—Light Color does not depend on any object's color you might have beneath the effect. As light intensity decreases, a bitmap-filled object's highlight color changes from its original color to white.

- **Intensity**   Use this slider to control the contrast of the emboss effect. Although the shadow object's color is not affected by intensity, the highlight object's color is.
- **Direction**   Use this slider to control the direction that light seems to cast on the emboss object(s). A Direction setting of 0° points the highlight at 3 o'clock, traveling counterclockwise. Therefore, if you need a highlight on an emboss effect at 11 o'clock (a very classic lighting position), set the Direction at about 120°.
- **Altitude**   This option is only available in Soft Edge mode and not Emboss. It changes the simulated position of a sun or light. Lower altitudes produce darker shapes and bevels, while higher values brighten and reduce the contrast between the shape and the bevel.

Creating Soft-Edge Bevel Effects

The other mode on the Bevel docker, Soft Edge, performs many more calculations than the Emboss mode and actually creates a bitmap image, masked by the control object, which you can adjust dynamically. The Shadow Color, Light Intensity (and Color), and Direction options on the docker produce predictable results, much like those you get when using Emboss mode, but because the Soft Edge mode is generated to bitmap format, the results look more detailed, refined, and almost photorealistic in appearance. In addition to having an Altitude slider in this mode, you have To Center as an available option in the Bevel Offset field. Here's what it does and how To Center works.

All soft-edge bevels are produced from the edge of a shape traveling toward its center. If, for example, you've created a circle that's 3" across and then type a Distance offset value in the num box in any amount less than 1.5", you'll see a dimensional, sloping bevel created inside the circle, with a flat top in the shape of the circle in its center. If, however, you type in a value greater than 1.5", the center of the object bevels to a point, and the front face of the object is entirely lost. The reason this happens is that the bevel effect travels toward the interior of the shape, and half of the 3" diameter of this circle is 1.5". Just keep in mind the size of the shape to which you apply a bevel effect to gain total control over the effect. If, on the other hand, you intend for the sides of the bevel to come to a point, you don't need to set values in the Distance field; you choose To Center, click Apply, and CorelDRAW creates the maximum-width bevel, meeting at a point inside the shape. You can create interesting marine creatures such as a starfish by using the Polygon tool to create the silhouette. Then you fill the object and choose To Center to auto-create a very lifelike composition.

Here are two different looks for the bevel effect: on the left, the Distance is set for Offset; on the right, To Center has been chosen.

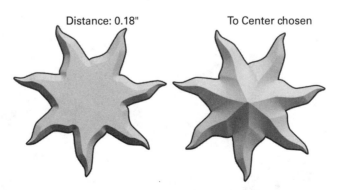

Distance: 0.18"   To Center chosen

Determining Altitude

Altitude determines the angle of the sun illuminating the bevel effect...if the sun were actually *involved* in creating the effect. Altitude is a simulation that does something a little different than Shadow and Light Color do to increase and decrease the contrast of the effect. At Altitude settings that approach 90°, you lessen the difference in brightness between the darkest and lightest areas in the bevel effect. Think of a coin on the sidewalk at high noon; you can't really see the embossed famous person on the coin because the bulges and recesses on the coin are fairly evenly lit. It's the same with the Bevel Altitude setting; smaller Altitude amounts cast the hypothetical sun closer to the hypothetical horizon, and you get more contrast on the bevel. If you want the bevel effect to have the greatest visual impact on your work, use a moderate Altitude value most of the time.

This chapter has shown you a lot of effects that do more to please than to stun your audience. Envelopes, lens effects, and bevels speak of a quiet elegance that strikes the viewer on a subliminal level. It's well worth your time to become proficient with these effects for the future when you need a touch of photorealism in a drawing—something that strikes the audience without hitting them over the head.

The following chapter takes you into two more embellishments—of the photorealistic variety—that can complete an "almost-done" composition you're not getting almost done! Transparencies are a treat to work with in version X8, and drop shadows don't just drop; they anchor your composition to the page so your design elements rise above the page, or walk into the sunset casting a hero's shadow. Bring some objects along; we're going to create new materials and new suggestions of surfaces they rest on using shadows.

PART VII

18 The Shape Editing Tools and Distortions

Once you've created an object, you might want to *edit* it, and that's the theme of this chapter. Whether it's a preset object you draw with the Rectangle tool, or manual design work with the Pen tools, not even a skilled illustrator is always satisfied with their first try. You'll learn various techniques in the pages that follow to massage that almost-perfect shape into *exactly* the shape you've envisioned. This chapter covers DRAW's tools and features for treating vector objects as though they're malleable in an organic way, and vector paths are as linear as a crumpled piece of paper. Often, creating an *approximation* of an object you need is a good first step. Then, with a pull here and a tug there, bulging an area or roughening an edge, you'll get quicker results than if you had built the object from scratch. You'll also see in this chapter that you can add visual complexity and embellishments that would be hard to achieve using other methods.

 Note Download and extract all the files from the Chapter18.zip archive to follow the tutorials in this chapter.

The Shape Edit Tool Group

Within the Shape Edit group on the Toolbox, you'll find Smear, Twirl, Attract, and Repel. These are incredibly dramatic and powerful tools that will make you feel as though you're dragging your finger through wet paint. Let's begin a survey from top to bottom in this group: the Shape tool, at the top, is such a fundamentally important tool in CorelDRAW that it's covered in Chapter 9 and several other chapters in this book, but not in this one. The group is shown here; draw an object and get set to have a lot of fun.

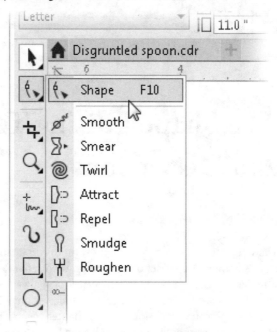

Using the Smooth Tool

The Smooth tool can undo accidental bumps and curves you've inadvertently created along a path. It can be used to produce better results than selecting nodes with the Shape tool and then using the Reduce Nodes slider because you might want some areas to remain rough, while needing to smooth other areas. As a smoothing tool, it gives you complete control over which areas receive smoothing.

Three controls on the Property Bar govern how the Smooth tool works:

- **Nib Size**   This control determines the size of your cursor.
- **Rate**   This box determines how quickly the tool responds. At a fast rate (a high value), scrubbing over a path produces immediate results; the curve is smoother and usually there are fewer nodes. When the tool is set to a low rate, you can be more selective and leisurely about smoothing your object.
- **Pen Pressure**   This option only works if you are using a tablet or a digitizing stylus. You set what pressure does with the tool. For example, you might want pressure set to determine the rate of the Smooth tool.

In the following illllustration you can see an example of the purposefulness of the Smooth tool. In the upper left is a design that was (unfortunately) drawn with the Freehand tool;

the B-Spline tool would have been a better choice. At the bottom, you can see the Smooth tool at work over areas that need the most help to create this design of a kidney-shaped retro coffee table. On the right, the design is realized.

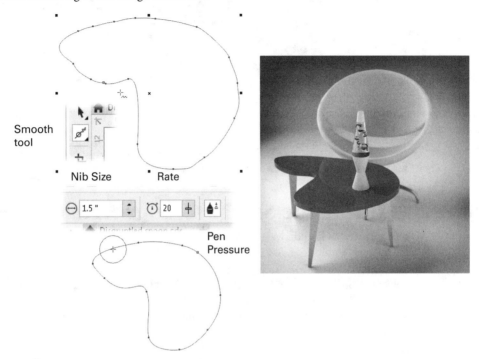

The Smear Tool

The Smear tool behaves like the Smudge tool's big brother (covered later). It offers more plasticity to areas you drag over and more control—and with a little practice, you can use a gallery of freeform shapes that look like anything but vector graphics. On the Property Bar, you have the following options:

- **Nib Size** Nib size determines the tool's diameter.
- **Pressure** Artists who use a mouse can use the num entry box or the flyout slider to set the tool's intensity.
- **Smooth and Pointy Smear buttons** Use one or the other type of smear to affect the end of a stroke. Smooth is good for natural, freeform distortion, whereas Pointy—an aesthetically severe effect—might be useful for embellishing machined parts and metal band logos.

- **Pen Pressure** Digitizing tablet users should click the Pen Pressure button to use physical pressure to add character to strokes.

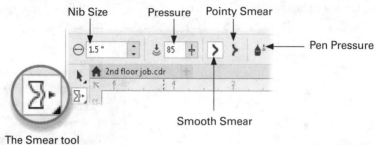

The Smear tool

In the following example, you'll get a feel for using the Smear tool in Smooth mode, to create a stylistic hairdo for a cartoon character who has no hair...yet.

Tutorial Adding the Smear to Your Artistic Career

1. Open Cartoon Guy.cdr. Most of the drawing is on a locked Layer 1. The top of his scalp is on Layer 2, unlocked. Select the scalp object (press CTRL-A, which is the shortcut for Select All).
2. Select the Smear tool; set the size of the tool to about ¾", the Pressure to about **85%**, and the style of the Smear to Smooth Smear on the Property Bar.
3. There is no "right" or "wrong" in this example; you're just experimenting. Try dragging from the fellow's scalp upward. Then try dragging on the area you just dragged. Repetition over an area can lead to quite intricate shapes.
4. Set the pressure lower (say, to **35**) and drag from the scalp away toward the top. You might want to drag repeatedly over this area; a pressure of 35 creates a bumpy skull, similar to the author's, as attested to in this illustration.

5. Try the Pointy Smear type and setting the Pressure to **100%**, and when the fellow's head is totally messed up, choose the Fill tool (toward the bottom of the Toolbox).

6. Drag from the base of the scalp upward and then click the start color node. When the mini pop-up color picker appears, click the down arrow to expand the box, click on the Eyedropper tool, and then sample a scalp color very close to where the start node is located.

7. Repeat Step 6, except choose the end color node and sample a medium mustard color for the hair. Adjust the start and end colors so a transition between scalp and blonde hair color is created. Figure 18-1 shows the finished piece. Write your boss's name at the top of the page, and then think twice about printing several copies, especially if you're on a network printer.

The Twirl Tool

The Twirl tool has clockwise and counterclockwise direction features on the Property Bar, in addition to options for setting the pressure and size of the tool. Depending on the size and pressure, you can create just about anything from a sink drain to a gentle swash on a typeface character. You can also get creative and apply a twirl to objects that you've already modified with other Shape Edit group tools.

FIGURE 18-1   **The Smear tool can quickly change parts of a path without the need to use the Shape tool.**

An unobvious technique to use with the Twirl tool—*and* the other Shape Edit tools—is to click, drag, and then hold the mouse button at the end of a stroke. Doing this increases the distortion at the end of the affected object and provides a novel effect.

Try this tool out to create a pinwheel effect in the following steps.

| Tutorial | ## Creating a Stylized Sun

1. Open Suntoon.cdr. The sunbeam object behind the face is a polygon object whose outer points were dragged inward with the Shape tool, in case you'd like to build one in the future.
2. Select the polygon object and then choose the Twirl tool from the Toolbox.
3. Set the Nib Size to ½" so it scales with the drawing and set the Pressure to about **60**. It's your call whether to twirl the sunbeams clockwise or counterclockwise.
4. Drag in a circular direction around the sunbeam object, as shown in the following illustration. If you want to create a little solar flare action, remain over an area (don't drag, just hold) for a moment or two.

The Attract and Repel Tools

These two tools in the Shape Edit group might also be called the Pull and Push tools, because that is what they do when you drag them over a selected object. To add to their versatility, for example, the effect of the Attract tool depends on whether you begin on the inside and drag outward or begin on the inside and drag inward. Either approach is valid with the Repel tool as well. There's an additional trick you can use with either tool: click, drag just a little to start the tool's effect, and then *hold* over an area of an object. Doing this sort of turns the Attract tool into a "Pucker" tool—especially visible on corners of rectangles and other sharp turns in paths—and the Repel tool becomes a "Bloat" tool.

Try this simple exercise to get an idea of the power of the Repel tool on a star shape. You'll turn it into an asterisk.

Tutorial Repelling a Polygon Object

1. Choose the Polygon tool from the Object group on the Toolbox.
2. Hold CTRL to constrain the shape to symmetrical and then drag a shape that's about 3" across.
3. Press F10 to get the Shape tool and then drag the node that's at about 1 o'clock toward the center of the object until it looks like a very spikey star. Fill it with any color. See Callout 1 in Figure 18-2.
4. Zoom in and then choose the Repel tool. Set the size of the nib to about ½" and the pressure to about **55%**.
5. Position the cursor carefully so it's inside the tip of the top point of the star. Then click-hold the mouse button until the preview outline of the intended effect doesn't get any larger. See Callout 2 in Figure 18-2.
6. Repeat Step 5 with the other four points. Then find a sentence that claims a new car will get 500 miles per gallon, put the asterisk after that statement, and then give the copywriter the bad news.

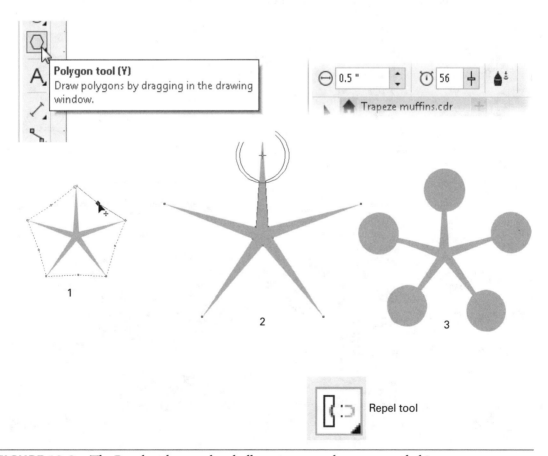

FIGURE 18-2   The Repel tool can make a bulbous area on a sharp-cornered object.

Using the Smudge Brush

The Smudge Brush is sort of a paint tool in a drawing program: you can dramatically alter shapes in a natural, painterly fashion, with results that would take hours using any other method. You move areas of a vector object by dragging from a starting point inside the object, dragging outward, or starting outside and dragging inside the object. The result is a little like the Eraser tool if you move object areas inward, and if you drag from the inside out, the result might remind you of dripping paint.

Applying Smudge to Shapes

Using the Smudge Brush, you can alter the outline shapes of open or closed paths by click-dragging across the outline path, in either an outward direction (to add to the object) or an inward direction (to create a recess in the object). As you drag, the path is altered according to your drag action and the shape settings of the Smudge Brush cursor. The following illustration shows a creative example of using the Smudge Brush: the rectangle is almost a puzzle piece now, the editing took less than five seconds, and the resulting path can be refined using the Shape tool or other CorelDRAW features.

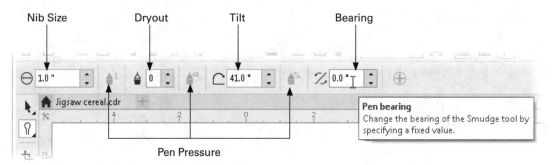

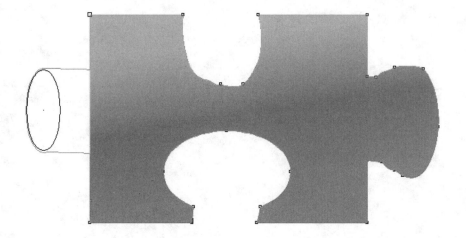

Tip As of version X8, you can now smudge shapes that have been applied with an effect (Envelope, Blend, Contour, Distortion, Extrude, or Drop Shadow). Smudging cannot be applied to objects in a group, bitmaps, or mesh-filled objects.

Choosing Smudge Brush Property Bar Options

The Smudge Brush works quite differently from other tools. You can control how the Smudge Brush effect is applied by varying tool properties such as the tilt, angle, and size of the nib; by adjusting how quickly the effect diminishes; or by using optional pressure settings, which are unavailable unless you are using a stylus and tablet.

While the Smudge Brush is selected, the Property Bar offers these options for controlling the shape and condition of your Smudge Brush cursor:

- **Nib Size** Nib Size can be set between hundredths of an inch up to 2 inches.
- **Pen Pressure** If you have a digitizing tablet and stylus that supports pressure, choose this option to have the Smudge Brush react to pressure you apply, increasing the width of the nib.
- **Dryout** This option sets a rate for the effect of gradually reducing the width of a smudge according to the speed of your click-drag action; it can be set between −10 and 10. Higher values cause your smudge to be reduced in width more quickly (as shown next), whereas a setting of 0 deactivates the Dryout effect. Interestingly, negative Dryout values make your stroke begin small and eventually widen as you click-drag.
- **Tilt** The Tilt value controls the elliptical shape of the Smudge Tool nib. Tilt is measured in degrees set between 15 (a flat-shaped nib) and 90 (a circular-shaped nib), as shown here. Tilt and Bearing values (discussed next) work in combination with each other to control the smudge nib shape.
- **Bearing** Bearing lets you set the angle of the cursor in circular degrees (0 to 359). The effects of changing Bearing are most noticeable at lower Tilt values—such as 15°, as shown here. It's the rotational angle of a *noncircular* tip.

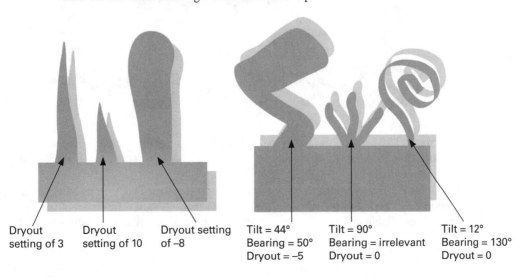

Dryout setting of 3   Dryout setting of 10   Dryout setting of −8   Tilt = 44° Bearing = 50° Dryout = −5   Tilt = 90° Bearing = irrelevant Dryout = 0   Tilt = 12° Bearing = 130° Dryout = 0

The Roughen Brush

To add a touch of character and imperfection to ultra-precise objects, you have the Roughen Brush.

The Roughen Brush alters the course of an outline path on an object, and depending on the setting you use on the Property Bar, you can achieve effects that range from lightning bolts to really gnarly lines to zigzag patterns, just by dragging on the edge of a shape. The options you have when using the Roughen Brush can be seen here on the Property Bar. They're similar to those of the Smudge Brush:

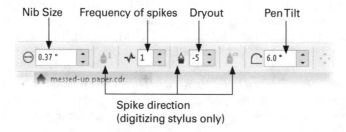

- **Nib Size** This sets the size of the Roughen Brush. It's usually a good idea to scale the nib in proportion to the selected object you want to roughen. By default, the scale of the nib is measured in inches.
- **Frequency** You'll see that the Roughen Brush creates irregularity on an object edge that is similar to the peaks and valleys of a mountain range—it varies the object outline in an "in and out" fashion. With low frequency values, the roughened object outline features

large, varying areas. With high frequency settings, you attain a zigzag effect. The range of frequency is from 1 to 10 (10 produces zigzags).

- **Dryout**   Like the Smudge Brush, the Roughen Brush can "dry out" at the end of a stroke you drag with the cursor. The range of Dryout effect is from –10 (the stroke tapers in the opposite direction in which you click-drag) to 10 (the stroke tapers and fades). At 0, the stroke remains consistent. The greater the Dryout setting (negative or positive), the more natural a roughened appearance you can achieve.
- **Tilt**   This property can be used in combination with stroking over areas that have already been roughened. At 0°, Tilt increases the irregularity of the spikes, often to a point of abstract, amateurish artwork. However, at high Tilt settings (such as 90°), dragging over an area that's already roughened can smooth out some of the jagginess and add a subtle, organic feel to a path segment.
- **Direction of spikes**   This feature is, by default, set to Automatic; it is not editable unless CorelDRAW is told (in Options) that you are using a digitizing tablet that supports pressure/direction. In default mode, spikes run on a tangent to the path you modify with the tool.

Try this basic tutorial to get a feel for the tool and learn a creative way to use it.

| Tutorial | # Roughing Out a Pumpkin's Smilie

1. Open Jack O Lantern.cdr. All objects except for the crescent moon smile are locked on Layer 1, and Layer 2 is chosen and unlocked.
2. Select the smile object (press CTRL-A to save choosing the Pick tool).
3. Choose the Roughen Brush and then on the Property Bar, set the Nib Size to ½" (for shark-scaled teeth—use a smaller size for less intimidating jaws). Set the Frequency to **1**, the Dryout to **0**, and the Tilt to about **8°**, in case you want to modify the toothy smile after you've completed the next step.
4. Drag the cursor over the top edge of the smile object, but start about ½" from the absolute left and end ½" before the right side. The Roughen Brush tends to mess up path areas where there is a sharp change in direction.
5. Perform Step 4 on the bottom smile object. Optionally, you can duplicate the smile object (select it and then press CTRL-C and then CTRL-V), fill it with yellow on the Color Palette, press SHIFT-PAGEDOWN to put the object behind the black smile, and then use the nudge keys up and left to offset its position, creating a highlight to the carved effect, as the pumpkin's eyes display in Figure 18-3.

Mastering Distortion Effects

The Distort tool in the Effects group on the Toolbox has three modes of operation, each producing a different effect you can also customize; plus there's a Preset selector on the Property Bar to get you introduced to some wild effects. The Distort tool and options are also *dynamic*, which means they create distortion without ruining your original. Distortion properties can be edited at any time, and they can be cleared from your shape, just like Envelopes. This "undo"

FIGURE 18-3 Creating an effect similar to a tailor's pinking shears with the Roughen Brush.

property makes the Distort tool unlike the Shape Edit tool group discussed at the beginning of this chapter.

Distortion effects also change your object without affecting its other properties, such as outline width and fill. Using distortion, the curve values and node properties are dramatically changed, and the more complex your object is to begin with, the more dramatic the Distortion effect will be. Adobe Illustrator users will feel right at home; although distortions are similar to Punk & Bloat, they go beyond this effect in variety and complexity, and when you're using CorelDRAW distortions, you can restore your objects at any time. Distortion effects are great for a number of illustration challenges, including organic-type effects. You can create flower shapes, zippers, swirly galaxies in space—not even the sky's the limit.

Using the Distort Tool and the Property Bar

Apply your distortions using the Distort tool, shown next, which is found in the Toolbox grouped with other effects tools and is used together with these Property Bar options.

Property Bar options for distortion

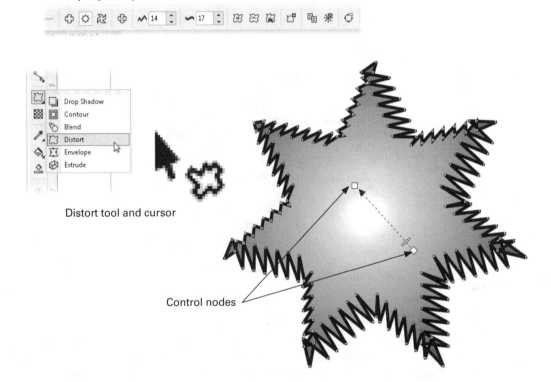

Distort tool and cursor

Control nodes

You'll notice three distortion modes: Push and Pull, Zipper, and Twister. With each mode, a different set of parameters is available. Amplitude and Frequency values can be varied in combination with certain other options (covered next) controlled interactively, or you can set these values on the Property Bar. Let's first take a look at the Property Bar when one of the modes, Zipper distortion, is chosen. All three modes offer slightly different options, but by reviewing Zipper mode, you'll get a handle on many of the options.

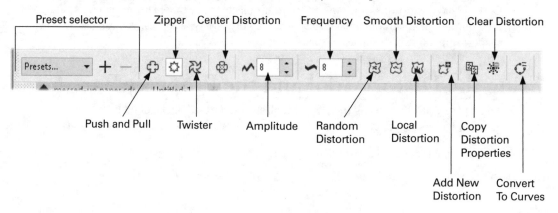

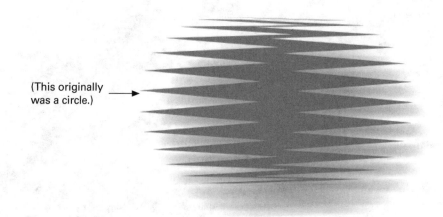

(This originally was a circle.)

Choosing Distortion Modes

If you've tried using the distortion effect, even just a little, you probably have a newfound appreciation for "steering" this effect—it's akin to slipping into a Ferrari right after your dad took the training wheels off your bike. However, the Distort tool will grow on you, and the intimidation factor will dwindle.

During a distortion session, interactive nodes (markers) provide much of the control over this effect. The nodes vary by the mode selected. The Distort modes are covered in the sections to follow in digestible, easy-to-assimilate, fun-size servings.

Push and Pull Distortion

Push and Pull distortions can inflate or deflate the slope of your shape's curves by amplitude. The *amplitude* value affects the *extent* of the effect, moving the curves of paths from an object's original path from shallow at low settings to severe at high settings. Think of an oscilloscope when you use these effects—it's all amplitude and frequency.

Amplitude can be set from 200 to –200 percent. Negative values cause the effect to distort the path away from the center origin of the object, which creates the "push" condition of the distortion. Negative values (which you can also define interactively with the Distort tool—it's fun and creatively therapeutic) can be used to illustrate flower petals, a cartoon splash into a pond, a thought balloon—all from beginning with a rectangle shape. Positive amplitude values cause the effect to be distorted toward the object's center origin, the "pull" condition. Again, if you use a rectangle as the target shape, you can almost instantly produce anything from a 1950s diner sign to a sleek, aerodynamic automobile or airplane, to a nice 3D visualization of a TV tube viewed in perspective. At an amplitude of 0, there is no distortion. Here, you can see the effects of both negative and positive Push and Pull amplitude settings.

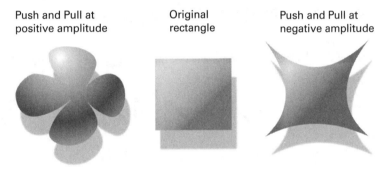

Push and Pull at positive amplitude   Original rectangle   Push and Pull at negative amplitude

Zipper Distortion

Zipper mode distorts the paths in your object to resemble a zigzag or stitching pattern. Here, amplitude can be set between 0 and 100 percent and can be used together with a frequency value and options for Random, Smooth, or Local distortion, as shown here:

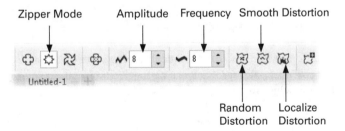

Zipper Mode   Amplitude   Frequency   Smooth Distortion

Random Distortion   Localize Distortion

Interactive markers are made up of an outer marker controlling the amplitude and a slider controlling frequency, which enables you to set the number of zigzags within a given distance. Both can be set within a range of 0 to 100 percent. You can see the dramatic effects of various amplitude and frequency values for a Zipper distortion in the next illustration. When beginning to work with the Distortion effects, you might prefer to use only the Property Bar to define an effect, but as you grow more comfortable with Distortion you'll surely want hands-on control by dragging the control handles directly with your cursor.

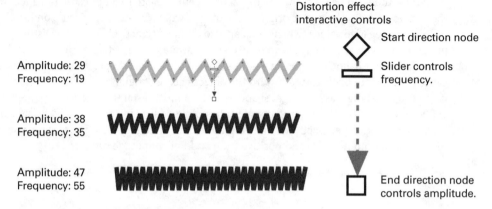

After the effect has been created, you can slant the zipper line by dragging the Start direction node vertically, left or right, as shown here:

Move the Start direction node left or right.

Tip   You can invert the direction of the zigzags on a line or closed shape by repositioning the control handles for the effect. For example, begin by placing the Start and End handles so they bisect the line that is affected. Then arrange the handles so both are above the line; notice where the peaks and valleys are on the line. Now move the Start and End handles so they're below the affected line. You'll see that where there were peaks there are now valleys, and vice versa.

In addition to amplitude and frequency, three other options are available for setting the shape and size of the zigzags. Each can be toggled on or off, so you can mix and match to create the following effects:

- **Random**   Choosing the Random option causes the zigzag Zipper distortion on your object's path to vary randomly between the current Amplitude values and zero. This creates the appearance of nonrepeating frequency and varied wave size, resulting in an uncontrolled distortion appearance. In the next illustration, you can see examples of Random set at 25 and then at 74. Notice where the interactive frequency marker is on the controls just above each object. You can slide this control instead of entering values on the Property Bar.

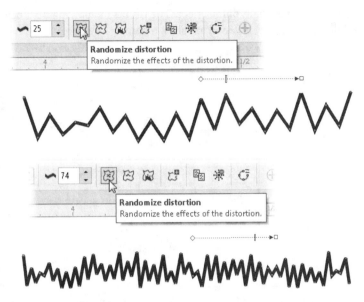

- **Smooth**   While the Smooth option is selected, the cusps of the zigzag Zipper distortion become rounded, instead of the default sharp corners normally seen. This is a great option if you need to simulate sound-wave frequencies and equipment monitors in hospitals. The next illustration shows *constant* (Random is toggled off) amplitude and variations in frequency when the Smooth option is active.

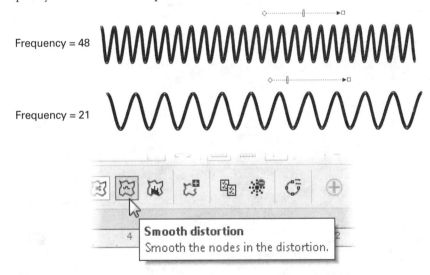

- **Local**   Using the Local distortion option has the effect of varying the Amplitude value of your Distortion effect around the center origin. At the center of the Distortion effect, Amplitude is at its maximum value. Amplitude then tapers to 0 as the distortion emanates from the center origin of the effect. The results of applying the Local distortion option while the frequency is varied are shown here.

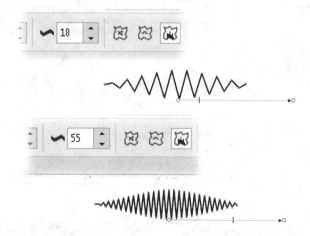

Tip To clear a Distortion effect, click Clear Distortion Effect in the Property Bar or choose Effects | Clear Distortion. If you've applied successive distortions, each distortion is cleared individually in order, from the last distortion applied to the first, so you can step out of the effect incrementally.

To bring all this Zipper talk down to a practical level, the following illustration shows two creative, commercial uses. On the left, the Zipper distortion is used as a coupon border, similar but more intricate than a burst you could use the Polygon tool to produce. The only finessing needed was to apply a contour to make the burst more colorful and pronounced. On the right, the diagram of a sewing pattern is gussied up a little by making the cut marks look as though real pinking shears were used.

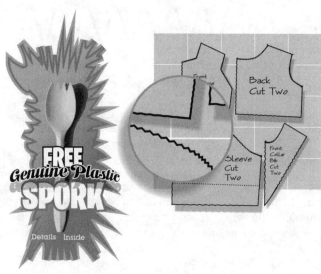

Twister Distortion

Twister distorts the outline paths and nodes of objects by rotating the outer areas around the center (which is largely undistorted) either clockwise or counterclockwise to achieve an effect much like a child's pinwheel toy. Twister options on the Property Bar include rotation direction, rotation amount, and degree of additional rotation.

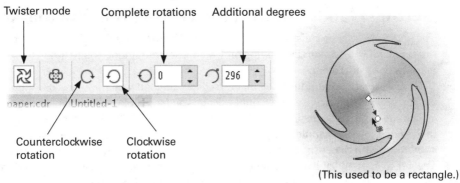

(This used to be a rectangle.)

Controlling a Twister distortion is simple; rotation can be clockwise or counterclockwise, but increasing the rotation really dramatizes the effect of this mode. Whole rotations can be set to a maximum of 9; additional rotations can be added up to 359°—nearly another full rotation. Figure 18-4 shows some of the widely differing effects that can result—it all depends on the number of rotations and the object used as the target for the effect.

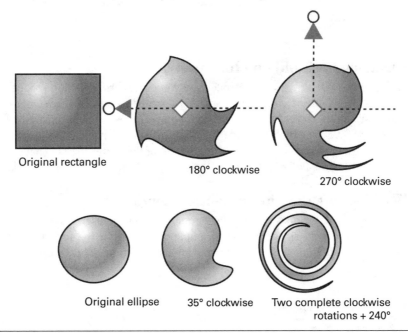

Original rectangle

180° clockwise

270° clockwise

Original ellipse

35° clockwise

Two complete clockwise rotations + 240°

FIGURE 18-4 Using simple objects and the Twister mode of the Distortion effect to create wild, organic shapes.

Note Objects applied with a Distortion effect can't be edited using the Shape tool unless the effect is cleared. However, you can *convert* a distorted shape to curves (CTRL-Q) and then edit away to get the shape you need.

Getting Hands On with the Distortion Tool Markers

The best way to shape a distortion is interactively, by dragging directly on the Distort tool markers with your cursor. Depending on which distortion mode you're using, these interactive markers serve different purposes.

There are different interactive markers, depending on which mode (Push and Pull, Zipper, or Twister) you've chosen, but basically you have a Start direction handle shaped like a diamond, which sets the center of the distort effect. The Start direction handle is connected to the End direction handle, which is used to define the direction of the effect and also the *amplitude* (with the Push and Pull and Zipper modes). Generally, interactive markers involve a center marker and at least one other, each joined by a directional guide. When Zipper distortion is being applied, a small extra slider appears between these two markers and controls the amount of *frequency* applied. In the case of Twister distortions, the outer marker serves as a handle for determining the degree angle and amount of rotation you apply to an object.

 Note To realign the center marker (the Start control node) with the center of the distortion, click the Center Distortion button in the Property Bar while the Distort tool and the distorted objects are selected. It's the button with the + symbol, to the right of the Twister button.

Changing Push and Pull Interactively

Push and Pull distortions are controlled using two markers: a diamond shape indicates the center of the distortion, and a square marker controls amplitude. The center marker can be moved around the object, but the amplitude marker movement is constrained to left or right movement. Dragging the amplitude marker left of center changes the negative amplitude values, causing the Push effect. Dragging it right of the center marker changes the positive values, causing the Pull effect. Figure 18-5 shows the effects of different marker positions:

Working with the Zipper Control Handles

Using Zipper distortion, the movable diamond marker represents the center origin, and the square marker to the right controls the amplitude value. Use the small rectangular slider on the dashed blue centerline to set frequency by moving it left or right. Dragging it right increases

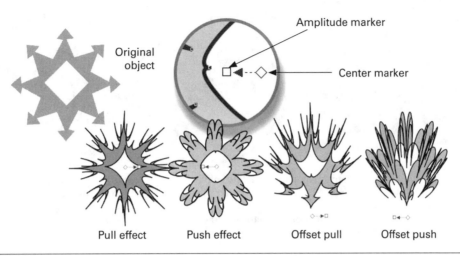

FIGURE 18-5   **Push and Pull distortions are controlled by a diamond shape and a square marker onscreen.**

the frequency, adding more zigzag shapes to your object's path, whereas dragging it left does the opposite. You also have the opportunity with Zipper, unlike the fixed positions of the markers in Push and Pull mode, to move the amplitude handle to slant the zigs and zags in a direction:

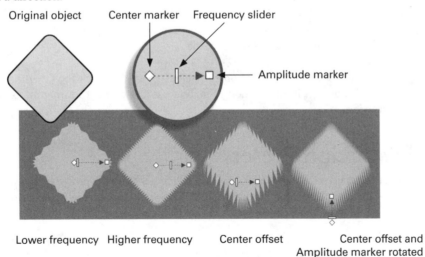

Tip   Exactly as with Envelopes, the Distortion effects can be copied using the Toolbox Eyedropper tool. Check Distortions in the Effects drop-down list on the Property Bar. You then hold SHIFT to toggle to the Paintbucket tool, and then click over an object to "fill" the object with the Distortion effect you copied.

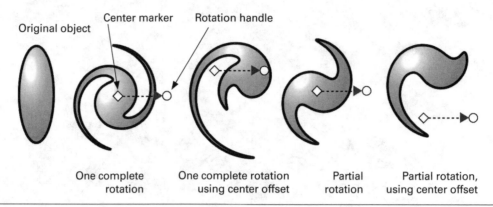

FIGURE 18-6 It's best to use the control handles to create Twister distortions.

Changing Twister Interactively

Controlling Twister distortions by dragging with your cursor over the markers is the most productive (and fun) way to apply this distortion mode since one click-drag enables you to set two properties at once, both of which have a dramatic effect on the distortion. The markers during a Twister distortion are a diamond-shaped center marker and a circular-shaped rotation handle. Dragging the rotation handle around the center marker causes distortion based on the angle of the guide between the center and rotation markers and the number of times the rotation marker is dragged completely around the center marker. You'll also see a dashed blue line connecting the markers. This provides a quick visual reference of the beginning angle of the Twister effect and the current angle of distortion you define. Figure 18-6 shows examples of Twister distortions and positions of the markers.

 Tip To copy a distortion to a new object, select an object, click the Copy Distortion Properties button in the Property Bar, and use the cursor to target an existing distortion.

Using Distortion Presets

The Property Bar Preset options for Distortion effects give you the power to apply, save, and delete saved distortions. Use the options on the Property Bar when the Distort tool is chosen, exactly as you use the Presets option with other effects in CorelDRAW.

Exploring Distortion Presets

When the Distort tool is the current tool selected, choosing a Preset from the list immediately applies a new Distortion effect to a selected object. If you've created a really awesome Distortion effect and you want to save the effect while the distorted shape in your document is selected, you can add it as a new Distortion Preset by clicking the Add button. The Delete button *permanently* removes a selected Distortion Preset from the list; therefore, think twice about ever clicking this button.

Between the Shape Edit and Distortion effects covered in this chapter, you should be well on your way to massaging an object or object group from something close to what you like to *exactly* what you like and need. Remember, these are dynamic effects and, as such, you don't permanently change that shape you've worked for hours on. And if you need to exchange data with a client or coworker who doesn't own CorelDRAW, you have two options:

- Take pity on them.
- Convert *a copy* of your effects work to curves (CTRL-Q) and then export the distorted or enveloped object to any number of file formats CorelDRAW supports. Effects are proprietary to CorelDRAW, but vector information can be used in other vector design programs and modeling programs or exported as typefaces—you name it.

This chapter has taken you through several processes by which you can create minor and big-time alterations to just about anything you draw; additionally, many of the operations apply to bitmaps you bring into the workspace. Use the command that best suits the task you have in mind, and use your judgment as to which operation will get you to your goal fastest. Personal computers are productivity enhancers: there's no need to labor over something when CorelDRAW and your PC can do it for you in less time.

The next stop on our tour of this vast continent called the Corel Graphics Suite is a little more fun with distortions, more fun still creating beveled objects, and a whole lot of fun getting deep into Corel's Lens Effects. In addition to Transparency, you can apply a Lens Effect property to make objects under the lens look like blueprints or a heat map, you can make parts of scenes look bloated or pickled, or you can suck the color out of an entire composition to create Grayscale Town!

No kidding! There are not a lot of things on Earth that are as fast and fun as what we cover in Chapter 19. C'mon, c'mon, turn the page! The ink's dry, so take your shoes off before coming in and relax!

19 Transparencies and Shadows

In our endeavors to make drawings more complete—to give the audience as detailed an illustration as possible—we rely on not just the silhouette of an object and its fill and texture, but also how an object *interacts* with its surroundings. There's more than meets the eye when it comes to replicating a scene or even a simple object. Wherever you have a light source, a solid object on a solid surface casts a shadow in the opposing direction. Even partially transparent objects leave their mark on a surface when illuminated from a direction. Similarly, what would our world be like if everything was 100 percent opaque? Sunglasses would be an impossibility, a room with a view would be false advertising, and even ice cubes would look suspicious! This chapter takes you through the CorelDRAW tools that assist you in creating transparent shapes and shadows cast by objects.

The Importance of Objects Interacting with the Scene

Here are a couple of illustrations to sell you on the importance of real-world phenomena. In the first illustration (open the file glass cube.cdr if you'd like to see how it was created), you can see a cube that's being illuminated from the right. There are no surprises, nothing of special interest, nothing being said artistically about a cube resting on a surface. In fact, the most interesting thing about this illustration is the cube's shadow—its softness contrasts with the hard lines of the cube, but you can do a *lot* better than this.

Here's the same cube, but it's made out of something; it's not simply covered with a texture (which is not necessarily a bad thing; see Chapter 12). As you can see, it's a material through and through. It might not be immediately obvious, but when you create a partially transparent object, you can see both its front and its back side, thus providing you with a more complete image of what you've drawn. If you create your drawing in a ¾ view, looking slightly downward, you can see all six faces of the cube. With solid cubes, the maximum number of sides viewable from a single angle is three.

Notice also that even a semitransparent object casts shadows. And shadows, in turn, aren't always 100 percent opaque; you can usually see details in the surface beneath the shadow. Shadows anchor a shape to the ground; they give you a visual clue as to where they are located relative to other objects in the scene. In the illustration here, the ball is not casting a shadow. No, it's not a vampire, but it's not a very complete illustration of a graphical idea, either. Is the ball floating? How close is it to the wall?

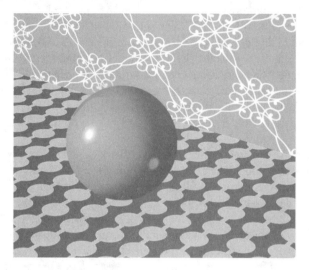

The answers to both these questions is immediately solved in this next illustration, where one of CorelDRAW's drop shadow effects was broken from the control object, converted to curves, and then split so the two pieces could give a reference point for the ball on both the floor and the wall. You can take a look at the pieces that make up the illustration by opening Shadows.cdr.

If the author has done his job, you're now sold on exploring how to create transparent shapes and shadows using DRAW in this chapter.

Clearing Things Up with the Transparency Tool

Transparency is an effect CorelDRAW users have leveraged for many years to illustrate scenes that have a very photorealistic look. The Transparency tool is quite different to use than the Transparency lens, as is the effect you achieve. You have *directions* for transparency such as Linear and Elliptical and also various operators (styles of transparency) available on the Property Bar to set how a partially transparent object interacts with the object below it.

One thing to keep in mind when working with transparency in a design is that this is the way you blend colors between objects. That's it; your work doesn't benefit from a totally transparent object—there has to be *some* influence from the object to which you apply transparency, and it's usually color. In a way, to think about transparency is to think about color blending.

One of the keys to creating amazing artwork using the Transparency tool is *the fill* that a semitransparent object has; in addition to uniform fills, fountain and pattern fills can also take on transparency. You put fills and transparency together, and you're talking seriously sophisticated compositions! Another key lies in how you approach a drawing in which you plan to feature partially transparent objects. To illustrate a real-world object, you need a few *nontransparent* objects in such a drawing, so don't overindulge in transparency when only certain parts of an illustration need the effect. In the illustration here, you can see what is today a fairly common button for a web page; it suggests glass. On the left, you can see a Wireframe view—not many objects went into this fairly convincing drawing of a glass button.

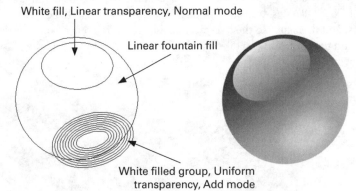

White fill, Linear transparency, Normal mode

Linear fountain fill

White filled group, Uniform transparency, Add mode

Using the Transparency Tool and Property Bar

The transparency effects discussed next are applied using the Transparency tool located in the Toolbox; the icon looks like a checkerboard, and in this version of the CorelDRAW Graphics Suite (CGS), it's a lone button and is not grouped with other effects.

While the Transparency tool is selected, the Property Bar displays all options to control the transparency effect. These options, as shown in Figure 19-1, can be used along with the object's interactive markers to produce phenomenally complex and fascinating compositions.

Often, the most rewarding way to discover and gain control over a feature in CorelDRAW or any program is to dive straight in. The following tutorial might seem a little challenging

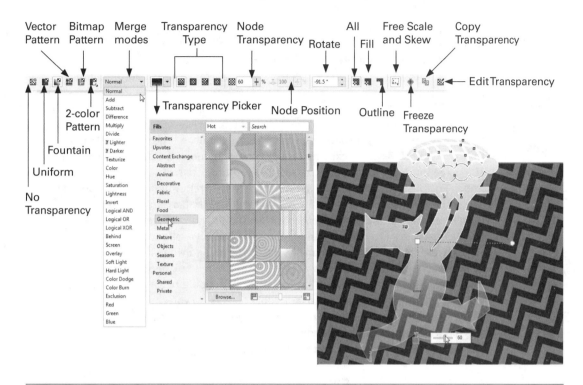

FIGURE 19-1   Use the Property Bar to customize a transparency object.

because an explanation of the transparency options is provided on the fly, sort of like getting directions *while* you're driving, but you might want the power of transparencies at hand *right now*, as we all do with valuable stuff. Follow along here to create a fairly realistic composition of a child's marble; transparency will take care of the shading and the highlights. This might remind you a little of Chapter 3's example, but the following tutorial is more of a comprehensive study of *how* transparency works in CorelDRAW. You can check out the Marble.cdr document to see and take apart the components at any time.

Tutorial   Creating a Dimensional Drawing Through Transparency

1. Create a circle (choose the Ellipse tool and then hold CTRL while you drag). Give it a Bitmap Pattern fill by first choosing the Fill tool. Click and hold on the Two-Color Pattern fill to display the Texture Fill icon on the Property Bar, click the Samples button (there is no need to click-hold to reveal the other categories of samples), and then choose the third pattern on the top row of the Fill picker. The texture is a pink agate-style fractal texture, perfect for making a kid's marble.

2. With the Pick tool, select the circle. Press CTRL-C and then CTRL-V to copy a duplicate of the circle directly above the original. Click the black color swatch on the color palette to give this duplicate a Uniform black fill.
3. Choose the Transparency tool. Click the Fountain Transparency button on the Property Bar.
4. Choose Elliptical Fountain transparency from the Property Bar and then choose If Darker from the Operator list on the Property Bar.
5. Click-drag the white transparency node (the Start node) a little toward 10 o'clock. Now, this transparency is going exactly the opposite as intended: a white node represents 100 percent transparency but you need 0 percent transparency (a black-colored node). Fortunately, if you click over the white transparency node, a mini pop-up with a Transparency slider saves you the trip to the Property Bar. Drag the slider from its current position at the far left to the far right for 100 percent transparency.
6. Click-drag the other node (the End node) to a position at about 5 o'clock on the edge of the circle object. Hover the cursor for a moment, and when the pop-up appears, drag its slider to the left, arriving at zero (0) transparency. Check out the illustration following Step 10 to get a better idea of where you should be now. The illustration of this marble tutorial is broken into individual objects, so you can better see the required steps. You'll see that the marble drawing is taking on some dimension and depth with this fountain-transparent object over it.
7. Create a circle that's about a tenth of the size of the original circle. Give it a white fill and no outline.
8. Set the Transparency Type to Fountain and the style to elliptical for the circle. Leave the Merge mode at the default of Normal.
9. The Start node should be in the center of the circle (click-drag it there if it's not), and it should be totally opaque (0 percent transparent), as indicated by white. If needed, use the pop-up slider to set it to 100.
10. Drag the End node to just inside the circle object; doing this ensures the object is 100 percent transparent at its edges, creating a perfect highlight object. Put it at the upper left of the marble drawing, and consider this a frenetic tutorial well done! See the following illustration if you haven't peeked ahead yet.

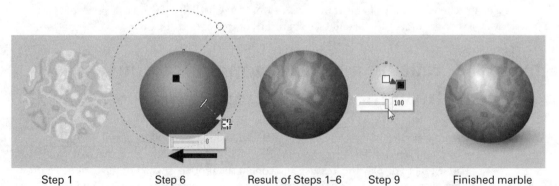

Step 1   Step 6   Result of Steps 1–6   Step 9   Finished marble
                                                                              illustration

Setting Transparency Properties

If you have experience with CorelDRAW's Fill tool, you're 99 percent of the way to mastering the transparency fill types with the Transparency tool. Because transparency isn't the same as an object's fill, the following sections take you through some unique properties. You can leverage wonderful design potential by choosing your transparency type according to what you need to design.

Uniform Transparency

Uniform transparency is the default for objects to which you assign this trait; the object will feature a flat and even transparency value. The way this semitransparent object blends with underlying objects is completely predictable. For example, if you assign a red rectangle and then a blue rectangle with 50 percent (the default) transparency and overlap them, yep, you'll see violet in the intersection.

Tip The Uniform transparency type has no Start and End nodes over the object as the other types do.

Fountain Fill Transparencies

Transparent objects that use any of the fountain fill direction types are exceptionally powerful for illustration purposes, as you'll see in a moment. What governs the degree of transparency at the Start and End points is the control nodes—not only their position relative to the object underneath but also *the brightness value* of the markers. Fountain fill transparencies are driven by *any of 256 shades, from black to white*. Let's use the Linear transparency type; if you understand this type, all the others (Elliptical, Conical, and so on) will become obvious. When you click-drag using Linear transparency on an object, the Start node is white, indicating full opacity, and the End node is black, indicating no opacity at all.

Trick Number One in creating an elegant fountain fill transparency is to change the degree of opacity at the Start and End points, which you can do using three methods:

- Reposition the Start and End nodes using the Transparency tool. If you position the markers way outside of the object, the transition between full and no opacity will be gradual and the outermost parts of the transparent object will be neither completely opaque nor completely transparent if you do this.
- Change the brightness; the nodes can have any of 256 shades of black. Let's say you have the Start and End nodes exactly where you want them; you like the angle of the fountain fill transparency. But you don't want the End (the black node) to be 100 percent transparent. You click-drag a deep shade of black from the color palette and then drop it onto the black End node. The end of the transparency then becomes mostly transparent, but not 100 percent.
- Use the mini pop-up controls that appear next to a selected transparency node to change the transparency value, by dragging from 0 (opaque) to 100 (transparent).

Trick Number Two is to choose the transparency object's color—any color is acceptable, but because this physical CorelDRAW *Official Guide* is in black and white, only black, gray, and white are used here to influence the objects visually below the transparency object. Here's an illustration: some black Paragraph Text is on the bottom of the drawing page. On top of it is a rectangle. On the left, the rectangle is filled with white, and a Linear fountain fill transparency is click-dragged from top to bottom. The text appears to be coming out of a fog. In the center, a 50 percent black fill is then applied to the rectangle and a different visual effect is achieved—the Paragraph Text still looks like it's in a haze, but more of it is legible toward the top. On the right, black is the fill for the rectangle, and now the top of the text is as illegible as the white rectangle example, but a different artistic sense of drama has been achieved. You now know two different methods for shading with fountain-type transparency fills: change the position of the transparency nodes, and change the color of the transparency object.

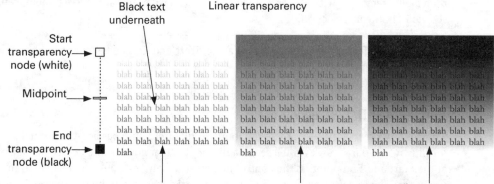

> **Tip** Although the transparency nodes can only be shades of black and white, the object *taking* the transparency can certainly be in color, or have any of the available fills in CorelDRAW, including bitmap patterns and fountain fills.

New Controls and Locations for Transparency Options

You still have two approaches to modifying an object's transparency in DRAW—using the Property Bar controls and the interactive markers (or nodes) on an object—but users of previous versions might be a little disoriented when trying to go through the same old moves to accomplish something. And for new users, the additional transparency effects were designed to be intuitive and easier to use than in previous versions. Here are a few of the more frequently used modification features, what they do, and where they are located:

- **Midpoint slider**   This slider controls where the 50 percent point in a transparency is located. It does *not* indicate where an object is 50 percent transparent, but it instead sets a relative 50 percent breakpoint because, as mentioned earlier, you can set the Start and End nodes to any brightness value you like. The midpoint slider is located on the Start-End line on the transparency object when selected. This feature is no longer on the Property Bar, but you can access by clicking the Edit Transparency button on the Property Bar, and then you can click-drag the midpoint, as shown in this illustration, to any point between the Start and End points.

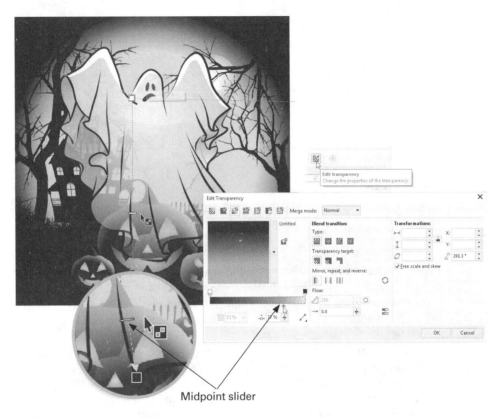

Midpoint slider

Tip   If no object is selected and you want to make any object partially transparent, the Transparency tool works as a selection tool in addition to controlling the transparency nodes. With the tool selected, click once to select the object to which you want to apply transparency, and then click-drag to create a Linear Fountain transparency that can then be modified using the Property Bar controls.

- **Rotate**   Some but not all transparency types will show any difference when you rotate their orientation. For example, a Linear Fountain transparency creates a different look when you rotate its orientation, but a perfectly circular Elliptical transparency, or 2-color transparency fill in an object, will look the same when you rotate it. You can rotate a transparency in three ways: by directly dragging on the End node above the object in the workspace, by changing the value in the Rotate spin box on the Property Bar, and via the

Transformations area of the Edit Transparency dialog. The following illustration shows an example of a Linear fountain fill with its transparency attribute changed.

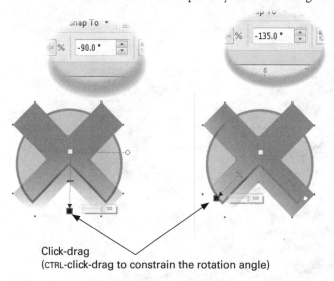

Click-drag
(CTRL-click-drag to constrain the rotation angle)

> **Tip** By default, when you hold CTRL and drag a control marker for a fountain-type transparency, you constrain the angle you're setting in 15° increments. You can also straighten a crooked Fountain transparency you've manually defined by CTRL-click-dragging.

- **Free Scale and Skew** As with the fill controls on objects, the transparency control nodes operate in 90° opposition to one another...*except* when you decide to activate the Free Scale and Skew button on the Property Bar, which adds a third handle and a white control node that can govern one dimension of a transparency while the End node controls the other. Free Scale and Skew can set the angle of an Elliptical transparency to any value, not just to the default 90°. This next illustration shows the difference between a default applied transparency and the same type of transparency after messing with it using the Free Scale and Skew feature. Dragging the Free Scale and Skew node away from the Start transparency node converts an Elliptical transparency type in its default circular state to an oval, and dragging in a circular direction around the Start node rotates the elliptical transparency.

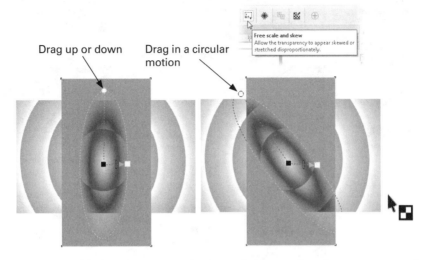

Drag up or down   Drag in a circular motion

Free scale and skew
Allow the transparency to appear skewed or stretched disproportionately.

The Free Scale and Skew feature can also be applied using the Edit Transparency dialog, but it's not as much fun as dragging the interactive nodes around.

- **Mirror, Repeat and Mirror, Reverse**   These options, which are exactly like the Fill options for fountain fills, are not located on the Property Bar like the Fill options are. You access them by selecting a transparent object and then clicking the Edit Transparency button on the Property Bar. You have a terrific visual of the proposed transformation in the Edit Transparency dialog, and the options are fairly self-explanatory. The biggest difference between the Repeat option and the Repeat and Mirror option is that the Mirror function tends to create "tubes" of transparency, whereas the simple Repeat function makes objects look like anything from shingles on a roof to a splash screen to a cartoon.

You can set the number of repeats within an object by dragging the End transparency node; when you click the Free Scale and Skew button on the Property Bar, you can also set the angle of distorted repeats in an object—and if you're determined, and take it slowly, you can also change the number of slanted repeats using the Freeform node.

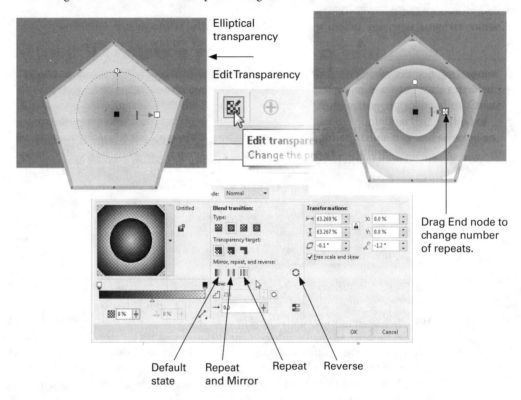

Let's kick back for a moment and run through some steps that demonstrate the practicality of a Linear transparency used in an illustration to imitate the "glass icon" reflective look.

Tutorial Creating a Reflection on a Shiny Surface

1. Get out US Quarter.cdr. The background patterned surface is locked, and all you need to do is play with the coin, which is a group of objects.
2. With the Pick tool, select the quarter and then hold CTRL while holding the top-center selection handle—you're going to drop a copy of this coin, but you're going to place the copy directly below the original, so both bottoms of the quarters line up perfectly.
3. Drag down on the selection handle. As soon as you can see the preview of where the duplicate is going to go, press the right mouse button and then release CTRL and the mouse buttons. The action is mapped out in the following illustration.

Hold CTRL and drag the top-center control node down.

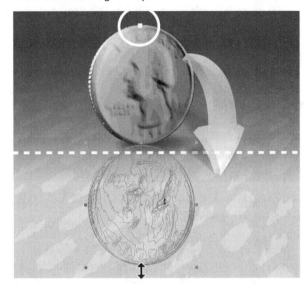

The mirror plane needs to be perfectly horizontal.

Right-click, then release CTRL to drop a mirrored copy.

4. Choose the Transparency tool and select the bottom, mirrored file (you can do this with the Transparency tool). Then, beginning at the very top of the upside-down file, drag down so that the 0 percent transparent area of this Linear transparency is at the top and the bottom is 100 percent transparent. Neat effect, eh? You're not quite done yet.

5. You neither want the top to be totally opaque nor the bottom totally transparent. The default for the Transparency tool can and should be modified to convey a little more convincing scene than opaque to transparent—that's not how you see reflections. Click the top transparency node to reveal the pop-up slider and change the value to about **23**. Then click the bottom transparency node and make the value about **96**. See the following illustration.

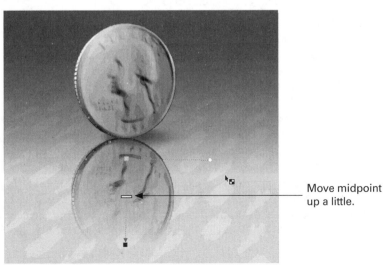

Move midpoint up a little.

6. Remember earlier when we talked about moving the control nodes to change the transparency effect? You might want to do this to make the effect seem more real to you (and your audience), but the alternative (moving the midpoint slider) is quicker and gets the task completed, as shown in this illustration. Just drag the slider up a little, and you've got yourself a U.S. quarter reflected in the floor. Incidentally, try the Lightness merge mode to heighten the reflection effect.

Tip For best results on your own with the preceding tutorial, create an object whose bottom side is a curve. Alternatively, with a drawing of a folder, make the bottom edge perfectly horizontal. Any object you draw or photograph resting on its corner with a convincing reflection is hard.

Creating a Better Reflection Using a Bitmap

Although the preceding reflection example produces a nice, clean reflection that diminishes in opacity as the top recedes from the scene, there's something missing from the drawing. Have you ever seen a perfect reflection? The answer is "no"—*no* surface is perfect in the world because nothing in the world is perfect, except for Krysten Ritter's hair.

Usually, there is a blur to a reflection, and by doing this on a composition, you'll see that the effect provides a lot more photorealism than without the blur. To do this blurring jazz, you can't perform it on vector shapes in CorelDRAW, but you can convert a copy of a group of objects into a bitmap and do all sorts of clever stuff with the bitmap. There's an additional perk to converting a copy of a drawing to a bitmap; there is a limit to the number of objects in a group that CorelDRAW can apply transparency to. The author learned this the hard way; DRAW popped me a "no can do" box when I tried to apply linear transparency to the two LED bulbs you'll be working with next. How *dare* DRAW refuse to apply this effects to more than 300 objects in a group?!

Okay, let's get real—and get to work.

Tutorial   Filtering a Bitmap Copy

1. Open LED Bulbs.cdr. The polygon pattern is locked; all you need to do is work with the bulbs groups of objects.
2. Make a copy of the bulbs using the drag-and-drop technique. One of the sets of bulbs will be converted to bitmaps, destroying the original vector art in the process.
3. With the Pick tool, select one of the bulbs. Then, while holding SHIFT to additively select, click the other bulb. Make sure the bulbs do not overlap one another.
4. Choose Bitmaps | Convert to Bitmap. In the Convert To Bitmap dialog, you can accept the default of 300 pixels per inch resolution, a nice resolution for printing your work. Also, make sure the Transparent box is checked in the Options area. Finally, *make sure you have a copy of your vector work.* "Convert to bitmap" *does not* mean "make a bitmap copy." Your work is literally converted to pixels. Are you good with that? Good. Click OK.
5. With the bitmap copy selected, choose Bitmaps | Blur | Gaussian Blur.
6. Drag the Radius slider in the dialog to about 33 pixels, and then click Preview to see what the effect might look like directly on the objects on the page. If you feel that's too

high an amount, drag the slider to the left and then click Preview. See the following illustration for a visual example of Steps 4–6.

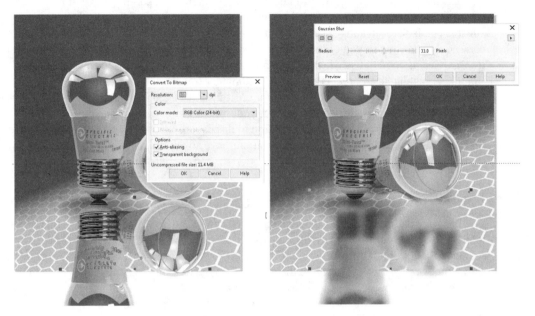

7. Choose the Transparency tool. Then, exactly like the previous tutorial, drag from the top to the bottom of the selected bitmap, and make adjustments to the midpoint and the Merge mode (Lightness works great in this example). In Figure 19-2, you can see the result of your hard work!

FIGURE 19-2   Use Transparency in combination with a filtered bitmap to create amazing reflections in your work.

Additional Fountain Transparency Types

You also have Elliptical, Conical, and Rectangular Fountain transparency types at hand when you design something you need to look more dimensional. The Elliptical transparency effect is fantastic for making spectacular highlights—brilliant but soft-edged highlights you commonly see when sunlight hits a highly polished metal or smooth plastic object. A Conical transparency is good to use when you need a pie-wedge-shaped area—and this, too, is good for simulating highlights and reflections. The Rectangular transparency type might not prove to be useful on a day-to-day basis, but it's great for creating soft-edged highlights to use as window panes and other right-angle geometric areas you want to emphasize visually.

Let's take a detour in this documentation to discuss *transparency operations*. Also called Merge modes and Blend modes, these operations have an additional effect on all objects with a transparency effect.

Using Transparency Operations (Merge Modes)

The Property Bar offers a list of *modes* so that you can set how your transparency colors interact with the colors of underlying objects. These options further the visual complexity of semitransparent objects. For example, a red plastic drinking glass on a yellow tablecloth will show some orange through it due to the nature of colors that mix as light passes through the glass. But the shadow cast by the nontransparent areas of the glass will not be the same shade of orange as the light we see through the glass—light in the real world is subtractive, and the shadow in such a scene would be almost brown. However, you don't have to calculate light properties or material properties when you choose the best Merge mode for your illustration.

The following definitions of Merge modes describe the effect you can expect with each mode; let's use "source" to refer to the top object that takes the transparency effect and "target" to refer to one or more objects below the transparency object that are overlapped by it. The "result" is the color you see in your drawing in the overlapping areas.

- **Normal**   Normal Merge mode is the default whenever a new transparency effect is applied to an object. Choosing Normal at 50 percent opacity usually produces predictable color blends between the source and target objects; for example, a pure yellow object at 50 percent Normal opacity over a pure red object yields orange as a result in overlapping areas. Similarly, and in traditional physical painting, a white source object produces a *tint* result over a pure color object (a pastel color), whereas a black source object produces a *shade* of the target object's color (if you're shopping for house paints, the salesperson will love this jargon).
- **Add**   The Add(itive) mode applies transparency in a similar fashion to Normal mode, except it whitens and brightens the result—seriously! In English, there's a subtle but distinct difference between "plus" and "added to"; similarly, Additive Merge mode moves the combined result of the target and source object colors in a positive direction in brightness value. The artistic result is good for adding subtle shading to composition areas; this is something painters through the centuries could not do without the added step of applying pure white because inks and pigments use the real-world subtractive color model.

- **Subtract**   This mode ignores the brightness value in the source object and is similar to mixing physical pigments. If you use Subtractive transparency mode on green and red objects and overlap them with a target blue object, the result color will be black.

- **Difference**   Remember color opposites on the color wheel? This is what Difference Merge mode does: it moves the result color to the difference (on the color wheel) between the source and target colors. For example, a red Difference transparency object over a yellow target object produces green areas. You'll see the Difference Merge effect most clearly if you put the object over an empty area of the drawing page. A red Difference object will cast cyan as the result on the page. This blending mode is for creating dramatic lighting effects—for example, you can shine a Difference Merge mode drawing of a shaft of theater spotlight on an object and get truly wonderful and bizarre lighting effects.

- **Multiply**   Multiply always produces a darker result color from merging the source and target objects. Its effect is similar to wood stain or repeatedly stroking a felt marker on paper. Several objects in Multiply Merge mode, when overlapped, can produce black, and this is perhaps the best mode for artists to re-create real-world shadows cast on objects. If the source object's color is lighter than the target object, the result is no change.

- **Divide**   The Divide mode produces only a lighter result color if neither the target object nor source object is black or white. Use this Merge mode to bleach and produce highlights in a composition by using a light color for the transparency object, such as 10 percent black.

- **If Lighter**   If the target color is lighter than the source transparency color, the area is replaced with the transparency object's color (that is, the source color). If the target color is darker than the source transparency shape, the result is this region shows no change in color.

- **If Darker**   The opposite effect of If Lighter. If the bottom (target) object's color is darker than the source object, this area takes the color of the top (the source, the transparency) object. There is no visible change if the target object is lighter than the source object.

- **Texturize**   This mode will not produce much of a change unless you fill the source object with a bitmap or pattern fill. However, if you fill the transparency object with a bitmap fill, the result is a shaded and patterned area. This mode removes the hue and saturation from the bitmap fill, leaving only brightness values—in effect, making your target object a shaded version of the original, sort of like merging a grayscale photograph over an object. This is a useful Merge mode when you do not want the target object to influence the result colors with any distinct hues. You can also use this mode to build up texture quickly and simulate real-world complexity in your composition.

- **Color**   This mode uses the hue and saturation values of the source color and the lightness value of the target color to create a result. This is the opposite of the Lightness Merge mode.

- **Hue**   The Hue Merge mode changes the result color to the hue of the target color, without affecting saturation or brightness in the result. This mode is useful for tinting compositions, and the target object colors are ignored in the result.

- **Saturation**   The Saturation Merge mode can be used to remove color from the result; it's quite nice at making black-and-white photographs from color images. This mode ignores hue and brightness components in the result. Try using shades of black as the transparency object's fill. Highlighting saturated target and source objects will produce no change in the result.

- **Lightness**   The target object's lightness values are calculated, ignoring hue and saturation. This is a great mode for brightening the result colors because the target object's colors are never changed, just the *lightness* (also called *value* and *brightness*).
- **Invert**   This Merge mode creates a result color that is the chromatic inverse of the target color. You can occasionally reproduce the look of a color negative using this mode—it moves the result color 180° on the color wheel. Using Invert Merge mode on the same colored target and source objects produces gray.
- **Logical AND, Logical OR, and Logical XOR**   The AND function includes similarity between the source and target objects; for example, two red ellipses that overlap and both have the AND transparency Merge mode appear not to be transparent at all but instead display 100 percent red where they overlap. This is a useful mode when you want only a color result in overlapping areas because AND creates no change outside of the overlapping result area. The OR operator is an exclusive operator; in other words, it excludes stuff. This is a good mode for clipping a color change, thus limiting it to areas only where the target and source objects overlap. You'll see nothing outside the overlapping areas when the target object has the OR operator. XOR is a Boolean math statement, based on something called a Truth Table, where certain conditions must be met to produce a result. You might not find a use for this transparency mode unless you use more than two objects in a design area; if both objects are similar or if neither object is similar, you'll get no result color. This operation only works if there is one differently colored object in the color calculation operation.
- **Behind**   You need two objects that have transparency for Behind Merge mode to work. Wherever the target object on bottom contains transparency, the source object with Behind mode fills the transparent bottom areas with its color(s). Therefore, the source object will appear invisible in areas where the target object has no transparency. Use this mode in your design work to fill in missing areas (transparent ones) in the target image without being apparent in areas that do not contain source object transparency.
- **Screen**   This Merge mode always returns a lighter color, or the source object is invisible if it is darker than the base object or if it's black. Screen is similar to (but a less intense effect than) Add Merge mode; the effect looks like bleach applied to a colored garment.
- **Overlay**   This mode examines the brightness value of the base color. If the result of combining the source with the base is greater than 128 on a brightness scale of 256, the result is a screened area. If the result is not as light as 128, the area is color multiplied. Highlights and shadow areas are preserved in the base image when you use this mode. You almost always achieve a result that has more visual contrast than the original when you use Overlay.
- **Soft Light**   Akin to Overlay Merge mode, except instead of screening and multiplying areas, the result is lightening and darkening, a less intense effect.
- **Hard Light**   Very similar to the screening and multiplying effect of the Overlay Merge mode, except highlight and shadow regions are *not* preserved. Use this mode if Overlay doesn't prove to be an intense enough effect for merging two color objects or images.
- **Color Dodge**   The base colors are brightened based on the colors used in the source object. Black produces no effect when used as a source color, whereas white can produce a near-white. The effect could be compared to adjusting the exposure of the base image by brightening and tinting the base image simultaneously while reducing overall contrast.

- **Color Burn**   The inverse effect of Color Dodge. White in the source object produces no effect above the base object; colors are reduced in exposure, increased in contrast, and black and darker shades of color in the source object appear to stain the base object.
- **Exclusion**   Similar to the Difference Merge mode, but instead of subtracting either the source or the base color (whichever is brighter) to arrive at a darker color, Exclusion Merge mode removes the color of the transparent areas in the resulting blend. When white is used in the source object, it inverts the underlying colors in the base object. Using black produces no effect.
- **Red, Green, and Blue**   Each of these Merge modes filters out a respective (RGB) channel, and the native color of the source object is ignored. This is a useful transparency mode for color correcting photographs you import to CorelDRAW; for example, if you put a Green transparency mode object over a portrait, and then play with the amount of transparency on the Property Bar, you can sometimes correct for harsh indoor (particularly cheap fluorescent) lighting.

Creating Multistage Transparencies

You might find you need a transparency object that's more complex than the Fountain types offered on the Property Bar; for example, a lens flare can add photorealism to an illustration, and this option doesn't seem to be on the Property Bar. However, the first place you might want to look for an exotic, complex multistage transparency is on the Transparency Fills picker on the Property Bar. (You can see the Transparency Fills picker in Figure 19-1.)

If you don't find what you envision, CorelDRAW's Transparency tool's power can be used to build a multistage fountain fill for an object, and then you can use the Transparency tool in a Merge mode operation that hides certain colors in the fountain fill. For example, if you want to create bands of transparency in an object, you drag shades of black from the color palette and drop them onto the marker connector, alternating with white markers. Remember, darker shades represent transparency, and lighter shades stand for opacity. You might want to reposition the new markers once you've added them; this is done by click-dragging with the Transparency tool. If your drop point for a new marker isn't exactly over the marker connector (the blue-dashed line), your cursor will turn into an international "no can do" symbol.

Pattern Transparencies

You can use pattern transparencies to create intricate detail by combining the transparency object and all the objects below it. The Transparency Type buttons on the Property Bar include Vector Pattern, Bitmap Pattern, and 2-Color Pattern transparency types. With any of these selected for the transparency type, the starting Transparency (the "Start") slider controls the percentage of transparency applied to brightness values in the chosen bitmap that are above 126 on a brightness scale of 0–255 (256 shades); the ending (the "End") Transparency slider controls the percentage of transparency applied to brightness values in the chosen bitmap that are below 128. When you double-click a custom transparency preset, it might take a moment to download the preset; you will *definitely* need an active Internet connection to work with the collection of transparency presets. If you click (don't double-click) on a thumbnail, a flyout appears where you can see the author of the preset, along with options for making this preset a Favorite and *liking* the preset, which is simply Corel's version of social networking.

Figure 19-3 shows Hawaiian shirt.cdr, a file you should feel free to experiment with, along with the options on the Property Bar when the Transparency tool is selected and the control nodes above the target object. You work with Scale, Rotate, and Skew in addition to setting the center point for the transparency a little differently than you do with the Fill tools, but you'll pick up the Rotate and Scale node—which looks like the Free Scale and Skew node in Fills—quick enough. It's suggested you choose Multiply Merge mode for the top object when you apply the transparency pattern. Clearly, CorelDRAW provides you not only with a robust feature set, but also with enough Hawaiian shirt patterns to last you several months of vacationing.

You don't need a tutorial to make a shirt decorated with a custom transparency. You select the light solid part of the shirt, open the Transparency Fills picker, and then drag your choice of fills to the selected object.

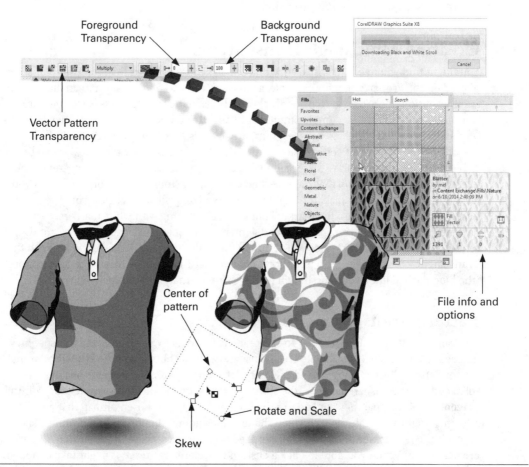

FIGURE 19-3   Use patterns as the basis for transparency to add visual complexity, simulating a woven texture, a painted one, or other engraved and embossed effects.

Using Transparency Freeze

In addition to the options on the Property Bar that are almost identical to the Fill tool's options—Copy Transparency, Apply To Outline, Fill, or All, and Edit Transparency—we have the option Freeze Transparency, which is much like freezing a lens effect. When you freeze a transparency object, the transparency object captures a composite of the target object's properties, combined with whatever was beneath the target object before you clicked the Freeze Transparency button on the Property Bar.

Tip   Deactivating the Freeze Transparency option (without ungrouping it) returns a transparent object to its current and active state. This means if you freeze the object, move it, and then unfreeze it, its interior will display whatever is *currently* under it.

Using the Drop Shadow Effect

With the Drop Shadow tool and the options available on the Property Bar when it is the active tool, you can create both shadows and glows, in drop shadow and cast shadow fashions (explained shortly). Although this section walks you through several variations, basically you have three different types of effects at hand when you use the Drop Shadow tool, as shown in Figure 19-4.

- **Drop shadows**   This shadow type creates the impression that you're viewing an object from the front and that the object is basically lit from the front. Drop shadows are a popular effect; however, they don't always bring out depth in a composition because the drop shadow suggests a face-front orientation of a scene—a viewpoint usually reserved for

Drop shadow   Perspective (cast) shadow   Glow

FIGURE 19-4   The drop shadow effect can add perspective and be used to light up a scene, not simply to make things cast shadows.

driver's license photos and wanted posters in the post office. However, drop shadows will indeed perk up a web page, because the audience expects a face-front orientation since we all tend to face the front of our monitors.

- **Cast shadows** This effect is sometimes called a *perspective shadow* in CorelDRAW. The effect suggests a shadow casting on the ground and travels to a scene's vanishing point. It visually suggests that the audience is looking *into* a scene from a perspective point and is not looking *at* an object placed *on* a scene, as drop shadows tend to do.
- **Glows** All effects created with the Drop Shadow tool are dynamically updated bitmaps, and, as such, they can look soft as shadows do on overcast days; they can also be put into Merge modes. Therefore, you take a blurry bitmap, put it in Multiply Merge mode, and you have a re-creation of a shadow. However, if you take that same blurry bitmap, give it a light color, and then put it in Normal or Add Merge mode, you have a glow effect. This is part of what CorelDRAW does when you use a Glow preset, and you have a lot of manual control over creating a shady or glowing look that perfectly suits a piece of work.

Like other effects in CorelDRAW, drop shadows maintain a dynamic link; any changes to the control object automatically update the shadow. A shadow's look—its position, color, opacity, and feathering—can be customized, plus you can manipulate the angle, stretch, and fade properties of shadows and glows.

Using the Drop Shadow Tool and Property Bar

The Drop Shadow tool—located and clearly marked in the Effects flyout on the Toolbox—is about as hard to use as click-dragging, and after you click-drag to create a custom shadow, you'll see a series of Property Bar options. The tool is found in the Toolbox with other interactive tools.

After an initial click-drag to add a drop shadow to an object, you'll notice the Property Bar lights up, and you now have a ton of options for refining what amounts to a sort of "default" drop shadow effect. Drop shadows can take one of two states: flat (drop) or perspective (cast). Depending on which state you use, the Property Bar options will change. Figure 19-5 handsomely illustrates a look at the Property Bar when a flat shadow is being applied.

Here's an introduction to shadow-making through a tutorial intended to familiarize you with the Property Bar options as well as with a little interactive editing. As with most of the effects in CorelDRAW, the onscreen markers for click-dragging to customize a shadow are very much like the markers for the Extrude fountain fill and other tool control handles.

Tutorial Working the Property Bar and Shadow-Making Markers

1. Create an interesting object to which you want to apply a shadow, and finish applying its fill and outline properties. If you deselect it, this is okay—a click on the object with the Drop Shadow tool selects it.

2. Choose the Drop Shadow tool, and notice that your cursor changes to resemble the Pick tool with a tiny Drop Shadow icon in its corner. If you don't do anything with the tool, the only option on the Property Bar is the Presets drop-down selector at the moment.

3. Click-drag from roughly the center of the selected object; continue holding down the mouse button so you can see some of the mechanics of this effect. Notice that a preview outline appears that matches your object. This indicates the position of the new shadow once you release the mouse button. Notice also that a white node has appeared in the center of the object, and that another node has appeared under the cursor as you drag it. A slider control has also appeared at the midpoint of a dotted guideline joining the two nodes.

4. Release the mouse button and *BAH-woing*! A drop shadow appears. This is a default shadow, colored black, and it has default properties.

5. Drag the slider control on the guideline between the two square-shaped nodes toward the center of your original object. This reduces the shadow's opacity, making it appear lighter and allowing the page background color—and any underlying objects—to become more visible.

6. To change the shadow color, click the Color selector on the Property Bar and then select a color. Notice that the color is applied; you can do some wild stage-lighting stuff by choosing a bright color for the shadow, but the opacity of the shadow remains the same.

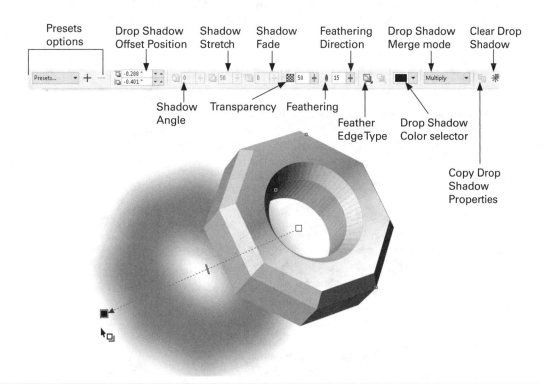

FIGURE 19-5 You might be a shadow of your former self after sifting through all the drop shadow options!

7. Drag the white node to the edge of one side of the original object. Notice the shadow changes shape, and the node snaps to the edge. This action changes a drop shadow to a perspective shadow.

8. Using Property Bar options, change the default Feathering value to **4** and then press ENTER. The shadow edges are now more defined. Increase this value to a setting of **35**, and notice that the shadow edges become blurry; you've gone from a sunny-day shadow to an overcast-day shadow.

9. Click the Fade slider control and increase it to 80. Notice that the shadow now features a graduated color effect, with the darkest point closest to the original object becoming a lighter color as the effect progresses farther away from your object. This is not only a photorealistic touch, but it also helps visually integrate a shadow into a scene containing several objects.

10. Click the Drop Shadow Stretch slider and increase it to 80. The shadow stretches further in the direction of the bottom node, and you've gone from high noon to almost dusk in only one step.

11. Click a blank space on the page to deselect the effect, or choose the Pick tool, and you're done. Take a break and hang out in the shade for a while.

Tip To launch quickly into the editing state of an existing drop shadow effect while using the Pick tool, click the shadow once to display Property Bar options or double-click the shadow to make the Drop Shadow tool the current tool.

Manually Adjusting a Drop Shadow Effect

After applying the drop shadow effect, you'll notice the interactive markers that appear around your shape. You'll see a combination Offset Position and Color node joined by a dotted line featuring an Opacity slider. If you're new to interactive controls, this illustration identifies these markers and indicates their functions.

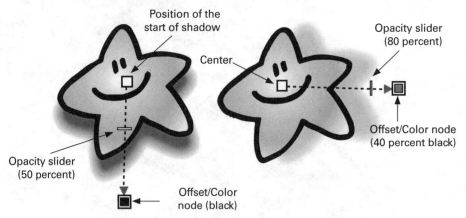

Position of the start of shadow

Center

Opacity slider (80 percent)

Offset/Color node (40 percent black)

Opacity slider (50 percent)

Offset/Color node (black)

Tip To change a selected drop shadow's color, click-drag any color swatch from the onscreen color palette onto the shadow's Color node.

Shadows as Glow Effects

CorelDRAW's drop shadow effect is not limited to making shadows; if you think about it, a blurry bitmap can also represent a glow effect by using a different Merge mode and color.

By default, whenever a new shadow is created, black is automatically the applied color. You can reverse this effect by applying light-colored shadows to dark-colored objects arranged on a dark page background or in front of a darker-colored object. Here, you can see a black compound path (the cartoon moon) on top of a Linear fountain-filled rectangle (black is the End color and 30 percent black is the Start color toward the moon) with a light-colored shadow effect applied. The result is a credible glow effect; there are also Glow Presets on the Property Bar when you use the Drop Shadow tool to give you a jump-start on creating glows.

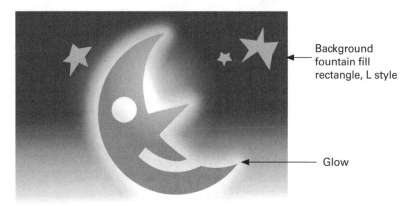

Background fountain fill rectangle, L style

Glow

This chapter has shown a lot of nonspecial effects. Keep in mind that transparencies and shadows aren't supposed to "wow" your audience, but rather speak of a quiet elegance that strikes the viewer on a subliminal level. It's well worth your time to become proficient with these effects for the future when you need a touch of photorealism in a drawing—something that strikes the audience without hitting them over the head.

20 Understanding and Working with Pixel-Based Images

Because people seldom photograph an object or a scene with exactly the elements they want in a composition, the field of retouching has thrived since the day a professional had something to sell using a photograph! This is why professionals trim photographs, and so can you, using the CorelDRAW features covered in this chapter. As objects, photographic areas that have been carefully cut out can be composited with other photos and vector shapes to add a whole new dimension to your posters, flyers, and fine art. Additionally in this chapter, Corel PowerTRACE, part of CorelDRAW, is demonstrated; you'll learn how to create a vector copy of a bitmap so you can scale and rotate it, edit it, and never lose details or resolution as bitmap images are prone to do.

 Note Download and extract all the files from the Chapter20.zip archive to follow the tutorials in this chapter.

Cropping a Placed Photograph

You can perform two types of cropping on placed photos: destructive (permanent) and nondestructive (you can undo what you've done). The Crop tool on the Toolbox performs destructive cropping. Unless you press CTRL-Z to undo a crop you don't like, you're stuck with your crop, and no exterior areas beyond the cropped image remain that you can expose later. With bitmaps, you need to import them (CTRL-I); you cannot File | Open a bitmap image. Cropping a photo involves several steps:

1. You define the area you want to crop by click-diagonal-dragging the Crop tool from one corner to the opposite corner.
2. You can redefine the crop by click-dragging the resulting bounding-box markers. The corner markers scale the proposed crop area proportionately, whereas the center markers are used to resize the proposed crop area disproportionately.

509

3. You can rotate the crop box, if, for example, you need to straighten a horizon. To do this, make a crop and then click inside the crop to put it into Rotate mode. You then drag on a corner double-headed arrow marker to rotate the crop. This doesn't rotate the photo itself, but rather the crop area.

4. You double-click inside the crop area to finish the crop. Figure 20-1 shows the elements you work with onscreen to crop a bitmap image.

If you'd like to use the photo the author used in these figures, you can find Unlucky balloon.png in the ZIP archive.

 Note To see the resolution of a placed bitmap image quickly, with the bitmap selected, look at the Status Bar, which names the file as well as tells you its color mode and current resolution. The rule is, as you increase bitmap dimensions, resolution decreases proportionately.

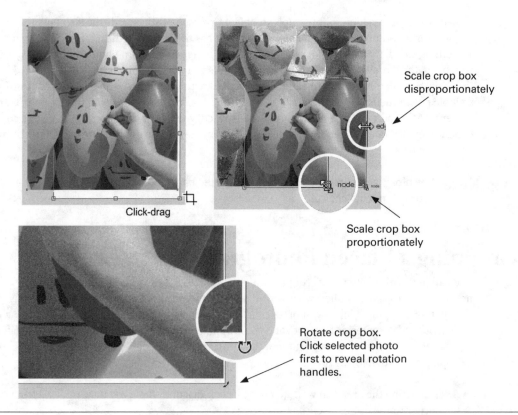

FIGURE 20-1 The Crop tool eliminates the exterior image areas of your defined crop area.

Nondestructive Cropping

In a nutshell, if you want to hide an area of a photo and not delete it as you do with the Crop tool, you use the Shape tool. Try this out with the Small apple1882_0435.jpg image by following the steps here.

Tutorial   Using the Shape Tool to Crop

1. Create a new (default-sized) document with landscape orientation. Place the image Small apple1882_0435.jpg in a new document by clicking the Import button on the Property Bar and then selecting the image from the location you downloaded it to. With the loaded cursor, click-diagonal-drag to place the image so it fills most of the page.
2. The crop you'll perform is to remove the distractions from the very top of the photo. Drag a horizontal guide to above the leaf on the apple, leaving just a little room without going into the shadow area.
3. From the Standard Bar, choose Snap To | Guidelines. With the Rectangle tool, begin click-dragging at the horizontal guide. Begin the click-drag to the left of the apple, but not so far to the right that it spoils the composition after you crop. Judge how far you will crop on top, and then click-drag from top to bottom left to define the crop on the left of the photo. You should stop dragging just about at the end of the apple's shadow. Peek ahead to the following illustration to get an idea of how to create the rectangle around the photo.
4. Drag a little down and to the right to create the bottom and right guides for dropping out of your rectangle. Like with the left edge, leave just enough space on the right side to balance your future crop with the other three sides of the rectangle.

Drag the horizontal guideline
to just above the apple leaf.

Disproportionate
scaling handle

Keep the crop fairly evenly away
from the subjects in the photo.

5. Give the rectangle a white outline while it is selected by right-clicking on the white color well on the color palette and then give it a 2-point outline using the num box on the Property Bar, just so you can see the rectangle when you edit the underlying photo. Right-click over the rectangle and then choose Lock Object from the pop-up context menu; see the next illustration.

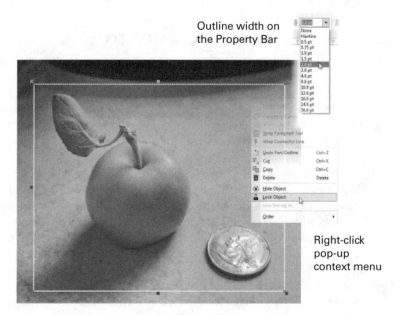

Outline width on the Property Bar

Right-click pop-up context menu

6. Choose the Shape tool from the Toolbox and then click on the photo to select it. The photo now has control node markers at each corner. These markers behave and operate exactly like control nodes on vector shapes.

7. Select one corner node of the photo and then drag it to the corresponding corner of the white rectangle, as shown in the illustration here. Like magic, the corner node of the photo magnetically aligns itself precisely with the corner of the rectangle. This is because the Snap To option is set to Guidelines (all four corners, in fact).

8. You're home free! Click-drag the remaining three corners to their corresponding positions around the rectangle. You can unlock and delete the rectangle now, and you have a clean, expertly executed, nondestructive crop. At any time, you can take the Shape tool and drag the image's four corner nodes way out until the original image is visible.

Masking Through Nondestructive Cropping

Go to the head of the class if you've already discovered that you can *add* control nodes to a placed photograph with the Shape tool! CorelDRAW "sees" a bitmap as an object that has a fill—specifically a bitmap fill. Therefore, this object can be shaped and reshaped by adding nodes and also by changing the segment property between nodes. The following sections take you through some advanced bitmap editing to trim around a photograph so it becomes a floating object in a composition.

Trimming Away Unwanted Image Areas

What you'll learn in this section goes way beyond the simple cropping of an image. You're going to trim the background away from an image of a trendy wristwatch, add a photographic element, put a new background behind the watch, and by the end of this section, you'll have designed a print advertisement. There are two nondestructive methods for removing the background from a photo's subject, and both techniques are described in this section. The elements of the poster have already been created for you, and shortly you'll see how to make a design with elements in front of and behind each other, just like you do with vector shapes, but using *photographs*.

To begin this design, you need to create a new document (portrait orientation, default page size) and import the image of the watch—a little smaller than the page size, but it can be scaled at a later time when needed. Then you use the Shape tool to trim the background.

Tutorial Background Removal, Technique 1

1. Click the Import button on the Property Bar, and then in the Import dialog, locate Splorch watch.png, choose it (over other brands), and then click Import.
2. Your cursor is loaded with the image: click-drag, and then release the mouse when the cursor reports that the width for the placed image is about 8 ½ inches.

Click-diagonal-drag to size and place.

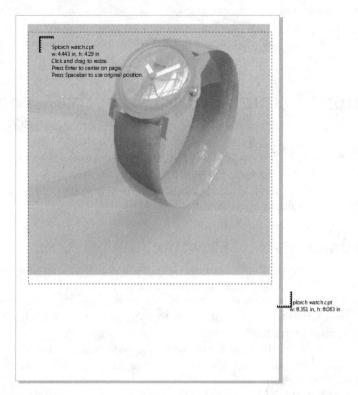

Splorch watch.cpt
w: 4.443 in, h: 4.29 in
Click and drag to resize.
Press Enter to center on page.
Press Spacebar to use original position.

plorch watch.cpt
w: 8.351 in, h: 8.063 in

3. Let's suppose that the ideal size for the picture should be 8 ½, but you didn't get the placement precisely at this size. No problem: with the Pick tool chosen, type **8.5** in the width field of the Object size box on the Property Bar and then press ENTER. Check the Document Grid box in the Snap To drop-down (on the Property Bar) and then use the Pick tool to precisely align the photo to the top center of the page.

4. Now that your photo is perfectly aligned for this mock composition, your mock boss tells you that he doesn't like the background. He wants to know if you can remove the background and put in a new one. And he also tells you that your answer should be "yes." The solution to your dilemma here begins with the following sentence. Choose the Shape tool. Begin by clicking the top-right node of the image, and then click-drag it toward the center of the image until the top and right edges touch the elegant wristband, as shown next. Clearly, you're not going to get where you want to go with only four control nodes because the geometry of the watch is far from perfectly rectangular. This is okay; you'll add nodes to the outline of the image in the

following step. Oh, and turn off Snap To | Document Grid now; you've done enough snapping for today.

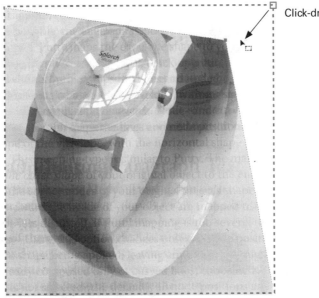

Click-drag

5. With the Shape tool, click a point on the outline of the photo where you want to change the direction of the line; near the upper-right corner of the photo is a good place to begin. Now, either double-click the segment, press the keyboard plus (+) key, or click the Add Node button on the Property Bar to add a node. While you're in the vicinity of the top of the watch, several additional points are needed. A quick way to add points in between existing points is to click a point repeatedly and press the + key.

6. Click-drag points so they visually coincide with the vertices of the curves on the fashionable wristband. It's okay if the lines between the nodes hide areas you want exposed. You'll want to frequently move a segment back and forth to see where the edge of the watch lies.

7. Click a straight line segment that should curve away from the photo. Then click the To Curve button on the Property Bar. The segment can now curve; click-drag the segment away from the photo, as shown next, until the red watch edge is apparent but the hideous muckish-colored background is not. You can also right-click a segment and choose To Curve from the pop-up menu.

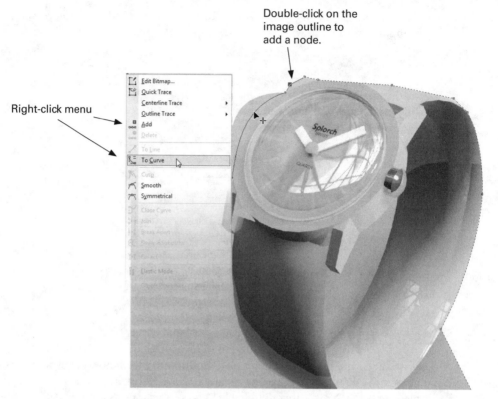

Double-click on the image outline to add a node.

Right-click menu

8. Once the outside of the watch has been manually masked, it's time to create a hole for the interior background white color, to remove it to a transparent state, exactly like the outside silhouette of the watch. Choose a line drawing tool; the Pen tool is fine for this example.

9. Set the View to Wireframe. You'll see a grayscale image of the watch, plus all the segments you draw are easy to see in this view. Why didn't you use this technique from the beginning, and why are you looking at the author that way? To show you more than one way to accomplish a task, of course. Some techniques work better than others, while some don't work at all. It depends on the photo, and like snowflakes and the washers you have in a jar in your workroom, no two are alike.

10. Trace along the edge of the wristband, as shown in the following illustration. With the Pen tool, the pattern of mouse gestures is to click-drag to create a curve segment, and just click to create a node that you decide will be the anchor for a curved or a straight segment.

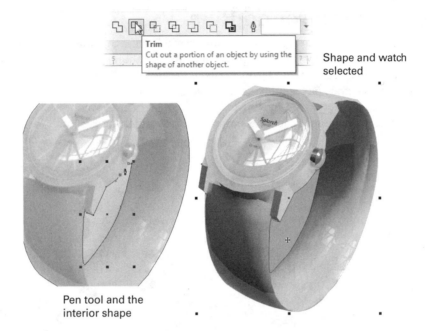

Shape and watch
selected

Pen tool and the
interior shape

11. Fill the selected inner shape with any color so it can be easily selected.
12. With both objects selected, click Trim on the Property Bar. By default, this will remove the path you drew, but the path is not deleted in the Merge mode. With the Pick tool, click the colored path and then press DELETE.
13. That's it; all it takes now is about 10 minutes of your time to work around the profile of the wristwatch, hiding areas and creating curve segments where needed. Yes, it's a lot of work, but so is putting on a tuxedo or gown to go and collect an industry award for outstanding design work (*prompt, hint, encouragement!*).

A good thing to do once you've trimmed away the nonessential watch parts, because the default color of the page is white, is to put a colored vector shape behind the composition to check your edge work. Make a rectangle, fill it with a dark color, and then press SHIFT-PAGE DOWN to put the rectangle to the back.

If you'd like to confirm the fact that the editing you performed is nondestructive, take the Shape tool and marquee-select several control nodes. Then drag them away from the center of the photo, as shown here. Then press CTRL-Z to undo this nondestructive *and unwanted* edit!

Tutorial Background Removal, Technique 2

There's no need for a step-by-step tutorial to explain the two other techniques for putting a mask around an imported bitmap. Running through short steps is not the way to our goal here, which is to create an ad for Splorch watches—which I've already designed for you so you only need concentrate on the elements of the design.

The second way you can isolate a foreground element from the background of a photo is to trace closely around the silhouette of the shape and then select both your closed path and the photo. Finally, you choose Intersect from the Property Bar, as shown next.

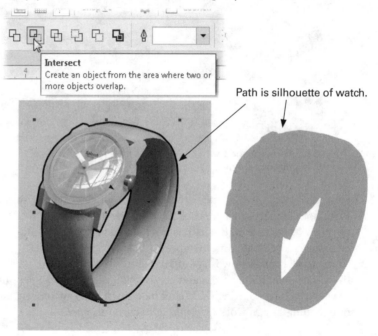

Path is silhouette of watch.

Background Removal, Last Technique!

In Chapter 9, we covered CorelDRAW's PowerClip feature. This masking technique is nondestructive, and a masked shape can be a vector object, vector group, or an imported bitmap. In Figure 20-2, you can see a small copy of the original image as imported with its "horrendous background," as your mock boss says. I've already masked this shape for you, and it's in the Splorch full page ad.cdr document, waiting for you to open it. To isolate the foreground "doodad," you carefully trace over the doodad (locking the photo is a great idea before you begin), unlock the photo after you've traced the outline, and with the photo still selected, choose Object | PowerClip | Place Inside Frame. With the special PowerClip arrow cursor, you click the outline drawing, and the photo then peeks out from inside the outline you drew. Again, see Chapter 9 for PowerClip details.

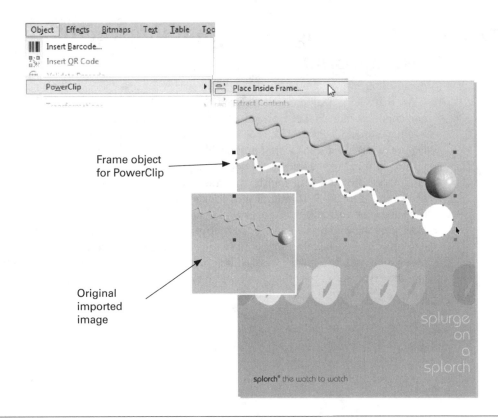

FIGURE 20-2   Clipping the exterior away from the main shape in a photo is easy and nondestructive using a PowerClip.

Compositions with Mixed Media

Creating this print ad is going to be fun...even though you're not getting paid for your work. Ah, but the invaluable experience! You're going to go beyond arranging and moving both bitmap and vector objects to laying out a finished art composition. What you'll see in the Splorch full page ad.cdr file is a nearly finished layout. The typeface family is called Bauhaus, and it should be in the "B" folder on your CorelDRAW disk or main folder. Unless the names of the fonts have changed recently, you'd be looking for TT0406M_.TTF and the other Bauhaus family members. If you want to install this font and play with the ad's text, install one or more members of the Bauhaus font family, unlock the text that was converted to curves in this file, delete the objects, and go to town.

Also in this ad design is the doodad element I mentioned a little earlier. Your task in this assignment is to make the watch look as though it's through the doodad—an abstract design element in keeping with the rest of the ad. After accomplishing this composition miracle, you'll add shadows to anchor the watch and the doodad to the page visually.

Tutorial # Composing a Design Using Vector and Image Shapes

1. Close that Welcome document in CorelDRAW and then open Splorch full page ad.cdr and choose Window | Tile Horizontally so you have a view of both your wristwatch work and the tutorial CDR file. This is one of the rare occasions when the tabbed document feature in DRAW doesn't work for duplicating objects as quickly or precisely as the old-fashioned Windows cascading windows configuration.

2. Hold CTRL and then drag your trimmed wristwatch into the advertisement window, as shown in Figure 20-3. This duplicates your work; it doesn't move it. You can save and then close the wristwatch image as a CDR file now.

3. Let's scale the watch and the doodad for optimum aesthetic size in the ad before working on a special effect that'll make the doodad go through the wristband, not just on top of it, or underneath. The doodad should be about 8.7" wide. If it's not, select it and then type **8.7** in the Object side width box. Press ENTER. Similarly, make the watch about 4.9" in width.

Window | Tile Horizontally

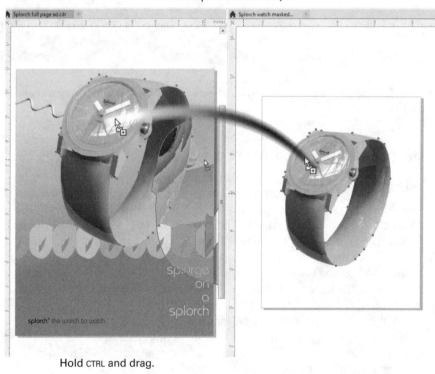

Hold CTRL and drag.

FIGURE 20-3 Duplicate your work in the advertisement window.

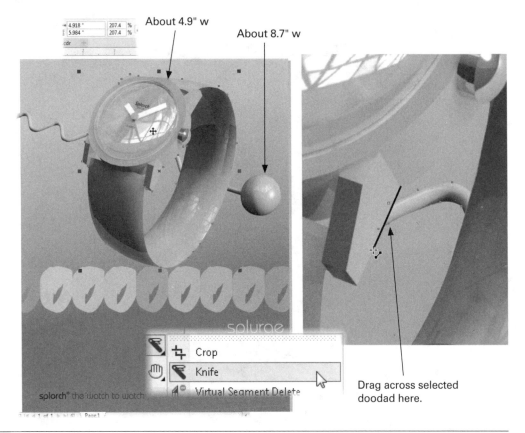

FIGURE 20-4 After scaling and positioning the objects, get out the Knife tool to slice the doodad shape.

4. Look at Figure 20-4 to see where a good position on the page is for the two masked pictures. Now, we'll be able to get exactly the same results by doing the following steps. Zoom into the area just below and to the right of the watch's stem.
5. Choose the Knife tool from the Toolbox group and then, with the doodad object selected, drag the Knife cursor across the doodad's stem, at an angle, exactly as you see in the figure.
6. The doodad object is now a left and right object. To create the illusion that the doodad is going through the inside of the wristband, with the Pick tool, select the right half of the doodad and then press SHIFT-PAGEUP to put the object at the top of the stack of objects on this document layer. See the next illustration.

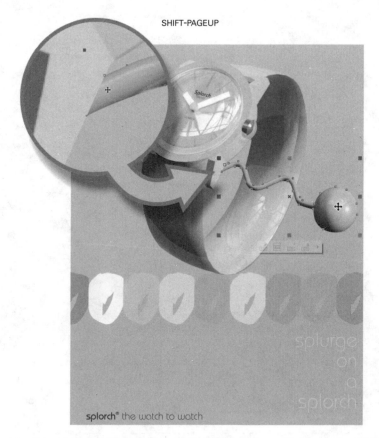

You could call it a day, and ask for your mock fee from your mock boss, but let's take the composition just one level higher in the photorealism realm. In the next section, you'll see how to add drop shadows to the watch and doodad so they are in the page, not just sitting on top of a color field.

The Easy Soft-Edge Shading Technique

Although CorelDRAW's Drop Shadow feature is terrific for making soft, photorealistic shadows of both the drop shadow and cast shadow variety, there is also a quick way to make a shadow of any shape you desire. You draw a shape, add a drop shadow to the bottom of the shape, and then select the shape you drew that's casting the shadow. Then, with the Transparency tool, you make the shape 100 percent invisible. Is that cool or what?!

Walk with me, as I show you how to finish the composition, and put you at the top of Really Good Designers heap:

1. With the Ellipse tool, make a circle about the size of the watch. Fill it with a medium gray so you can see it, and then remove the outline.
2. With the Drop Shadow tool, begin your drag to produce the shadow at the bottom of the circle. See callout "a" in the following illustration.

3. Choose the Transparency tool with the circle selected, and then drag the transparency slider on the pop-up to 100 percent. See callout "b" in the following illustration.

4. With the Pick tool, drag the shadow to beneath the watch, as shown in callout "c," and then press CTRL-PAGEDOWN until the shadow is beneath the watch. See the nifty illustration now!

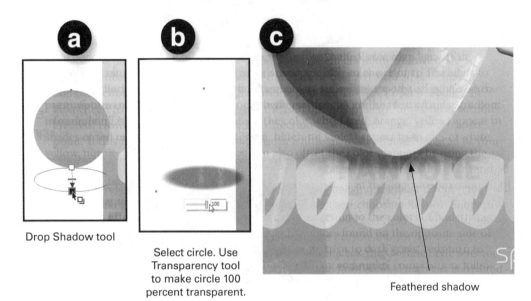

Drop Shadow tool

Select circle. Use Transparency tool to make circle 100 percent transparent.

Feathered shadow

5. At your leisure, you might want to decrease the opacity of the shadow, or make it more oval in shape, or increase the feathering to make the shadow softer. Use the Pick tool for shape changing, and use the controls on the Property Bar to change the properties of the shadow.

6. You're in the home stretch now! With the Pick tool, drag and then right-click the shadow to drop a copy of it. Scale it and work with the transparency and feather amounts after you place it below the doodad sphere. You'll need to use CTRL-PAGEDOWN to move the duplicate shadow to beneath the sphere.

7. Why not, with the Pen tool, draw a wavy shape like the stem on the doodad, right above the wristband on the watch, so the doodad appears to be casting a shadow on the wristband? It's possible to blur the shadow like the two other shadows, but I think we've had enough retouching adventures with this example. Besides, an object very close to a different object casts a sharper shadow when a light casts shadows. Hey, in art, usually if it looks right, it is right. If your work looks like Figure 20-5, you did *great. More* than great! In fact, look in a mirror real quick— you might be *me!*

FIGURE 20-5 Text, vector art, and imported photos can all be added to a single, unified composition.

Working with Alpha Channels and Image Transparency

The following sections explain how you can trim your subject out of an image background, why certain file types are imported with transparency, and what transparency really means in your CorelDRAW work. More features than you might imagine are available for working with bitmaps directly in CorelDRAW; for *exceptionally* tricky image-editing assignments, Chapter 21 covers some of Corel PHOTO-PAINT.

Working with Partial Transparency

Both Alpha Channel transparency and Image Layer transparency offer more than simply 100 percent opaque or 100 percent transparent areas. With 24-bit images, you can have 256 levels of opacity in any area of the image, and this leads to some fascinating visual effects that you can create. You'll work shortly with an image that has semitransparent areas, but right now, it's time to learn how to *build* semitransparent areas into an image that has none but should have them. Bob's Beer, a fictitious microbrewery, has an image of a bottle in PNG file format that is surrounded by transparency. Let's say Bob wants the bottle to sit in front of a background that has his name repeated far too many times. Visually, his name should partially show through the neck of the bottle where there's only tinted glass and no beer.

The following tutorial shows you how to trim away the top quarter of the bottle, the most transparent part. Then you'll see how to make this area only partially opaque so some of the background shows through. And to top it off, you'll see how to build a cast shadow from the bottle onto the "ground" in the composition.

Tutorial   Creating a Photorealistic Glass Effect

1. Open the file Bob's Background.cdr, and then click the Import button and choose Bob's Beer.png (it's a domestic beer, but you'll import it anyway). Click Import and then with the loaded cursor, click-diagonal-drag until the bottle is placed in the image as shown here.

2. With a Pen tool (the Bézier Pen works fine in this example), create a shape that fits in the top part of the glass, from the fill line to the bottle's lip, staying slightly inside the neck of the beer bottle so the edge is not part of the trimming operation you'll perform in a moment. You should fill the shape after creating it to better see what you're doing in the following steps—any color is fine.

3. Select the shape but not the bottle. Choose Object | Shaping | Shaping to display the Shaping docker. Choose Intersect from the selector drop-down list, and then check Leave Original Target Object. Now uncheck the Leave Original Source Object box. Click the Intersect With button and then click the bottle. The shape is deleted because it's the source object, and you didn't choose to leave it. Apparently the bottle has not changed, but there is a perfect cutout duplicate of the top of the bottle resting on top

of an unchanged bottle; you're halfway there—you need to trim away part of the bottle using the new intersect shape now.

4. Click the spot formerly occupied by your drawn object to select the product of the intersect operation in Step 3 (don't worry; it's hard to see that it's a separate object). Choose Trim from the Shaping docker's drop-down list, check Leave Original Source Object, and uncheck Leave Original Target Object. Click the Trim button and then click the bottle, and the beer bottle is now actually two separate pieces. See the following illustration for the docker settings for Steps 3 and 4. Now it's on to transparency.

Separate object (not obvious)

5. Select the top part shape and then choose the Transparency tool from the Toolbox; the little wine glass that's about to tip over icon. Click the Uniform Transparency button on the Property Bar, and then drag the Opacity slider on the Property Bar to about 50 percent. As you can see next, your editing work resulted in quite a convincing illustration. You can see Bob's logo in the background peeking through semitransparent glass; the background is even tinted a little from the green of the object on top of it.

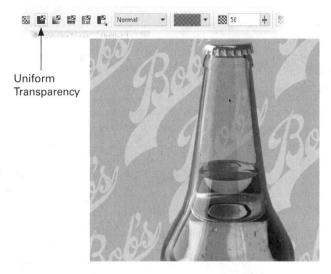

Uniform
Transparency

6. Here's the *pièce de résistance*: with the bottle selected and not the semitransparent piece, choose the Drop Shadow tool. Click toward the bottom of the bottle image to define an anchor for the shadow and then drag up and to the right.

7. Click-drag the end marker of the shadow so the shadow ends closer to the bottle. Then, because the bottle should be casting a deep green (not black) shadow, click the Shadow Color flyout on the Property Bar and then choose something like hex value 20800D. Because it works pretty well in this case, you can just type in the value. Click OK to get back to your work. Also consider increasing the opacity of the shadow by dragging the Drop Shadow Opacity slider on the Property Bar up to 70 percent or so.

8. Well, oops. The area you trimmed in Step 4 is not part of the shadow—there's a hole in the shadow where there should be a lighter green, because a shadow cast by green glass through beer would be a little darker than a shadow cast through green glass alone. No problem; you can draw a fill shape for the missing part of the shadow, as shown here, fill the shape with a lighter green than the bottle shadow's color, and then give it about 50 to 60 percent Uniform transparency.

Blending Photos with Transparency

Let's imagine in the tutorial challenge coming up next that the Tree.png file you'll be working with was created by masking everything except the tree in the photo, and then you saved it as a PNG file with transparency using PHOTO-PAINT.

You know now that an image can have transparent areas, and you know that you can use CorelDRAW's Transparency tool to make any object on a page *partially* transparent. The steps that follow show you how to perform surreal, completely professional photo retouching with two images you graft onto one another with only one CorelDRAW tool.

Tutorial Creating a Transition Between Two Images

1. Press CTRL-N to create a new file; accept the default standard letter page size, and define it as Portrait orientation.
2. Import ThumbsUp.jpg. You'll want to click-drag the loaded cursor after clicking Import to scale the imported image to the 11" height of the page.

3. Import Tree.png. PNG files can (in some cases) retain image resolution information, so all you need to do is click the loaded cursor on the page.

4. With the Pick tool, position the tree so its trunk fits over the thumb in the underlying photo.

5. Choose the Transparency tool from the Toolbox.

6. Click-drag downward, starting from around the thumbnail area in the underlying photo to just above the trunk on the tree. You should see the amazing transformation between the guy's thumb and the trunk of the tree. If the beginning and end points for this Linear transparency aren't perfect, you can adjust the start and end points with the Transparency tool cursor. Because you performed this edit interactively, you'll see that the Property Bar states that this is a Fountain Transparency style and that the Linear Transparency type button is depressed automatically.

7. Unfortunately, the guy's thumb doesn't taper toward the top like the tree trunk does; some of the thumb is visible, ruining the special effect. Choose the Bézier Pen tool from the Toolbox, and then draw a closed shape whose right edge matches the contour of the tree trunk's left side. Fill it with the same color as the background of the thumb photo—choose the Color Eyedropper tool from the Toolbox, click over the background, and then click the paint bucket cursor on the shape you drew. See Figure 20-6 for the exact location of this edit in the photo.

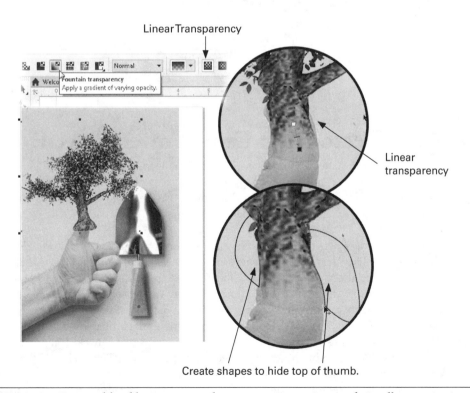

FIGURE 20-6   Create a blend between two photos to present unique and visually arresting imagery.

8. Perform Step 7 on the right side of the thumb, after drawing a second shape.

9. Remove the outline of both shapes (select them both) by right-clicking the No Fill color well on the Color Palette.

10. Read Chapter 10 on working with text because this image would make a terrific magazine cover.

Bitmaps to Vector Art: Using PowerTRACE

You can export both vector art and bitmaps to bitmap file format, but once in a while, you'll need to go the other way: taking a bitmap and making vector art from it. Many design professionals are faced daily with clients who want to use their logo for a truck sign or a high-resolution print ad, but all they can provide the designer is a really pathetic GIF copy from their web page.

Fortunately, designers don't have to reconstruct logos by hand—Corel PowerTRACE is a highly accurate utility that often produces a vector equivalent of a placed bitmap that requires no hand-tweaking afterward. What PowerTRACE does is simple: it creates a vector version of the selected bitmap. *How* PowerTRACE does this is not easy to explain, but if you understand the "how," you'll be better prepared to choose the right option before making a vector copy of an imported bitmap. In a nutshell, PowerTRACE examines the bitmap based on the criteria you specify in the dialog and then seeks edges in the bitmaps that show a clear and marked difference in color and/or brightness between neighboring pixels. PowerTRACE then creates a vector line at this neighboring region, continues to create a closed path (with the Centerline option chosen, it creates open paths), and fills the path with the closest color match to the pixels inside the area it creates. The following sections take you through the operation of PowerTRACE and offer suggestions on settings as well as when and why you'd use this handy feature.

Bitmap Conversions for Logo Alterations

Sometimes you'll want to use PowerTRACE to rework an existing logo that's in bitmap format. Many times—and the next tutorial prepares you for "many times"—the existing logo of your client is a total mess. They can't find the original because they fired the previous art director/custodian. Additionally, the only copy they have of a logo that they want not only reproduced, but also edited, is a GIF image they downloaded from the website. They want new text to reflect the new ownership—the former boss and custodian fired himself. And you want a better design than the half-hidden, sorry picture you have to work with. As you can see in the next illustration, the logo is a GIF file; it looks to be sampled from only 12 colors, and diffusion dithering was used to fake the additional colors. The close-ups reveal that the text has severely jagged edges, and one of the colors isn't even a color, but rather a pattern of two colors to simulate a color that fell outside of the limit of unique colors (*color space*).

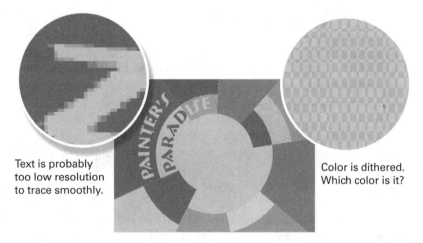

Text is probably
too low resolution
to trace smoothly.

Color is dithered.
Which color is it?

Yep, you have just the tools you need in DRAW to repair and revise the logo. You also need a strategy for revising the piece. Fortunately, the best and fastest solutions for this work are covered in the following tutorials. Is that convenient, or *what*?

PowerTRACE Options

This logo, placed in Painter's Paradise.cdr, is probably the hardest one you'll encounter professionally to use PowerTRACE on for cleanup work and alterations. If you succeed at this fictitious example, your *paying* gigs will be a charm. The steps are not hard, but the order of the steps and the strategy will be a little bit of a challenge. Let's get familiar with Corel's PowerTRACE as the first step to acquiring and vectorizing most of this design—the part that machine and man can tease out of this poor bitmap. Choose Bitmaps | Outline Trace to begin this adventure.

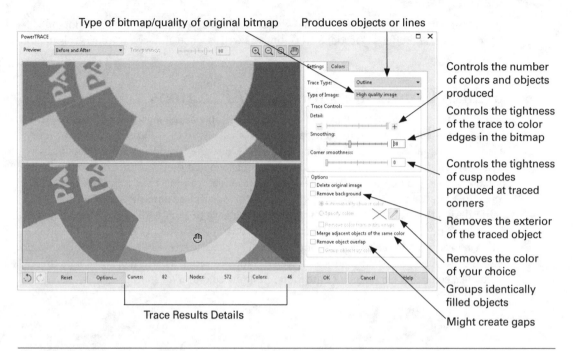

Type of bitmap/quality of original bitmap   Produces objects or lines

Controls the number of colors and objects produced

Controls the tightness of the trace to color edges in the bitmap

Controls the tightness of cusp nodes produced at traced corners

Removes the exterior of the traced object

Removes the color of your choice

Groups identically filled objects

Might create gaps

Trace Results Details

FIGURE 20-7   Use the features and settings in PowerTRACE to create an optimized group of vector objects based on the bitmap.

This logo has too much dithering, and the edges are fuzzy. Now, ordinarily, this would call for a lot of smoothing and not much detail, but this produces a lower number of unique colors, and you don't want that. Therefore, PowerTRACE should be set for less smoothing and greater precision. As you can see here, the logo has a transparent background, because Options | Remove Background has been checked. The final product, therefore, will include a little something special with no extra time spent by you removing the white background by hand. Once you are in the interface for tracing, there's some ground to cover regarding the options you set, which will have a definite impact on the quality of the trace. Figure 20-7 is reviewed in detail next.

- **Trace Type**   In addition to Quick Trace, you can choose Outline or Centerline from this drop-down. Outline is the method that produces objects based on areas of similar color in the bitmap. Centerline is a good option when your source bitmap is calligraphy or a technical drawing; this option generates open paths to which you can assign different widths and styles after the trace is placed on the page.
- **Type of Image**   Both Centerline and Outline Trace have options—you'll be using Outline Trace, which has the most options for helping PowerTRACE understand what type of graphic is to be traced. This usually has an impact on accuracy, limiting image noise and other things. Depending on your choice—from Line Art to High Quality Image—PowerTRACE can render a few objects or hundreds. You can customize the way TRACE evaluates a bitmaps image by altering parameters, and you can also use an

"inappropriate" setting for your imported image. No two images are alike, and you might be surprised at the hi-fi rendering of a piece of clipart you trace using the Line Art setting, for example.

- **Colors** On this tab, you can set the number of unique colors PowerTRACE evaluates, from 1 (which renders a stencil of your original) to a varying maximum of unique colors, which you can limit by typing in a value. You can specify the color mode for the trace; you'd choose CMYK, for example, if you needed a trace that could be sent as an EPS file to a commercial printer. Generally, your best bet is the RGB color mode. You can also sort the colors to be used by how frequently they appear in the original bitmap or by similarity. Additionally, if you intend to replace a color when you edit the traced result, you can do so by clicking a color well and then clicking Edit.

- **Settings** This tab is used to define how tightly and accurately you want PowerTRACE to render the bitmap as a vector object.

- **Detail** You set the overall complexity of the trace with this slider. Higher values instruct PowerTRACE to evaluate the bitmap carefully, whereas lower Detail settings can produce a stylized, posterized trace with fewer colors and many fewer groups of objects.

- **Smoothing** This setting controls both the number of nodes along paths and, to a lesser extent, the number of objects the trace yields. A higher smoothing value is good when your bitmap import is a GIF image that contains a lot of noise, dithered colors, and jagged edges.

- **Corner Smoothness** Use this setting depending on the visual content of your imported bitmap. For example, a photo of a sphere probably doesn't require any corner smoothness. However, a photo of a bird's feather will certainly have a lot of abrupt color and geometry changes—you'd want to use a very low Corner Smoothness setting to represent accurately the sharp turns and corners that make up a feather.

- **Remove Background** Usually you'll want to check this box. When an imported image such as this logo is floating in a background of white, Remove Background doesn't make the background a huge white rectangle. Optionally, any color can be removed from the final trace by clicking the Specify Color button and then using the Eyedropper to choose a color from the preview window.

- **Merge Adjacent Objects of the Same Color** This option makes one object instead of several if the bitmap contains areas of almost identical color in neighboring regions.

- **Remove Object Overlap** Most of the time, you'll want to leave this box unchecked. If you do choose to enable Remove Object Overlap, there might be visible gaps between the resulting grouped vector shapes, making it hard to put a solid background behind your trace without the background color or texture peeking through. This option must be chosen before you can use Group Objects by Color.

- **Group Objects by Color** This is a handy feature that automatically groups identically colored objects after you click OK to make the trace. You can then choose a different color and apply it to the entire group or delete an entire group of objects identically filled, and you don't have dozens of objects that can be accidentally moved lying all over the page.

- **Trace Results Details** This area on the dialog predicts how many objects (curves), how many nodes, and how many different colors are produced. As a guideline, if the results show more than 200 objects will be created in the case of single object, think twice. It's a large number of objects to edit, and the resulting trace will possibly be a challenge to work with.

The Colors Tab in PowerTRACE

Before you decide on the best setting for this example's image, click the Colors tab in PowerTRACE and benefit from this nugget of advice. Yes, you *could* set the Detail slider to a value lower than the maximum. You *could* also choose a different type of image from the Type of Image drop-down. However, doing either of these things reduces both the number of nodes *and* the maximum number of colors PowerTRACE renders.

The following is an example of how using a less-than-optimum trace setting can result in missing parts of small areas, such as text, and poor color matches.

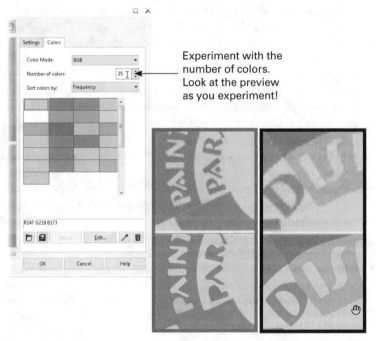

Experiment with the number of colors. Look at the preview as you experiment!

Low-quality trace   High-quality trace

I estimated, through trial but no error, that 24 unique colors will produce all the colors in this GIF image fairly accurately with the best typeface quality. Because this is not a real-world assignment, go ahead and press OK after you've set the options shown.

As you can see in the following illustration, the severely dithered color at about 2 o'clock in the design was traced with a pretty darned close color match to the GIF. To figure out what a dithered color should represent, use the Eyedropper tool, set at a 5×5 pixel sampling area, and then click over an area of dithering that shows several colors. I moved a filled rectangle from the eyedropper sample next to the same area in the PowerTRACE, in the next illustration. Wow, that's a close match to the averaged sample of the colors in the dithered area.

If a trace of a dithered area of your own GIF file does not match the trace, the solution is just around the corner: you sample the original GIF's dithered area at a 5×5 pixel range, and then with the Fill tool, you fill the miscolored object.

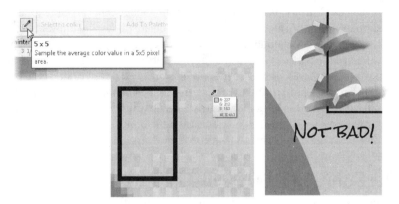

There are a few more steps that are needed to repair, restore, and revise this vector copy of the poor GIF logo. In the next section, I'll run down the problem and then the solution.

Lines, Curves, and Excess Nodes

Even with settings that provide a "tight trace," you will encounter, including in this example, too many nodes along a path, especially at corners. Also, there will be small, unconnected pieces of the trace in areas you won't see unless you go to View | Wireframe. When curves aren't curvy enough and lines that should be straight look like a branch on a maple tree, following this succinct but extraordinary set of solutions will help:

- **Too many nodes on a path**   It's possible that the result of the trace will be a group of objects; it's a good idea to select the trace and then press CTRL-U to Ungroup. With the Shape tool, marquee-select this area so that only the excess nodes and not the useful ones are modified. On the Property Bar, drag the Reduce noise slider until you preview the deleted nodes on your drawing, and then release the slider. You can see the effect in this illustration.

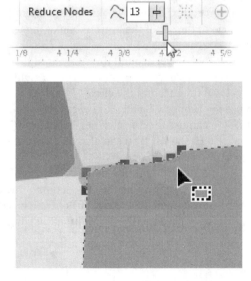

- **A curve is bumpy or lopsided**   Again, the Shape tool can enhance a path that is supposed to be perfectly curvy. Manually delete nodes you know are superfluous—a curve might have a node at its center, but not six or seven! You can then either drag at the center of the curve to increase or decrease its curvature, or drag to one side or the other to correct the curve's slope. For more precision, click a cusp node at the beginning or the end of the curve segment, and then drag the control handle and the control point to perfect the curve. To make lines into straight lines, marquee-select the beginning and end nodes (hold SHIFT and then click on node, then the other), and then right-click and choose To Line from the context menu (the pop-up menu).

The Solution to Messed-Up Text

I'm going to play the client for a moment and tell you that I don't care what font you use to replace the text, but it should be "fat" (or "bold" in the words of a designer) and should say "Pigment Pals," which is the new name for the paint emporium.

You'd want to replace the text regardless of a word change; the text as traced is just too spindly and "hand drawn" in appearance. This is not PowerTRACE's fault. The less-than-great text is a result of the original GIF expressing the text in a mere handful of pixels. You can't trace great text from 17 pixels (or whatever)! Here are the steps for replacing the tracings with real text.

Tutorial   Making New Text Along a Curve

1. Drag a vertical guide and a horizontal guide out of the rulers to estimate where the center of all the colored arcs and text in this vector image is.
2. Choose the Ellipse tool. Hold CTRL-SHIFT to trace a perfect circle from the inside out.
3. Drag from the intersection of the guides while holding the modifier keys. When the circle appears to be sitting on the baseline of the word "Paradise," release the mouse button and keys. Now with the Pick tool, move the circle until it rests under the arc of the vector text in the trace. You might notice that the center of the circle is not the center of the arced text, but that's okay for the moment. It's of importance right now to fit the circle to the arc of the bottom line of the text (the word "Paradise"). Keep the circle selected.
4. With the Text tool, hover around the circle until the cursor turns into an insertion (vertical) bar with a curvy segment to its lower right. This indicates you can type now, and the text will flow around the circle. Type **PALS**.
5. You can use the Property Bar right now to center the text relative to the original "Paradise." You can use the Offset slider on the text (it should be selected) to move the text to the right or the left. You can also marquee-select the nodes of the text using the Shape tool and drag the characters.
6. Choose a good font from the enormous collection of typefaces that come with CorelDRAW. If you sift through the "B" section of the collection, you'll find Bremen Bold (it's probably named TT1231M_.TTF), which is the font used in the original design (you'd really have no way of intuiting this). Even places such as What the Font

would have a hard time divining the font used in this small GIF file. You install a font merely by double-clicking on it to preview it and then clicking Install. To improvise here, I chose to install Kabel Bd (TT0166M_.TTF). Choose a typeface from the installed fonts list (you *don't* have to restart DRAW when you install a font while it's running), and choose the Kabel font. You can see in the following illustration that a real font is much better than the traced one.

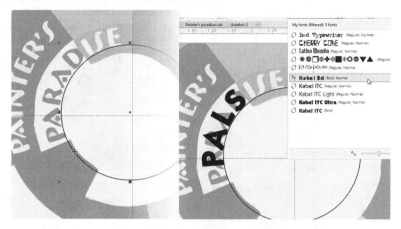

7. Repeat Steps 3–6 to create the word PIGMENT to the top of PALS.
8. Because text along a curve cannot be directly filled using the Eyedropper tool, do this: create a circle or a rectangle, and then sample and apply the original text color to the circle or rectangle. The color is then added to the document palette (the short string of swatches at the bottom of the interface). You can delete the object you created to fill now.
9. Select the text and then click the swatch on the document palette. This fills both the text *and* the circle that it is bound to. No problem.
10. CTRL-click over the circle to select it but not the text. On the color palette, first left-click the "x" swatch (the "no fill" swatch) and then right-click the x to remove any outline color or width.
11. Seriously consider pressing CTRL-S and naming your file at this point. Don't close it; there's one more set of steps.

I was personally not happy with the overall design. I felt an additional arc with a unique color would finish off the design. The location of this new element can be seen in the illustration to follow. Here's how to make much more money with an assignment such as this one, and don't laugh. It's common knowledge that if a company makes more than $1,000 a year, they know nothing about logos.

Get out the Ellipse tool and let's go:

1. Drag a circle from the center of the arcs until you reach the innermost arc at the bottom of the design.
2. With the Pick tool, drag and drop this circle at the next outer ring of the bottom arc; see the following illustration for a visual description of this.

3. With the Pen tool, trace an area that matches both the top and bottom arc and that butts against the left and right shapes using a straight line.

4. With the closed shape selected, choose Window | Dockers | Color.

5. Fill the shape using any color you like. For the moment, it's okay as long as it's filled. Filling a shape a second time is easier than filling an empty object.

6. Pick a nice color from the HSB field and Hue slider and then drag and drop the "after" swatch at the bottom of the two-color onto the object to be filled on the page.

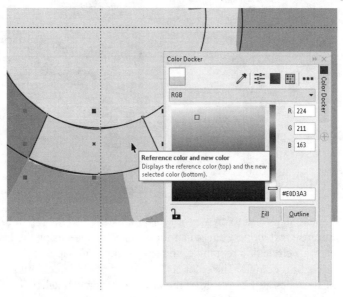

7. Clean the drawing up by deleting guides and unnecessary objects—that sort of stuff. Figure 20-8 shows the finished trace. Although it's partially automatic, it shows off an awful lot of your newfound skills too.

FIGURE 20-8 Use different techniques and approaches to make a great vector logo from whatever a client tosses your way.

PowerTRACE for Traditional Artists

Many different types of users are attracted to CorelDRAW. Logo and other graphics designers are one category of visual communicators. However, CorelDRAW's tracing feature also appeals to artists who come to the digital world of illustration after years of work with physical pens, pencils, and inks.

If you have a scanner, and have, for example, a pen and ink cartoon, PowerTRACE makes child's play out of re-creating your cartoon as scalable vector art, to which you can apply color fills with a smoothness and precision that enhances your cartoons and can elevate them to the status of Fine Art. Seriously!

Cartoon sneaker drawing.png is a fairly high-resolution scan to get you started with a specific workflow you can adopt with scans of your own drawings. One important issue is removing pencil or other marks on the physical paper before you scan; use a kneaded eraser, and even if the paper doesn't come completely clean, the following steps show you a novel way to use PowerTRACE to remove stray marks.

Here's how to create a digital cartoon suitable for exporting as either vector or bitmap art to any size you need; this is a perk you don't have when working with only physical tools.

Tutorial Digi-tooning

1. In a new document, select Landscape orientation, click the Import button on the Standard Bar, and then choose Cartoon sneaker drawing.png. Place it by click-dragging the loaded cursor so it fills the page.
2. Click Bitmaps, and then choose Outline Trace | Line Art.

 Note Occasionally, you'll receive an attention box stating that the bitmap size is too large and that, if you choose not to resize the bitmap, the trace process might be on the slow side. This is your artistic call: if you want the pen strokes to look extremely faithful to the author's original cartoon, click Keep Original Size. If you're in a hurry, click Reduce Bitmap.

---

3. In the PowerTRACE window, choose a medium amount of Detail, about 25 percent Smoothing and no Corner Smoothness, check Remove Background, and then click the Colors tab. Set the number of colors to **2**. Doing this generates almost entirely black objects with the exception of one or two areas that are totally enclosed, which should produce a white fill inside a black object. Check Remove Color From Entire Image to get rid of superfluous white areas. To make the dark areas truly black, choose the Colors tab and click on the almost-black color. Click Edit, and make R, G, and B equal to zero for a pure black. Check Delete Original Image, click OK, and you'll see that the pencil marks that are not entirely a black color disappear from the trace.

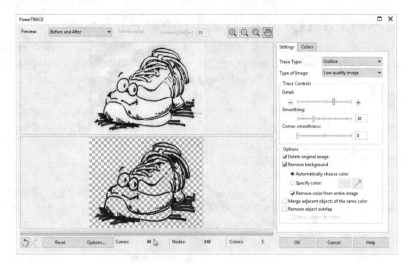

4. Choose Window | Dockers | Object Manager. Create a new layer and then drag its title on the list to below Layer 1. You can rename these layers **Coloring** and **Trace** by clicking to select the name and then clicking a second time to open the title for editing—type anything you like in the field. Lock the tracing layer.

5. Using the Pen tool you're most comfortable with for creating free-form shapes, create objects that represent the different areas of the cartoon you'd like to color in. For example, the treads of the sneaker would look good in several different shades of warm gray. The solution would be to use the Mesh fill on this object you draw—see Chapter 15 for thorough documentation of object fills. The top of the sneaker could be an interesting Linear Fountain fill, traversing from deep orange at the bottom to a bright yellow at the top. Another great thing about coloring your work digitally is that you never have to decide on a final color.

Linear Fountain fill

Mesh fill

FIGURE 20-9 Make a hybrid drawing from traditional ink to digital fills in CorelDRAW.

6. You continue this process until you've "colored inside the lines" and filled as much of the drawing as you see fit artistically. You can see a logo mockup in Figure 20-9 for a children's footwear store. Clearly the drawing has an organic sense about it—the opposite of the sterile and flawless "computer art" we see occasionally—and yet this is CorelDRAW computer art, with a little ingenuity added to create a symbiosis between the physical and traditional elements.

You can take a look at how this drawing was completed if you open Sneaky kids finished .cdr.

This chapter has been an introduction to how imported bitmaps can happily coexist and help enhance your vector work in CorelDRAW. As you move on to Chapter 21, you're going to graduate to *Advanced* Bitmap Editing. Corel PHOTO-PAINT doesn't get all the attention it really deserves; it's indispensible for photo retouching and exporting animations—if it's pixel-based, it's PHOTO-PAINT. Come see how great image editing enhances your overall skills as a CorelDRAWing kinda individual.

21 Common Image-Editing Techniques Using PHOTO-PAINT

Photography tells a different story than the vector graphics you create in CorelDRAW. Although vector drawings can look crisp, powerful, and brilliant in coloring, photographs typically mirror more of a literal human story. Digital images deliver emotional content through soft tones, an intricate latticework of highlights and shadows, and all the photorealistic qualities that portray the world as we're accustomed to seeing it. Understandably, the tools you use to edit a digital photo or other bitmap image are different from those you use to edit paths in CorelDRAW. This is where PHOTO-PAINT enters the scene to round out your creative toolset.

This chapter introduces you to the fundamentals of *bitmap images*—how to measure bitmaps, how to crop them to suit a specific output need, and ultimately how to make your original photo look better than when it came off the camera.

 Note Download and extract all the files from the Chapter 21.zip archive to follow the tutorials in this chapter.

The Building Block of Digital Photos: The Pixel

We all use the word occasionally in a humorous context in conversations, but seldom is an explanation or *definition* of a pixel provided in a way that is useful when you need to alter a digital photograph. A *pixel*—an abbreviation for *pic*ture *el*ement—is the smallest recognizable unit of color in a digital photograph. It is *not* a linear unit of measurement; a pixel doesn't have to be square in proportions, and it's not any specific color. Now that you know what a pixel *isn't*, read on to learn what a pixel *is*, and how understanding its properties will help you work with PHOTO-PAINT's tools.

Pixels and Resolution

A pixel is a *placeholder* in a bitmap image; as such, it has no fixed size you can measure the same way you'd measure the length of a 2-by-4 piece of wood (which is usually 2" by 4"). It's hard to discuss a pixel with a friend or co-worker without any sort of *context* because these pixel units cannot exist unless they're within a background, which is usually called the *paper* or the *canvas,* which in PHOTO-PAINT is an imaginary grid into which you assign units of colors with the Paint tool or the Fill tool. When you open a digital photograph, the paper is predefined by the capability of the digital camera; the *resolution* of your photographs are of a fixed size.

Resolution is expressed as a fraction, a ratio: how many *pixels per inch* there are expresses image resolution, in much the same way that *miles per hour* expresses speed. We often call this resolution *dpi* (dots per inch), owing to the visual similarity between dots of ink on a printed page and the pixels of color we see on a monitor. Bitmap images are also called *resolution-dependent* images because once a photo has been taken or a paper size defined for a PHOTO-PAINT painting, you cannot change the resolution without distorting the visual content of the picture. Here's an example that shows the use of resolution when you click the New Document title on the Get Started welcome screen, press CTRL-N, or choose File | New:

1. In the Create a New Image dialog, you're offered a Preset Destination setting of PHOTO-PAINT Default, which, as you can see here, is 5 inches in width by 7 inches in height. However, this is not a *complete* description of how large the default paper size is in real-world units. How many *pixels* will be created per inch? Without knowing the resolution, the paper size is as meaningful as how many grapefruits per inch will fit on the page! Fortunately, below the Height and Width fields, you see the Resolution field, set to the default of 72 dpi.

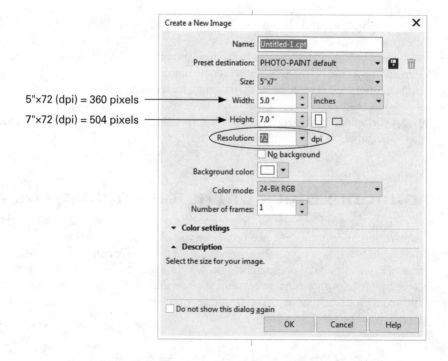

5"×72 (dpi) = 360 pixels

7"×72 (dpi) = 504 pixels

2. Aha! Now we can discover the number of pixels in the new document. Knowing this can be important for just about all types of work because you always presume a fixed screen resolution with the audience; therefore, images destined for a website, for example, are measured in absolute number of pixels in width and height for graphics. In this example, 504 pixels wide might make a good logo at the top page of a website; in 2017, many people who browse the Web run a screen that displays 1280×1024 pixels or higher, so this default image size is a little more than one-third the width of an audience's screen.

Image Resolution

Any PHOTO-PAINT document resolution can be great for web graphics, but *not* so good for printing. The finite number of pixels in the resolution-dependent bitmap image can be the culprit. Figure 21-1 shows, on the left, a CorelDRAW illustration of a child's paint box. In this book, the drawing looks crisp around the edges and smooth in its transitions from neighboring tones. It was a graphic suitable for printing as a bitmap because it was exported at a high resolution (300 dots per inch) for printing in this book. On the right, however, is an illustration of the same paint box, with the imaginary bitmap grid shown, but it was exported at desktop icon size (about 19-by-19 pixels), and the loss of image detail is evident at its resolution of 72 pixels per inch.

Resolution, Pixel Count, and Printing

It's a frequently asked question, and one whose answer is not precise: what is the resolution needed for a photograph to make a good print?

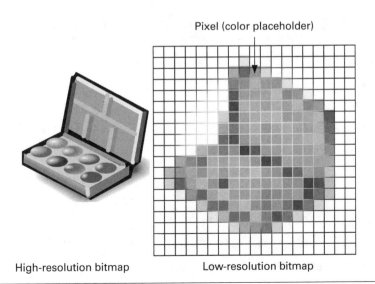

Pixel (color placeholder)

High-resolution bitmap   Low-resolution bitmap

FIGURE 21-1 The number of pixels in a bitmap, combined with the image's resolution, determines whether an image is suitable for printing.

To answer a question with a question: how good is "good"? Also, how large is the print you need? Of lesser importance but still something to think about is, how large are the individual sensors on your camera? PHOTO-PAINT can't do anything about the quality or resolution of your camera, but in general, the more pixels you have, the better the detail, and the larger the print you can make that has fine details. This details stuff will become more clear in a moment when you see a chart of camera capability and the corresponding image size.

Tip Scanning a physical photograph doesn't provide the best sampling of color pixels to produce a terrific photograph, but it *does* ensure that you have a *sufficient* number of pixels (an image's *pixel coun*t) to print the scanned photo.

Keep in mind that this chapter was written in 2016, and the speed of technology development might contradict some of this info by next month! The movement, even with many professional photographers, from a digital SLR camera to a mobile device (such as Apple's iPhone) has been due not just to portability (spontaneity, the ability to photograph where a larger camera is impractical) but to quality as well. Last year's iPhone could capture 12 megapixels (MP) using a quality lens and sensor array. Almost all of today's digital cameras are capable of taking full-frame pictures that can be printed to inkjet printers at 12" by 18" in high quality. Digital cameras measure the number of pixels in width and height of the picture's frame in *megapixels* (a million pixels equal a megapixel). For example, for about the same price as an unlocked iPhone (under $600), the Canon EOS Rebel T6 EF-S can take approximately 18.70 megapixels. The width of a frame is 5184 pixels, and the height is 3456 pixels. When these numbers are multiplied, the result is 17,915,904 pixels, almost exactly 18 MP.

Depending on the make and model of your digital device, you can take photos that vary in maximum print size. The following table provides the maximum printable dimensions for different megapixel-capable cameras and corresponding resulting image quality:

Sensor	Resolution	Excellent Print Quality (300 dpi)	Good Print Quality (200 dpi)	Poor Print Quality (150 dpi)
3 MP	2048×1536	7"×5"	10"×8"	14"×11"
4 MP	2464×1632	8"×6"	12"×8"	16"×12"
6 MP	3008×2000	10"×8"	15"×10"	19"×13"
8 MP	3164×2448	12"×8"	16"×12"	22"×16"
10 MP	3872×2592	13"×9"	19"×13"	26"×17"
12 MP	4290×2800	15"×10"	21"×14"	28"×18"
16 MP	4920×3264	17"×11"	24"×16"	32"×22"
36 MP	7360×4912	24"×16"	36"×24"	48"×32"
42 MP	7952 x 5304	27"×18"	40"×30"	54"×36"
50 MP	8688×5792	30"×20"	44"×29"	58"×39"

Note What you can conclude from the preceding chart is that resolution decreases as physical size of a print increases. Given the critical factor of viewing distance, most of the time you can get away with printing a very low resolution image to, say, the size of a billboard. Because we see billboards from far away, no one notices the pixilated quality of the image.

Print size at 1-to-1 resolution can be far greater than computer screen resolution, and that's why digital photos can be enlarged to a great extent while retaining focus and clarity. This is because even the largest computer monitor resolution of 2560×1440 pixels yields a count of only 3.67 megapixels.

The maximum print sizes listed in the previous table are not hard-and-fast dimensions, but are guidelines for print output for two reasons:

- The dots that inkjet printers render are imprecise. They are more like *splats* than dots as the print head sprays color onto the page.
- There is flexibility when printing to home inkjet printers because *image dimensions are inversely proportional to image resolution*. You can see from the previous chart that if your home inkjet can print 200 to 300 dpi, you have some wiggle space for the final print size.

The math for calculating maximum resolution goes like this: most affordable inkjet printers advertise a high-quality resolution of about 720 dpi. The documentation might claim that the printer offers "enhanced resolution of 1440 dpi," but usually this enhancement is only rendered in one direction, height or width, depending on your print layout. The *true* resolution is always the lower number when two are offered in the inkjet printer's documentation. Manufacturers of inkjet printers, makers of inks, and other printing experts agree that the ideal resolution for printing (in dots per inch) requires about one-third this number (in pixels per inch) for the image to be printed, so 720 dpi divided by 3 is 240 dpi.

In PHOTO-PAINT, you can change the resolution of an image, thereby changing its real-world dimensions, *without changing the pixel count*. If you *change* the number of pixels in an image, the image appears sharper when it's made smaller, but appears blurred when it's enlarged. For example, a photo that is 3" by 3" at 300 pixels per inch (ppi) is *exactly equal* to a 6"-by-6" image at a resolution of 150 ppi. Both images have the *same number* of pixels, but the print *dimensions* and *resolution* have been changed inversely proportionately.

Let's walk through an example of how to determine a photo's resolution and then adjust it for printing.

Tutorial Resizing a Photograph

1. In PHOTO-PAINT, open Late Graduate.png, a photo that has been somewhat contrived to demonstrate a technique in this chapter.
2. Let's say you need to print this photo at inkjet high quality. You decide to settle for a good-to-excellent print—let's say 240 pixels/inch in resolution. That's a resolution the author often uses on his own inkjet. To check the resolution of the current foreground

document, with the Object Pick tool, right-click over the document and then choose Document Properties from the context menu.

Tip To display rulers around the edges of a document, press CTRL-R. To hide rules, press CTRL-R again to toggle them off. If the rulers don't display the units you need, right-click over either ruler and then choose Ruler Setup from the context menu.

Well, oops. This photo is a nice 8" by 11", but it's of insufficient resolution to print at the desired 240 ppi, as shown here. It *can* print with high quality and great image fidelity, but the physical output dimensions need to be decreased to *increase* the resolution.

3. Right-click over the photo and then choose Resample from the context menu. The Resample (Image menu item) box does more than resample an image; it can also *resize* an image, and the two terms are very different. *Resizing* is the action of decreasing or increasing image resolution, affecting image dimensions inversely, and the result is an image that has the same number of pixels. *Resampling* (covered in this chapter) involves *changing the number of pixels* in the image. Original pixel colors are moved around the grid—some are duplicated, some removed—and the resulting color pixels are a new color based on an average of neighboring original color pixels. Resampling changes original image data and occasionally blurs or creates unwanted harsh edges in image areas.

4. Click to check the Maintain Original Size box, and make sure the Maintain Aspect Ratio box is checked. Then type **7** in the Height field. Because the photo was doctored for this example, the photo is now a perfect 7" by 5", smaller than its original dimensions. As the dimensions decreased, as shown in Figure 21-2, the photo's resolution increased and is now more than adequate for inkjet printing. Save the file if you like ducks, or college, or both, and then print it to see what image resolution does for digital images: it *improves* them.

FIGURE 21-2   Resolution is inversely proportional to image dimensions.

 Note There is a little disagreement in the imaging community about screen resolution: whether it should be measured at 72 or 96 pixels per inch, the standard that Microsoft put forth with Windows 95. The answer to this disagreement is, when you're measuring pixels for screen display, *it makes absolutely no difference*. Screen resolution, regardless of how you measure it, is a fixed size, so a 300-pixel-wide bitmap might look larger or smaller depending on the screen resolution you use for display, but it doesn't change the number of pixels in width or the total pixel count of a bitmap when you display it on your monitor.

Resampling and Resizing Photos

At times, you absolutely *have* to upscale a photo; you might not have a better image and you can't retake the scene or person's portrait. When you increase the number of pixels in a photo, you're *not* increasing image detail—all the details in the scene were captured when you took the photo. PHOTO-PAINT adds pixels by duplicating existing pixel colors and then averages the colors a little to make a smooth photo transition between neighboring pixels in the resampled photo *if* you leave Anti-alias checked in the Resample dialog.

How much larger you can make a photo before the individual pixels become apparent depends on the visual content of the photo. Pictures of intricate machinery and images of lots of differently colored small objects such as leaves do not upsample nearly as well as, say, a photo of soft clouds on an overcast day. If you need to make a photo 150 percent of its original size, usually you can get away with this without taking any additional steps. However, if you need to print a picture from the Web that's only 300 pixels wide, for example, you have two things going for you in this endeavor:

- Inkjet printers tend to smooth out small rough areas in a digital image because ink spreads on the printed page, blending flaws together. Don't count on this factor; it's an assistant, but a small one.
- PHOTO-PAINT can sharpen edges in the resampled photo while keeping large areas of similar colors smooth in appearance.

Tip PHOTO-PAINT has several sharpening filters under Effects | Sharpen. PHOTO-PAINT's Help system provides a good general explanation of the Sharpen filters; launch any of them and then click Help button in the filter dialog. Generally, when in doubt, choose Unsharp Mask to add some crispness to resampled photos. Unsharp Mask provides good sharpening without an overwhelming number of options you need to learn. Click the Preview button in any of the filter dialogs to toggle the effect on and off within the document window for comparison.

Figure 21-3 shows a small JPEG photograph; let's pretend for the purposes of working through a tutorial that you own this condo and want to time-share it. And you want to print postcard-size images to hand out in addition to using the image on your website.

350 pixels wide   Zoom to 800 percent

FIGURE 21-3   Unless some corrective steps are taken, this small photo would print with huge, clearly visible color pixels.

Tip The Zoom tool (Z) affords you the opportunity to get in very close to an image area to view and edit. However, if you're not familiar with resolution-dependent bitmap editing, a zoomed-in view of a photo might look coarse and your instinct might be to soften the image. Periodically check the document title bar: after the name of the file, there's an @ symbol followed by your current viewing resolution. If the zoom factor is greater than 100 percent, this document is not displaying as your audience will see it. To quickly zoom a document to 1:1 (a 100 percent viewing resolution), double-click the Zoom tool on the Toolbox.

The following set of steps is a "worst-case" scenario—you will almost certainly be able to enlarge photos so they become print-worthy by resampling up to 150 percent or so; you won't have to make the *gross* sort of enlargement and image corrections shown in these steps. However, as you'll soon see, the High Pass effect you'll use does, indeed, enhance a copy of the small JPEG photo to a usable state.

Tutorial Making a Thumbnail Image Suitable for Printing

1. Open Hollywood-5203.jpg in PHOTO-PAINT. With the Object Pick tool, right-click over the image and then choose Resample from the context menu.
2. In the Width field, type **7**, and then click an insertion point in the Resolution | Horizontal field. Make sure the Maintain Aspect Ratio and Anti-alias check boxes are checked, and then type **240** in the box. Click OK to resample the photo.
3. Press CTRL-D. This places a duplicate object above the original.
4. At 100 percent viewing resolution, clearly the photo needs a little edge sharpening without sharpening the larger smooth areas. Press F7 if the Object Manager docker isn't docked to the window or isn't visible. You're going to duplicate this image and put the copy on top of the original. This is an unusual thing to do—and *to be able to do*—but PHOTO-PAINT has advanced image-editing features that let you change and merge image areas (called *objects)* so the pixels in objects can have different colors while being aligned to the imaginary grid in the document identically.
5. Click the Object 1 thumbnail on the Object list to select it—you want to edit this, not the Background object.
6. Choose Effects | Sharpen | High Pass. Wherever sharp transitions between pixel colors appear in the photo, edge details are retained and strengthened. Wherever there is little color difference between neighboring pixels (called *low-frequency* areas), the visual information is filtered out, leaving a light gray area with almost no color. The higher the percentage you specify (use **100** in this example), the less original color is retained. The greater the radius (use about **12** in this example), the greater the distance this filter examines from neighboring pixels to filter out areas of little detail difference.

This tends to result in sharp edges in the photo with smooth color areas where there's little or no detail, such as a clear sky. Click OK to apply these settings.

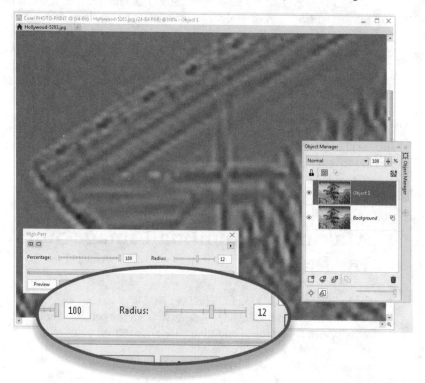

7. Beyond the strong edges in Object 1, this object doesn't look as though it will contribute much to enhancing the enlarged image, but the correct answer is, "Yes, it will!" Here's a simple explanation of why Overlay mode will turn this largely gray object into a perfect "lens" to sharpen the underlying Background photo. The brightness values in a photo (the tones, not the colors) are usually calculated on a scale of 0 to 255, with 255 representing the brightest area (pure white has a brightness of 255). Overlay Merge mode can be thought of as a filter: Overlay mode objects that have a brightness greater than 128 lighten (bleach, screen) objects under them, whereas brightness pixel values less than 128 darken (multiply) the underlying pixels. The High Pass filter made most of the pixels in this object neutral gray—which has no effect in Overlay mode on the underlying pixels. However, the *edge details* in Object 1 are darker and lighter than the underlying, corresponding Background areas. Choose Overlay from the Merge Mode drop-down list.

8. Objects do not have to be 100 percent opaque. This Overlay mode object contributes a little too strongly to the overall picture; click the Transparency combo box at the top right of the Object docker to reveal the slider and then drag the slider left to about **29%**, or whatever value looks best in the document window.

Without High
Pass object

High Pass object
in Overlay mode

FIGURE 21-4   Use PHOTO-PAINT filters and objects to strengthen and smooth image areas selectively.

9. You can choose to save this file right now as a PHOTO-PAINT (CPT) or Adobe Photoshop (PSD) document, and the objects will retain their order using these special image file formats. And you can now print the composition. However, if you'd like to standardize the image so it can be saved to practically any file format (PNG, JPEG, TIFF, and others) and thus shared with most other computer users, with the Object Pick tool, right-click on either object on the Object Manager docker and then choose Combine | Combine All Objects With Background.

As you can see for comparison in Figure 21-4, without the High Pass copy of the image in Overlay mode, on the left, the pixels dominate the image in visual importance. On the right, however, with the duplicate object you filtered and merged with the original, it's a fairly photogenic image…given that you enlarged it to almost *23 times* its original file size!

Automation: Recording Your Cropping and Resampling

It's almost a foregone conclusion that if you work at a small- to medium-size business, you have dozens if not hundreds of photos that need some sort of alterations and uniformity so they'll look consistent in size when you make a catalogue or web page. Cropping is a separate process from resizing photos in PHOTO-PAINT, but the good news is that if your photos are even remotely similar in subject matter, you can record your cropping and resampling moves and then play this recorded script back on an entire folder of images. No errors, no recalculations, and you might have a free hand to eat your sandwich as you work through lunch.

Evaluating a Crop Area for a Collection of Photos

PHOTO-PAINT's Crop tool does only one thing perfectly well: it eliminates areas of a picture outside the crop rectangle you drag before double-clicking or pressing ENTER to finalize the crop. You are free before finalizing to reposition, reset, and move the crop rectangle. The Crop tool resizes an image area, and depending on whether you've chosen Custom on the Property Bar, the Crop tool can possibly resample an image (but you might not be happy with an upsampled photo). Therefore, if you want to enlarge or decrease the number of pixels in the finished version, you must perform the additional step of resampling *before* saving a copy of the photo.

The imaginary company in this scenario (leading up to a tutorial) specializes in exotic minerals—no common quartz or hematite to be found on their website—and the photographer took seven pictures whose visual content is more or less all in the same position from photo to photo. Your mission is to crop out the bottom pedestal and place a card in all the photos to favor the mineral itself. You also want to reduce the size of all the pictures, all sized to exactly the same dimensions, so the collection of minerals can be featured on a web page. Because Windows 7, 8, and 10 can display large thumbnails of common image file formats such as PNG, you can easily preview the contents of an entire folder of images to better see which individual photo needs the most height or width to then apply a suitable crop for all the images.

Figure 21-5 is a view of the folder of mineral pictures as seen from the File | Open An Image window in PHOTO-PAINT, with Extra Large Icons chosen from the drop-down list.

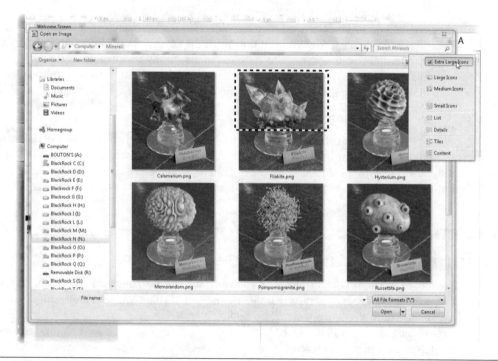

FIGURE 21-5 Out of the many images you need to resample and crop, choose the one that requires the loosest cropping as the basis for your automation recording.

The overlay of the dotted line shows that the Fliakite.png image requires the greatest width of all the files—this is something you can detect by eye. Therefore, when you begin the tutorial, you'll begin by choosing Fliakite.png as the image on which you'll record your cropping and resampling edits.

Tutorial   Recording Your Edits

The following set of steps guides you simultaneously through recording and editing the resampling and cropping process. Playing the saved recording back on a folder is quite simple and covered in a following section. If you have a real-world need to crop and resample scores of images, and your boss or client wanted them yesterday, you're going to have your solution and the images completed sooner than anyone might imagine! Locate the images you downloaded at the beginning of this chapter; put only the mineral PNG files in a unique folder.

1. Choose Windows | Dockers | Recorder (CTRL-F3).
2. Choose File | Open (CTRL-O) and then open Fliakite.png from the folder to which you copied the seven PNG files.
3. Click the red button on the Recorder docker; you're recording now. Choose the Crop tool from the Toolbox.
4. Drag a rectangle around the top of the image, excluding the glass pedestal from your crop.

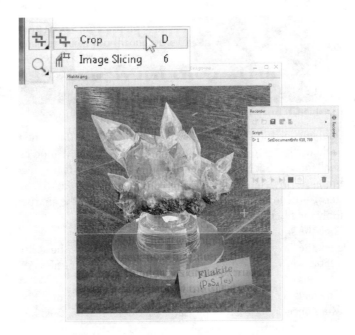

5. Press ENTER to finalize the crop (double-clicking inside the document does the same thing).
6. Press v (Object Pick tool) and then right-click over the image and choose Resample.

7. Three or possibly four thumbnails across a conservatively sized web page of 800 pixels wide means the width to resample this image should be about 200 pixels. Choose Pixels from the Image Size units drop-down list and then type **200** in the Width field. The height will automatically scale down in proportion.

8. Because you're not measuring in real-world units, but instead in number of pixels, you don't have to specify 72 or 96 dpi for the resampled image. On the Web, a screen pixel is an absolute, unchangeable size. Additionally, if you change the dpi setting now, you'll need to go back and again specify the width as 200 because you've changed the resolution value. If the percentage field reads approximately 32%, you're good to go— click OK to apply.

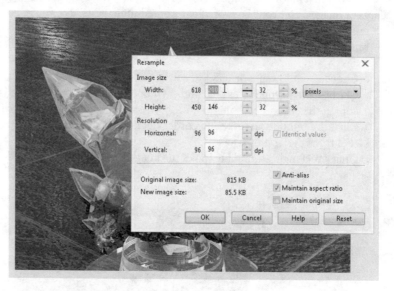

9. Double-click the Zoom tool to move your view to 100%. The resampled image could use just a touch of Effect | Sharpen | Sharpen, a good choice for extremely small images. Set the Edge Level to about **26%**; this is the degree of sharpening with emphasis on neighboring pixels that have dissimilar colors. Set the Threshold to **0** (zero)—the lower the value, the more pronounced the sharpening effect. Click OK to apply the filter.

10. Click the square Stop button on the Recorder docker.

11. Click the Save button on the Recorder docker, name the script, and then choose a location on your hard disk where you keep important files.

Note The Save icon on the Recorder and other dockers is of a floppy disk. Floppy disks were once used to store digital media before DVDs, CDs, air travel, and horses were invented.

You can close the Fliakite file without saving changes. In the following section, you'll run the recorded script on this image and save it, so your work that's not done yet will be automatically done for you in a moment.

The Fun Part: Playing Back Your Script

The following steps will seem anticlimactic; the bulk of the work you have ahead of you is accomplished merely by filling out a few fields in the File | Batch Process dialog and clicking Play.

1. Choose File | Batch Process.
2. Click Add File. Navigate to where you stored the mineral images. Select all of them by clicking on one file to place your cursor inside the file box and pressing CTRL-A, and then click Import.
3. Click Add Script. Look at the default path where PHOTO-PAINT saves scripts at the top of the box. The default location is under *your user account* | Appdata | Roaming | Corel (in case you lose a file in the future). Click the name of the script you saved in the previous tutorial and then click Open.
4. In the Options field, click the drop-down list and then choose On Completion: Save As New Type.
5. Save To Folder is an important choice if you want to find the processed images later! Because you'll be saving to JPEG, it's okay to save the processed images to the same folder as the originals, which are in the PNG file format, and will not be overwritten by the batch process.
6. You'll probably want the JPEG file type for the resampled photos if this is a website display. Click the Save As Type drop-down list and then choose JPG-JPEG bitmaps.

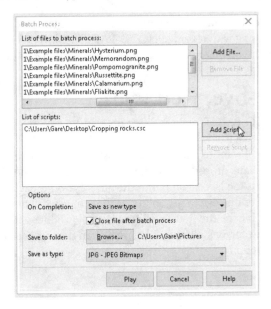

7. Click Play, and you're done!

Back in CorelDRAW, use the Extrude tool for a fancy website banner. When you select the multiple files for import into CorelDRAW from the destination folder to which you saved your batch processing, you can simply click the page to place the images, one at a time, at 100 percent their size, and in no time you'll look like a miracle worker to your boss. And if you're self-employed, you can look in your bathroom mirror and say, "Darn, I'm good!" (Keep in mind this is a PG-rated book.)

Fun and Fantastic Image-Retouching

If you've ever seen a fantastic, unbelievable image in a magazine, the chances are it was retouched using an image editor, PHOTO-PAINT being one of the best ones on the software market. The next sections will run you through a basic retouching assignment, an ambitious one, and an over-the-top exercise that will trigger several variations of your own invention in the future. Come along and play with people's faces!

Ridding a Photo of the Red-Eye Effect

Even with digital cameras, when you use a flash and the subject is a human—and they have their eyes open for a change—you're probably going to get a red dot where their beautiful blue eyes should be. This is because the flash is bouncing off the blood-rich retina in the individual's eyes. In the future, you probably want to angle the flash so it bounces off (ideally) a white ceiling onto the subject, but when you have a bum photo like the one shown in the upcoming illustration, thank goodness you're reading the right chapter for the remedy.

It's really quite simple: PHOTO-PAINT's Red-Eye Removal tool makes quick work of removing red eye, and more refined work than you could do manually with the Paint tool. Let's take a quick ride through the next steps to make this wedding photo perfect, and then we'll get to messing with it using PHOTO-PAINT's Objects feature and some tricky masking techniques. More on that in a moment. Let's use the Red-Eye Removal tool now.

Tutorial   **Bye-bye, Red Eye**

1. In PHOTO-PAINT, open the Two dressed-up guys.png file and then choose the Red-Eye Removal tool from the Toolbox.
2. Now, you'll want to choose a soft brush to avoid hard edges in the restoration, so on the Nib shape drop-down in the Property Bar, click the 50 pixel diameter nib. Because 50 pixels is too large, zoom into the guy's eye on the left of the photo and hover the cursor over one eye to get an idea of how much you need to reduce the diameter. A suggestion here: the Red-Eye Removal tool produces the most natural results when the size of the cursor's nib is a little larger than the red-eye area, and a little larger than the subject's pupil.

3. Set the diameter to 12 (because I said so) and then set the Tolerance to the maximum of 5 to ensure that all the red will be replaced by a blackish color.

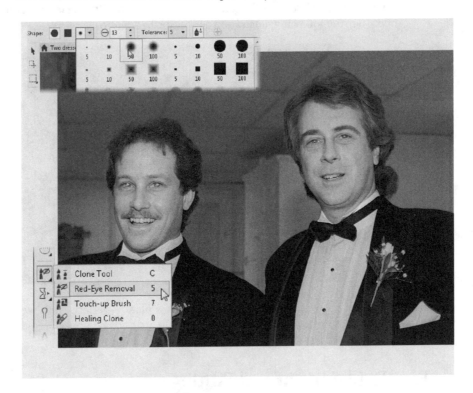

4. Zoom in (push away from yourself with the mouse wheel) if you haven't done so already, and then with the cursor, click on the red area of one of the guy's eyes. As you can see in the following illustration, the tool does a pretty good job of restoring the handsome guy's peepers to a semblance of normality.

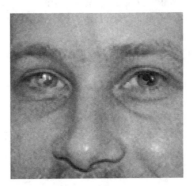

5. The excitement is all downhill from here: you just click the Red-Eye Removal tool on the guy's other pupil, and then do this twice more for the other guy's pupils.
6. Save the file as "Two good-looking guys" in the native CPT file format and leave the file open. See the following illustration of the finished photo.

That didn't take much, did it? The picture is now picture-perfect. Next, we'll use our imagination and some PHOTO-PAINT features that are as of yet undiscovered to make the two guys into twins. How's that for digital mischief?

Face Replacement and Editing

The guy on the left in the photo has a better smile than the guy on the right. So what do you say we make both guys have not only the same smile but the same face? Head replacement has been the sport of "Brand P" users for decades, and there's absolutely no reason why you can't do the same stunt with the same finesse in PHOTO-PAINT. You've got a good teacher here!

First, you need to make a copy of the left guy's face; let's call him Dave. To do this, I recommend a soft brush nib and the Brush Mask tool. Just follow my lead here.

Tutorial ## Selecting a Face

1. Zoom into Dave's face. Choose the Brush Mask tool, and instead of creating marquee lines, use the Mask Overlay feature from the Mask menu. Now, the first time you stroke over an area, a tinted mask appears over places you have not stroked. So the idea is to clear all the tint overlay from Dave's face in order to select it.

2. Before beginning with the Paint Mask tool, make sure you click the green + button on the upper left of the Property Bar; doing this adds to each stroke you make instead of starting over each time you release the mouse button! You can also subtract from the mask (add to the selection) by holding SHIFT while painting over the mask.

3. You want to select a little more than Dave's face, because you'll be scaling it and rotating it over the other guy's face (let's call him Phil), and it's easier to erase excess face than to try to add to it after it has been selected.

4. Once the face area has been revealed (not masked, not protected from editing), get out Window | Docker | Object Manager. Click the bottom-left button for Thumbnail Extents mode, the author's preference for displaying objects on the Object Manager's list. Doing this helps you more clearly see what's where in the file.

5. Right-click over any area of the photo and then choose Copy from Mask. The tinted overlay disappears and Dave appears to have a rectangle around his head. But no; a duplicate of his head is surrounded by translation handles. You can see Dave's spare head on the Object Manager.

6. With the Object Pick tool, drag the object to over Phil's head, as shown in the next illustration. The composition is beginning to look surreal already, isn't it?

Save this file now as "Two Dressed-up Guys Retouched" and keep the PNG file open. If you *must* close the file because you're late for bowling league night or something, save it in the PHOTO-PAINT file format because it can accept objects whereas the PNG file format cannot.

Now that the face has been copied and repositioned, it's time for some pinpoint plastic surgery to totally integrate Dave II's head onto Phil's one head.

Tutorial Getting A Head with PHOTO-PAINT

1. Once the copy of Dave's head is approximately centered over Phil's face, reduce the opacity of the object on the Object Manager so you can see both part of Phil's face and Dave's face to line up the mouth and eyes and possibly widen the face. Here's the deal with the modes for transforming an object in PHOTO-PAINT: when an object is selected, it's in Move (Translate) mode. Click the object a second time and it's in Rotate and Skew mode: in a specific mode you manipulate the properties of the edit by click-dragging the control handles that bound the object. One more click, and Rotate becomes Distort mode, where you can drag on the handles independent of one another. Finally, another click puts the mode into Perspective, which is not used at all in this tutorial, but it's great for making head objects look funny. (Do this on your own time!) See Figure 21-6.

2. There's no shorter way to put this step other than "massage the head object"; first rotate the duplicate head so its angle matches the angle of Phil's head. Use the Distortion mode to unevenly increase the height of the face—the right side, facing closer to the camera, should probably be a little larger than the left side. Finally, move the face

Scale (Position
and Size)

Distort

Perspective

Rotate/Skew

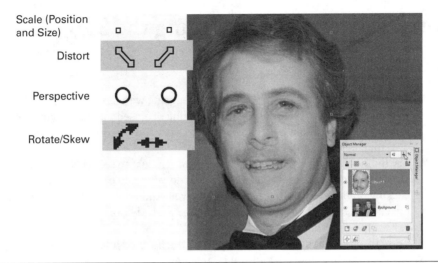

FIGURE 21-6   Use different Object modes to correct, rotate, and distort the chosen object.

around in Position and Size mode. Once you have the face looking a lot like the one shown in the next illustration, it's time for two more touchups.

Earlier, I recommended that you select (remove mask) to just outside of Dave's face for a little leeway when scaling and positioning the rotated face. Now that we're in the home stretch, it's time to remove a little of the excess surrounding Dave's second face here. Also, we don't want flawlessly identical twins; ideally they should have slightly different features and expressions, and that's a job for the Liquid Smear tool. Let's finish up, get this guy off the operating table, and send him a bill.

Tutorial # Erasing and Liquefying the Subject

1. Choose the Eraser tool from the Toolbox. On the Property Bar, the ideal settings for this example are as follows:
   - **Nib size** 20.
   - **Flatten nib** +90. You don't want to go erasing with a pointy nib!
   - **Transparency** 14, for just a little blending of erased into underlying areas.
   - **Feathering** About 60. You want a very, very soft erasure to make the image retouching look undetectable.

2. Try hiding the Background image for a moment, just to see what the outer edge of Dave's duplicate face looks like; how much do you need to remove? You hide a layer by clicking on the eye icon to the left of the layer. And oddly, the layer doesn't mind being poked in the eye. Then, click the vacant area to the left of the Background image to restore the eye (visibility) icon.

3. Erase the areas that clearly don't belong in the finished image. Dave's hair beneath his right ear can be removed, and you might even want to try restyling the front of Dave's hair by removing just a little of the Object 1. See Figure 21-7.

4. The object no longer needs to be on top of the background. With the Object Pick tool, right-click over the Object title on the Object Manager and then choose Combine | Combine Objects with Background.

5. Press CTRL-S to save. Now it's on to some very minor but highly noticeable editing. Choose the Liquid Smear tool, and before beginning, here's some advice: Define a nib size a lot larger than the area you intend to alter. Small Smear sizes look fake, and when

FIGURE 21-7   Erasing superfluous areas further helps disguise telltale edges in this photo-phakery.

they don't look fake, they look ugly. Try to get the effect you need with "broad strokes" so the transition between edited and original areas is gradual, thus making your work subtle. Set the Nib size to about 59 pixels in diameter and keep the pressure at about 50 percent. Make sure the Smooth Smear button is clicked.

6. With small but smooth (not jerky) strokes, pull the Dupli-Dave's nose down ever so slightly. We're looking for variations on the faces of twins, not caricatures. Push his nostrils just a little toward the tip of his nose, and perhaps raise the eyebrows just a little. Get ready to press CTRL-z to undo any mistakes, because this is a very powerful PHOTO-PAINT tool.

7. Reduce the pressure to about 20, and increase the nib diameter to about 120. Pull the hairline down ever so slightly so the twins don't have identical haircuts.

8. You're done. Examine and revel in your terrific work. Now these twins can eat a 2-for-1 meal on the house, and only pay for one tuxedo.

Flipping Images, with a Twist

Let's cover another common retouching need. A problem can occur when you try to accomplish something seemingly as simple as mirroring a photograph. This is going to be your first step into the league of the pros with invisible image retouching.

Many objects that you photograph in the real world—in particular, portraits of people—are bilaterally symmetrical: when you look in the mirror, you recognize yourself because even though your image is horizontally flipped, the right and left side of your face looks pretty much the same. This reality usually allows you to flip a photograph when you need, for example, your subject looking to the right instead of the left. The fly in the ointment, however, is when your subject is wearing a garment that has text on it; similarly, when a building in the background has a sign, or there's only one shirt pocket on a garment—these flipped images will have something in them that looks clearly wrong to the audience.

 Note The image you'll work with is not sharp. It was taken with a cheap camera at a planned event with children who played with water balloons. You'll be happy to know that our DSLR is safe and dry at home.

The following steps venture into the area of PHOTO-PAINT objects: how you can lift an area, copy it to a new object, and then flip the background but not the new object—which in this example is the text on a child's T-shirt. Retouching is not this simple; you will have a little edgework to clean up before considering the task completed, but with a little guidance, you'll learn a technique now that can be applied to a number of different retouching needs down the road:

1. Open Two Kids.png in PHOTO-PAINT. On the Object Manager docker, you need to convert this "normal" bitmap image into an object-capable one so the objects can be flipped independent of one another. Click the From Background icon at the right of the thumbnail, and the name of the item now changes to "Object 1". Once a photo is an object, you can perform many PHOTO-PAINT feats not possible with a standard JPEG or other image file.

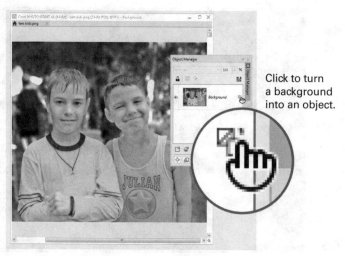

Click to turn a background into an object.

Feather amount

FIGURE 21-8   Copy the image area that you *don't* want to flip to a new object in the document.

2. Choose the Freehand Mask tool from the Toolbox; if it's not visible, click-hold on the third-from-top icon on the Toolbox (usually the Rectangle Mask tool) to reveal the entire group of Masking tools, and then choose the Freehand tool.
3. On the Property Bar, set the Feather value to about **6** pixels. Feathering softens a selection, so inside and outside the edge of a selection mask there are pixels that are *partially* selected. Having an area partially selected might sound strange (like an egg being partially broken), but the effect ensures smooth and seamless retouching work.
4. Choose Mask | Show Mask Marquee and uncheck Mask | Mask Overlay. Drag around the word "Julian" on (Julian's) T-shirt to select it; double-click when you're done, and the image area is now available for editing. If you don't include the entire name on your first try, click the Additive Mode button on the Property Bar and use the Freehand Mask tool to add to the existing mask.
5. Right-click inside the dashed indicator lines for the mask area, and then choose Copy From Mask from the context menu, as shown in Figure 21-8. On the Object Manager docker, you'll now see a new thumbnail at the top of the list of objects, titled "Object 2."

 Tip   Pressing CTRL-SHIFT-H reveals and hides an object marquee onscreen. CTRL-H alternately hides and shows mask marquees—*not* the same thing as the dotted lines running around objects.

6. Click the Object 1 entry on the Object list to make it the current editing object. Then, choose Object | Flip | Horizontally.
7. Click the Object 2 entry on the Objects docker, choose Lightness merge mode from the Object Manager's drop-down list—a good mode for making underlying areas fade away only if the top affecting object has lighter corresponding pixels—and then move the object over Julian's chest at left on the image with the Object Pick tool.

8. Evaluate the composition for a moment. What needs to be done now is to remove some of the backward text on Object 1 to keep it from showing through. A straight paint color won't do the job because the image area has varying tones of color from the texture of the T-shirt. Choose the Clone tool from Toolbox; it's the Toolbox icon with the two brushes.

9. The Clone tool picks up an image area you define by right-clicking and then applies the image area to a different area when you drag, based on the diameter and hardness you set for the tool. On the Property Bar, choose Medium Soft Clone from the drop-down list.

10. Click on Object 1 to choose it for editing, and then hide Object 2 by clicking the Visibility (the eye) icon to the left of its thumbnail.

11. Right-click with the Clone tool just below the name on Julian's T-shirt. You're choosing a sampling area that's close in tone and color to the area you want to hide.

12. Drag, ever so slowly, slightly, and carefully over the backward lettering on the T-shirt to get a feel for the Clone tool. When you release the mouse button, the sampling point for the Clone tool snaps back to its original position. Therefore, release the mouse button when you see that the traveling sampling point is getting mighty close to an undesired area for sampling. Work from the outside inward, resampling frequently to match the original tones of the light shirt. Periodically, unhide Object 2 to see how much work you need to do and what areas are not necessary to clone away. See Figure 21-9.

13. When you think you're finished cloning, restore the visibility of Object 2. You might be done, but you might want to refine the edges of Object 2 with the Eraser tool. If so, continue on to Step 14.

14. Click Object 2 to select it for editing. Choose the Eraser tool, and then on the Property Bar, choose a soft tip from the Presets drop-down list and set the size to about **35** pixels in diameter.

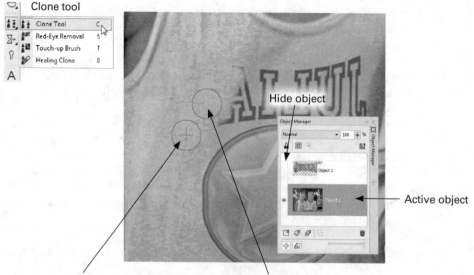

Right-click to set the sample point, then stroke over the area to be retouched.

FIGURE 21-9   Use the Clone tool to visually integrate the areas in Objects 2 and 1.

15. Zoom into the editing area and then drag over any areas whose brightness doesn't match the edge of the object. The work in progress and the illusion shown here look pretty convincing.

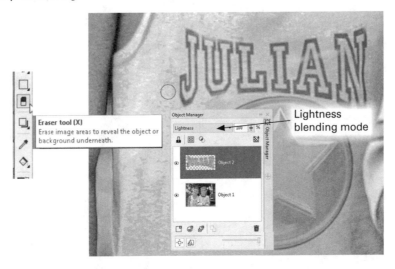

16. Optionally, you can standardize this image's data by combining all objects—as you did in the Hollywood condo example. Right-click over either object title on the Object docker and then choose Combine | Combine All Objects With Background. The following illustration shows the visual payoff.

Consider what you've learned in this chapter: you now know how to repeat actions on an entire folder of images; you can scale, crop, and flip pictures; and you have a basic handle on all the sophisticated editing you can perform using transparency, objects, and merge modes. But the biggest payoff is an ironic one: a good photo retoucher's work *should* go unnoticed!

22 Creating Animations in PHOTO-PAINT

You have a *lot* more power than you might expect once you begin investigating all the effects, the exquisitely cobbled brushes, the modes for compositing objects—and the capability to make *animations*. This chapter takes you through two examples of animations you can create if you have multiple drawings in CorelDRAW as the subject matter, and a clip of video from which you can pull frames. Although PHOTO-PAINT is perfectly capable of importing AVI files, I'd recommend that you take a whole three minutes and download and install a third-party utility that snags and saves frames from a video. The utility is free, and it is the simplest way I've ever seen to get stock for an animated GIF from movie stills. The URL can be found a little later in this chapter.

This is a fun and ambitious chapter, so let's start with an ambitious venture, but one that's not overwhelming and involves using CorelDRAW—remember that program from earlier chapters?

Creating an Animated GIF

GIFs had a waning popularity on the Web only a few years ago, giving way to Flash files. However, due to the relative insecurity of Flash videos (they can be hacked to make an exploit booby-trap), the MPEG-4 format has become the standard for high-resolution videos with sound. You see MPEG-4 videos all the time on YouTube and other websites with breaking news stories, and they are also used as tutorial files for specific software.

The good news is that there has been a resurgence of GIF animations, which are by their nature short in length and therefore very pointed in their message. Today you can see banners and movies that are only 15 frames in length, and they serve as almost a totally new visual communication device because of software such as PHOTO-PAINT.

An additional marvelous thing about animated GIFs is that they can play on any device without a special codec or plug-in. GIFs are native to HTML code, and they play on any web device. In contrast, it's estimated in 2016 that about half the web audience is using mobile devices, and Flash media will not play on handheld Internet devices. This is motivation enough to play with PHOTO-PAINT, the program that comes free in the Corel Graphics Suite. You owe it to yourself to perform some creative messing around with it!

The following sections take you through some CorelDRAW and PHOTO-PAINT moves for creating a sample animation.

Playing with a Paper Airplane

When you design an animation, you follow a checklist—the same as you do when gathering resources for any composition. The example in this section is a paper airplane, which has already been drawn for you as a CDR file. Let's pretend that a travel agent wants you to put a web banner on their site advertising the fact that children under 12 fly free this month only (or some similar offer). The concept is to fly a paper airplane across a sky, with a tag attached that spells out the offer.

The sky photo has been provided for you in the ZIP archive for this chapter, but the paper airplane CorelDRAW illustration is blank—it needs something written on the tag—so it's off to CorelDRAW to begin the next tutorial. The tag is intentionally blank: feel free to work with the file, take it apart and learn from it, and use it as part of your own composition with a different slogan written on it. Let's begin!

Tutorial   Adding Text and Exporting a CorelDRAW Drawing

1. Open Paper Airplane.cdr in CorelDRAW and then zoom into the tag area.
2. With the Text tool, type **Kids Fly Free** (or whatever you like) over the tag area. You can put a line break after "Kids" to avoid running over the tag's hole in this area.
3. With the text selected with the Pick tool, choose a contrasting color for the text, such as bright yellow, by clicking the color well on the color palette.
4. On the Property Bar, choose a light-hearted typeface such as Comic Sans MS, bold. Scale the text up or down so it nearly fits inside the tag area.
5. Choose the Envelope tool from the effects group of tools on the Toolbox, and then distort the text a little, as shown in Figure 22-1. The drawing is at an angle to an imaginary camera, so the text shouldn't be perfectly parallel to the screen.
6. Select all the objects and then click the Export button on the Standard Bar. In the Export dialog, choose PNG-Portable Network Graphics (*.PNG) from the Save As Type drop-down list. Make **Paper Airplane.png** the name for the file, choose a hard drive location for the bitmap file, and then click Export.

FIGURE 22-1   Don't export with the text you've added looking too perfect!

7. In the Export dialog, make sure the export resolution is 96 dpi; otherwise, the airplane will be far too large for the GIF animation (see the following Note). Check the Transparency box if it's not already checked. Finally, look to see if the export file width is 513 pixels—choose Pixels as the Transformation | Units setting if it's not already. Click OK to export, and after CorelDRAW makes a bitmap copy of the illustration, you're finished and can close CorelDRAW and launch PHOTO-PAINT.

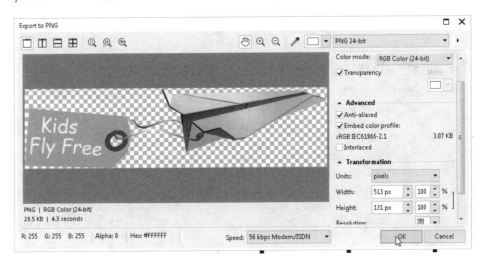

Note You didn't have to set a lot of options in the Export dialog because the CorelDRAW file was carefully set up and the airplane scaled to a predetermined size that made the tutorial work easily. When exporting drawings to be used as bitmap versions in PHOTO-PAINT, you begin your drawing with a new file in CorelDRAW whose resolution is 96 dpi, the same as your screen and the same resolution as graphics you see in your internet browser. In the Create a New Document dialog, type **96** in the Rendering Resolution field and you're good to go. Then you set the units in CorelDRAW to pixels by choosing from the Units drop-down on the Property Bar. Keep in mind that GIF animations have to be small in dimension. For example, the airplane is about 500 pixels wide because the composition you'll make is about that width. When you draw a foreground object, you keep it to the width you want it to be, measured in pixels, for your final composition. Then, exporting the drawing to the correct pixel width and height is a simple and nearly automatic process. Measuring is a pain, so when you set up your document for web export, it's a pain you only have to endure once when you begin a new drawing.

Animation: Defining Frames and Basic Setup

You'll move procedurally, which means "not at breakneck speed," through the next sections; you need to build each frame of a GIF animation one at a time—PHOTO-PAINT doesn't perform "tweening" to auto-create intermediate animation frames. First on your to-do list is to import the Background image, Sky.png, and then turn the document into a movie by adding frames with the same sky background. Then you'll place and copy the paper airplane file so you can progress with an animation: you flatten each frame when the airplane is in a certain position, and then change its position in each frame. You're going to create an animation of the airplane traveling from left to right, thus creating an *animation cycle* that will play indefinitely on a web page. You'll create six frames of animation as the airplane travels from camera left to an exit at camera right, and it will pause in the middle of the frame so audiences can clearly read the text.

Let's get moving!

Tutorial Building a GIF Animation: Part 1

1. In PHOTO-PAINT, press CTRL-O and then choose Sky.jpg from your hard drive.
2. You need to measure the background so the movie file you create is the same size. This is a mock assignment, and a web banner would certainly be much smaller in dimensions, but you can do that on your own later. Right-click over the image, choose Document Properties from the context menu, and as you can see in the illustration, the sky image measures 504 pixels wide by 360 pixels tall. You can close the box, remember those dimensions, and then close the Sky.png image. As mentioned in Chapter 21, if you measure pictures in pixels, you can ignore the resolution (for example, 96 pixels per inch). Pixels are not an absolute size, but they *are* an absolute value.
3. Choose File | New. In the Create a New Image box, choose 504 by 360 @ 72 dpi, because this is exactly the dimensions of the Sky.png image. The airplane drawing you exported to PNG scales perfectly to the background. Number of Frames should be set to 2, even though this is a six-frame animation. There's a neat trick you can do to add frames after the first two have had the sky image placed into the frame.

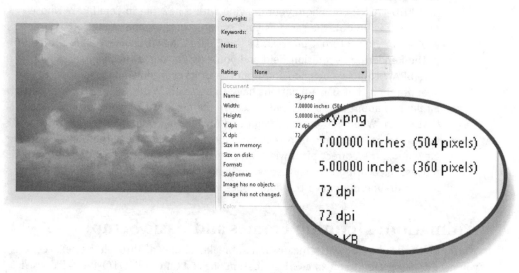

4. Choose Window | Dockers | Movie to display the docker you'll need to create the necessary frames. Also open Windows | Dockers | Object Manager. This docker is necessary for placing objects and merging them with the background sky image to complete a frame. Note that the frames on the Movie docker list are set to a 200-millisecond duration. Duration can be changed, and you'll do so a little later; a millisecond is a tenth of a second, about the duration of a 16th note in music (at an average tempo of 60 beats per minute). This is also evaluated as the minimum time it takes for a human to recognize a picture.

5. To populate six frames with the background clouds, click the first frame on the Movie docker. Then click the Insert from File button at the bottom of the docker (see the following illustration), and a dialog appears where you can choose the Sky.png image as long as the path to the file is correct. From there, a final dialog pops up asking you whether the picture should go after or before the currently selected frame. After is fine, so click OK to apply the command.

6. Keep doing this until you have six frames with a background of the sky. If there are extra blank frames, click the frame to select it, and then press the trash icon on the bottom right of the Movie docker.

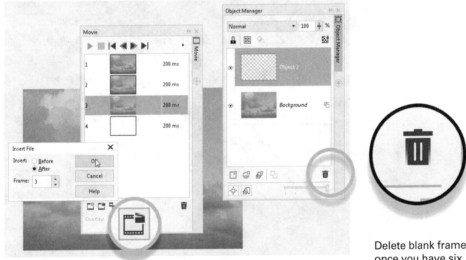

Insert From File button

Delete blank frames once you have six background frames.

7. With the first frame chosen on the Movie docker, double-click it, and it'll take on a red outline to indicate it's active. Now you can import Paper Airplane.png. Because you exported this PNG file with transparency, it's now an object with a transparent background, and is easy to animate against the sky image. Let's strategize for a moment:

you should position the airplane so that only its nose sticks out of the left of the frame. Why? Because the last frame will have it departing at the right of the animation. This way, you'll have a looping animation.

8. Just click without moving the mouse, and the paper airplane illustration should appear, sized correctly because you measured both the plane and the sky photo earlier. Copy this airplane as long it is an object in the composition; you'll need it for successive frames, and copying it is easier than importing it time and again.

9. Go to the next frame by double-clicking its thumbnail of the Movie docker. Choose Edit | Paste | Paste as a New Object, and you have a brand-new copy of the airplane you can move.

10. Move it to the position you need, and then right-click and choose Combine | Combine
    Objects With Background. See the following illustration.

Right-click over a thumbnail.

Tip If you want precision in the airplane's progress from left to right, choose to display
rulers (see the following illustration) and then drag vertical guides to create
vertical intervals for the lane movement.

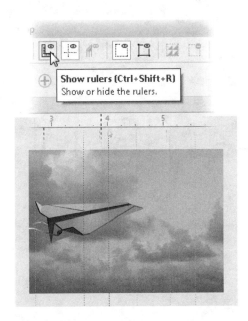

11. You can use the Overlay feature rather than guides to see how the airplane progresses from left to right. SHIFT-click the two frames you want to compare (it's okay to choose a frame that's not flattened), move the Overlay slider to 100% in this example, and then move the airplane object to your liking. Finally, use the Combine right-click menu option to flatten the frame after you're happy with its position. See Figure 22-2.

12. Finish filling all six frames. Frame 3 or 4 should probably be the complete airplane view with the tag message. Later, you'll learn how to extend the display time of this frame to drive the deal home with the viewer and potential client.

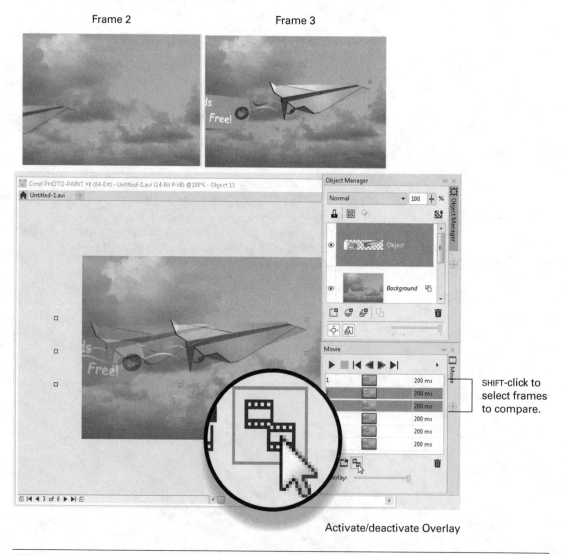

Frame 2   Frame 3

SHIFT-click to select frames to compare.

Activate/deactivate Overlay

FIGURE 22-2   An entertaining animation keeps movement predictable between frames.

13. Frame 6 is of importance, too. You want all of the tag to the left of the plane to be out of frame on the left. Why? Because when this animation loops. If you followed the directions earlier, the tip of the nose of the plane is in view. So to loop the animation, the last frame needs the airplane to be mostly if not all out of sight.

14. Do *not* save your work, because for reasons unknown, PHOTO-PAINT will insist on saving any work in progress as an AVI, PSD, or GIF file, and you are not ready to finish the file to any of these file formats. Just hang in there; the hard work is done.

Just for fun, you can check the accuracy of your work. The Movie docker has controls like you'd find on a TV remote. You can play, stop, and go to the first and/or last frame. Press the Stop button when you're finished entertaining yourself and get ready to export your work.

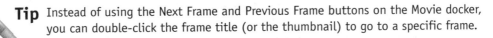

Tip Instead of using the Next Frame and Previous Frame buttons on the Movie docker, you can double-click the frame title (or the thumbnail) to go to a specific frame.

Tutorial Building a GIF Animation: Part 2

1. Now that the frames all have content in them and there are no objects in the composition (but only backgrounds), go to the frame where the plane and message are centered with the text easy to read, probably frame 3 or 4. Double-click that thumbnail frame on the Movie docker and you're all set to make a different display time for that frame's default of 200 ms.

2. Click the "200 ms" title for this frame to select it for editing and then type in **800**. Press ENTER, and PHOTO-PAINT automatically tags "ms" at the end and you're all set. Four-fifths of a second is plenty of time for the audience to see the message. Also, this GIF will continuously loop (coming up next), adding more time for the sales pitch sandwiched in between the light entertainment. See the following illustration.

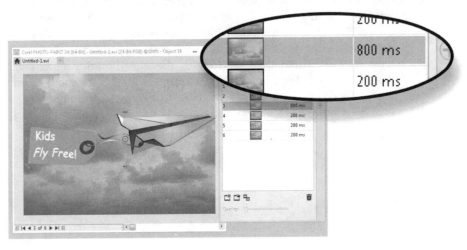

Finishing the Animation

The following steps take you through timing; as mentioned earlier, the frame where you get a good view of the message you typed on the tag needs to be a longer duration. Follow these steps to put the finishing touches on the animation, and then you'll see how to export it to GIF file format.

Tutorial Exporting an Animation

1. Choose File | Save As, and choose GIF - GIF Animation (*.gif) as the file format you want from the Save As type drop-down list. Choose a file location, give the file an appropriate name, and then click OK to enter a couple more dialogs where you specify color depth and the means by which certain colors are averaged to produce a relatively small file size.

2. In the Convert to Paletted dialog, you set the type of dithering and color palette used in your animation frames. You'll see that if you type 256 in the Colors box, many options are dimmed. This is because if you export an image at the maximum color range of the GIF file format, which is 256, the other options for dithering and the color palette used are a moot point. You can't enhance something at its maximum quality, so to speak. GIFs have a maximum of 256 unique colors, and these palettes help preserve the delicate shading of the cloud photo and some of the fountain fills used in the CorelDRAW airplane drawing.

3. Try out the Adaptive palette for this type of composition. Adaptive emphasizes the most frequently used colors and averages them a little while ignoring smaller, almost dismissible color pixels. Besides, one sure way of optimizing a palette to reduce colors is by previewing all of them. Choose one from the drop-down; if the preview looks like the floor on a subway, move to the next method.

4. Because any of these images has more than 256 unique colors, you'll want to use dithering as a method for keeping the excess areas from being moved to the closest but flat color area—which is pretty unattractive. Choose Adaptive as the Palette, and then choose Ordered from the Dithering drop-down. Ordered dithering is also called pattern dithering, and the result looks like a woven pattern, but only with images that have, say, 10,000 unique colors. Honestly, the other dithering options will increase the size of the saved file (although they can produce handsome, subtle changes), and the number of colors in the images is so close to 256 that ordered dithering will be virtually invisible. Click the OK button, and you're off to the GIF Animation Options dialog.

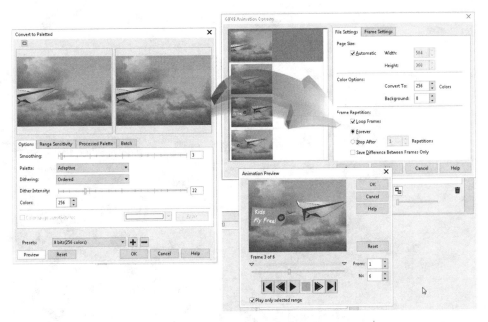

5. Of paramount importance in this dialog is the Frame Repetition area. Put a check in the Loop Frames box, click the Forever button, and you've completed all the relevant options for this animation. Oh, you can preview the animation at a small size by first clicking Preview and then using the remote control buttons at the bottom of the Animation Preview box.

6. Stop! Be sure you read this step two or three times. Before you click OK and export the GIF to any location (I suggest your Desktop), your work in assembling this animation will all go away after you close PHOTO-PAINT. You can choose to keep the file open and keep PHOTO-PAINT open until you've perhaps done a second, better (or different) version of the paper airplane. You can save your work as a PDF file, which in theory you could crop frame by frame and repeat the process in this section of this chapter (hint: it's irritating, tedious work). You could save the animation as an AVI file, but opening the file to work with it typically results in missing frames and duplicate frames—it's a train wreck of an imported file with frames, but it's your best option for saving most of your work here.

7. Click OK, and then drag the GIF file into an internet browser window to watch it play!

Figure 22-9 Shameless Plug

Are you ready for the cutting-edge, totally trendy movie GIF animation now? Sure you are! Because you read the previous section, a lot of the steps will be a snap, crackle, and pop!

Movie Animations

Naturally, to create a movie animation, you need a movie clip. And you then need to pick key frames—frames of a definitive graphics event, such as one frame of a guy with his head in profile and the next frame of his head turned to the camera. Animated GIFs taken from video frames are all the rage and almost the standard for playing brief video clips on the Web. Everything from fashion to silly, surreal videos are found in e-zine articles and on banners. So turning a short video clip into a compelling, attractive GIF is our next stop in this chapter.

Limitations and Workarounds for GIF Movies

Let me be frank for a moment. Acquiring a video clip is not easy. For example, the tutorial video you'll use in this chapter is pretty poor, but serviceable. In fact, I did several things you should avoid. So, here are some tips to keep in mind:

- Be close to your subject. Frame them so the action takes place where you want it. Also, if possible, use a tripod, because frame-to-frame jitter, especially with a 12-frame GIF file, spoils the presentation a little. My problem with the video Duchess.mp4 is that our Siamese stops being interesting if you get too close to her performing strange things, as you'll soon see.

- I used a digital zoom on my now ancient flip camera. Digital zooms on *any* camera suck, even the iPhone 6. You lose focus, and noise (similar to grain on analog cameras) is visible. You therefore need to find a predictable subject and use a tripod.

- Try to get good separation between the foreground subject and the background. Use good lighting so that you use the whole spectrum of brightness.

- If at all possible, try to get the first and last frame very similar in composition so the film loops in a natural and expected way. I was not so lucky with Duchess as my subject, but I have a workaround for a looping video that begins and ends in different places I'll share with you later.

Essentially, use the rules of good photography for good cinematography. What I did to this short MP4 file was to sharpen the edges, brighten certain areas, and then apply a toon filter using a video editor to trace the edges in the video, ever so slightly (8 percent), to bring out a little more foreground motion. Finally, I reduced the size of the video from the native 1290×720p to 720×480p to make the file smaller for you to download. Plus, it's a more suitable size for the internet.

You'll need to download and install a small, easy-to-use program off the Web, because PHOTO-PAINT will not import MPG4 videos. Also, it's not a fun task to browse through hundreds of stills to find exactly the one you want.

Go to http://paul.glagla.free.fr/imagegrab_en.htm and download the ImageGrab file. It's in a ZIP archive that includes a setup file. Once you answer a few questions about file location and whether you want it on your Start menu, you're almost all set to capture frames from the Duchess video.

Seriously consider donating a few bucks to Paul Glagla and his work. This is the most recent ImageGrab program, and it's dated six years ago (but works in Windows 10 and earlier). Help this fellow make more, better, and more frequent releases if you like the program. The file you're downloading is freeware and not for commercial use.

Let's begin at the beginning by picking out, say, 12 key frames to bring into PHOTO-PAINT.

Tutorial Capturing and Saving Video Frames

1. Open ImageGrab. You can actually drag and drop the Duchess.mp4 video into the main viewing window to load it. ImageGrab is fussy about file extensions and wants MPEG-4 as an extension, not MP4. Tough. Just drop it onto the video area. Alternatively, if you want to jump ahead to the compiling part (which you already did in the previous tutorial), you can use the Duchess stills I snagged in the ZIP file.

2. Look ahead to Figure 22-3. The first thing you need to do is click the Options button to set the location of saved files. I'm choosing my Desktop, as you can see here (because everything else in the world is on my Desktop), and I've typed 01 in the Number From entry box. This is because we're only snatching 12 frames, and I don't want to have to work with or renumber files named 000023.bmp, for example. Finally, choose BMP as the file format for saves instead of the lossy JPEG file format to ensure the video is as good as can be when it is compressed when it's exported from PHOTO-PAINT as a GIF.

Captures a frame from the video and saves it to the location you set in Options.

Captures a frame from the video but doesn't save it.

Settings. Choose the save location.

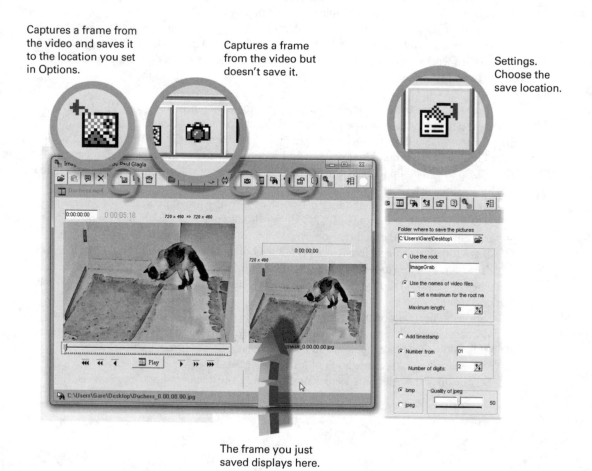

The frame you just saved displays here.

FIGURE 22-3   It's easy to get frames from a video with a utility such as ImageGrab.

3. You're good to go. Drag the timeline slider under the main preview window back and forth a little to force a preview image, and then drag it to frame 1. I think that's a good picture to begin the GIF animation with (and so do you!). Click the Grab The Current Video Frame To Picture button (without saving it). Generally, because you don't have the destination folder readily at hand, it's best to save a file to screen and then save it to file. This saves renumbering and the accidental overwriting of a file you like. Right-click over the small thumbnail the program just generated and choose Save to File (F7). If you look closely under the small thumbnail, the green area tells you what the file name will be.

4. Let me explain what this GIF will be so you can scout down the best keyframes. Duchess loves the small rug next to the door to the garage. In this clip I was lucky enough to capture, she goes under the rug and then reappears on the other side. So drag the slider forward a little until you find a good frame of Duchess beginning to go under the rug at about 12 o'clock in the frame. When you click the picture with the plus sign icon, the small preview thumbnail goes to the left of the main window and you've saved the photo.

5. Repeat this action at keyframes. I counted about 12 good ones, and there's a folder in the ZIP file for this chapter that you can use. Of particular interest is toward the end of the video where she looks at me and then looks away. It's a nice touch for the end of a silly film clip.

6. You can exit ImageGrab without saving settings or anything. Go locate your stills and start PHOTO-PAINT.

An Anticlimax with Fantastic Results

You already know how to place an image on a background of a multiframe document, and how to export this document to GIF. So this section is a small review of the steps you'll have permanently committed to memory after working through them using the video of my cat.

Creating the Video Animation Sequence

1. In PHOTO-PAINT, choose File | New. You already know (because I told you) that the image dimensions are 720 pixels wide by 480 high, so enter these settings in the Create a New Image dialog and then enter **12** for the number of frames. Unlike the airplane image earlier, these frames aren't static, so they can't be copied and pasted onto new backgrounds.

Click OK to display the empty document window, and make sure both the Object Manager and Movie docker are onscreen. See the following illustration.

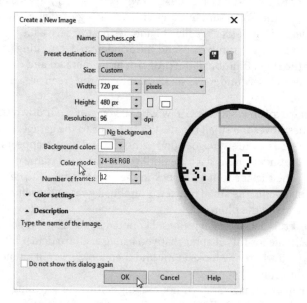

2. Double-click the first frame thumbnail on the Movie docker to make sure the first image you place is in the first frame. It's marked with an "a" in Figure 22-4.

Tip You can drag frames up and down on the Movie docker to relocate them in time—which sounds like a new show on the Syfy network, doesn't it?

---

3. Click the Import button, which is about in the middle of the Standard Bar. Go find the first still image in your sequence. For me, it's Duchess0000.bmp. Click File | Import, and your cursor is now loaded with a 720×480 image ready to be placed in a 720×480 frame. Although you can click almost anywhere in the frame to place the image, be sure to make it a definitive (not moving) click. PHOTO-PAINT gets impatient when you hesitate, and a misplaced frame is the result. See callout "b" in Figure 22-4.

Tip If you think you have an excellent mastery of your mouse or stylus, you can select more than one image file when you choose to import an image. The cursor then becomes loaded with successive images that you click one at a time into frames after you flatten the current image and then move on to highlight the next frame on the Video docker.

---

4. On the Object Manager, right-click and then choose Combine | Combine Objects With Background. Frame 1 is now finished.
5. Repeat Steps 2–4 for the rest of the images you captured, making certain they are in sequence and you don't accidentally place duplicates in new Movie docker slots.
6. Once you have the stills tagged in the Video docker, play the sequence, and you might notice that two frames need time adjusting.

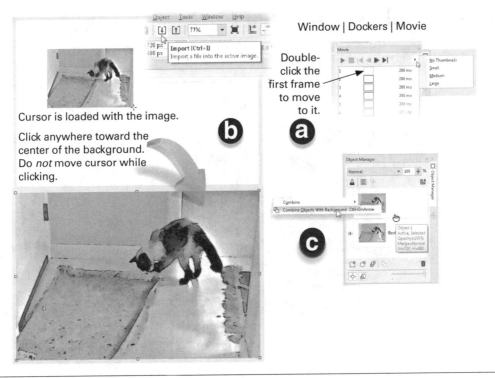

FIGURE 22-4 Add the frames you saved as new objects in PHOTO-PAINT.

Timing Is Everything

You'll notice that because the video sequence doesn't loop perfectly, Duchess begins at the right of the rug, and the video ends with her in the middle of the rug, more toward my camera. You cannot (do not want to) sweat for hours trying to find stills or use the Liquefy brush to get her to match the first and last frames. And ping-ponging the stills will result in a 23-frame file that looks like a 1980s cat food commercial, and really pushes it in terms of what is an acceptable file size for GIFs—with broadband these days, a 1MB to 2MB GIF is not a problem.

Let's rethink the ending, then. Why not just put a short hold on the last frame, so the audience can gander a little at a still image of a cat that is under a rug half the time? A "hold" of say 800 ms is a good amount of time in this example to stay on frame 12 before looping back to frame 1. A fade to black would work, too, telling the audience (instead of strongly hinting) that the video is over. But let's stick with the hold and see how you feel about it.

Hold On to That Cat!

1. Click the frame 12 entry box that reads 200 ms at the moment.
2. Type **800** in it, as shown in the next illustration.

3. One more edit in timing would make the video a little more interesting. Duchess doesn't spend very much time under the rug—she believes that all games are time trials—and it would be neat if she stayed "undercover" for just a little longer. Therefore, go to frame 3 or 4, or wherever your frames show a lumpy carpet, and change the length of the frame to 400 ms. See the next illustration. Through trial and error—mostly error—I came up with times for this video (and no two videos are alike) of

800 ms to create a pause and 400 ms to create a brief delay. Play with the timing on this stuff. A lot of GIF animators don't have the features that PHOTO-PAINT does.

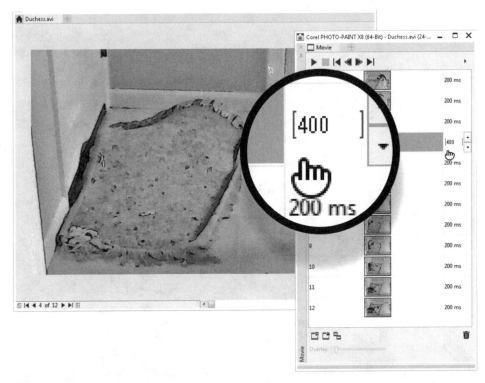

4. It's on to the export part of the tutorial. Really, the only difference between exporting the airplane example and this one is, I think, an optimized palette, and it needs lot less dithering intensity (try 22%). This image, by the nature of its content, doesn't need a lot of "faking" different colors via dithering.

5. Do it! Export the file, play it in an internet browser, and then invite some friends over and tell them, "See? I *told* you the internet is made of cats!"

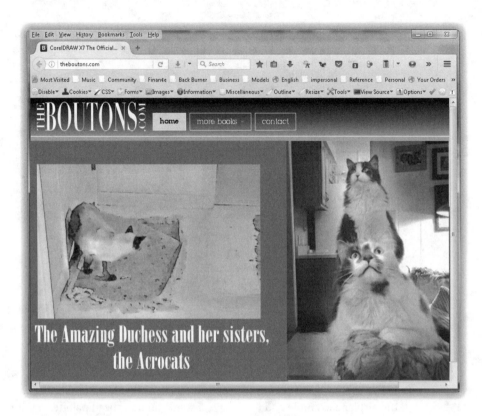

You owe yourself a big pat on the back (don't try this by yourself) for getting through this chapter. Imagine: you now not only have quite a few advanced image retouching tricks tucked under your belt, but you know how to make a visually rich GIF animation with a moving object that loops continuously. This is a *lot* better than learning how to make a GIF animation that blinks static text such as "My First Website 101" on and off.

Now that you know how to make, save, and change movie frames, you have weeks if not years of experimenting to be done with new ideas and different animation objects of your own. And you *can* save an animation to AVI in addition to the GIF file format—you can choose these from the Save As type drop-down list when you select File | Save and Save As. This means that creating titles and (minor) special effects for larger projects is a possibility.

You've probably noticed that the left side of the book you're holding is a tad heavier than the right side at this moment. Or if you're reading the e-book version of this *Official Guide,* you might notice that the left side of your reading device is heavier. Perhaps not.

In either event, this means you're almost at the end of the book. But not *exactly* the end, because I have some closing thoughts and suggestions on where to go from here. The next chapter is a short one, but it's long on advice that can be best given by the fellow who wrote all those pages beneath your left thumb.

23 Final Thoughts: Where Do We Go from Here?

Everyone is new to CorelDRAW, regardless of the version. It's an adventure for the pro and the beginner alike, and hopefully I didn't leave out anything in the steps, the notes, the text, or the discovery process. As you close this book and hunker down into another personal episode with CorelDRAW, it's crucial to your growth as a designer to keep your senses keen and your eyes open. See what you see, and not what you *think* you see; we're easily misled by preconceived notions about what the world that surrounds us truly looks like, as odd as that sounds. I credit this nugget of wisdom to Betty Edwards, author of *Drawing on the Right Side of the Brain*.

I left such specific, sometimes profound revelations for the end of the book, because this is, after all, *CorelDRAW X8: The Official Guide*. Indulge me with this chapter, and in return I'll gift you with some "good stuff" you'll need to keep in mind (and question) long after you've put this book back on your shelf—or turned your iPad off.

No Skipping: You'll Lose Points!

While learning how to set up CorelDRAW so it operates to your best advantage, do *not* take the attitude of, "Yeah, yeah, I know about the Pen tool, so I'll skip this section." First of all, there are *eight* tools for drawing in CorelDRAW, and each was designed for a specific purpose. I bought a book on vector graphics once in 1991, and I closed the cover far too soon out of a giddy feeling of self-confidence that I knew everything about Pen tools. I then fired up my screaming 386, loaded CorelDRAW version minus 3 or something…and was completely lost. I expect your experience might be a little like mine. For example, Chapter 7 is a pretty authoritative one on how paths are created with the drawing tools, and you'll be missing out on valuable information if you gloss over it. I went into writing this book not presuming anything, and as a reader, you shouldn't either.

Let's make learning CorelDRAW X8 an excursion, an *adventure*. Feel free to open this book at any point, but like with any adventure, you must travel with provisions, such intangibles as a positive attitude, a concept, a proficiency with your computer, and an eagerness to learn.

And last but not least, you should have a desired direction, so you don't travel too many side roads, as interesting and valuable as they might be. I've tried to make this book travel from the general to the specific, to fork and branch into specialized powers in CorelDRAW from the trunk of this book, the basic understanding of vector graphics. The following sections further describe the structure of this *Official Guide,* which will be useful when you have a question about a tool, your career, and the possible hurdles this book will get you through.

Closing Thoughts

CorelDRAW X8: The Official Guide must end somewhere, but this *doesn't* mean your learning experience is also at an end. If I've done my job, you now have an appetite for more. Seriously, though, this *Official Guide* was not the beginning of your computer graphics education—you began when you developed enough of an interest in graphics to go out and look for a book— and it is not the end of your education either. I'll be back with a version X9 book in good time, but until then, be sure to keep this book handy because there are user manuals and then there are guides—this book doesn't focus on what things are in CorelDRAW, but rather what you can *create* with them.

Guiding Yourself After All Is Written and Read

You have probably heard at least once in your life the difference between *knowledge* and *wisdom.* Knowledge resides in a vacuum; you need to take its lid off and wave the container around a few times before the contents settle into wisdom.

This has similarly been my experience writing documentation about computer software. I believe that some facts are good, but facts need to be *contextualized*—they need to germinate— before they can become a part of a solution to a goal set before you.

CorelDRAW X8: The Official Guide would not be a guide at all if it did not *lead* you someplace. For example (and a poor one at that), you come to a dead end when the instructions for using a tool consist only of the following:

1. To draw a circle, choose the Ellipse Tool, hold CTRL, and then drag.

We would be in a lot of trouble if the instructions for operating a chainsaw were this presumptuous.

Circles are *fine* to draw, but seldom do they represent a *complete* artistic idea. In CorelDRAW, complex, visually interesting compositions often begin with simple shapes, so a tutorial needs to reflect this. As a complete idea—and a complete tutorial in which drawing a circle is *in context*— let's try drawing a crescent moon:

1. Create a circle by holding CTRL while dragging with the Ellipse tool.
2. Choose the Pick tool, and then drag the circle above and to the left of the circle's original position on the page. Before releasing the mouse button, tap the right mouse button to drop a copy of the circle above the original.
3. Marquee-select both circles, and then on the Property Bar, click the Trim button.

4. Move the circle away from the resulting object; by default, the object that does the trimming remains on the page.
5. While the crescent moon is selected, click an appropriate swatch on the vertical color palette.
6. Press CTRL-S to save your work for a time when you've mastered fills and other CorelDRAW features to make this a moon in a cloudy sky with silhouettes of trees, and perhaps a figure carrying an ominous sack…. Okay, you get the picture.

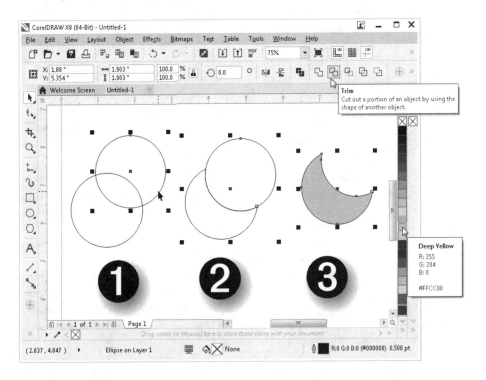

Learning from Life

In the same way that you must occasionally take your face away from the monitor to catch a breath of fresh air, you should also seriously consider taking a day or two off from the computer. Go outdoors, visit a friend you respect and haven't spoken with in a while, and even stick your head into a continuing education classroom that looks interesting. The creative mind is always looking for outside stimulation. You see a beautiful scene, your mind filters it, and you eventually express what you feel about this scene, using CorelDRAW, PHOTO-PAINT, or even (gasp!) a pencil and paper. When the creative urge strikes (and it has historically been a very strong urge), you should do two things.

The Concept Drives the Artwork

Realize firmly in your mind what the *concept* is. It can be as commercial as a stunning graphic to sell a car, or as personal as a graphic that tells your spouse that you love her.

A concept is an elusive thing. Many people presume that a concept is, for example, getting an elephant to stand on one leg next to a washing machine. This describes what someone wants to see visually in a composition, but it is *not* the concept. Why is the elephant there? Why is the elephant next to a washing machine? If there's no reason, there's no concept, and as we would traditionally say, it's "back to the drawing board."

A fair example of a concept (I don't want to give away *too* many free concepts!) would be of a clown, in color, walking down an urban street that's in black and white. The picture is saying that there is humor amid the cold, serious world; *that's* the concept. Do you see the difference between the clown and the elephant?

Also, you will get the most out of CorelDRAW if you bring along the right *attitude*. If you are serious, somber, and intent on conquering a new application, you will defeat the purpose of learning to work with a design program. Work can be *fun*—Leonardo da Vinci was an extremely light and fun guy (or so Mona said)—and getting into the *spirit* of self-expression is essential.

Look Around and Then Catalog Your Ideas for Later!

Gather stock photography, but also gather stock ideas—and write them down. There's a yin/yang to ideas. You give an idea life, but the idea also provokes you on an emotional level, and then more ideas are created. There's nothing sadder than sitting down in front of CorelDRAW or PHOTO-PAINT without an idea. It's time wasted that's better spent examining the geometric complexity of a flower, or how clouds can create specific moods.

We, as a civilization, are so caught up in the day-to-day machinery we call a working life that we often deprive ourselves of inspiration and really good ideas. After this book has been written, I will, weather permitting, mow the lawn, inspect all the flowers my wife Barbara has planted, look at the sky, look at an insect crawling around for food—and then open DRAW or another application and see where these impressions of life lead. To be an artist means being able to see life with the widest vision you permit yourself, and then filter what you're thinking about what you saw into a graphical composition. It doesn't get much easier than that. Don't feel intimidated about the outcome of your work. Simply immerse yourself without shame or fear of public acceptance of your work, and gaze upon what you've done as a way of expressing yourself.

Learning How to Learn

It's not easy to instinctively know how to learn. Schools tend to make you recite instead of invent, and we tend to be conditioned, not taught, by even the best-meaning (but opinionated) scholars. I feel differently about books than any other medium of communication, because you, the reader, have the option of closing the book and taking a break any time you feel like it. Additionally, *CorelDRAW X8: The Official Guide* is a dialog between an artist and someone who wants more out of their art. Yet this is also a tutorial book—above all things—so this puts the author in the position of being a fellow artist second and an "information vendor" first. Hopefully, I've set a conversational tone in this book, but not at the expense of the primary goal, which is teaching.

CorelDRAW X8: The Official Guide is the (lucky!) 29th book I have written—along with some talented coauthors and a magnificent staff of editors—on computer graphics. I'd have to look on Amazon to see how many CorelDRAW books I've written! Through the years, I've received mail from friends and readers with questions, and a scattered complaint here and there. Like other artists, I depend on feedback to influence what I document, and how I communicate with you, the reader. The most useful feedback I've received has been on how users approach this book.

Your personal goal while learning CorelDRAW is to try to make using it second nature to you. Because software is designed by people, it's inescapable that there will be some preferences the engineer put in the program, and you need to get to know the engineer through what they did. This means meeting the software halfway, as odd as this might sound. When someone tells me that Adobe Illustrator is a lot easier to master than CorelDRAW, I ask them to return to their mothership. The second thing I do, which is much more important, is to remember that all design software forces the artist to work in an idiosyncratic way. I look at wizards working with audio software and am amazed at how their hands look like a blur as they gracefully move around the keyboard. Is it magic? Not at all. They've reached a compromise with the program, a treaty that teaches the user to accept the rules of the software. And before you know it, CorelDRAW will become more transparent to you. There will be fewer layers, fewer hurdles between what you think and what winds up on the page.

Attitude Is Everything

You will know you have arrived at a new creative stratum when you are drawing something and are concentrating on your work rather than on the tool you are using. Many of CorelDRAW's Toolbox tools serve more than one function, depending on your mouse gestures and any keyboard modifiers you are pressing. Therefore, after you have taken time to develop a skill, you will feel as though the CorelDRAW and PHOTO-PAINT workspaces are something *different* from a standard computer program interface. They are responsive, *truly* intuitive to use, and give the feedback artists need when they use physical media. If you find yourself becoming immersed in CorelDRAW for hours on end, do not freak. You are simply in your element, doing what it is that brings an idea to life.

You will find more than you imagine in DRAW if you allow for some yin and yang to occur. That is, you command CorelDRAW X8 to perform certain calculations, but also leave yourself open to letting the *application's* features influence your work and your ideas. You will quickly discover new purposes for tools; the Corel Community forum has new posts almost daily about something strange and wonderful a designer has discovered. CorelDRAW is literally as extensible as your own curiosity allows it to be.

Get excited about all the unrealized possibilities you have before you as you work through this book. It is not just an artist's prerogative to have a passion about waking up each morning and contemplating all the great new stuff you will accomplish; it's what you came to the party for, so revel in it! I have been working with CorelDRAW for a quarter century (taking breaks once in a while) and do not feel I have plumbed its depths. Do not see it as intimidating, but rather as a source for *excitement.* You have wrapped presents under the tree *every day.*

Tutorials Unlock Many Doors

I've heard from many readers who never actually perform the tutorials; instead, they skip around in the book looking for a magic recipe or technique here and there. For many users, this approach works when they need to quickly solve a specific problem. But the most "successful" readers, the ones who have increased their overall relationship with art, and increased their skill level, are practicing something prudent and quite common. They are the ones who found time to sit with the book for an hour or two and work their way through a chapter. Like most things in life, mastery of an art comes from *doing*. It's only then that the principles behind the steps become tangible. If you've passed over chapters on your way to this paragraph, please invest in your own talent and work completely through a favorite chapter. Follow the steps, and then do something similar with images of your own. Make the knowledge truly yours.

Also, it should be known that *authors* actually read sometimes, too, and even a tutorial-based book has some "good stuff" lodged between the pages that might not be a formal set of steps to arrive at a finished piece. What we do when we discover a nugget of wisdom is outlined in (you guessed it) a tutorial.

Tutorial Indexing a Nugget of Wisdom in a Book

1. Take out a pad of fluorescent sticky notes.
2. Detach one leaf.
3. Place it between the pages in the book that contain a morsel of interest.

For all the information organized into procedures found in this book, however, please *don't* treat this *Guide* as a workbook. I've tried to make this book an excellent *resource* tome as well as a book on art.

Okay, Gary. Why'd You Write This Book?

A really good question to ask of a book is, what was the motivation for the author to write it? Well, I'm just passionate about teaching others, and my greatest feat is to mold a reader into an artist who is *better* than me! Why *not* share? It's a far better question than "Why share?"

Whether you are a design enthusiast who simply wants to make community bulletins and attractive flyers for the Boy Scouts, or a designer in a large enterprise who is forced to measure output in volume, you might not immediately know where you're going creatively. But, especially as fine artists who are looking for that "special something" to redefine their work, we all pack toolkits for our artistic voyages, both virtual and physical. You've seen in this book that CorelDRAW is not only a necessary part of your computer graphics toolkit, but that it should be located at the *top* of the toolkit.

I have had the privilege in my career of never having to write about an application that I did not believe in. Bringing all the examples in this book, as well as the tricks, tips, techniques, and secrets, together involved being able to learn correctly. But it also took accommodating design software as capable as CorelDRAW as the vehicle of my expression. You've got the right application, you've got the right book, and now it's simply up to you to create your own gallery of ideas.

That is really as hard as it gets with the tutorials in this book; you are guided toward a goal, you can modify the goal to suit scores of personal artistic needs, and the end goal is as simple or as ambitious as the situation calls for. The CorelDRAW interface provides no mysteries, but only things you have not discovered yet. And incidentally, the chapter I wrote on PHOTO-PAINT should be easier than you'd expect, because the layout of the program, the UI, is nearly identical in how the goodies and functions of a lot of the tools are positioned. So if you read up on CorelDRAW, you'll be that much more ahead when you decide to paint and retouch.

The intention of this book is to work the element of discovery into a creative *process:* you pick up the knowledge of how a tool or feature works, you discover several purposes for the tool, and finally you take your newfound wisdom and apply it—to realize an idea on paper.

The thing we call *skill* lies outside of the *Official Guide's* curriculum: skill comes with time and practice. If you take the time, this book will provide you with the *other* stuff so that your footing is sound in a new application, and your bearings are based first on knowledge and eventually on instinct.

The only hitch to having an active, fertile imagination is that putting all your gems down on paper is too slow, and you might forget an idea or two—especially if you're like me. Fortunately, there's a program called CorelDRAW, and once you're comfortable and then proficient with it, your ideas will fill page after page. And you and everyone around you will share the wonder of bringing an idea to life.

Index